262/5653

Susan D'Ambros

561-338-5260

Rd already

① ✓
⑧
③ ✓
④ ✓
⑮

⑯

_____
       ch.
1, 2, 3, 4, 15, 16
17, 18, 19, 6

_____
Reel
⑪ 12, 13, 14 ⑰

CRISIS INTERVENTION HANDBOOK

Second Edition

CRISIS INTERVENTION HANDBOOK

Assessment, Treatment, and Research

SECOND EDITION

Edited by

Albert R. Roberts, Ph.D.

OXFORD
UNIVERSITY PRESS

2000

OXFORD
UNIVERSITY PRESS

Oxford New York
Athens Auckland Bangkok Bogotá Buenos Aires Calcutta
Cape Town Chennai Dar es Salaam Delhi Florence Hong Kong Istanbul
Karachi Kuala Lumpur Madrid Melbourne Mexico City Mumbai
Nairobi Paris São Paulo Singapore Taipei Tokyo Toronto Warsaw
and associated companies in
Berlin Ibadan

Copyright © 2000 Oxford University Press

Published by Oxford University Press, Inc.,
198 Madison Avenue, New York, New York 10016
http://www.oup-usa.org

Oxford is a registered trademark of Oxford University Press

Library of Congress Cataloging-in-Publication Data
Crisis intervention handbook : assessment, treatment,
and research / edited by Albert R. Roberts.—2nd ed.
    p. cm.
Includes bibliographical references and index.
ISBN 0-19-513365-X
    1. Crisis intervention (Mental health services)—Handbooks, manuals, etc.
2. Community mental health services—Handbooks, manuals, etc.
I. Roberts, Albert R.
RC480.6.C744 2000
616.89′025—dc21   99-048950

9 8 7 6 5 4 3 2

Printed in the United States of America
on acid-free paper

Foreword

Unlike the usual stresses and conflicts that are a part of everyday life at home and at work, acute crisis episodes frequently overwhelm our traditional coping skills and result in dysfunctional behavior, "going to pieces," intense fears, and a highly anxious state, also known as a state of disequilibrium. This handbook focuses on acute crisis episodes and psychiatric emergencies and the step-by-step crisis intervention strategies used by crisis counselors. Each chapter focuses on a different major crisis-precipitating event, such as turbulent divorces, adolescent suicides, airplane crashes and fatalities of family members, date rape on the college campus, shootings in the public schools, battering of women and their children, polydrug abuse, HIV-positive women, patients in intensive care units, and adults who are survivors of incest. This book includes many illuminating case studies that illustrate how best to intervene in the aftermath of a crisis episode or traumatic event.

The acute and situational crises experienced by millions of individuals and families has been escalating in intensity and frequency. Crisis intervention programs and strategies can limit the debilitating impact of acute crisis episodes as they maximize opportunities for crisis stabilization and resolution.

The first edition of the *Crisis Intervention Handbook* was published over ten years ago in 1990 and was a major success. It was a main selection in the prestigious Behavioral Science Book Club. Dr. Roberts and the 34 chapter authors have done such a thorough job of updating the chapters that the end result is a completely remodeled book. Over two-thirds of the 21 comprehensive chapters are brand new and specially written for this second edition. This is the only interdisciplinary crisis intervention book with prominent contributors from counseling psychology, clinical psychology, psychiatric mental health nursing, pediatrics, public health, and clinical social work. Whenever you read a book by Dr. Albert R. Roberts, you do so in clear anticipation of excellence. In this book, Dr. Roberts has surpassed my high expectations.

Dr. Roberts has always been an innovator and clinical research professor in the forefront of futuristic treatment planning. In 1999, Professor Roberts completed his six-level continuum on the duration and severity of domestic violence based on 501 cases. Now as we begin the 21st century, Dr. Roberts has updated and expanded the first edition of his authoritative handbook. The *Crisis Intervention Handbook* is a masterful sourcebook of practical significance, bridging crisis theory and assessment to evidence-based practice. This book provides well-written, detailed, up-to-date, thorough, and practical best practices. I predict that this authoritative volume will become the classic definitive work on crisis intervention for the important years ahead.

As editor of this volume, Dr. Roberts has selected as the chapter authors an outstanding cast of 34 internationally recognized experts in the rapid assessment and treatment of crisis episodes. Each chapter provides the reader with a comprehensive and practical application of Roberts's seven-stage crisis intervention model to the key components of acute and situational crises. This second edition of 21 original chapters includes 15 brand new chapters and 6 thoroughly revised chapters. This is the first handbook on crisis intervention to incorporate into each chapter a section on resilience, protective factors, and the strengths perspective. Also, 15 of the chapters each apply two or more case studies to the seven stages in Roberts' Crisis Intervention Model.

This all-inclusive resource provides everything mental health clinicians, crisis counselors, healthcare specialists, crisis intervenors, and trained volunteers need to know about crisis intervention. This book is a stunning achievement and landmark work.

Ann Wolbert Burgess, RN, CS, D.N.Sc., FAAN., DACFE
van Ameringen Professor of Psychiatric-Mental Health Nursing
School of Nursing, University of Pennsylvania
Philadelphia

Acknowledgments

I want to express my sincere gratitude to the authors who contributed their expertise and original chapters to this book. I am also appreciative of the anonymous reviewers' important insights and technical suggestions.

Grateful acknowledgment goes to my exceptional editor, Joan Bossert (Editorial Director, Academic Books at Oxford University Press) for her deep commitment to this second edition and her editorial wisdom and care for detail. This book also owes a debt to the late Lilian Schein, longtime director of the Behavioral Science and Nursing Book Clubs. Ms. Schein helped me plan the first edition and taught me to appreciate interdisciplinary clinical practice. Cynthia Garver, Production Editor at Oxford University Press, deserves special mention for all her hard work.

My wife Beverly deserves special thanks and appreciation for thoroughly editing and proofreading several chapters and co-authoring chapter eight. Most important, Beverly's patience with me for the lost weekends during 1999 and for the overflowing numbers of books, files, and papers in several rooms of our house went way beyond the call of duty of a marital partner.

I dedicate this book to my late parents, Evelyn and Harry Roberts, who gave me unconditional love, emotional strength, and encouragement. They instilled within me a deep conviction to pursue knowledge, overcome adversity, and thrive to set realistic short-term and long-term goals; to aid and support vulnerable groups; and to persevere in all my occupational and family endeavors. I am forever devoted and appreciative of everything they did for me and my brother during our childhood and adolescence.

Both of them demonstrated superior inner strength after being diagnosed with cancer. At a time when women had only a 10% chance of a two- to five-year survival from breast cancer and mastectomy, my mother lived sixteen years. During his two years with the intense pain of prostrate cancer, my father rarely complained and bravely persevered. Their quiet fighting spirit, courage, and resilience serve to make them role models for all persons in medical and psychological crisis.

I also dedicate this book to Dr. Viktor Frankl, psychiatrist, author of *Man's Search for Meaning*, and founder of logotherapy. When I was a young adult, his book helped me cope, survive, and master depression in the aftermath of my parents' deaths. His work continues to sustain and motivate many others.

Contents

**Part III: Crisis Intervention and Crisis Prevention
With Victims of Violence**

Contributors

The Editor

Albert R. Roberts, Ph.D., D.A.C.F.E., is a Professor of Social Work and Criminal Justice at Rutgers–The State University of New Jersey, Piscataway. He previously taught at the Indiana University School of Social Work in Indianapolis. He is an Editorial Adviser to Oxford's Professional Reference and Academic Trade Division. Dr. Roberts is the founding Editor in Chief of the journal *Crisis Intervention and Time-Limited Treatment*, and is also the Editor of the Springer Publishing Company's Series on Social Work and the Series on Family Violence. He has authored, edited, or coedited 20 previous books, and he has more than 100 published articles and book chapters to his credit. Dr. Roberts serves on the editorial boards of *The Justice Professional*, the *Journal of Human Behavior in the Social Environment*, the *Journal of Social Work Research and Evaluation*, and the *Journal of Police Hostage Negotiations*. Four of his recent books are *Visions for Change: Crime and Justice in the Twenty-first Century* (1999), *Battered Women and Their Families: Intervention Strategies and Treatment Programs* (1998), *Helping Battered Women: New Perspectives and Remedies* (1996), and *Crisis Intervention and Time-Limited Cognitive Treatment* (1995).

Dr. Roberts is an active member of the National Association of Social Workers (NASW) and the Council on Social Work Education (CSWE), a fellow of the American Orthopsychiatric Association, and a lifetime member of the Academy of Criminal Justice Sciences (ACJS). He is also a member of the New Jersey Supreme Court's Probation Advisory Board.

During the past two decades, Dr. Roberts has served as project director or consultant on several research, training, and evaluation projects, including the National Victim Assistance Training Academy of the U.S. Department of Justice, the National Organizational Survey of Crisis Intervention Units and Centers, and the National Institute of Justice–funded study on the Effectiveness of Crisis Intervention With Crime Victims, at the Victim Services Agency in New York City.

Chapter Authors

Alan L. Berman, Ph.D., Executive Director, American Association of Suicidology, Washington, DC; Professor Emeritus, Department of Psychology, American University, Washington, DC

Linda L. Black, Ph.D., Associate Professor, Department of Educational Psychology, Counseling, and Special Education, Northern Illinois University, DeKalb

Mary Boes, D.S.W., M.P.H., M.S.W., Associate Professor, Department of Social Work, University of Northern Iowa, Cedar Falls

Ann Wolbert Burgess, R.N., C.S., D.N.Sc., F.A.A.N., Van Ameringen Professor of Psychiatric–Mental Health Nursing, School of Nursing, University of Pennsylvania, Philadelphia; Associate Editor, *Crisis Intervention and Time-Limited Treatment*; and former Chairperson of the National Research Council's Panel on Research on Violence Against Women

Jacqueline Corcoran, Ph.D., Assistant Professor and Clinic Director, School of Social Work, University of Texas at Arlington

Elaine P. Congress, D.S.W., Professor and Director of the Doctoral Program, Graduate School of Social Service, Fordham University, New York City; Associate Editor, *Crisis Intervention and Time-Limited Treatment*; and President, New York City Chapter of NASW

Ellis P. Copeland, Ph.D., Professor of School Psychology, Division of Professional Psychology, University of Northern Colorado, Greeley

Sophia F. Dziegielewski, Ph.D., Professor and Director, B.S.W. Program, School of Social Work, University of Central Florida, Orlando

Yvonne M. Eaton, L.S.W., Clinical Supervisor, Community Integration, Inc. Crisis Services, Erie, Pennsylvania; and Clinical Director, Erie County Critical Incident Stress Management Team

Barb Ertl, M.S., C.T.S., Critical Incident Stress Management Team Coordinator, Erie County Critical Incident Stress Management Team, Erie, Pennsylvania

George S. Everly Jr., PhD., FAPM, CTS, Cofounder, International Critical Incident Stress Foundation, Inc., Ellicott City, Maryland; Adjunct Professor of Psychology, Johns Hopkins University and Loyola University of Baltimore, Maryland

Donald K. Granvold, Ph.D., Professor, School of Social Work, University of Texas at Arlington

Gilbert J. Greene, Ph.D., Professor, College of Social Work, The Ohio State University, Columbus; Book Review Editor, *Crisis Intervention and Time-Limited Treatment*, and Editor of the first double issue on Constructivist/ Systemic Approaches to Crisis Intervention and Brief Therapy, Vol. 4, Nos. 2–3 (1998)

Thomas K. Gregoire, Ph.D., Assistant Professor, College of Social Work, The Ohio State University, Columbus

David A. Jobes, Ph.D., Professor, Department of Psychology, Catholic University of America, Washington, DC; former President, American Association of Suicidology

Jeffrey M. Lating, Ph.D., Clinic Director, Union Memorial Hospital, Baltimore, Maryland

Mo-Yee Lee, Ph.D., Assistant Professor, College of Social Work, The Ohio State University, Columbus

Sarah Lewis, M.S.W., Ph.D. Candidate, School of Social Work, The Florida State University, Tallahassee

Jan Ligon, Ph.D., Assistant Professor of Social Work, Department of Social Work, College of Health and Human Sciences, Georgia State University, Atlanta

Gordon MacNeil, Ph.D., Associate Professor, School of Social Work, The University of Alabama, Tuscaloosa

Catherine E. Martin, M.A., Doctoral candidate, Department of Psychology, Catholic University of America, Washington, DC

Virginia McDermott, R.N., B.A., Medical-Surgical Nurse, Cardiac Care Unit, Allen Memorial Hospital, Waterloo, Iowa

Jeffrey T. Mitchell, Ph.D., C.T.S., Cofounder and President, International Critical Incident Stress Foundation, Inc., Ellicott City, Maryland; Associate Professor, Emergency Services Department, University of Maryland at Baltimore County, Maryland

Diane Harrison Montgomery, Ph.D., Professor and Dean, School of Social Work, The Florida State University, Tallahassee

Scott Newgass, M.S.W., Clinical Instructor in Social Work, Yale University Child Study Institute, and Coordinator, Regional School Crisis Prevention and Response Program, New Haven, Connecticut

M. Sean O'Halloran, Ph.D., Professor of Counseling Psychology, Clinic Director, Psychological Services Clinic, Division of Professional Psychology, University of Northern Colorado, Greeley

Allen J. Ottens, Ph.D., Associate Professor and Chair of counseling faculty, Department of Educational Psychology, Counseling and Special Education, Northern Illinois University, DeKalb

Gerald T. Powers, Ph.D., Professor and Director, Doctoral Program, School of Social Work, Indiana University, Indianapolis

Judy Rheinscheld, M.S.W., Scioto Paint Valley Mental Health Center, Fayette County Clinic, Washington Court House, Ohio

Beverly Schenkman Roberts, M.Ed., Director, Mainstreaming Medical Care Program, The Arc of New Jersey, North Brunswick

David J. Schonfeld, M.D., Associate Professor of Pediatrics and Child Study, Department of Pediatrics and Institute for Child Study, Yale University School of Medicine and Yale–New Haven Hospital; and Director, Regional School Crisis Prevention and Response Program, New Haven, Connecticut

Amy L. Shewbert, B.A., Research Assistant, Psychological Management Services, Lubbock, Texas

Norman M. Shulman, Ed.D., Clinical Assistant Professor, Department of Neuropsychiatry and Behavioral Science at the Texas Tech University School of Medicine; Licensed Psychologist, Psychological Management Services, Lubbock, Texas

Chris Stewart, Ph.D., Assistant Professor, School of Social Work, The University of Alabama, Tuscaloosa

Rhonda Trask, M.S.W., Clinical Social Worker, Newark, Ohio

Pamela Valentine, Ph.D., Assistant Professor of Social Work, Department of Public Policy and Political Science, The University of Alabama, Birmingham

Kenneth R. Yeager, Ph.D., C.C.D.C. III E, Clinical Director, The Ohio State University Hospitals East Talbot Hall, Columbus; Assistant Clinical Professor, The Ohio State University Medical School, Columbus

Introduction

The first edition of this book (published in 1990) was a major success, and the editor has kept the same framework with five main sections. However, this is basically a new book, with 16 brand-new specially written and designed chapters. The remaining five original chapters were thoroughly updated and revised by the original authors.

Since the publication of the first edition, crisis intervention practices and programs have changed considerably. Professional and public interest in crisis intervention, crisis response teams, crisis management, and crisis stabilization has grown tremendously in the past decade, partially due, no doubt, to the prevalence of acute crisis events impacting on the lives of the general public. The focus of this book is on crisis intervention services for persons who are victims of natural disasters; school-based and home-based violence; violent crimes, such as homicide, aggravated assault, sexual assault, domestic violence, and date rape among college students; and personal or family crises, such as the death of a loved one, incest, life-threatening medical conditions, divorce, suicide and suicide attempts, and drug abuse.

Suicide prevention programs and other 24-hour crisis hotlines provide valuable assistance to callers who are contemplating suicide and related self-destructive acts. These telephone hotlines are operational nationwide, usually staffed by trained graduate students and volunteers. The programs that are accredited by the American Association of Suicidology require all crisis hotline workers to complete a minimum of 40 hours of training and 20 hours of supervised hotline experience.

Hundreds of thousands of persons in distress turn to health care, family counseling, and domestic violence and mental health facilities throughout the United States for help in resolving crisis situations. Many crises are triggered by a life-threatening event, such as acute cardiac arrest, attempted murder, criminal homicide, motor vehicle crashes, child custody battles, drug overdoses, psychiatric emergencies, sexual assaults, woman battering, suicide, and/or community disasters. Crisis events and situations can often be critical turning points in a person's life. They can serve as a challenge and opportunity for rapid problem resolution and growth, or as a debilitating event leading to sudden disequilibrium, failed coping, and dysfunctional behavior patterns. In addition, given the limitations imposed on crisis intervenors and clinicians by the requirements of managed care groups, the use of brief treatment has become more widespread.

INDIVIDUAL VERSUS GROUP CRISIS INTERVENTION

There is debate in the field of crisis intervention among competing professional groups. The primary debate stems from each professional group's somewhat different crisis intervention model, and the groups' different training and educational requirements for certification. The nature of the debate is complicated by the fact that in the professional literature read by the involved professional groups and organizations, crisis intervention has been defined in different ways, including different concepts and parameters of intervention. *This handbook applies a unifying model of crisis intervention while building on the strengths of each model.*

At the core of the debate among professionals in the crisis intervention field is the definition and scope of the assistance provided by professionals *immediately* after the crisis event has occurred, and the definition and scope of the assistance provided by professionals in the short-term period (several weeks) following the crisis event. Also key to the debate is the level of training and expertise of the professionals who provide the *immediate* assistance. This issue is further compounded by the fact that there are two overarching categories of crisis events: *private events* that impact individuals or families (e.g., a suicide attempt, an HIV diagnosis, divorce, woman battering, or the untimely death of a close family member), and *public events* that impact groups of individuals (e.g., a shooting at a school or in the workplace, a devastating tornado, or an airplane crash). A complicating factor in the latter category is the involvement and intrusion of the news media at a time when the affected individuals may want to be left alone to deal with the crisis situation. This handbook will address and clarify these issues.

Some authorities have mistakenly defined *crisis intervention* as grief counseling, hostage negotiations, or observing and collecting evidence at the crime scene of a domestic violence incident. Other authorities define crisis intervention to include disaster relief work and emergency medical services performed by paramedics, firefighters, emergency medical technicians (EMTs), airport security officers, flight attendants, and airline baggage handlers, as well as trained volunteers. Other authorities contend that crisis intervention is synonymous with the work of crisis response teams consisting of trained mental health professionals, victim advocates, law enforcement specialists, and clergy (2-day training and follow-up debriefings by the trainers from the National Organization for Victim Assistance [NOVA]). Finally, the third and largest group of authorities (including the editor of this book) have operationally defined crisis intervention as immediate, short-term, and applied through rapid assessment protocols; bolstering coping methods, psychosocial adaptation, solution-focused, timely crisis resolution. In general, the expectation is that the crisis intervenor (also referred to as the crisis clinician, crisis counselor, psychologist, or social worker) has completed a graduate degree in clinical, community, or school psychology; guidance and counseling; pastoral counseling; psychiatric–mental health nursing; or social work. As part of the master's or doctoral program, the mental health professional has acquired basic counseling, crisis intervention, and clinical practice training and skills, as well as field practicum experience.

In chapter 1, and subsequent chapters, the authors focus on the extensive step-by-step, eclectic model of crisis intervention (interchangeable with the term *crisis counseling*). There is much confusion among the general public regarding the definition of crisis intervention among mental health professionals in the aftermath of traumatic events, such as mass shootings in the schools, airplane disasters, and murders in the workplace. Frontline crisis workers and emergency services personnel are well trained and effective in rescuing survivors and defusing potentially disastrous situations. The average citizen is not aware of the vital work of crisis clinicians after the work of first responders/frontline crisis workers is completed. Because of a strong code of ethics and confidentiality safeguards, it would be a violation for social workers and psychologists to issue press releases or engage in interviews with journalists. Chapter 4, by Everly, Lating, and Mitchell, focuses on Critical Incident Stress Debriefing for emergency services personnel, firefighters, and police officers after individuals in the disaster receive medical attention and are stabilized. Jeff Mitchell and George Everly are the founders of the International Critical Incident Stress Foundation, and critical incident stress and trauma debriefing teams.

The controversy in this field developed as a result of rigid adherence to one model or approach rather than using an eclectic perspective that recognizes and accepts the most effective components of each model. *This is the first comprehensive handbook that prepares the crisis intervenor for rapid assessment and timely crisis intervention in the twenty-first century.* Emotional and psychological first aid (also known as critical incident debriefing, frontline first response, and crisis stabilization) can be effectively administered by trained volunteers, including emergency service workers. *However, crisis intervention or crisis counseling is much more extensive than critical incident debriefing and crisis stabilization, usually requiring considerably more time (usually 4 to 6 weeks) and graduate-level courses in a mental health discipline.* Since crisis intervention is a multidisciplinary field, the editor is more concerned with the graduate courses and training seminars completed, and the skills of the crisis intervenor, than with the particular academic discipline with which the crisis clinician is identified.

There are two primary phases to crisis intervention. The initial phase occurs either immediately after the acute crisis episode or disaster has occurred or within 48 hours of the event. This phase is generally referred to as defusing the crisis and securing safety, crisis stabilization, emotional first aid, or crisis management. This phase is usually standard operating procedure for statewide crisis response teams (who have been trained by the American Psychological Association disaster task force, the International Critical Incident Stress Foundation, and/or the American Red Cross), law enforcement agencies, hospitals and medical centers, and correctional agencies.

The specific nature of the intervention varies depending on the type of crisis event that has occurred. An example is the need for crisis intervention brought on by violence in the workplace, in which a disgruntled employee returns to his former place of business and shoots his former supervisors and/or coworkers. In this scenario, the initial intervention revolves around providing emergency medical services for the shooting victims, as well as crisis stabilization for the victims and coworkers, particularly those who were at the scene and witnessed the shooting. The first activity of the crisis team is to meet with the key people who are in charge at the site where the crisis event occurred to establish the plan of action. Next, the crisis team assembles the victims and observers to the crisis event (who have been medically stabilized) to provide a debriefing and to clarify the facts surrounding the event (e.g., has the shooter been taken into custody? has a telephone hotline been set up for family members who want to know what is happening?); identify postcrisis problems; provide an overview of what to expect emotionally in the aftermath of the crisis event; and describe where victims and observers can go for individual counseling and support. The team also facilitates individual and group discussions to help the parties involved to ventilate and process the event. Finally, the crisis team communicates with the supervisors to help them understand how to identify and facilitate their employees' recovery by referral to a licensed mental health professional.

Although the crisis team approach described here is the recommended response to an institutional or natural disaster, it is not always available and depends on the readiness and proactive stance of the community in which one lives and works. Every community should have access to trained crisis intervenors, either locally or through a consulting contract with a crisis team from a nearby city. The most commonly used models for group crisis intervention—emotional first aid, crisis and disaster management—were developed by Jeff Mitchell, George Everly, David Schonfeld, and Scott Newgass. These two models will be applied in chapters 4, 9, and 16.

The most popular model for individual crisis intervention is generally known as *crisis intervention* or *crisis counseling*, which takes place during the days and weeks immediately after the crisis event. This phase or type of crisis intervention is commonly utilized by clinical social workers and psychologists in group private practices, crisis intervention units of community mental health centers, child and family counseling centers, and hospital settings. Various practice models have been developed to assist clinicians in working with persons in crisis including the three-step model (assessment, boiling down the problem, coping alternatives). This book will consistently utilize the Roberts seven-stage crisis intervention model, which is applied as an intervention framework for providing crisis counseling. This thorough and sequential model can facilitate early identification of crisis precipitants, active listening, problem solving, effective coping skills, inner strengths and protective factors, and effective crisis resolution. The Roberts seven-stage model consists of the following:

1. Assess lethality and mental health status.
2. Establish rapport and engage the client.
3. Identify major problems.
4. Deal with feelings.
5. Explore alternative coping methods and partial solutions.
6. Develop an action plan.
7. Develop a termination and follow-up protocol.

This handbook was written for frontline crisis workers, graduate students, and clinicians who work with individuals, families, and communities in crisis. Crisis theory and practice principles cut across several professions, including counseling, social work, psychology, psychiatric nursing, psychiatry, law enforcement, and victim assistance. Therefore, an interdisciplinary approach has been used in compiling and editing this book. This volume is a collaborative work, with original chapters written by prominent clinical social workers, health social workers, clinical nurse specialists, clinical psychologists, counseling psychologists, community psychologists, and victim advocates. Each practice chapter (chapters 5 through 19) begins with one to three case studies or vignettes, followed by sections that present an introduction; the scope of the problem; and the research literature related to resilience and protective factors for specific high-risk groups (e.g., depressed adolescents, incest survivors, stressed-out college students, battered women, chemically dependent individuals). The main part of each chapter includes a framework for the practice of crisis intervention with a specific target group. Several detailed cases and case commentaries are included in each chapter to demonstrate the steps in the operation of the seven-stage crisis intervention model. Also highlighted in each chapter are clinical issues, controversies, roles, and skills. Many of the chapters conclude with summaries and predictions for the future use of crisis intervention with a particular target group, such as callers to a 24-hour mobile crisis unit, college students in crisis, women with AIDS, adolescent suicide attemptors, victims of violent crimes, victims of community disasters, and substance abusers.

Although the primary focus of this book is crisis intervention in the United States, some of the chapters do include a discussion of personal and family crises and community disasters in other countries. Chapter 20 (by Corcoran and Roberts) reviews studies on the effectiveness of suicide prevention centers in Canada, England, Japan, Taiwan, and Germany, as well as the United States. Suicide prevention by e-mail has been shown to be effective through the network of Samaritans mutual aid in Australia, England, and Hong Kong. Chapter 20 also includes information on crisis intervention studies conducted with groups of clients in Italy, Switzerland, Canada, and the United States who had psychiatric emergencies.

In Chapter 4, Everly, Mithcell, and Lating, the founders of Critical Incident Stress Management (CISM), apply their group crisis intervention model to community disasters—for example, the bombing of the U.S. Embassy in Nairobi; a nationwide crisis intervention system for postwar Kuwait; and crisis intervention services for families of victims of the TWA 800 air disaster that occurred over Long Island, New York.

In Chapter 10 there is a discussion of school shootings, potentially violent situations, and crisis prevention, as well as group crisis intervention models in the aftermath of school fatalities in the United States. Chapter 9 focuses on a statewide school crisis prevention team and crisis response program that has helped thousands of children and adolescents during the past decade. These chapters contain valuable information for mental health professionals worldwide, by providing detailed information on how to plan and implement individual crisis intervention, schoolwide notification systems, classroom interventions, training and support for schoolteachers and guidance counselors, and crisis intervention in resource rooms. No nation is immune from the shootings at schools and at work that have received extensive attention in the media. An example of a horrendous act of violence, in what could have been viewed as an unlikely location for mass murder, occurred in Sterling, Scotland on March 13, 1996. A disgruntled former school custodian, angry because he had been fired, returned to the elementary school where he had worked, killing a teacher and 16 children and injuring many other children before turning the gun on himself. The police and emergency services staff brought the injured victims to the three infirmaries (hospitals) in the area. In the aftermath of this horrific school disaster, no crisis intervention teams were available to provide assistance to the grieving family members and the recovering victims.

Recognizing the necessity of having mental health professionals mobilized to respond quickly if a disaster occurred in their local community, the American Red Cross in the 1990s developed cooperative agreements with the American Counseling Association, the American Psychological Association, and the National Association of Social Workers in order to facilitate the development of mental health and crisis response teams to provide immediate intervention. As a result, within 24 hours of a major disaster in the United States (such as a plane crash of tornado) community crisis response teams are on the scene, providing crisis intervention services.

This volume is intended to be a key resource for professionals who are called upon to intervene with individuals and groups in crisis. There is a very strong interest in the application of crisis theory and crisis intervention techniques among professionals practicing in school, family, health, mental health, victim assistance, and group private practice settings. This book has been designed primarily for frontline crisis workers (e.g., clinical psychologists and social workers at outpatient mental health centers, psychiatric–mental health nurses, social work case managers, and clinicians skilled in crisis management after a community disaster), clinicians in managed care settings, and graduate students who need to know the latest steps and methods for intervening effectively with persons in acute crisis. This book will also be useful as the primary text in courses such as crisis intervention, crisis counseling, crisis intervention and brief treatment, social work practice II, and mental health practice, and as the supplementary text in health social work, introduction to human services, psychiatric nursing, and community psychology.

I

OVERVIEW

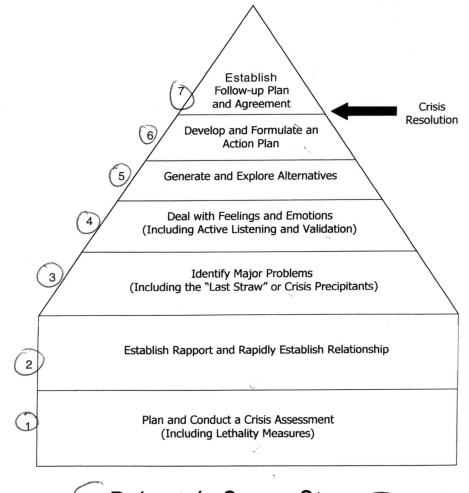

7 — Establish Follow-up Plan and Agreement

6 — Develop and Formulate an Action Plan

← Crisis Resolution

5 — Generate and Explore Alternatives

4 — Deal with Feelings and Emotions (Including Active Listening and Validation)

3 — Identify Major Problems (Including the "Last Straw" or Crisis Precipitants)

2 — Establish Rapport and Rapidly Establish Relationship

1 — Plan and Conduct a Crisis Assessment (Including Lethality Measures)

Roberts's Seven-Stage Crisis Intervention Model

1

An Overview of Crisis Theory and Crisis Intervention

ALBERT R. ROBERTS

Some crisis situations are personal, such as the death of a loved one or being the victim of a rape, a robbery, or a severe battering incident; others are triggered by a traumatic event, such as an airplane crash, flood, hurricane, or tornado. Both individual and community-wide traumatic events can cause widespread crisis for dozens, hundreds, or even thousands of people.

Sudden Death of a Spouse and Child

Joe begins to barbecue the hamburgers for tonight's dinner. His wife and their two daughters are expected home in about 20 minutes. His older daughter had a track meet, and his wife and younger daughter went to watch her. The phone rings, and Joe is informed by a police officer that his wife and older daughter have been killed by a drunken driver who sped through a red light and smashed into their car two blocks from their house. His life will never be the same.

Deaths and Injuries Related to Plane Crash

At 9:00 A.M. one morning, the pilot of a malfunctioning air force attack jet tried unsuccessfully to make an emergency landing at Indianapolis International Airport. The out-of-control jet clipped the top of a nearby bank building, then rammed into the lobby of a Ramada Inn and exploded, killing 10

3

people and injuring several others. This tragic accident resulted in hundreds of persons in crisis: those injured in the explosion, the family members of the dead and injured, the guests and surviving employees at the hotel who witnessed the horror, and the employees and customers at the bank building that was struck by the plane, even though no one at the bank was physically hurt.

Woman Battering

Judy B., a 27-year-old surgical nurse, was a survivor of wife battering. She and Ray had been married for 6 years, and they had two children. As Ray's drinking increased, so did his beatings. The final straw was a violent attack in which Ray punched Judy many times in her face. The day following this last assault, after looking at her swollen face in the mirror, Judy went to a gun store and purchased a handgun. As she drove home looking at the gun by her side, she finally decided to seek help. She called the battered women's shelter hot line and said, "I'm afraid that I'm going to kill my husband."

Forcible Rape

Mary R. was a 22-year-old college senior when she was raped. At 11 P.M. one evening Mary had just left the health sciences library at the university and was walking the three long blocks to the parking lot where her car was parked. She recalls her reactions a week later: "I was sort of in shock and numb. It was a terrifying, painful, and degrading experience. It was something you don't expect to happen. But it could have been much worse. He held a knife to my throat while raping me. I thought he was going to kill me afterward. I'm glad to be alive."

Robbery

John A., a 24-year-old blind male, was a victim of robbery. John was returning to his apartment in the Bronx following an afternoon appointment with his physician when he was robbed. John recalled what took place: "A guy came up to me and pressed the cold barrel of his gun on my neck. He said if I don't give him what I got he would shoot me and the dog. I gave him the $21 I had. Nobody helped me. Everybody's afraid to intervene. They're afraid because they know the guy will get off or be put on probation and may come after them.

About a week after the robbery, I woke up sweating and had a serious asthma attack. I was hospitalized for a week. Now I try not to visit friends or my cousin in Manhattan. I go out a lot less. I stay home and listen to the radio or TV most of the time."

Broken Romance, Depression, and Alcoholism

Liz, a 21-year-old college senior, is very depressed. She and her fiancé have just broken up, and she feels unable to cope. She cries most of the day, feels agitated, and isn't sleeping or eating normally. Since the beginning of the relationship a year ago, Liz has become socially isolated. Her family strongly dislikes her fiancé, and her fiancé discouraged her from spending time with her friends. Liz now doubts that she will find a job upon graduation in 3 months and is considering moving home. She comes from a large family, with parents who are very much involved with the other children. Thoughts of moving back home and losing her independence, as well as the broken romance and the lack of a support system, have immobilized Liz, who has cut all her classes for the past week. She has not talked with friends or family about the breakup, and she is "holed up" in her room in the dormitory, drinking herself into a stupor and refusing to eat or leave the building even for a walk.

Joe, Judy, Mary, John, and Liz are experiencing crisis reactions in the aftermath of highly stressful hazardous events. The initial crisis reaction in the aftermath of the sudden death of a loved one or being the victim of a violent crime is usually a series of physiological and emotional reactions. Some common reactions and symptoms after traumatic and crisis events include overwhelming feelings of anxiety, despair, and hopelessness, guilt, intense fears, grief over sudden losses, confusion, difficulty concentrating, powerlessness, irritability, intrusive imagery, flashbacks, extreme suspiciousness of others, shame, disorientation, loss of appetite, binge drinking, sleep disturbances, helplessness, terror, exhaustion, losses or lapses of religious beliefs, and/or shattered assumptions about personal safety. Persons experiencing traumatic events or an accumulation of stressful life events usually attempt to understand and reduce their symptoms, to regain control of their environment, and to reach out to their support system (e.g., a significant other). Sometimes the person's internal and external coping methods are successful, and an acute crisis episode is averted; at other times vulnerable individuals and groups fail in their attempts to cope, and crisis episodes escalate.

Chapters 1 through 4 of this book link crisis theory to practice. The emphasis in the first four chapters is placed on the application of individual and group crisis intervention paradigms and models to facilitating crisis resolution. Chapter 1 links the past to the present state-of-the-art knowledge of conceptualizing crisis theory, crisis reactions, and crisis intervention practices. Chapter 2 integrates Roberts's seven-stage crisis intervention model with solution-based therapy and a strengths perspective. Chapter 3 develops a continuum of stress and crisis episodes ranging from low-level somatic distress to cumulative and catastrophic acute crisis episodes. The last chapter in this section, chapter 4, focuses on the application of Everly, Mitchell, and Lating's group crisis intervention model: critical incident debriefing with survivors of community disasters.

Chapters 5 through 19 apply Roberts's seven-stage model of crisis assessment and intervention to particular high-risk groups and situations such as the following:

- early adolescents who have experienced a significant loss
- adolescents with suicidal gestures
- crises on the college campus
- battered women in crisis
- crisis related to separation, divorce, and child custody
- HIV-positive women in crisis
- persons in medical crisis presenting at intensive care units
- persons presenting with life-threatening injuries at a hospital emergency room
- persons experiencing psychiatric crises and coming to the local mental health center or emergency room
- a series of crises experienced by incest survivors
- people experiencing mental health–related crises and being helped by a frontline 24-hour mobile crisis team

This is the first comprehensive handbook to consistently apply a comprehensive seven-stage crisis intervention model to a wide range of clients in acute crisis.

SCOPE OF THE PROBLEM AND PREVALENCE ESTIMATES

We live in an era in which traumatic events and acute crisis episodes have become far too prevalent. Each year, millions of people are confronted with traumatic crisis-producing events that they cannot resolve on their own, and they often turn for help to 24-hour telephone crisis hotlines; crisis units of community mental health centers; and outpatient, hospital-based programs.

During the past two decades, thousands of crisis intervention programs have been established throughout the United States and Canada. There are over 1,400 grassroots crisis centers and crisis units affiliated with the American Association of Suicidology or a local community mental health center. Altogether there are also over 9,000 victim assistance programs, rape crisis programs, child sexual and physical abuse intervention programs, police-based crisis intervention programs, and battered women's shelters and hotlines. In addition, crisis services are provided at thousands of local hospital emergency rooms, hospital-based trauma centers and emergency psychiatric services, suicide prevention centers, and pastoral counseling services.

Crisis centers and hotlines provide information, crisis assessments, intervention, and referrals for callers with such problems as depression, suicide ideation, psychiatric emergencies, chemical dependency, AIDS, sexual dysfunction, woman battering, and crime victimization. Because of their 24-hour availability, they can provide immediate, though temporary, assistance. Some crisis victims do not have a caring friend or relative to whom they can turn; they often benefit from an empathetic, active listener. Even when significant others are available to aid the person in crisis, hotlines provide a valuable service by linking the caller to appropriate community resources.

The large number of documented calls to crisis hotlines—an estimated 4.3 million calls annually—indicates the importance of these programs (Roberts & Camasso, 1994). The first national organizational survey of crisis units and centers yielded a response from 107 programs (Roberts, 1995). The researcher's summary findings indicated that a total of 578,793 crisis callers were handled by the crisis centers and programs in the 1-year period directly prior to receipt of the mailed questionnaire, or an annual average of 5,409 callers per crisis intervention program. In 1990, 796 crisis intervention units and programs (affiliated with a community mental health center) were in operation throughout the United States, and the annual average number of callers received by each program was 5,409. As a result of multiplying the average number of callers by the number of programs, Roberts (1995) estimated the annual number of callers to be sightly over 4.3 million. If we broaden our estimate to all national and local 24-hour crisis lines, including those for crime victims, battered women, sexual assault victims, troubled employees, adolescent runaways, and child abuse victims, as well as the crisis intervention units at mental health centers, the total estimate would be approximately 35 to 45 million crisis callers per year.

CRISIS REACTIONS AND CRISIS INTERVENTION

A *crisis* can be defined as a period of psychological disequilibrium, experienced as a result of a hazardous event or situation that constitutes a significant problem that cannot be remedied by using familiar coping strategies. A crisis occurs when a person faces an obstacle to important life goals that generally seems insurmountable through the use of customary habits and coping patterns. The goal of crisis intervention is to resolve the most pressing problem within a 1-to 12-week period using focused and directed interventions aimed at helping the client develop new adaptive coping methods.

Crisis reaction refers to the acute stage, which usually occurs soon after the hazardous event (e.g., sexual assault, battering, suicide attempt). During this phase, the person's acute reaction may take various forms, including helplessness, confusion, anxiety, shock, disbelief, and anger. Low self-esteem and serious depression are often produced by the crisis state. The person in crisis may appear to be incoherent, disorganized, agitated, and volatile or calm, subdued, withdrawn, and apathetic. It is during this period that the individual is often most willing to seek help, and crisis intervention is usually more effective at this time (Golan, 1978).

Crisis intervention can provide a challenge, an opportunity, and a turning point within the individual's life. According to Roberts and Dziegielewski

(1995), crisis clinicians have been encouraged to examine psychological and situational crises in terms of "both danger and opportunity" (p. 16). The aftermath of a crisis episode can result in either a highly positive or a highly negative change. Immediate and structured crisis intervention guided by Roberts's seven-stage model facilitates crisis resolution, cognitive mastery, and personal growth, rather than psychological harm.

A divorce, a robbery, a broken engagement, being the victim of a domestic assault, and being the close relative of a person killed in an automobile accident or a plane crash are all highly stressful occurrences that can result in an active crisis state. The persons involved may exhibit denial, intense anxiety, and confusion; they may express anger and fear, or grief and loss, but they can all survive. Crisis intervention can reduce immediate danger and fear, as well as provide support, hope, and alternative ways of coping and growing.

Persons in acute crisis have had similar reactions to traumatic events, from initial feelings of disruption and disorganization to the eventual readjustment of the self. During the impact phase, survivors of victimization and other crisis-producing events often feel numb, disoriented, shattered, fearful, vulnerable, helpless, and lonely. The survivors may seek help, consolation, and advice from friends or professionals within several hours or days after the traumatic or stressful life event.

Helping a person in crisis—whether it be in the aftermath of a violent crime, a suicide attempt, a drug overdose, a life-threatening illness, a natural disaster, a divorce, a broken romance, or an automobile crash—requires exceptional sensitivity, active listening skills, and empathy on the part of the crisis intervenor. If a hotline worker, crisis counselor, social worker, or psychologist is able to establish rapport with the person in crisis soon after the acute crisis episode, many hours of later treatment may be averted.

DEFINING A CRISIS AND CRISIS CONCEPTS

Crisis may be viewed in various ways, but most definitions emphasize that it can be a turning point in a person's life. According to Bard and Ellison (1974), crisis is "a subjective reaction to a stressful life experience, one so affecting the stability of the individual that the ability to cope or function may be seriously compromised" (p. 68).

It has been established that a crisis can develop when an event, or a series of events, takes place in a person's life and the result is a hazardous situation. However, it is important to note that the crisis is not the situation itself (e.g., being victimized); rather, it is the person's *perception of and response to* the situation (Parad, 1971, p. 197).

The most important precipitant of a crisis is a stressful or hazardous event. But two other conditions are also necessary to have a crisis state: (a) the individual's perception that the stressful event will lead to considerable upset and/or disruption; and (b) the individual's inability to resolve the disruption by previously used coping methods (see the Glossary p. 513).

Crisis intervention refers to a therapist entering into the life situation of an individual or family to alleviate the impact of a crisis to help mobilize the resources of those directly affected (Parad, 1965).

In conceptualizing crisis theory, Parad and Caplan (1960) examine the fact that "crises have a peak or sudden turning point"; as the individual reaches this peak, tension increases and stimulates the mobilization of previously hidden strengths and capacities. They urge timely intervention to help individuals cope successfully with a crisis situation. Caplan (1961) states that "a relatively minor force, acting for a relatively short time, can switch the balance to one side or another, to the side of mental health or the side of mental ill health" (p. 293).

There is a general consensus among clinical social workers and psychologists that the following characterize a person in crisis:

1. Perceiving a precipitating event as being meaningful and threatening
2. Appearing unable to modify or lessen the impact of stressful events with traditional coping methods
3. Experiencing increased fear, tension, and/or confusion
4. Exhibiting a high level of subjective discomfort
5. Proceeding rapidly to an active state of crisis—a state of disequilibrium

The term *crisis* as it has been described here is applicable to most of the clients of the social workers, psychologists, and professional counselors who prepared chapters for this handbook. The definition of a crisis stated previously is particularly applicable to persons in acute crisis because these individuals usually seek help only after they have experienced a hazardous event and are in a vulnerable state, have failed to cope and lessen the crisis through customary coping methods, and want outside help.

Foundation Assumptions and the Crisis Theory Framework

The conceptual framework for crisis intervention practice presented in this handbook incorporates the basic principles of crisis theory. The crisis intervention specialization is built on a basic knowledge of crisis theory and practice. Crisis theory includes a cluster of principles upon which crisis clinicians and researchers usually agree. In this book the prominent authorities on crisis intervention demonstrate the application of the crisis intervention process and practices to special groups at high risk of crisis. But first it will be helpful to summarize the foundation principles of crisis theory and to place them in a step-by-step crisis management framework.

Basic Tenets of Crisis Theory

As mentioned earlier, a crisis state is a temporary upset, accompanied by some confusion and disorganization, and characterized by a person's inability to cope with a specific situation through the use of traditional problem-solving methods. According to Naomi Golan (1978), the heart of crisis theory and practice rests in a series of basic statements:

- Crisis situations can occur episodically during "the normal life span of individuals, families, groups, communities and nation." They are often initiated by a hazardous event. This may be a catastrophic event or a series of successive stressful blows which rapidly build up a cumulative effect. (p. 8)

- The impact of the hazardous event disturbs the individual's homeostatic balance and puts him in a vulnerable state. (p. 8)

- If the problem continues and cannot be resolved, avoided, or redefined, tension rises to a peak, and a precipitating factor can bring about a turning point, during which self-righting devices no longer operate and the individual enters a state of a disequilibrium . . . (an) active crisis. (p. 8)

Duration of the Crisis

Persons cannot remain indefinitely in a state of psychological turmoil and survive. Caplan (1964) noted, and other clinical supervisors have concurred, that in a typical crisis state equilibrium will be restored in 4 to 6 weeks. However, the designation of 4 to 6 weeks has been confusing. Several authors note that crisis resolution can take from several weeks to several months. To clarify the confusion concerning this period, it is useful to explain the difference between restoring equilibrium and crisis resolution.

Disequilibrium, which is characterized by confusing emotions, somatic complaints, and erratic behavior, is reduced considerably within the first 6 weeks of crisis intervention. The severe emotional discomfort experienced by the person in crisis propels him or her toward action that will result in reducing the subjective discomfort. Thus, equilibrium is restored, and the disorganization is time limited.

Viney (1976) aptly describes crisis resolution as restoration of equilibrium, as well as cognitive mastery of the situation and the development of new coping methods. Fairchild (1986) refers to crisis resolution as an adaptive consequence of a crisis in which the person grows from the crisis experience through the discovery of new coping skills and resources to employ in the future. In this handbook, crisis intervention is viewed as the process of working through the crisis event so that the person is assisted in exploring the traumatic experience and his or her reaction to it. Emphasis is also placed on helping the individual do the following:

Make behavioral changes and interpersonal adjustments.
Mobilize internal and external resources and supports.
Reduce unpleasant or disturbing affects related to the crisis.
Integrate the event and its aftermath into the individual's other life experiences and markers.

The goal of effective crisis resolution is to remove vulnerabilities from the individual's past and bolster him or her with an increased repertoire of new coping skills to serve as a buffer against similar stressful situations in the future.

HISTORICAL DEVELOPMENT

As far back as 400 B.C., physicians have stressed the significance of crisis as a hazardous life event. Hippocrates himself defined a crisis as a sudden state that gravely endangers life. But the development of a cohesive theory of crisis and approaches to crisis management had to await the twentieth century. The movement to help people in crisis began in 1906 with the establishment of the first suicide prevention center, the National Save-a-Life League in New York City. However, contemporary crisis intervention theory and practice were not formally elaborated until the 1940s, primarily by Erich Lindemann and Gerald Caplan.

Lindemann and his associates at Massachusetts General Hospital introduced the concepts of crisis intervention and time-limited treatment in 1943 in the aftermath of Boston's worst nightclub fire, at the Coconut Grove, in which 493 people perished. Lindemann (1944) and colleagues based the crisis theory they developed on their observations of the acute and delayed reactions of survivors and grief-stricken relatives of victims. Their clinical work focused on the psychological symptoms of the survivors and on preventing unresolved grief among relatives of the persons who had died. They found that many individuals experiencing acute grief often had five related reactions:

1. Somatic distress
2. Preoccupation with the image of the deceased
3. Guilt
4. Hostile reactions
5. Loss of patterns of conduct

Furthermore, Lindemann and colleagues concluded that the duration of a grief reaction appears to be dependent on the success with which the bereaved person does his or her mourning and "grief work." In general, this grief work involves achieving emancipation from the deceased, readjusting to the changes in the environment from which the loved one is missing, and developing new relationships. We learned from Lindemann that people need to be encouraged to permit themselves to have a period of mourning and eventual acceptance of the loss and adjustment to life without the parent, child, spouse, or sibling. If the normal process of grieving is delayed, negative outcomes of crises will develop. Lindemann's work was soon adapted to interventions with World War II veterans suffering from "combat neurosis" and bereaved family members.

Gerald Caplan, who was affiliated with Massachusetts General Hospital and the Harvard School of Public Health, expanded Lindemann's pioneering work in the 1940s and 1950s. Caplan studied various developmental crisis reactions, as in premature births, infancy, childhood, and adolescence, and accidental crises such as illness and death. He was the first psychiatrist to relate the concept of homeostasis to crisis intervention and to describe the stages of a crisis. According to Caplan (1961), a crisis is an upset of a steady state in which the individual encounters an obstacle (usually an obstacle to significant life goals) that cannot be overcome through traditional problem-solving activities. For each individual, a reasonably constant balance or steady state exists between affective and cognitive experience. When this homeostatic balance or stability in psychological functioning is threatened by physiological, psychological, or social forces, the individual engages in problem-solving methods designed to restore the balance. However, in a crisis situation, the person in distress faces a problem that seems to have no solution. Thus homeostatic balance is disrupted, or an upset of a steady state ensues.

Caplan (1964) explains this concept further by stating that the problem is one in which the individual faces "stimuli which signal danger to a fundamental need satisfaction . . . and the circumstances are such that habitual problem-solving methods are unsuccessful within the time span of past expectations of success" (p. 39).

Caplan also described four stages of a crisis reaction. The first stage is the initial rise of tension that comes from the emotionally hazardous crisis-precipitating event. The second stage is characterized by an increased level of tension and disruption to daily living because the individual is unable to resolve the crisis quickly. As the person attempts and fails to resolve the crisis through emergency problem-solving mechanisms, tension increases to such an intense level that the individual may go into a depression. The person going through the final stage of Caplan's model may experience either a mental collapse or a breakdown, or may partly resolve the crisis by using new coping methods. J. S. Tyhurst (1957) studied transition states—migration, retirement, civilian disaster, and so on—in the lives of persons experiencing sudden changes. Based on his field studies on individual patterns of responses to community disaster, Tyhurst identified three overlapping phases, each with its own manifestations of stress and attempts at reducing it:

1. A period of impact
2. A period of recoil
3. A posttraumatic period of recovery

Tyhurst recommended stage-specific intervention. He concluded that persons in transitional crisis states should not be removed from their life situation, and that intervention should focus on bolstering the network of relationships.

In addition to building on the pioneering work of Lindemann and Caplan, Lydia Rapoport was one of the first practitioners to write about the linkage of modalities such as ego psychology, learning theory, and traditional social casework (Rapoport, 1967). In Rapoport's first article on crisis theory (1962), she defined a crisis as "an upset of a steady state" (p. 212) that places the individual in a hazardous condition. She pointed out that a crisis situation results in a problem that can be perceived as a threat, a loss, or a challenge. She then stated that there are usually three interrelated factors that create a state of crisis:

1. A hazardous event
2. A threat to life goals
3. An inability to respond with adequate coping mechanisms

In their early works, Lindemann and Caplan briefly mentioned that a hazardous event produces a crisis, but it was Rapoport (1967) who most thoroughly described the nature of this crisis-precipitating event. She clearly conceptualized the content of crisis intervention practice, particularly the initial or study phase (assessment). She began by pointing out that in order to help persons in crisis, the client must have rapid access to the crisis worker. She stated: "A little help, rationally directed and purposefully focused at a strategic time, is more effective than more extensive help given at a period of less emotional accessibility" (Rapoport, 1967, p. 38).

This point was echoed by Naomi Golan (1978), who concluded that during the state of active crisis, when usual coping methods have proved inadequate and the individual and his or her family are suffering from pain and discomfort, a person is frequently more amenable to suggestions and change. Clearly, intensive, brief, appropriately focused treatment when the client is motivated can produce more effective change than long-term treatment when motivation and emotional accessibility are lacking.

Rapoport (1967) asserted that during the initial interview, the first task of the practitioner is to develop a preliminary diagnosis of the presenting problem. It is most critical during this first interview that the crisis therapist convey a sense of hope and optimism to the client concerning successful crisis resolution. Rapoport suggested that this sense of hope and enthusiasm can be properly conveyed to the client when the interview focuses on mutual exploration and problem solving, along with clearly delineated goals and tasks. The underlying message is that client and therapist will be working together to resolve the crisis.

Seeking Help

In the late 1960s the suicide prevention movement took hold, and suicide prevention centers were established across the United States. From the outset, the initial request for help was generally made via a telephone hotline, a practice that continues to the present day. Aided by funding from the National Institute of Mental Health's Center for Studies of Suicide Prevention, these centers grew from 28 in 1966 to almost 200 by 1972. They built on Caplan's crisis theory and the work of Edwin Schneidman and Norman Farberow at the Los Angeles Suicide Prevention Center (Roberts, 1975, 1979).

An enormous boost to the development of crisis intervention programs and units came about as a result of the community mental health movement. The availability of 24-hour crisis intervention and emergency services was considered a major component of any comprehensive community mental health center (CMHC). As a prerequisite to receiving federal funding under the Community Mental Health Centers Act of 1963, CMHCs were required to include an emergency services component in their system plan. During the 1970s the number of CMHCs that contained crisis intervention units grew rapidly, more than doubling from 376 centers in 1969 to 796 as of 1980 (Foley & Sharfstein, 1983).

What motivates people in crisis to seek help? Ripple, Alexander, and Polemis (1964) suggest that a balance of discomfort and hope is necessary to motivate a distressed person to seek help. Hope as defined by Stotland (1969) is the perceived possibility of attaining a goal.

The crisis clinician knows that coping patterns differ for each of us. The crisis clinician also knows that for an individual to suffer and survive a crisis (such as losing a loved one, living through an earthquake or a tornado, attempting suicide, or being sexually assaulted), he or she must have a conscious purpose to live and grow. Each individual in crisis must define his or her own purpose. Persons in crisis need to ventilate, to be accepted, and to receive support, assistance, and encouragement to discover the paths to crisis resolution.

It is useful for the client to understand the specific personal meaning of the event and how it conflicts with his or her expectations, life goals, and belief system. Thoughts, feelings, and beliefs usually flow out freely when a client in crisis talks. The crisis clinician should listen carefully and note any cognitive errors or distortions (overgeneralizing, catastrophizing) or irrational beliefs. The clinician should avoid prematurely stating rational beliefs or reality-based cognitions for the client. Instead, the he or she should help the client to recognize discrepancies, distortions, and irrational beliefs. This is best accomplished through carefully worded questions such as "How do you view yourself now that you realize that everyone with less than 5 years' seniority got laid off?" or "Have you ever asked your doctor whether he thinks you will die from cancer at a young age or what your actual risk of getting cancer is?"

CRISIS INTERVENTION MODELS AND STRATEGIES

Several systematic practice models and techniques have been developed for crisis intervention work. The crisis intervention model applied in this book builds on and synthesizes those developed by Caplan (1964), Golan (1978), Parad (1965), Roberts (1991, 1998), and Roberts and Dziegielewski (1995). All of these practice models and techniques focus on resolving immediate problems and emotional conflicts through a minimum number of contacts. Crisis-oriented treatment is time limited and goal directed, in contrast to long-term psychotherapy, which can take several years to complete.

Crisis intervenors should "adopt a role which is active and directive without taking problem ownership" away from the individual in crisis prematurely (Fairchild, 1986, p. 6). The skilled crisis intervenor should display acceptance and hopefulness in order to communicate to persons in crisis that their intense emotional turmoil and threatening situations are not hopeless, and that, in fact, they (like others in similar situations before them) will survive the crisis successfully and become better prepared for potentially hazardous life events in the future.

In order to become an effective crisis intervenor, it is important to gauge the stages and completeness of the intervention. The following seven-stage paradigm should be viewed as a guide, not as a rigid process, since with some clients stages may overlap.

Roberts's (1991) seven-stage model of crisis intervention (Figure 1.1) has been utilized for helping persons in acute psychological crisis, acute situational crises, and acute stress disorders. The seven stages are as follows:

1. Plan and conduct a thorough assessment (including lethality, dangerousness to self or others, and immediate psychosocial needs).
2. Make psychological contact, establish rapport, and rapidly establish the relationship (conveying genuine respect for the client, acceptance, reassurance, and a nonjudgmental attitude).
3. Examine the dimensions of the problem in order to define it (including the last straw or precipitating event).
4. Encourage an exploration of feelings and emotions.
5. Generate, explore, and assess past coping attempts.

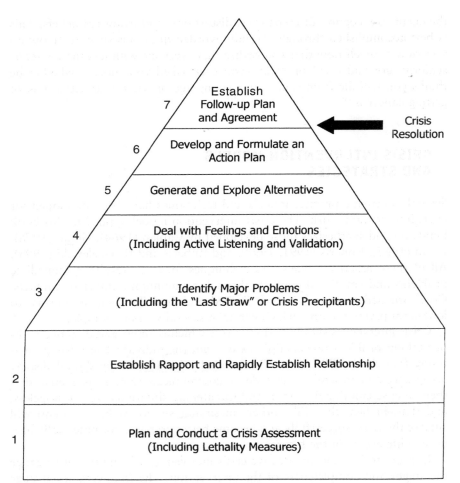

Figure 1.1   Roberts's Seven-Stage Crisis Intervention Model

6) Restore cognitive functioning through implementation of action plan.
7) Follow up and leave the door open for booster sessions 3 and/or 6 months later.

1. *Plan and conduct a thorough psychosocial and lethality assessment.* In many cases, stages 1 and 2 occur at the same time. However, first and foremost, basic information needs to be obtained in order to determine whether the caller is in imminent danger. Crisis clinicians are trained to perform an ongoing, rapid risk assessment with all clients in crisis. Crisis counselors, psychologists, and social workers encounter a full range of self-destructive individuals in crisis, including those who have taken potentially lethal drug

overdoses, depressed and lonely callers who have attempted suicide, and impulsive acting-out adolescents threatening to injure someone. In cases of imminent danger, emergency medical or police intervention is often necessary. All suicide prevention and other 24-hour crisis hotlines have access to paramedics and emergency medical technicians, poison control centers, the police, and the emergency rescue squad. It is critically important for the crisis intervenor to be in close contact with the crisis caller before, during, and after medical stabilization and discharge.

In many other crisis situations, there is some potential for danger and harm. As a result of potential danger to crisis callers with a history of reckless driving, binge drinking, chemical dependency, bi-polar disorder, explosive anger, passive aggressive behavior, schizophrenia, and/or preoccupation with suicidal thoughts or fantasies, it is imperative that crisis intervenors use stages 1 through 7 of Roberts's model as a guide to crisis intervention. Assessments of *imminent danger and potential lethality* should examine the following factors:

- Determine whether the crisis caller needs medical attention (e.g., drug overdose, suicide attempt, or domestic violence).
- Is the crisis caller thinking about killing herself or himself? (Are these general thoughts, or does the caller have a specific suicide plan or pact, with the location, time, and method specified?)
- Determine whether the caller is a victim of domestic violence, sexual assault, and/or other violent crime. If the caller is a victim, ask whether the batterer is nearby or likely to return soon.
- Determine whether any children are in danger.
- Does the victim need emergency transportation to the hospital or a shelter?
- Is the crisis caller under the influence of alcohol or drugs?
- Is the caller about to injure herself or himself (e.g., self-injurious behaviors or self-mutilations)?
- Inquire whether there are any violent individuals living in the residence (e.g., assaultive boarders or perpetrators of elder abuse or sibling abuse).

If time permits, the risk assessment should include the following (recognize that a client who is in imminent danger needs to go immediately to a safe place):

- In domestic violence situations, determine the nature of the caller's previous efforts to protect herself or her children, in order to determine her ability to protect herself.
- In order to fully assess the perpetrator's threat in cases of domestic violence, inquire into the batterer's criminal history, physical abuse history, substance abuse history, destruction of property, impulsive acts, history of mental disorders, previous psychiatric diagnosis, previous suicide

threats or gestures, stalking behavior, and erratic employment or long
periods of unemployment.
- If the caller is a victim of a violent crime, is there a history of prior visits
to the hospital emergency room for physical abuse, drug overdose, or
suicide attempts?
- Are there any guns or rifles in the home?
- Has anyone recently used a weapon against the caller?
- Has the caller received any terroristic threats, including death threats?
- Determine whether the caller is suffering from major depression, intense
anxiety, phobic reactions, agitation, paranoid delusions, acute stress disorder, adjustment disorder, personality disorder, post tramatic stress disorder (PTSD), and/or sleep disturbances.

2. *Make psychological contact and rapidly establish the relationship.*
This second stage involves the initial contact between the crisis intervenor
and the potential client. The main task for the clinician at this point is to
establish rapport by conveying genuine respect for and acceptance of the
client. The client also often needs reassurance that he or she can be helped
and that this is the appropriate place to receive such help. For example,
sufferers of obsessive-compulsive disorders (OCDs) and phobias, such as agoraphobia, often believe that they will never get better. This is often the case
when they have been misdiagnosed with a psychosis or personality disorder
by a crisis clinician who has never seen patients with OCD or agoraphobia.
If the crisis clinician has helped many other clients suffering from agoraphobia, he or she should describe the situation of a previous client who at one
point could not even leave his room for a 4-month period and now is married and successfully working 5 days a week outside of his home.

3. *Examine the dimensions of the problem in order to define it.* It is
useful to try to identify the following: (a) the "last straw," or the precipitating event that led the client to seek help; (b) previous coping methods; and
(c) dangerousness or lethality. Crisis counselors should explore these dimensions through specific open-ended questions. The focus must be on *now* and
how rather than *then* and *why.* For example, key questions would be: "What
situation or event led you to seek help at this time?" and "When did this
event take place?"

4. *Encourage an exploration of feelings and emotions.* This step is closely
related to examining and defining the dimensions of the problem, particularly the precipitating event. It is presented here as a separate step because
some therapists overlook it in their attempt to make rapid assessment and
find the precipitating event. It is extremely therapeutic for a client to ventilate and express feelings and emotions in an accepting, supportive, private,
and nonjudgmental setting.

The primary technique for identifying a client's feelings and emotions is
through *active listening.* This involves the crisis intervenor listening in an

empathic and supportive way to both the client's reflection of what happened and how the client feels about the crisis event.

5. *Explore and assess past coping attempts.* Most youths and adults have developed several coping mechanisms—some adaptive, some less adaptive, and some inadequate—as responses to the crisis event. Basically, an emotionally hazardous event becomes an emotional crisis when the "usual homeostatic, direct problem-solving mechanisms do not work" (Caplan, 1964, p. 39). Thus, attempts to cope fail. One of the major foci of crisis intervention involves identifying and modifying the client's coping behaviors at both the preconscious and the conscious level. It is important for the crisis intervenor to attempt to bring to the conscious level the client's coping responses that now operate just below the surface, at the preconscious level, and then to educate the client in modifying maladaptive coping behaviors. Specifically, it is useful to ask the client how certain situations are handled, such as feelings of intense anger, loss of a loved one (a child or spouse), disappointment, or failure.

Solution-based therapy should be integrated into crisis intervention at this stage. This method emphasizes working with client strengths. The client is viewed as being very resourceful and having untapped resources or latent inner coping skills from which to draw upon. This approach utilizes specifically explicated clinical techniques (e.g., the miracle question, the partial miracle question, the scaling technique) appropriate for crisis intervention practice. Solution-focused therapy and the strengths perspective view the client as resilient. The resilient person generally has sufficiently high self-esteem, a social support network, and the necessary problem-solving skills to bounce back, cope with, and thrive in the aftermath of stressful life events or traumatic events.

Integrating strengths and solution-focused approaches involves jogging clients' memories so they recall the last time everything seemed to be going well, and they were in a good mood rather than depressed and/or successfully dealt with a previous crisis in their lives. These are some examples of components in a solution focused approach:

- How would you have coped with the divorce or death of your parents when you were in a good mood?
- Write a letter to your parents, letting them know that you are setting a specific goal for yourself in order to make them proud of the values and ambition they instilled within you.
- If your deceased parents are in heaven looking down on you, what could you do to make them proud?

See chapters 2 and 12 for thorough applications of crisis intervention and brief solution-focused therapy with suicidal, abused, unemployed, and drug-addicted clients.

It is important to help the client to generate and explore alternatives and previously untried coping methods or partial solutions. If possible, this involves collaboration between the client and the crisis intervenor to generate alternatives. It is also important at this stage to explore the consequences and client's feelings about each alternative. Most clients have some notion of what should be done to cope with the crisis situation, but they may well need assistance from the crisis clinician in order to define and conceptualize more adaptive coping responses. In cases where the client has little or no introspection or personal insights, the clinician needs to take the initiative and suggest more adaptive coping methods. Defining and conceptualizing more adaptive coping behaviors can be a highly productive component in helping the client resolve the crisis situation.

6. *Restore cognitive functioning through implementation of an action plan.* The basic premise underlying a cognitive approach to crisis resolution is that the ways in which external events and a person's cognitions of the events turn into personal crisis are based on cognitive factors. The crisis clinician who uses a cognitive approach helps the client focus on why a specific event leads to a crisis state (e.g., it violates a person's expectancies) and, simultaneously, what the client can do to effectively master the experience and be able to cope with similar events should they occur in the future. Cognitive mastery involves three phases. First, the client needs to obtain a realistic understanding of what happened and what led to the crisis. In order to move beyond the crisis and get on with life, the client must understand what happened, why it happened, who was involved, and the final outcome (e.g., being locked out of one's house, a suicide attempt, death of an adolescent, a divorce, a child being battered).

Second, it is useful for the client to understand the event's specific meaning: how it conflicts with his or her expectations, life goals, and belief system. Thoughts and belief statements usually flow freely when a client in crisis talks. The crisis intervenor should listen carefully and note any cognitive errors or distortions (overgeneralizing, catastrophizing) or irrational beliefs. The clinician should avoid prematurely stating the rational beliefs or reality-based cognitions for the client. Instead, the clinician should help the client discover distortions and irrational beliefs. This can be facilitated through carefully worded questions such as "Do you still want to move out of state now that you know that the person who raped you and brutally killed his previous two victims will be executed today in the electric chair?" or "Have you ever asked your doctor whether he thinks you will die from a heart attack at a young age?"

The third and final part of cognitive mastery involves restructuring, rebuilding, or replacing irrational beliefs and erroneous cognitions with rational beliefs and new cognitions. This may involve providing new information through cognitive restructuring, homework assignments, or referral to others who have lived through and mastered a similar crisis (e.g., a support group for widows, for rape victims, or for students who have been confronted with school violence).

2. *Follow up*. At the final session the client should be told that if at any time he or she needs to come back for another session, the door will be open and the clinician will be available. Sometimes clients cancel their second, third, or fourth appointment prior to resolving the crisis. For example, a client who was raped at knifepoint is up half the night prior to her appointment with her clinician. She mistakenly thinks her nightmares and insomnia are caused by the clinician. In actuality, she has not come to grips with her vulnerabilities and fears that the rapist will return. The clinician, knowing that victims of violent crimes often go into crisis at the anniversary of the crime—exactly 1 month or 1 year after the victimization—informs the client that she would like to see her again, and that as soon as she calls she will be given an emergency appointment the same day.

CRISIS INTERVENTION UNITS AND 24-HOUR HOTLINES

Where can persons in crisis turn for help? How do they find the phone number of the crisis intervention program in their area? Police officers and hospital emergency room staff are available 24 hours a day, 7 days a week. In fact, on weekends and at night they are often the only help available. The police or an information operator can give a person in crisis the name of a local hotline, a community crisis center, the crisis intervention unit at the local community mental health center, a rape crisis center, a battered women's shelter, or a family crisis intervention program that provides home-based crisis services. In addition, many large cities have information and referral networks funded by the United Way, the Community Service Society, or the American Red Cross. These information and referral (I and R) services give crisis callers the phone numbers of community agencies in their localities. Unfortunately, because of limited resources, some of these information and crisis lines are available only from 8:30 A.M. to 5:00 P.M.

The information and referral services throughout the United States, which number in excess of 30,000, operate under different organizational auspices, including traditional social service agencies, community mental health centers, public libraries, police departments, shopping malls, women's centers, travelers' aid centers, youth crisis centers, and area agencies on aging (Levinson, 1999). The goal of information and referral networks is to facilitate access to services and to overcome the many barriers that obstruct entry to needed resources (Levinson, 1988, p. 7). According to the United Way of America, "I and R is a service which informs, guides, directs and links people in need to the appropriate human service which alleviates or eliminates the need" (1980, p. 3).

Some information and referral networks are generic and provide information to the public on all community services, including crisis centers. Others are more specialized and focus on meeting the needs of callers such as those who are depressed and have suicide ideation, children and youths in crisis, women in crisis, survivors of violent crimes, runaways and homeless youths, or the elderly.

The *primary objective* of a crisis intervention program is to intervene at the earliest possible stage. Thus, given the immediacy and rapid response rate of telephone crisis counseling and referrals, 24-hour crisis lines generally meet their objective (Waters and Finn, 1995). With the development of crisis centers nationwide, there has been a considerable increase in the use of the telephone as a method of rapid crisis assessment and management. The 24-hour telephone crisis service maximizes the immediacy and availability of crisis intervention. It also provides anonymity to the caller while allowing the intervenor to assess the risk of suicide and imminent danger. The telephone crisis intervenor is trained to establish rapport with the caller, conduct a brief assessment, provide a sympathetic ear, help develop a crisis management plan, and/or refer the caller to an appropriate treatment program or service. In most cases effective crisis resolution can be facilitated by suicide prevention hotlines as long as they provide referral and follow-up services.

Waters and Finn (1995) have identified and discussed the goals of 13 types of crisis hotlines for special and high-risk groups:

- Career-oriented and job information hotlines
- Employee assistance hotlines
- Information and referral hotline for dementia caregivers
- Kidline
- Media call-ins
- Police emergency calls (911)
- Substance abuse crisis lines
- Suicide prevention hotlines
- Teen lines
- Telephone reassurance programs for the elderly
- Telephone crisis treatment for agoraphobia
- University-based counseling hotlines
- 24-hour availability for telephone therapy with one of the 300 licensed family therapists, psychologists, or social workers on call

Suicide Prevention and Crisis Centers

Suicide prevention services began in London England, in 1906 when the Salvation Army opened an antisuicide bureau aimed at helping persons who had attempted suicide. At about the same time, the Reverend Harry M. Warren (a minister and pastoral counselor) opened the National Save-a-Life League in New York City. Over the years the league's 24-hour hotline has been answered by full-time staff, by trained volunteers, and, in a few instances, by consulting psychiatrists who have served on the agency's board of directors.

In the 1960s and early 1970s, federal funding was made available as a result of the Community Mental Health Centers Act of 1963 and by the National Institute of Mental Health (NIMH). Between 1968 and 1972, almost 200 suicide prevention centers were established (Roberts, 1979, p. 398). In the United States and Canada that number now has increased more than sevenfold. See chapters 2, 5, 6, 15, and 16 for detailed examinations of crisis intervention and follow-up treatment of depressed children, youth, and adults, and of persons with suicide ideation and prior suicide attempts.

At about the same time that 24-hour suicide prevention centers were developing and expanding, crisis units of community mental health centers were also being established throughout the United States. The overriding goal of both types of crisis intervention programs was rapid assessment and early intervention for potentially suicidal callers. There was an emphasis in the late 1960s and throughout the 1970s on 24-hour telephone crisis intervention, outreach to clients in the community, and, on a more limited scale, 24-hour mobile crisis units, which were part of the community mental health centers. See chapters 15 and 16 for a detailed examination of two 24-hour mobile crisis intervention units currently saving numerous lives in the communities of Erie, Pennsylvania, and Atlanta, Georgia.

National Domestic Violence Hotline

A 24-hour, toll-free, national domestic violence hotline became operational in February 1996. Operated by the Texas Council on Family Violence in Austin, this crisis phone line provides immediate crisis assessment and intervention, as well as referrals to emergency services and shelters throughout the United States. The national hotline received an initial $1-million-dollar grant from the U.S. Department of Health and Human Services, and its annual budget is $1.2 million per year.

In January 1997 the Center for Social Work Research at the School of Social Work of the University of Texas at Austin completed the first evaluation study of the National Domestic Violence Hotline (NDVH; McRoy, Danis, and Lewis, 1997). The high frequency of incoming calls to the NDVH—61,677 calls during its first 6 months of operation—is an important initial indicator of success. The volume of calls far exceeded expectations.

The hotline has an electronic phone-tracking system that monitors the number of incoming calls, the average length of calls, the busiest call times, and the number of calls received from all the different area codes. The NDVH also has an internal database consisting of the information logs the hotline workers complete on each caller.

The national hotline averaged 300 calls per day, with the highest volume days handling more than 2,000 calls. Calls are distributed throughout the

United States, with all 50 states represented. The highest and the lowest use states, based on phone bills, are as shown in Table 1-1.

Another important measure of effectiveness is the extent to which hotline workers linked domestic violence callers in crisis to community resources such as an emergency shelter. During the first 6 months of operation, 89% of the 24,441 referrals were made to shelters for battered women. In addition, 80% of the shelters receiving referrals from the national hotline have indicated that they operate their own local 24-hour hotline (Lewis, Danis, and McRoy, 1997).

There seem to be two primary reasons for the high visibility and large number of calls. First and foremost, the national hotline is highly visible due to public service announcements made in conjunction with television movies on domestic violence and other major media campaigns. Second, the hotline provides immediate information for women who plan to move or are in transit to another state to escape from the batterer, and thus most likely are unfamiliar with shelters and transitional housing in a different area.

It is important to point out that the phone bill by design protects callers' anonymity. No information provided by phone records can be connected to identifiable information on actual callers.

In-depth interviews were conducted with all hotline workers to determine what they considered the most important crisis intervention technique they provided to callers. The three most important crisis services or techniques were actively listening, making referrals, and being empathetic with callers (Lewis, Danis, and McRoy, 1997, p. c13).

Table 1.1   Volume of Calls From the 15 States With the Highest and Lowest Utilization

States	Number
Highest Use	
1. California	8,645
2. Texas	7,151
3. New York	4,433
4. Florida	2,873
5. Pennsylvania	2,353
6. Ohio	2,268
7. New Jersey	2,223
Lowest Use	
1. Virgin Islands	21
2. Puerto Rico	91
3. North Dakota	104
4. Vermont	107
5. South Dakota	120
6. Alaska	132
7. Wyoming	150
8. Rhode Island	150

Child Abuse Hotlines and Referral Networks

Childhelp USA operates a national tollfree (1-800-4-A-Child) child abuse hotline dedicated to the prevention of physical and emotional abuse of children. It is staffed 24 hours a day with professional crisis counselors and serves the United States, Canada, U.S. Virgin Islands, and Puerto Rico. Between its inception in 1982 and the end of 1999, it had received more than 2 million calls. It utilizes a database of 55,000 resources.

A number of states, cities, and counties have developed hotlines for reporting suspected cases of child abuse and neglect. Early case finding and rapid investigation and intervention can lead to resolving crisis situations and preventing further child maltreatment. Many communities have also developed parental stress hotline services, which provide immediate intervention for potentially abusive parents who are at risk of injuring their child. These crisis intervention hotlines offer supportive reassurance, advice, and nonjudgmental listening from trained volunteers. The hotlines are usually available on a toll-free basis, 24 hours a day, 7 days a week.

Respite centers or crisis nurseries are available in most large cities to provide parents in crisis with temporary relief from child care. For example, New York City's Foundling Hospital has a crisis nursery where parents can take their children and leave them overnight when they fear they may lose control and inflict injury.

Rape Crisis Programs

Programs for rape crisis have been developed by medical centers, community mental health centers, women's counseling centers, crisis clinics, and police departments. Social workers at rape crisis organizations provide crisis intervention, advocacy, support, education, and referral to community resources. Crisis intervention generally involves an initial visit or accompaniment from a social worker, crisis counselor, or nurse while the victim is being examined in the hospital emergency room. Although follow-up is often handled through telephone counseling, in-person counseling sessions may take place when the victim is in distress. In several parts of the country, rape crisis programs have begun support groups for sexual assault victims. See chapter 11 for a comprehensive review of assessment and crisis intervention strategies for rape and incest survivors.

Battered Women's Shelters and Hotlines

A number of state legislatures have enacted legislation that provides special grants, contracts, and city/county general revenue funding for hotlines and shelters for victims of domestic violence. There are crisis intervention services for battered women and their children in every state and major metropolitan area in the country. The primary focus of these services is to ensure the women's safety, but many shelters have evolved into much more than just a place for safe lodging. Crisis intervention for battered women generally entails a 24-hour telephone hotline, safe and secure emergency shelter (the average length of stay being 3 to 4 weeks), an underground network of volunteer homes and shelters, and welfare and court advocacy by student interns and other volunteers (Roberts, 1998). Shelters also provide peer counseling, support groups, information on women's legal rights, and referral to social service agencies.

In some communities, emergency services for battered women have been expanded to include parenting education workshops, assistance in finding housing, employment counseling and job placement for the women, and group counseling for batterers. In the all-too-often neglected area of assessment and treatment for the children of battered women, a small but growing number of shelters provides either group counseling or referral to mental health centers, as needed. For a more complete discussion of crisis intervention practices with battered women and their children, see chapter 8.

Case Example

The Victim Services Agency in New York has a 24-hour crime victim and domestic violence hotline, staffed by 68 counselors and 20 volunteers, that responded to approximately 71,000 callers in 1998. The following is a case illustration of a battered woman who required many calls, hours of commitment from the crisis worker, and case coordination to resolve her life-threatening situational crisis.

Jasmine

An emergency call was received at 8:00 one morning from Jasmine, the 15-year-old daughter of Serita, who begged the crisis worker to help her mom, frantically explaining, "My mom's live-in boyfriend is going to kill her." The crisis worker reported that the daughter described previous incidents of violence perpetrated by the boyfriend. Jasmine described a serious argument that had erupted at 6:00 that morning, with loud yelling from the boyfriend, who threatened to kill Serita with the gun he had recently obtained, while pointing it directly at her.

The crisis worker tried to build rapport with the terrified girl, asking where her mother was and whether she could be reached by phone. Jasmine replied that her mother had escaped temporarily to a neighbor's apartment as soon as the boyfriend stormed out of the apartment following a visit from the police, which had occurred a few minutes before Jasmine made her phone call to the Victim Services Agency.

Jasmine gave the worker the neighbor's phone number, and the worker called Serita there. The neighbor had called the police at 6:45 A.M. because of the yelling and fighting in the nearby apartment. The boyfriend had previously told Serita that if anyone ever called the police, he would kill her. After the police were called by the neighbor, Serita knew that her boyfriend's violent temper would become even worse. She was terrified to go to a local battered women's shelter, fearing that he would track her down and kill her.

Serita had a sister living in Georgia, who was willing to take her and Jasmine in on a temporary basis. The advantage of staying with her sister was that Serita had never talked to her boyfriend about where her sister lived, telling him just that it was "down South," and had never mentioned her sister's last name, which was different from Serita's. She believed he would never be able to find her if she traveled so far away from New York.

The worker needed to quickly coordinate plans with Travelers' Aid to provide a bus ticket for Serita and her daughter to travel to Georgia that evening. Serita obtained an Order of Protection, and the police took the batterer's keys to the apartment. For a period of time during the afternoon, the batterer watched the apartment from across the street.

A taxi cab (which had a special arrangement with Victim Services) was called to take Serita and Jasmine to Travelers' Aid to pick up the bus ticket for her trip to Georgia. The driver needed to wait until the boyfriend left the area before arriving at the apartment. The crisis worker felt that secrecy was necessary to avoid the inevitable confrontation that would have ensued if the boyfriend had seen Serita leaving the apartment with all her luggage.

Serita's escape from the batterer was handled flawlessly; she reached Georgia, with the batterer unaware of her plans or her intended destination. Serita and Jasmine stayed with Serita's sister until her Section 8 housing paperwork was transferred from New York to Georgia.

The next chapter, by Gilbert Greene, Mo-Yee-Lee, Rhonda Trask, and Judy Rheinscheld demonstrates through case illustrations how to tap into and bolster clients' strengths in crisis intervention. The chapter demonstrates how to integrate Roberts's seven-stage crisis intervention model with solution-focused treatment in a stepwise manner. The crisis clinician utilizing this integrated strengths approach serves as a catalyst and facilitator for clients discovering their own resources and coping skills. Greene et al. systematically bolster their clients by emphasizing the person's resilience, inner strengths, and ability to bounce back and continue to grow emotionally. This highly practical overview chapter aptly applies the strengths-based approach to a diverse range of clients in crisis situations.

I firmly believe that crisis intervention which focuses on the client's inner strengths and resilience, and that seeks partial and full solutions will become the short-term treatment of choice during the first quarter of the twenty-first century.

SUMMARY

It is clear, in reviewing current progress in applying time-limited crisis intervention approaches to persons in acute crisis, that we have come a long way in the past decade. Crisis intervention is provided by several hundred voluntary crisis centers and crisis lines; by most of the 790 community mental health centers and their satellite programs; and by the majority of the 9,000 victim assistance, child abuse, sexual assault, and battered women's programs, available throughout the country. In addition, crisis services are provided at thousands of local hospital emergency rooms, hospital-based emergency psychiatric services, suicide prevention centers, crisis nurseries, local United Way–funded information lines, and pastoral counseling services. The crisis services that have proliferated in recent years are often directed toward particular groups, such as rape victims, battered women, adolescent suicide attemptors, victims of school violence as well as students who were in the building but were not directly harmed, separated and divorced individuals, abusive parents, and victims of disasters. The increased development of crisis services and units reflects a growing awareness among public health and mental health administrators of the critical need for community crisis services.

This handbook provides an up-to-date, comprehensive examination of the crisis model and its application to persons suffering from an acute crisis. Most social workers, clinical psychologists, marital and family therapists, and counselors agree that crisis theory and the crisis intervention approach provide an extremely useful focus for handling all types of acute crisis. Almost every distressed person who calls or visits a community mental health center, victim assistance program, rape crisis unit or program, battered women's shelter, substance abuse treatment program, or suicide prevention program can be viewed as being in some form of crisis. By providing rapid assessments and timely responses, clinicians can formulate effective and economically feasible plans for time-limited crisis intervention.

REFERENCES

Aguilera, D. C., & Messick, J. M. (1982). *Crisis intervention: Theory and methodology*. St. Louis, MO: C. V. Mosby.

Bard, M., & Ellison, K. (1974, May). Crisis intervention and investigation of forcible rape. *The Police Chief, 41,* 68–73.

Bellak, L., & Siegel, H. (1983). *Handbook of intensive brief and emergency psychotherapy*. Larchmont, NY: CRS.

Burns, D. D. (1980). *Feeling good*. New York: New American Library.

Caplan, G. (1961). *An approach to community mental health*. New York: Grune and Stratton.

Caplan, G. (1964). *Principles of preventive psychiatry*. New York: Basic Books.

Fairchild, T. N. (1986). *Crisis intervention strategies for school-based helpers.* Springfield, IL: Charles C. Thomas.

Foley, H. A., & Sharfstein, S. S. (1983). *Madness and Government: Who Cares for the Mentally Ill?* Washington, D.C.: American Psychiatric Press.

Golan, N. (1978). *Treatment in crisis situations.* New York: Free Press.

Halpern, H. A. (1973). Crisis theory: A definitional study. *Community Mental Health Journal, 9,* 342–349.

Kadushin, A., & Martin, J. A. (1988). *Child welfare services* (4th ed.). New York: Macmillan.

Levinson, R. (October 1, 1999). Personal Communication.

Levinson, R. W. (1988). *Information and referral networks.* New York: Springer.

Lewis, C. M., Danis, F., and McRoy, R. (1997). *Evaluation of the National Domestic Violence Hotline.* Austin: University of Texas at Austin, Center for Social Work Research.

Lindemann, E. (1944). Symptomatology and management of acute grief. *American Journal of Psychiatry, 101,* 141–148.

Meichenbaum, D., & Jaremko, M. E. (1983). *Stress reduction and prevention.* New York: Plenum.

Parad, H. J. (1965). *Crisis intervention: Selected readings.* New York: Family Service Association of America.

Parad, H. J. (1971). Crisis Intervention. In R. Morris (Ed.), *Encyclopedia of social work* (Vol. 1, pp. 196–202). New York: National Association of Social Workers.

Parad, H. J., & Caplan, G. (1960). A framework for studying families in crisis. *Social Work, 5*(3), 3–15.

Rapoport, L. (1962). The state of crisis: Some theoretical considerations. *Social Service Review, 36,* 211–217.

Rapoport, L. (1967). Crisis-Oriented Short-Term Casework, *Social Service Review* 41, 31–43.

Ripple, L., Alexander, E., & Polemis, B. (1964). *Motivation, capacity, and opportunity.* Chicago: University of Chicago Press.

Roberts, A. R. (1975). *Self-Destructive Behavior.* Springfield, IL: Charles C. Thomas.

Roberts, A. R. (1979). Organization of suicide prevention agencies. In L. D. Hankoff & B. Einsidler (Eds.), *Suicide: Theory and clinical aspects* (pp. 391–399). Littleton, MA: PSG Publishing.

Roberts, A. R. (1984). *Battered women and their families.* New York: Springer.

Roberts, A. R. (1991). Conceptualizing crisis theory and the crisis intervention model. In A. R. Roberts (Ed.), *Contemporary perspectives on crisis intervention and prevention* (pp. 3–17). Englewood Cliffs, NJ: Prentice-Hall.

Roberts, A. R. (1995). Crisis intervention units and centers in the united states: A national survey. In A. R. Roberts (Ed.), *Crisis intervention and time-limited cognitive treatment* (pp. 54–70). Thousand Oaks, CA: Sage.

Roberts, A. R. (1998). *Battered women and their families: Intervention strategies and treatment programs* (2nd ed.). New York: Springer.

Roberts, A. R., & M. Camasso (1994). Staff turnover at crisis intervention units and programs: A national survey. *Crisis Intervention and Time-Limited Treatment, 1*(1), 1–9.

Roberts, A. R., & S. F. Dziegielewski. (1995). Foundation skills and applications of crisis intervention and cognitive therapy. In A. R. Roberts (Ed.), *Crisis intervention and time-limited cognitive treatment* (pp. 3–27). Thousand Oaks, CA: Sage.

Slaby, A. E. (1985). Crisis-oriented therapy. In Frank R. Lipton & Stephen M. Goldfinger (Eds.), *Emergency psychiatry at the crossroads* (pp. 21–34). San Francisco: Jossey-Bass.

Stotland, E. (1969). *The psychology of hope.* San Francisco: Jossey-Bass.

Tyhurst, J. S. (1957). The role of transition states—including disasters—in mental illness. In *Symposium on preventive and social psychiatry* (pp. 1–23). Washington, DC: Walter Reed Army Institute of Research.

United Way of America. (1980). *Information and referral: Programmed resource and training course.* Alexandria, VA: Author.

Viney, L. L. (1976). The concept of crisis: A tool for clinical psychologists. *Bulletin of the British Psychological Society, 29,* 387–395.

Waters, J., & Finn, E. (1995). Handling client crises effectively on the telephone. In A. R. Roberts (Ed.), *Crisis intervention and time-limited cognitive treatment* (pp. 251–189). Thousand Oaks, CA: Sage.

2

How to Work With Clients' Strengths in Crisis Intervention

A Solution-Focused Approach

GILBERT J. GREENE
MO-YEE LEE
RHONDA TRASK
JUDY RHEINSCHELD

Through a review of literature, theory, and case examples, this chapter will address the following:

- How to use solution-focused therapy in working with the strengths of clients in crisis
- How to structure a solution-focused/strengths-based approach to crisis intervention in a stepwise manner
- How to consistently engage clients in "change talk" and not stay stuck in "problem talk"
- How to co-construct with clients outcome goals that include a future without the presenting problem
- How to develop homework tasks that are consistent with enhancing client strengths

According to Roberts (1991), a crisis is "a period of psychological disequilibrium, experienced as a result of a hazardous event or situation that constitutes a significant problem that cannot be remedied by using familiar coping strategies" (p. 4). Crisis intervention tends to view the precipitating event as overwhelming the client's usual coping skills (strengths); consequently, these coping skills are inadequate to meet the challenge of the precipitating event. The Chinese translation of the word *crisis* consists of two separate characters that literally mean "danger" and "opportunity." Crisis intervention views the provision of services to clients in crisis as an "opportunity" for clients to learn new coping skills. In fact, the literature has consistently stressed that clients need to develop new resources and coping skills in order for crisis intervention to be successful (Roberts and Dziegielewski, 1995; Roberts, 1996; Kanel, 1999). The emphasis throughout the crisis intervention literature has overwhelmingly been on how to help clients develop new coping skills.

People in crisis also have the "opportunity" to further identify, mobilize, and enhance the strengths (coping skills) they already have. Some scholars have stated that crisis intervenors should also identify and work with clients' personal strengths (Parad & Parad, 1990; Puryear, 1979; Roberts, 1991); however, the crisis intervention literature lacks a clear explication of how to specifically operationalize doing this. One possible source for information on how to operationalize working with clients' strengths in crisis intervention is the *strengths perspective* (Rapp, 1998; Saleeby, 1992, 1997).

The strengths perspective views clients as having the resources and coping skills for successfully handling crisis situations but they are not using them, are underusing them, or are not aware that they are using them (Saleebey, 1997). The job of the clinician using this approach is to help clients tap into the resources within themselves (Saleebey, 1997). A clinician, therefore, does not change people but serves as a catalyst for clients discovering and using their own resources to accomplish their goals (Saleeby, 1997). General guidelines for the clinical use of the strengths perspective have been discussed in the literature (Cowger, 1994; Rapp, 1998); however, a more specific operationalization of its use in conducting and facilitating the therapeutic conversations that make up clinical practice generally and crisis intervention specifically is lacking.

One approach to clinical practice that emphasizes working with client strengths is *solution-focused therapy*, which has been developing since the 1970s and emphasizes working only with client strengths (de Shazer, 1985; de Shazer et al., 1986), This approach provides specifically defined clinician behaviors that are very appropriate for operationalizing a strengths perspective in the practice of crisis intervention. Like the strengths perspective, solution-focused therapy views clients as being very resourceful and assumes they have all they need to solve their problems (Walter & Peller, 1992). Only recently, however, has the use of solution-focused therapy in operationalizing the strengths perspective been discussed in the literature (DeJong & Miller, 1995). There has been some discussion of crisis intervention within the provision of solution-focused therapy (Berg & Miller, 1992b; Berg, 1994; DeJong & Berg, 1998), but solution-focused therapy as the primary treatment approach for crisis intervention has not been discussed, and certainly not within a context of the strengths perspective.

Both the strengths perspective (Rapp, 1998; Saleeby, 1997) and solution-focused therapy (Selekman, 1997) view clients as resilient. *Resilience* has been defined as a person's ability not only to cope with, survive, and bounce back from difficult and traumatic experiences and situations but also to continue to grow and develop psychologically and emotionally (Walsh, 1998). However, in the crisis intervention literature, the emphasis has consistently been on helping people return only to their precrisis level of functioning (Fraser, 1998); such a perspective is not completely consistent with client resilience. Fraser (1998) proposes that clinicians should consistently view a crisis as a catalyst for clients experiencing growth and development beyond a precrisis level of functioning. The literature does not contain a discussion of operationalizing working with clients' strengths and powers of resilience in the provision of crisis intervention services. The purpose of this chapter is to present such an operationalization so that clients in crisis have the opportunity not only to develop new coping skills but also to identify, mobilize, and enhance those strengths and coping skills they already have but may have forgotten or may be underutilizing.

CRISIS INTERVENTION AND SOLUTION-FOCUSED THERAPY

Crisis Intervention

A crisis can result from situational stressors, transitional changes, or disasters (Parad & Parad, 1990). The degree to which an event is experienced as a crisis depends on how the person perceives it; a crisis for one person may not be a crisis for another (Roberts & Dziegielewski, 1995). A crisis occurs when a precipitating event disrupts an individual's or a family's usual ways of functioning, resulting in their experiencing a sense of disequilibrium (Roberts, 1991; Parad & Parad, 1990). When in this state, people experience a variety of strong feelings, such as vulnerability, anxiety, powerlessness, and hopelessness (Parad & Parad, 1990). At this point a person may resort to increasing the use of his or her usual coping strategies or trying some new strategies in a trial-and-error manner to attempt to deal with the crisis situation (Ewing, 1990). If these additional efforts are unsuccessful, the person experiences increasing tension and is at risk for major disorganization of his or her functioning (Caplan, 1964).

After 4 to 6 weeks, clients will, with or without treatment, experience either a return to their previous equilibrium or a new equilibrium that may leave them coping better or worse than prior to the crisis (Parad & Parad, 1990). The primary purpose of crisis intervention is to accelerate the return to equilibrium and at least prevent individuals from stabilizing at a new, regressed level of equilibrium. There are various models of crisis intervention. One of the most complete models is the seven-stage approach developed by Roberts (1991): (1) assess lethality and safety needs; (2) establish rapport and communication; (3) identify the major problems; (4) deal with feelings and provide support; (5) explore possible alternatives; (6) assist in formulating an action plan; and (7) follow up.

A central idea in crisis intervention is that because of their disequilibrium and emotional distress, clients will take steps that they otherwise might have resisted prior to the crisis and in the process develop new coping skills (Ewing, 1990; Parad & Parad, 1990; Roberts, 1991). Client change in crisis intervention is accomplished by various in-session and between-session activities. One clinician activity in the session involves challenging the client's negative self-talk or irrational beliefs by the use of "carefully worded questions" (Roberts, 1991, p. 8). The purpose of such questions is to get the client to replace the negative, irrational self-talk with positive, rational self-talk. The clinician also works with the client to identify alternative courses of action for successfully dealing with the crisis. After various alternatives have been identified, the clinician and the client develop an action plan for implementing them. An action plan involves carrying out specific *tasks*, "primarily by the client, but also by the worker and significant others, designed to solve specific problems in the current life situation, to modify previous inadequate or inappropriate ways of functioning, and to learn new coping patterns" (Golan, 1986, p. 323). Tasks are specific actions that must be performed in order for the client to achieve his or her treatment goal (reestablish equilibrium; Fortune, 1985; Golan, 1986; Levy & Shelton, 1990). Most tasks are performed by the client between sessions in the form of "homework assignments," but some are done within the treatment situation. Successfully performing therapeutic tasks should result in the client feeling, thinking, or behaving in new and different ways. In crisis intervention, clinicians should "encourage clients to think of alternative ideas, coping methods, and solutions" (Roberts, 1991, p. 12). However, when they are under the stress of helping clients deal with the crisis, clinicians are often tempted to jump in quickly to offer solutions and advice.

A clinician who offers advice to and generates solutions for a client may quicken crisis resolution but does not foster client empowerment. Clients often do not respond as quickly as clinicians would like. However, clients are more likely to generate their own solutions, and thus feel empowered, if clinicians show patience. Perhaps clinicians would be less likely to "rescue" (Friesen & Casella, 1982) clients and more likely to reinforce client strengths, even in a crisis, if they had a specific model to guide them in such situations. One therapeutic model that lends itself to working with client strengths in crisis situations is solution-focused therapy.

Solution-Focused Therapy

Solution-focused therapy views change as inevitable and continuous (Kral & Kowalski, 1989). This approach presumes that there are fluctuations in the client's presenting problem such that it does not remain constant in severity;

at times the problem is either not present or at least is less frequent or intense than at other times (Berg & Miller, 1992b). The task of a clinician using a solution-focused approach is to work collaboratively with the client to identify what she or he is already doing that contributes to the diminishing of the problem. Solution-focused therapy, therefore, emphasizes identifying and amplifying clients' strengths and resources used in solving or reducing the frequency and/or intensity of the presenting problem. This therapeutic approach assumes that clients ultimately possess the resources and capabilities to resolve their problems (de Shazer, 1985). Solution-focused therapy, therefore, is a nonpathologizing approach to working with clients.

In solution-focused therapy the emphasis is on finding solutions rather than solving problems. The solution-focused therapist is a catalyst for the client, enlarging and increasing the frequency of solution patterns rather than decreasing problem patterns; the focus is on "what is happening when things are going well" instead of "what is happening when the problem is present." Solution-focused therapy's emphasis on strengths and solutions helps build the expectation that change is going to happen (de Shazer et al., 1986). According to de Shazer et al. (1986), the more the therapeutic discourse concerns alternate futures and solutions, the more clients expect change to occur. The clinician's focus is on asking clients questions that achieve solutions through encouraging "change talk" (Weiner-Davis, 1993) or "solution talk" as opposed to "problem talk" (Walter & Peller, 1992). Change talk involves clients identifying either positive changes that have occurred in the problem or exceptions to the problem, or their no longer viewing the situation as problematic (Weiner-Davis, 1993). Gingerich, de Shazer, and Weiner-Davis (1988) found that when clinicians intentionally engage in change talk, clients are more than four times as likely to discuss change in their next speaking turn. This is in keeping with an assumption of solution-focused therapy that a small change is all that is necessary to elicit a larger change (O'Hanlon & Weiner-Davis, 1989; Walter & Peller, 1992), thus resulting in a positive self-fulfilling prophecy instead of a negative one.

Solution-focused therapy assumes that clients really do want to change rather than seeing them as resistant. Clients not changing is viewed as their way of letting the clinician know how to help them. Asking the client to do more of what he or she is already capable of doing can strengthen the therapeutic relationship because the clinician is not asking the client to do something unfamiliar (Molnar & de Shazer, 1987); the client is likely to get the message that he or she is okay and is not deficient or in need of "fixing." According to Berg and Jaya (1993), when clinicians focus on working with clients and respecting their way of solving problems, the clients will offer clinicians many opportunities to learn from them. Adaptation to the way clients see their situation not only is respectful but also promotes cooperation in therapy. It is the clinician's responsibility to be sensitive to the client's worldview and try to fit with it as closely as possible.

Solution-focused therapy is appropriate for use with clients in crisis because it is known to produce quick and dramatic changes. Solution-focused therapy is also especially useful with clients in crisis because the therapist usually begins in the present and focuses on joining and understanding the client's view of the problem. After the problem is defined as concretely and specifically as possible, the clinician moves the focus to discussion of solutions. A basic tenet of solution-focused therapy is that one does not need to know the cause or function of a problem in order to resolve it (O'Hanlon & Weiner-Davis, 1989). This is consistent with crisis intervention, in which a clinician does not have to know everything about the client's problem and the goal in order to successfully provide crisis intervention as soon as possible (Gilliland & James, 1993).

A SOLUTION-FOCUSED APPROACH TO CRISIS INTERVENTION

The structure of a solution-focused approach to crisis intervention, which has some overlap with Roberts's model of crisis intervention, described earlier, is the following: (1) join with the client; (2) elicit the client's definition of the problem; (3) elicit the client's desired outcome goal; (4) identify solutions; (5) develop and implement an action plan; (6) conduct termination and follow-up. The solution-focused crisis worker assesses lethality and safety needs from the very first contact with the client. Assessing lethality and safety needs, however, is not listed as a separate step here because it is done in the course of joining, defining problems, and identifying goals and solutions. The solution-focused crisis worker relies heavily on the use of questions during the interview to identify and amplify client strengths, successes, and solutions. In this regard, the primary intervention is the use of questions.

Step 1: Joining

According to Berg (1994), joining involves "what the worker needs to do in the engagement phase in order to establish a positive working relationship" (p. 51). Joining is comparable to Roberts's stages 2 and 4. For joining to occur, the crisis clinician must use a number of skills, including empathy (identifying and reflecting the client's feelings), support, acceptance, tracking, matching and mirroring nonverbal communication, and using the client's language. Joining is done throughout the crisis intervention work but is especially important in the beginning. To facilitate joining, Berg recommends that the clinician should avoid confronting clients and provoking defensiveness, avoid getting into debates and arguments with clients, and when appropriate take a "one-down position" and see the client as the "expert" on her or his situation (p. 53).

 (one-down position)

In this phase the crisis worker also should immediately begin assessing the extent to which the client is a threat to him- or herself or to others or is being threatened by others. Such an assessment is certainly an initial focus and should continue throughout the crisis work. Ensuring client safety is analogous to stage 1 (assessing lethality) of Roberts's model of crisis intervention (1996). In the solution-focused crisis intervention model discussed here, assessing lethality, which includes ensuring client safety, is viewed not as a separate step but as a theme continuing throughout the crisis work; the crisis worker performs these activities as the crisis work unfolds.

Step 2: Defining Problems

Although the approach described in this chapter emphasizes "solutions," the first interview usually begins with the client describing the problem(s) that precipitated seeking crisis services. At this point the client may want to talk about the problematic situation and the accompanying painful feelings. The crisis worker can begin the interview by asking, "What kinds of concerns are you having now for you to want to see someone like myself?" Instead of using the word *problem,* the crisis worker may want to use *concern* or *issue* as a way to normalize the crisis event the client is experiencing. In this way, the crisis worker moves away from pathologizing the crisis and conveys the message that such an event can be a part of life, although mostly unexpected, that calls for extra effort to find a solution. A question many therapists use when beginning a first interview, which should not be used, is: "What brings you here today?" This question can reinforce a sense of external locus of control, which most clients already are experiencing (Frank, 1982). Since all clinical work should be empowering to clients (reinforcing an internal locus of control), clinicians should choose their words carefully.

When the client mentions a number of problems, the crisis worker should ask the client to prioritize them. This prioritizing could be done by the worker saying the following: "You have mentioned several problems you are having now. I find it very helpful to work on one problem at a time, whenever possible. Which of the problems you just mentioned do you want to focus on first in our work together?" It is important for problems to be defined as specifically (concretely and behaviorally) as possible in terms of who, what, when, where, how, and how often. Once the worker thinks the client has defined the problem as specifically as possible for now, the worker should ask the client to define his or her goal(s). Some clients, however, have a greater desire to ventilate and may still want to keep focused on problem talk. When this occurs, it is best to not push clients to define goals and solution talk until they are ready.

Step 3: Setting Goals

In solution-focused therapy, setting goals receives more emphasis than defining problems (de Shazer, 1985). A goal describes a desired future state for the client in terms of how she or he will be feeling, thinking, and behaving differently. Like problems, goals should be set by the client and defined as specifically as possible (de Shazer, 1988). Clients are much more likely to cooperate (not resist) in the clinical situation when the focus of the work is on their goals rather than those set by the clinician (Berg & Gallagher, 1991).

Often when clients are asked what their goal is, they might say something like: "I want to stop being depressed" or "I want to get rid of my depression." Goals, however, should be stated in the positive rather than the negative, such as, "What do you want to be feeling instead?" or "How do you want to be feeling differently?" (Walter & Peller, 1992). Goal setting involves clients representing to themselves a future reality that does not contain the presenting problem. The more they describe in detail how they want to be feeling, thinking, and behaving differently in the future, the more real these become (Walter & Peller, 1992).

The Miracle Question and the Dream Question

Sometimes clients have trouble setting a goal with sufficient specificity. A clinician can use the *miracle question* or the *dream question* to facilitate such specificity. An example of the miracle question is the following:

> Suppose that after our meeting today you go home and go to bed. While you are sleeping a miracle happens and your problem is suddenly solved, like magic. The problem is gone. Because you were sleeping, you don't know that a miracle happened, but when you wake up tomorrow morning, you will be different. How will you know a miracle has happened? What will be the first small sign that tells you that a miracle has happened and the problem is resolved? (Berg & Miller, 1992a, p. 359)

The *dream question*, which is an adaptation of the miracle question, is illustrated in the following:

> Suppose that tonight while you are sleeping you have a dream. In this dream you discover the answers and resources you need to solve the problem that you are concerned about right now. When you wake up tomorrow, you may or may not remember your dream, but you do notice you are different. As you go about starting your day, how will you know that you discovered or developed the skills and resources necessary to solve your problem? What will be the first small bit of evidence that you did this? (Greene, Lee, Mentzer, Pinnell, & Niles, 1998)

The miracle question was adapted for use in the following cases.

Domestic Violence

An anonymous woman called, and her voice was barely audible. She sounded exhausted, lethargic, hopeless, and depressed. She began the call by saying she lives with a man who is very abusive. He beat her up yesterday, claiming he must discipline her. He makes her write out her mistakes on paper 100 times, and then she must write him a formal apology promising not to do it again. When he goes to work, he locks all doors, windows, and cupboards and the refrigerator. He allows her to eat only one meal a day and withholds that if she is being punished.

Worker: Suppose that while you are sleeping tonight a miracle happens and your problem is suddenly solved. Like magic the problem is gone. Because you were sleeping, you don't know that a miracle happened, but when you wake up tomorrow, you will be different. How will you know a miracle happened? What will be the first small sign that tells you that a miracle has happened and the problem is resolved?

Client: He would be out of the house, and I would be here safe.

Worker: What would your being safe look like?

Client: I would be free to go about the house as I please and do what I want to do. I might even leave the house and walk to the store.

Worker: What would you do at the store once you were there?

Client: I might call my sister and talk to her, which I haven't done in months.

Worker: What would you talk to her about?

Client: I'd probably tell her what a no-good SOB Bill is, and then she would help me figure out how to get out of the house for good.

Worker: What would need to happen for even a small part of this miracle to happen?

Client: Well, I'd have to have a plan. A plan that would let me sneak out of the house when Bill is at work.

Worker: Have you ever done this before? (questions on past successes)

Client: Yes, a long time ago.

Worker: How did you do that at that time?

Relationship Questions

Based on a systems perspective, individuals never exist alone. Besides asking clients to establish concrete, precise indicators of change for themselves through the use of miracle questions, it is also helpful to ask what their

significant others think or might think about their problematic situation and
progress (Berg, 1994). Establishing multiple indicators of change helps clients develop a clearer vision of a desired future appropriate to their real-life
context. Examples are: "What would your mother (or husband, friend, sister, etc.) notice that's different about you if they didn't know that a miracle
had occurred?"

Harrassment

An anonymous woman called feeling hopeless, helpless, and angry. She is a
lesbian who is being harassed and discriminated against by coworkers because of her lesbianism. She feels trapped because she enjoys her work and
does not want to leave, but she is also sick of the harassment. Recently, someone has begun following her and driving by her house all night. She believes
it is a coworker but has no proof. The client reports feeling extremely fearful
and has no idea what to do.

Worker: Suppose that while you are sleeping tonight a miracle happens
          and your problem is suddenly solved, like magic. The problem is
          gone. Because you were sleeping, you don't know that a miracle
          happened, but when you wake up tomorrow, you will be differ-
          ent. How will you know a miracle happened? What will be the
          first small sign that tells you that a miracle has happened and the
          problem is resolved?

Client: I would be able to wake up, not in fear, and I would be able to
          go to work, enjoy my work and my coworkers, and I would be
          treated like any other normal decent human being, without being
          treated like some freak with the plague.

Worker: That's a big miracle! What will be the first small sign that tells
          you a miracle has happened? (Focus on small, concrete behavior
          instead of the big, grandiose solutions)

Client: Well, first, I'll wake up with no fear.

Worker: What would your partner notice about you if you wake up with
          no fear?

Client: Well, she'll probably feel that I am more relaxed . . . umm, proba-
          bly less tense.

Worker: What will she notice you doing when you are more relaxed
          when you wake up in the morning?

Client: Umm, I'll be in a good mood, maybe joke around a little bit, and
          get both of us a good breakfast (a smile on her face). Isn't that
          nice?

Worker: What would it take for you to start acting as if you wake up
          with no fear?

Client: I would need to know I was safe.

Worker: What would you need to do in order to feel safe?

Client: I would probably need to get the police involved. And maybe I could tighten up my security, you know, buy a deadbolt lock and a saber-toothed tiger (ha-ha!).

Worker: See, you have some great ideas to help yourself! (Compliment) What will you do first? (Assisting client to develop a concrete plan to make her feel safe)

Step 4: Identifying Solutions

After the client describes in detail a future without the problem(s), the crisis worker uses exception questions, coping questions, and questions about past successes to assist the client to identify solutions that are conducive to realizing the envisioned future. At the same time, the crisis worker uses scaling questions to help the client quantify and evaluate his or her situation and progress.

Scaling Questions

Scaling questions allow for quantifying the client's problem and goal, which can be helpful not only in evaluating the client's situation and progress but also is an intervention itself (Greene, 1989). Scaling questions ask the client to rank the problem and goal on a scale of 1 to 10, with 1 as the worst the problem could possibly be and 10 as the most desirable outcome. The clinician usually begins each meeting by asking the client where he or she is on the 1 to 10 scale of the problem/goal continuum. When clients rank themselves higher on the scale in subsequent meetings, even slightly, the clinician asks what she or he has been doing to make this happen (Berg, 1994). This is a way to help the client notice what has been helpful, which may otherwise go unnoticed. The following case illustrates the use of scaling questions.

Grief and Loss

A woman called saying she needed to talk. Her father died yesterday. The client is upset but goes on to say that her main problem is the fact that her divorce will be final any day. She was married for 3 years and has two children under the age of 3. Her husband left her with the children and has moved in with another woman. The client says she does not know how she will make it.

Worker: I'm amazed that you've kept yourself going for the past 6 months.

Client: Yeah, me too. I guess things have been worse.

Worker: They've been worse than even now?

Client: Yeah, when he first left I was at an all-time low.

Worker: If I were to ask you to rate the way you're handling this situation on a scale of 1 to 10, with 1 being 6 months ago and 10 being where you want to get to, where would you say you're at today?

Client: I'd say I'm at a 3 or 4.

Worker: Wow, that's pretty impressive given what you've been through. How have you gotten yourself from a 1 to a 4?

Client: Well, I decided I've got to keep myself going for the kids. I've been taking classes to get my GED, even though I'm not very good at math.

Worker: Your kids give you energy to move on and to start planning for your future.

Client: Yes, I think so.

Worker: What would need to happen in order for you to move from a 4 to a 5? (Using the scaling question to help the client identify solutions)

Client: Well, I haven't thought about that. . . . Maybe if I get support from my own family . . . like if they baby-sit my babies when I am preparing for the exam.

Worker: Who in your family can possibly baby-sit your children? (Be specific)

Client: Maybe my sisters.

Worker: How will they know that you need their help?

Client: Well, maybe I need to talk to them. . . . We have pretty good relationships with each other.

Exception Questions

When clients first see a crisis clinician, they usually start talking about their crisis situation and their corresponding feelings (the presenting problem). In keeping with solution-focused therapy's assumption that there are fluctuations in how the client experiences the problem, the clinician asks questions to learn when the problem does not exist or at least is less frequent or intense. In regard to this Kral and Kowalski (1989) state: "The therapist's job is not to initiate change, but to punctuate the differences between the complaint pattern and the pattern of the exceptions (change) thereby making explicit the 'naturally' occurring variations which are in the direction of the desired solution" (p. 73). The assumption is that during these times the client is usually doing something to make things better, and the clinician asks further questions to discover what the client is doing. After "doing more of what works" comes "do more of the same," making the exception the rule

(Kral & Kowalski, 1989). The next case provides an illustration of identifying exceptions.

Maintaining Sobriety

Jane is extremely disappointed by and ashamed of her recent fall from sobriety. She has been sober for 19 months but yesterday got into a big argument with her ex-husband and spent the evening in a bar getting drunk.

Worker: You were able to stay sober for 19 months?

Client: Yeah, but what good is it? I wasn't sober last night!

Worker: It sounds like you felt drinking would be a way for you to deal with the stress of your ex-husband?

Client: Yeah, that's usually when I always got my drunkest, when he and I would get into one of those fights.

Worker: How many times during the last 19 months did you argue with your ex-husband and not drink?

Client: Well, there have been a few times.

Worker: How did you manage to not drink during those times?

Client: Well, one thing that kept me from drinking is going to my AA meetings. I really count on those people for support.

Worker: How did you know to go to an AA meeting when you had these arguments with your ex and you did not drink?

Client: I just told myself if I don't go to a meeting and talk to someone I'm going to drink. And I got myself away from him.

Worker: That's very smart thinking on your part. Is this something you're willing to do again in the future?

Client: Well, I think I can, especially with the help of the program.

Past Successes

Sometimes clients initially have difficulty identifying exceptions to their presenting problem in their current lives or their recent past. When this situation occurs, the clinician can ask about times in the past when the client successfully handled the same or similar situations and how she or he was able to do so (Berg & Gallagher, 1991). In regard to the presenting problem, the clinician can even ask the client about exceptions that occurred years earlier. If the client cannot come up with any exceptions, the clinician can ask about an exception to similar problems in the past. The idea is to find out what solutions have worked in the past and to apply them to the current crisis situation. The following case illustrates the use of identifying past successes.

A Suicidal Client

The anonymous client was a 58-year-old woman who reported feeling depressed and suicidal. She began having these feelings at Christmas, when an argument developed between her sister and mother. The client stated that she had spent several years and much effort trying to mend these relationships, and she now fears it has all been for nothing. The argument also brought up the many issues of her childhood, and now she finds it necessary to deal with these issues again. The client says she is so depressed that she is contemplating suicide.

Worker: Have you ever felt suicidal in the past?

Client: Yes, about 25 years ago.

Worker: Did you make a suicide attempt then?

Client: No, somehow I got out of it.

Worker: How did you do that?

Client: A doctor put me on antidepressants for a while. I also keep busy walking and exercising. Talking to friends also was very helpful.

Worker: How did you keep from thinking about those family problems?

Client: I just kept occupied.

Worker: Are you doing any of those things now that you did then?

Client: No, but I guess I could.

Worker: What is one small thing you could start with?

Coping Questions

Oftentimes clients in crisis will state that nothing is going right, that they can find nothing positive in their lives, and that they are unable to identify any exceptions, either present or past. Such clients can feel hopeless about themselves and their future (Berg & Miller, 1992b). The crisis worker needs to recognize such negativity as a sign of great desperation and a signal for empathetic help. In such a situation, the client could perceive the clinician's focus on the positive as being artificial and imposing. The coping question can be quite effective with these clients in crisis who see little possibility for positive changes (Berg & Miller, 1992b). Coping questions can be an impetus for clients feeling a sense of empowerment because they start to become aware of resources they did not know they had or had forgotten (Berg, 1994). The following example illustrates the use of coping questions.

The Desperate Single Mom

Loraine was a 26-year-old unemployed single mother with a 7-year-old, "impossible" boy, Teddy. According to Loraine, she had never been able to handle Teddy, who never listened and destroyed almost everything. Recently, Teddy set fire at the apartment and inappropriately touched a 5-year-old girl. Loraine claimed that she had a very bad relationship with Teddy, had not talked to him for a long time, and was on the verge of giving up. Loraine was very depressed and became agitated when the worker tried to get her to think about positive changes in the mother-child relationship, which seemed to be impossible to Loraine. The worker used the coping questions instead.

Worker: If I ask you to rank your relationship with Teddy on a scale of 1 to 10, with 1 as the worst scenario both of you can get to and 10 as the best possible relationship that both of you can have, how would you rank your relationship with Teddy now?

Client: I have to say it would be in the minus range.

Worker: Sounds like the situation is really bad. I just wonder what have you been doing to keep it from getting worse? You know, the situation can be much worse; how do you keep it from getting any worse?

Client: I do pay attention to him sometimes. I don't ignore him totally, even though sometimes I feel so depressed and overwhelmed it's all I can do to pay attention to what's going on with me.

Worker: So how are you able to do that—to take care of Teddy some of the time even though you are feeling so bad you don't feel like it?

Client: I just do it. I am his mother, and I do have responsibility for him. I really don't know how I do it. I let things go for a while, but eventually I just tell myself I've got to take care of Teddy, since no one else can. I know I should be doing a better job of being a mother, but right now I feel like I can barely take care of myself.

Worker: That's really something that you are able at times to get yourself to do what you have to do for Teddy even though you don't feel like it. Using the same 1 to 10 scale, with 1 meaning you don't want to take care of him at all and 10 meaning that you would do whatever you have to in order to take care of Teddy and keep him from getting into trouble, how would you rank yourself?

Client: I would say around 7.

Worker: That's pretty high. When was the last time you were able to take care of Teddy and keep him from getting into trouble? (Exception questions)

Compliments

Many clients seeing a clinician for the first time expect to be judged and criticized, and they may be prepared to defend themselves (Wall, Kleckner,

Amendt, & duRee Bryant, 1989). Complimenting clients is a way to enhance their cooperation rather than elicit defensiveness and resistance. Compliments do not have to be directly related to the presenting problem but can be related to whatever the client is doing that is good for him or her, that he or she is good at or aspires to (Berg & Gallagher, 1991, p. 101). Such compliments, therefore, are feedback to clients about strengths, successes, or exceptions. Clients are usually surprised, relieved, and pleased when they receive praise from the clinician. A consequence of therapeutic compliments is that clients are usually more willing to search for, identify, and amplify solution patterns. The following provides an example of using compliments.

Relationship Issues

Betty was hysterical when she called and asked for advice. She is a single mother of four children. Betty must work full-time to support her children and often feels guilty about the time she spends away from them. Betty's guilty feelings intensified today when she came home from work to find her 7-year-old daughter and 9-year-old son involved in "sexual play." She is feeling very inadequate as a parent.

Worker: Wow, this must feel terribly overwhelming for you. I want to commend you on your strength and courage in calling here today.

Client: Well, I don't know how strong I am. Look what a mess my kids are in. And it's all my fault. If I didn't have to work so much, this probably wouldn't be happening.

Worker: What have you said to your children about your working?

Client: They know I work to feed 'em, clothe 'em, and keep this shack over their heads.

Worker: That is a lot of responsibility: working, raising four children as a single parent, keeping food on the table, clothing on the children, and a home together. It takes a lot of energy, skill, and motivation to do that. I really admire you for being able to do all that.

Complimenting clients is helpful at any time during the interview but especially toward the end of a session as a preface to giving clients homework assignments or tasks. However, clients in crisis often are overwhelmed by their problematic situations and tend to be pessimistic. The crisis worker has to be careful not to overcompliment, which the client may perceive as superficial and insincere. Compliments should be based on what clients have actually done or mentioned in the interview.

Step 5: Develop and Implement an Action Plan

Tasks or homework assignments are also used in solution-focused therapy but in different ways than in other crisis intervention models. As mentioned earlier, solution-focused therapy assumes clients are already doing to some extent or are capable of doing whatever is needed for problem resolution and goal attainment. Therefore, tasks in solution-focused therapy involve the client identifying solutions and/or doing more of them (Walter & Peller, 1992). Tasks are based on thoughts, feelings, and behaviors that the client has used in the past or is using in the present (Molnar & de Shazer, 1987). The following are some commonly used solution-focused tasks.

Formula First Session Task

Between now and next the time we meet, we[I] would like you to observe, so that you can describe to us[me] next time, what happens in your [pick one: family, life, marriage, relationship] that you want to continue to have happen. (de Shazer, 1985, p. 137)

Clients in crisis situations often feel that nothing is going right for them and that they are losing control of their lives. This task helps refocus clients' attention to something they are doing *well* rather than problems or failures. This change of focus can lead to clients realizing that there still is something working in their lives, and thus they can have some sense of control of their life situation (Berg, 1994).

The name of this task comes from its successful use at the end of the first session with a wide variety of clients regardless of presenting problem (de Shazer et al., 1986). The formula first session task is especially useful with clients who present vaguely defined problems and are not responsive to the clinician's attempt to define them more concretely and specifically. In one follow-up survey on the use of the formula first session task, 89% of clients reported at the next session that they noticed things they wanted to continue, and 92% of these clients said that at least one was something "new or different" (de Shazer et al., 1986, p. 217).

Keep Track of Current Successes

Identify the ways you are able to keep doing _____ (behaviors which are exceptions to the problem behavior). (Molnar & de Shazer, 1987, p. 356)

or

Pay attention to and keep track of what you do to overcome the temptation or urge to . . . (perform the symptom or some behavior associated with the problem). (Berg & Gallagher, 1991, p. 101; Molnar & de Shazer, 1987, p. 356)

The purpose of this task is to help clients focus on what skills and abilities they have and use them to improve their situation. The more specific and detailed the clients are in making these descriptions, the more likely they are in anchoring such behaviors into their behavioral repertoire. Furthermore, the more they notice the connections between their behavior and positive outcomes, the more likely they are to have a sense of control over their problematic situation.

Prediction Task

Oftentimes the client experiences the problem as outside her or his control. The client is able to identify exceptions but believes that she or he has no control over these occurrences. In the prediction task the client is asked to predict or rate something, e.g., "First thing each morning rate the possibility of ____ (an exception behavior) happening before noon" (Molnar & de Shazer, 1987, p. 356). The purpose of this task is to help clients realize that the exception behaviors may be much more within their control than they think. By asking a client to keep a careful record of what he or she predicted and how the day actually turned out will produce important insights into the client's ability to make what appears to be a random or spontaneous exception into a deliberate one (Berg, 1994). The crisis worker can then encourage the client to do more of such deliberate exception and ultimately making the exception into the rule.

Pretend the Miracle Has Happened

This task asks the client to pick a day when he or she is to pretend that a miracle has happened and the problem or crisis that brought him or her for help is solved. The worker should encourage the client to do everything that he or she would do if the miracle had happened and to keep track of what he or she notices that is different about himself or herself and how other people react to him or her (Berg, 1994). The purpose of this strategy is for clients to have a reason to have good feelings and successes in a way they otherwise would not. Clients do not need to wait for a miracle to happen before they can experience good feelings, thoughts, and behaviors that are associated with a problem-free situation. This task allows clients to learn that they can turn a desired "fantasy" into a reality.

Solution-focused tasks have been shown to be effective in a wide variety of problem situations. The important issue for the worker, however, is to find a good fit between the client's circumstances and strengths and the task assignment. The worker has to judge whether the task appears to make sense to the client and the client's readiness to engage in the specific task assignments.

Step 6: Termination and Follow-Up

A person in a crisis situation usually experiences significant disequilibrium. Crisis intervention attempts to prevent a person from stabilizing at a regressed level of functioning and preferably helps a person reestablish equilibrium with increased coping abilities. An important criterion for termination is for the client to return to the previous level of functioning, if not a higher one, rather than having all of his or her problems solved. In this regard, a solution-focused approach shares a philosophy with crisis intervention with respect to termination. A solution-focused approach perceives that life is full of problems to be solved, and it is simply not realistic for clients to solve all their problems before terminating the case. Instead, specific goal achievement is identified as the criterion for termination. Therefore, at termination, the worker assists clients to review their specific goals, assess their readiness for termination, and anticipate possible future setbacks. Scaling questions are frequently used in the process. The following examples illustrate the process.

The Doubtful Single Father

John was a 37-year-old single father with a 9-year-old son, Justin, who has been diagnosed as having attention deficit hyperactivity disorder. The father has learning difficulties of his own and did not finish high school. John is separated from Susan, Justin's mother, who has some serious "mental problems" and "poor parenting skills." Justin chose to live with his father. In addition to the separation and the stresses of single parenting, John's mother died recently and he became very depressed. Two months ago he got drunk, and the apartment caught on fire, apparently because of a lighted cigarette. Luckily, no one got hurt. The Children Services Department got involved because of suspected child neglect. John had six sessions of crisis intervention and made tremendous improvement. Although John was still lacking confidence in his parenting, both John and the worker thought termination was in order at this time.

Worker: John, suppose when we first started meeting, your ability to take care of Justin was at 1 and where you wanted your parenting ability to be was at 10. Where would you say you are at today between 1 and 10? (Evaluating progress)

Client: I would say I am at maybe 6 or 7.

Worker: That's a lot of progress. Looking back, what have you done to help yourself to be an adequate parent?

Client: Well, I keep telling myself that I don't want to mess up the life

	of my son. Later on when I thought about it, I didn't dare to think about what would happen if I'd set the apartment on fire.
Worker:	So, you remind yourself a lot that you don't want that to happen again. What else have you been doing that's helpful?
Client:	Hey, the list that we came up with helps me a lot (client referred to a checklist that the worker developed with him about things that he should do regarding adequate parenting). I put it on the fridge so I can see it every day.
Worker:	I'm glad to hear that. What else have you been doing with Justin that's helpful? (Try to get a behavioral description of the interaction between father and son)
Client:	With Justin. . . . Oh, I guess I do more things with him. He really likes it.
Worker:	You know, you have made terrific progress since we started. I just wonder on a scale of 1 to 10, with 10 meaning you have every confidence that you will keep up with your progress and 1 meaning you have no confidence at all to maintain the changes, where would you put yourself between 1 and 10 today? (Evaluating confidence to maintain the changes)
Client:	I don't know, maybe 5. Sometimes I have doubts about whether the situation would go back again.
Worker:	So, you're a little bit uncertain. What would it take for you to move from a 5 to a 6?
Client:	Maybe I just have to keep doing what I've been doing. Well, it's good to have someone reminding me, I guess.
Worker:	Who may be a good person to remind you?
Client:	Let me think. My sister is really concerned about Justin and me. She would probably like to help if I ask her.
Worker:	How easy would it be for you to talk to her about this?
Client:	Very easy; there should be no problem.
Worker:	I want to ask you a slightly different but very important question. What would be the earliest sign to you that you are starting to go backward? What would your sister notice about you that would tell her that you are beginning to slip?

The primary task at termination is for clients to evaluate and consolidate their progress. It is important for clients to know what is working for them so they can connect their own action to the successful outcomes. In this way, life is no longer a series of crises that are out of their control. They can actively participate in creating solutions and enhance their skills and competencies as a result of the experience. The emphasis is no longer on deficits; instead, clients' strengths are recognized and celebrated. The use of the compliment is especially important for clients who have successfully coped with a crisis. A general guideline is for clients to own and take full credit for their successes.

Besides evaluating and celebrating positive progress, it is important to assist clients to go beyond current successes and develop indicators that will tell them when they may need help in the future. A solution-focused approach views problems as both normal and inherent in human living. Therefore, helping clients to ameliorate all their problems is less realistic than helping clients to recognize times when they will need help again and/or giving them the skills for dealing with new problematic situations when they occur.

Sometime after termination of crisis intervention, the crisis worker, whenever possible, should contact the client to see how well she or he is doing (Roberts, 1991, 1996). The length of time between termination and follow-up will vary, but follow-up usually should occur within 1 month (Roberts, 1991, 1996). At termination the worker should inform the client that he or she will want to make a follow-up contact and seek permission to do so. Such a contact can help support and consolidate the client's continued successes, solutions, and strengths. In addition, during a follow-up contact the worker can make a referral for longer term clinical work if the client requests it. Most therapeutic approaches do not make follow-up an explicit component, and solution-focused therapy is no exception. The authors of this chapter, however, agree with Roberts in this regard.

SUMMARY AND CONCLUSION

Although crisis intervention and solution-focused therapy come from distinct therapeutic traditions, they do have commonalities. For instance, crisis intervention perceives most crises as self-limiting in that the state of disequilibrium usually lasts 4 to 6 weeks (Parad & Parad, 1990). Consequently, crisis work tends to be immediate, short-term, and intense. A solution-focused approach also emphasizes a rapid and brief response to clients' help-seeking effort.

Although a solution-focused approach assumes clients already have resources and strengths and that the purpose of intervention is to help clients successfully deal with their presenting problem(s) by utilizing what they bring with them to the treatment situation, it does not deny that at times a more direct approach may be necessary. A solution-focused approach encourages clients to look for exceptions to the problem and do more of the exception-maintaining patterns. A crisis event, however, may be so novel that new coping and problem-solving skills are needed. In a solution-focused approach, if no exceptions can be found, clients are encouraged to do something different. In fact, one of the basic tenets of solution-focused therapy is "If it works, do more of it. If it doesn't work, don't do it again, do something else" (de Shazer et al., 1986, p. 212). In addition, even a solution-oriented crisis worker may need to actively provide concrete services, practi-

Soluth — hen dint

cal support, information, and other interventions that will help alleviate clients' immediate disequilibrium in their life situation—actions that are not emphasized in a typical solution-focused approach. The authors of this chapter, however, encourage crisis workers, whenever possible, to not use a direct approach too quickly before trying a solution-focused approach. A more direct approach may quickly resolve the presenting crisis but may not leave the client with a greater sense of strength, competence, and empowerment.

Experience, skilled judgment, flexibility, and individualized treatment may best describe the wisdom required in using a solution-focused approach to crisis intervention. For many years now, the crisis intervention literature has recognized the "opportunity" inherent in a crisis situation: A person can experience notable personal growth if the situation is handled successfully (Caplan, 1964). This chapter adopts a strengths perspective operationalized by the use of solution-focused therapy integrated with crisis intervention. It is assumed that clients, in spite of their crisis situation, come with a diverse repertoire of strengths and skills that they are not currently noticing. In solution-focused crisis intervention, clients are assisted in discovering and amplifying their strengths and resources—an intervention approach that envisions clients' new learning and strengths through the passage of life. This approach provides clinicians with a systematic way to work with clients' strengths and resilience to help them handle crises and experience personal growth and development.

The authors believe that a solution-focused approach to crisis intervention is the treatment of choice in the majority of crisis situations. Currently, there are no well-designed studies documenting the effectiveness of a solution-focused/strengths-based approach to crisis intervention. However, one of the authors in a previous job at a crisis hotline documented that shortly after introducing solution-focused techniques to the staff, the time spent on the telephone with chronic callers decreased from 1,000 minutes to 200 minutes in a 1-month period. Only future research can shed light on what this dramatic decrease means and whether it can be attributed to the use of a solution-focused approach.

ACKNOWLEDGMENTS   Portions of this chapter are adapted from G. J. Greene, M. Y. Lee, R. Trask, & J. Rheinscheld (1996), Client strengths and crisis intervention: A solution-focused approach. *Crisis Intervention and Time-Limited Treatment*, 3, 43–63.

REFERENCES

Berg, I. K. (1994). *Family based services: A solution-focused approach.* New York: Norton.

Berg, I. K., & Gallagher, D. (1991). Solution focused brief treatment with adolescent substance abusers.

In T. C. Todd & M. D. Selekman (Eds.), *Family therapy approaches with adolescent substance abusers* (pp. 93–111). Boston: Allyn and Bacon.

Berg, I. K., & Jaya, A. (1993). Different and same: Family therapy with Asian-American families. *Journal of Marital and Family Therapy, 19*, 31–38.

Berg, I. K., & Miller, S. D. (1992a, June). Working with Asian American clients: One person at a time. *Families in Society, 356–363.*

Berg, I. K., & Miller, S. D. (1992b). *Working with the problem drinker: A solution-focused approach.* New York: Norton.

Caplan, G. (1964). *Principles of preventive psychiatry.* New York: Basic Books.

Cowger, C. D. (1994). Assessing client strengths: Clinical assessment for client empowerment. *Social Work, 39*, 262–268.

Dattilio, F. M., & Freeman, A. (1994). *Cognitive-behavioral strategies in crisis intervention.* New York: Guilford.

DeJong, P., & Berg, I. K. (1998). *Interviewing for solutions.* Pacific Grove, CA: Brooks/Cole.

DeJong, P., & Miller, S. D. (1995). How to interview for client strengths. *Social Work, 40*, 729–736.

de Shazer, S. (1985). *Keys to solution in brief therapy.* New York: Norton.

de Shazer, S. (1988). *Clues: Investigating solutions in brief therapy.* New York: Norton.

de Shazer, S., Berg, I. K., Lipchik, E. Nunnally, E., Molnar, A., Gingerich, W., & Weiner-Davis, M. (1986). Brief therapy: Focused solu-

tion development. *Family Process, 25*, 207–221.

Ewing, C. P. (1990). Crisis intervention as brief psychotherapy. In R. A. Wells & V. J. Giannetti (Eds.), *Handbook of the brief psychotherapies* (pp. 277–294). New York: Plenum.

Fisch, R., Weakland, J. H., & Segal, L. (1982). *The tactics of change: Doing therapy briefly.* San Francisco: Jossey-Bass.

Fortune, A. E. (1985). The task-centered model. In A. E. Fortune (Ed.), *Task-centered practice with families and groups* (pp. 1–30). New York: Springer.

Frank, J. D. (1982). Therapeutic components shared by all psychotherapies. In J. H. Harvey & M. M. Parks (Eds.), *Psychotherapy research and behavior change* (pp. 5–38). Washington, DC: American Psychological Association.

Fraser, J. S. (1998). A catalyst model: Guidelines for doing crisis intervention and brief therapy from a process view. *Crisis Intervention and Time-Limited Treatment, 4*, 159–177.

Friesen, V. I., & Casella, N. T. (1982). The rescuing therapist: A duplication of the pathogenic family system. *American Journal of Family Therapy, 10*, 57–61.

Gilliland, B. E., & James, R. K. (1993). *Crisis intervention strategies* (2nd ed.). Pacific Grove, CA: Brooks/Cole.

Gingerich, W., de Shazer, S., & Weiner-Davis, M. (1988). Constructing change: A research view of interviewing. In E. Lipchik (Ed.), *Interviewing* (pp. 21–32). Rockville, MD: Aspen.

Golan, N. (1986). Crisis theory. In F. J. Turner (Ed.), *Social work treatment: Interlocking theoretical approaches (pp. 296–340). New York: Free Press.

Greene, G. J. (1989). Using the written contract for evaluating and enhancing practice effectiveness. *Journal of Independent Social Work, 4,* 135–155.

Greene, G. J., Lee, M. Y., Mentzer, R. A., Pinnell, S. R., & Niles, D. (1998). Miracles, dreams, and empowerment: A brief therapy practice note. *Families in Society, 79,* 395–399.

Hoff, L. E. (1995). *People in crisis: Understanding and helping* (4th ed.). San Francisco: Jossey-Bass.

Kanel, K. (1999). *A guide to crisis intervention.* Pacific Grove, CA: Brooks/Cole.

Kiser, D. J., Piercy, F. P., & Lipchik, E. (1993). The integration of emotion in solution-focused therapy. *Journal of Marital and Family Therapy, 19,* 233–242.

Kral, R., & Kowalski, K. (1989). After the miracle: The second stage in solution focused therapy. *Journal of Strategic and Systemic Therapies, 8,* 73–76.

Levy, R. L., & Shelton, J. L. (1990). Tasks in brief therapy. In R. A. Wells & V. J. Gianetti (Eds.), *Handbook of the brief therapies* (pp. 145–163). New York: Plenum.

Molnar, A., & de Shazer, S. (1987). Solution focused therapy: Toward the identification of therapeutic tasks. *Journal of Marital and Family Therapy, 5,* 349–358.

O'Hanlon, W. H., & Weiner-Davis, M. (1989). *In search of solutions: A new direction in psychotherapy.* New York: Norton.

Parad, H. J., & Parad, L. G. (1990). Crisis intervention: An introductory overview. In H. J. Parad & L. G. Parad (Eds.), *Crisis intervention book 2: The practitioner's sourcebook for brief therapy* (pp. 3–68). Milwaukee, WI: Family Service America.

Puryear, D. A. (1979). *Helping people in crisis.* San Francisco: Jossey-Bass.

Rapoport, L. (1970). Crisis intervention as a mode of brief treatment. In R. W. Roberts & Robert H. Nee (Eds.), *Theories of social casework* (pp. 265–312). Chicago: University of Chicago Press.

Rapp, C. A. (1992). The strengths perspective of case management with persons suffering from severe mental illness. In D. Saleebey (Ed.), *The strengths perspective in social work practice* (pp. 45–58). New York: Longman.

Rapp, C. A. (1998). *The strengths model: Case management with people suffering from severe and persistent mental illness.* New York: Oxford University Press.

Roberts, A. R. (1990). Overview of crisis theory and crisis intervention. In A. R. Roberts (Ed.), *Crisis intervention handbook: Assessment, treatment and research* (pp. 3–16). Belmont, CA: Wadsworth.

Roberts, A. R. (1991). Conceptualizing crisis theory and the crisis intervention model. In A. R. Roberts (Ed.), *Contemporary perspectives on crisis intervention and prevention* (pp. 3–17). Englewood Cliffs, NJ: Prentice-Hall.

Roberts, A. R. (1996). Epidemiology and definitions of acute crisis in American society. In A. R. Roberts (Ed.), *Crisis management and brief treatment: Theory, technique, and applications* (pp. 16–33). Chicago: Nelson-Hall.

Roberts, A. R., & Dziegielewski, S. F. (1995). Foundation skills and applications of crisis intervention and cognitive therapy. In A. R. Roberts (Ed.), *Crisis intervention and time-limited cognitive treatment* (pp. 3–27). Thousand Oaks, CA: Sage.

Saleeby, D. (Ed.). (1992). *The strengths perspective in social work practice.* New York: Longman.

Saleeby, D. (Ed.). (1997). *The strengths perspective in social work practice* (2nd ed.). New York: Longman.

Selekman, M. D. (1997). *Solution-focused therapy with children: Harnessing family strengths for systemic change.* New York: Guilford.

Wall, M. D., Kleckner, T., Amendt, J. H., & duRee Bryant, R. (1989). Therapeutic compliments: Setting the stage for successful therapy. *Journal of Marital and Family Therapy, 15,* 159–167.

Walsh, F. (1998). *Strengthening family resilience.* New York: Guilford.

Walter, J. L., & Peller, J. E. (1992). *Becoming solution-focused in brief therapy.* New York: Brunner/ Mazel.

Weiner-Davis, M. (1993). Pro-constructed realities. In S. Gilligan & R. Price (Eds.), *Therapeutic conversations* (pp. 149–160). New York: Norton.

Crisis Intervention for Persons Diagnosed With Clinical Disorders Based on the Stress-Crisis Continuum

ANN WOLBERT BURGESS
ALBERT R. ROBERTS

All mental health professionals, including crisis clinicians, will benefit from applying our seven-level stress-crisis continuum. By determining the level and category that the person in crisis presents with, clinicians will be in an optimal position to determine whether crisis intervention, cognitive-behavioral therapy, medication, inpatient hospitalization, or other treatment modalities are appropriate. This chapter delineates and discusses a stress-crisis continuum consisting of seven levels to be used in conjunction with persons diagnosed with clinical disorders. Burgess and Roberts's first two levels are identified as somatic distress–crisis and transitional stress–crisis. In both, the stress symptomatology is usually reduced with brief crisis intervention and primary mental health care treatment. Levels 3, 4, and 5 seem to have occurred with increasing frequency during the 1990s. Individuals suffering from level 3 (traumatic stress–crisis) benefit from individual and group crisis-oriented therapy; level 4 (family crises) benefits from case management, and crisis treatment with forensic intervention; level 5 (mentally ill persons in crisis) benefits from crisis intervention, case monitoring, and day treatment; level 6 (psychiatric emergencies) benefits from crisis stabilization, hospitalization, and/or legal intervention; and level 7 (catastrophic traumatic stress crises) involves multiple successive traumatic events in combination with level 4, 5, or 6 stressor and requires crisis stabilization, grief counseling, social support, and symptom resolution. The application of Burgess and Roberts's stress-crisis continuum can optimize treatment planning, symptom reduction, and cost-effective outcomes in the context of a managed care health system.

Managed care is emerging as the dominant model of care as we begin the twenty-first century, and mental health practice is envisioned as a system based on principles of management and competition. Feldman (1992) asserts that managed mental health care systems have a great potential to save insurance carriers money by reducing inpatient stays and purchasing therapists' treatment more cost-effectively. Lazarus (1995) points out that an important component in preparing for practice in an era of managed competition is a continuum-of-care model that matches treatment modality with severity of symptoms.

If it is true that history repeats itself, writes Arthur Lazarus (1994), then it is no accident that some managed mental health care programs of the 1990s resemble community mental health practice in the 1960s and 1970s. Prevention, outreach, team care, and case management are crucial to the operation of managed care programs, just as they were to community mental health. Treatment protocols indicate a resurgence of group and family therapy with individual counseling, strongly resembling that provided in community mental health centers: brief, symptom focused, and crisis oriented (Lazarus, 1994).

As we enter the twenty-first century, legislators, policy makers, and health care administrators have an intensified interest in issues related to the quality of patient care, patterns of utilization of services, costs, and benefits. Every day, millions of individuals and families experience acute crisis episodes. These individuals are not able to resolve their crises on their own; as a result, many seek help from a mental health professional in their community.

We believe that to compete in the managed mental health care arena, crisis intervention will be a critical component. To practice crisis intervention requires a theoretical conceptualization of the stress-crisis continuum, the assessment and classification of levels of stress-crisis, and an empirical basis to the interventions.

Patricia Kelley confronts the challenge of the managed care world and narrative constructivist psychotherapy (1998). She notes that as managed care pushes for time-limited treatment, DSM-IV diagnosis, concrete problem definition, specific goals, and preapproved treatment plans based on evidence-based outcome models, the constructivist therapies seem at odds with the approach. Such therapies are based on a world that is nonlinear, denies the possibility of objectivity, and holds multiple views of reality with no fixed truths. Kelley argues for optimism and outlines ways to improve the fit between narrative therapy and managed care.

This chapter presents a classification paradigm for assessing emotional stress and acute crisis episodes in terms of seven levels that fall along a stress-crisis continuum. This classification is an adaptation and expansion of Baldwin's (1978) crisis classification. The seven levels are somatic distress, transitional stress, traumatic stress–crisis, family crises, serious mental illness, psychiatric emergencies, and catastrophic/cumulative crises (See Baldwins Table 2.1). With advancement from level 1 to level 7, the internal conflicts of the client become more serious and chronic.

For example, the closing case in this chapter illustrates cumulative levels of ongoing stress and crises that interact with a somatic distress and traumatic event: the diagnosis of HIV. The woman was an adopted child (transitional stress), and her sexual identity (transitional stress) was also an issue for her over the years. Much of her substance abuse and suicidal intent (psychiatric emergency) numbed her confusion over developmental issues, including her employment disruption (transition stress) and physical assaults with female partners (transitional stress–crisis). The male patient assault (traumatic stress–crisis) precipitated her involvement in the legal system (transitional stress). Her HIV-positive status (somatic and traumatic event) remains her most immediate precursor to a series of acute crisis episodes.

Each of the seven types of crisis is presented with defining characteristics and suggested treatment modalities consistent with the managed mental health care objective of cost-effective and time-efficient clinical care. Cost-effectiveness measures of managed mental health and substance abuse services should be based on clearly delineated and measurable parameters. For example, what specific behavioral measures will indicate functional improvement of client groups receiving "x" number of crisis intervention sessions? Equally important from the insurance company's perspective is whether a client's improvement is predictable and within the guaranteed claim allowance or, ideally below, current claim costs.

THEORETICAL FRAMEWORK

The clearest framework for the description of a psychological/biological stress continuum is the model reported by the Institute of Medicine study of stress and human health (Elliot & Eisdorfer, 1982). There are three primary elements in the model, the activators/stressors, the reactions, and the consequences, which can be referred to as the "x-y-z sequence" (Elliot & Eisdorfer, 1982). Activators/stressors, which are the focus of this typology, may be internal or external events or conditions—such as depressive symptoms, a serious illness, death of a family member, violent crime victimization, child abuse, recurring psychosis, or a suicide attempt—that are sufficiently intense to evoke some change in the individual. Reactions include both biological and psychosocial responses to the activator/stressor. Consequences are the prolonged and cumulative effects of the reactions, such as physical and/or mental distress. The model attends to individual differences and variations throughout the sequence through its conceptualization of mediators, which are the filters and modifiers in the sequence (Elliot & Eisdorfer, 1982). Added to the model are interventions designed to reduce stress and symptomatology between reactions and consequences. This model suggests a dynamic, interactive process across the stress continuum between an individual and the environment (Lowery, 1987, p. 42).

Burgess and Roberts's (1995) stress-crisis continuum is an eclectic classification developed in 1995 and expanded from earlier models (Baldwin, 1978; Elliot & Eisdorfer, 1982).

LEVEL 1: SOMATIC DISTRESS

Case Example

Mrs. Gardner, a 30-year-old widow, was admitted to a psychiatric unit with numerous physical complaints, including urinary incontinence, nausea, generalized pain, and dizziness. The patient was about to be married for the second time and experienced severe symptoms while writing wedding invitations. Her fiancé's brother had been killed suddenly in an automobile accident while working at his job on the railroad several weeks before the patient's admission. This death was similar to that of the patient's first husband, who was killed in an automobile accident 1 year after their marriage. As a child, the patient had enuresis frequently until age 7. Although the diagnosis of multiple sclerosis was ruled out at this admission, this diagnosis might still show up in later years.

Initially, Mrs. Gardner showed no distress over her symptoms. She was able to give up the catheter when other patients exerted negative reinforcement for this behavior. After this milieu intervention, Mrs. Gardner was able to control her own urine. She concurrently began to talk to the psychiatric nurse about her fear of losing her fiancé as she had lost her first husband, which was causing her to fear another marriage. The nurse helped the patient connect this dynamic understanding to the multiple somatic symptoms she experienced prior to admission, especially the urinary incontinence. Mrs. Gardner was discharged with no recurrence of the symptoms. She and her second husband continued attending couples counseling on an outpatient basis after their marriage.

Such crises are defined by somatic distress resulting from (a) a biomedical disease and/or (b) minor psychiatric symptoms. The mental health issue may or may not be clearly identified. Examples of this type of crisis precipitant include biomedical diagnoses such as cancer, stroke, diabetes, and lupus, as well as minor psychiatric states such as somatization, depression, and phobia or anxiety. The patient's response to this level of stress-crisis is generally anxiety and/or depressive symptoms. The etiology of the crisis is biomedical, that is, there is generally an immune system suppression, a physical health disequilibrium, or, in minor psychiatric symptomatology, an unresolved dynamic issue.

Primary care providers generally see this type of somatic stress–crisis. Physical health symptoms bring the patient to a physician or nurse-practitioner. A physical examination with laboratory testing can generally identify patients with a clear medical diagnosis. Those patients without a biomedical diagnosis may move into the first group at a later time with additional physical symptoms.

Patients without a confirmed medical diagnosis may report physical complaints ranging from a specific set of pain symptoms related to the head, back, abdomen, joints, or chest, or pain during menstruation or intercourse; gastrointestinal symptoms such as bloating, nausea, vomiting; sexual symptoms; and pseudoneurological symptoms such as body weakness, loss of sensation, fatigue, and impaired concentration (American Psychiatric Association, 1994). In the case example, Mrs. Gardner had serious physical symptoms that were connected, in part, to an unresolved grief issue.

Both patients with and without a medical diagnosis can respond with minor psychiatric symptoms of anxiety and depression. Mechanic (1994) argues for a close connection between physical and mental health care in an integrated system in order to address the common comorbidities between physical and mental disorders. That is, a medical diagnosis of cancer or diabetes can easily increase a person's stress level leading to the development of depressive symptoms.

Research

Approximately half of all mental health care is provided by the general medical sector (Regier, Narrow, Rae et al., 1993). Studies indicate that utilization of primary care ambulatory services increases with patients who present with physical symptoms with underlying psychosocial issues. These studies suggest that 40 to 60% of all visits involve symptoms for which no biomedical disease can be detected (Barsky, 1981; Van der Gaag & Van de Ven, 1978). Bodily symptoms or negative mood may result from stress and/or psychosocial problems.

The prevalence of depressive symptomatology in primary care patients ranges from 3.4 to 5.4% (Hoeper, Nyez, Cleary et al. 1979; Barrott, Barrott, Oxman et al., 1988) compared with 4% for major depressive disorder (Blacker, Clare, & Thomas, 1979). Perez-Stable and colleagues (1990) found depression prevalent not only in medical patients but especially in the disadvantaged public sector.

Untreated minor psychiatric symptoms can be costly for a primary care facility. When patients with negative laboratory results complain of vague somatic symptoms, they may be referred to as *somatizers*. Miranda and colleagues (1991) examined the prediction from Mechanic's (1994) attribution theory of somatization that somatizers who are under stress will overuse ambulatory medical services. As hypothesized, life stress interacted with somatization in predicting number of medical visits; somatizers who were under stress made more visits to the clinics than did nonsomatizers or somatizers who were not under stress. Although stress affected somatizers most, stress was predictive of increased medical utilization for all patients. These results suggest that psychological services intended to reduce overutilization of outpatient medical services might be best focused on stress reduction and be most beneficial to somatizers and persons with negative mood states.

The etiology of stress and medical illness is being studied in the stress/immune response research (Lowery, 1987). One program of research that addresses the stress-illness linkages by examining central arousal, immune changes, and clinical outcomes, albeit with different populations, is the work of Levy and colleagues. In a series of studies Levy et al. (1987, 1990) found that breast cancer patients who were rated as less well adjusted to their illness, that is, expressing more distress, had lower levels of natural killer (NK) cell activity than did patients who were less distressed. Moreover, lower NK activity was associated with cancer spread to the axillary lymph nodes. In a sample of healthy individuals (Levy et al., 1991), younger subjects (18 to 29 years of age) who reported more perceived stress were more likely to have lower NK activity and lower levels of plasma beta endorphins, and reported more infectious morbidity.

Intervention

Patients with a defined medical illness will be treated with medical and nursing protocols appropriate to the illness. For patients without a clear medical diagnosis, the intervention strategy is symptom reduction, which requires the use of brief self-report assessment tools to first detect psychiatric symptomatology that is distressing but does not meet criteria for the *Diagnostic and Statistical Manual* (American Psychiatric Association, 1994, DSM-IV). The early treatment of psychiatric symptomatology has been shown to reduce symptoms and interrupt the progression to major psychiatric disorder (Miranda & Munoz, 1994).

An intervention of choice in level 1 somatic distress–crisis is education. Teaching patients about their illness, symptoms, and subsequent health care has long been a priority in health care practice. The method of teaching may be self-tutorial, as in watching videotapes or reading written materials, or individually taught by a nurse or health care provider or through a group method of learning. One teaching method, described by Miranda and Munoz (1994), reports on an 8-week cognitive-behavioral course that was intended to teach patients to control negative moods. The course was similar to cognitive-behavioral therapy.

LEVEL 2: TRANSITIONAL STRESS CRISIS

Case Example

Mary, age 8, is the only child of parents who have been married 12 years. The mother indicated that it took 4 years to get pregnant with Mary. The pregnancy was complicated by a 69-pound weight gain, chronic indigestion, and a blood sugar level of 160 (the mother was told she had gestational diabetes). Mary was born at term; forceps were used because she was in the occiput-posterior head presentation (described by the mother as "sunny-side up"); the delivery was complicated by shoulder dystocia. Mary was large for gestational age, with a birth weight of 10 pounds 13 ounces. At less than 24 hours of age, Mary had a generalized tonic-clonic seizure that lasted about 10 minutes. She continued to have intermittent seizures and was treated with Valium and phenobarbital. She became seizure free, and blood workups were negative. Skull films were negative except for bilateral hematomas from the forceps. Mary was continued on phenobarbital until 8 months of age. She was off anticonvulsants from 8 months until 15 months of age. Mary also had a heart murmur.

At age 8, neuropsychological testing revealed "a pattern of deficits consistent with right hemisphere atrophy and subsequent attention deficit disorder (ADD) with mild hyperactivity." Mary's primary ADD symptoms included visual distraction, slower processing speed, perceptual-motor disorganization, and impulsive response pattern. Both parent and teacher checklists reflect a high level of attentional problems, distractibility, impulsive behavior, and moderate behavior problems in both the home and the school settings. Mary's self-esteem is high; however, her ADD symptoms create considerable learning problems, and she is at continued risk for underachievement in the classroom. Her functioning was legally determined to be a result of neonatal head trauma.

Such crises reflect stressful events that are generally anticipated and reflect life transitions over which the child or adult may or may not have substantial control. Defining characteristics of transitional stresses are that there is disruption of the anticipated developmental event or role. The stressor is generally identified; the event is developmental in nature in that many people experience it. The transition is anticipated, and time is available to prepare for the changes that occur.

Transition stresses include normative events around parenthood such as infertility or premature birth; childhood such as birth injury, hyperactivity, or illness; adolescence such as teen pregnancy or school problems; adulthood such as work disruption or chronic illness; and legal issues such as litigation. The individual's response is the development of personality trait rigidity and loss of personal flexibility. The etiology of the crisis is the failure to master developmental tasks.

The case example describes a medical problem in a normative life event of childbirth. The transition stress results from interruption and delay in the normal neurobiological development of infancy into childhood. Mary's hyperactivity and academic problems are linked to a birth injury, something she and her mother had no control over. Additionally, this injury has the capacity to compromise mastery of the developmental tasks of childhood, adolescence, and adulthood.

Erikson (1963) attributed a central or nuclear conflict to each of the eight developmental life issues. His theory further states that a relatively successful resolution of the basic conflicts associated with each level of development provides an important foundation for successful progression to the next stage. Whatever the resolution of these conflicts—mastery or failure—the result significantly influences personality development. Thus, in transitional stress, there is the potential to fail to master a developmental task.

J. S. Tyhurst (1957) studied transition states—migration and retirement—in the lives of persons experiencing sudden change during civilian disaster. Based on his field studies on individual patterns of responses to community disaster, Tyhurst identified three overlapping phases, each with its own manifestations of stress and attempts at reducing it: a period of impact, a period of recoil, and a posttraumatic period of recovery.

Intervention

There are several useful interventions for transitional stress. The primary task of the crisis counselor during time-limited individual sessions is to educate the patient to an understanding of the changes that have taken or will take place and to explore any psychodynamic implications of these changes. Support is provided as needed, and anticipatory guidance is used to help the individual plan an adaptive coping response to problems that have resulted from the transition. Crisis intervention techniques are used if the event occurs without anticipatory information.

A second intervention is the use of group approaches. Following the brief individual therapy, the client is referred to self-help groups specific to the transition issue (e.g., parents without partners, parents of children with chronic illness). Self-help groups assist those experiencing a similar life transition (e.g., preretirement groups, childbirth preparation groups, group approaches to college orientation).

LEVEL 3: TRAUMATIC STRESS CRISIS

Case Example

Carol had been on maternity leave for 2 months and needed to return to work. She was a single parent who also had a 4-year-old boy and a 7-year-old girl, and she depended on the income she made as an assistant manager at a local restaurant, where she had worked for the past 5 years. Carol placed an ad for a baby-sitter in the newspaper. A woman called about the ad, set up an appointment, and the next day came to the house for an interview. Carol could not be there, so she had her mother come to the house to talk with the woman. The woman introduced herself to Carol's mother, who was holding the month-old baby. She seemed like a pleasant, competent woman and was well dressed. She said she didn't need the money but wanted to spend her time doing something she enjoyed. She said she had two teenage children of her own but missed taking care of an infant. Carol's mother wanted to see how she held a baby, so she handed the baby to the woman. At that moment the telephone rang, and Carol's mother went to the other room to answer it. As soon as she was out of sight, the woman left the house and drove off with the baby. When Carol's mother returned to the room, no one was there. She ran to the door just as the woman was driving away.

Carol's mother immediately called the police, who arrived within 5 minutes. Carol arrived shortly after and was told of her baby's kidnapping. She was devastated and at first blamed her mother. After this incident, Carol's mother began having nightmares and couldn't sleep. Carol, who could barely function, had to send the other children to their father's house to live temporarily.

The news media were immediately involved, and 4 days later the baby was recovered through a tip to a hotline. The abductor's husband's work associates had visited the baby and were suspicious when they noted it did not look like a newborn. They had heard the media announcement about the kidnapping and called the hot line. The abductor was a master's-prepared psychotherapist who had faked a pregnancy as a way to halt divorce proceedings. She pled guilty and spent 1 year in a psychiatric hospital plus 4 years on probation.

Such crises are precipitated by strong, externally imposed stresses. They involve experiencing, witnessing, or learning about a sudden, unexpected, and uncontrollable life-threatening event that overwhelms the individual. Other examples of traumatic crises include crime-related victimization of personal assault, rape, and sexual assault, arson, or hostage taking; victimization by natural disaster; being the victim of a serious vehicular accident or plane crash; sudden death of a partner or family member; accidents with physical dismemberment; and receiving a life-threatening medical diagnosis such as cancer. One of the most recent traumatic stress–crises events was the right-wing terrorist truck bombing of the federal office building in Oklahoma City in which 82 men, women, and children died. The trauma, stress, and crisis reactions of the hundreds of survivors and family members of the deceased will be remembered for years. The community was totally united, and hundreds of caring citizens came to the aid and support of the survivors. In addition, the FBI quickly mobilized and apprehended the two terrorists responsible for the bombing.

The individual's response in the midst of a disaster or traumatic event is intense fear, helplessness, and behavior disorganization. Usual coping behaviors are rendered ineffective due to the sudden, unanticipated nature of the stress. There may be a refractory period during which the person experiences emotional paralysis and coping behaviors cannot be mobilized.

In the case example, the infant's grandmother directly experienced the abduction by offering the infant to the abductor to hold and then leaving the room to answer a telephone call. The infant's mother experienced the trauma by learning about the abduction when she returned home. The women were unable to process the information about the trauma, and thus the dysfunctional symptoms developed. Until the infant was returned, the mother and grandmother were unable to cope with daily activities.

Research

Lindemann and his associates at Massachusetts General Hospital introduced the concepts of crisis intervention and time-limited treatment in 1943 in the aftermath of Boston's worst nightclub fire, at the Coconut Grove, in which 493 people perished. Lindemann (1944) and colleagues based their crisis theory on their observations of the acute and delayed reactions of survivors and grief-stricken relatives of victims. Their clinical work focused on the psychological symptoms of the survivors and on preventing unresolved grief among relatives of the persons who had died. They found that many individuals experiencing acute grief often had five related reactions: somatic distress, preoccupation with the image of the deceased, guilt, hostile reactions, and loss of patterns of conduct.

Furthermore, Lindemann and colleagues concluded that the duration of a grief reaction appears to be dependent on the success with which the bereaved person does his or her mourning and "grief work." In general, this grief work refers to achieving emancipation from the deceased, readjusting to the changes in the environment from which the loved one is missing, and developing new relationships. People need to be encouraged to permit themselves to have a period of mourning and eventual acceptance of the loss and adjustment to life without the deceased. If the normal process of grieving is delayed, negative outcomes will develop.

In the 1970s, the trauma of rape was introduced into the literature through the term "rape trauma syndrome" (Burgess & Holmstrom, 1974). Rape trauma consists of an acute phase of disorganization followed by a longterm phase of reorganization. A wide range of somatic, cognitive, psychological, and social symptoms are noted in both phases.

The trauma suffered by the victim affects her family, her social network, and the community. Recovery from rape is complex and influenced by many factors, including prior life stress, style of attack, relationship of victim and offender, number of assailants, pre-existing psychiatric disorders, the amount of violence or the sexual acts demanded, and postrape factors of institutional response to the victim, social network response, and subsequent victimization. Clinicians should consider all these factors in assessing and identifying victims who are at high risk for slow recovery from rape and who will remain vulnerable to many life stresses for a long time.

The pioneering work of Charles R. Figley and members of the Consortium on Veteran Studies (Figley, 1978) provides insight into the level 3 crisis of war combat. Figley suggests that combat includes four major elements that make it highly traumatic: a high degree of dangerousness, a sense of helplessness in preventing death, a sense of destruction and disruption, in both lives and property, and a sense of loss. Moreover, the long-term emotional adjustment to combat follows four stages: recovery, avoidance, reconsideration, and adjustment.

Intervention

Crisis reaction refers to the acute stage, which usually occurs soon after the hazardous event and includes the neurobiology of trauma. During this phase, the person's acute reaction may take various forms, including helplessness, confusion, anxiety, shock, disbelief, and anger. Low self-esteem and serious depression are often produced by the crisis state. The person in crisis may appear to be incoherent, disorganized, agitated, and volatile or calm, subdued, withdrawn, and apathetic. It is during this period that the individual is often most willing to seek help, and crisis intervention is usually most effective at this time (Golan, 1978).

Tyhurst recommended a stage-specific intervention. He concluded that persons in a traumatic crisis state should not be removed from their life situation, and intervention should focus on bolstering the network of relationships.

Cognitive-behavioral therapy to assist in the information processing of trauma (Burgess & Hartman, 1997) is a treatment recommended for rape-related posttraumatic stress disorder and depression. Also termed *cognitive processing therapy* (Resick & Mechanic, 1995), this treatment is time-limited and effective. Other modalities to consider include pharmacotherapy with antianxiety medication to help with the longterm physiological symptoms of posttraumatic stress disorder. In addition and/or following individual trauma work, patients are referred for stress reduction/relaxation treatment, crisis or self-help groups, and psychoeducation groups.

Strategic solution-focused therapy (Quick, 1998) combines the principles and techniques of strategic therapy and solution-focused therapy. In this approach, the therapist clarifies problems, elaborates solutions, identifies and evaluates attempted solutions, and designs interventions that include validation, compliment, and suggestion components. The pragmatic principle of doing what works and changing what is not working is the goal for both the client and the therapist. See chapter 2 for detailed information.

A promising therapeutic technique designed by Francine Shapiro, eye movement desensitization and reprocessing (EMDR), incorporates key aspects of many of the major therapeutic modalities. The basic underlying principles derive from an information-processing model that aims to directly access and process dysfunctional perceptions that were stored in memory at the time of the traumatic event. The state-dependent perceptions are considered primary to the development of posttraumatic stress symptoms. Additional, rigid thoughts are assumed to be caused by earlier life experiences that are dysfunctionally stored. The primary goal of EMDR is to release clients from the nonadaptive bonds of the past, thereby providing them with the ability to make positive and flexible choices in the present. Current research on EMDR substantiates its ability to rapidly and effectively process the targeted event and attendant traumatic information. The eight phases of treatment are considered necessary to resolve the trauma (Shapiro, 1998).

LEVEL 4: FAMILY CRISIS

Case Example

Meredith, age 23, first met Willis, age 29, when he came to the apartment she shared with a roommate hairdresser, to have a haircut. According to Willis, they felt an instant chemistry, and they began dating. From the beginning they isolated themselves from others, and when Meredith and her roommate parted, Willis asked Meredith to move in with him. Meredith ignored a nagging internal warning that this was not a good decision. For example, on their first date, Willis showed Meredith, a mental health counselor, his psychiatric record. She later said his diagnosis should have been a red flag to her: borderline personality disorder with antisocial, dependent, and passive-aggressive features. He also had a history of a drinking problem.

Willis believed he had found his future marriage partner; Meredith did not. After several months, she met another man she wanted to date and told Willis, whose reaction was worse than she imagined. He became depressed and began cutting himself and leaving blood on tissues around the apartment and writing "I love you" in blood on the wall. He begged her not to leave.

As Meredith began dating her new boyfriend, Willis obtained his address and telephone number. He began to write threatening letters. The boyfriend ended the relationship by leaving town. Willis continued to mail Meredith notes and greeting cards, pleading with her and then berating her. Detectives told Willis they could not arrest him, since his letters had been written before the new state stalking law took effect. They suggested he enter a psychiatric hospital.

Meredith left town, but within months Willis located her. She found a balloon and get-well card taped to her car and noticed two holes in the front windows of her apartment. When police arrested Willis, they found a stun gun, rope, latex gloves, duct tape, and a pocketknife in his car. He pled no contest to his 16-month obsession with his ex-girlfriend.

Some emotional crises result from attempts to deal with primary interpersonal situations that develop within the family or social network (e.g., relational dysfunction). These relate back to developmental tasks and level 2 transitional crisis. If unresolved, the family crises reflect a struggle with a deeper, but usually circumscribed, developmental issue that has not been resolved adaptively in the past and that represents an attempt to attain emotional maturity. These crises usually involve developmental issues such as dependency, value conflicts, sexual identity, emotional intimacy, power issues, or attaining self-discipline. Often a repeated pattern of specific relationship difficulties occurs over time in those presenting with this type of crisis (Baldwin, 1978). The crisis may be directed internally or externally, as in chronic abuse.

Examples of family crises include child abuse, the use of children in pornography, parental abductions, adolescent runaways, battering and rape, homelessness, and domestic homicide. The individual's response to this level of crisis is chronic fear, an inability to protect the self and others, and a type of learned helplessness. The etiology of the crisis relates to the neurobiology of chronic trauma. There is often undisclosed relationship abuse and divided family loyalty.

In the case example, the potential dangerousness of the male partner, Willis, is clearly noted. His psychiatric diagnosis of personality disorder suggests an unresolved developmental power issue as noted by his stalking.

Research

It is important to note that every type of emotional crisis involves an interaction of an external stressor and a vulnerability of the individual. However, it is in level 4 crisis that there is a shift from a primarily external locus of stress that produces the crisis to an internal locus determined by the psychodynamics of the individual and/or preexisting psychopathology that becomes manifest in problem situations. Child abuse and battering within a domestic violence context are prime examples of family crises. Both are interpersonal situations that exist around long-term relationships. See chapter 20 for a review of the research on child abuse and crisis intervention.

Intervention

In family violence, the goals of intervention in level 4 crises are to help individuals restabilize their lives, strengthen their interpersonal relationships, and deter psychiatric symptomatology. First the crisis state, if there is one, must be resolved. All abuse must cease, and children and adults must be safe. The survivors must adapt to immediate losses and changes created by the disclosure of abuse and the protective response by others. The dysfunction in the family system must be addressed.

Roberts's (1995, 1996) seven-step crisis intervention model is implemented. This model offers an integrated problem-solving approach to crisis resolution. The steps include assessing lethality and safety needs; establishing rapport and communication; identifying the major problems; dealing with feelings and providing support; exploring possible alternatives; assisting in formulating an action plan; and conducting follow-up.

Recovery services are to aid survivors in resolving the long-term issues. Stress reduction interventions are of two types: (a) those designed to help the individual prevent or manage stress, and (b) those aimed at eliminating or reducing the potency of the stressor. Techniques to consider include physical activity to discharge repressed energy; nutrition therapy to enhance physiological recovery; spiritual support for persons who value religious beliefs to promote a sense of integrity with the natural world; relaxation to counter hypervigilance; pleasure activities to promote a sense of fun and humor; and expressive activities such as reading, art, and music.

A variety of psychoeducational and therapeutic interventions have been developed to change perpetrator behavior, many of which have produced an actual decrease in violent or exploitive behavior. Generally, interventions include components designed to increase the knowledge and skills of the perpetrator with regard to anger control, mediation, communication, and family roles. See chapter 8 on domestic violence interventions.

Group models are often helpful. For example, narrative theory provides a useful framework for brief group treatment of persons in crisis because it proposes that understanding of experience is gained through social discourse. Groups offer persons in crisis a new context for attributing meaning to critical events (Laube, 1998).

LEVEL 5: SERIOUS MENTAL ILLNESS

Case Example

Mrs. Dee, age 32, was referred to the mental health clinic by her case manager. When she arrived, clinging to her were her four children: Doddy (age 2), Bryant (age 3), Katie (age 5), and Sally (age 6). The children were unkempt and waiflike. Mrs. Dee, chain-smoking cigarettes, stated that she wanted some Valium for her nerves. Mrs. Dee lives in the project with her husband, Jim. She and her family (namely, three sisters, a younger brother, father, and mother) have been known to the multiservice health center for more than 15 years. Mrs. Dee, upon questioning, revealed that she felt things were just getting to be too much this morning, and she decided to call her case manager. Although she did not describe herself as depressed, questioning revealed that she was hearing voices telling her not to eat because the food was poisoned. She had lost 20 pounds in the last month, and her sleeping was erratic because she felt the neighbors were able to see through her walls. She, as well as the children, looked emaciated. Although the children clung to their mother, she seemed to ignore them.

Three months earlier, Mrs. Dee had had a hysterectomy. She was upset with the home care she received after the surgery. She had been promised homemaker services, but when the homemakers came to the apartment, they quit the next day, which she attributed to the fact that they were Black and she was White Irish. A month later she got into a row with her father, who was an alcoholic. Her husband, who was out of work, was at home most of the day or out playing baseball. During this time, her three sisters were in and out of her apartment, as was her brother. All her siblings were on drugs or were drinking. Two sisters had children and presently the state was stepping in to remove the children from their mothers because of neglect and multiple injuries that could not be accounted for.

Shortly after her return home from the hospital after the hysterectomy, Mrs. Dee slashed her wrists. She was taken to an emergency ward, where her wrists were stitched. She refused to talk to a psychiatrist. Homemaker help was sent to her house, but she refused to let the homemaker enter her house. She did develop a relationship with a nurse, and she recounted a life full of struggle. Her first child was born when she was 16. She married 2 years later and had another child, followed by a divorce, then marriage to her present husband and two more children. She had difficulty with her husband, who often beat her. During this time a social worker came to the house, and eventually all these children were placed in a home and later were given up for adoption. Thus, Mrs. Dee forbade any investigation into the records at this time for fear her present four children would be taken away. She claimed that she had been abused by the authorities and that her children were removed from her against her will. The current stressor of the hysterectomy and its unresolved meaning reactivated underlying psychotic symptoms and heightened the multiproblem nature of this family.

Such crises reflect serious mental illness in which preexisting problems have been instrumental in precipitating the crisis. Or the situation may involve a state in which the severity of the illness significantly impairs or complicates adaptive resolution. There is often an unidentified dynamic issue.

Other examples of serious mental illness include diagnoses of psychosis, dementia, bipolar depression, and schizophrenia. The patient response will be disorganized thinking and behavior. The etiology is neurobiological.

The case example indicates that Mrs. Dee was experiencing perceptual difficulties and paranoid thinking. An unresolved issue for her was related to the hysterectomy and the psychological meaning of the end to her childbearing.

Intervention

The clinician needs to be able to diagnose the mental illness and adapt the intervention approach to include appreciation of the personality or characterological aspects of the patient. Persons with long-term and recurring severe mental illness require a mix of traditional medical and long-term treatments that are helpful in sustaining their function and role. Roberts's (1991, 1995, 1996) crisis intervention model may be used to reduce symptoms in an acute crisis.

The crisis therapist responds primarily in terms of the present problem of the patient, with an emphasis on problem-solving skills and environmental manipulation. The therapist gives support but is careful not to produce or reinforce dependency or regression by allowing the therapeutic process to become diffuse. The therapist acknowledges the deeper problems of the client and assesses them to the degree possible within the crisis intervention context, but does not attempt to resolve problems representing deep emotional conflict. Through the process of crisis intervention, the patient is helped to stabilize functioning to the fullest extent possible and is prepared for referral for other services once the process has been completed.

Case monitoring and management are indicated, as well as an assessment for inpatient hospitalization or sheltered care. Medication will be needed for psychotic thinking. Continuity of care is critical with this level of crisis and is generally accomplished through the case manager. Other services should include referral for vocational training and group work.

LEVEL 6: PSYCHIATRIC EMERGENCIES

Case Example

Mr. Mars, age 65, was admitted to a psychiatric unit following a suicide attempt. According to his history, he had two older sisters and several older half siblings. His mother, who had glaucoma, died in her 90s of a cause unknown to the patient; his father died at age 66 of prostate cancer. Mr. Mars described himself as the "bully" in his family and felt distanced from siblings and parents.

Mr. Mars enlisted in the Marine Corps after high school and served in World War II combat. After the war, he returned home and worked 20 years as a truck driver, then for 8 years as a prison guard. He and his wife had no children. Prior to his diagnosis of diabetes, he drank beer regularly and enjoyed the company of his tavern friends. He had many interests prior to his work retirement, belonging to community groups, the Marine Corps League, and the VFW, and he was chairman of his church picnic.

Mr. Mars was first hospitalized at age 48 with complaints of inability to sleep, no interest in work, suicide ideation, thoughts of wanting to hurt his wife, a peculiar preoccupation with numbers, lack of appetite, and weight loss. His recent diagnosis was diabetes mellitus, which was seen as a precipitant to the depression. He was diagnosed with psychotic depressive reaction and treated with Elavil, Trilafon, and group therapy and discharged after 6 weeks. Mr. Mars continued outpatient counseling and pharmacotherapy for a year. Counseling notes indicate he discussed his contemplated suicide at the time of hospitalization, displayed no insight into his condition, regretted not having children, always worked hard, had little communication with his wife, talked on a very superficial level, and had passive aggressive behavior (e.g., waiting weeks to get even for a perceived wrong).

Mr. Mars's history of medical problems included diabetes, high blood pressure, and glaucoma. He had a transurethral resection of the prostate for a benign condition. His second psychiatric hospitalization occurred following the laceration of his left wrist and arm, which required surgical correction. On admission, he stated, "I wanted to end it all . . . too many things in too little time." That evening he had eaten dinner around 6 P.M. and had a graham cracker snack at 10 P.M. While his wife was at choir practice, he cut his arm several times with a razor blade and "held it over the bathtub hoping to pass out and die." When nothing happened, he cut his arm several more times. He said that after retiring he "couldn't enjoy it like I wanted; I'm stuck in the house and bored." His stated goals for hospitalization were to "straighten out, get better and get the hell out of here."

Mrs. Mars stated her husband did not give her any indication he was depressed or was thinking of harming himself. She had gone to choir practice, and when she returned found her husband over the bathtub with several deep lacerations; she called the ambulance. Mrs. Mars described her husband as selfish and self-serving, showing no consideration for others. She said they argued frequently and that he did not talk about his feelings. They had been married 40 years. Mrs. Mars reported that when they argued, her husband would hold a grudge and not talk to her for days.

Psychiatric emergencies involve crisis situations in which general functioning has been severely impaired. The individual is rendered incompetent, unable to assume personal responsibility, and unable to exert control over feelings and actions that he or she experiences. *There is threat or actual harm to self and/or others.*

Examples of psychiatric emergencies include drug overdose, suicide attempts, stalking, personal assault, rape, and homicide. The individual presents with a loss of personal control. The patient's level of consciousness and orientation, rationality, rage, and anxiety all affect the level of cooperation he or she may give to the immediate assessment of the need for emergency intervention.

The etiology of these crises focuses the self-abusive component to suicide attempts and drug overdoses. Aggression toward others suggests a need for dominance, control, and sexualized aggression.

The case example illustrates serious suicidal intent on the part of Mr.

Mars. Of interest is the denial by Mrs. Mars of any warning signs. By history it was learned that Mr. Mars was trying to dispense some of his money to a favorite niece when Mrs. Mars interceded. While in the hospital, he tried to run away from a group activity and into a river. Three weeks after admission, he successfully hung himself in a bathroom at 12:30 A.M., between 30-minute unit checks.

Intervention

The clinician needs to be confident in his or her skills at managing a client's out-of-control behavior and/or must have adequate assistance available (see chapter 16). When an emergency presents itself, with appropriate cooperation, questions need to be raised and answered regarding the location of the patient, exactly what the patient has done, and the availability of significant others. In the case of a suicide attempt, the clinician's immediate task, to assess the lethality of the act, is greatly aided by published lethality scales. Where medical-biological danger has been determined to exist or where sufficient data for that determination are not available, emergency medical attention is required. Dangerous and volatile situations should be handled by police and local rescue squads, who can provide rapid transportation to a hospital emergency room. Rapid medical evaluation is an essential first step in resolving a current and future suicidal crisis (Jobes & Berman, 1996).

Psychiatric emergencies are the most difficult type of crisis to manage because there may be incomplete information about the situation, the patient may be disruptive or minimally helpful, and there is an immediacy in understanding the situation in depth in order to initiate effective treatment. Patient assessment is greatly facilitated when informants with some knowledge of the precipitating events accompany the patient; in many instances they can be helpful in planning appropriate psychological and medical services (see chapters 15, 16, and 18).

The basic intervention strategy for level 6 psychiatric crisis involves the following components: (a) rapidly assessing the patient's psychological and medical condition; (b) clarifying the situation that produced or led to the patient's condition; (c) mobilizing all mental health and/or medical resources necessary to effectively treat the patient; and (d) arranging for follow-up or coordination of services to ensure continuity of treatment as appropriate. It is in this type of psychiatric emergency that the skills of the crisis therapist are tested to the limit because he or she must be able to work effectively and quickly in highly charged situations and to intervene where there may be life-threatening implications of the patient's condition (Burgess & Baldwin, 1981; Burgess & Roberts, 1995).

Police or emergency medical technicians are often called to transport the patient to a hospital or jail. Medication, restraint, and/or legal intervention are all indicated for psychiatric emergencies.

LEVEL 7: CATASTROPHIC CRISIS

Case Example

A young bisexual woman in her mid-30s was admitted to a psychiatric hospital following a serious suicide attempt. A number of stressful events had occurred over a 3-month period. She began drinking heavily when her partner moved out of her apartment; she had a car accident during a snowstorm; later her car was stolen, and she began "drinking around the clock." She could not control herself and took a leave of absence from her computer analyst job. She was hospitalized briefly at the local psychiatric hospital. Three weeks after that hospitalization, one evening she was drinking with a man she met at a bar. He drove her home, and they continued drinking in her apartment. The man wanted sex, but she refused, and he forced the situation. After he left the apartment she called a friend to take her to a local hospital, where a rape examination revealed vaginal lacerations. On returning home, the woman continued drinking and, while intoxicated, slashed her wrist with a broken glass. She again called her friend, who took her back to the hospital, where she received 10 sutures; later she was transferred to the psychiatric hospital.

The next day the woman requested discharge against medical advice. She returned to her apartment and went on an extended drinking bout for another 6 weeks, during which she was also very suicidal. About the time she brought a legal suit against one of the male patients and the psychiatric hospital for simple assault, blood tests revealed that she was HIV-positive.

Level 7 has two or more level 3 traumatic crises in combination with level 4, 5, or 6 stressors. Classifying an individual into one of the preceding levels of crisis is dependent upon the nature, duration, and intensity of the stressful life event(s) and one's perception of being unable to cope and lessen the crisis. Sometimes a crisis is temporary and quickly resolved; at other times it can be life-threatening and extremely difficult to accept and resolve (e.g., having AIDS or a multiple personality disorder, or losing all family members due to a disaster).

In summary, the lack of an up-to-date classification model for determining levels of emotional crises has resulted in a significant gap to advancing the development of crisis theory. The revised and expanded Baldwin (1978) crisis typology is presented to increase communication between therapists and other crisis care providers in clinical assessment, treatment planning, and continuity of health care within a managed care context.

REFERENCES

American Psychiatric Association. (1994). *Diagnostic and statistical manual of mental disorders* (4th ed.). Washington, DC: Author.
Baldwin, B. A. (1978). A paradigm for the classification of emotional crises: Implications for crisis intervention. *American Journal of Orthopsychiatry, 48,* 538–551.
Barrott, J. E., Barrott, J. A., Oxman,

T. et al. (1988). The prevalence of psychiatric disorders in primary care practice. *Archives of General Psychiatry, 44,* 1100–1108.

Barsky, A. J. (1981). Hidden reasons some patients visit doctors. *Annals of Internal Medicine, 94,* 492.

Burgess, A. W., & Baldwin, B. A. (1981). *Crisis intervention theory and practice.* Englewood Cliffs, NJ: Prentice-Hall.

Burgess, A. W., & Hartman, C. R. (1997). Victims of sexual assault. In A. W. Burgess (Ed.), *Psychiatric nursing: Promoting mental health* (pp. 425–437). Stamford, CT: Appleton & Lange.

Burgess, A. W., & Holmstrom, L. L. (1974). Rape trauma syndrome. *American Journal of Psychiatry, 131,* 981–986.

Burgess, A. W., & Roberts, A. R. (1995). The stress-crisis continuum. *Crisis Intervention and Time-Limited Treatment, 2*(1), 31–47.

Caplan, G. (1961). *An approach to community mental health.* New York. Grune & Stratton.

Caplan, G. (1964). *Principles of preventive psychiatry.* New York: Basic Books.

Elkin, J., Shea, T., Watkins, J. et al. (1989). National Institutes of Mental Health treatment of depression collaborative research program: General effectiveness of treatment. *Archives of General Psychiatry, 46,* 971–982.

Elliott, G. R., & Eisdorfer, C. (1982). *Stress and human health.* New York: Springer.

Enthoven, A. C. (1993). The history and principles of managed competition. *Health Affairs, 12* (suppl), 24–28.

Escobar, J. I., Rubio-Stipec, M., Canino, G., & Karno, M. (1989). Somatic symptoms index (SSI): A new abridged somatization construct. *Journal of Nervous and Mental Disease, 177,* 140–146.

Feldman, S. (1972). *Managed mental health services.* Springfield, IL: Charles C. Thomas.

Figley, C. (1978). *Stress disorders among Vietnam veterans: Theory, research and treatment implications.* New York: Brunner/Mazel.

Golan, N. (1978). *Treatment in crisis situations.* New York: Free Press.

Hoeper, E. W., Nyez, G. R., Cleary, P. D. et al. (1979). Estimated prevalence of research diagnostic criteria mental disorders in primary medical care. *International Journal of Mental Health, 8,* 6–13.

Hollon, S. D., DeRubeis, R. J., Evans, M. D. et al. (1992). Cognitive therapy and pharmacotherapy for depression singly and in combination. *Archives of General Psychiatry, 49,* 774–781.

Jobes, D. A., & Berman A. L. (1996). Crisis assessment and time-limited intervention with high risk suicidal youth. In A. R. Roberts (Ed.), *Crisis management and brief treatment: Theory, practice and research* (pp. 53–69). Chicago: Nelson-Hall.

Kelley, P. (1998). Narrative therapy in a managed care world. *Crisis Intervention and Time-Limited Intervention, 4,* 113–123.

Laube, J. J. (1998). Crisis-oriented narrative group therapy. *Crisis Intervention and Time-Limited Treatment, 4,* 215–226.

Lazarus, A. (1994). Managed care: Lessons from community mental health. *Hospital and Community Psychiatry, 45*(4), 30–31.

Lazarus, A. (1995). Preparing for practice in an era of managed competition. *Psychiatric Services, 46*(2), 184–185.

Levy, S. M., Herberman, R. B., Whiteside, T., et al. (1990). Perceived social support and tumor estrogen/progesterone receptor status as predictors of natural killer cell activity in breast cancer cell patients. *Psychosomatic Medicine, 52,* 73–85.

Levy, S. M., Herberman, R. B., & Winkelstein, A. (1987). Natural killer cell activity in primary breast cancer patients: Social and behavioral predictors. Paper presented at the Annual Meeting of the American Society of Clinical Oncology.

Lindemann, E. (1944). Symptomotology and management of acute grief. *American Journal of Psychiatry, 101,* 141–148.

Lowery, B. (1987). Stress research: Some theoretical and methodological issues. *Image, 19*(1), 42–46.

Mechanic, D. (1994). Integrating mental health into a general health care system. *Hospital and Community Psychiatry, 45,* 893–897.

Miranda, J., & Munoz, R. (1994). Intervention for minor depression in primary care patients. *Psychosomatic Medicine, 56,* 136–142.

Miranda, J., Perez-Stable, E., Munoz, R. F., Hargreaves W., & Henke C. J. (1991). Somatization, psychiatric disorder, and stress in utilization of ambulatory medical services. *Health Psychology, 10*(1), 46–51.

Perez-Stable, E., Miranda, J., Munoz R. F. et al. (1990). Depression in medical outpatients: Underrecognition and misdiagnosis. *Archives of Internal Medicine, 150,* 1083–1088.

Quick, E. K. (1998). Strategic solution focused therapy: Doing what works in crisis intervention. *Crisis Intervention and Time-Limited Intervention, 4,* 197–214.

Regier D. A., Narrow W. E., Rae, D. S. et al. (1993). The de facto US mental and addictive disorders service system: Epidemiologic Catchment Area prospective 1-year prevalence rates of disorders and services. *Archives of General Psychiatry, 50,* 85–94.

Resick, P., & Mechanic, M. (1995). Cogitive processing therapy with rape victims. In A. R. Roberts (Ed.), *Crisis intervention and time-limited cognitive treatment* (pp. 182–198). Thousand Oaks, CA: Sage.

Roberts, A. R., (Ed.). (1991). *Contemporary perspectives on crisis intervention and prevention.* Englewood Cliffs, NJ: Prentice-Hall.

Roberts, A. R., (Ed.). (1995). *Crisis intervention and time-limited cognitive treatment.* Thousand Oaks, CA: Sage.

Roberts, A. R. (1996). The epidemiology of acute crisis in American society. In A. R. Roberts (Ed.), *Crisis management and brief treatment* (pp. 13–28). Chicago: Nelson-Hall.

Shapiro, F. (1998). Eye movement desensitization and reprocessing (EMDR): Accelerated information processing and affect-driven constructions. *Crisis Intervention and Time-Limited Interventions, 4,* 145–157.

Tyhurst J. S. (1957). The role of transition states—including disasters—in mental illness. In *Symposium on social and preventive psychiatry.* Washington, DC: Walter Reed Army Institute of Research.

Van der Gaag, J., & Van de Ven, W. (1978). The demand for primary health care. *Medical Care, 16,* 299.

4

Innovations in Group Crisis Intervention

Critical Incident Stress Debriefing (CISD)
and Critical Incident Stress Management (CISM)

GEORGE S. EVERLY, JR.
JEFFREY M. LATING
JEFFREY T. MITCHELL

Crises are affecting an ever-increasing number of businesses, schools, and communities, and mass disasters are becoming virtually epidemic. For example, the lifetime prevalence for trauma exposure has been estimated to be about 60% for males and about 51% for females in the United States (Kessler, Sonnega, Bromet, Hughes, & Nelson, 1995); the prevalence for trauma exposure for children and adolescents has been estimated to be about 40% (see Ford, Ruzek, and Niles, 1996); and the lifetime prevalence of criminal victimization as assessed among female HMO patients has been estimated to be 57% (Koss, Woodruff, & Koss, 1991).

As a result of these disturbing trends, formalized crisis intervention programs have been recommended and instituted in larger numbers than ever before (see chapter 1). For example, in 1989 the International Critical Incident Stress Foundation (ICISF) formalized an international network of crisis response teams that utilize a standardized group crisis intervention model and share access to centralized international coordination. This network now consists of over 300 crisis response teams with approximately 10,000 trained crisis team members worldwide. The ICISF network, which represents the largest crisis intervention system of its kind in the world, gained United Nations affiliation in 1997.

In 1992, the American Red Cross initiated its disaster mental health network, which as of 1999 had approximately 2,000 active disaster mental health personnel throughout the United States. In 1996, the Occupational

Safety and Health Administration (OSHA, 1996) recommended that health care and social service organizations implement a comprehensive program of medical and psychological support services for employees who experience or witness violence at the workplace. Similarly, OSHA (1998) later recommended that such postincident response programs, including postincident debriefing and counseling, also be made available to the employees of late-night retail establishments. In addition, OSHA has specifically noted that an emerging trend in crisis response is the utilization of comprehensive, multicomponent Critical Incident Stress Management (CISM) programs in order to "provide a range or continuum of care tailored to the individual victim or the organization's needs" (OSHA, 1998, p. 8). Crisis intervention programs are not confined to civilian populations; they have been implemented by the United States military as well. The U.S. Air Force has mandated that crisis response teams be trained and available at every U.S. Air Force base to respond to any psychological crises that might arise (AFI 44153). Similarly, the U.S. Coast Guard Policies and Procedures (COMDTINST 1754.3) has mandated that multicomponent crisis intervention programs be established in each geographic region for which the U.S. Coast Guard has responsibility.

As the need for crisis intervention services has grown, so, too, has the need for innovation in these services. Three such innovations are the Two-Factor Model of acute crisis, Critical Incident Stress Debriefing (CISD), and CISM. The Two-Factor Model is a phenomenological innovation, whereas CISD and CISM are applied innovations. These three innovations, as well as case examples, shall be reviewed in this chapter.

A TWO-FACTOR MODEL OF ACUTE CRISIS

Before introducing the aforementioned methods of group crisis intervention, let us begin with a brief introduction to the nature of the acute crisis response. The conceptual exploration and potential theoretical integration of the acute crisis response is not a new endeavor. More than 100 years ago, the psychologist Pierre Janet formulated a systematic therapeutic approach to posttraumatic psychopathology that recognized the various stages and evolutions of posttraumatic stress reactions. Janet contended that the cognitive appraisal of the traumatic event combined with emotional reactivity determined the degree, nature, and severity of psychological impact. In a later integrated conceptual delineation, Kardiner (1941) described posttraumatic stress as a physioneurosis, a term that encompasses the intricate connections of biological and psychological substrates. Almost 40 years after Kardiner's psychophysiological formulation of posttraumatic stress, the American Psychiatric Association (APA, 1980) operationalized posttraumatic stress disorder (PTSD) under the rubric of an anxiety disorder, combining more basic physiological constituents with higher order cognitive and affective processes. The APA criteria (APA, 1980, 1987, 1994) conceptualized PTSD within three symptom clusters that occur following exposure to a traumatic event. These symptom clusters are (a) intrusive psychological reexperiencing of the traumatic event; (b) psychological numbing to, or reduced involvement with, the external environment; and (c) autonomic nervous system (ANS) hyperreactivity and/or hyperfunction (although recent data suggest that the physiological arousal is not limited to the ANS).

Everly (1995) has posited that these symptom clusters may be blended into a two-factor "neurocognitive" phenomenological core. The two factors are:

1. A *neurological hypersensitivity*, which results in a pathognomonic proclivity for *neurologic arousal* (Everly, 1990; van der Kolk, 1988) existing within the limbic circuitry and primarily affecting amygdaloid and hippocampal cells (Everly, 1995).
2. A *psychological hypersensitivity* in the form of intrusive cognitive recollection of some uniquely meaningful aspect of the trauma. This psychological hypersensitivity may be viewed as some form of violation or contradiction of the individual's worldview (or Weltanschauung) regarding safety, security, or sense of self. Moreover, the individual is unable to assimilate the traumatic event into his or her idiosyncratic worldview (Bowlby, 1969; Everly, 1995; Janoff-Bulman, 1992; Lifton, 1988; Wilson, 1989).

Factor 1: Neurological Hypersensitivity

We will now briefly review each of these factors. As mentioned previously, Kardiner's (1941) term *physioneurosis* captured the inextricable combination of biological and psychological phenomena. More specifically, he purported five consistent clinical features of posttrauma syndromes:

1. Exaggerated startle reflex and irritability
2. Atypical dream experiences
3. A propensity for explosive and aggressive reactions
4. Psychic fixation upon the trauma
5. Constriction of personality functioning

Reviewing Kardiner's criteria, as well as DSM criteria, it is apparent that the core physiological mechanisms of a trauma reaction involve arousal of the central nervous system (CNS), the autonomic nervous system (ANS), and sundry neuroendocrine effector mechanisms (Everly, 1995). Moreover, van der Kolk (1988) views PTSD as a pathological inability to modulate arousal, which is also consistent with Kardiner's original perspective. Therefore, PTSD may represent CNS neurological hypersensitivity (in the form of "ergotropic tuning" or preferential sympathetic nervous system responsiveness) and hyperfunction (in the form of hypertonus, reactive hyperphasic amplitude, or both). Robert Post (1985, 1986; Post & Ballenger, 1981) has proposed the term *behavioral sensitization* to reflect the condition in which extreme stress, including psychosocial stressors, may render the neurological tissues of the limbic system hypersensitive to subsequent excitation. Post (1992) has since postulated that psychosocial stressors may be capable of creating a form of neurological sensitization that may be encoded at the level of gene expression. Thus, an individual suffering from posttraumatic stress may experience neurological hypersensitivity in the following forms:

1. Altered neuronal structural and intraneuronal function such as an augmentation of excitatory postsynaptic receptors and/or a decrease in inhibitory receptors (see Gray, 1982; Joy, 1985; Nutt, 1989; Perry, Southwick, & Giller, 1990; Post & Ballenger, 1981).
2. An augmentation of available excitatory neurotransmitters, such as norepinephrine (Davidson & Baum, 1986; Murburs, McFall, & Veith, 1990; Krystal et al., 1989); dopamine (Kalivas & Duffy, 1989); and glutamate (McGeer & McGeer, 1988; Palkovits, Lang, Patthy, & Elekes, 1986).
3. A decrease in inhibitory neurochemicals, such as gamma-aminobutyric acid (GABA; Biggio, 1983; Drugan et al., 1989; Gray, 1982; Krnjevic, 1983; van Gelder, 1986).

Excessive stimulation of CNS mechanisms may, in extreme cases, result in a well-documented phenomenon known as *excitatory toxicity.* In essence, excitatory toxicity entails massive release of excitatory neurotransmitters (primarily glutamate, but likely norepinephrine, aspartate, dopamine, and others as well), which in high enough concentrations may become "excitotoxins" capable of damaging or possibly destroying the neural substrates they serve. Neural excitatory toxicity within hippocampal, septal, and corpus callosum cells may account for some of the memory and concentration dysfunctions (Everly & Horton, 1989), aggressive behavior, and diminished family or social interaction or bonding, as well as posttrauma alexithymia (Henry, 1993). In fact, recent data have suggested reduced hippocampal volume in individuals with combat-related PTSD and in individuals with PTSD related to childhood physical and sexual abuse (Bremner et al., 1995; Bremner et al., 1997). As noted previously, overarousal in PTSD is not limited to the CNS; neuroendocrine hyperactivity (elevated circulating catecholamine levels) is considered a core feature of PTSD (Davidson & Baum, 1986; Mason et al., 1986). The data are, however, less conclusive regarding endocrine involvement of the hypothalamic-anterior pituitary-adrenal cortical (HPAC) axis (Davidson & Baum, 1986; Mason et al., 1986; Pitman & Orr, 1990; Rahe et al., 1990; Schaeffer & Baum, 1984).

Factor 2: Psychological Hypersensitivity

As mentioned earlier, the essence of a traumatic reaction from a psychological perspective is likely predicated on the violation of the individual's worldview as it pertains to safety or security, as well as the person's inability to assimilate the traumatic event into his or her perception of the self and/or the world. Janoff-Bulman (1988) described certain core assumptions about how people view the world and themselves with regard to invulnerability. More specifically, these assumptions are (a) that the world is benevolent (i.e., people are inherently good, and good things happen); (b) that events in the world are meaningful (i.e., events make sense); and (c) that the self is positive and worthy (i.e., good things happen to good people). Naturally, a traumatic event seriously threatens these core assumptions, and from the cognitive as well as existential perspectives, treatment consists of reestablishing an organized, integrated set of assumptions.

Other noted scholars have also addressed the psychological hypersensitivity associated with PTSD. For example, developmentalist John Bowlby (1969) noted that individuals need to create working models of the environment (called the *environmental model*) and of one's self (i.e., one's resources, proficiencies, etc., called the *organismic model*). Attainment of life's goals, including safety and security, requires continual and functional interaction between the models.

Robert Lifton (1988) has written extensively about survivors of trauma and their struggles to master and assimilate traumatic events into some meaningful context. One of his 10 formulated principles relevant to the study of psychological trauma specifically addresses the importance of meaning. According to Lifton (1988), "without addressing this idea of meaning . . . we cannot understand post-traumatic stress disorder" (p. 10).

Abraham Maslow's (1954) proposed hierarchy of human needs (physiological needs, safety, affiliation, self-esteem, and self-actualization) posits that the foundation of motivation is the need to satisfy basic physiological needs (e.g., food, water). He defined safety as freedom from fear, having security, protection, and the need for structure and order. The remainder of the hierarchy involves the need to belong and be loved, the need for self-esteem, and finally becoming self-actualized. Maslow maintained that one cannot progress to a higher level in the hierarchy until one has satisfied the need at the preceding level, which leads to some individuals "getting stuck" and spending a lifetime pursing a rudimentary need. As we know, trauma is the antithesis of order, protection, and security. No matter which higher order Maslovian need level one has reached prior to being traumatized, the trauma serves to return the individual back to a quest for safety. Therefore, concepts such as personal growth are suppressed until the safety need can once again be satisfied.

Existentialist Viktor Frankl (1959) argued that the failure to discover meaning and a sense of responsibility in one's life is the core of psychopathology. As Frankl explained in his exposition of logotherapy, he who loses the "why" to live may lose the "how" as well. Indeed, trauma may have a devastating impact because it produces a violation or contradiction to both the meaning and the sense of responsibility that one may have previously found in life. Frankl did, however, adhere to Nietzsche's famous motto, "That which does not kill me, makes me stronger." This statement helps to provide an optimistic cognitive foundation to help in reintegrating one's worldview or Weltanschauung.

CRITICAL INCIDENT STRESS DEBRIEFING

The "modern era" of crisis intervention has existed since the mid-1940s, built upon the work of Lindemann (1944) and the subsequent work of Caplan (1964), according to Roberts (in chapter 1 of this volume). Since that time, crisis intervention has become "a proven approach to helping people in the pain of an emotional crisis" (Swanson & Carbon, 1989, p. 2520).

For the most part, the history of crisis intervention has been built upon individual applications, that is, one-on-one applications. However, as crisis interventions were applied to large-scale crises and mass disasters, the need for more efficient tactics became clear. The tactic of *group* crisis intervention, which had its roots in the military and later the emergency services, emerged as an innovation to the field. One model of group crisis intervention was developed by Jeffrey T. Mitchell (1983), who built upon the historical tenets of crisis intervention combined with the insights gained through group therapeutic applications (Yalom, 1970). Mitchell formulated a specific model of group crisis intervention referred to as Critical Incident Stress Debriefing (CISD; Mitchell & Everly, 1996). A review of relevant literature reveals the CISD model of group crisis intervention to be an effective tactic (Everly & Boyle, 1999; Everly & Mitchell, 1999; Everly & Quatrano-Piacentini, 1999; Everly, Boyle, & Lating, 1999).

CISD is designed to mitigate the psychological impact of a traumatic event and accelerate recovery from acute symptoms of distress that may arise in the immediate wake of a crisis or a traumatic event. A very important component of CISD is identifying individuals who may require professional mental health follow-up after the event. The formal CISD process is a seven-phase group meeting or discussion in which individuals who have been affected by a traumatic event are given the chance to talk about their thoughts and emotions in a controlled and rational manner. The debriefing process has been carefully structured to flow in a nonthreatening manner from the cognitively oriented process of human experience through a more emotionally oriented experience, and then back to an educative, cognitive process. It is important to note that despite having both psychological and educative elements, the debriefing process should not be considered psychotherapy. We will now briefly review the formal stages of the CISD process, which usually takes 1 to 3 hours to complete.

Introduction Phase

The introduction to the CISD is absolutely critical for success; it sets the tone for the subsequent phases. If the introduction is mishandled, it is likely that the remainder of the debriefing will be awkward and difficult. The following are several objectives that should be achieved during the introduction:

- Explain the purpose of the meeting.
- Explain and give an overview of the process.
- Motivate the participants.
- Assure confidentiality.
- Explain the guidelines (e.g., no tape recorders or notes, talk only for yourself).
- Point out the team members.
- Answer questions or concerns.

The concept that drives the introduction is the attempt to anticipate logistical and psychological barriers to the group discussion and to establish guidelines to minimize or eliminate them.

Fact Phase

Typically, the most natural thing for a distressed individual to discuss is a description of the facts of an incident. Facts are, in essence, a collection of impersonal items. A discussion of facts is not likely to engender the type of distress that a more personal discussion of feelings would. To assist participants in talking about an incident in the fact phase, the leader of the debriefing may say something like this:

> The CISD team wasn't present during the incident. We only know some bits and pieces of what happened. It would be helpful to our understanding if you would tell us *who you are, what your role was during the incident, and, briefly, what happened from your perspective*. It doesn't matter if what you experienced is different from what everyone else experienced. You all had an important part to play in the situation, and it would help everyone to have a big picture constructed by putting all your pieces of the incident together. If you choose not to speak, that is OK; just shake your head, and we will pass over you. For the sake of organization, we will start on my left [or right] and proceed around the room. Again, what we need to know from you is (a) who you are, (b) what was your job or

involvement during the incident, and (c) what happened from your perspective?

The group participants will then begin to tell their stories. The exact order of telling the story is irrelevant; the last to arrive at the scene might be the first to speak. As others present their pieces, ideally the story comes together. The concept that drives the fact phase is the notion, as Sir Francis Bacon stated, that "information is power."

Thought Phase

The thought phase begins when the CISD team leader asks each of the participants to express their *first thoughts* or *most prominent thought* concerning the traumatic event. This phase serves as a transition between the impersonal outside facts and that which is becoming more internal, close, and personal. It is quite difficult to respond to questions about thoughts without some discarding of emotion entering the discussion. CISD teams should expect this leakage of emotion as a natural by-product of the debriefing process. Emotional comments during the thought phase should be considered a sign that the process is working and on schedule.

Reaction Phase

The reaction phase is typically the most emotionally powerful of all phases. However, if the introduction, fact, and thought phases have been performed well, then the reaction phase will flow easily and naturally. The CISD team will typically experience a quieting of their interactions with the group during this phase. In fact, most of the talking during this stage is done by the participants. The discussion at this point is freewheeling. Whoever wants to speak may do so; there is no longer a specified order to the discussion (i.e., systematically going around the room) as during the fact and thought phases. The questions that trigger most of the discussion in the reaction phase are:

- What was the worst thing about this situation for you personally?
- If you could erase one part of the situation, what part would you choose to erase?"
- What aspect of the situation causes you the most pain?

The concept that drives this phase is that of cathartic ventilation with a potential for emotional abreaction.

Symptom Phase

This phase serves as another transition. The objective is to begin to move the group back from the emotionally laden content of the reaction phase toward more cognitively oriented material. Stopping the debriefing at this juncture would leave people in a charged emotional state, which could possibly be distressing. A debriefing is always continued to the end to complete the process and to restore people to the cognitive level.

The symptom phase is initiated when the team asks the participants to describe any cognitive, physical, emotional, or behavioral experiences they may have encountered at the scene of the incident, as well as symptoms that followed subsequently. The concept that drives this phase is consensual normalization and attacking the myth of unique weakness or vulnerability.

Teaching Phase

The teaching phase evolves naturally after the symptoms phase. It begins by acknowledging several of the symptoms just described in the symptom phase and reaffirming to the group that those symptoms are normal, typical, or predictable after the type of incident they experienced. Other team members forewarn the group about possible symptoms they might develop in the future. The team may then spend time providing stress management strategies such as instructions on diet, exercise, rest, talking to one's family, and a range of other topics. The teaching phase is very cognitive in its approach. It is designed to bring the participants further away from the emotional content they had worked through in the reaction phase.

Reentry Phase

This is the last, and possibly the most important, phase of the formal debriefing. It is used to clarify issues, answer questions, make summary statements, and accelerate homeostasis, sometimes thought of as psychological closure. The participants in the debriefing will need to do the following:

1. Introduce any new material they wish to discuss.
2. Review old material already discussed.
3. Ask any questions.
4. Discuss anything they wish that would help them bring closure to the debriefing.

The debriefing team will need to do the following:

1. Answer any questions posed.
2. Inform and reassure as needed.
3. Provide appropriate handouts.
4. Provide referral sources as appropriate for psychological assessment, therapy, and so on.
5. Make summary comments.

The summary comments made by the CISD team are usually words of respect, encouragement, appreciation, support, and direction. Every CISD team member should make a summary statement in the last few minutes of the debriefing, but the essence of this phase is the identification of homogenizing themes that may be used to facilitate closure and provide a psychological uplift.

CRITICAL INCIDENT STRESS MANAGEMENT

Having reviewed the nature of the group crisis intervention known as Critical Incident Stress Debriefing (CISD), let us now move to an analysis of another innovation in the field of crisis intervention: Critical Incident Stress Management (CISM). As innovative and useful as the CISD has proven, we believe that crisis intervention must be multifaceted to maximize its effectiveness (Everly & Mitchell, 1999). This is the essence of CISM.

CISM is a comprehensive, integrative, multicomponent crisis intervention system. It is considered comprehensive because it consists of multiple crisis intervention components that functionally span the entire temporal spectrum of a crisis. CISM interventions range from the precrisis phase through the acute crisis phase, and into the postcrisis phase (see Figure 4.1). CISM is also considered comprehensive in that it consists of interventions that may be applied to individuals, small functional groups, large groups, families, organizations, and even communities. The seven core components of CISM are defined in the following and are summarized in Table 4.1.

1. Precrisis preparation. This includes stress management education, mental preparedness training, stress resistance, and crisis mitigation training for both individuals and organizations.
2. One-on-one crisis intervention/counseling or psychological support throughout the full range of the crisis spectrum (this is the most widely used of the CISM interventions). Typically, this form of intervention consists of one to three contacts with an individual who is in crisis. Each contact may last anywhere from 15 minutes to 2 hours, depending on the nature and severity of the crisis.
3. Disaster or large-scale incidents, as well as school and community support programs, including demobilizations, informational briefings, and "town meetings" and staff advisement.
4. Critical Incident Stress Debriefing (CISD) refers to the ICISF model (Mitchell & Everly, 1996), a seven-phase, structured group discussion, usually provided 1 to 10 days after an acute crisis and 3 to 4 weeks after the disaster in mass disasters. It is designed to mitigate acute symptoms, assess the need for follow-up, and, if possible, provide a sense of postcrisis psychological closure.

5. Defusing. This is a three-phase, structured small-group discussion provided within hours of a crisis for purposes of assessment, triaging, and acute symptom mitigation.
6. Family crisis intervention, as well as organizational consultation.
7. Follow-up and referral mechanisms for assessment and treatment, if necessary.

Specific guidelines for these interventions, summarized in Table 4.1, can be found in Everly and Mitchell (1999) and Mitchell and Everly (1996).

Just as one would never attempt to play a round of golf with only one golf club, one would not attempt the complex task of intervention within a crisis or disaster with only one crisis intervention technology. Because crisis intervention, generically, and CISM, specifically, represent a subspecialty within behavioral health, one should not attempt application without adequate and specific training (see Koss & Shiang, 1994). CISM is not psychotherapy, nor a substitute for psychotherapy. CISM is a form of psychological "first aid."

APPLICATION OF MODELS TO CASE STUDIES

To understand how the comprehensive and integrative CISM model works from a temporal perspective, the following case examples will provide intervention recommendations that may be offered during the precrisis phase, the acute crisis phase, and the postcrisis phase (see Figure 4.1).

Case 1

The line of thunderstorms happened suddenly and seemed remarkably isolated. The 65 children and 38 staff at the relatively secluded Willow Park Day Care Center never saw it coming. The thunderstorms spawned several tornadoes of mainly low magnitude in the surrounding vicinity. The tornado near the day care center was the most powerful, with winds of close to 200 miles per hour. When it touched ground, it demolished the roof of the building while most of the children were napping. The collapsed roof immediately killed 14 of the children, and three of the staff, and left 7 other children trapped in the rubble for 8 to 12 hours while two shifts of emergency workers, as well as excavation experts from the next town, worked feverishly to rescue them. Despite the best efforts of the rescue workers, two of the trapped children suffered massive injuries and died.

For this tragic event, CISM services would likely be offered to both the emergency service (EMS) workers and to the civilians. Upon being informed of the incident, a CISM team would be dispatched to the scene.

Table 4.1 Critical Incident Stress Management (CISM): The Seven Core Components

Intervention	Timing	Activation	Goals	Format
1. Precrisis preparation	Precrisis phase	Anticipation of crisis	Set expectations; improve coping	Groups Organizations
2. Individual crisis intervention (1:1)	Anytime Anywhere	Symptom driven	Symptom mitigation; return to function, if possible; referral, if needed; stress mgmt.	Individuals
Large groups: 3a. Demobilizations & staff consult. (rescuers); 3b. Group info. briefing for schools, businesses, and large civilian groups	Shift disengagement; or, Anytime postcrisis	Event driven	To inform, and consult; to allow for psychological decompression; stress mgmt.	Large groups Organizations
4. Critical Incident Stress Debriefing (CISD)	Postcrisis (1–10 days; at 3–4 weeks for mass disasters)	Usually symptom driven; can be event driven	Facilitate psychological closure; symptom mitigation; triage	Small groups
5. Defusing	Postcrisis (within 12 hrs)	Usually symptom driven	Symptom mitigation; possible closure; triage	Small groups
Systems: 6a. Family CISM; 6b. Organizational consultation	Anytime	Either symptom driven or event driven	Foster support, communications; symptom mitigation; closure, if possible; referral, if needed	Families Organizations
7. Follow-up; referral	Anytime	Usually symptom driven	Assess mental status; access higher level of care	Individual Family

Source: Everly, G., & Mitchell, J. (1999). Critical Incident Stress Management (CISM): A new era and standard of care in crisis intervention (2nd ed.). Ellicott City, MD: Chevron Publishing.

EMS Workers

It is hoped that the EMS workers would have received an introduction to the appropriate expectations about acute stress disorder and its management as part of their precrisis professional preparation. However, even with ample psychological preparedness, few EMS workers are actually prepared for the horrific psychological devastation that occurs when a group of children perishes. When the CISM team arrives at the scene, its initial duties would include not intruding on the rescue efforts but providing support to the oper-

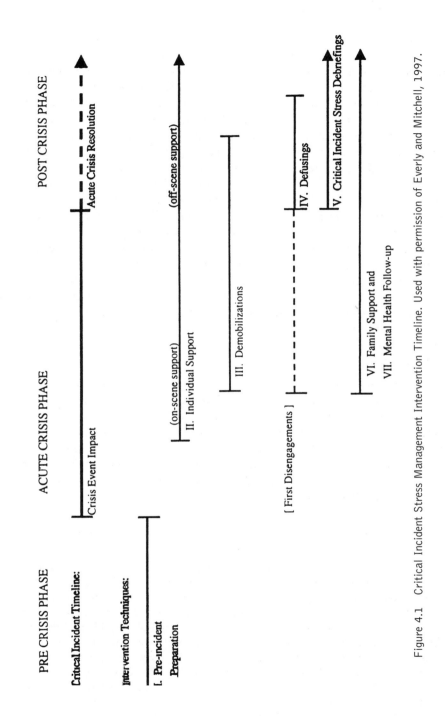

Figure 4.1 Critical Incident Stress Management Intervention Timeline. Used with permission of Everly and Mitchell, 1997.

ation as requested. The CISM team members may provide acute one-on-one support for those with clear evidence of functional impairment during the rescue efforts. Several models of one-on-one interventions may be employed (Everly & Mitchell, 1999; Roberts, 1991, 1996). Given the nature and severity of this trauma, for the workers completing their initial shift (and with the prospect of returning to the scene the next day), a demobilization area should be established where the workers can decompress and receive information for 10 to 20 minutes. A 30-minute defusing intervention may then be done to help mitigate the effects of acute trauma if deemed necessary. Approximately 1 week after the acute rescue assignment (when the out-of town rescuers are back home), debriefings would be conducted with those involved in the operation to assist them in normalizing their reactions, to put the incident in perspective, and to challenge irrational beliefs. A separate debriefing would be conducted with those from out of town who have since returned home. Also, the CISM team would want to make consultations with families available for those in need. It is also very important that follow-up services such as employee assistance programs (EAPs) or community mental health referrals are made available for those workers for whom the crisis intervention services described here are insufficient.

Civilians

For the civilians involved in the disaster, such as the day care staff or relatives of the victims, one-on-one interventions, family support, and follow-up referrals to mental health professionals are likely to be the most relevant CISM components. "Town meetings" and group informational briefings (Everly & Mitchell, 1999) can be held for civilians and the community at large. Within a few days of the event, social support services may be offered. A week to 10 days after the completion of the event, the CISD may be utilized for the civilians most severely impacted.

Case 2

It was 9:58 A.M. on a morning in May, seemingly no different than most days in this small midwestern town. However, appearances can be deceiving. Two blocks away from the town's second-largest insurance building, 35-year-old David G., a recently unemployed auto and truck mechanic, sat passively in his car, contemplating what the next several hours would bring. He had fleeting, emotional thoughts about his mother, who passed away suddenly less than 2 months ago. He had described her to others as his only "true friend." He also continued to seethe about the rejection he encountered 2 days ago, when his girlfriend of 3 years, 28-year-old Angela, told him that she no longer wanted to see him. David, who did not have a history of violence, warned her following the breakup that he would not allow her to embarrass him and ruin his life. She refused to take his calls since the breakup, but David had decided that he would be heard. When his watch signaled 10:00 A.M., David slowly, yet purposefully, approached the building.

What happened next could only be described as a nightmarish blur. When David was questioned by the receptionist in the empty lobby regarding the purpose of his visit, he calmly removed the 9-millimeter pistol he had concealed under his jacket and shot her twice in the chest, killing her instantly. Seemingly void of emotion, he proceeded onto the elevator and then to Angela's crowded work area, where he located her talking to several of her colleagues while they were on a break. Unfortunately, she did not notice him until he was less than 10 feet away. Without uttering a word, David shot Angela three times, also killing her instantly. He then placed the weapon under his chin and with a single pull of the trigger ended this grisly, shocking, and tragic ordeal.

A highly efficient and well-organized EAP or in-house crisis team that may be part of a human resources department would likely provide initial support services. This, for example, may include two counselors trained in CISM who may be dispatched and who arrive at the scene within 2 to 4 hours after the shooting.

EMS Workers

This type of event, albeit devastating in its own right, typically does not result in inordinate functional impairment on the part of seasoned EMS personnel, who have received extensive psychological preparedness precrisis training. The CISD intervention and possible follow-up referrals should, however, be available for EMS workers who may experience functional difficulty with this event. Given the 2 to 4 hour time lag before the arrival of the counselors, any support service that the EMS workers need would come from resources connected with their respective organizations.

Civilians

In this type of crisis, interventions for the employees will be critical. The CISM counselors will likely begin by making themselves available for one-on-one interventions with those who were most directly involved in the incident and for those most clearly decompensated. Given the magnitude of this type of event within a company, a defusing may be done, and a CISD should be scheduled within a week's time. Moreover, in this type of incident in a relatively large company, it is important to have a group informational briefing that allows for dissemination of accurate information about the events and alleviation of concerns about security and safety for affected employees. Included within this briefing should be guidelines on how individuals may access "local" professionals who may be used for follow-up should individuals and/or families have further concerns about the incident. Indeed, follow-up services will be vitally important in this type of event.

As is clear from these examples, CISM covers the crisis spectrum, from preincident training to postincident follow-up. Every crisis is unique. Therefore, although it may not be feasible, or at times even efficacious, to provide the interventions exactly as described here, these suggestions allow the reader to have a better applied sense of CISM. Take, for example, the second case study. Should this insurance company be considered negligent for not having provided precrisis training for its employees? Clearly, in a high-risk industry, such as banking, the issue of negligence might be raised; however, should this be the case for businesses such as insurance companies? We would like to think not; however, incidents like the World Trade Center bombing, the Oklahoma City bombing, and the recent rash of school shootings may lead us to reconsider our response to this question.

CONCLUSIONS AND SUMMARY

As noted earlier, CISM represents an integrated multicomponent crisis intervention system. This systems approach underscores the importance of using multiple interventions combined in such a manner as to yield maximum impact to achieve the goal of crisis stabilization and symptom mitigation. Although in evidence since 1983 (Mitchell, 1983), this concept is commonly misunderstood, as evidenced by recent articles by Rose and Bisson (1998) and Snelgrove (1998), who argue that the CISD group intervention should not be a stand-alone intervention. This point has, frankly, never been in contention. The CISD intervention should be viewed as one component within a larger functional intervention framework. Admittedly, some of the confusion surrounding this point was engendered by virtue of the fact that in the earlier expositions, the term *CISD* was used to denote the generic and overarching umbrella program/system, while the term *formal CISD* was used to denote the specific seven-phase group discussion process. The term *CISM* was later used to replace the generic *CISD* and to serve as the overarching umbrella program/system, as noted in Table 4.1 (see Everly and Mitchell, 1999).

Similarly, there is a misconception that evidence exists to suggest that CISD/CISM has proven harmful to its recipients (e.g., see Snelgrove, 1998); however, this is a misrepresentation of the extant data. The investigations that are frequently cited to suggest such an adverse effect simply did not use the CISD or CISM system as prescribed (Dyregrov, 1998), a fact that often is unreported or overlooked (e.g., see Rose & Bisson, 1998; Snelgrove, 1998).

A careful review of literature in the area of crisis intervention reveals a body of literature fraught with inconsistent terminology (Everly & Mitchell, 1999); inconsistent standards for training and practice (Dyregrov, 1998;

Koss and Shiang, 1994; Mitchell & Everly, 1998); poorly defined and poorly controlled outcome investigations (Everly, Flannery, & Mitchell, in press; Dyregrov, 1998; Everly & Mitchell, 1999; Mitchell & Everly, 1998); and even the possibility of "political" or guild issues (Dyregrov, 1998)—all of which apparently serve to hinder a more rapid refinement of the field. Nevertheless, the specific effectiveness of CISD and/or CISM programs has been empirically validated through thoughtful qualitative analyses, controlled investigations, and even meta-analyses (Everly, Boyle, & Lating, in press; Everly & Boyle, in press; Everly & Quatrano-Piacentini, 1999; Flannery, 1998; Mitchell & Everly, 1998; Everly & Mitchell, 1999; Mitchell & Everly, in press; Everly, Flannery, & Mitchell, in press; Dyregrov, 1997). Unfortunately, this fact is often overlooked (e.g., see Rose & Bisson, 1998; Snelgrove, 1998). Flannery and his colleagues have applied the CISM model to violence in the workplace with strikingly beneficial results (Flannery, 1998). His Assaulted Staff Action Program (ASAP) stands as the gold standard for violence-oriented crisis intervention programs and has been validated through well-controlled empirical investigations.

In sum, no one CISM intervention is designed to stand alone, not even the widely used CISD. Efforts to implement and evaluate CISM must be programmatic, not unidimensional (Mitchell & Everly, in press). While the CISM approach to crisis intervention is continuing to evolve, as should any worthwhile endeavor, current investigations have clearly demonstrated its value as a tool to reduce human suffering. Future research should focus upon how the CISM process can be made even more effective to those in crisis.

Although the roots of CISM can be found in the emergency services professions dating back to the late 1970s, CISM is now becoming a "standard of care" in many schools, communities, and organizations well outside the field of emergency services (Everly & Mitchell, 1999). By standard of care, we mean a generally recognized procedure or pattern of practice. Whereas some standards of care are mandated, others emerge, or evolve, through widespread recognition and utilization. Clearly, CISM has emerged over the last 17 years as the most widely used comprehensive crisis intervention system in the world for community-wide disasters.

REFERENCES

American Psychiatric Association. (1980). *Diagnostic and statistical manual of mental disorders* (3rd ed.). Washington, DC: Author.

American Psychiatric Association. (1987). *Diagnostic and statistical manual of mental disorders* (3rd ed., rev.). Washington, DC: Author.

American Psychiatric Association. (1994). *Diagnostic and statistical manual of mental disorders* (4th ed.). Washington, DC: Author.

Biggio, G. (1983). The action of stress, beta carbones, diazepam, Ro15-1788 on GABA receptors in the rat brain. In G. Biggio & E.

Costa (Eds.), *Benzodiazepine recognition and site ligands* (pp. 105–119). New York: Raven.

Bowlby, J. (1969). *Attachment and loss: Vol. 1. Attachment.* New York: Basic Books.

Bremner, J. D., Randall, P., Scott, T. N., Bronen, R. A., Seibyl, J. P., Southwick, S. M., Delaney, R. C., McCarty, G., Charney, D. S., & Innis, R. B. (1995). MRI-based measurements of hippocampal volume in combat-related posttraumatic stress disorder. *American Journal of Psychiatry, 152,* 973–981.

Bremner, J. D., Randall, P., Vermetten, E., Staib, L., Bronen, R. A., Mazuré, C., Capelli, S., McCarthy, G., Innis, R. B., & Charney, D. S. (1997). Magnetic resonance imaging–based measurement of hippocampal volume in posttraumatic stress disorder related to childhood physical and sexual abuse: A preliminary report. *Biological Psychiatry, 41,* 23–32.

Caplan, G. (1964). *Principles of preventive psychiatry.* New York: Basic Books.

Davidson, L., & Baum, A. (1986). Chronic stress and post-traumatic stress disorders. *Journal of Consulting and Clinical Psychology, 54,* 303–308.

Drugan, R. C., Murrow, A. L., Weizman, R. et al. (1989). Stress-induced behavioral depression associated with a decrease in GABA receptor–mediated chloride ion influx and brain benzodiazepine receptor occupancy. *Brain Research, 487,* 45–51.

Dyregrov, A. (1997). The process of psychological debriefing. *Journal of Traumatic Stress, 10,* 589–604.

Dyregrov, A. (1998). Psychological debriefing: An effective method? *Traumatologye, 4*(2), Article 1.

Everly, G. S. (1990). Post-traumatic stress disorder as a "disorder of arousal." *Psychology and Health: An International Journal, 4,* 135–145.

Everly, G. S., & Boyle, S. (1999). Effectiveness of Critical Incident Stress Debriefing (CISD): A meta-analysis. *International Journal of Emergency Mental Health, 1*(3), 165–168.

Everly, G. S., Boyle, S., & Lating, J. (1999). The effectiveness of psychological debriefings in vicarious trauma: A meta-analysis. *Stress Medicine, 15,* 229–233.

Everly, G. S., Flannery, R., & Mitchell, J. (in press). CISM: A review of literature. *Aggression and Violent Behavior: A Review Journal.*

Everly, G. S., & Horton, A. M. (1989). Neuropsychology of PTSD. *Perceptual and Motor Skills, 68,* 807–810.

Everly, G. S., & Mitchell, J. T. (1997). *Critical Incident Stress Management (CISM): A new era and standard of care in crisis intervention.* Ellicott City, MD: Chevron.

Everly, G. S., & Quatrano-Piacentini, A. (1999, March). The effects of CISD on trauma symptoms: A meta-analysis. Paper presented to the *APA NIOSH Work, Stress and Health '99: Organization of Work in a Global Economy* conference, Baltimore.

Ford, J. D., Ruzek, J., & Niles, B. (1996). Identifying and treating VA medical care patients with undetected sequelae of psychological trauma and post-traumatic stress disorder. *NCP Clinical Quarterly, 6,* 77–82.

Flannery, R. B. (1998). *The Assaulted Staff Action Program: Coping with the psychological aftermath of violence.* Ellicott City, MD: Chevron.

Frankl, V. (1959). *Man's search for meaning.* Boston: Beacon.

Gray, J. (1982). *The neuropsychology of anxiety.* New York: Oxford University Press.

Henry, J. P. (1993, February). Alexithymia and PTSD. Paper presented to the Fifth Montreux Congress on stress, Montreux, Switzerland.

Janoff-Bulman, R. (1988). Victims of violence. In S. Fisher and J. Reason (Eds.), *Handbook of life stress, cognition and health* (pp. 101–113). New York: Wiley.

Janoff-Bulman, R. (1992). *Shattered assumptions.* New York: Jason Aronson.

Joy, R. (1985). The effects of neurotoxicants on kindling and kindled seizures. *Fundamental and Applied Toxicology, 5,* 41–65.

Kalivas, P. W., & Duffy, P. (1989). Similar effects of cocaine and stress on mesocorticolimbic dopamine neurotransmission in the rat. *Biological Psychiatry, 25,* 913–928.

Kardiner, A. (1941). *The traumatic neuroses of war.* New York: Hoeber.

Kessler, R. C., Sonnega, A., Bromet, E., Hughes, M., & Nelson, C. (1995). Posttraumatic stress disorder in the National Comorbidity Survey. *Archives of General Psychiatry, 52,* 1048–1060.

Koss, M., & Shiang, J. (1994). Research on brief psychotherapy. In A. Bergin and S. Garfield (Eds.), *Handbook of psychotherapy and behavior change* (pp. 664–700). New York: Wiley.

Koss, M. P., Woodruff, W., & Koss, P. G. (1991). Criminal victimization among primary care medical patients. *Behavioral Sciences and the Law, 9,* 45–46.

Krnjevic, K. (1983). GABA-mediated inhibitory mechanisms in relation to epileptic discharges. In H. Jasper & N. van Gelder (Eds.), *Basic mechanisms of neuronal hyperexcitability* (pp. 249–263). New York: Liss.

Krystal, J. H., Kosten, T. R., Southwick, S. et al. (1989). Neurobiological aspects of PTSD. *Behavior Therapy, 20,* 177–198.

Lifton, R. J. (1988). Understanding the traumatized self. In J. P. Wilson, Z. Harel, & B. Kahana (Eds.), *Human adaptation to extreme stress* (pp. 7–31). New York: Plenum.

Lindemann, E. (1944). Symptomatology and management of acute grief. *American Journal of Psychiatry, 101,* 141–148.

Maslow, A. H. (1954). *Motivation and personality.* New York: Harper.

Mason, J. W. et al. (1986). Urinary free cortisol in PTSD. *Journal of Nervous and Mental Disorders, 174,* 145–149.

McGeer, E., & McGeer, P. (1988). Excitotoxins and animal models of disease. In C. Galli, L. Manzo, & P. Spencer (Eds.), *Recent advances in nervous system toxicology* (pp. 107–131). New York: Plenum.

Mitchell, J. T. (1983). When disaster strikes . . . The critical incident stress debriefing process. *Journal of Emergency Medical Services, 8*(1), 36–39.

Mitchell, J. T., & Everly, G. S. (1996). *Critical Incident Stress De-*

briefing: An operations manual. Ellicott City, MD: Chevron.

Mitchell, J. T., & Everly, G. S. (1998). Critical Incident Stress Management: A new era in crisis intervention. *Traumatic Stress Points,* Fall, vol. 1, no. 1, 6–7, 10–11.

Mitchell, J. T., & Everly, G. S. (in press). CISM and CISD: Evolution, effects and outcomes. In B. Raphael & J. Wilson (Eds.), *Psychological debriefing.* Cambridge: Cambridge University Press.

Murburs, M., McFall, M., & Veith, R. (1990). Catecholamines, stress and PTSD. In E. Giller (Ed.), *Biological assessment and treatment of Post-Traumatic Stress Disorder* (pp. 29–64). Washington, DC: American Psychiatric Press.

Nutt, D. (1989). Altered central a-2 adrenoreceptor sensitivity in panic disorder. *Archives of General Psychiatry, 46,* 165–169.

OSHA. (1996). *Guidelines for preventing workplace violence for healthcare and social service workers.* OSHA 3148-1996. Washington DC: U.S. Department of Labor.

OSHA. (1998). *Recommendations for workplace violence prevention programs in late-night retail establishments.* OSHA 3153-1998. Washington, DC: U.S. Department of Labor.

Palkovits, M., Lang, T., Patthy, A., & Elekes, L. (1986). Distribution and stress-induced increase of glutamate and aspartate levels in discrete brain nuclei of rats. *Brain Research, 373,* 252–257.

Perry, B. D., Southwick, S. M., & Giller, E. L. (1990). Adrenergic receptor regulation in post-traumatic stress disorder. In E. Giller (Ed.), *Biological assessment and treat-*

ment of post-traumatic stress disorder (pp. 87–114). Washington, DC: American Psychiatric Press.

Pitman, R. K., & Orr, S. P. (1990). Twenty-four hour urinary cortisol and catecholamine excretion in combat-related post-traumatic stress disorder. *Biological Psychiatry, 27,* 245–247.

Post, R. (1985). Stress, sensitization, kindling, and conditioning. *Behavioral and Brain Sciences, 8,* 372–373.

Post, R. (1986). Does limbic system dysfunction play a role in affective illness? In B. Doane & K. Livingston (Eds.), *The limbic system.* New York: Raven.

Post, R. (1992). Transduction of psychological stress into the neurobiology of recurrent affective disorders. *American Journal of Psychiatry, 149,* 999–1010.

Post, R., & Ballenger, J. (1981). Kindling models for progressive development of psychopathology. In H. Van Pragg (Ed.), *Handbook of biological psychiatry* (pp. 609–651). New York: Marcel Dekker.

Rahe, R. H., Karson, S., Howard, N. S., Rubin, R. T. et al. (1990). Psychological and physiological assessments on American hostages freed from captivity in Iran. *Psychosomatic Medicine, 52,* 1–16.

Roberts, A. R. (1991). Conceptualizing crisis theory and the crisis intervention model. In A. R. Roberts (Ed.), *Contemporary perspectives on crisis intervention and prevention* (pp. 3–17). Englewood Cliffs, NJ: Prentice-Hall.

Roberts, A. R. (1996). Epidemiology and definitions of acute crisis in American society. In A. R. Roberts (Ed.), *Crisis management and brief treatment* (pp. 16–33). Belmont, CA: Wadsworth.

Rose, S., & Bisson J. (1998). Brief early psychological interventions following a trauma: A systematic review of the literature. *Journal of Traumatic Stress, 11,* 698–710.

Schaeffer, M. A., & Baum, A. (1984). Adrenal cortical response to stress at Three Mile Island. *Psychosomatic Medicine, 46,* 227–237.

Snelgrove, T. (1998). Debriefing under fire. *Trauma Lines, 3*(2), 3–11.

Swanson, W. C., & Carbon, J. B. (1989). Crisis intervention theory and technique. In *The Task Force Report of the American Psychiatric Association Treatments of Psychi-atric Disorders* (pp. 2520–2531). Washington, DC: APA Press.

van der Kolk, B. (1988). The trauma spectrum. *Journal of Traumatic Stress, 1,* 273–290.

van Gelder, N. M. (1986). The hyper-excited brain: Glutamic acid release and failure of inhibition. In R. Schwarz & Y. Ben-Ari (Eds.), *Excitatory amino acids and epilepsy* (pp. 331–347). New York: Plenum.

Wilson, J. P. (1989). *Trauma, transformation, and healing.* New York: Brunner/Mazel.

Yalom, I. (1970). *Theory and practice of group psychotherapy.* New York: Basic Books.

II

CRISIS ASSESSMENT AND
INTERVENTION MODELS
WITH CHILDREN AND YOUTH

5

Crisis Intervention With Early Adolescents Who Have Suffered a Significant Loss

M. SEAN O'HALLORAN
ELLIS P. COPELAND

This chapter uses three examples to examine crisis intervention with early adolescents. We will identify important developmental considerations in assessment, planning, and intervention, and will apply Roberts's (1996) seven-stage crisis intervention model in working with significant losses in the lives of youth. The losses we focus on are the death of loved ones, divorce, and the impact of exposure to violence outside the home; however, many of the issues we address can be generalized to other types of crises.

Adolescence is a time of significant physical, social, and psychological change (Arnett, 1999). Because change occurs rapidly during this phase of life, writers in the field of adolescent psychology often divide this time into three periods: early adolescence, from about the age of 11 to 14; middle adolescence, from about 15 to 18; and late adolescence, roughly from 18 through 21 (Steinberg, 1996). We will focus on the first of these, early adolescence. (11–14)

Some of the fundamental developmental tasks of adolescents include developing a sense of identity, including clarification of values and a sense of purpose. Erik Erikson (1959, 1963, 1968) wrote extensively on adolescent identity, and the reader is referred to his work on the eight stages of psychosocial development. During a time of already rapid change, the adolescent who is facing a crisis may be more seriously impacted than a person at a different developmental stage. Arnett (1999), examining historical views on adolescence, refers to this as a time of "modified storm-and-stress," empha-

101

sizing that conflict with parents, mood disruptions, and engaging in risky behaviors are common to many, though certainly not all adolescents during this time of change. It is critical for anyone doing crisis intervention to have an awareness of the distinct cognitive, social, and biological capacities of this age-group and to create interventions that bear these factors in mind.

We will include, where pertinent, discussions of techniques drawn from time-limited therapies. Given that we live during a time in which brief and solution-focused therapy models are advocated because they are often effective within a short time, and because many of our clients are unable to pursue the therapy they need due to insurance restrictions, it is important to be aware of these techniques. McFarland (1995) notes that "brief therapy can be defined as no more therapy than necessary" (p. 4), and, indeed, crisis intervention focuses on quickly helping a person in crisis to return to normal functioning.

We use three cases to illustrate issues in crisis intervention with early adolescents.

Case 1

Jenny, a 13-year-old White girl, has suffered a series of significant losses. This past year her parents divorced, following several years of progressive deterioration of her father's health as a result of alcoholism; most recently, her beloved grandmother died. Jenny has become increasingly withdrawn from friends and family, less involved in school activities, and more worried about her appearance; she has lost nearly 10 pounds. Her brothers have noticed that Jenny spends more time alone in her room and has stopped going to their baseball games. Feeling that relationships end in tragedy and that there is little she can control, Jenny avoids closeness and seeks to control her life through rigorous diet and exercise.

The model discussed by Roberts to help intervene in a crisis situation works very well for Jenny's situation and also demonstrates how time-limited therapies can be helpful in assisting an early adolescent who is forced to cope after a series of losses.

The case of Esperanza permits us to demonstrate the utility of Roberts's model in stabilizing an adolescent in crisis after an unexpected and serious loss, the death of a beloved parent.

Case 2

Esperanza is a 12-year-old Mexican American girl. Five months ago, her parents were snowmobiling in the mountains when the snowmobile spun out of control and they were thrown off. Her mother was hurt, but she recovered quickly. Her father broke his neck and died. Since then, Esperanza has had great difficulty sleeping and concentrating. The academic work she once took great pride in has suffered, and her grades have dropped so precipitously that she may not pass seventh grade. She is very depressed and is alternately either very passive or very aggressive at school. She has told several people she is close to that she wants to die.

In this case, special attention must be paid to the issue of Esperanza's lethality. In her case, a lethality assessment, which is the first step in Roberts's model, is combined with the second step, that of relationship building. This case demonstrates how the application of Roberts's model provides a heuristic and sensible approach to assisting an early adolescent after a tragedy.

The case of Peter allows us to examine the utility of Roberts's model following a tragic and catastrophic event where the early adolescent does not perceive that he can ask for help until a later date.

Case 3

It appeared to be a routine Tuesday morning at Franklin Middle School. Yet, shortly before noon a call came to the principal's office concerning a shooting at the high school; there were a number of victims. By 1:00 P.M. enough information had been gathered to confirm that a high school student who had been critically injured has a 12-year-old brother, Peter, who attends Franklin Middle School. The principal asked the school counselor to call Peter's parents, but the counselor's phone attempts were not successful. The principal was ready to announce to the middle school staff and students that a tragedy had occurred at the nearby high school. Her instincts told her that she should isolate Peter and three other students before making the announcement. By 2:00 P.M. it was confirmed that Peter's older sister was dead.

This case is one in which the counselor will need to convey genuine respect for, and acceptance of, the client in order to offer the reassurance that Peter can be helped and that his time with the counselor is the appropriate time and place to receive such help.

CRISIS IN THE LIVES OF EARLY ADOLESCENTS

Crises impact the lives of many American youths as a result of experiences as close to home as child abuse and divorce and as distant, for some, as Hurricane Hugo, the massacre at Columbine High School, and wars throughout the world. Natural and human-made events precipitate crises in humans; we are exposed to these events daily, either personally or through the media. Terr (1990) distinguishes between Type I crises, in which an acute single event (for example, the Columbine shootings) precipitates a crisis, and Type II crises, which are responses to seemingly unremitting and prolonged events (e.g., repeated episodes of abuse or family violence). Most discussions of crisis intervention, including ours, focus on the first of these, which Roberts (1996) refers to as an "acute situational crisis" (p. 17). He defines this as follows:

> A sudden and unpredictable event takes place . . . ; the individual or family members perceive the event as an imminent threat to their life, psychological well-being, or social functioning; the individual tries to cope, escape the dangerous situation, gain necessary support from a significant other or close relative or friend, and/or adapt by changing one's lifestyle or environment; coping attempts fail and the person's severe emotional state of imbalance escalates into a full-blown crisis (p. 17).

We will discuss immediate, short-term responses to difficult and intense events, including acute psychological crises, acute situational crises, and acute stress disorders (Roberts, 1996). It is important to distinguish this from longer term psychotherapy; as Greenstone and Leviton (1993) put it, "Crisis intervention is to emergency medicine what a medical practice is to a psychotherapy practice" (p. 3). In many cases, crisis intervention may be precisely what is needed to assist an adolescent in crisis, but it is important to remember that, in other situations, more intensive therapy or ongoing support will be needed. It is essential to assess each individual's specific needs carefully, and to remember that access to longer-term psychotherapy may be especially important for individuals who have experienced prolonged and repeated crises (Terr's Type II crises). Crisis intervention may be very useful if an early adolescent has experienced a violent episode, if such an event has happened to someone close to them, or if personal loss has occurred through the death of a loved one or through the sense of loss that accompanies divorce.

SCOPE OF THE PROBLEM AND CLINICAL CONSIDERATIONS

Among early adolescents, crises can take many forms, and their impact can vary greatly among individuals. Particular vulnerabilities and risk factors will be discussed later, but it is important to note that no adolescent is protected by gender, culture, or socioeconomic status from the effects of a crisis. In this chapter, we will use examples that focus on crises due to the impact of violence outside the home or to loss following the death of a loved one or the divorce of parents.

Violence in the home (child abuse or domestic violence) clearly has major impacts on early adolescents, but we do not address this specific topic here because it is the subject of another chapter in this volume. Violence is all too common in the lives of youth, whether by direct exposure in their communities, homes, or schools or through indirect exposure to the media, which often target youth with violent images and violent content. Violence claimed the lives of nearly 25,000 young people in the United States between 1985 and 1995, an increase of 66% over a 10-year span (OJJDP, 1997). Outside of their homes, American youth also regularly experience violence in their communities. Each day 13 young people under the age of 20 are the victims of homicides, and many of these are killed by firearms (CDF, 1999). Violence is pervasive in school settings as well: approximately three quarters of students report knowing of incidents of physical attack, robbery, or bullying on school property, and 12% of those surveyed have themselves been victims of such incidents at school (Poe-Yamagata, 1998). Tragically, most recently there has been an alarming increase in deadly violence in school (Cloud, 1999).

Other crises are all too common in the lives of early adolescents in this country. In the United States today, there are approximately 30 million young people between the ages of 10 and 17; in the 1995 census nearly 15 million were between the ages of 14 and 17. More than half of all marriages of these children's parents end in divorce. Thus, millions of early adolescents are growing up in homes where divorce has occurred, and it is likely that more than half of all children will live in a single-parent home at some point in their lives (Dryfoos, 1998). Parental divorce can induce a crisis in children, but it does not always do so: Recent research indicates that children's response to divorce is not uniform.

Divorce, although it is a family crisis, may also be seen as an opportunity for positive change. Among some children, there may be little difference on measures of psychosocial adjustment than for their peers from intact families, and some studies actually found higher scores on adjustment measures in children from divorced families. Some of the predictors of positive postdivorce adjustment include good communication and lack of overt conflict between parents, good psychological adjustment of parents, good parenting skills (including displays of warmth and appropriate limit setting), healthy accommodation to the stresses inherent in change, and support from family and friends. However, there is also evidence that divorce can take a serious toll on the lives of children, often related to difficulties in the factors discussed here (Twaite, Silitsky, & Luchow, 1998), with the greatest problems often manifest within the first 2 years after the divorce (Hetherington, 1989).

The death of a parent is one of the most significant and serious losses one can experience in a lifetime, especially for an early adolescent who is still dependent on the care of a parent. Data indicate that nearly 1.5 million youth in the United States lose a parent to death by the age of 15 (Silverman & Worden, 1992). In a recent study of 80 minority youths aged 9 through 17, 65% had lost a father, with causes of death of parents in this study including, in descending order, natural death, homicide, and accidents (Thompson, Kaslow, Kingree, King, Bryant, & Rey, 1998). The bonds of attachment at this age are very strong, and such writers as Bowlby (1980) and Worden (1996) have explored the impact of parental death on children and adolescents in depth. Worden (1996) examined the risk factors for high levels of emotional and behavioral problems in bereaved children. Some of the common risk factors evident at 4 months, 1 year, and 2 years after the death include low self-esteem, having experienced a sudden death, the presence of health problems in the surviving parent, depression and fear about the safety of the parent, high levels of family stress and change, and a passive coping style.

ASSESSMENT OF VULNERABILITIES AND RISK FACTORS

It is difficult to predict how a child or adolescent will react to a crisis. As the early adolescent develops, the path of his or her life is marked by thousands of events that vary in the magnitude, duration, and the meaning they have for the person. Why one individual reacts markedly differently to a similar life event than another individual is the question at the heart of stress research and is critical to identification of how one will react to a crisis event. Unlike adults, children and younger adolescents are subject to many events over which they have little control; therefore, what they perceive as stressful is often different from what an adult might perceive, and is also likely to be different from the perceptions of older adolescents (Brooks-Gunn, 1992). Early adolescence has been viewed as a highly stressful period specifically in relation to its "age-graded experiences," including physical, cognitive, and social changes that mark the middle school or junior high school years (Swearingen & Cohen, 1985). During this period, the early adolescent must cope with many stressors, including puberty, new experiences, increased responsibilities, and future-oriented plans and goals. Financial hardship of the family, educational disability, illness, and so on only increase an early adolescent's vulnerability to a crisis event.

Adolescents cope with stressors in many ways, and identifying risk factors that predispose individuals to cope in a dysfunctional way in a crisis situation is an important domain of research. The greatest amount of research has focused on internal cognitive or biological factors. The research indicates that individuals' expectations about the world and attributions about the causes of events have particularly important effects on responses to acute stressors; it also has identified specific biological or physiological correlates of susceptibility to crisis.

For example, Seligman (1995) has studied the attributions that children make to both positive and negative events. His results indicate that children who are more vulnerable to crisis tend to make specific and external attributions to positive events (e.g., the teacher gave me a good grade) and global and internal attributions when a negative event occurs (e.g., my inability to act led to the tragedy). Lazarus (1993) also argues that how a child appraises a stressful situation or crisis event is critical to her or his coping process and subsequent adjustment. Catanzaro and Mearns (1990) focus on the importance of one's mood and ability to regulate mood states. Consistent with cognitive theory, what people think will happen when they experience a negative event has important implications for the development of a healthy or unhealthy psychological and/or physical response. Garmezy (1987) noted that biological disposition and temperament are associated with how individuals may cope with a stressful or crisis situation. Fox (1992) found that children who demonstrate greater left frontal lobe activation, associated with attention and verbal strategies, may be better able to regulate their emotions than children who show greater activity in the right frontal lobe. Other styles more reflective of temperament (such as a depressive, stress-reactive, or psychosomatic style) may also reflect the potential for a negative outcome following a crisis event.

At least some aspects of risk factors can also vary with gender. A study by Rossman (1992) revealed that certain emotion regulation coping had a significant blocking effect on the negative reactions to stress. However, girls used the coping responses of social support (e.g., peers and parents) and distress expression (e.g., self-blame) significantly more often than boys, who typically used humor and anger expressions (e.g., ventilation).

Other sociocultural factors may also be important. For example, most research on "at-risk" adolescents has focused on inner city and urban adolescents, but rural areas represent distinctly different social and economic characteristics than urban areas. According to Miller and Luloff (1981), rural areas are defined socioculturally, occupationally, and ecologically. The sociocultural dimension is a set of values, including social conservatism, provincialism, and fatalism. Forrest (1988) found that rural youth experience high levels of stress, especially isolation and loneliness. Further, she found that limited resources coupled with concerns about anonymity when seeking mental health care compound the problem of intervention in rural communities.

RESILIENCE AND PROTECTIVE FACTORS

Although research into what makes an individual react in a dysfunctional manner to an acute stressor is important in attempting to understand why some individuals are more especially susceptible to crisis, by itself this research offers a limited view of the process considered here. Recently, work on the other side of this process—how people maintain mental health—has begun to gain greater prominence. Researchers have particularly responded with studies of resilient persons, or children who grew up in aversive environments yet became productive, caring adults. Mash and Dozois (1996) defined the resilient child as one who manages to avoid negative outcomes and/or achieve positive outcomes despite being at significant risk for the development of psychopathology, and as one who displays sustained competence under stress and shows recovery from trauma. Resilient individuals cope well in spite of great stressors; however, even resilient individuals may become overwhelmed if supports are lost and/or stressors increase.

Recent work in this area identifies a range of internal psychological and external social or familial forces that contribute to resilience. For example, Blocker and Copeland (1994) found that the trait of social responsiveness, including cooperation and participation, most discriminated between resilient and nonresilient high-stressed youths: Resilient adolescents were involved in more activities, spent more time on academic pursuits, and spent fewer hours alone than their nonresilient peers. Werner and Smith (1992) found that adolescent males who had realistic educational plans and adolescent females with good self-esteem were the most likely to develop into well-adapted adults. Turner, Norman, and Zunz (1995) defined protective factors of resilience along personality dimensions: self-esteem, self-efficacy, intellectual capabilities, an easy temperament, good social and problem-solving skills, a sense of humor, the ability to separate from a "toxic" environment, and empathy. Other protective factors that have been found to contribute to resilience include an adequate identification figure, a sense of curiosity, a sense of self, social responsiveness, and representational competence (Blocker & Copeland, 1994). Significantly, the specific factors that may be most important to a given individual can vary with gender (Werner & Smith, 1992) and probably with other factors as well.

The ultimate goal in the study of resilience is to design interventions that better reduce risk factors and/or increase protective factors; such interventions could have implications for crisis intervention. Sadly, interventions that successfully promote resilience are less documented than identification of protective factors that contribute to resilience. Seligman's (1995) work offers a promising solution. Finding that an optimistic attributional style is a hallmark of resilience, Seligman developed a cognitive training program for children that combats pessimism when children are faced with adversity or crisis; promotes a temporary, specific, and impersonal explanatory style to negative events and a permanent, pervasive, and personal explanatory style to positive events; teaches disputing and decatastrophizing of adversities; and boosts social skills. Specifically, a child would be trained to attribute negative events to transitory external circumstances while crediting successes to personal and stable positive characteristics.

CASE EXAMPLES

We now examine three case studies in light of Roberts's (1990, 1996) seven-stage model of intervention. These stages are (1) assess psychosocial needs and, especially, lethality, (2) establish rapport, (3) identify major problems,

(4) deal with feelings, (5) explore alternatives, (6) generate an action plan to put these alternatives into practice, and (7) conduct follow-up. Each case study shows how Roberts's seven-stage model was applied.

Esperanza, Parental Death

Esperanza is a 12-year-old Mexican American girl. She lives on a small ranch with her family, who raise llamas. She has three older sisters (ages 18, 16, 15), a younger brother (age 10), and a horse named Cookie. Her mother Ana is 41 and co-owns an insurance business with her sister and brother. Her father, Michael, ran the family business until his death 5 months ago. Ana and Michael were snowmobiling in the mountains when their snowmobile spun out of control and they were thrown off. Her mother broke her leg and received other minor injuries, but she recovered quickly. Her father broke his neck and died.

In the first few months after Michael's death, Esperanza and her siblings openly mourned his loss and took great care of their mother, who alternated between constant weeping and then worrying for her children. Because of Ana's injuries, the older children took care of the cleaning, cooking, and ranch work. The eldest, Camille, who was in her first year of college, decided to take a semester off to help her family; she ran things quite smoothly and was very efficient in helping the other children get ready for school and complete their homework and chores. The other sisters, Luisa and Margaret, although devastated by their father's death, spent a lot of time together and decided to begin an ambitious project of gathering family memorabilia to dedicate to their father's memory. The youngest child, Martin was often distracted and sad but felt his family was very helpful to him; he spent a lot of time with his male cousins at his aunt and uncle's house, a few miles from home.

After her father's death, Esperanza had great difficulty sleeping and concentrating. She complained of stomachaches to her older sister, who gave her several over-the-counter medications to soothe her stomach and told Esperanza not to bother their mother. The academic work in which she once took great pride suffered; her grades dropped so precipitously that she was in danger of not passing seventh grade. She was alternately very passive or very aggressive at school. She told Luisa that she wanted to die. She thought everyone else was "managing" better than her. Esperanza also told Luisa that she felt responsible for their father's death and that she thought their mother was very angry at her.

Luisa was alarmed at this. She spoke with Camille and Margaret, who agreed they needed to speak to their mother, who, though now mostly recovered and back at work, seemed very distant at times. Ana immediately went to Esperanza, who denied feeling suicidal. However, Esperanza cried for hours after this and kept repeating that it was her fault her father died. Ana, who is devoutly Catholic, contacted her parish priest, a warm, thoughtful person with a reputation for being available during times of crisis. He came to the house and spoke with the entire family about how they were doing; finally, he spoke with Esperanza in the presence of her mother. Esperanza was inconsolable and wailed that she wanted to be with her father, and that her father might forgive her if she could be with him. No one was able to determine why Esperanza felt so responsible and at last the priest recommended Ana call a counselor he knew at a university about 30 minutes from their town. He mentioned that this counselor was an expert in working with grieving children. Esperanza and Ana made an appointment and met with the counselor a few days later.

Given the concern expressed by those close to Esperanza (that she was considering suicide and seemingly inconsolable), it was essential for her counselor to quickly establish a relationship with her. Doing so required, of course, empathy, respect, and genuineness (Roberts, 1996; Rogers, 1965). Given that Esperanza had expressed a wish to die, it was also critical to assess her lethality. Esperanza is 12 years old and is probably within the third stage of cognitive development, the formal operational stage (Piaget, 1968). At this stage, thinking is logical and children are able to understand abstractions. Of particular relevance here, children of this age can understand that death is not a reversible process (Husain & Vandiver, 1984; Webb, 1993), and thus Esperanza's wish to die had to be treated seriously. Worden (1996) also discusses the fact that while it is uncommon for children to express suicidal ideation when a parent dies, their threats must be taken seriously.

Many writers, Worden included, are aware that those who care for a child may hesitate in asking about suicidal ideation, fearing they may suggest ideas to the child. Worden recommends a gentle inquiry to initiate the discussion. Following Roberts (1996), the first stage in crisis intervention is to assess lethality, which includes an assessment of danger to self and others and attending to immediate psychosocial needs. The second stage of this model focuses on establishing rapport and rapidly building the relationship. Both steps were attended to in the first half of the counseling session when the counselor made it clear to Esperanza that she knew why those who loved her had referred Esperanza to counseling and that other people came to the counselor's office to talk about painful losses. While she was sensitive to Esperanza's acute sense of loss, the counselor began an assessment of lethality after exploring Esperanza's feelings about being sent to counseling. James (1989) recommends that counselors make clear why the child is being seen in counseling. Explaining the role of the counselor and the participation of parent and child in planning treatment will do much to demystify the process of counseling and give the child and parent a sense of control. This is particularly important in cases like Esperanza's because bereaved children commonly feel that they have less control over events than nonbereaved children

(Worden & Silverman, 1996). To the extent possible, a counselor will want to help a child feel that he or she has some control and choice in counseling.

In the second half of the first session, the counselor met with the entire family, except for Martin, who was on a camping trip with his cousins. The family members were asked about what they would like changed in their current situation. They emphasized their concern for Esperanza and her expression of suicidal ideation. The counselor chose to use a solution-focused approach to assess Esperanza's suicidal ideation (Softas-Nall & Francis, 1998). It was a surprise to the family that the basis for Esperanza's desire to die was related to her certainty that her mother was angry at her and blamed Esperanza for the death of her husband. Ana was shocked that Esperanza felt responsible, and she reassured her daughter that she could not allow herself to feel responsible. She was able to correct Esperanza's misperception that she had "made" her parents go snowmobiling on the fateful day. Ana told her that her father had made up his mind that he wanted to go and, as usual, he teased Esperanza that he could not go because he had "so much work to do." Clearing up this misperception did not lessen Esperanza's agony over her father's death, but it did help her feel that she was not responsible. It was helpful to have the family gathered because they could provide support for Esperanza, which was important in helping her through this crisis. Esperanza admitted she had just wanted to die to get away from her painful feelings, but she did not have a specific plan for killing herself. After Esperanza promised she would not kill herself and did not have a plan or specific means of committing suicide, the session ended with scheduling an appointment to meet again in a few days.

In the next session, after determining once again that Esperanza was not in imminent danger, her counselor began to accomplish the tasks set forth in the third stage of Roberts's model. This stage focuses primarily on identifying the major problems or events that precipitated the crisis. In some cases it may be helpful to identify problems and to rank them by priority so as to clarify a focus and address potentially harmful aspects of the problem. However, Esperanza made it clear that her crisis was about one problem and one problem only: her father's death.

Discussion of this tremendous loss led naturally into the fourth stage, expression of feelings. Esperanza was assisted in exploring her feelings using the fundamental counseling skills discussed in many elementary counseling skills books such as those by Cormier and Cormier (1998) or by Egan (1998). The skills included active and empathic listening, paraphrasing important content, reflecting feelings within the context of events the client is discussing, clarifying confusing or ambiguous statements, and summarizing both content and feelings. Esperanza was also helped by the counselor's use of more direct "action" skills (Cormier & Cormier, 1998), including gentle confrontation between verbal and nonverbal behaviors. For example, at one point Esperanza said, "Everyone is handling this better than me; my sisters don't miss him at all," whereupon she laughed, while at the same time tears fell from her eyes. Her counselor gently confronted the discrepancy between Esperanza's tears and her incompatible expression of laughter. Esperanza admitted she did not believe her sisters were managing as well as they seemed, but their concentration on a project to memorialize their father made Esperanza feel "left out."

Many techniques designed to help children express their feelings about loss are discussed in the works of prominent writers in the field (e.g., James, 1989; Webb, 1993; Worden, 1996). A few techniques that Esperanza found helpful included writing a letter to her father and reading it in session while she was invited to explore her feelings, going to the site of the accident and planting a small tree in his memory, and looking at photographs of her family, especially a few special ones of times she spent with her father on the farm and doing things together at horse fairs. Esperanza, a talented young adolescent, said she wanted to create a collage with color copies of the photographs. She began to work on this project with the counselor on a weekly basis because she did not want to take it home, fearing that it might upset her mother. In a subsequent family session, Esperanza discussed her project. Upon hearing about it her mother cried, but with the counselor's attention to the feelings of mother and daughter, both felt closer to each other as they were able to talk about how the loss impacted them. Ana asked Esperanza to bring the project home so they could work on it together. Esperanza was excited to do this and to feel that she was doing something special with her mother.

This collage project gives an example of what Roberts recommends in the fifth stage of his model, which focuses on generating and exploring adaptive coping strategies in crisis. Very often, a client is too distressed to develop good coping strategies; initially this was certainly the case with Esperanza. Husain and Vandiver (1984) note that the adolescent who feels suicidal finds coping difficult and is emotionally strained. Using the basic counseling skills noted earlier, Esperanza's counselor mentioned that many young people who have suffered the death of a parent may go through a time when they cry, feel sad, and have trouble concentrating. Worden and Silverman (1996) caution against labeling these symptoms depression because they are normal in the first year following parental death and often lessen by the first anniversary: We need to exercise caution in using the term *depression* to describe a normal response. Esperanza's counselor helped her to see that her responses were normal but that it was very important to either develop new coping resources or find a way to use the resources that helped her in difficult situations in the past. Esperanza's counselor gave her several examples of children in her age-group with whom she had worked and of some of the things they did to help themselves cope. Esperanza was very interested in hearing about what others in her position had done. She had confidence in this counselor, who clearly had experience in working with others who were grieving the loss of a parent.

Esperanza's counselor asked her to describe how she had coped in the past when something bad had happened or when nothing seemed to be going right. Esperanza recalled that when her cousin's parents divorced it was a very hard time for her, too, because she felt very close to her aunt and uncle. She prayed to God to help her through this time; she focused a lot of attention on helping her cousin, who was very sad; and she rode horses a lot and cleaned the barn. With her counselor's help, Esperanza generated lists of ways in which she might cope now, one list each for helping herself (a) inside, (b) being with others, and (c) doing things. Both Esperanza and her counselor brainstormed on items they could place under each heading. It helped to put three large pieces of paper on the wall of the room and to use a marker to write ideas as they emerged. Under the heading "Helping myself inside," Esperanza wrote "Pray." She has prayed since her father's death, but initially it was for God to make him well, then for God to take her to her father. Now she wrote, "Pray to God to help me through this hard time" and "Pray to God to give me strength." Her counselor also suggested "Listening to the relaxation tape," which she had made at Esperanza's request and which had helped relieve her stomach pains. Esperanza added "Drawing and painting in my journal" because she enjoyed artistic expression. Under the second list ("Helping myself by being with others"), there were many items, including spending more time with her little brother, helping her older sister to cook, reestablishing riding lessons, arranging outings with one or two friends or cousins at a time, and staying with her godparents for an overnight. Esperanza's counselor took it as a very positive indicator of her progress that Esperanza was willing to spend time with others because, since her father's death, she had been isolated and withdrawn from those who could offer support. Esperanza was clear that she was not ready to spend time with more than a few people at a time, and her counselor agreed that she was respecting her own limits and taking a step in the right direction. It was the collage of her family and special times with her dad that Esperanza put under the last coping category ("Helping myself by doing things").

It was in the sixth stage of Roberts's model, developing an action plan, that Esperanza became stuck. Having ideas, as Esperanza did, is essential, but these ideas need to be planned and executed to help restore functioning in the client (Roberts, 1996). Initially Esperanza was excited to begin taking some steps in items related to all three categories. She had no trouble creating goals and developing intermediate steps (Cormier & Cormier, 1998), but, when asked by her counselor which activity she would do this week, Esperanza became stuck in indecision. Outside of counseling, Esperanza sought the advice of her mother and sisters, but she did not like any of their suggestions and became surly when she was encouraged to follow her own plan. In counseling, Esperanza pushed her counselor to choose for her. When she refused, Esperanza became annoyed and said people were no longer being helpful to her. She wondered why she should try if everyone else was giving up. This change in mood was remarkable.

Her counselor told her a story of a girl she had worked with whose brother had died; this girl also went through a time of indecision and inaction. Esperanza was relieved to hear that this other girl had also found it hard to accept that she had the right to be happy and to move on with her life after surviving her brother in a car accident. This client, like Esperanza, was smart and creative but thought that if she went on with her life she might forget her brother, and that having fun would be akin to betraying him. As Roberts (1996) notes, it can be helpful to clients to know that we have worked with others who have had difficulties in executing plans, and it is equally helpful for them to know that these clients ultimately succeeded in overcoming their self-imposed obstacles.

Esperanza did worry that she would begin to forget details from her life with her father, and she still worried at times that if she had not told her parents to go snowmobiling he would still be alive. After further clarification and expression of her feelings, Esperanza decided she would focus on completing the collage so that her fear about forgetting her dad could be laid to rest. She also said she wanted to begin praying that day, twice daily, for God to continue giving her strength and to help her believe she did not have anything to do with the accident. Thus, after exploring the difficulty in implementing her plans, Esperanza was more readily able to continue with a course of action.

The last stage of the crisis intervention deals with follow-up. Worden and his colleagues on the Child Bereavement Project (Worden, 1996; Worden & Silverman, 1996) found that recently bereaved children were no more or less disturbed than the matched nonbereaved controls on a variety of psychological measures. However, when the data were examined 1 and 2 years after the death of a parent, there were significant differences between bereaved children and the control group of nonbereaved children. In particular, adolescent boys (ages 12 through 18) who did not show much difference 1 year after the death of a parent did indicate that they were more withdrawn and had slightly more social problems than controls. The preadolescent girls had no more problems than the nonbereaved control group at 1 year after the parental death, but there were significant changes by 2 years, including more anxiety and depression. This extensive study has implications for mental health professionals and others who work with children. We must be aware of the long-term effects of losing a parent, and know that problems may not appear until 1 or 2 years after the death. Esperanza made very good progress in therapy. After only 4 months of regularly working together, she and her counselor agreed to terminate their regular sessions and moved to periodic check-ins. Because her counselor was aware of the research of the Child Bereavement Project, she encouraged Esperanza to meet with her every couple of months for a while to check in. The counselor met with Esperanza six times over the next 2 years and also met with the entire family four times to keep apprised of how everyone else was doing. Nearly 14 months after her father's death, Camille, the eldest, began to develop insomnia and frequent periods of sadness. Having anticipated that one of the other children in the family might later experience more grief over the father's death, Esperanza's counselor encouraged Camille to meet with a counselor at the university she attended.

At 2 years and 4 months after her father's death, Esperanza felt that she was functioning well. She had good support from family and friends, was earning excellent grades in school, and had won several statewide equestrian events of which she was very proud. She told her former counselor that in the future she might want to come back to counseling, but right now she was too busy having a full and satisfying life, and even periodic follow-up no longer seemed necessary.

Jenny: Parental Divorce, Paternal Alcoholism, Death of Grandmother

Jenny is a white, middle-class, 13-year-old American girl of high average intelligence whose parents, Bill and Emily, both age 40, divorced a year ago following several years of progressive deterioration of Bill's health and increased absences from home due to alcoholism. For the last 2 years, Jenny's mother had become increasingly involved in her work as an administrator for a health care network and had to take complete care of family finances.

Prior to the separation, when her dad seemed to be getting worse, Jenny was able to talk to her mother and grandmother about her sadness for and anger at her father. Her father had participated in several treatment programs but never followed through on aftercare for very long, lapsing again into alcoholism. After the last treatment failure, Emily filed for divorce. Jenny had tried to talk to her mother about her feelings, but Emily had grown bitter about Bill and responded, "Your father can't get beyond his problems, but we can do better than that, and it is time to move on." Jenny felt she could not talk to her mother and instead turned to her grandmother, who provided significant emotional support and comfort.

Two months ago, Jenny's beloved grandmother died; following this, Jenny became increasingly withdrawn from friends and family and less involved in school activities. Although Jenny became quieter and seemed mostly sad, she had several angry outbursts at her mother and her two younger brothers, ages 10 and 8. She frequently woke at night crying and complained to her mother that she was afraid to go back to sleep in case the nightmares would return. She dreamed that she was hiking up a mountain with family and friends, but that whenever she turned around she had lost someone; in the dream she was alone on the mountain with the cold night approaching. Over the last month, she had also become increasingly preoccupied with her appearance and had lost 8 pounds. Her mother worried that Jenny was eating less and was spending too much time running and swimming. Jenny's brothers noticed that she spent more time alone in her room and had stopped going to their baseball games.

Jenny's mother was worried about her daughter. At the recommendation of the school counselor, Emily set up an appointment for them with a counselor in the community. Early in crisis intervention it is essential to assess lethality and establish rapport with a client (Roberts, 1996). Although the counselor encouraged her, Jenny was reluctant to disclose her feelings, saying there was nothing anyone could do because her grandmother was gone and her dad was too sick to care. Her counselor was quickly able to establish a relationship with Jenny by respecting and acknowledging her hopelessness that anything would change regarding the death of her grandmother, her father's alcoholism, and her parents' divorce. She affirmed the myriad feelings such losses engendered such as sadness, anger, guilt, and anxiety and pointed out that sometimes people feel sick and tired and may act out (Worden, 1996), but that such feelings are normal. The counselor encouraged help-seeking behavior and emphasized that others have found it useful to talk about losses in counseling and to develop coping strategies. She also mentioned that she had worked with many people who have suffered losses and that, although each person is different, people do have some similar experiences when such terrible losses occur.

Jenny cried as she told her counselor that her grandmother was "the one person who believed in me, no matter what. My dad checked out a while ago and has not done much with us kids the last couple of years, and now my mom has to work so much. I know Mom loves us, but she has so much to do, and Gram was always there for me." Jenny feared that the people she loves would leave her through illness or death and thought that maybe it is better to be alone: she reasoned that "everyone leaves for some reason, and if I don't depend too much on other people, I won't be so sad if something bad happens." Her counselor accurately paraphrased Jenny's concerns. Using open-ended questions, she probed further and discovered that Jenny's fear of losing people was part of the reason she had withdrawn from friends. Jenny said that sometimes she wished she could be with her grandmother. The counselor inquired further, and Jenny stated that if she were dead, she would be with her grandmother. Her counselor asked if Jenny had thought about suicide. Jenny said she had, but that she would never do it because she knew how sad it would make her mother. The counselor conducted a brief assessment, asking Jenny about how she had thought of killing herself. Jenny was vague, saying, "I don't know, maybe a lot of aspirin." The counselor asked Jenny to scale her suicidal ideation on a scale from 1 to 10, with one being "not at all" to 10 being "very serious" (see Softas-Nall & Francis, 1998). Jenny responded, "It's 1. I could never really do that. It is against my religion, and my Gram would think it was awful. I would never do that to her or my mom." The counselor reflected back that, even in death, Jenny's grandmother's opinion was very important.

Although the reason for seeking services focused on Jenny's response to her grandmother's death, the counselor was also aware of the divorce and wanted to explore that as well. Webb (1991, 1993) notes that in complicated grief, like Jenny's, stresses that are superimposed on one another will affect each person differently, but the combined impact of multiple stressors is more likely to lead to greater problems, such as fragmentation of coping abilities. Bowlby (1980) also discusses the increased likelihood of developing disorders under these circumstances.

In the third stage of the crisis intervention model, it is important develop a focus for intervention. The counselor examined the number and significance of the recent losses Jenny experienced and noted that her grandmother's death was the most recent in a series of losses. Roberts (1996) discusses the importance of identifying the precipitating event that leads a client to seek help; this may be the "last straw," but many events led to the crisis, the problems must be prioritized so that a central focus can be developed. Jenny's counselor asked her to identify the important events that led to her being in counseling. Jenny expressed anger, saying she has had enough to deal with and she is tired of so many bad things happening. Her counselor asked an open-ended question: "What are the losses you are thinking of right now?" Jenny explained about her father's increasing withdrawal from home, the nights spent away from his family, the loss of his job, her mother becoming so busy and preoccupied with work, her parents' divorce, and the humiliation of her family needing to move into a smaller house because of financial problems.

Her counselor acknowledged and further explored Jenny's feelings. Jenny said the divorce was hard on her because her mom was so sad, but that her father had been "missing" for a long time, so it was better than staying married. She had not been able to talk about the divorce much, except with her grandmother, and she still found it hard to believe her parents were not married anymore: "I had such a great childhood and I kept thinking if Daddy could only find a better hospital he could be better and things could be like they were." With such a long list of events, Roberts (1996) notes that it may be helpful to rank them by priority so as to clarify a focus. Jenny identified her grandmother's death and her parents' divorce as the most serious concerns to her at this time.

Once the major problems have been identified, it is important to encourage and explore feelings, which is the focus of the fourth intervention stage. Throughout counseling, Jenny's counselor used active listening and other basic skills to develop a relationship and to encourage Jenny to express her feelings. The counselor consistently linked past experiences with the present through use of such basic counseling skills as paraphrasing, reflection, and open-ended questions. Although talking was a common vehicle for expression, Jenny loved to paint and write poetry, and these modes of expression were very useful in helping her work through her feelings. The current literature offers many strategies that can be useful in helping children of different ages to work through grief (e.g., see James, 1989; Landreth, 1991; Webb, 1993; Worden, 1996).

Jenny angrily admitted she "closed" herself off from her father and spent less time with him because he yelled a lot and was mean, but that she spent more time with people who were "good" to her, such as her grandmother and friends. Her feelings about moving to a smaller house included embarrassment at having to move from " a big house with a pool where my friends could hang out to a little house with a tiny yard that had so few rooms that my brothers have to share a room. But, even though it is really hard to move, it is better than having to leave my school and friends." Jenny also spent time writing in her journal and doing artwork, which she found relaxing. Although these activities had helped her to cope in the past, now Jenny worried that she was being "too sad" and that her friends would not want to be around her anymore.

The counselor mentioned that sometimes when young women are distressed and things seem out of control, they try to control what is within their own reach, such as weight. Jenny mentioned that her cheerleading coach, trying to be helpful, suggested that exercise improved her own mood; thus Jenny, looking for ways to feel better, began to exercise more and more. A few friends had noticed that she looked thinner and complimented her on it, whereupon Jenny thought cutting out sweets and dieting might help her lose the few pounds she had gained over the winter.

Although the fourth stage of the crisis intervention model focuses on exploring and expressing feelings, it would be erroneous to think such exploration occurs only at that stage. Throughout the counseling process, it is imperative that a counselor be attuned to the child's needs and respond in an empathic way. In the fifth stage, emphasis is placed on assessing past coping attempts, developing alternatives, and designing specific solutions. While listening to Jenny, her counselor was particularly attentive to ways Jenny coped effectively so as to reinforce any adaptive behaviors and cognitions. With her counselor's help, Jenny explored how she handled such past stressors as her parents' divorce, the move to a smaller house, and her father's alcoholism. As noted earlier, Jenny found it helpful to spend less time with her father when he was in a bad mood and more time with people who were "good" to her, such as her grandmother and friends. She had also reframed the move to a smaller house as not so bad because it was better than having to leave her friends and school, and she often wrote in a journal and did artwork. All these approaches had been useful, but Jenny complained they were not working well anymore; furthermore, she had lost one of her strongest supporters. Roberts (1990) notes that clinicians may need to take the initiative when clients have little insight or if they are emotionally distressed. Jenny felt dismayed that her former coping strategies were either unavailable or that she could not seem to use them effectively.

It can be helpful to hear what other clients have done in the past, and so her counselor asked Jenny if she would like to know something about how other clients whose parents were divorced or who had experienced losses coped. Because Jenny seemed interested, her counselor told her about a boy whose favorite uncle, who was also his godfather, had died. The boy talked about feelings as Jenny did, and then he came up with a way to let go of some of his problems. One technique was to imagine he was inhaling his anger and pain deep into his lungs; then he exhaled all of those feelings into a balloon, which he took outside and released into the air to let the feelings go. He also wrote a letter to his uncle about many of the wonderful things they had done together and read this to his counselor; afterward they explored how he felt doing this and what he found helpful. Jenny's counselor then asked Jenny to imagine she was a counselor; what would she recommend, as coping strategies, to a 13- or 14-year-old who was dealing with so many losses? Jenny found this amusing and insisted on sitting in her counselor's chair as she took on the role of a directive list maker. Jenny quickly wrote a list of ideas, including spending time with close friends; talking to your family; writing down feelings on sticky-notes and putting them on a wall and making a poem of them; painting feelings and using pictures and words cut from magazines to create a collage of how you feel now and what you want to change to feel better; doing things that are relaxing; taking bubble baths; watching movies that make you laugh; and exercising.

One "coping" strategy the counselor felt needed to be addressed was with exercise and weight loss. She expressed her concern that this strategy might be exacerbating the problem. Jenny, who felt very good about losing weight, argued that she had been a bit overweight and that exercise was healthy. Because her counselor had previously worked with clients with eating disorders, she was aware of the futility of arguing about weight. Instead, she focused on the effectiveness or lack thereof of using diet and excessive exercise to feel better about herself. Jenny admitted she felt tired and had problems concentrating if she did not eat breakfast or lunch and that, although she enjoyed exercise, it was starting to feel all-consuming to her.

Her counselor asked "On a scale of 1 to 10, with 1 being tired and 10 being very energetic, where are you?"

      Jenny: I'd like to say 8, but I feel like a 4 today.

Counselor: OK, what would it take to move that to a 5 or 6?

      Jenny: Get some sleep!

Counselor: How can you do that today?

Jenny: Hmm. I woke up hungry, so if I ate more and exercised a bit less, I think I would have more energy.

Counselor: What are you willing to do today to move in that direction?

Jenny: I will eat dinner and just go for a short bike ride instead of riding for 2 hours. That way I will have time to relax before I go to bed.

The focus moved away from weight and food and on to how to help Jenny feel more energetic. She already had some of the solutions to her own problems.

Jenny and her counselor talked about divorce, depression, eating disorders, loss, and grief. Jenny also read educational material related to these concerns. Through talking, doing artwork, and writing poetry, she began to understand that many of her feelings of loneliness, anger, sadness, and depression were rooted in the significant losses she had suffered, and that it is normal to have difficulties when such things happen. Jenny was encouraged to talk about her feelings in counseling and to think about how she could reconnect with people who are important to her, especially people who she saw as "believing in her." Jenny thought she would like to spend more time with her mother's younger sister and to see her best friends more often.

After Jenny and her counselor spoke with Jenny's mother, aunt, and school counselor, all agreed that Jenny had suffered many losses and that she needed their help. Jenny's aunt arranged her schedule so she could meet with Jenny one evening a week, and they spent time together taking hikes, going to movies, or having pizza. Jenny's mother made plans to shift responsibilities at work so she had fewer evening meetings, and she spent that time with her children. Emily was also more sensitive to her daughter's feelings and created opportunities to encourage Jenny to share her thoughts and feelings. Emily also suggested that Jenny speak to one or two of her closest friends so they would know what had been going on. Jenny agreed to do this and found that her friends had been worried about her and were eager to help. The school counselor, apprised of the cheerleading coach's recommendation, considered ways he could consult with school personnel on helping children with loss and grief.

In the sixth step of the crisis intervention model it is important to move from generating ideas to developing and implementing an action plan. As Jenny began to feel better about herself, felt listened to, and had more energy, she had little trouble implementing her plans. As noted earlier, she is quite bright and likes to make lists. Jenny began with creating artwork to better express, understand, and manage her feelings. Some of her collages expressed much anger and overwhelming sadness, yet others indicated hope and looking toward the future. She wrote a poem about losses and changes that was later published in a book, and she felt particularly proud of turning her grief and anger into hope and a published work.

In the follow-up stage of crisis intervention, which took place at 1- and 2-month follow-up sessions, Jenny was functioning well. She was satisfied that counseling had helped her through a difficult period of her life.

Peter: Tragic Death of a Sibling

Peter is a White, upper-middle-class, 12-year-old early adolescent who comes from an intact family who have been active members of the community. Peter lives with his parents, Judy and Paul, ages 43 and 45, respectively, and his older sister, Cheryl, age 16. Judy is part owner of an interior design company, a business she and two others started 9 years ago. Paul, a civil engineer, has been employed by the Army Corps of Engineers for 20 years. Three grandparents all live in the same state. Peter's maternal grandmother died 2 1/2 years ago following surgical complications.

The week after spring break, Peter was in his history class at Franklin Middle School. Midway through the class, Peter was called to the office, where he and three other students were told of a tragedy at Southridge High School. Apparently, three students had brought weapons into the high school and began firing indiscriminately at students and staff shortly before the noon hour. Each of the four middle school students has a brother or sister at the high school who either was known to be wounded or was not accounted for. The four students exhibited diverse emotions; Peter sat baffled and withdrawn and asked few questions. At 2:30 P.M., Paul, Peter's father, arrived at school, hugged Peter, and left the building quickly. Peter was told of his sister's death by his parents at 5:00 P.M. on the day of the catastrophe.

Three weeks after the tragedy, Peter's parents remained in shock and provided little support for him. Peter appeared to be fine and, after a 7-day absence from school, had returned to his classes at Franklin Middle School. Extended family and neighbors have been very involved with the family, yet Peter had spent most of his time with his grandfather, Clay, his mother's father. Peter and Granddad talked a great deal, yet they seldom spoke directly about Cheryl, as Judy and Paul are obviously not ready to actively deal with the murder of their daughter.

Media attention remained intense. The scale of the tragedy (6 students murdered and 14 seriously injured) led to national and international coverage. One positive result was that significant funds were made available for mental health counseling for students, teachers, and their families who were affected by the Southridge tragedy. A month before school was scheduled to end, Judy and Paul were encouraged by a school social worker to take Peter to see a counselor. Peter resisted yet later consented to please his parents. The counselor reviewed fears, concentration, sleep, safety, and somatic complaints for three sessions. Peter denied any concerns and told his grandfather, who had been taking him to the appointments, that he did not want to return for a fourth session. Clay conveyed Peter's desires to Judy and Paul, and counseling was terminated by the parents at the end of the school year.

Two months passed, with Judy and Paul beginning to see the benefits of mental health counseling. The two took advantage of couple counseling and a grief support group. Judy was engaged in individual therapy. Talk of Cheryl in the household was no longer taboo. As the parents began their recovery, Paul returned to his job and Judy increased her working hours to 30 a week. Judy's partners, seeing a definite improvement, encouraged her to travel on an out-of-state business trip for a 4-day period. When Peter was told that his mother would be leaving on a business trip, a tantrum followed, and he was sick the next day with a fever. Judy rescheduled her trip for 3 days the following week and did leave town without incident from Peter.

Peter was now reporting somatic concerns and a fear of ghosts to his grandfather, and he was certain that another tragedy was going to follow in the fall. When Clay was briefly hospitalized for a medical problem, Peter became anxious and inconsolable. Judy and Paul decided it was time for Peter to return to a counselor. They selected a new counselor, with crisis expertise, and scheduled an appointment.

Although Judy related the tragedy and the problems of the spring and summer, Peter's presenting problem in counseling was his grandfather's medical problems. He appeared sad and upset, and he cried briefly. Peter then stated that what was happening to his grandfather was "not fair." The counselor simply allowed Peter to talk about his grandfather. A consistent issue was that grandfather "has been there for me." After listening attentively and empathetically to Peter's concerns, the counselor began to talk about "problems that we feel we have little control over." The counselor recognized that it took a lot of courage for Peter to come to counseling, and that counseling was the appropriate place for him to explore the problems that he could and could not control.

After the counselor conveyed genuine respect for and acceptance (Roberts, 1996), Peter began to relax in the session. He began to talk of his birthday at the end of the month and of going back to school. Peter's increased acceptance of the counseling process enabled the counselor to begin examining the dimensions of the tragedy and the subsequent problems. They began to discuss the tantrum over the summer. In an open manner, consistent with an early adolescent, Peter related that he was mad at his mother for leaving. He was saddened by his grandfather's condition. When the counselor asked if he was afraid, he simply said, "Maybe." Examining previous coping methods, Peter noted that he used to be a good problem solver, that he believed in God, he liked music, and he made friends easily. Over the summer, however, he spent a lot of time alone, playing video games and listening to music.

The discussion of God enabled the counselor to explore the death of Peter's sister and any cognition of lethality. Peter noted that his sister was "with God." The two briefly discussed how she died, and the counselor asked if Peter would like to be "with God." Peter said that his time will come, and we really don't know when. Peter spontaneously declared that "death is awful, and young kids shouldn't die." Peter later noted that he doesn't want anyone he loves to die in the near future. They ended the session by briefly talking about Peter's grandfather and his medical concerns.

Two sessions later found Peter, now 13 years old, starting eighth grade at the middle school. Judy asked to see the counselor before the session began and explained that Peter was experiencing a difficult start to the school year. The second day of school, he was sent home for fighting. In the session, Peter readily admitted that he fought with another boy in his class. Peter externalized (Seligman, 1995) the problem and noted that the other boy should not be making jokes about blondes. He then started crying and said that his grandfather had to "go back for more testing. It is just not fair. Why us?" He was anxious and agitated and could not see the point. He changed the subject to ask, why did someone at his sister's funeral say that "God works in strange ways?" Peter was encouraged to explain his feelings and explore whether he wants to believe in a God who allows such sorrow.

The counselor asked Peter if he still believed in God. After Peter said yes, the counselor asked Peter to explore the role that God has played in his life. The discussion of God enabled Peter to talk about his grandmother's death, his sister's tragic death, and his grandfather's problems. Peter's eyes were wet as he discussed his grandmother, who had been filled with life, and his sister, whom he used to tease with blonde jokes. After a smile came to his face, Peter stated that he was ready to talk about his sister. He began to relate the tragic events of the spring as the counselor listened in an empathic and supportive manner.

Assessing previous coping attempts allowed the counselor to examine methods that worked for Peter in the past and to identify ones that may be adaptive for him in the future. Peter related that he used to do all of his homework, he was a good problem solver, he liked the stories in church, and he enjoyed music and friends. He recalled that, following his sister's death, he simply did not know what to do and felt numb and helpless. He stated that he now believes that a number of his friends are "too weird." He related a story about a moment of silence at his school to mark the 6-month anniversary of the shootings at Southridge High, and how he had wanted to make contact with another student whose brother was murdered that tragic day. Peter was able to initiate contact after the moment of silence. He felt sad that the boy appeared very isolated, yet he remembered how he often feels and realizes that he is making a choice not to be so isolated. He recalled the summer when he only wanted to play video games and listen to music. Peter emotionally related that he was still reluctant to talk because two of his favorite people to talk with are now dead. The counselor reflected his sadness concerning the intensity of grief Peter has experienced at such a young age.

Peter spent two sessions talking about his sister and the tragic events of Southridge High. The counselor paraphrased important content and encouraged Peter to explore the story and his feelings with greater intensity each session. Peter saw that his mother was benefiting from her own work in therapy and that his father was becoming far more open to discussions. His grandfather was still visiting the house a great deal, and Peter could see the relationship between Clay and his father improving. The counselor decided that Peter was ready for stage 5, generating and exploring adaptive coping strategies.

As Peter gained insight into his thoughts and feelings concerning his sister's death, he began to expand the issues he needs to explore. He described an ebb and flow of emotions: One moment he was fine, and the next he was sad. He realized that his concentration in school was "not normal" and that he periodically had trouble sleeping, as some thoughts were intrusive. He was bothered by his mother's trips out of town, and he still worried about his grandfather's health. He asked his mother to check in more often when she is out of town and asked his grandfather to be honest with him about his failing health. Peter was now willing to admit he is sometimes fearful of the events he cannot control. He still wanted God "to make it all well," yet the youth director at church helped him to see that God may just want Peter to focus on making himself well. Peter felt that he was doing just that by talking to his counselor and making new friends whom he can talk with. Peter decided to spend less time playing video games and to discard all his aggressive games; he was proud that he made this decision without the incidence of his mother or father. He was still having trouble relating to some kids in school, yet he was convinced that being safe is more important than fighting to make a point.

Exploring fears, denial, isolation, worries, emotions, and events he could not control enabled Peter to move to stage 6, developing an action plan. He saw the difference between the external events he cannot control and the steps he could take to regain a more realistic perspective of control. He developed a system to manage his homework and again began to feel like homework was something he could complete on a daily basis. Completing his work helped him to gain a greater sense of control. Following the 6-month anniversary of Cheryl's death, Judy and Paul turned their daughter's room into a guest bedroom. Two pictures of Cheryl remained in the room, and Peter decided to "take his grieving to the guest room." He related that once a week he went into the room to cry, but that sometimes he left the room with a smile on his face. Judy and Paul became more active in church, and Peter decided to become a member of the confirmation class. He joined the group a few sessions late yet was convinced he could keep up with the work required. He renewed his interest in soccer and began to play weekends with a community team. Peter made the decision to reengage in life.

The final session of crisis intervention found Peter feeling successful: he was able to mediate a conflict in school, work on homework for an extended period of time, and enjoy his involvement in sports. Through his work in church, he began to thank God for the time he enjoyed with his grandmother and with Cheryl. He realized that the tragedy changed "everyone" in the community. He understood that his grief for his sister will not end in the near future, yet he felt ready to terminate counseling.

One and one half years after counseling was terminated, Peter was ready to enter high school. He decided to attend Southridge High School even though a new high school has opened and adolescents in his neighborhood have been given an option to go there. He reported that he misses his sister and still, at times, grieves her death.

SPECIAL CONSIDERATIONS

There are many considerations one should bear in mind in working with early adolescents who have suffered a serious loss. Each child is unique, and counselors should expect to find significant individual differences in personality style and temperament that can alter responses to acute stressors. It is important to understand further that all of these responses are shaped by biopsychosocial, cultural, and familial influences. It is not within the scope of this chapter to explore these influences in depth, but we wish to highlight the importance of developmental stages, cultural issues, and the differences between youths coping with single episodes and with a series of crises, as well as ethical considerations in working with youth.

First, as noted early in this chapter, adolescence can be divided into three periods. However, the developmental characteristics representative of each time period are not always completely consistent with a child's chronological age. For example, a 13-year-old early adolescent eldest child whose parent died may "grow up quickly" because he or she must take on additional responsibilities in the home. This child may have characteristics more similar to those of an older adolescent of 15 or 16 years. Likewise, a child who has suffered a crisis may regress and seem much younger than his or her chronological age. The implications for intervention may include using approaches that are often designed for younger children, such as play therapy. Successful interventions thus need to include careful assessments of each individual's stage of cognitive and emotional development, and must design and apply specific techniques in response to this assessment.

Second, cultural differences, which influence a myriad of behaviors, attitudes, values, and family structures, must also be taken into consideration in working with early adolescents. For example, in the first case, it was clear that Esperanza's and Martin's godparents played an important role in their support systems, and this will not be true in all families. In many cases, we must assess early on culturally variable definitions of family membership and use the client's definition of family in choosing who to treat and who to include in any intervention. It may also be the case that the values of one culture conflict with the counselor's. For example, many counselors might view Camille's choice to stay home as "codependent" or "enmeshed" behavior; such counselors might have suggested that she should return to college to resume her studies rather than take a semester off to help at home. However, Camille's family and community do not share this view: They value maintenance of the family and the individual's commitment to the family above a temporary delay in an individual's education. Note that our point is *not* that the counselor should assume a homogeneous, stereotypic set of culturally determined values for any group of people; there is great variation within all groups. Rather, it is essential to examine one's own cultural assumptions and remain open to the likelihood that these are not appropriate for all people. This will often be particularly important during Roberts's stages 5 and 6, when the counselor and the client are working to frame goals and develop plans to implement these goals. The complexity and importance of this issue warrant special consideration by the reader. We strongly recommend examining the literature focusing more extensively on the relations among adolescents, family, and culture (DeGenova, 1997; Gopaul-McNichol & Thomas-Presswood, 1998; Herring, 1997; McGoldrick & Giordano, 1996; Ponterotto, Casas, Suzuki, & Alexander, 1995; Powell, 1983).

Although discussed earlier, it is also important to draw attention to the differences between clients who present with a single crisis episode, such as Esperanza, and those who present with a series of crises, such as Jenny. In *Helping Bereaved Children*, Webb (1993) discusses a case of two children dealing with the dual losses of parents, who were separated, as well as with the death of a beloved godfather. In complicated bereavement cases such as these, Webb notes that expressions of grief are similar following divorce and death, but that there are differences that can lead to complex reactions. One difference is the intense anger a child may feel about the divorce, coupled with the self-blame for the failed marriage and often with a hope that parents will reunite. When someone dies, grief reactions will vary greatly, in part due to the degree of closeness one had with the person who died. In Jenny's case, she was very close to her grandmother and openly grieved more after her death than she did when her parents divorced. However, her reaction was complex, perhaps due, in part, to her unresolved grief and mixed feelings over her parents' divorce. Worden (1996) also notes that children may feel a need to hide their mourning in a divorce situation because of conflict between parents. This was certainly the case with Jenny, whose mother was not very supportive of her grieving the divorce but was much more attentive when Jenny's grandmother died.

Finally, there are ethical and legal issues specific to work with minor children that often must be in the forefront of the counselor's mind. In many cases, minor children are not legally able to give informed consent for treatment. Informed consent requires an understanding of psychotherapeutic treatment and an ability to make decisions about recommended interventions (Orton, 1997). The age at which children are considered competent to give informed consent varies by state, but in most cases children need the permission and signature of their parents. In divorce situations, this can be complicated by the fact that, if both parents have custody, both must grant permission for the minor child to be seen in therapy. Thus, the child's ability to receive needed services may be compromised if either parent is unwilling to permit psychological treatment. It is important for counselors to know who the custodial parent or parents are, and obtaining proof of custody is recommended (Thompson & Rudolph, 1996).

There is also the issue of willingness to participate on the part of the minor child, which can be seriously impacted by the stresses and conflicts that are typical of early adolescent development. For example, an adolescent child (as in the case of Peter) may be referred to therapy but may not want services and may be resentful about being "forced" into counseling. Furthermore, early in therapy there must be an explicit discussion among all parties regarding confidentiality, including such issues as what a counselor must report to parents even when a minor is adamant that he or she does not want a parent to be informed (i.e., abuse or a child threatening to do harm to him- or herself or another person). There must also be a discussion with parents about permitting a counselor or child not to disclose information to them about counseling sessions. Counselors must be aware of their professional code of ethics and the laws in their state about the age of consent, the rights and limits to confidentiality, and the rights to privacy (Orton, 1997). The earlier these issues are addressed, the better for all parties concerned. Addressing these issues early on in an intervention is important not just for ensuring a counselor's compliance with ethical and legal requirements but also for establishing rapport and trust during the early stages of intervention that makes work in the later stages possible. Adolescents are particularly likely to view unexpected (from their perspective) exposure of information as a fundamental violation of trust, which can compromise any form of intervention.

CONCLUSION

Crisis intervention is a critical and necessary resource for early adolescents. The counselor skilled in crisis intervention can assist in stabilization and intervention to prevent immediate crises from becoming long-standing problems. Crisis intervention is a more cost-effective and time-effective way of dealing with problems than long-term therapy, although it is clear that in some cases long-term therapy is necessary.

Counselors working with early adolescents in crisis need to be especially aware of the impacts of developmental issues on individual responses to acute stressors: Individuals in this age-group vary widely, although it must be assumed that all are struggling with complex and pervasive changes in most aspects of their lives. An awareness of this struggle must be built into any approach to crisis intervention. One important force influencing the course of early adolescent change is an individual's cultural context; counselors need to be aware of this and of their own cultural preconceptions. Applying Roberts's model of intervention with issues like these in mind has the potential for successful outcomes in many, and perhaps most, instances.

ACKNOWLEDGMENTS   We wish to acknowledge the editorial and research assistance of Carrie Merscham and Cynthia Hazel, and the insightful comments and suggestions of Douglas Bamforth.

REFERENCES

Arnett, J. J. (1999). Adolescent storm and stress, reconsidered. *American Psychologist, 54,* 317–326.

Blocker, L. S., & Copeland, E. P. (1994). Determinants of resilience in high-stress youth. *High School Journal, 77,* 287–293.

Bowlby, J. (1980). *Attachment and loss: Vol. 3. Loss.* New York: Basic Books.

Brooks-Gunn, J. (1992). Growing up female: Stressful events and the transition to adolescence. In T. M. Field, P. M. McCabe, & N. Schneiderman (Eds.), *Stress and coping in infancy and childhood* (pp. 119–145). Hillsdale, NJ: Lawrence Erlbaum.

Catanzaro, S. J., & Mearns, J. (1990). Measuring generalized expectancies for negative mood regulation, coping, and dysphoria among college students. *Journal of Counseling Psychology, 41,* 34–44.

Children's Defense Fund. (1999). *Key facts on youth, crime, and violence.* Washington, DC: Author.

Cloud, J. (1999, May 31). Just a routine school shooting. *Time, 153,* 34–43.

Cormier, W. H., & Cormier, L. S. (1998). *Interviewing strategies for helpers* (3rd ed.). Pacific Grove, CA: Brooks/Cole.

DeGenova, M. K. (1997). *Families in cultural context.* Mountain View, CA: Mayfield.

Dryfoos, J. G. (1998). *Safe passage: Making it through adolescence in a risky society.* New York: Oxford University Press.

Egan, G. (1998). *The skilled helper* (6th ed.). Pacific Grove, CA: Brooks/Cole.

Erikson, E. (1959). Identity and the life cycle. *Psychological Issues, 1,* 1–171.

Erikson. E. (1963). *Childhood and society.* New York: Norton.

Erikson, E. (1968). *Identity: Youth and crisis.* New York: Norton.

Forrest, S. (1988). Suicide and the rural adolescent. *Adolescence, 14,* 119–133.

Fox, N. A. (1992). Frontal brain symmetry and vulnerability to stress. In T. M. Fields, P. M. McCabe, & N. Schneiderman (Eds.), *Stress and coping in infancy and childhood* (pp. 83–100). Hillsdale, NJ: Lawrence Erlbaum.

Garmezy, N. (1987). Stress, competence, and development: Continuities in the study of schizophrenic adults, children vulnerable to psychopathology, and the search for stress-resistant children. *American Journal of Orthopsychiatry, 57,* 159–174.

Gopaul-McNichol, S., & Thomas-Presswood, T. (1998). *Working with linguistically and culturally different children*. Boston: Allyn and Bacon.

Greenstone, J. L., & Leviton, S. C. (1993). *Elements of crisis intervention*. Pacific Grove, CA: Books/ Cole.

Herring, R. D. (1997). *Counseling diverse ethnic youth*. New York: Harcourt Brace.

Hetherington, E. M. (1989). Coping with family transitions: Winners, losers, and survivors. *Child Development, 60,* 1–14.

Husain, S. Y., & Vandiver, T. (1984). *Suicide in adolescents and children*. New York: Spectrum.

James, B. (1989). *Treating traumatized children*. New York: Free Press.

Kelley, B. T., Huizinga, D., Thornberry, T. P., & Loeber, R. (1997). *Epidemiology of serious violence*. Washington, DC: U.S. Department of Justice, Office of Justice Programs, Office of Juvenile Justice and Delinquency Prevention.

Landreth, G. (1991). *Play therapy: The art of the relationship*. Muncie, IN: Accelerated Development.

Lazarus, R. S. (1993). Coping theory and research: Past, present, and future. *Psychosomatic Medicine, 55,* 234–247.

Mash, E. J., & Dozois, D. J. (1996). Child psychopathology: A developmental-systems perspective. In E. J. Mash & R. A. Barkley (Eds.), *Child psychopathology* (pp. 3–60). New York: Guilford.

McFarland, B. (1995). *Brief therapy and eating disorders*. San Francisco: Jossey-Bass.

McGoldrick, M., & Giordano, J. (1996). *Ethnicity and family therapy* (2nd ed.). New York: Guilford.

Miller, M. K., & Luloff, A. E. (1981). Who is rural? A typological approach to the examination of rurality. *Rural Sociology, 46,* 608–625.

Orton, G. L. (1997). *Strategies for counseling with children and their parents*. Pacific Grove, CA: Brooks/ Cole.

Piaget, J. (1968). *Six psychological studies*. New York: Vintage Books.

Poe-Yamagata, E. (1998). *School crime and victimization, 1993*. Washington, DC: Office of Juvenile Justice and Delinquency Prevention.

Ponterotto, J. G., Casas, J. M., Suzuki, L. A., & Alexander, C. M. (Eds.). (1995). *Handbook of multicultural counseling*. Thousand Oaks, CA: Sage.

Powell, G. (Ed.). (1983). *The psychological development of minority group children*. New York: Brunner/Mazel.

Rice, F. P. (1999). *The adolescent: Development, relationships, and culture*. Boston: Allyn and Bacon.

Roberts, A. R. (1990). An overview of crisis theory and crisis intervention. In A. R. Roberts (Ed.), *Crisis intervention handbook: Assessment, treatment, and research* (pp. 3–16). Belmont, CA: Wadsworth.

Roberts, A. R. (1996). Epidemiology and definitions of acute crisis in American society. In A. R. Roberts (Ed.), *Crisis management and brief treatment* (pp. 16–35). Chicago: Nelson-Hall.

Rogers, C. (1965). *Client-centered therapy: Its current practice, implications, and theory.* Boston: Houghton Mifflin.

Rossman, B. B. R. (1992). School-age children's perceptions of coping with distress: Strategies for emotional regulation and the moderation of adjustment. *Journal of Child Psychology and Psychiatry and Allied Disciplines, 33*(8), 1373–1397.

Seligman, M. E. P. (1995). *The optimistic child.* Boston: Houghton Mifflin.

Silverman, P., & Worden, W. (1992). Children's reactions in the early months after the death of a parent due to cancer. *Journal of the American Academy of Child and Adolescent Psychiatry, 31,* 215–232.

Softas-Nall, L., & Francis, P. C. (1998). A solution-focused approach to a family with a suicidal member. *Family Journal: Counseling and Therapy for Couples and Families, 6*(3), 227–230.

Steinberg, L. (1996). *Adolescence.* New York: McGraw-Hill.

Swearingen, E. M., & Cohen, L. H. (1985). Measurement of adolescents' life events: The Junior High Life Experiences Survey. *American Journal of Community Psychology, 13,* 69–85.

Terr, L. (1990). *Too scared to cry.* New York: HarperCollins.

Thompson, C. L., & Rudolph, L. B. (1996). *Counseling children.* Pacific Grove, CA: Brooks/Cole.

Thompson, M. P., Kaslow, N. J., Kingree, J. B., King, M., Bryant, L., & Rey, M. (1998). Psychological symptomatology following parental death in a predominantly minority sample of children and adolescents. *Journal of Clinical Child Psychology, 27*(4), 434–441.

Turner, S., Norman, E., & Zunz, S. (1995). Enhancing resiliency in girls and boys: A case for gender specific adolescent prevention programming. *Journal of Primary Prevention, 16,* 25–38.

Twaite, J. A., Silitsky, D., & Luchow, A. K. (1998). *Children of divorce.* New Jersey: Jason Aronson.

Webb, N. B. (1991). *Play therapy with children in crisis.* New York: Guilford.

Webb, N. B. (1993). *Helping bereaved children.* New York: Guilford.

Werner, E. E. (1990). Protective factors and individual resilience. In S. Meisel & J. Shonkoff (Eds.), *Handbook of early childhood intervention.* Cambridge: Cambridge University Press.

Werner, E. E., & Smith, R. S. (1992). *Overcoming the odds: High-risk children from birth to adulthood.* Ithaca, NY: Cornell University Press.

Worden, J. W. (1996). *Children and grief.* New York: Guilford.

Worden, W. J., & Silverman, P. R. (1996). Parental death and the adjustment of school-age children. *Omega: Journal of Death and Dying, 33,* 91–102.

6

Adolescent Suicidality and Crisis Intervention

DAVID A. JOBES
ALAN L. BERMAN
CATHERINE E. MARTIN

Case Scenarios

Tom is a troubled 17-year-old high school senior. Since the divorce of his parents the previous year and a recent breakup with his girlfriend of 3 years, Tom had become increasingly depressed and reckless in his behavior. His attendance at school had become irregular, and his increased use of alcohol, marijuana, and LSD had alarmed some of his close friends. At a recent high school dance Tom was arrested for being drunk and disorderly and for carrying a concealed weapon. Friends reported that Tom had been waving a loaded handgun at his head and placing the muzzle of the gun in his mouth.

Lisa is a 12-year-old seventh grader whose school guidance counselor referred her to a psychologist for an evaluation. Lisa had become quite despondent since the recent death of her beloved grandfather. One of her teachers contacted the guidance counselor after Lisa had turned in a five-page poem entitled "Grandpa and Me in Heaven." The poem depicted a fantastic journey into "sweet death," which culminated in a "heavenly reunion" with her grandfather. When her parents were contacted, they reported that they had recently found a shoe box full of pills and pictures of her grandfather in Lisa's bedroom closet.

Bill, a 20-year-old college junior, was found by a roommate hanging by a belt in the closet of their dorm room. The roommate (who was supposed to be away for the weekend) entered the room only moments after Bill had begun to hang from the belt, and his immediate intervention probably saved Bill's life. The roommate reported that Bill had become increasingly depressed since he had recently "come out" to his parents about being gay. Bill's parents were enraged by this news and had threatened to disown him if he "did not get such a silly notion out of his head."

The acute suicidal crisis is produced by a unique synergy of intrapersonal, environmental, social, and situational variables. As a response to life crises, suicide and self-destructive behaviors are seen among people of every age, sex, race, religion, and economic and social class. Because patients may respond to life crises with suicidal behaviors, clinicians must be prepared to face the immediate tasks of assessing possible self-harm behavior while concurrently protecting against that possibility. Often these tasks must be accomplished under conditions of incongruent expectations and goals. Suicidal people tend to defy the health professional's expectation that fostering and maintaining life is a shared goal of patient and doctor (Hoff, 1995). Suicidal individuals are typically brought to treatment by others under conditions of acute and volitional threat to life. These are not characteristics of the "good patient"; instead, these qualities bring tension and instability to (and potentially impede) the necessary working alliance with the caregiver (Vlasak, 1994). Thus, working with depressed and suicidal people can be a frightening and difficult undertaking. Indeed, the assessment, treatment, and general management of an acute suicidal crisis are perhaps among the most difficult challenges faced by any mental health professional, despite attempted suicide being one of the most frequently encountered of all mental health emergencies (Roberts, 1991; Schein, 1976).

Completed suicide is a complex and relatively rare (low-base-rate) event. Ideally, clinicians would like to be able to "predict" future occurrences of suicidal behavior and thereby make appropriate interventions. Attempts to construct inventories and use psychological tests to predict suicide (in a statistically valid and reliable manner) have thus far failed. Since completed suicide occurs relatively infrequently, most instruments tend to identify a prohibitive number of "false positives" (i.e., the identification of individuals as suicidal who do not complete suicide). Clinicians are therefore forced to make interventions based on inexact and subjective calculations of potential "suicide risk" (see Berman & Jobes, 1991; Jobes & Berman, 1993).

Nevertheless, clinicians can strengthen their ability to effectively assess and intervene by increasing their understanding of suicidal behaviors. The tragic finality of suicide demands that clinicians develop a knowledge base and a level of competence in suicide risk assessment and intervention. As suicidologists point out, suicidal impulses and behaviors are largely temporal, transient, and situation specific. Suicide intent is state dependent and tends to wax and wane, disappear and return (Berman & Jobes, 1991). Empirical research indicates that most people who kill themselves give some form of prior warning (see Shafii, Carrigan, Whittinghill, & Derrick, 1985) and often desire an outcome other than the termination of their biological existence (Shneidman, 1994). The crisis clinician is thus in a pivotal position. Accurate risk assessment and appropriate interventions can make a life-or-death difference. Making a lifesaving difference is perhaps all the more poignant when the object of assessment and intervention is a young person.

Many hold the view that youthful years should be a carefree time of inno-
cence, play, and exciting exploration. Adolescents are commonly viewed as
not yet acquainted with the hardship and responsibility of adulthood (Group
for the Advancement of Psychiatry Committee on Adolescence, 1996). This
culturally enforced avoidance and denial regarding the nature of adolescence
and its connection to suicidal behavior might contribute to the lack of appropriate response to the adolescent suicide attempter (Berman & Jobes,
1991). Crisis clinicians must struggle with the incongruity between this commonly held view and direct evidence that for some youngsters life may be
filled with intense turmoil and abject despair.

SCOPE OF THE PROBLEM

In 1996 there were 30,903 certified suicides in the United States. A total of
4,358 of these deaths, or approximately 14%, were of young people between
the ages of 15 and 24. The age-specific rate of youthful suicide (12/100,000
for 15- to 24-year-olds) is somewhat lower than rates for adults ages 25 to
44 (15) and 45 to 64 (14.3). However, between 1950 and 1996 the suicide
rate for youth aged 15 to 24 increased from 4.5 to 12/100,000 (almost tripled), making suicide the third leading cause of death (behind only accidents
and homicide) for young people between the ages of 15 and 24 (National
Center for Health Statistics, 1998). Suicide is the second leading cause of
death for young people between the ages of 15 and 19 (American Association of Suicidology, 1997).

Over five times more adolescent males than females complete suicide in
the United States. In contrast, females are four times as likely to make nonfatal attempts as males. The suicide rate among males between the ages of 15
and 24 has more than tripled since the mid-1950s. The suicide rate for men
in this age range remains double the overall rate of suicide in the United
States (National Center for Injury Prevention, 1995). (The gender differences
in suicidal behaviors observed in adolescents, with some variations, tend to
remain fairly consistent across the adult life span. For all ages, completed
suicide is a primarily male activity, particularly among the elderly.) Whereas
approximately 4,358 American youth between the ages of 15 and 24 completed suicide in 1996, as many as 2 million teenagers may make nonfatal
attempts at some point in their teenage lives (Smith & Crawford, 1984).
One plausible explanation for these observed sex differences lies in the differential choices of methods employed. In 1996, 62.5% of young people
between the ages of 15 and 24 used firearms to complete suicide (National
Center for Health Statistics, 1998), a 40% increase above the rate in 1970
(Berman & Jobes, 1995). Whereas the majority of both sexes use guns to
complete suicide (in 1996: 65% of males and 47% of females; National
Center for Health Statistics, 1998), the overwhelming majority of nonfatal

suicidal behaviors consist of ingestion overdoses, better than 80% of which are effected by females. The ingestion of poisons, the lethality of which depends on a number of factors, including the greater chance of rescue and intervention given the time necessary for toxic action, accounted for only 267 suicide deaths in 1990.

Suicidal death among adolescents also is more common among Whites than Blacks, with White males accounting for the majority (71% in 1996) of all youth suicides. However, 15- to 24-year-old Black youth account for a greater proportion of all Black suicides (21% in 1996) than 15- to 24-year-old White youth account for all White suicides (11% in 1996). Although suicide rates among Black adolescents are lower than for White adolescents, for Black males between the ages of 15 and 19 the suicide rate increased 165% between 1980 and 1992 (National Center for Injury Prevention, 1995). For all youth, the highest rates are recorded for youth living in the western, primarily intermountain, states.

CRISIS INTERVENTION: ROBERTS'S SEVEN-STAGE MODEL

Effective intervention and treatment of suicidal people always begins with a thorough assessment and subsequent interventions based on that assessment. Through all phases of working with a suicidal patient, ongoing risk assessment is an imperative. In general practice, clinicians must be prepared to face a range of potential suicidal crisis situations. These crises may range from that of a telephone call from a desperate patient who has just ingested a potentially lethal overdose; to that of a borderline personality in an unstable, intense, and dramatically shifting mood state; to that of a patient in session simply stating vague suicidal ideation and hopelessness, in a context of a history of impulsive acting out.

As described by Roberts (1991), clinicians may effectively respond to an individual in crisis by working through seven stages of intervention: (a) assessing lethality and safety needs, (b) establishing rapport and communication, (c) identifying the major problems, (d) dealing with feelings and providing support, (e) exploring possible alternatives, (f) formulating an action plan, and (g) providing follow-up. Roberts's seven-stage model was developed to apply broadly to a range of crises, but it is clearly applicable to specific interventions with suicidal youth.

Stage 1: Assessing Lethality

An assessment of the overall lethality (i.e., dangerousness) of a crisis situation is the starting point for any crisis intervention effort. The assessment of lethality may perhaps be best understood as a process of psychiatric triage that leads to three treatment options: (1) emergency psychiatric treatment, (2) outpatient counseling/psychotherapy, and (3) basic emotional support, validation, reassurance, or education. In the case of suicide lethality assessment, clinicians are faced with two primary scenarios—the imminently dangerous situation and the potentially dangerous situation.

Imminent Danger

In some cases, crisis intervention may need to begin with a suicidal patient who has already initiated a suicide attempt. In the imminently dangerous situation, the clinician must be fully prepared to respond to the individual whose suicide attempt may require prompt first aid and/or medical treatment. The patient's level of consciousness and orientation, rationality, and agitation will affect the level of cooperation he or she may give to the immediate assessment of the need for emergency intervention. With appropriate cooperation, questions need to be raised and answered (by the patient or the person making the contact) with regard to the location of the patient, exactly what the patient has done, and the availability of significant others. The clinician's immediate task, to assess the lethality of the attempt, can be aided by the availability of published lethality scales (Smith, Conroy, & Ehler, 1984). Where it is determined that medico-biological danger exists, or where sufficient data for that determination are not available, emergency medical intervention is required. As discussed by Hoff (1995), imminently dangerous situations should be handled by police and rescue squads, which can assure rapid transportation to a hospital emergency room—prompt medical evaluation is crucial. In addition to using lethality scales, one can assess potential lethality by accessing a hospital with a poison control center that can be called for specific overdose information. The exact amount of drug needed to effect a fatal overdose may be difficult to ascertain because the effects vary according to the size of the person, the amount and kind of drug taken, and the person's tolerance for a drug. Generally, sleeping pills, major tranquilizers, tricyclic antidepressants, and aspirin or acetaminophen are dangerous overdose drugs (especially in combination with alcohol). One rule of thumb is that a lethal dose is 10 times the normal dose; in combination with alcohol, only 5 times the normal dose may result in death (Hoff, 1995). It is useful for the clinician to have ready access to emergency phone numbers for the police, emergency rescue squad, hospital emergency rooms, and poison control centers. Needless to say, it is essential to maintain active communication with the client while these procedures are being effected. As part of this communication, the clinician should begin to structure the client's expectations through clear directives about what will happen, thus increasing the chances of establishing a therapeutic alliance with both paramedics and emergency personnel. Future treatment may be facilitated by the presence of the clinician during the medical crisis. Close contact and follow-up after the immediate medical danger is resolved assure that the patient is not simply treated and discharged without a crisis prevention plan in place.

Potential Danger

In contrast to imminently dangerous suicide crises, clinicians more typically encounter suicide crisis situations that are *potentially* dangerous. In these situations clinicians must be prepared to intervene in crises where there is active suicidal ideation but an attempt has not yet been made (but could be made in the near future). In these circumstances, intensive one-to-one clinical contact that fully addresses stages 2 through 6 in Roberts's model is necessary.

Stage 1 lethality assessments of the three initial cases of Tom, Lisa, and Bill reveal three moderately to highly suicidal youth. Bill, who was found hanging in an imminently dangerous situation by his roommate, is obviously the most lethal of the three. However, Tom's depression, reckless behavior, substance abuse, and access to a gun clearly put him at high risk as well. Finally, although Lisa's level of risk is somewhat less extreme, her suicidal preoccupation and her cache of medication for overdosing are distinct causes for concern.

Stage 2: Establishing Rapport and Communication

The importance of the clinical relationship (and the techniques used to enhance it) in the suicidal crisis cannot be overestimated. A number of authors have discussed the difficulties inherent in working with a suicidal individual (Farberow, 1970; Shneidman, 1980; Hendin, 1981). As Shneidman (1980) has observed, working with a highly suicidal person demands a more active and directive kind of involvement. Particularly in a crisis, the ability to make interpersonal contact is critical, and a supportive working relationship must be rapidly established. Hipple and Cimbolic (1979) have noted that suicidal clients must know (and feel) that they are talking with someone who is actively interested in their well-being. Any technique or approach that potentially strengthens the relationship and connectedness should therefore be employed. Eye contact, posture, and other nonverbal cues may be used to express a level of interest, concern, and involvement. Empathic listening, mirroring of feelings, emotional availability, honesty, warmth, and caring can help foster a sense of trust and a willingness to examine possibilities other than self-destruction. Empathy and support are crucial, but it is important to remember that suicidal adolescents often feel out of control. Accordingly, a more active and directive role than would normally be seen in ongoing individual psychotherapy can provide valuable reassurance and structure in a time of crisis.

There are some unique aspects to developing rapport and communication with a suicidal youth. Young people inherently bring to the suicidal crisis a unique set of developmental and emotional issues that may complicate effective assessment and intervention. Adolescence and young adulthood can be a time of tremendous change and turmoil. As Berman (1984) has discussed, adolescents are developmentally caught between childhood and adulthood, which engenders the conflictual task of separating from the world of parents and family, while simultaneously and paradoxically seeking protection from and inclusion within the family system. Accordingly, potential mistrust of adults further complicates the assessment of the young person's emotional status. An example of youthful distrust can be seen when a young person tells a friend about his or her suicidal thoughts with the clear understanding that the peer is not to betray this confidence to an adult. Youthful distrust of adults has been indirectly substantiated in the empirical literature. One recent study of a youthful sample of completed suicides revealed that 83.3% had made suicidal threats in the week prior to their deaths; of these, half made their suicidal intention known only to a peer or sibling (Brent et al., 1988).

Other developmental forces also increase the assessment challenge. With limited life experience, youth tend to be more focused on the present rather than the future. When a young person experiences stress, there may be a limited view of future possibilities—momentary and immediate solutions may become appealing (Berman, 1984). Adolescents characteristically have a limited capacity to delay gratification. Plainly stated, if something is wrong, the adolescent may want it fixed immediately. As Cantor (1976) has pointed out, the situation is further complicated by suicidal fantasies that may be common among adolescents. This combination of adolescent impulsivity, poor problem-solving skills, and suicidal fantasies (of escape and relief from pain) can become a recipe for lethal action. Additionally, adolescents are highly vulnerable to peer influence and are often eager to imitate role models as they seek to develop their own sense of identity. It is therefore important to assess and intervene in youthful crises with a keen awareness of the unique developmental issues of the population.

Stage 3: Identify the Major Problems

Identifying the major problems that may underlie a suicidal crisis is best accomplished through a thorough assessment interview. Ideally, an assessment interview should draw upon theory, the strength of the therapeutic relationship, and empirical/clinical knowledge specific to suicidal individuals. Theoretical knowledge provides a conceptual frame and foundation, while the therapeutic relationship (alliance) becomes the vehicle of assessment and treatment. Empirical and clinical knowledge is used to assess key variables that bear on the assessment of suicide risk. In the course of the assessment interview, it is essential for the clinician to listen closely, make direct inquiries, and assess and evaluate key variables.

Clues to Suicide

The clinician must listen carefully for signs, symptoms, or clues that may indicate suicidal intent. Often the clinician is alerted by a patient's direct or indirect comment or nonverbal behavior. The vast majority of suicidal people provide clues to their self-destructive feelings. Close scrutiny of the patient is essential because the clinician must determine whether the youth shares some commonality with those who have acted out their suicidal fantasies (Berman & Jobes, 1991). As Hipple and Cimbolic (1979) have discussed, the suicidal individual may make only veiled or disguised verbal references to suicidal feelings. The clinician must be alert for veiled threats such as "Sometimes it's just not worth it; I feel like giving up"; "I'm so tired, I just want to sleep"; or "People would be a lot happier if I weren't around." As well, other communications (e.g., diaries, journals, school essays, drawings, poems) often contain valuable, nonverbal clues to the adolescent's ideational focus.

Asking About Suicide

The assessment of suicide risk fundamentally requires direct inquiries about suicidal thoughts and feelings. Simply stated, vague suicidal comments should *always* elicit a direct question from the clinician as to whether the patient is thinking about suicide (e.g., "Sometimes when people feel depressed they contemplate suicide. Are you thinking about killing yourself?"; "Do you feel like hurting yourself or ending your life?"; "You sound pretty hopeless. Have you been considering suicide?").

Even for the experienced clinician, asking directly about suicide can be unsettling. Accordingly, there may be a tendency to underestimate the seriousness of the situation and a strong temptation to avoid asking directly about suicide. Frequently, potential helpers fear that a direct inquiry might introduce a dangerous new option not previously considered by the patient (i.e., planting a seed for suicide in the patient's mind).

Avoidance and fear are understandable reactions to suspicions of suicide, but experts in the field strongly support the value of direct inquiry (Hipple & Cimbolic, 1979; Beck, Rush, Shaw, & Emery, 1979; Pope, 1986; Curran, 1987; Alberts, 1988; Berman & Jobes, 1991). Critically, direct inquiry gives the potentially suicidal individual permission to discuss feelings that may have seemed virtually undiscussable. Direct inquiry can bring great relief to the patient—at last the inner battle of life or death can be openly discussed and explored in a safe, supportive, and accepting climate. Moreover, direct inquiry opens the doors for further assessment, potentially bringing out otherwise veiled resistances. The expression of resistances in the therapeutic context may alert the clinician to the distinct possibility of suicidal urges in the client, signaling an interpersonal alienation common to the suicidal character. It is our experience that when clinicians are sensitive and attentive to their suspicions of suicide, they are more often correct than incorrect (i.e., suicide will probably have been at least a consideration for the client).

If the client is genuinely not considering suicide, the dyad can easily move on from the topic of suicide to other areas of inquiry. On the other hand, if the client is considering suicide and the counselor avoids direct inquiry, the client may interpret the counselor's behavior as clear evidence of a lack of caring, therefore confirming his or her sense of both unlovability and the impossibility of receiving help. Hopelessness may thus be reinforced, and the risk increases accordingly.

Assuming that the clinician has attended to suicidal clues and the client has affirmed some degree of suicidal thoughts or feelings upon direct inquiry, the clinician must determine whether there is an imminent danger of suicidal behavior at potential risk to the life of the client. The degree and immediacy of suicide risk must be evaluated for both clinical and legal/ethical purposes. When voluntary hospitalization is refused in extreme cases, the law often allows involuntary hospitalization (commitment) when there is evidence of clear and imminent danger to self or others (these considerations being defined by statute in each state). Therefore, the clinician must establish whether the risk of suicide is acute and immediate or chronic and long-term. Is this indeed a crisis situation with a risk of a suicide attempt in the immediate or near future? Is there sufficient upset, agitation, and emotional energy to create an immediately dangerous situation?

Approximately 80% of all suicides occur when the individuals are in a state of acute impulsive crisis. Only a small percentage of suicides are methodical or planned (especially among youthful populations). It can be reassuring to both the client and the clinician to know that most cases are those of *transient* crises. Getting through the crisis phase provides the young person the opportunity to consider more constructive and reversible options for coping. Therefore, one of the most important aspects of suicide assessment, the temporal evaluation of imminent versus long-term risk of self-harm, is essential to further assessment, intervention, and treatment.

The final determination of imminent danger depends on the assessment of key variables or "risk factors" that reflect the degree of suicide risk. It is important to assess the following (not necessarily in the following order): (a) psychological intent, (b) the suicide plan, (c) the history of previous suicidal behavior, and (d) clinical risk variables.

Assessing Psychological Intent

Many attempts have been made to operationally define the concept of suicide (see Jobes, Berman, & Josselson, 1987; Jobes, Casey, Berman, &

Wright, 1991; Rosenberg et al., 1988; Shneidman, 1994). Most define suicide as a death that is self-inflicted and intended. By definition, an individual who dies by a self-inflicted accidental death does not intentionally seek the end of his or her life, whereas the aim or purpose of one who completes suicide is escape and/or death.

Clearly, the motive of ending one's existence versus that of receiving more attention from a loved one reflects very different kinds of suicidal intent. It is therefore critical to assess the psychological intention, purpose, motive, or goal of the suicidal individual—what does the option of suicide *mean* to the youth? As Berman and Jobes (1991) have discussed, the stated intent of a suicidal motive in young people is often interpersonal and instrumental. In general, the intended goals of youthful suicidal behavior involve an effort to escape the experience of pain, helplessness, hopelessness, and the emotions and cognitions associated with the suicidal state. For some, this means seeking relief through death; for others, relief may be sought through changes in others' behavior, effected by gambling with life.

Assessing the Suicide Plan

The presence or absence of a plan to attempt suicide is critical to ascertain. The plan reflects both the desired and the expected consequences of suicidal behavior and therefore provides one of the best indicators of what may actually come to pass (Berman & Jobes, 1991). Again, direct inquiry about a potential suicidal plan is necessary. If a plan is acknowledged, it is important to assess its lethality. Suicidal plans generally reveal the relative risk in that the degree of intent is typically related to the lethality of the potential method (e.g., using a gun or hanging infers higher intent, whereas overdosing or cutting infers lower intent).

Empirical research indicates that there tends to be a relationship between level of intent and the lethality of a method identified in the suicidal plan. Indeed, Brent (1987) found that a robust relationship appeared to exist between medical lethality and suicide intent in a study of youthful attempters. In general, lethal plans tend to be concrete and specific and involve dangerous methods. Risk increases when there is evidence of a carefully thought-through and articulated self-harm strategy. Similarly, the availability of lethal means (such as guns or lethal quantities of medications) about which the youngster is knowledgeable also increases the suicide risk. A plan that minimizes the chance of intervention and rescue reflects a greater suicide risk. Conceptually and empirically, the potential for rescue has been found to be central to two well-respected instruments that were constructed specifically to assess the lethality of suicide attempts (see Weissman & Worden, 1972; Smith et al., 1984). Simply put, the less likely that someone will be able to intervene, the greater the risk. Under the heading of rescue, the reversibility of a chosen method and the discoverability of an attempt must be differentially evaluated. A much higher level of suicide intent and lethality is reflected in an attempter who plans to use an irreversible method (e.g., a gun) in a place with little likelihood of discovery (e.g., a remote wooded area). For example, suicide risk may be assessed as low in a case of a vague plan involving the ingestion of pills in front of parents, versus high in a case where an individual has access to a large quantity of barbiturates and plans to ingest them after the parents leave the house.

In summarizing various elements of the assessment of a suicide plan, the clinician must evaluate the lethality and availability of the proposed method and the specificity of the self-harm strategy. Moreover, the clinician must evaluate the probability of postattempt discovery and whether efforts could be made to reverse the impact of the potential suicide act (e.g., pumping the stomach after an overdose). Assessment of the various aspects of a potential plan is perhaps the best means of evaluating suicidal intent and imminent risk of self-harm.

It should be noted that perhaps the majority of suicidal acts by youth are impulsive and unplanned. That does not in any way decrease their potential lethality, particularly if a lethal weapon is accessible at the time of urge and impulse. In the context of the other levels of assessment, the absence of a plan simply means the clinician lacks but one significant source of information.

Assessing Suicide History

Another variable that bears significantly on suicide risk is the presence or absence of a suicidal history. The risk and dangerousness increase significantly when there is *any* previous history of suicidal ideation, gestures, and particularly previous attempts. Risk increases if a previous attempt was recent, if a potentially lethal method was used, or if an effort was made to avoid rescue. Multiple past attempts, particularly if these occurred within the last 12 months and if one or more was potentially lethal, significantly increase the risk of further suicide attempts and of ultimate completion. The clinician should note the contingent reinforcers to prior behaviors to determine what was learned by the client in consequence to these events. In addition, the history of suicidal events in the client's family is an important area of inquiry for assessing the client's level of exposure to suicide and its legacies of possible imitation and modeling and/or possible biological causes to suicidal vulnerability.

Assessing Clinical Risk Variables

It is helpful for the clinician to have a working knowledge of additional risk variables for suicide that have been identified in the empirical literature. Research conducted over the past 25 years has provided practitioners with valuable information concerning various correlates of increased suicide risk (Garland & Zigler, 1993).

As described by Beck and his colleagues (Beck, Resnik, & Lettieri, 1986; Kovacs, Beck, & Weissman, 1975), for example, hopelessness may be one of the single best indicators of suicide risk. A profound sense of hopelessness and helplessness about oneself, others, and the future has been closely linked to depressive conditions and suicide (Rush & Beck, 1978). Other clinical indicators of suicide may include the following: dramatic and inexplicable affective change; affect that is depressed, flat, or blunted; the experience of recent negative environmental changes (losses); feelings of isolation or emptiness; and experience of extreme stress, free-floating rage, agitation, and fatigue.

Young people can be very sensitive to the various interpersonal pressures and expectations of others, including parents, siblings, peers, coaches, teachers, and girlfriends or boyfriends. Murray's (1938) construct of "presses" may be applied to suicidal youth to identify a range of additionally experienced pressures that may be less socioculturally bound, such as genetic factors, physical danger, chance events, alcohol or substance abuse, and psychopathology. As Berman and Jobes (1991) have noted, it is important to examine predisposing conditions, precipitating factors, and psychopathology in the assessment of those forces that may affect the suicidal youth.

Biological and sociocultural forces create a range of predisposing conditions that impinge upon on the suicidal adolescent. The suicidal youth often experiences blows to self-esteem, sense of self, and ability to cope (Berman & Jobes, 1991). These may be the direct result of growing up in a stressful family and having conflictual interpersonal relationships. Research has indicated that the parents of suicidal adolescents have conflictual relationships than do controls, including threats of separation and divorce, additionally the parents have more often experieneced an early loss of one of their parents (Stanley & Barter, 1970; Corder, Shorr, & Corder, 1974; Miller, Chiles, & Barnes, 1982). Further, suicidal youth have more frequent and serious interpersonal problems with peers, are more interpersonally sensitive, and are less likely to have a close confidant (McKenry, Tishler, & Kelley, 1982; Tishler & McKenry, 1982).

Adolescent suicides often are linked to a significant precipitating event, particularly an acute disciplinary crisis or a rejection or humiliation (Shaffer, 1988). It is important to note that such events (e.g., a fight with one's parents, a breakup of a relationship, being teased) are common to the experience of all adolescents and thus must be considered within the broader context of each adolescent's vulnerability to respond with increased suicidality to such stressors. The crisis clinician must be attentive to evidence of psychopathology, because perhaps as many as 90% of adolescent suicide completions involve youth with retrospectively diagnosable mental disorders (cf. Berman & Jobes, 1991; Shaffer, 1988). Empirical research has confirmed that certain types of psychopathology are correlated with suicidal behavior—in particular, mood disorders, especially manic-depressive illness or bipolar spectrum disorders (Garfinkel, Froese, & Hood, 1982; Robbins & Alessi, 1985; Brent et al., 1988); schizophrenia (McIntire, Angle, Wikoff, & Schlicht, 1977); and personality disorders, especially borderline and antisocial (Alessi, McManus, Brickman, & Grapentine, 1984; Berman & Jobes, 1991). Similar to adults, substance abuse disorders (both alcohol and drugs) are often implicated in adolescent suicides and may be comorbid with the preceding disorders (Brent et al., 1988; Garfinkel et al., 1982). The clinician must therefore be particularly sensitive to young people who show any evidence of psychopathology who may be in distress but may not reveal suicidal intention.

Imminent risk for self-harm behavior appears most reactive to conditions that threaten a breakdown in usual coping mechanisms and, consequently, which increase loss of behavioral control. In addition to a variety of psychopathological disorders, as noted earlier, the clinician needs to be alert for significant changes in behavior, particularly if they involve increased reliance on alcohol or drugs. Levels of rage and anxiety also are good measures of the adolescent's ability to maintain control. In addition, behavioral change and/or loss of control often alienate the adolescent from significant others who otherwise could serve to buffer or protect him or her from untoward consequences of thinking designed simply to impulsively end painful affect. Again, hopelessness tends to increase and/or be reinforced under these interactional conditions.

Stage 4: Dealing With Feelings and Providing Support

As Shneidman (1994) has discussed, the suicidal person fundamentally seeks to escape unendurable psychological pain. Critically, the feeling of pain that drives the suicidal situation must be understood idiosyncratically—what is painful to one person may not be painful to the next. Therefore, it is essential that the clinician be empathetically connected to the youth's subjective experience of pain. Connecting with the pain can be achieved through careful and thoughtful listening, emotional availability, and warmth; it may be shown by eye contact, posture, and nonverbal cues that communicate genuine interest, concern, and caring. However, as Curran (1987) has discussed, a suicidal youth may be unwilling or unable to communicate painful feelings. This, of course, is a formidable problem for the accurate assessment of risk. It may be necessary in emergency situations to confer with friends and family who may be aware of the youth's recent emotional status. A teacher or best friend may be able to provide critical information concerning recent behaviors, changes in mood, and potential losses in the young person's life. Whether the information comes directly from the young person or from a friend, parent, or teacher, it is important to try to infer an accurate assessment of the subjective pain. It should be noted, however, that such contacts might adversely affect a therapeutic relationship after the crisis is resolved.

Even though emotional pain is difficult at any age, young people may experience it especially intensely. It is critical that the clinician respect the depth and degree of pain reported by a youth. Self-reports of extreme emotional pain and trauma should not be dismissed as adolescent melodrama. The experience of pain is acute and real to adolescents and potentially life-threatening. As discussed earlier, young people tend to be present oriented and lack the years of life experience that may provide the perspective needed to endure a painful period. It is therefore critical that the clinician appreciate this perhaps limited worldview.

Simply stated, the risk of suicide increases as subjectively perceived psychological pain increases. Accordingly, it may be useful to have the suicidal youth actually rate his or her pain or hopelessness (e.g., ranging from 0 equaling absolutely no pain to 10 equaling absolutely unendurable pain). A subjective rating can be especially useful in helping to understand the young person's degree of pain. It also can help make the suicidal experience more concrete and less abstract for both the youth and the counselor. Moreover, the subjective rating can provide an ongoing barometer of suicide risk, allowing changes and improvements to be tracked beyond the initial crisis and throughout the course of treatment.

Stage 5: Exploring Possible Alternatives

In the course of crisis work it is important to explore possible options and alternative ways of coping (other than suicide). The exploration of possible alternatives typically requires a thorough evaluation of negative forces in the young person's life, as well as positive influences—what are the relative strengths and weaknesses of the individual? Various expectations and pressures can become overwhelming to the young person in the midst of a suicidal crisis, making effective problem solving difficult, if not impossible. The intensity of one particularly salient pressure can potentially outweigh other objective strengths, resources, and abilities. For example, among adolescents who complete suicide, there is a subgroup of seemingly outstanding victims who "seemed to have it all." In such cases various abilities, skills, and strengths may be irrelevant when extraordinarily high standards and an expectation of continued success or perfection rigidly define the individual's self-worth. Such a compulsive demand may defend against an underlying fragile sense of self. Accordingly, an unacceptable performance such as a grade of C on an exam, easily interpreted as the equivalent of an F, could actually precipitate a suicide attempt to thwart the experience of unacceptable feelings. Operationally, the clinician needs to directly ask a youth about the pressures and worries he or she is experiencing and perhaps rank order them to better ascertain their relative importance to the youth. Among these pressures is the adolescent's perceived "fit" within his or her family. Suicidal adolescents often talk of feeling responsible for family problems and conflicts. Some even consider their expendability as a way of freeing their family to move beyond current impasses. Conversely, it is critical to identify and assess the potential strengths, coping skills, and resources available to the young person. Reflecting back strengths and resources to the youth may provide some comfort in the midst of a crisis and underscore alternative means of coping. The risk of suicide is significantly lessened when there is evidence of internal (e.g., cognitive) and external (e.g., interpersonal) resources for coping with conflict and stress (Berman & Jobes, 1991).

The need to explore alternatives in the cases of Tom, Lisa, and Bill is abundantly clear. Tom, a troubled youth reeling out of control, is a suicide waiting to happen. At the time of his arrest, Tom was primarily dealing with his losses and depression by abusing substances and acting out. As an intelligent and generally popular teenager, with friends and family willing to support him, Tom had notable personal and interpersonal resources at his disposal but seemed unable to ask for help. Lisa, struggling to overcome the loss of her beloved grandfather, seemed to be living in a romanticized fantasy world of death and reunion. Her concerned parents were at a loss regarding how to help their daughter work through her grief. Bill, overwhelmed by his parents' hostile reaction to his homosexuality, sought escape from his unbearable feelings. In hindsight, it would seem that Bill, who had only just begun to explore his sexual identity in a gay support group on campus and in psychotherapy at the college counseling center, perhaps came out to his parents prematurely. In each of these three cases, we see individuals suffering through painful losses and debilitating feelings, yet in each case there are resources and potentials for alternative ways of coping.

Stage 6: Formulating an Action Plan

Having thoroughly assessed the risk of suicide, the clinician is in a position to formulate an action (treatment) plan of intervention. As described by Hoff (1995) and others, a series of strategic steps needs to be initiated to ensure the patient's immediate safety and shift the patient's focus from crisis to resolution.

Removing the Means

The first goal should be to immediately reduce the lethality of the situation. This is best accomplished by literally removing the means from the client's access or, at a minimum, delaying access to available means. Pills should be flushed down the toilet or given to others to monitor and dispense; guns and/or other weapons should be removed from the home. Where available, parents or significant others need to be involved in all efforts to safeguard the environment.

Negotiating Safety

One of the clinician's most effective interventive tools involves the negotiation of the patient's safety. Generally, the concrete goal of these negotiations is to ensure the patient's physical safety by establishing that the patient will not hurt him- or herself for a specific period of time. The more concrete and specific the understanding, the better. Typically, the patient will agree to maintain his or her safety until the next clinical contact, at which point a new understanding can be negotiated. The clinician must remember to keep these agreements time limited and renewable. The clinician should also remember that a "contract" with a psychologically wounded (narcissistically injured) teenager does not necessarily guarantee the patient's safety because early wounds may have severely affected the youth's trust and trustability.

Future Linkage

The clinician and the patient must create a crisis game plan that orients the patient toward the future. Long-term goals should be established and operationalized with the patient in short-term steps. This may be accomplished by identifying when the next clinical contacts will occur. Plans for activities and social contacts may be made as well. Scheduling phone contacts to touch base can also be planned. It is critical that the suicidal patient has something to look forward to. Future linkage helps orient the patient to a different and hopefully better future, creating a distance from the immediate crisis.

Decrease Anxiety and Sleep Loss

If the suicidal youth is acutely anxious and/or not able to sleep, the suicidal crisis may become worse. Medication may be indicated as an emergency intervention. However, dosages must be closely monitored and linked to ongoing psychotherapy so that the medication is not used for an overdose. Other symptoms that may exacerbate the patient's ability to benefit from verbal intervention and/or threaten the patient's ability to maintain control must be continuously monitored and treated accordingly.

Decreasing Isolation

The patient must not be left alone in the midst of a suicidal crisis. It is critical that a trustworthy friend or family member remain with the patient through the crisis phase. Efforts must be made to mobilize friends, family, and neighbors, making them aware of the importance of ongoing contact with the suicidal youth. In cases where friends or family are unavailable (or unwilling), hospitalization may be necessary.

Hospitalization

When the risk of suicide remains unabated and high, and the patient is unable to negotiate his or her safety, hospitalization becomes the necessary intervention. Simply stated, stabilization through hospitalization can provide the patient with a safe environment and a chance to remove him- or herself from the environment that produced the suicidal crisis.

Stage 7: Providing Follow-Up

Beyond emergency medical treatment and crisis intervention, after crisis resolution, ongoing counseling and psychotherapy follow-up are essential. In this era of managed care, the prevailing reimbursement structure does not lend itself to providing comprehensive follow-up care following an acute suicidal crisis. In light of the research indicating the importance of follow-up care in treating the suicidal adolescent, these policies should be examined for cost-effectiveness and should be revised accordingly (Brent & Perper, 1995). The absence or amelioration of an immediate crisis is not synonymous with the decision to not provide ongoing psychotherapy. It is important for the clinician to remember that people who have used suicidal behavior to respond to life crises in the past are prone to use such behaviors in future life crises. As the final phase of crisis resolution, the clinician must ensure that follow-up evaluation and treatment are arranged and that a strategic, preventive treatment plan is in place to circumvent potential future suicidal crises.

Various treatment modalities with suicidal clients have been discussed in the literature (see Berman & Jobes, 1991). These modalities range from longer term individual treatment (Hendin, 1981; Jobes, 1995; Toolin, 1962), to shorter term individual models (Beck & Beck, 1978; Getz, Allen, Myers, & Linder, 1983), to group treatment (Comstock & McDermott, 1975; Farberow, 1976; Hipple, 1982). Family therapy may be particularly helpful with youthful populations (Alanen, Rinne, & Paukkonen, 1981; Richman, 1979, 1986). In addition, ongoing pharmacotherapy may be useful in stabilizing mood and intrusive psychopathological symptoms. It is beyond the scope of this chapter to delineate the many aspects and variants of ongoing inpatient and outpatient psychotherapy with the suicidal adolescent. However, it is imperative that the clinician familiarize him- or herself with the increasing array of effective short- and long-term intervention strategies available to treat the depressed and suicidal adolescent, if the alarming increase in suicide among adolescents is to be halted and reversed.

CASE STUDY OUTCOMES

Tom, Lisa, and Bill were three high-risk youth in serious suicidal crises that could have had tragic outcomes. Thankfully, each case received appropriate and effective crisis intervention. Following Tom's arrest, his high school guidance counselor, with the support of his parents, arranged to have him hospitalized. He received intensive psychiatric treatment for his depression and substance abuse, and after 4 weeks he was discharged to the care of an outpatient psychotherapist. After 6 months of therapy and regular attendance at AA and NA meetings, Tom finished his remaining semester of high school and was accepted to a local community college.

After the poem episode, Lisa began to meet with a psychologist in both individual and family sessions. Recognizing her creativity, her therapist used art therapy and encouraged her to continue to write poetry about her feelings. Family therapy was helpful in working through the mourning of the grandfather, since the family had not really dealt with his death. In addition, family work led to an improved relationship between Lisa and her father, who had long been jealous of her special relationship with her grandfather (his father).

Bill was hospitalized for 3 days after his aborted hanging. After discharge, Bill continued to pursue therapy in the counseling center and also continued to attend the gay support group. Bill's parents were horrified by, and felt intensely guilty about, his suicide attempt. Although they continued to disapprove of Bill's lifestyle, they nevertheless refrained from threatening to disown him and avoided discussing the topic with him. About 3 months after his suicide attempt, Bill began dating someone from his support group, and he was markedly less depressed by the end of the school year.

SUMMARY

This chapter has examined the complexities of youthful suicide, a phenomenon that has exhibited dramatic increases over the past 40 years. Although accurate clinical prediction of suicide is virtually impossible, practitioners can nevertheless optimize their capacity to effectively respond to youthful suicide crises by informing themselves of, and developing skills in, suicide risk assessment and interventive strategies. Roberts's (1991) seven-stage model of crisis intervention has been used to illustrate one approach to working with a suicidal youth in crisis. By assessing lethality, establishing rapport, identifying major problems, dealing with feelings, exploring alternatives, formulating an action plan, and providing follow-up, a crisis clinician can make an intervention that may help save the life of a young person in a suicidal crisis.

REFERENCES

Alanen, Y. O., Rinne, R., & Paukkonen, P. (1981). On family dynamics
and family therapy in suicidal attempts. *Crisis, 2,* 20–26.

Alberts, F. L. (1988). Psychological assessment. In D. Capuzzi & L.
Golden (Eds.), *Preventing adolescent
suicide* (pp. 189–211). Muncie, IN:
Accelerated Development.

Alessi, N. E., McManus, M., Brickman.,
A., & Grapentine, L. (1984). Suicidal behavior among serious juvenile offenders. *American Journal of
Psychotherapy, 141,* 286–287.

American Association of Suicidology.
(1997). *Youth suicide fact sheet.*
(Available from the American Association of Suicidology, Suite 408, 4201
Connecticut Avenue, NW, Washington, DC 20008)

Beck, A. J., & Beck, A. T. (1978). Cognitive therapy of depression and suicide. *American Journal of Psychotherapy, 32,* 201–219.

Beck, A. T., Resnick, H. L. P., & Lettieri, D. J. (Eds.), (1986). *The prediction of suicide,* 2nd edition, Bowie,
Md: The Charles Press.

Beck, A. T., Rush, A. J., Shaw, B. F., &
Emery, G. (1979). *Cognitive therapy
of depression.* New York: Guilford.

Berman, A. L. (1984). The problem of
teenage suicide. Testimony presented
to the United States Senate Committee on the Judiciary Subcommittee
on Juvenile Justice.

Berman, A. L. (1986). Adolescent suicide: Issues and challenges. *Seminars
in Adolescent Medicine, 2,* 269–277.

Berman, A. L., & Jobes, D. A. (1991).
*Adolescent suicide: Assessment and
intervention.* Washington, DC: American Psychological Association.

Berman, A. L., & Jobes, D. A. (1995).
Suicide prevention in adolescents
(age 12–18). *Suicide and Life-Threatening Behavior, 25*(1), 143–154.

Brent, D. A. (1987). Correlates of the
medical lethality of suicide attempts
in children and adolescents. *Journal
of the American Academy of Child
and Adolescent Psychiatry, 26,*
87–91.

Brent, D. A., & Perper, J. A. (1995). Research in adolescent suicide: Implications for training, service delivery,
and public policy. *Suicide and Life-
Threatening Behavior, 25(2),* 222–
230.

Brent, D. A., Perper, J. A., Goldstein, C.
E., Kolko, D. J., Allan, M. J., All-
man, C. J., & Zelenak, J. P. (1988).
Risk factors for adolescent suicide.
Archives of General Psychiatry, 45,
581–588.

Cantor, P. (1976). Personality characteristics among youthful female suicide
attempters. *Journal of Abnormal Psychology, 85,* 324–329.

Comstock, B., & McDermott, M.
(1975). Group therapy for patients
who attempt suicide. *International
Journal of Group Psychotherapy, 25,*
44–49.

Corder, B. F., Shorr, W., & Corder, R.
F. (1974). A study of social and psychological characteristics of adolescent suicide attempters in an urban,
disadvantaged area. *Adolescence, 9,*
1–16.

Curran, D. K. (1987). *Adolescent suicidal behavior.* Washington, DC:
Hemisphere.

Farberow, N. (1970). The suicidal crisis
in psychotherapy. In E. Shneidman,
N. Farberow, & R. Litman (Eds.),
The psychology of suicide. New
York: Science House.

Farberow, N. L. (1976). Group therapy
for self-destructive persons. In J. J.
Parad, H. L. P. Resnik, & L. G.
Parad (Eds.), *Emergency and disaster
management: A mental health sourcebook.* Bowie, MD: Charles Press.

Garfinkel, B. D., Froese, A., & Hood, J. (1982). Suicide attempts in children and adolescents. *American Journal of Psychiatry, 139,* 1257–1261.

Garland, A. F., & Zigler, E. (1993). Adolescent suicide prevention: Current research and social policy implications. *American Psychologist, 48*(2), 169–182.

Getz, W. L., Allen, D. B., Myers, R. K., & Linder, K. C. (1983). *Brief counseling with suicidal persons.* Lexington, MA: Lexington Books.

Group for the Advancement of Psychiatry Committee on Adolescence. (1996). *Adolescent Suicide* (Rep. No. 140). Washington, DC: American Psychiatric Press.

Hendin, H. (1981). Psychotherapy and suicide. *American Journal of Psychotherapy, 35,* 469–480.

Hipple, J. (1982). Group treatment of suicidal clients. *Journal for Specialists in Group Work, 7,* 245–250.

Hipple, J., & Cimbolic, P. (1979). *The counselor and suicidal crisis.* Springfield, IL: Charles C. Thomas.

Hoff, L. A. (1995). *People in crisis.* Menlo Park, CA: Addison-Wesley.

Jobes, D. A. (1995). Psychodynamic treatment of adolescent suicide attempters. In J. Zimmerman and G. Asnis (Eds.), *Treatment approaches with suicidal adolescents.* New York: Wiley.

Jobes, D. A., & Berman, A. L. (1993). Suicide and malpractice liability: Assessing and revising policies, procedures, and practice in outpatient settings. *Professional Psychology: Research and Practice, 24*(1), 91–99.

Jobes, D. A., Berman, A. L., & Josselson, A. R. (1987). Improving the validity and reliability of medicolegal certifications of suicide. *Suicide and Life-Threatening Behavior, 17,* 310–325.

Jobes, D. A., Casey, J. O., Berman, A. L., & Wright, D. G. (1991). Empirical criteria for the determination of suicide manner of death. *Journal of Forensic Sciences, 36,* 244–256.

Kovacs, M., Beck, A. T., & Weissman, A. (1975). The use of suicidal motives in the psychotherapy of attempted suicides. *American Journal of Psychotherapy, 29,* 363–368.

McIntire, M. S., Angle, C. R., Wikoff, R. L., & Schlicht, M. L. (1977). Recurrent adolescent suicidal behavior. *Pediatrics, 60,* 605–608.

McKenry, D., Tishler, C., & Kelley, C. (1982). Adolescent suicide: A comparison of attempters and non-attempters in an emergency room population. *Clinical Pediatrics, 21,* 266–270.

Miller, M. L., Chiles, J. A., & Barnes, V. E. (1982). Suicide attempters within a delinquent population. *Journal of Consulting and Clinical Psychology, 50,* 491–498.

Murray, H. A. (1938). *Explorations in personality.* New York: Oxford University Press.

National Center for Health Statistics. (1998). *Vital statistics of the United States* (Vol. 47, No. 9). Washington, DC: U.S. Government Printing Office.

National Center for Injury Prevention. (1995). *Suicide in the United States: 1980–1992.* Washington, DC: U.S. Government Printing Office.

Pope, K. S. (1986). Assessment and management of suicidal risk: Clinical and legal standards of care. *Independent Practitioner, 6,* 17–23.

Richman, J. (1979). Family therapy of attempted suicide. *Family Process, 18,* 131–142.

Richman, J. (1986). *Family therapy for suicidal people.* New York: Springer.

Robbins, D., & Alessi, N. (1985). Depressive symptoms and suicidal behavior in adolescents. *American Journal of Psychiatry, 142,* 588–592.

Roberts, A. R. (1991). *Contemporary perspectives on crisis intervention and prevention*. Englewood Cliffs, NJ: Prentice Hall.

Rosenberg, M. L., Davidson, L. E., Smith, J. C., Berman, A. L., Buzbee, H., Gantner, G., Gay, G. A., Moore-Lewis, B., Mills, D. H., Murray, D., O'Carroll, P. W., & Jobes, D. (1988). Operational criteria for the determination of suicide. *Journal of Forensic Sciences, 32,* 1445–1455.

Rosenberg, M. L., Smith, J. C., Davidson, L. E., & Conn, J. M. (1987). The emergence of youth suicide: An epidemiological analysis and public health perspective. *Annual Review of Public Health, 8,* 417–440.

Rush, A. J., & Beck, A. T. (1978). Cognitive therapy of depression and suicide. *American Journal of Psychotherapy, 32,* 201–219.

Schein, H. M. (1976). Suicide care: Obstacles in the education of psychiatric residents. *Omega, 7,* 75–82.

Shaffer, D. (1988). The epidemiology of teen suicide: An examination of risk factors. *Journal of Clinical Psychiatry, 49,* 36–41.

Shafii, M., Carrigan, S., Whittinghill, J. R., & Derrick, A. (1985). A psychological autopsy of completed suicide in children and adolescents. *American Journal of Psychiatry, 142,* 1061–1064.

Shneidman, E. S. (1980). Psychotherapy with suicidal patients. In T. B. Karasu & L. Bellak (Eds.), *Specialized techniques in individual psychotherapy*. New York: Brunner/Mazel.

Shneidman, E. S. (1994). *Definition of suicide*. New York: Wiley.

Smith, K., Conroy, R. W., & Ehler, B. D. (1984). Lethality of suicide attempt rating scale. *Suicide and Life-Threatening Behavior, 14,* 215–242.

Smith, K., & Crawford, S. (1984). Suicidal behavior among "normal" high school students. *Suicide and Life-Threatening Behavior, 16,* 313–325.

Stanley, E. J., & Barter, J. J. (1970). Adolescent suicidal behavior. *American Journal of Orthopsychiatry, 40,* 87–96.

Tishler, C., & McKenry, P. (1982). Parental negative self and adolescent suicide attempters. *Journal of the American Academy of Child Psychiatry, 21,* 404–408.

Toolin, J. M. (1962). Suicide and suicide attempts in children and adolescents. *American Journal of Psychiatry, 118,* 719–724.

Vlasak, G. J. (1994). Medical sociology. In S. Perlin (Ed.), *A handbook for the study of suicide* (pp. 131–146). New York: Oxford University Press.

Weissman, A., & Worden, W. (1972). Risk-rescue rating in suicide assessment. *Archives of General Psychiatry, 26,* 553–560.

7

Crisis Intervention at College Counseling Centers

ALLEN J. OTTENS
LINDA L. BLACK

This chapter's focus is on the application of Roberts's (1996) seven-stage model to the delivery of crisis intervention services at college and university counseling centers. Roberts's model is especially relevant, given several compelling reasons for providing crisis intervention as a therapeutic modality in this setting and with this particular clientele.

First, traditional-age college students often encounter crises—death of a parent, dating violence, relationship dissolution, and threats to academic performance, to name a few—that threaten their accomplishing critical developmental tasks. These tasks include concretizing personal values, establishing emotional control, acquiring self-confidence, achieving independence, and shaping relationship skills.

Second, college counselors are witnessing the encroachment onto campuses of "real-life" problems like the AIDS epidemic (Hayden, 1994), hate crimes and violence (Downey & Stage, 1999), sexual violence (Ottens & Hotelling, in press), and coping with the aftermath of serial murders (Archer, 1992). There is also the perception among college mental health practitioners that the recent cohorts of students are presenting with significantly more serious emotional and behavioral problems (O'Malley, Wheeler, Murphy, O'Connell, & Waldo, 1990). Bishop (1990), who predicted that the increasing severity of students' problems is unlikely to abate, recommended that the college counseling center should strive to provide effective crisis response services.

Furthermore, Ottens and Fisher-McCanne (1990) pointed out that crisis

152

intervention as a form of brief therapy is highly compatible with both college students' characteristics and institutional needs. With regard to the former, most clients at college counseling centers meet the criteria suited to brief therapeutic interventions: acute problem onset, previous good adjustment, ability to relate, and high initial motivation (Butcher & Koss, 1978). From an institutional standpoint, crisis intervention, with its brief duration (typically 3 to 12 weeks), makes sense as counseling centers face lengthening waiting lists and set limits on the number of sessions available.

The chapter is organized around two composite case examples of relatively common types of crises encountered by college counselors. We discuss the particulars of each case and present clinical information relevant to the crisis issues. Finally, using the case examples as templates, we guide the reader through the seven stages of the Roberts (1996) model, demonstrating how the model can be adapted for brief, crisis-oriented therapy within the college context.

ACQUAINTANCE RAPE

Tamika

Hesitantly, Tamika, a 18-year-old African American freshman, requests services for problems with concentration and insomnia. She states that she has felt unsettled and "creepy" for the past 3 weeks. Haltingly, she reports that she is experiencing a vague sense that something awful has happened to her, although she has no distinct memory of any traumatic event. Tamika is concerned that she can not remember events following a recent sorority-fraternity party. She adds that she remembers going to the party and then waking up naked the next morning, dazed and confused, in an unfamiliar bedroom. She admits to drinking alcohol while at the party but is adamant that she was not drunk. According to Tamika, her sorority sisters told her she left the party around 10 P.M. with a member of the host fraternity. She was not seen after that time.

Trembling, she discloses that she is scared that the fraternity acquaintance, someone she vaguely remembered from her freshman orientation group, may have spiked her drink with a "roofie," one of the street names for Rohypnol, an illegal tranquilizing drug. She has heard frightening rumors about this crime becoming more frequent at campus parties and local bars. She is at times tearful, angry, and scared. In the absence of any clear memory of the evening's events, she has assumed that she was sexually "taken advantage of" and has no one to blame but herself. She arrived at this conclusion because in the past couple of weeks she heard through the campus grapevine that her fraternity acquaintance has a reputation as a sexual predator.

Since earlier in the week she has found it increasingly difficult to cope with the uncertainty of what happened to her. She is skipping classes, neglecting her grooming, and avoiding friends. She tells the on-call counselor that she feels "tainted" due to being sexually victimized. Compounding the problem, Tamika feels completely isolated, unable to reach out to friends or family for fear of being stigmatized or criticized.

Definitions and Clinical Considerations

When a student like Tamika presents with an acquaintance rape–precipitated crisis, the university counselor needs to consider and incorporate into the intervention plan various facts and implications that are germane to both the general problem of campus acquaintance rape and specifically to its impact on African American women.

Acquaintance rape has been defined as "nonconsensual sex between adults who know each other" (Bechhofer & Parrot, 1991, p. 12). It is contrasted with *date rape,* which is a narrower term that refers to nonconsensual sex between partners who date or who are on a date (Bechhofer & Parrot, 1991). Although these definitions appear straightforward, the campus crisis counselor needs to be aware that it is often difficult to draw distinctions between consensual and nonconsensual sex and who is an acquaintance or a stranger. The definitional distinctions should not obscure the fact that there are important differences in impact and recovery between stranger and acquaintance rape. One complication is that acquaintance rape victims, as opposed to stranger rape vicitims, are more likely to levy blame against themselves (Koss, Dinero, & Seibel, 1988). This self-blame is associated with postassault depression (Frazier, 1990), as well as symptoms of anxiety and slower recovery time (Katz, 1991). Acquaintance rape can leave the victim feeling socially ostracized and unable to even talk about the assault for fear of not being believed (Koss, Gidycz, & Wisniewski, 1987). The victim may delay seeking treatment (Sorenson & Brown, 1990) or may underuse professional help resources (Sugarman & Hotaling, 1991).

In this vignette, the clinical picture and intervention plan are complicated by the apparent use of a "date rape drug" that further traumatizes the victim. Rohypnol and gamma hydroxybutyrate (GHB) are two powerful illegal sedatives that have made their way onto some U.S. campuses. Rohypnol, known by such street names as "la rocha," "roachies," and "roofies," is colorless, odorless, and tasteless but has strong amnesiac and disinhibiting effects (Zorza, in press). Within 30 minutes of ingestion, the victim experiences muscle relaxation and drowsiness. Rohypnol leaves the victim incapacitated and unable to resist sexual exploitation (Zorza, 1998). With Tamika, the counselor must keep in mind that sedative-induced acquaintance rape may require a longer and more painful road to recovery. Unlike rape survivors who were conscious during the assault, those who were drugged simply cannot know how they might have been exploited; as a result, they may experience profound shame or guilt (Zorza, in press).

Unfortunately, there is a dearth of data on the prevalence of courtship violence for African American college students (Clark, Beckett, Wells, & Dungee-Anderson, 1994). Yet the campus crisis counselor must be aware of several crucial factors. First, the counselor must be alert to any tendency to view forced sexual encounters against African American women as less serious offenses (Foley, Evancic, Karnik, King, & Parks, 1995). Second, as a result of our society's racist and segregationist history, African Americans have tended to be exposed to more violence than White Americans and hence are at greater risk for using or experiencing violence in interpersonal relationships. Finally, any dating or relationship violence among African American students can be viewed as ultimately having a negative impact on the future of the African American family; such violence undermines the positive effects of relationship and family that have been protective buffers against oppression (Clark et al., 1994).

Scope of the Problem

One of the most cited and ambitious studies of sexual victimization among college students was conducted by Koss et al. (1987). In their survey of over 6,000 students at 32 U.S. colleges, they found alarmingly high incidence and prevalence rates of sexual violence perpetrated against women respondents. For example, from their data Koss et al. calculated a victimization rate of 83 per 1,000 women who, within just 6 months preceding the survey, reported a sexual experience that met legal definitions of rape or attempted rape. Perhaps their most distressing finding was that 84% of the women who were raped knew their assailants.

Miller (1988) surveyed women students at North Carolina State University and found that 27% of their sample had been physically or psychologically pressured into intercourse. Finley and Corty (1993), at a midwestern university, concluded from their survey results that "by the time they were in junior and senior years, about a third of the women reported having been victims [of forced sexual assault] and about a third of the men reported being perpetrators" (p. 116). Generally, estimates cited by researchers of the incidence and prevalence rates for sexual assault at U.S. colleges are in the 15 to 25% range (e.g., Frintner & Rubinson, 1993; Malamuth, Sockloskie, Koss, & Tanaka, 1991; Schwartz & DeKeseredy, 1997).

It was no surprise to the college crisis counselor that Tamika's assailant was known to her, or even that the rape was associated with a fraternity party. Although there is not a definitive answer as to whether fraternity members are more prone to committing rape than other college men (Koss & Cleveland, 1996), student development research, both qualitative and quantitative, suggests that the college crisis counselor should at least be prepared to inquire whether a client's rape and attendance at a fraternity function are connected. For example, Copenhaver and Grauerholz (1991) found that fraternity members resort to the "party method" as a means for sexual exploitation. Fraternity parties are often unsupervised events where the members control the structure of activities and drinking is encouraged. Schwartz and DeKeseredy (1997) have put forth peer-support models suggesting that the bonding, secrecy, shared traditional values toward women, and narrow concepts of masculinity promote sexual victimization of women on campus.

Major Vulnerabilities and Risk Factors

Although not a cause of sexual assault or acquaintance rape per se, alcohol is frequently linked to such aggressive acts. In a representative study, Muehlenhard and Linton (1987) found that over 50% of the men and over 50% of the women who reported sexual assault on a date had been drinking. It should be kept in mind that alcohol, not illegal sedatives, is the most common date rape drug. However, college crisis workers must absolutely avoid making value judgments about the drinking behavior of an acquaintance rape victim and refrain from blaming the victim, even when the victim, as in Tamika's case, is an underage drinker. The counselor must remember that when a male acquaintance brings a sedative to a party in order to spike drinks, he is committing a premeditated criminal act. As Abbey, McCauslan, and Ross (1998) have pointed out, the vulnerability resides in the manner in which certain males exploit situational variables:

> A sexually predatory male who has stereotypic beliefs about gender roles and rape is inclined to view women as sexual objects, seek out and exploit all opportunities for sexual encounters, and misperceive friendliness as a sexual come-on because this is what he is hoping to find. He then feels comfortable forcing sex, especially if he feels led on or can attribute his actions to the effects of alcohol. (p. 186)

Indeed, the rape-supportive attitudes and personality characteristics of the male perpetrator are a major consideration in terms of the factors that place college women at risk. The rape-supportive attitudes allow perpetrators to psychologically denigrate women, to provide justification for exploiting women, and to discount the seriousness of their own behavior. In their review of the literature on college men and rape, Berkowitz, Burkhart, and Bourg (1994) pointed out that sexually aggressive men are found to possess hypermasculine and antisocial personality characteristics. Hypermasculine males are likely to harbor callous attitudes toward women and to treat them with anger and rejection; an antisocial orientation has been linked to college men's coercive sexuality. In his interviews with college men who had committed date rape, Kanin (1985) found the men to be constantly on the prowl for sexual partners and willing to use any verbal or physical strategy to get sex.

The college crisis counselor should be aware that, since Tamika is a freshman student, she is at a higher risk of sexual assault. Freshmen women in their first few weeks on campus are especially vulnerable because they haven't caught on to the social "rules" (Bohmer & Parrot, 1993). This last point is crucial. College dating relationships are governed by unwritten "scripts" or rules that often reflect a power differential in favor of the male. When the male is older, pays for the date, provides transportation, and arranges the dating location, the implicit rules are set into motion for an exploitable sexual opportunity (Muehlenhard & Linton, 1987).

It is not unusual for young women to enter college with histories of childhood or adolescent sexual assault experiences. The crisis worker should, at some point, very tactfully ascertain whether Tamika's recent acquaintance rape is a revictimization experience. Women with a history of sexual victimization tend to be at a higher risk for being sexually revictimized by a college date or acquaintance (Gidycz, Coble, Latham, & Layman, 1993; Gidycz, Hanson, & Layman, 1995). From a preventive perspective, the crisis counselor should begin considering postvention procedures with Tamika so that she does not become more "victimizable."

Resilience and Protective Factors

After an acquaintance rape on campus, tertiary prevention efforts should be mobilized to limit the damage inflicted by the incident (Benson, Charlton, & Goodhart, 1992). These efforts may involve the college's health center, campus security personnel, residence halls, counseling center, campus ministry office, women's resource center, and judicial affairs office.

In the first vignette, Tamika came to the university's counseling center several weeks after the assault. This was an important first step on her part because victims of acquaintance rape may not label their experience as rape or may be too ashamed to seek help. The college crisis worker began brief individual counseling to help Tamika begin the stabilization process and to drain off intense emotions. It is important to consider the gender and value orientation of the crisis worker as factors that will influence recovery (Petretic-Jackson & Jackson, 1990). A male counselor, despite his clinical skill and compassion, may not be trusted. Likewise, the counselor must convey warmth and acceptance and be free of bias toward the victim. The counselor also must be careful about overidentifying with the victim, lest she or he zealously try to rescue the client or take over the recovery (Petretic-Jackson & Jackson, 1990).

The crisis counselor talked with Tamika about possible health consequences of her assault. With the counselor's assistance, Tamika made contact with a physician on the university's health staff who is particularly sensitive to the needs of physically and sexually assaulted women. The physician will perform tests and an examination to check for injuries, possible pregnancy, or sexually transmitted diseases. Confidentiality and respect for the client must be essential priorities. The counselor must not divulge information about Tamika's situation without her consent; and the counselor and Tamika must establish a collaborative relationship—the counselor cannot compel her to take any preventive or remedial action, no matter how "good" it might be for her.

Individual counseling may give way to group counseling for survivors of sexual assault. When a college or university offers this counseling service, clients find the healing environment and sense of bonding with other survivors to be especially therapeutic. The group provides an outlet for the expression of feelings and for their validation by other group members, which is important for recovery (Burkhart, 1991).

The residence hall staff can be enlisted to perform important tertiary prevention functions. It may be necessary to provide safer housing for an acquaintance rape victim or to arrange a move to a different residence hall. In Tamika's case, the residence hall staff consulted with her roommate and hall friends to help them respond to Tamika in positive ways and to educate them about how Tamika might feel as she recovers from the assault. The friends were helped to accept Tamika's changed moods and need for personal space and to listen empathically as she disclosed at her own pace.

The college crisis worker should consider the role that spirituality or church involvement might play in recovery and be aware of its particular value for African American clients in crisis (Kanel, 1999). Although Tamika was not comfortable discussing her feelings with the minister of her church back home, she did accept a referral to an African American member of the campus ministry. Some colleges have a women's resource center that may offer alternative therapies and growth activities such as dance, painting, or other expressive arts. Some women (and certainly a small percentage of acquaintance rape victims) may seek redress through the campus judicial affairs office. These officers can counsel students about options available through the code of conduct policies and procedures for handling the case sensitively and appropriately. For some women the successful prosecution of a case against their assailant brings a powerful sense of empowerment and satisfaction that other women may have been helped.

CRISIS INTERVENTION: APPLICATION OF THE MODEL (TAMIKA)

Tamika, an African American freshman, appears as a walk-in for counseling services. She begins by describing problems during the past 3 weeks with insomnia and inability to concentrate on her schoolwork. She reports having felt unsettled, "creepy," and weepy for no apparent reason. She also reports having a vague impression that something very wrong happened to her. Slowly, she provides more details about her feelings and symptoms. She says that about 3 weeks ago, she had been at a fraternity party, where she met an acquaintance from a class and had only one drink with him. She remembers virtually nothing beyond that point, except for waking up the next morning in a strange bed. Later, she heard rumors about drinks being spiked at local bars with a substance known as "roofies." Ever since the apparent rape, Tamika has found it difficult to cope. She has been skipping class, avoiding friends, and dressing in baggy, unattractive clothes. She has been withdrawing from friends and is preoccupied with thoughts of having done something wrong.

Stage 1: Establish Rapport and Relationship

Tamika's initial request for a female, African American counselor is honored. The counselor communicates caring and warmth both verbally and nonverbally. In an accepting manner, the counselor allows Tamika to express her feelings and describe the sequence of events. To quell some of Tamika's anxiety, the counselor briefly answers her questions about confidentiality and the effects of "date rape drugs" like Rohypnol. The counselor allows Tamika to disclose her story through gentle questions and encouragers; she doesn't sidetrack Tamika by focusing unnecessarily at this point on her academic difficulties.

Stage 2: Conduct a Thorough Assessment, Including Immediate Psychosocial Needs

Given the emerging clinical picture, the Roberts (1996) model suggests assessing for dangerousness to self or others and for the client's immediate psychosocial needs. In this case, the salient issue is to determine immediate psychosocial needs. Rating Tamika across the three dimensions of the Triage Assessment Form (Myer & Ottens, 1994), the counselor arrives at a score of 26, suggesting the need for a more directive counseling approach in order to help her cope. Health, physical safety, and social support are identified as the three most pressing needs. The counselor assists in facilitating a referral for Tamika to an empathic physician at the university health center. Next, the counselor determines that Tamika is not being harassed or stalked by her assailant and that she is apparently safe remaining in her residence hall room. Social support is found to be available from Tamika's older sister whom she trusts, and plans are set for the sister to come to campus during the weekend.

Stage 3: Identify Major Problems

The event that precipitated Tamika's visit to the counseling center occurred only a day previously. At that time she felt ready to tell her roommate about the events at the party. The roommate, however, reacted with shock, "How could you have let this happen to you? Don't you know that you've been *raped*?" This insensitive remark shocked Tamika into awareness—finally someone had provided her with the word that matched her experience.

With a complicated crisis event such as a drug-induced acquaintance rape, the crisis worker can expect a host of problems and issues to emerge. Tamika feels compelled to focus on several concerns that tend to muddle the picture: What should I tell others so they won't think the wrong thing about me? How am I going to make up the schoolwork I've missed? How could I have been so naive? Among Tamika's expressions of shame, indecision, and worry, the counselor takes note of one that has potential for focusing their work. When Tamika says, "I want to get this mess out of my life and just get on with things," the counselor leans forward and asks the focusing question, "And how would that happen? How can we help you recover?"

Without much difficulty, Tamika puts forth two possibilities—getting a handle on her feelings (e.g., fear, anger, sadness, guilt) and regaining a sense of control over her life. The counselor, who is also concerned about Tamika's withdrawal and disengaging coping choices, adds a third possibility, which is widening the helping net around her.

Toward the close of this counseling session, the counselor and Tamika engage in the following dialogue:

Counselor: Tamika, can you tell me if there was any other time in your life when you felt this way, that is, wanting to get over a terrible mess and get on with things?

Client: (*pausing to think*) Maybe the closest to this is when I was a junior in high school and my favorite teacher, Mrs. Adams, was killed in a car crash. She was my music teacher.

Counselor: That's very sad. . . . How did you manage to carry on after that?

Client: Well, eventually I figured God had a plan in this tragedy. I got myself another piano teacher and practiced harder to get better. I wanted to do my best to, you know, to honor her memory.

Counselor: To me that's an indication of exceptional maturity on your part. The way you took a positive meaning from her accident, does that tell us anything about your capacity to do something like that under the present circumstances?

This brief dialogue seems to be a key step in bringing the problem into focus and forging a working alliance between client and counselor.

Stage 4: Deal with Feelings and Emotions

During the early counseling sessions, Tamika is able to ventilate feelings and self-statements. She is fearful of meeting her assailant at some other campus function. She feels simultaneously angry at him and at herself. A number of times, she expresses disgust with herself, such as, "Something must be wrong with me. It's my fault for hanging out in the wrong places." The counselor is aware that, if adhered to, these blaming self-statements could slow Tamika's recovery. Eventually, the responsibility for the assault needs to be placed on the assailant himself. However, during the early sessions, the counselor allows Tamika to express her feelings without being censored. The counselor also helps Tamika to "unpack" or clarify vague emotional sensations, such as her feeling "creepy."

Stage 5: Generate and Explore Alternatives

Fortunately, the college campus and local community contain a number of resources to help Tamika become a survivor of the assault. Initially, the counselor takes a more directive approach given Tamika's isolation, intrusive thoughts, and disengagement. This approach involves suggesting and prioritizing (with input from Tamika) several appropriate resources in order to expand the net of support and caring around her. The student health center, her residence hall staff, and an older, trusted sister are quickly identified. Continued individual counseling is suggested, with referral to a sexual assault survivors' group in the near future.

A list of helping resources can be generated, and that is often the easiest part. In this case, care must be taken to answer Tamika's ongoing questions about confidentiality. She must be given assurances about the sensitivity of the helping resources. The counselor acts to mobilize helping resources and may serve as an advocate in order to cut "red tape" that could unnecessarily delay Tamika's getting medical attention or an appointment with residence hall staff.

Stage 6: Develop and Formulate an Action Plan

Several sessions of individual counseling have helped stabilize Tamika. During the sessions Tamika has begun telling the narrative of her assault, and this has initiated the process of normalizing her emotional reactions and reframing them as part of the recovery process. One of the important functions of crisis resolution at this stage is to identify and examine self-blaming statements. As healing progresses, there is a shift from recalling and recounting the trauma to exploring the *meaning* of the traumatic event and how it can be incorporated into the self-system (Funderburk, in press). Journaling, relaxation exercises, and continuing use of her support network (older sister, close friend from home) are part of Tamika's therapeutic adjunctive activities. At the suggestion of a friend and the encouragement of the counselor, Tamika also began kick-boxing lessons that were held in the campus recreation center.

Tamika accepts referral into a trauma recovery group that is held in a safe off-campus location. Some group members are students from campus; about two thirds are adult women from the local community. In the group, sharing, bonding, and support are important healing factors. The group itself becomes a safe vessel in which the initial meaning attached to the assault is deconstructed and reconstructed. Tamika's perception of herself as "tainted" or stigmatized becomes transformed into, "I'm not someone who is 'spoiled' through and through. My recovery and strength give me power over an event that I did not cause. I feel in control when I prevent *him* from winning."

Stage 7: Conduct Follow-Up

Recovery from an acquaintance rape—especially a drug-induced one—is an ongoing, difficult process. Group counseling with supportive family and friends and self-empowering extratherapeutic activities (journaling, kick-boxing) become part of a multipronged healing strategy. The message that Tamika is internalizing is "living well is the best revenge."

The crisis intervention with Tamika has proceeded with a focus on the here and now and on the future (Roberts, 1990). Now the crisis counselor schedules occasional "check-ins" and monitors Tamika's progress and participation in her healing activities. During the check-ins, the counselor performs a brief assessment using the Clinician-Assisted PTSD Scale (Blake et al., 1995) to monitor symptoms. At the follow-up sessions, the counselor inquires into Tamika's current academic, social, spiritual, cognitive, and emotional functioning.

THE IMPOSTOR PHENOMENON

Megan, the "Impostor"

Megan, a 20-year-old second-semester sophomore, attends a large public university. She is enrolled in a prelaw curriculum. A serious, high-achieving student (GPA of 3.60 on a 4.0 scale), Megan has set her sights on a lucrative corporate legal career.

Megan presents herself as a walk-in client at her university counseling center. She is in obvious distress, expressing worry that she will fail an important midterm exam. She harbors serious self-doubts about her ability to eventually perform as a lawyer. When the on-call counselor inquires about recent events that might have precipitated her fear, Megan responds, "I've been worrying about this big accounting exam next week and how I'll mess it up. I couldn't get the worry out of my mind. It just kept building, and I kept telling myself: 'You've got to ace it! This is your chance to prove yourself!' I had no confidence in my ability to apply all these complicated accounting principles. After all, If I'm going to be a corporate lawyer, I've got to be able to handle this kind of pressure. Then it dawned on me: I've gotten by all along because courses have been easy, and I've been able to charm my way to good grades. With this accounting test, you either know it or you don't, and I don't. I'm afraid everybody else will find out I don't have what it takes."

After relating that her academic accomplishments are due to luck and an ingratiating personality, Megan slumps in her chair and sobs quietly. She says she hasn't been sleeping well for the past week in anticipation of this exam; additionally, her racing thoughts seem to have a mind of their own. Because she believes that her academic situation and emotional state are out of her control, she remarks that she doesn't know if she can continue living this way.

She considers a host of impulsive coping options: changing majors, dropping out of school, avoiding her friends on campus, and hatching plans to deceive her parents. Interspersed between Megan's pressured description of these ill-conceived plans are numerous self-deprecating statements such as "I can't continue fooling myself and others like this" and "I knew eventually others would find out about me."

Definitions and Clinical Considerations

The impostor phenomenon (IP) is described by Clance and Imes (1978) as an internal experience of intellectual phoniness prevalent among a select group of women in clinical and college settings. The impostor experience persists despite independent, objective, and tangible evidence to the contrary.

Clance and O'Toole (1988) describe the female impostor experience as being cyclical. The cycle begins when the student faces an exam, project, or task that involves external evaluation. The individual experiences great self-doubt and fear that, as in Megan's case, may be expressed as generalized anxiety, psychosomatic complaints, or sleep disturbance. It is important for the university crisis counselor to keep in mind that "impostors" are actually high achievers who may attempt to cope by overpreparing or by procrastinating, only to end up in a frenzied rush to catch up. The cycle ends with the impostor likely to have successfully completed the test or project. When she is praised or rewarded for her success, she discounts the recognition, which further feeds into her self-doubt and belief that suffering leads to success. And so the cycle repeats itself.

Impostors tend to be introverted and feel terrorized by failure. The intellectual inauthenticity these women describe often leads to the fear of being publicly unmasked as a fake. This fear led to Megan's choosing impulsive and dysfunctional coping methods.

Scope of the Problem

Clance and Imes (1978) found a higher prevalence of IP among women than among men. Clance and Imes interacted with 150 high-achieving women from a variety of disciplines at both graduate and undergraduate levels. These women all had external evidence of success (degrees, awards, high test scores), yet they felt like impostors. Common clinical symptoms included lack of self-confidence, depression, generalized anxiety, and low frustration tolerance with respect to meeting personal standards (Clance & Imes, 1978; Matthews & Clance, 1985).

The failure to internalize success was initially viewed as unique to females (Clance & Imes, 1978), but college counselors must be aware that IP may be just as prevalent in males (Topping & Kimmel, 1985). The research has been equivocal with regard to gender differences in the expression and prevalence of IP (Thompson, Davis, & Davidson, 1998). King and Cooley (1995), in a study of 127 undergraduates, found that higher levels of IP for females were associated with greater family achievement orientation, higher grade point averages, and more time spent on academic endeavors. However, these results need to be interpreted with caution because of the use of imprecise measures of academic achievement (e.g., GPA) and achievement orientation. The college counselor should bear in mind that when a study uncovers a greater prevalence of IP among females, it may be an artifact of gender role stereotyping or parental messages regarding success (King & Cooley, 1995).

Thompson et al. (1998) compared impostors and nonimpostors from a sample of 164 undergraduates. The impostors evidenced higher levels of anxiety, lower self-esteem, and a greater need for perfectionism. One finding of particular relevance for college counselors from this study is the tendency of impostors to overgeneralize—that is, to equate academic failure with failure as a person. Carver and Ganellen (1983) reported this tendency to overgeneralize to be a powerful predictor of depression in college students. Returning to the vignette, if the college counselor has not already assessed for it, he or she should be sure to ask Megan about depressive symptomatology.

Major Vulnerabilities and Risk Factors

Clance and Imes (1978) and Matthews and Clance (1985) suggest that IP develops within the dynamic interactions of the family of origin. Clance (1985) hypothesized that the family context may provide four essential elements in the development of IP. First, in childhood, the imposter believes that her abilities are unique and atypical in her family. Second, the feedback she receives from outside the family system conflicts with feedback from within the system. Third, she is not recognized or praised for accomplishments by family members. Finally, family members communicate that success and intelligence should come with little effort.

The crisis counselor needs to be mindful of the role assigned to the IP sufferer within the family and how that role impacts current thoughts and feelings. Clance and O'Toole (1988) suggested that the IP sufferer has received either of two messages from her family: You are not the bright one, or you are the bright one and success will come easily to you. King and Cooley (1995) considered it possible that IP females in their study received parental messages that implied academic achievement was due to effort rather than talent. Such messages might impress upon females that they inherently have less of "what it takes."

King and Cooley (1995) presented data that support the hypothesis that a family environment emphasizing achievement is associated with higher levels of IP. They recommend obtaining students' perceptions of the importance of achievement in their families of origin. Miller and Kastburg (1995) interviewed six women employed in higher education settings who came from blue-collar family backgrounds. Although IP was not an issue for all six, for some of the women IP dogged them as a "lifelong charade." This is very preliminary evidence suggesting that socioeconomic status (SES) might impact the degree of IP present.

Crisis counselors should be mindful and inquire about the IP sufferers' perceptions of achievement orientation in their families of origin and recollections of parental messages about achievement and ability. A gauge of the families' SES level might also fill out the clinical picture, as well as ascertaining whether the IP client is the first in the family to attend college.

Resilience and Protective Factors

Megan's request for assistance and support should be viewed by the college crisis worker as an invitation to intervene in the IP cycle. Typically, impostor feelings are not presented in a forthright manner by the client. Persons suffering from IP usually do not seek assistance due to the potential for shame and embarrassment of being found out. Therefore, it is critical to establish an empathic, nonauthoritarian, therapeutic alliance (Clance & O'Toole, 1988) that allows for identification and emergence of these feelings.

Megan presented at the counseling center with feelings of intense anxiety and a sense of dread prior to her accounting exam. This is significant because the IP sufferer customarily moves away from others who could help. Clance and O'Toole (1988) described this movement away as an attempt to isolate oneself in order to deal with the fear and shame that accompany IP. The alert counselor begins by establishing a supportive and inclusive relationship. The nonjudgmental, accepting relationship reduces Megan's tendency to isolate herself. This relationship may provide the basis for a later referral into a support group.

CRISIS INTERVENTION: APPLICATION OF THE MODEL (MEGAN)

Step 1: Establish Rapport and Relationship

Megan, a prelaw student, is a walk-in client at her university's counseling center. She is panicking over an upcoming accounting exam. She describes her symptoms, which include an inability to concentrate and spiraling anxiety. "I've got to do well on this test," she repeats, while emphasizing the importance of grades, given her career ambition of becoming a corporate lawyer. During this initial contact, the counselor communicates her concern about Megan's fear of failing by intermittent eye contact, voice tone, and physical proximity. Establishing rapport is crucial, since the counselor surmises that Megan, like other IP clients, may be ashamed to ask for help—an act tantamount to admitting failure. Instead of weakness, the counselor strives to frame Megan's help-seeking in terms of hopefulness and strength of character:

> Counselor: I'm optimistic about your ability to prevent events from getting out of control. In fact, coming here to talk to someone suggests that you knew this was the right thing to do.
>
> Client: Well, I felt like I had nowhere else to turn.
>
> Counselor: But isn't there always the option of "toughing it out" in isolated silence? Instead you seem to be making a more proactive choice.

Step 2: Conduct a Thorough Assessment, Including Immediate Psychosocial Needs

The event triggering Megan's panic was the thought that she might not possess the necessary self-confidence for a law career, especially if such a thing as an accounting exam could disquiet her so. She then connected this thought to a realization that there was nothing of intellectual substance to her—she had gotten by through luck and charm. With this information, the counselor establishes the initial clinical impression that Megan presents with the imposter phenomenon (IP). It becomes evident to the counselor that Megan's modal coping style is to overachieve and motivate herself through worrying. Through probes and brief history taking, the counselor defines the scope and duration of the problem. Actually, feeling phony is a long-standing concern for Megan, but it appears now in bold relief given the stressor of the big exam. The nature of IP is such that Megan is likely to struggle to acknowledge previous success and personal strengths despite evidence to the contrary.

The counselor assesses Megan's current functioning utilizing the Triage Assessment Form (TAF; Myer & Ottens, 1994). This assessment reveals most dysfunction in the cognitive domain—the intrusiveness of her self-doubts and how her self-evaluation differs from the reality of her accomplishments. The TAF score of 18 suggests a collaborative approach can be used with Megan at this stage of treatment. The counselor also made note of Megan's offhand comment, "I don't know if I can continue living this way." Later in this initial session, the counselor came back to that comment in order to "unpack" its meaning, since it might be an indirect reference to suicidal ideation:

> Counselor: Megan, a few minutes ago you said that you didn't know if you can continue living this way. Is that an expression of just how out of control this situation has gotten?
>
> Client: Absolutely. If this is what important exams are going to do to me, I don't want any more of it. I mean, I can't continue to freak out over every test.
>
> Counselor: I want to be sure I understand exactly what you mean. Are you saying to me that your approach to taking tests has to change—that you don't want to continue freaking out whenever there's a test?
>
> Client: Yes, that's what I mean.
>
> Counselor: As opposed to saying, "I can't continue living this way" when somebody has plans to hurt themselves?
>
> Client: (*face reddens*) You mean suicide? Oh, no, that's not anything I'm even thinking about.

Step 3: Identify Major Problems

In this case the precipitating event, the upcoming accounting exam, was quickly established. The problems needing to be addressed were intertwined: How to attenuate the symptoms of anxiety and effectively prepare for the exam?

During this stage, Megan is allowed to express her feelings, which are a mix of catastrophizing about the test outcome and self-doubting personal criticisms. Besides the raw feelings, the counselor also listens for Megan's beliefs about her intellect, work ethic, and attributions for her previous successes. Knowing that IP may have a familial component, the counselor tunes into family messages about success and expectations of Megan's gender.

Step 4: Deal With Feelings and Emotions

There are two distinct aspects to this component of the crisis intervention model. The counselor strives to allow Megan to freely express her feelings, to cathart, and to tell the "story" about her current crisis situation. To this end, the counselor relies on standard active listening skills—accurate paraphrasing, minimal encouragers (Egan, 1998), reflecting feelings, summarizing, and reassurances. These complementary counselor responses not only allow the client's dysfunctional style to unfold but also are the basis for establishing a working alliance (Kiesler, 1988). Very cautiously, the counselor at this stage will work "anticomplementary" responses into her dialogue with the Megan. Anticomplementary responses include advice giving, interpretations, reframes, and probes. Such responses are designed to begin the process of challenging the client's maladaptive cognitive and behavioral choices (Kiesler, 1988). Such confrontative interventions loosen Megan's maladaptive schemas, help her consider behavioral options, and question her attributions of failure and success. The judicious blending of complementary (supporting or bonding) responses and anticomplementary (challenging or frustrating) responses is thought to constitute an interplay that is fundamental to the therapy process (Hanna & Ottens, 1995). The following is a probing response typical of this stage:

> Client: (*emphatically*) I can't afford to take this test lightly. I'll try psyching myself up—"You've *got* to prove yourself on this test! You *can't* screw it up! What if you fail?"
>
> Counselor: Consider this for a moment—will your success on the test be *because of* or *in spite of* that kind of self-talk?

Step 5: Generate and Explore Alternatives

The crisis counselor must deal with the immediate concern of how Megan will cope with the upcoming test. Beyond that, the larger questions of dealing with the distorted view of her personal competency and possible familial dynamics may be issues for later counseling work. The counselor is aware that IP clients devalue their opinions and overvalue those of the "authority." Hence, a collaborative approach is used to brainstorm ways to handle the exam. All options are "fair game." Eventually, three options are seriously discussed that are the opposite of Megan's initial avoidant, impulsive choices: (a) Join a study group with some laid-back friends; (b) provide tutoring for her roommate, who is seriously struggling with accounting, since one actually learns best by teaching another; (c) practice a rapid relaxation technique (Ottens, 1984) to lower anxious arousal while studying.

Stage 6: Develop and Formulate an Action Plan

For the short term, that is, to manage the crisis of the upcoming accounting exam, the counselor and Megan adopt a three-pronged approach. First, they draw up a behavioral contract that includes the three coping choices outlined previously. Second, they identify the types of sabotaging self-talk Megan might use to negate the contract (e.g., "Why waste my time helping my roommate?" "This won't work!"). Third, the counselor makes an explicit commitment to be there to help: "Megan, I want you to know that as long as you are committed to working on this contract, I will do all that I can to help and support you. This truly is a 50–50 effort on both of our parts."

There are also longer-term considerations, because for the IP client there will always be another test, term paper, or important evaluation that will be cause for self-doubt. Even if Megan excels on the big exam, it will be easy for her to discount her success or to attribute it to external factors. Hence, continued intervention is recommended in order to target her beliefs around themes of negative self-efficacy, perfectionism, and the use of worry as a self-motivator. She also has the belief that others can somehow see into her and spot her as a phony. In subsequent sessions, the counselor will address these issues, as well as familial achievement expectations. Group counseling is an option, especially if the group is composed of other women who share these IP beliefs.

Stage 7: Conduct Follow-Up

Brief, crisis-oriented therapy in this case consisted of 10 individual counseling sessions. Megan elected not to join a group at this time but kept this idea in mind as a later option. The counselor and Megan agreed to schedule a follow-up session during the second week of the next semester.

At that follow-up session, the counselor must note whether Megan has fallen back into the IP cycle. The counselor will want to (a) assess the fluidity or rigidity of Megan's cognitions, (b) discuss future stressors, (c) inquire into how she is rehearsing to handle those stressors, (d) assess her relationships with peers, and (e) learn what evidence she now uses for gauging performance.

CONCLUSION

Several themes emerge from the vignettes of Tamika and Megan. First, the concerns facing both women need to be addressed by the counselor in a sensitive, knowledgeable, and culturally aware manner that demonstrates an understanding of the potential impact that gender, ethnicity, and/or family history can have on the presentation and maintenance of symptoms. Second, the crisis worker in a college counseling center should be cognizant of the personal context in which these symptoms emerge (e.g., client's potential for self-blame, desire for perfection, cultural expectations—sexually and academically—for young women). Third, the potential for students to isolate from those who could help them needs to be understood in terms of students' developmental needs for autonomy, personal competency, and self-definition. In both vignettes the potential for isolation was high. The availability of a caring professional allowed each client to engage in a process of stabilization that was facilitated by following the crisis intervention model (Roberts, 1996). Finally, there is the need for ongoing training and education so that counselors can keep abreast of issues facing today's college population. This training builds competency into the counseling staff and makes for more effective service delivery.

Crisis-oriented interventions are a critical and valuable resource for college students. By definition, the college crisis counselor is the initial contact person and stabilization resource who can serve as the conduit to a myriad of campus and community services. Appropriate crisis intervention and follow-up on the college campus support a student's efforts to balance the academic and emotional demands of college, as well as allowing the counselor an effective strategy to manage a burgeoning caseload.

REFERENCES

Abbey, A., McCauslan, P., & Ross, L. T. (1998). Sexual assault perpetration by college men: The role of alcohol, misperception of sexual intent, and sexual beliefs and experiences. *Journal of Social and Clinical Psychology, 17,* 167–195.

Archer, J. (1992). Campus in crisis: Coping with fear and panic related to serial murders. *Journal of Counseling and Development, 71,* 96–100.

Bechhofer, L., & Parrot, A. (1991). What is acquaintance rape? In A. Parrot & L. Bechhofer (Eds.), *Acquaintance rape: The hidden crime* (pp. 9–25). New York: Wiley.

Benson, D., Charlton, C., & Goodhart, F. (1992). Acquaintance rape on campus: A literature review. *Journal of American College Health, 40,* 157–165.

Berkowitz, A. D., Burkhart, B. R., & Bourg, S. E. (1994). Research on college men and rape. In A. D. Berkowitz (Ed.), *Men and rape: Theory, research, and prevention programs in higher education.* New Directions for Student Services, No. 65. San Francisco: Jossey-Bass.

Bishop, J. B. (1990). The university counseling center: An agenda for the 1990's. *Journal of Counseling and Development, 68,* 408–413.

Blake, D., Weathers, F. W., Nagy, L., Kaloupek, D., Klauminzer, G., Charney, D., & Keane, T. M. (1995). The development of a clinician-administered PTSD scale. *Journal of Traumatic Stress, 8,* 75–90.

Bohmer, C., & Parrot, A. (1993). *Sexual assault on campus: The problem and the solution.* New York: Lexington Books.

Burkhart, B. R. (1991). Conceptual and practical analysis of therapy for acquaintance rape vicitms. In A. Parrot & L. Bechhofer (Eds.), *Acquaintance rape: The hidden crime* (pp. 287–303). New York: Wiley.

Butcher, J. N., & Koss, M. P. (1978). Research on brief and crisis-oriented therapies. In S. L. Garfield & A. E. Bergin (Eds.), *Handbook of psychotherapy and behavior change* (2nd ed.; pp. 725–767). New York: Wiley.

Carver, C. S., & Ganellen, R. J. (1983). Depression and components of self-punitiveness: High standards, self-criticism, and overgeneralisation. *Journal of Personal-*

ity and Social Psychology, 48, 1097–1111.

Clance, P. R. (1985). The imposter phenomenon: Overcoming the fear that haunts your success. Atlanta: Peachtree.

Clance, P. R., & Imes, S. A. (1978). The impostor phenomenon in high-achieving women: Dynamics and therapeutic intervention. Psychotherapy: Theory, Research, and Practice, 15, 241–247.

Clance, P. R., & O'Toole, M. A. (1988). The impostor phenomenon: An internal barrier to empowerment and achievement. Women and Therapy, 6, 51–64.

Clark, M. L., Beckett, J., Wells, M., & Dungee-Anderson, D. (1994). Courtship violence among African American college students. Journal of Black Psychology, 20, 264–281.

Copenhaver, S., & Grauerholz, E. (1991). Sexual victimization among sorority women: Exploring the link between sexual violence and institutional practices. Sex Roles, 24, 31–41.

Downey, J. P., & Stage, F. K. (1999). Hate crimes and violence on college and university campuses. Journal of College Student Development, 40, 3–9.

Egan, G. (1998). The skilled helper (6th ed.). Pacific Grove, CA: Brooks/Cole.

Finley, C., & Corty, E. (1993). Rape on campus: The prevalence of sexual assault while enrolled in college. Journal of College Student Development, 34, 113–117.

Foley, L. A., Evancic, C., Karnik, K., King, J., & Parks, A. (1995). Date rape: Effects of race of assailant and victim and gender of subjects

on perceptions. Journal of Black Psychology, 21, 6–18.

Frazier, P. A. (1990). Victim attribution and post-rape trauma. Journal of Personality and Social Psychology, 59, 298–304.

Frintner, M. P., & Rubinson, L. (1993). Acquaintance rape: The influence of alcohol, fraternity membership, and sports team membership. Journal of Sex Education and Therapy, 19, 272–284.

Funderburk, J. R. (In press). Group counseling for survivors of sexual assault. In A. J. Ottens & K. Hotelling (Eds.), Sexual violence on campus in the twenty-first century. New York: Springer.

Gidycz, C. A., Coble, C. N., Latham, L., & Layman, M. J. (1993). A sexual assault experience in adulthood and prior victimization experiences: A prospective analysis. Psychology of Women Quarterly, 17, 151–168.

Gidycz, C. A., Hanson, K., & Layman, M. J. (1995). A prospective analysis of the relationships among sexual assault experiences. Psychology of Women Quarterly, 19, 5–29.

Hanna, F. J., & Ottens, A. J. (1995). The role of wisdom in psychotherapy. Journal of Psychotherapy Integration, 5, 195–219.

Hayden, J. (1994). HIV testing on campus: The next step. Journal of College Student Development, 35, 208–211.

Kanel, K. (1999). A guide to crisis intervention. Pacific Grove, CA: Brooks/Cole.

Kanin, E. J. (1985). Date rapists: Differential sexual socialization and relative deprivation. Archives of Sexual Behavior, 14, 219–231.

Katz, B. L. (1991). The psychological impact of stranger versus non-stranger rape on victims' recovery. In A. Parrot & L. Bechhofer (Eds.), *Acquaintance rape: The hidden crime* (pp. 251–283). New York: Wiley.

Kiesler, D. J. (1988). *Therapeutic metacommunication.* Palo Alto, CA: Consulting Psychologists Press.

King, J. E., & Cooley, E. L. (1995). Achievement orientation and the impostor phenomenon among college students. *Contemporary Educational Psychology, 20,* 304–312.

Koss, M. P., & Cleveland, H. H. (1996). Athletic participation, fraternity membership, and date rape. *Violence Against Women, 2,* 180–190.

Koss, M. P., Dinero, T. E., & Seibel, C. A. (1988). Stranger and acquaintance rape: Are there differences in the victims' experience? *Psychology of Women Quarterly, 12,* 1–24.

Koss, M. P., Gidycz, C. A., & Wisniewski, N. (1987). The scope of rape: Incidence and prevalence of sexual aggression and victimization in a national sample of higher education students. *Journal of Consulting and Clinical Psychology, 55,* 162–170.

Malamuth, N. M., Sockloskie, R. J., Koss, M. P., & Tanaka, J. S. (1991). Characteristics of aggressors against women: Testing a model using a national sample of college students. *Journal of Consulting and Clinical Psychology, 59,* 670–681.

Matthews, G., & Clance, P. R. (1985). Treatment of the impostor phenomenon in psychotherapy clients. *Psychotherapy in Private Practice, 3,* 71–81.

Miller, B. (1988). Date rape: Time for a new look at prevention. *Journal of College Student Development, 29,* 553–555.

Miller, D. G., & Kastberg, S. M. (1995). Of blue collar and ivory: Women from blue-collar backgrounds in higher education. *Roeper Review, 18,* 27–33.

Muehlenhard, C. L., & Linton, M. A. (1987). Date rape and sexual aggression in dating situations: Incidence and risk factors. *Journal of Counseling Psychology, 34,* 186–196.

Myer, R. A., & Ottens, A. J. (1994). Assessment for crisis intervention on college campuses. *Crisis Intervention, 1,* 31–46.

O'Malley, K., Wheeler, I., Murphy, J., O'Connell, J., & Waldo, M. (1990). Changes in level of psychopathology being treated at college and university counseling centers. *Journal of College Student Development, 31,* 464–465.

Ottens, A. J. (1984). *Coping with academic anxiety.* New York: Rosen.

Ottens, A. J., & Fisher-McCanne, L. (1990). Crisis intervention at the college campus counseling center. In A. R. Roberts (Ed.), *Crisis intervention handbook: Assessment, treatment, and response* (pp. 78–100). Belmont, CA: Wadsworth.

Ottens, A. J., & Hotelling, K. (Eds.) (In press). *Sexual violence on campus in the twenty-first century.* New York: Springer.

Petretic-Jackson, P., & Jackson, T. (1990). Assessment and crisis intervention with rape and incest victims: Strategies, techniques, and case illustrations. In A. R. Roberts (Ed.), *Crisis intervention hand-*

book: Assessment, treatment, and research (pp. 124–152). Belmont, CA: Wadsworth.

Roberts, A. R. (1990). An overview of crisis theory and crisis intervention. In A. R. Roberts (Ed.), Crisis intervention handbook: Assessment, treatment, and research (pp. 3–16). Belmont, CA: Wadsworth.

Roberts, A. R. (1996). Epidemiology and definitions of acute crisis in American society. In A. R. Roberts (Ed.), Crisis management and brief treatment: Theory, technique, and applications (pp. 16–33). Chicago: Nelson-Hall.

Schwartz, M. D., & DeKeseredy, W. S. (1997). Sexual assault on the college campus: The role of male peer support. Thousand Oaks, CA: Sage.

Sorensen, S. B., & Brown, V. B. (1990). Interpersonal violence and crisis intervention on the college campus. In H. L. Pruett & V. B. Brown (Eds.), Crisis intervention and prevention (pp. 57–66). New Directions for Student Services, No. 49. San Francisco: Jossey-Bass.

Sugarman, D. B., & Hotaling, G. T. (1991). Dating violence: A review of contextual and risk factors. In B. Levy (Ed.), Dating violence: Young women in danger (pp. 100–118). Seattle: Seal Press.

Thompson, T., Davis, H., & Davidson, J. (1998). Attributional and affective responses of impostors to academic success and failure outcomes. Personality and Individual Differences, 25, 381–396.

Topping, M. E., & Kimmel, E. B. (1985). The impostor phenomenon: Feeling phony. Academic Psychology Bulletin, 7, 213–226.

Zorza, J. (1998). Rohypnol and GHB: Terrifying date-rape drugs. Sexual Assault Report, 2, 17–30.

Zorza, J. (In press). Drug-facilitated rape. In A. J. Ottens & K. Hotelling (Eds.), Sexual violence on campus in the twenty-first century. New York: Springer.

III

CRISIS INTERVENTION AND
CRISIS PREVENTION WITH
VICTIMS OF VIOLENCE

8

A Comprehensive Model for Crisis Intervention With Battered Women and Their Children

ALBERT R. ROBERTS

BEVERLY SCHENKMAN ROBERTS

Case Scenarios

Do you know what some women get for their birthdays? A black eye, a punch in the ribs, or a few teeth knocked out. It's so frightening because it doesn't just happen on their birthday. It may be every month, every week, or even every day. It's so frightening because sometimes he abuses the kids, too. Or maybe she's pregnant and he kicks her in the stomach in the same spot where, just a few minutes ago, she felt the baby moving. It's so frightening because the woman doesn't know what to do. She feels so helpless. He's in control. She prays he'll come to his senses and stop. He never does. She prays he won't hurt their kids. He threatens to. She prays he won't kill her. He promises he will. (Haag, undated)

We were married 13 years. It was okay until the past 5 years and he started to hit me to hurt me. He was doing drugs. He was usually high or when he couldn't get drugs, he'd hit me cause he couldn't have it. We'd get in an argument because he'd want money and I'd say no and that's how it would start. He punched and kicked me. Usually I had a black eye and black and blue marks on my legs. He used to steal my money—he stole my Christmas money and my food stamps. He tried to say someone broke into the house, but I knew he had it.

My ex-husband drank every day, especially in the summer. He is very violent. I fear for my life that one day he will get me alone and kill me. He hated my little dog because I spoiled him. He would tell me that he was going to drop kick him (he only weighed 4 pounds). I had to give my dog away because I didn't want him to hurt it. I had to give up my family and friends for the same reason. He broke my nose without even thinking twice. He also tried to strangle me a couple of times and he didn't let go until I faked passing out. I've had to fake a blackout, and that is the only reason I am alive. For all he knew, I could have been dead when he left me lying there on the floor.

The description of the fear, anguish, and physical injuries to which battered women are repeatedly subjected comes from Al Roberts's research files. Case illustrations are included in this chapter to acquaint crisis intervenors, social workers, nurses, psychologists, and counselors with the painful history of the women they will be counseling and assisting. Increasingly, battered women are turning to emergency shelters, telephone crisis intervention services, mental health centers, and support groups for help. Recognition of the need for and actual establishment of crisis intervention services for victims of the battering syndrome has increased dramatically since the 1970s.

The most promising short-term interventions with battered women include 24-hour crisis hotlines, crisis-oriented support groups, shelters for battered women, and/or therapy. Although only a small number of research studies have been conducted on the effectiveness of different types of crisis services for battered women, one research article analyzing 12 outcome studies demonstrated positive outcomes. Tutty, Bidgood, and Rothery (1993) studied outcomes of 76 formerly battered women in Canada after completion of a 10 to 12-session support group. They found significant improvements in self-esteem, locus of control, and decreases in stress and physical abuse 6 months after treatment (Tutty, Bidgood, & Rothery, 1993). Gordon (1996) examined 12 outcome studies on the effectiveness of intervention by community social services, crisis hotlines, women's groups, police, clergy, physicians, psychotherapists, and lawyers. In summary, it seems that battered women consistently found crisis hotlines, women's groups, social workers, and psychotherapists to be very helpful. In sharp contrast, the battered women respondents reported that usually police, clergy, and lawyers are *not* helpful to different types of abused women (Gordon, 1996).

This chapter will examine the alarming prevalence of woman battering, risk factors and vulnerabilities, precursors to crisis episodes, and resilience and protective factors. In addition, the following types of crisis intervention programs will be discussed: early intervention by police-based crisis teams and victim assistance units; assessment and detection in the hospital emergency room; electronic technology to protect battered women in imminent danger; specific intervention techniques used by crisis hotlines and battered women's shelters; and short-term treatment for the victim's children. The chapter will also discuss the importance of referrals.

SCOPE OF THE PROBLEM

Woman battering is one of the most life-threatening, traumatic, and harmful public health and social problems in American society. Recent estimates indicate that each year approximately 8.7 million women have been victims of some form of assault by their partner (Roberts, 1998; Straus & Gelles, 1991; Tjaden & Thoennes, 1998). Partner violence continues to be the single greatest health threat to American women under the age of 50. On an annual basis, more women sustain injuries as a result of domestic violence than from the combined total of muggings and accidents (Nurius, Hilfrink, & Rafino, 1996).

Women who suffer the most severe injuries require treatment in hospital emergency rooms and hospital trauma centers. It is estimated that 35% of emergency room visits are made by women who need emergency medical care as a result of domestic violence–related injuries (Valentine, Roberts, & Burgess, 1998).

A study published in the *Journal of the American Medical Association* found that up to one in five pregnant women are abused by their partners during pregnancy, with prevalence rates ranging from 0.9 to 20.1% (Gazmararian et al., 1996). Battering during pregnancy endangers both the woman and the fetus, with some of the risks being "miscarriage, preterm labor, chorioamnionitis, low birth weight, fetomaternal hemorrhage, abruptio placentae, and in some cases fetal death or neonatal death" (Carlson & McNutt, 1998, p. 237).

The frequency and duration of violence range from women who are hit once or twice (and make a decision to end the relationship immediately) to women who remain in the relationship and are beaten with increasing frequency for an extended period, which may last for many years (Roberts & Burman, 1998). Petretic-Jackson and Jackson (1996) and Walker (1985) found a strong correlation between women who had suffered chronic abuse and the onset of bipolar disorder, anxiety disorder, posttraumatic stress disorder (PTSD), panic disorder, and/or depression with suicide ideation.

A telephone survey of 16,000 persons from across the nation (8,000 women and 8,000 men) provided research findings on the prevalence, incidence, and consequences of violence against women, including rape and physical assault (Tjaden & Thoennes, 1998). The researchers found that physical battering is widespread among American women of all racial and ethnic groups. The following are Tjaden and Thoennes's major findings:

52% of surveyed women said they were physically assaulted as a child by an adult caretaker and/or as an adult by any type of perpetrator.

1.9% of surveyed women said they were physically assaulted in the previous 12 months.

18% of women surveyed said they experienced a completed or attempted rape at some time in their life, and 0.3% said they experienced a completed or attempted rape in the previous 12 months.

Although there were only 7 emergency shelters for battered women in 1974 (Roberts, 1981), by 1998 there were more than 2,000 shelters and crisis intervention services coast-to-coast for battered women and their children (Roberts, 1998). Through crisis intervention, many women are able to regain control of their lives by identifying current options and goals and by working to attain those goals. The children of battered women may also be in crisis, but their plight has sometimes been overlooked as the domestic violence programs focused their efforts on emergency intervention for the women. The progressive programs now incorporate crisis intervention for children (as well as for the mothers) in the treatment plan.

Battered women are usually subjected to a prolonged pattern of abuse coupled with a recent severe attack; by the time the victim makes contact with a shelter, she is generally in need of both individual crisis intervention and a crisis-oriented support group. Abused women are subjected to an extended period of stress and trauma that results in a continual loss of energy. The woman is in a vulnerable position, and when a particularly severe beating takes place or when other factors occur (e.g., the abuser starting to hurt the children), the woman may be thrust into a state of crisis (Young, 1995).

Effective treatment for battered women and their children in crisis requires an understanding of crisis theory and the techniques of crisis intervention. According to Caplan (1964), Janosik (1984), and Roberts (1996a), a crisis state can occur rapidly when the following four things happen:

1. The victim experiences a precipitating or hazardous incident.
2. The incident is perceived by the woman as threatening to her or her children's safety, and as a result tension and distress intensify.
3. The battered woman attempts to resolve the situation by using customary coping methods and fails.
4. The emotional discomfort and turmoil worsen, and the victim feels that the pain or anguish is unbearable.

At this point of maximum discomfort, when the woman perceives the pain and torment as unbearable, she is in an active crisis state. During this time there is an opportunity for change and growth, and some women are mobilized to seek help from a 24-hour telephone crisis intervention service, the police, the hospital emergency room, or a shelter for battered women.

The emphasis in crisis assessment is on identifying the nature of the precipitating event and the woman's cognitive and affective reaction to it. The five most common precipitating events that lead battered women in crisis to seek the help of a domestic violence program are (a) an acute battering incident resulting in serious physical injury; (b) a major escalation in the degree of violence, for example, from shoving and slapping to attempted strangulation or stab wounds; (c) an impairment in the woman's hearing, sight, or thought process as a direct result of severe batterment; (d) a high-profile story in the news media about a woman who was brutally murdered by her partner after suffering in silence for many years; and (e) a serious abusive injury inflicted on the woman's child. Often the precipitating event is perceived by the woman in crisis as being the final incident, or "last straw," in a long history of violence (Edington, 1987; Podhorin, 1987; Roberts, 1998; Schiller-Ramirez, 1995).

Crisis intervention with battered women needs to be done in an orderly, structured, and humanistic manner. The process is the same for victims of other violent crimes, but it is particularly important to respond quickly to abused women because they may continue to be in danger as long as they remain in a place where the batterer can locate them. Crisis intervention activities can result in the woman either returning to her precrisis state or growing from the crisis intervention so that she learns new coping skills to use in the future (Roberts, 1998).

BATTERED WOMEN AT HIGH RISK OF CRISIS EPISODES

For some women, the effects of partner abuse can be short-term, with a quick recovery, while for others the result is chronic dysfunction and mental health disorders. Domestic violence researchers have found that among women who are battered for many years, those who receive the most severe forms of injury seem to have the highest risk for the following difficulties: nightmares and other sleep disturbances, reenactment of trauma, major depression, posttraumatic stress symptoms, substance abuse, self-destructive behavior, psychosexual dysfunction, and/or generalized anxiety disorder. Research studies indicate that, in general, these women's mental health problems were not present early in the relationship but developed as a result of the repeated acts of violence (Gleason, 1993; Woods & Campbell, 1993).

Posttraumatic stress disorder (PTSD) may occur when an individual perceives an event as life-threatening to herself or significant others. Characteristic features of PTSD identified in the clinical literature are as follows:

1. Integration of the traumatic experience by reexperiencing the traumatic event (through recurrent and/or intrusive thoughts, flashbacks, nightmares, or other intense reactions)
2. Management of subsequent stress (increased arousal and hypervigilance)

3. Facilitation of affective expression
4. Determination of the meaning of victimization (Petretic-Jackson & Jackson, 1996, p. 210)

As a result of one or more severe battering incidents, some battered women have had their cognitive schemas or mental maps altered. According to Valentine, under extreme duress, the battered woman's schema is imprinted strongly with a survival message that guides the victim even after the crisis is passed. Victims are then left with the chore of either assimilating that event into their previously existing schemas or altering their schemas to incorporate this terrifying event. She states that "PTSD symptoms consist of intrusive thoughts [nightmares], hypervigilance [i.e., startle responses], and avoidance [i.e., blunted affect to avert all reminders of the incident]" (see chapter 11, this volume).

Crisis intervention and time-limited treatment with battered women must be approached with empathy, sensitivity, and caution. When an abused woman is suffering from PTSD, if the crisis intervenor asks the woman to "reexperience" the violent event, the counselor may inadvertently precipitate a retraumatization rather than the intended therapeutic opportunity (Petretic-Jackson & Jackson, 1996). Before crisis intervention is initiated, it is critically important to create a safe, highly flexible, empowering environment where symptom relief strategies are emphasized. If avoidance, startle overreactions, and nightmares are the primary presenting problems, the crisis intervenor may well facilitate the narrative and storytelling process by utilizing experiential techniques, art therapy, poetry, photographs, and/or police reports.

Stress management techniques can build on the battered woman's inner strengths and potential for positive growth. Examples of these techniques are progressive relaxation, guided imagery, refocusing one's attention on external reality, good nutrition, developing a support system, and using "dosing"—"a technique in which attention is alternately shifted toward and away from the traumatic experience" (Petretic-Jackson & Jackson, 1996, p. 210). Many battered women seem to have developed very limited affective expression as a result of suppressing their emotions. In addition, because battered women generally suppress feelings of anger, they may suddenly express rage a year or two after leaving the batterer.

Many battered women who experienced three or more traumatic and severe battering incidents often take a long time to gain a sense of control of their environment. Their self-esteem, trust in men, and cognitive assumptions are often shattered. The survivor's low self-esteem, weak decision-making skills, intrusive thoughts, and flashbacks often result in a series of acute crisis episodes. The crisis intervenor or counselor needs to help the woman build trust while bolstering her self-esteem. This is done through modeling, reframing, stress inoculation, relaxation techniques, exercise, thought stopping, encouraging journal entries, solution-based therapy, and cognitive restructuring.

TRAUMATIC BATTERING EVENTS, LEGAL ACTION, MEDICAL INJURIES, AND SLEEP DISTURBANCES AS PRECURSORS TO CRISIS EPISODES

Several types of traumatic, life-threatening mental health and legal events or situations often can precipitate a crisis. These include:

- A battered woman sustaining a life-threatening injury (e.g., a concussion, multiple stab wounds, a miscarriage, or strangulation).
- A child being severely physically or psychologically harmed by the batterer.
- The victim obtains a restraining order or files for divorce, and her taking legal action enrages the batterer, resulting in stalking, terroristic threats, and/or a rapid escalation of the battering incidents.
- A battered woman encounters explicit kidnapping or terroristic death threats against herself, her children, and/or her elderly parents.
- The batterer has already made explicit death threats against the formerly battered woman, and he is soon to be released from prison or a residential drug treatment program.

In Roberts's (1996b) study of 210 battered women, the majority of the participants interviewed had experienced one or more severe beatings. The outcomes of these beatings were manifested in anxiety, depression, sleep disturbances, panic attacks, and intrusive thoughts. The following are illustrations of sleep disturbances:

Somebody chases me or is trying to kill me. I can't remember the last pleasant dream I had.

I have nightmares about him burning up the house. I keep dreaming that the kids and I were trapped in the house with flames all around us and we couldn't get out. I would see his face in the flames, point at us and laughing while we are crying and in pain.

I have the same nightmare a few times a week. I see this guy who looks like my former boyfriend (drug dealer who was shot 3 years ago by the Newark police). He is raising up out of the casket, and he said he loved me and is coming back to stab me to death so I can join him in hell. I wake up screaming, shaking, and sweating. A lot of times I can't fall asleep even though I'm mentally and physically exhausted. The next day at work I'm very jumpy and afraid to talk to any of the men in the office. When my supervisor asks me something, I get this flashback and am reminded of my nightmare and I start crying. I go into the ladies room sometimes for an hour and cry and cry, and then leave work early. I go home and try to calm down by smoking cigarettes and talking with my daughter.

In crisis intervention work with battered women, clinicians must be prepared to understand a range of potential precipitants and precursors. Crisis clinicians need to be aware of the aftermath of traumatic events, common triggering incidents, and precursors to crisis episodes in order to provide battered women with the most appropriate interventions.

RESILIENCE AND PROTECTIVE FACTORS

The previous section examined high-risk groups and trauma, sleep disturbances, and other precursors to crisis episodes. Those groups of individuals with preexisting risk factors and trauma histories have difficulty recovering. In sharp contrast, some abused women have significant inner strengths, also known as *resilience* and *protective factors*, that have been found to mediate and lessen the impact of stress related to battering. The most common protective factors include high self-esteem, a social support network, and cognitive coping skills. One of the most important components of maximizing a battered woman's recovery is accomplished through believing in the client and helping her to realize her strengths. Many battered women feel trapped, socially isolated, and overwhelmed by the physical and emotional pain they have endured. Crisis intervenors and counselors can help the woman to recognize alternative coping strategies.

During the past decade, a growing number of crisis intervenors, counselors, social workers, and psychologists have recognized that a strengths perspective that builds on the resilience of individuals is much more fruitful to helping clients grow and change in positive directions than the previous 50 years of emphasis on pathologizing the client (Saleebey, 1997). The strengths perspective of crisis intervention utilizes empowerment, resilience, healing and wholeness, collaboration, and suspension of disbelief. *Empowerment strategies* create opportunities for individuals and communities (Roberts & Burman, 1998). *Resilience* focuses on accelerating growth and identifying inner capabilities, knowledge, and personal insights. *Healing* refers to the ability of the body and mind to resist disease and chaos. The resilience literature incorporates a strong belief that individuals have self-righting tendencies and a spontaneous inclination toward healing and survival (Saleebey, 1997; Weil, 1995). *Collaboration* refers to clients, counselors, crisis intervenors, and family members all working together to help strengthen the client. *Suspension of disbelief* refers to the ending of pessimism and cynicism and the affirmation of belief, learned optimism, self-protective strategies, a sense of humor, and commitment to change.

An integrated approach to crisis intervention combines Roberts's (1996a) seven-step crisis intervention practice model with solution-based therapy. Gilbert Greene and Mo-Yee Lee, in chapter 2 of this book, provide a detailed discussion with several case applications of an integrated model of solution-based therapy. This practice model emphasizes building on and bolstering one's inner strengths, protective factors, latent coping skills, and positive attributes. It systematically reinforces the importance of realistic goal setting, identifying and explicating the positive exceptions in situations or behavior patterns, and the importance of the dream and miracle questions. We firmly believe that crisis intervention based on enhancing positive coping skills, rediscovering the exceptions and positive alternatives to crisis situations, building on and optimizing the client's bright spots and inner strengths, and seeking partial and full solutions will become common practice during the twenty-first century.

Tedeschi and Calhoun (1995) interviewed over 600 college students who had recently experienced significant stressful life events, including a parent's death, being the victim of a crime, or receiving an accidental injury. The goal of their research was to determine which personality factors might lead to personal growth when an individual is confronted with a crisis situation. The researchers identified the characteristics of extroversion, openness, agreeableness, conscientiousness, and having an "internal locus of control" as benefiting persons in crisis by allowing them to find some positive outcome connected to what might otherwise be viewed as a devastating circumstance. For instance, those who indicated growth from the traumatic experience were more likely to report that they had experienced positive change (i.e., developing a new area of interest, forming a new relationship, or enhancing one's spiritual beliefs).

Some battered women develop positive coping strategies, whereas others develop negative and potentially self-destructive coping strategies. Examples of positive coping strategies include using formal and informal social support networks, seeking informational support, and requesting help from a shelter for battered women. Examples of negative coping mechanisms are dependence on alcohol or drugs or suicide attempts.

Positive coping strategies help women to facilitate their own survival and expedited recovery. The core focus of Lazarus and Folkman's (1984) conceptualization and application of the coping process is based on how an individual makes an appraisal of the stressful event. Appraisal takes place when an individual experiences an event and determines that it is "excessive relative to resources." There are two levels of appraisal related to coping responses:

1. Primary appraisal is viewed as the first level, wherein a person evaluates whether the event has the potential to cause harm (i.e., physical injury), to instill fear, or to interfere with a goal. More specifically, the individ-

ual decides whether a particular situation is at risk. The outcome reflects the individual's assessment of the stressful life event and the significance of the event for that individual's well-being.

2. When the event is perceived as harmful or threatening, the individual
enters into secondary appraisal, wherein the available resources for
coping are examined. When a person is confronted with a circumstance
that is perceived as threatening or harmful, the person "enters into secondary appraisal" when she makes efforts to cope with the event (e.g.,
leaving the violent home immediately and living with a relative or at a
shelter). (Lazarus & Folkman, 1984)

Battered women in crisis who are contemplating leaving the violent relationship are confronted by both internal and external barriers. Recent legislation, policy reforms, and federal funding initiatives have resulted in increased funding for transitional housing, job training, and concrete services
for battered women. These societal and community-wide changes have empowered and improved the economic status of some battered women who
were trapped by poverty, limited welfare checks and food vouchers, no employment skills, a lack of affordable housing, and no affordable child care.
However, these policy changes and reforms are not enough.

As noted by Carlson (1997), the following four internal barriers often
keep the battered woman trapped in a recurring pattern of acute crisis episodes: "low self-esteem; shame and self-blame for the abuse; poor coping
skills; and passivity, depression, and learned helplessness" (p. 292). Carlson
(1997) proposed an intervention model grounded in both an ecological perspective and Lazarus and Folkman's (1984) stress and coping paradigm. This
practice model should be used by licensed mental health clinicians who are
also trained in domestic violence (Carlson, 1997). The intervention is summarized as follows:

- Practice orientation: nonjudgmental acceptance, confidentiality, and a
  belief in self-determination of the client
- Engagement and developing a collaborative relationship
- Assessment (based on Petretic-Jackson and Jackson [1996], as discussed
  earlier in this chapter)
- Intervention: development of a safety plan, increasing information, enhancement of coping, enhancement of problem-solving and decision-
  making skills, and reducing isolation by increasing social support

Unfortunately, although it is important to study the correlation between
coping methods in facilitating crisis resolution among battered women, there
is a dearth of research in this area. A thorough review of the research related
to crime victimization and the connection between cognitive appraisal, attributions, and coping mechanisms indicates no conclusive findings (Wyatt,
Notgrass, & Newcomb, 1990; Frieze & Bookwala, 1996; Frazier & Burnett,

1994; Johnson, 1997). Examples of specific strengths are high self-esteem, having a devoted mother, conscientious performance at work or a job training program, or having a social support network.

Much of the professional literature on this topic focuses on the cognitive resources individuals employ when coping with unexpected, stressful life events (Lazarus & Folkman, 1984; Folkman & Lazarus, 1985). Coping has been defined by Folkman (1984) as "cognitive and behavioral efforts to master, reduce, or tolerate the internal and/or external demands that are created by the stressful transaction" (p. 843). These demands include perceptions of potential loss and/or harm, at which time the individual evaluates choices for coping via problem-focused and emotion-focused strategies. Problem-focused strategies are based on the use of problem-solving and action plans, whereas emotion-focused strategies utilize the control of negative or distressing emotions.

CRISIS INTERVENTION BY POLICE-BASED CRISIS TEAMS AND VICTIM ASSISTANCE UNITS

Surveys of police departments around the United States indicate that approximately 80 to 90% of the police officers' time is spent on service calls, also known as order maintenance activities, for such incidents as assaults among family members, neighbor disputes, bar fights, traffic accidents, and individuals who are drunk and disorderly. The police may have the skills to intervene and resolve a dispute among neighbors, a bar fight, or a traffic accident, but they are rarely skilled in providing crisis intervention and follow-up counseling with victims of domestic violence (Roberts, 1996b, 1990).

In recognition of the large amount of time police spend responding to repeat family violence calls and their lack of clinical skills, a growing number of police departments have developed crisis intervention teams staffed by professional crisis clinicians and/or trained volunteers.

Victims often turn to their local city, county, or township police department when confronted with the unpredictable injuries or life-threatening danger posed by domestic violence. As a result of the *Thurman* case (in which a battered woman was awarded $2.3 million in her lawsuit against the Torrington, Connecticut, police department for its failure to protect her from her violent husband), more police departments have been responsive to calls from domestic violence victims. Police can respond quickly to domestic violence calls and can transport the victim to the local hospital emergency room or the battered women's shelter. In some cities, police receive backup from the crisis team, which arrives at the home or police department shortly after the police transport the victim to police headquarters. The first such crisis team began in 1975 at the Pima County District Attorney's Office in

Tucson, Arizona. The acceptance of and growing reliance on this program by the Tucson Police Department is revealed by the significantly increased number of police referrals to the crisis team—there were a total of 840 police referrals in 1977, compared with 4,734 referrals in 1984. It should be noted that these figures reflect referrals for all types of crime victims, but most referrals are for domestic violence cases. Since violence in the home constitutes a considerable percentage of police calls, abused women are frequent beneficiaries of this innovative system.

The following description of the program in Tucson will illustrate the intervention procedures utilized by victim assistance programs:

> The Pima County Victim Witness Program has received national recognition for providing immediate crisis intervention to battered women and other crime victims. It also has served as a model for similar programs in other cities. The program was initiated in 1975 with a grant from the Law Enforcement Assistance Administration (LEAA). The grant-funded program was so successful that, when the grant expired, city and county officials agreed to pay for its continuation. The crisis intervention staff uses two police vehicles (unmarked and radio equipped) to travel to the crime scene. The mobile crisis teams are on patrol every night between 6:00 P.M. and 3:00 A.M. At all other times they are contacted via a beeper system (Roberts, 1990).
>
> Domestic violence cases are potentially the most dangerous for the crisis counselors. The staff members work in pairs, generally in a team of a male and a female. They are given an intensive training program in which they are taught self-defense, escape driving, and how to use a police radio, as well as crisis intervention techniques.

During the mid-1980s through the 1990s, a small but growing number of police departments developed a program to provide immediate crisis counseling to victims of domestic violence, as well as victims of other violent crimes such as rape. The crisis intervention team provides the following services: crisis counseling, advocacy, transportation to and from medical centers and shelters, and referrals to social service agencies. The majority of clients, over the years, have been battered women.

The crisis intervention team staff are civilian employees, trained volunteers from the community, or clinical social workers (e.g., New York City collaborative programs between Victim Services and NYPD; Austin, Dallas, and Houston Police Departments; Plainfield, New Jersey, Police Department). A crisis team (always working in groups of two) is notified of a crisis situation via the police radio, and the crisis counselors usually meet the police at the crime scene. The police, after determining that the counselors will not be in danger, may leave the home. The clinicians utilize a basic crisis intervention model of assessing the situation, discussing the options, forming a plan of action, and aiding the victim in implementing the plan. The New York and Texas programs have between 3 and 18 full-time staff members and two to four graduate student interns each semester, as well as trained volunteer workers.

The programs are funded by city or state criminal justice grants, city or county general revenue grants, and federal Violence Against Women grants. Initially, all of the budgets came from a combination of state and city grants. In its first year of operation, the Houston crisis intervention program was budgeted at $159,000. The amount had increased to $351,000 by the program's third year of operation.

As of 1998, similar programs had been developed under the auspices of the police departments in many cities, including South Phoenix, Arizona; Santa Ana, San Diego, and Stockton, California; Indianapolis, Indiana; Detroit, Michigan; Omaha, Nebraska; Las Vegas, Nevada; East Windsor, Plainsboro, South Brunswick, and South River, New Jersey; Rochester, New York; Memphis, Tennessee; and Salt Lake City, Utah. However, there are still many communities that have not initiated this type of program. It is hoped that the success of these 24-hour crisis intervention programs will encourage other localities to establish a similar type of service.

VOCATIONAL TRAINING FOR BATTERED WOMEN

Thousands of battered women in large urban areas have been trapped in an intergenerational cycle of poverty, violence, and a dearth of marketable job skills. As part of President Clinton's welfare-to-work initiative, battered women's programs in some cities have developed job training programs specifically for women who were previously abused by their partner. For example, Victim Services in New York City initiated two innovative employment skills training programs. Victim Services' first welfare-to-work training program, Project RISE, began in New York City in late 1997 to help victims of domestic violence who have been recipients of welfare enter the workforce with good-paying jobs. Project RISE provides 6-month training programs to teach formerly battered women word processing computer skills (specifically, Microsoft Word and Excel). The second innovative program, Project Superwomen, assists domestic violence survivors to obtain nontraditional employment in blue-collar positions (which traditionally were held solely by men) that offer a stable income and benefits but do not require advanced training. The women receive 3 months of training to prepare them to work in building maintenance positions, which have the advantage of flexible hours and, often, rent-free housing. The women learn such skills as replacing broken locks; handling light plumbing repairs; and spackling, sanding, and painting apartment walls.

ASSESSMENT AND INTERVENTION
IN THE EMERGENCY ROOM

A visit to the emergency room may provide the initial opportunity for some victims to recognize the life-threatening nature of the violent relationship and to begin making important plans to change their situations. At a growing number of large hospitals in urban areas, crisis assessment and intervention are being provided to battered women by emergency room staff.

A recommended way for emergency rooms to handle detection and assessment of batterment is through an adult abuse protocol. Two of the pioneers in the development of these protocols are Karil Klingbeil and Vicky Boyd of Seattle, who in 1976 initiated plans for emergency room intervention with abused women. The social work department of the Harborview Medical Center in Seattle developed an adult abuse protocol that provides specific information on the assessment to be made by the involved staff—the triage nurse, the physician, and the crisis clinician. Using a protocol serves two purposes. First, it alerts the involved hospital staff to provide the appropriate clinical care; second, it documents the violent incident so that if the woman decides to file a legal complaint, "reliable, court-admissible evidence" (including photographs) is available (Klingbeil & Boyd, 1984).

Although this protocol was developed for use by emergency room crisis clinicians, it can easily be adapted for use by other health care personnel. The following case example describes how the adult abuse protocol has been successfully used.

Case Example

Mrs. J was admitted to the emergency room accompanied by her sister. This was the second visit within the month for Mrs. J and the emergency room triage nurse and social worker realized that her physical injuries were much more severe on this second visit. Mrs. J was crying, appeared frightened, and in spite of the pain, she constantly glanced over her shoulder. She indicated that her husband would follow her to the emergency room and that she feared for her life. The social worker immediately notified Security.

Mrs. J indicated that she just wanted to rest briefly and then leave through another entrance. She was four months pregnant and concerned about her unborn child. She reported that this had been the first time Mr. J had struck her in the abdomen. The social worker spent considerable time calming Mrs. J in order to obtain a history of the assaultive event. Consent for photography was obtained and Mrs. J indicated that she *would* press charges. "The attack on my child" seemed to be a turning point in her perception of the gravity of her situation, even though Mr. J had beaten her at least a dozen times over the previous two years.

While the social worker assisted in the history taking, a physician provided emergency medical care: several sutures over the right eye.

With Mrs. J's permission, an interview was conducted with her sister who agreed to let Mrs. J stay with her and also agreed to participate in the police reporting. When Mrs. J felt able, the social worker and sister helped her complete necessary forms for the police who had been called to the emergency room.

Although the physician had carefully explained the procedures and rationale to Mrs. J, the social worker repeated this information and also informed her of the lethality of the battering, tracing from her chart her last three emergency room visits. Mrs. J was quick to minimize the assaults but when the social worker showed her photographs from those visits, documenting bruises around her face and neck, she shook her head and said, "No more, not any more." Her sister provided excellent support and additional family members were on their way to the emergency room to be with Mrs. J. When the police arrived Mrs. J was able to give an accurate report of the day's events. . . . She realized there would be difficult decisions to make and readily accepted a follow-up counseling appointment for a Battered Women's group. (Klingbeil & Boyd, 1984, pp. 16–24)

It should be noted that all cases are not handled as easily as this one. The two aspects of Mrs. J's situation that led to a positive resolution were (a) the immediate involvement of emergency room staff and their discussion with the patient of her history and injuries, and (b) the availability of supportive relatives.

Before the woman leaves the emergency room, the crisis clinician should talk with her about whether to return home or to seek refuge with friends, with family, or at a shelter for abused women. The emergency room staff should be able to provide names and phone numbers of referral sources. It is helpful if the pertinent information is printed on a small business-size card (which is easy to tuck away in a pocket or purse) and given to all abuse victims, as well as to suspected victims (Klingbeil & Boyd, 1984). Even if a woman refuses to acknowledge that her current bruises are the result of batterment, she may decide to keep the card for future use.

Merely having an adult abuse protocol does not ensure that it will be used. A study conducted by Flaherty (1985) at four Philadelphia hospitals found that the protocol was used selectively, mainly for victims who volunteered that they had been battered. The medical staff thus ignored the opportunity to help batterment victims who were not able to volunteer the information. The researchers cited the following reasons for underutilization of the protocol:

1. Some physicians and nurses did not regard battering as a medical problem.
2. Some of the emergency room staff believed that it would be an invasion of privacy to ask a woman questions about how she was injured.
3. Many viewed completing the protocol as an additional burden when they were already overworked.

Of those medical personnel who did recognize batterment as a legitimate problem, the most frequently used intervention technique was the tear-off list of referral sources, which was printed at the bottom of the protocol.

There is a crucial difference between Flaherty et al.'s Philadelphia study and the procedures described previously by Klingbeil and Boyd (1984) in Seattle. The Philadelphia study requested the cooperation of nurses and physicians but did not involve medical crisis clinicians. In contrast, the Harborview Medical Center protocol was created and implemented by the hospital's social work department. It emphasized a multidisciplinary team approach, with the social workers taking the lead role in conducting screening and assessment, often talking to the victim while the physician provided medical treatment.

The information just presented would indicate that the involvement of medical social workers is advisable and perhaps necessary in successfully implementing a crisis assessment and intervention system with battered women in the hospital emergency room.

INTERVENTION TECHNIQUES USED BY TELEPHONE HOTLINES AND BATTERED WOMEN'S SHELTERS

Battered women in crisis may reach out for help in any of a number of ways. The initial contact is generally by telephone, making the phone a lifeline for many women. Violence often occurs late in the evening, on weekends, or on holidays, and shelter staff are usually available 24 hours a day to respond to a crisis call. But a woman in crisis who has just been brutally beaten probably does not know the name or phone number of the local shelter. A frequent scenario is that of a woman and her children hastily escaping from home late in the evening and fleeing to a neighbor's home to make an emergency call for help. Not having the number of the local shelter, these women generally contact the police, a toll-free statewide domestic violence hotline, or the city- or community-wide crisis hotline (which aids people in all types of crisis). If the woman contacts the community-wide hotline, there is generally a brief delay while the worker gathers some basic information and then gives the caller the phone number of the closest shelter. An alternative is for the crisis intervenor to take the caller's phone number and have the shelter worker call her back.

When a battered woman in crisis calls a hotline, it is essential that she be able to talk immediately to a trained crisis clinician—not be put on hold or confronted with an answering machine or voice mail. If she is not able to talk to a caring and knowledgeable crisis intervenor, she may just give up, and a valuable opportunity for intervening in the cycle of violence will have been lost. In these situations time is of the essence; if the violent male is still on the rampage, he is likely to search for her, thereby endangering not only his mate but the neighbor as well.

Hotline workers distinguish between a *crisis call*—one in which the woman is in imminent danger or has just been beaten—and other types of calls in which the individual is not in immediate danger but is anxious or distressed and is seeking information or someone to talk to. The overriding goal of crisis intervention is ensuring the safety of the woman and her children. To determine whether the call is a crisis call, the worker asks such questions as:

- Are you or your children in danger now?
- Is the abuser there now?
- Do you want me to call the police?
- Do you want to leave, and can you do so safely?
- Do you need medical attention?

Programs have different policies regarding transporting women who need refuge but have no way to get there. Although some shelters will send staff to pick up the woman at her home, it is more common for shelter policy to prohibit staff from doing so because of the possibility of the staff member being attacked by the abuser. In cities that have a crisis intervention team affiliated with the police department (e.g., New York City, or Plainsboro and East Windsor, New Jersey), the shelter staff can contact the police, who investigate the situation and radio for the victim advocate or crisis counselor to transport the victim and her children to the shelter. Many times the police themselves are prevailed upon to provide the transportation. Another alternative is for the victim advocate from the shelter to meet the battered woman at the local hospital emergency room.

Once the urgent issues pertaining to the woman's physical safety have been resolved, the crisis intervenor can begin to help the victim talk about her situation and discuss possible courses of action. Throughout this process it is important for the crisis intervenor to remember that he or she can present different alternatives, but the client must make her own final decisions in order to be empowered.

The following is a step-by-step guide to intervention with battered women (originally developed by Jones, 1968), which is included in the training manual prepared by the Abuse Counseling and Treatment (ACT) program in Fort Myers, Florida. It is referred to as the A-B-C process of crisis management—the A referring to "achieving contact," the B to "boiling down the problem," and the C to "coping with the problem."

A. Achieving contact
   1. Introduce yourself: name, role, and purpose.
   2. If a phone call, ask the client if she is safe and protected now.

3. Ask the client how she would like to be addressed: first name, sur-
name, or nickname; this helps the client regain control.
4. Collect client data; this breaks the ice and allows the client and
clinician to get to know each other and develop trust.
5. Ask the client if she has a clinician or if she is taking any medication.
6. Identify the client's feelings and ask for a perception check.
B. *Boiling down the problem*
1. Ask the client to describe briefly what has just happened.
2. Encourage the client to talk about the here and now.
3. Ask the client what is the most pressing problem.
4. Ask the client if it were not for said problems, would she feel better
right now.
5. Ask client if she has been confronted with a similar type of problem
before, and if so, how she handled it then. What worked and what
didn't?
6. Review with the client what you heard as the primary problem.
C. *Coping with the problem*
1. What does the client want to happen?
2. What is the most important need—the bottom line?
3. Explore what the client feels is the best solution.
4. Find out what the client is willing to do to meet her needs.
5. Help the client formulate a plan of action: resources, activities, time.
6. Arrange follow-up contact with the client.

Careful recruitment and thorough training of crisis intervention staff is
essential to a program's success. It is also necessary for an experienced clinician to be on call at all times for consultation in difficult cases. In addition
to knowing what to say, clinicians need to learn about the tone of voice and
attitude to be used while handling crisis calls. Crisis clinicians are advised to
speak in a steady, calm voice, to ask open-ended questions, and to refrain
from being judgmental.

A shelter's policies and procedures manual, should include guidelines for
crisis staff. For example, the ACT program in Fort Myers, Florida, has developed a 45-page training manual, which includes sections on shelter policies
and procedures, referral procedures, and background information on domestic violence that discusses both the victims and the abusers. The ACT manual
explains the wide variation in the emotional reactions of the women who
call for help. The client's speaking style may be "fast, slow, hesitant, loud,
barely audible, rambling, loss of words, [or] normal." Her emotional reaction may be "angry, highly upset, hysterical, withdrawn, laughing, calm, icy,
guilty, or a combination of these" (Houston, 1987, p. 5). No matter what
characteristics the caller exhibits, the crisis clinician's task is to try to help
the victim cope with the immediate situation. However, the guidelines also
advise crisis clinicians to avoid the pitfall of believing they need to provide
the caller with immediate, expert solutions to her problems. Crisis clinicians

should not subject themselves to guilt feelings if they cannot help an abused woman resolve her situation. If the clinician suspects child abuse or neglect, he or she is required to notify the supervisor and then report the suspected abuse to the appropriate agency (Houston, 1987).

Shelter staff are confronted with a dilemma when the caller is an abused woman who is under the influence of drugs or alcohol or who has psychiatric symptoms. Although such women are victims of batterment, they also have a significant problem which the staff are not trained to treat. Shelter policy generally requires crisis intervenors to screen out battered women who are under the influence of alcohol or drugs, but there are exceptions. At Womanspace (in central New Jersey), women with drug or alcohol problems are accepted provided they are simultaneously enrolled in a drug or alcohol treatment program (Hart, 1999). Likewise, it is the crisis clinician's responsibility to determine whether a woman's behavior is excessively irrational or bizarre or whether she is likely to be a danger to herself or others. If a woman is suspected of having psychiatric problems, she is generally referred to the psychiatric screening unit of a local hospital or to a mental health center for an evaluation.

TELEPHONE LOG

Battered women's shelters usually maintain a written record of all phone calls, whether or not they are crisis calls. In addition to seeking such routine information as name, address, phone number, marital status, and ages of children, the form may include the following: (a) the questions "Are you in immediate danger?" "Do you want me to call the police?" and "How did you get our number?"; (b) action taken by the crisis clinician; and (c) follow-up action (Hart, 1999). Shelters, which are often overcrowded, may also have a section of the form on which the counselor can indicate whether the family is able to be housed immediately, is to be referred to another shelter or safe home, or needs to be put on a waiting list.

Womanspace developed a one-page telephone log form, which on the front asks many of the questions just listed, and on the reverse side contains further screening questions and an explanation of their shelter's policies. An example is the following printed statement, which explains the program's policy on weapons (Hart, 1999):

We do not allow weapons in the shelter.
We ask that you not bring a weapon or anything that may be used as a weapon with you.
Do you own a weapon?
If yes, do you agree to let us keep it in a safe place for you?

The advantage of printing this and other procedural statements on every telephone form is to ensure that all crisis workers impart the same basic information. At the bottom of each form is a list of nine of the most frequently used telephone numbers, including those of three area police departments. The advantage of having these numbers on every form is that during a crisis, they are always readily available, and valuable time is not lost searching for them.

ART THERAPY

Art therapy has been used effectively with women as well as children who have been subjected to domestic violence. As part of a comprehensive treatment approach in shelters for battered women and their children, art therapy can help victims (including young children) communicate their painful experiences in a nonverbal manner that is less threatening than traditional talk therapy. The goal of art therapy is to deal with the violence that took place, while also empowering the mother and enhancing her parenting skills. It is helpful in initiating the healing process for the mother and her children to have the opportunity to communicate what has occurred through their drawings (Riley, 1994).

Art therapy is also helpful when working with young children who have limited verbal ability. The following illustration shows how art therapy was used in a family session with a battered 23-year-old mother and her 4-year-old son:

> Although this child was not able to draw complete figures and fully describe the reason that brought him to the shelter, he was able to tell a story about the images he created. He said that the figure on the upper right was sneaking up on the smaller round circle directly to the left of it, which he identified as a "rock star." He said that the first figure bit the rock star in the leg. This very young boy was able to articulate the same story theme that his mother expressed in more detail. His mother explained through her picture that the four-year-old had bitten the abuser's leg when the abuser last attacked the mother. (McGloughlin, 1999, p. 53)

INDIVIDUALIZED TREATMENT FOR CHILDREN

Battered women who seek temporary shelter to escape from the violence at home generally have children who come to the shelter with them. The children often feel confused, afraid, and angry. They miss their father and do not know if or when they will see him again. It is not uncommon for children to be misinformed or uninformed about the reason they were suddenly uprooted from their home, leaving their personal possessions, friends, and school to stay at a crowded shelter. Similarly, the children may not realize that all of the other children have come to the shelter for the same reason.

Moreover, large numbers of these children have at one time or another also been victims of physical abuse. The 1986 Annual Report from the Family Violence Center in Green Bay, Wisconsin, provided data on child abuse committed by the batterer. The center found that close to half (73) of the 148 abusers of the women had on one or more occasions also beaten their children (Prelipp, 1987).

The following is a true story written by Lisa, a 10-year-old girl who came to a shelter after her father's violent attack on her mother.

My Life, by Lisa

One day around two months ago my mom and dad got into a fight. First, my mom and I come home from the mall. We had a really nice time there. But, when we came home our nice time got to be terrible. I knew they were going to get into a fight so I went into my bedroom and did my homework. I knew he was going to talk to her about something, but I didn't know what. Then I heard my mom start screaming and I went to the door and asked what was wrong. My dad said, "Oh, nothing is wrong. Go do your homework." But I knew something was wrong so I went and prayed to God. My dad was really mean that night. I hated him so bad. My mom did not deserve to get hurt. I love her more than anything else in the entire world. Then I heard my mom scream something but I didn't understand what she said because my dad covered her mouth with his hand. Afterward she told me she said call the cops. Anyway, I went back to the door by the bedroom and told my mom I needed help on my homework, but I didn't. I just wanted my mom to come out of the bedroom because I was afraid. Then they both came out. And I hugged my mom and went to bed. Then my dad started to strangle my mom. So I went out and told my dad to stop. He told me to go back to the bedroom and go to sleep. So, I did. But I was so stupid. Then I heard my mom screaming. So I went back into the living room and he was kicking my mom. He wouldn't stop, he kept kicking her in her arm and legs. I told him to stop. He told me to go back to bed but I said, No! Then he took his guitar and was gonna hit her over the head. But I went on top of my mother. He told me to get off. But I said, No. So he put down the guitar, then he got her ice for her arm. Then I went to sleep crying. The next morning I didn't go to school and she didn't go to work. Then he called up the house and talked to her for a while. He threatened to kill her. So we left to go to the shelter. And here I am *now*. (Arbour Disabuse, 1986).

This girl was fortunate in that her mother brought her to the Jersey Battered Women's Service in northern New Jersey, which has a carefully developed counseling program for battered mothers and their children. Sadly, however, there are still a number of shelters that offer only basic child care services; they do not provide the art therapy and crisis counseling needed to help children deal with the turmoil of recent events (Alessi & Hearn, 1998).

Nevertheless, innovative techniques for helping children have been incorporated into the programs of the more progressive shelters. St. Martha's Hall, a shelter in St. Louis, Missouri, provides counseling for the children, and also requires mothers to participate in parenting classes and to meet with the coordinator of the children's program about establishing family goals and meeting the child's individual needs. The program also provides opportunities for mother and child to participate jointly in relaxing recreational activities (Schiller-Ramirez, 1995).

Two other types of intervention—coloring books and groups for children—are used at some shelters.

Coloring Books as Part of an Individualized Treatment Approach

Some shelters utilize specially designed coloring books that discuss domestic violence in terms children can understand. Laura Prato of the Jersey Battered Women's Service in Morristown, New Jersey, has created two coloring books (Prato, undated), one for children aged 3 to 5 entitled *What Is a Shelter?* and another for 6- to 11-year-olds called *Let's Talk It Over*. In addition to the children's books, Prato has written two manuals for shelter workers that serve as a discussion guide for counselors. The books contain realistic, sensitive illustrations that depict the confused, sad, and angry emotions the children are feeling. They are illustrated in black and white so that the children can color the pictures if they wish. Funding for preparation and printing of the books and manuals came from the New Jersey Division of Youth and Family Services. The purpose of the coloring books and the way in which they are to be used are explained in the introduction to the counselors' manuals. The manuals state that the books are used as part of the intake and orientation process for all children who stay at the shelter. The stated objectives of the books are as follows:

- To provide assurances of the child's continued care and safety
- To encourage children to identify and express their feelings
- To provide information needed for children to understand what is happening in their families.
- To provide information that will improve each child's ability to adapt to the shelter setting
- To begin to assess the individual child's needs and concerns

The clinicians' manuals stress the importance of how the book is presented to the child, as shown in the following passage:

The process surrounding the use of the orientation books is extremely important. It is likely to be the initial contact between the counselor and the newly arrived family and one that will set the tone for future interactions. Consistent with the JBWS Children's Program philosophy, this initial meeting communicates respect for mother and child and acceptance of their feelings. (Prato, undated)

Before meeting with the child, the clinician meets privately with the mother to show her the book, explain its purpose, and ask for her permission to read the book to her child. The clinicians are advised to read any available intake information prior to meeting with the child so that they are better able to "anticipate the individual child's special concerns and place the child's responses in a meaningful context" (Prato, undated). The books have been prepared in a way that encourages the child's active participation. Throughout both books there are several places where the child can write his or her thoughts on the page. For example, one of the pages in *Let's Talk It Over* focuses on a child staying at a shelter who misses her father. The caption under the picture states:

Many children at the shelter think a lot about their fathers, and that's okay. You may not see your father for a while until everyone in your family has a chance to think about things carefully. The little girl in the picture is wondering about her father.... What questions do you think she is asking?

There is a place on that page for the child's response to the question. The response could be written by the child or dictated to the counselor, who would write it in the book. On the next page is a large blank space and a caption that reads, "You may use this page to draw a picture of your father." Books such as those developed by the Jersey Battered Women's Service are very appropriate in helping children cope with the crisis that has led to their staying at the shelter.

GROUP TREATMENT FOR CHILDREN

Another way to help children cope is through therapeutic groups such as the approach developed at Haven House, a shelter for battered women and their children in Buffalo, New York. Alessi and Hearn (1998) initiated the group approach when they observed the maladaptive ways in which the children at the shelter reacted to the crisis they were experiencing. The children tended to be aggressive and attempted to resolve problems through hitting. They had considerable anxiety, "biting their fingernails, pulling their hair, and somaticizing feelings as manifested by complaints of headaches and 'tight' stomachs" (Alessi & Hearn, 1998, p. 163). They had ambivalent feelings toward their fathers, loving them as well as hating them.

The two group leaders established a six-session treatment program for children ages 8 to 16 focusing on the following topics: "(1) the identification and expression of feelings; (2) violence; (3) unhealthy ways to solve problems; (4) healthy ways to solve problems; (5) sex, love and sexuality; and (6) termination and saying goodbye" (Alessi & Hearn, 1998, p. 167). To provide an indication of the scope of the group sessions, the following summarizes the content of the session on violence.

The purpose of the session on violence is to give children an opportunity to explore and express feelings about the violence in their families and how it has affected them. This helps children break down their denial and minimization of the problem. It also gives them a chance to learn that other families have similar problems and that many families do not. The following questions are presented to each of the children for reflection and discussion:

1. Why did you come to Haven House?
2. Do you think it's right for a man to hit a woman or a woman to hit a man, and why?
3. Do you think it's right for a parent to hit a child, and why?
4. How do you think you've been affected by the violence in your family?
5. Do you think you'll grow up to be violent or accept violence in intimate relationships?

The children are always given homework to keep the session alive between meetings. For example, after the discussion on violence, they are asked to develop a minidrama on family violence to be presented the next week. Following the session on healthy problem solving, they are asked to prepare a list of healthy ways of coping with their problems (Alessi & Hearn, 1998).

TECHNOLOGY TO PROTECT BATTERED WOMEN

During the 1990s, some battered women in imminent danger seem to have benefited from different types of technology, including alarm/security systems; panic alarms in conjunction with electronic bracelets; cell phones preprogrammed to 911 for an emergency police response; and instant cameras that provide an immediate photographic record documenting the assault and battery.

A few corporations, notably B.I., Inc., T.L.P. Technologies, Inc., ADT Security, and Transcience, have developed electronic monitors to protect women from domestic abuse. T.L.P. Technologies created an alarm system that is fully operational "even when the phone lines are down and when there is no electrical power" (Roberts, 1996c, p. 93). Law enforcement officers install the system in the abused woman's residence. The system includes a radio transmitter with a battery backup, a remote panic or motion-detector device, and an antenna. When the woman is in danger, she transmits an alarm directly to the police radio channel, unlike with other systems, in which a private security company serves as an intermediary (Roberts, 1996c).

ADT established the AWARE Program, which stands for Abused Women's Active Response Emergency Program, in 1992; by 1997 the program was operational in 150 cities across the United States. The women who participate in this program are selected by prosecutors, law enforcement officials, and shelter directors, and they receive an electronic emergency pendant, worn around the neck, donated by ADT. If the batterer is endangering the woman at her home, she activates the pendant, sending a silent alarm to ADT, which notifies the police to respond to the emergency alarm. Each city police department, in collaboration with the prosecutor's office, establishes its own criteria for participation in the AWARE Program, but typically all women who receive the pendant must "(1) be in imminent danger, (2) have a restraining order against the abuser and (3) be willing to prosecute the abuser and testify against him in a court of law", if he is apprehended as a result of the use of the ADT security system" (ADT, 1999). Through the AWARE Program, ADT installs a security system at the woman's residence, and each woman receives a pendant that is operational within a radius of 100 feet from her home system. (Whenever the woman is more than 100 feet from her home, the pendant does not work; therefore, this system offers excellent protection in the home but not at work or other community locations.)

In addition to the ADT pendant system, a number of prosecutors' offices and battered women's shelters have made arrangements with mobile phone companies to provide abused women with preprogrammed cell phones, so that they can press one button to be automatically connected to the 911 police emergency system. This offers women protection when they are away from home. Although no system is foolproof, these electronic devices provide battered women with increased security.

It is the high cost of electronic devices that has prevented *all* battered women who are in danger from having access to enhanced protection through the latest technology. Because of funding limitations (and the fact that the women are generally not financially able to purchase expensive equipment on their own), criminal justice agencies and battered women's shelters are forced to allocate these scarce resources to women whom they determine are at the highest risk for a life-threatening assault. Usually, these devices are reserved for women who are living apart from the batterer and who have obtained a restraining order (also known as an order of protection) from the court. Local battered women's shelters, in cooperation with law enforcement agencies, may be able to contact manufacturers directly and discuss the possibility of donations of some equipment, or a reduced cost if bulk purchases are made. Statewide and community-wide domestic violence coalitions may also target their fund-raising activities toward the acquisition of these electronic devices.

It is vitally important that battered women receive both short-term emergency assistance and long-term security services. Electronic pendants and other electronic technology should be initiated widely to protect the safety of thousands of women who have been severely battered, who have left the violent relationship, and who are still fearful that an abuser will return to harm her again. Funding for these devices should be provided by government agencies and corporate sponsors. Research studies should be conducted to learn which emergency electronic devices provide the most protection for women who have been battered, as well as the drawbacks to particular devices (Roberts, 1996c).

High-intensity Polaroid cameras are being used by police departments and hospital emergency rooms to document the injuries perpetrated by the batterer. Photos that carefully document the woman's injuries are extremely valuable when the case goes to court and may serve to prevent future, more lethal, assaults either because the batterer will be sent to prison on the basis of the indisputable evidence documented in the photographs or because the judge will issue a harsh warning of a prison sentence if he ever assaults the woman again.

Some police officers carry the Spectra instant point-and-shoot camera with them on domestic violence calls, to make a photographic record of the injuries as well as the overall scene at the home (e.g., a knife or gun on the table; children disheveled and crying; damage to doors, walls, or furniture due to the batterer's rampage; a phone cord ripped out of the wall). The advantage of using an instant camera is that the officers can be certain they have accurately photographed the injuries and the disarray at home before leaving the scene.

Similarly, emergency room staff are using these cameras when examining women who admit to being abused or are suspected of being a victim of abuse. Physicians, nurses, or social workers employed in the emergency room are often the first to see the woman following a severe assault. Some abused women with severe injuries go straight to the emergency room without contacting the police. The significant role of medical personnel in identifying victims of domestic violence cannot be overemphasized. Dr. Elaine Alpert, of the Boston University School of Medicine, has stated the importance of hospital personnel taking instant photos of the battered woman's injuries:

> Often, the image, taken on-the-spot, may serve as the only visible evidence that violence has taken place. Cigarette burns, scratches, welts, bite marks, bruises and cuts heal and disappear. But the photo reveals, conclusively, that abuse did take place—and can serve as a crucial piece of incriminating

evidence in civil or criminal proceedings against the batterer. (Poremba, 1997, p. 7)

REFERRAL

Knowledge of referral sources is essential when intervening on behalf of abused women in crisis situations. It is just as important for the police, hospitals, and human service agencies to know about and refer to programs helping battered women and their children as it is for staff at domestic violence treatment programs to refer clients to appropriate community resources.

It is frequently determined that the battered woman needs a variety of services, such as job training and placement, low-cost transitional housing, day care, and ongoing counseling; therefore, referral should be made to the appropriate service providers. In its 1995 year-end report, St. Martha's Hall in St. Louis itemized the agencies to which its clients had been referred (Schiller-Ramirez, 1995). Most women were referred to three or more agencies, and several clients were given nine or more referrals, depending on their individual needs. The most frequently used referral sources were as follows:

Legal aid
Medical care
Careers for Homemakers
Job bank
Day care programs
Women in Need (WIN), long-term housing for single women
Alcoholics Anonymous
Women's Self-Help Center, providing counseling and support groups
St. Pat's, a Catholic social service agency that finds low-cost housing and
    provides classes in budgeting money and other life skills

Examples of other, less frequently used, referral sources were

A shelter in another state	Dental care
Alateen	GED program
Al Anon	Crisis nursery
Literacy Council	Victim Services
Big Brothers	Red Cross

There are two ways in which programs providing crisis intervention services can facilitate the referral process: (a) by publicizing their services to the population at large and to other service providers, and (b) by becoming knowledgeable about community services needed by their clients and in some instances accompanying them to the appropriate agencies.

Publicize the program through the following methods:

1. Print brochures that describe the program's services, and have business cards that provide the program's name and phone number. These materials should be made available in large quantity to police officers, emergency room staff, and other potential sources of referral to the program.
2. Participate in interdisciplinary workshops and seminars on family violence so that the program can become widely known. In addition, this enables the staff to learn about appropriate programs to which their clients can be referred.
3. Attend in-service training programs for police officers, countywide hotline staff, emergency room staff, and others to discuss referral of abused women and to resolve any problems in the referral process which may have occurred.
4. Alert the public through newspaper articles and public service announcements on radio and television, with the program's phone number prominently mentioned.

Become familiar with community resources: Information for crisis clinicians on appropriate referral sources should be available in several ways:

1. The phone number of the most urgently needed agencies—such as the police, victim assistance program, drug/alcohol treatment programs, and psychiatric screening unit—should be readily available, preferably printed on each intake sheet or telephone log form.
2. The program's training manual should contain a section on the most frequently used referral sources. For example, the manual of the ACT program in Fort Myers, Florida, contains eight pages of often-used referral sources, which list the address, phone number, office hours, and services provided for each source.
3. Most major metropolitan areas have a comprehensive resource guide (published by the local United Way or an affiliate such as Call for Action) that provides a comprehensive listing of all of the community services in that area. All programs serving abused women and their children should have a copy of and be familiar with their community's resources handbook.

The way in which referrals are made is extremely important, since it may affect the outcome. All too often, victims in crisis do not follow through in making the initial contact with the referral agency. Clinicians and advocates at St. Martha's Hall and other shelters provide support by accompanying the client to the agency in order to demonstrate how to obtain services. This is viewed as a positive alternative to the often intimidating and frustrating experience encountered by women who are given a referral but are expected to fend for themselves.

SUMMARY AND CONCLUSION

A number of important issues and techniques relating to crisis intervention with battered women and their children have been examined in this chapter. Specific methods for crisis intervention in different settings have also been discussed. As increased numbers of women in acute crisis seek help, crisis clinicians and victim advocates must be prepared to respond without delay. Crisis intervention for battered women and their children may do much to alleviate the emotional distress and anguish experienced by those exposed to the trauma of domestic violence. Because of their experience and specialized training, crisis clinicians and medical social workers can play a vital role in assisting women and children in crisis.

Law enforcement officers, victim advocates, hospital emergency room staff, and clinicians at citywide crisis lines and battered women's shelters often come in contact with abused women who are experiencing a crisis. Effective crisis intervention requires an understanding by these service providers of the value and methods of crisis intervention, as well as the community resources to which referrals should be made. Battered women are often motivated to change their lifestyle only during the crisis or postcrisis period. Therefore, it is important for service providers at community agencies to offer immediate assistance to battered women in crisis. With an estimated 8 million couples involved in battering episodes annually, policy makers and program developers should give priority to expanding urgently needed crisis-oriented and follow-up services for battered women and their children.

REFERENCES

ADT (1999). Aware program brochure. Washington, D.C.: ADT is a Tyco International Company.

Alessi, J. J., & Hearn, K. (1998). Group treatment of children in shelters. In A. R. Roberts (Ed.), *Battered women and their families* (2nd ed., pp. 159–173). New York: Springer.

Arbour, D. (1986, December). *Disabuse Newsletter*, p. 4. Morristown, NJ: Jersey Battered Women's Service.

Arbour, D. (1987, February 12). Director, Jersey Battered Women's Shelter, Morristown, NJ. Personal communication.

Caplan, G. (1964). *Principles of preventive psychiatry*. New York: Basic Books.

Carlson, B. E. (1997). A stress and coping approach to intervention with abused women. *Family Relations, 46*, 291–298.

Carlson, B. E. & McNutt, L. (1998). Intimate partner violence: Intervention in primary health care settings. In A. R. Roberts (Ed.), *Battered women and their families* (2nd ed., pp. 230–270). New York: Springer.

Edington, L. (1987, February 19). Executive Director, *Sojourner,* Indianapolis, IN. Personal communication.

Flaherty, E. W. (1985, February). *Identification and intervention with battered women in the hospital emergency department: Final report.* Philadelphia: Philadelphia Health Management Corp.

Folkman, S. (1984). Personal control, and stress and coping proceses: A theoretical analysis. *Journal of Personality and Social Psychology, 46,* 839–852.

Folkman, S., & Lazarus, R. S. (1985). If it changes it must be a process: Study of emotion and coping during three stages of college examination. *Journal of Personality and Social Psychology, 48,* 150–170.

Frazier, P. A. & Burnett, J. W. (1994). Immediate coping strategies among rape victims. *Journal of Counseling and Development, 72,* 633–639.

Frieze, I., & Bookwala, J. (1996). Coping with unusual stressors: Criminal victimization. In M. Zeidner et al. (Eds.), *Handbook of coping: Theory, research and applications* (pp. 303–321). New York: Wiley.

Gazmararian, J. A., Laxorick, S., Spitz, A. M., Ballard, T. J., Saltzman, L. E., & Marks, J. S. (1996). Prevalence of violence against pregnant women. *Journal of the American Medical Association, 275,* 1915–1920.

Gleason, W. J. (1993). Mental disorders in battered women: An empiri-cal study. *Violence and Victims, 8,* 53–68.

Gordon, J. (1996). Community services available to abused women in crisis: A review of perceived usefulness and efficacy. *Journal of Family Violence. 11(4),* 315–329.

Greene, G. J. & Lee, M. (1996). Client strengths and crisis intervention: A solution focused approach. *Crisis Intervention and Time-Limited Treatment, 3(1),* 43–63.

Haag, R. (Undated). The birthday letter. In S. A. Prelipp (Ed.), *Family Violence Center, Inc. Training Manual.* Green Bay, WI: mimeographed.

Hart, P. (June, 1999). Executive Director, Womanspace, Lawrenceville, NJ. Personal communication.

Houston, S. (1987). *Abuse Counseling and Treatment, Inc. (ACT) Manual.* Fort Myers, FL: ACT.

Janosik, E. H. (1984). *Crisis counseling.* Belmont, CA: Wadsworth Publishers

Johnson, K. (1997). Professional help and crime victims. *Social Service Review, 71,* 89–109.

Jones, W. A. (1968). The A-B-C method of crisis management. *Mental Hygiene, 52,* 87–89.

Klingbeil, K. S., & Boyd, V. D. (1984). Emergency room intervention: Detection, assessment and treatment. In A. R. Roberts (Ed.), *Battered women and their families: Intervention strategies and treatment programs* (pp. 7–32). New York: Springer.

Lazarus, R. S. & Folkman, S. (1984). *Stress, appraisal and coping.* New York: Springer.

McGloughlin, M. (May, 1999). Art therapy with battered women and their children. M.A. thesis, Eastern

Virginia Medical School, Norfolk, Virginia

Nurius, P., Hilfrink, M., & Rafino, R. (1996). The single greatest health threat to women: Their partners. In P. Raffoul and C. A. McNeece (Eds.), *Future issues in social work practice* (pp. 159–171). Boston: Allyn and Bacon.

Petretic-Jackson, P., & Jackson, T. (1996). Mental health interventions with battered women. In A. R. Roberts (Ed.), *Helping battered women: New perspectives and remedies* (pp. 188–221). New York: Oxford University Press.

Podhorin, R. (1987, February 12). Director, Womanspace, Inc., Lawrenceville, NJ. Personal communication.

Poremba, B. (Ed.). (Spring 1997). Instant evidence: Break the cycle of family violence. Cambridge, MA: Polaroid Corporation.

Prato, L. (Undated). *What Is a Shelter?; Let's Talk It Over; What Is a Shelter? A ShelterWorker's Manual; Let's Talk It Over: A Shelter Worker's Manual*. Morristown, NJ: Jersey Battered Women's Service.

Prelipp, S. (1987, February 13). Director, Family Violence Center, Green Bay, WI. Personal communication.

Riley, S. (1994). *Integrative approaches to family art therapy*. Chicago: Magnolia Street Publishers.

Roberts, A. R. (1981). *Sheltering battered women*. New York: Springer.

Roberts, A. R. (1988). Crisis intervention: A practical guide to immediate help for victim families. In A. Horton & J. Williamson (Eds.), *Abuse and religion* (pp. 6066). Lexington, MA: D. C. Heath.

Roberts, A. R. (1990). *Helping crime victims*. Thousand Oaks, CA: Sage.

Roberts, A. R. (1996a). Epidemiology and definitions of acute crisis in American society. In A. R. Roberts (Ed.). *Crisis management and brief treatment: Theory, technique and applications* (pp. 16–33). Chicago: Nelson-Hall.

Roberts, A. R. (1996b). A comparative analysis of incarcerated battered women and a community sample of battered women. In A. R. Roberts (Ed.), *Helping battered women: New perspective and remedies* (pp. 31–43). New York: Oxford University Press.

Roberts, A. R. (1996c). Police responses to battered women. In A. R. Roberts (Ed.), *Helping battered women* (pp. 85–95). New York: Oxford University Press.

Roberts, A. R. (Ed.). (1998). *Battered women and their families* (2nd ed.). New York: Springer.

Roberts, A. R. & Burman, S. (1998). Crisis intervention and cognitive problem-solving therapy with battered women: A national survey and practice model. In A. R. Roberts (Ed.), *Battered women and their families: intervention strategies and treatment programs* (2nd ed., pp 3–28). New York: Springer.

Saleebey, D. (1997). *The strengths perspective in social work practice* (2nd ed.). White Plains, NY: Longman.

Schiller-Ramirez, M. (1995). *St. Martha's Hall year end report 1994*. St. Louis, MO: St. Martha's Hall.

Straus, M., & Gelles, R. (1991). *Physical violence in American families*. New Brunswick, NJ: Transaction Books.

Tedeschi, R. G. & Calhoun, L. G. (1995). *Trauma and transformation growing in the aftermath of suffering*. Thousand Oaks, CA: Sage.

Tjaden, P., & Thoennes, N. (1998). Battering in America: Findings from the National Violence against Women Survey. *Research in Brief* (60–66). Washington, DC: National Institute of Justice, U.S. Department of Justice.

Tutty, L., Bidgood, B. and Rothery, M. (1993). Support groups for battered women: Research on their efficacy. *Journal of Family Violence, 8*, 325–343.

Valentine, P. V., Roberts, A. R., & Burgess, A. W. (1998). The stress-crisis continuum: Its application to domestic violence. In A. R. Roberts (Ed.), *Battered women and their families* (2nd ed., pp. 29–57). New York: Springer.

Walker, L. E. (1985). Psychological impact of the criminalization of domestic violence on victims. *Victimology: An International Journal, 10*, 281–300.

Weil, A. (1995). *Spontaneous healing*. New York: Knopf.

Woods, S. J. & Campbell, J. C. (1993). Posttraumatic stress in battered women: Does the diagnosis fit? *Issues in Mental Health Nursing, 14*, 173–186.

Wyatt, G. E., Notgrass, C. M., & Newcomb, M. (1990). Internal and external mediators of women's rape experiences, *Psychology of Women Quarterly, 14*, 153–176.

Young, M. A. (1995). Crisis response teams in the aftermath of disasters. In A. R. Roberts (Ed.). *Crisis intervention and time-limited cognitive treatment* (pp. 151–187). Thousand Oaks, CA: Sage.

9

School Crisis Intervention, Crisis Prevention, and Crisis Response

SCOTT NEWGASS
DAVID J. SCHONFELD

Vignette 1

A fourth-grade boy is fatally wounded by his cousin while playing with a gun that they find at home. Uncomfortable with addressing the child's death, the school administrators decide not to discuss it with the boy's classmates until after finding someone who can advise them on how to handle such a situation. Several days later, they identify a consultant who can visit the class.

Over the phone, they request that the consultant meet during the upcoming visit with the student who had pulled the trigger to advise them on whether referral for mental health counseling is indicated. They inform the consultant that since the death, the other students have been calling him "murderer," and the school has therefore transferred the boy to another school. Given this limited information, the consultant advises over the phone that referral to mental health counseling is appropriate given the circumstances and suggests that it is not necessary to wait until the visit in a few days in order to assess the child directly.

The consultant arrives at the school about a week after the death has occurred. The child's desk remains unchanged. When the consultant meets several of the students as they return from recess, they explain that they do not wish to discuss what happened and are reluctant to carry on any conversation. Several students begin crying loudly as the consultant is introduced. With some difficulty, the students are encouraged to begin discussing their classmate's death and their reactions to it.

A school staff member working late on Friday afternoon is notified by a parent that one of the school's third-grade students has just been injured by a gunshot wound to the face. The child's brother, who is in the fourth grade at the school, had been playing with a handgun that accidentally discharged. The principal is notified, and he immediately contacts the other members of the crisis team. The crisis team talks over the phone for the rest of the evening and begins making plans while the principal and the school social worker go to the hospital to offer support to the family. Using the school crisis telephone tree, the entire school staff is contacted over the weekend and notified about an emergency staff meeting on Monday morning prior to the start of the school day.

On Monday morning, the crisis team meets early and discusses its plans; it is joined by consultants from the Regional School Crisis Prevention and Response Program. A staff meeting is held immediately after this meeting, just before the children's arrival. Staff members are encouraged to talk about their reactions to the recent events and are provided advice on how to facilitate discussions within their classrooms. Notification announcements are distributed, and all teachers agree to read the announcement during the homeroom period.

Several children arrive at school with copies of the local newspaper that carries a banner headline story about the tragedy. Rumors are already beginning to surface among the youngsters. Many of the children are just hearing about the situation from their peers as they arrive at school.

During the homeroom period, at a predetermined time, each class is informed of the incident by its teacher, who then facilitates a discussion. Mental health staff join the teacher in leading the discussions in the English and Spanish classes of the two children who were involved in the event. The children are encouraged to express their thoughts and feelings; misinformation is corrected (e.g., according to one rumor the child intentionally shot his sister over a minor disagreement) and concerns answered (e.g., several students volunteer that their parents have advised them to avoid their classmate because he has a gun and may try to kill them). Ultimately, most of the classes decide that they want to do something to show their support for the family. Students begin working on cards, banners, and letters to send to the student in the hospital, as well as cards of support for the student who fired the gun.

Several parents arrive at the school throughout the course of the day because of the impact that this accident has had on the community. A number of these parents do not speak English as their native language. Bilingual staff are available to provide direct support or translation services. A room is identified for parents to come and meet with others so that they have an opportunity to express their upset and concern, as well as to receive some direction on how they can contribute to their children's adjustment during this time. The Child Development–Community Policing Program holds a community meeting at the school to discuss handgun violence.

Over the next several weeks, many staff members talk about their own distress—some because of the recent events, some because the crisis has triggered memories of prior losses. The staff form a mutual support group that continues for several weeks after the crisis. The crisis team provides ongoing evaluation of the needs of students, staff, and parents. The boy who pulled the trigger returns to class the following week and is welcomed back by his classmates. His sister subsequently recovers and is also welcomed back to school. On follow-up, the school staff report that the management of the crisis has led to increased respect for the new principal and has brought them closer as a school community.

(Vignette 3)

A 14-year-old girl is the unintended victim of a shooting outside her house. One month later, a classmate commits suicide during the school day. Another month passes, and another classmate kills himself during a 3-day weekend.

The first incident presented several obstacles to the school's attempts to provide services; the death took place at the beginning of a week's vacation, and the student, recently transferred into the school, had developed only a small network of friends and acquaintances. When the students returned to school the following week, the staff made announcements in each classroom and offered support services for any students wanting to discuss their reactions to the news or the circumstances of community violence.

When the second student died, several hundred students utilized the support room services over the course of several days. Multiple staff members were assigned from other schools by the coordinator of counseling services of the district crisis team to assist with the interventions. While interventions took place in classrooms and the support rooms, a group within the school initiated by the crisis team began to plan how to reach out to the parents community in an attempt to prevent further suicides. The media coordinator accepted all calls from the press and provided complete information about the interventions taking place, including information on warning signs of suicidality and suggestions for parents on how to discuss this situation with their children. Students began leaving graffiti messages on the locker of the student who had recently died, as well as on the locker of the student who had died a month previously. After discussion with the crisis team about memorialization, the principal announced that messages left on the two students' lockers would be allowed to remain until the following weekend, at which time they would be removed. Parents of children who utilized support room services were contacted directly by telephone concerning the level of intervention their child received and whether or not follow-up with an outside agency for ongoing therapy might be helpful.

Following the third death, another suicide, the school again provided support room services and began to delegate mental health staff to assist in the classroom interventions. Several parents called the school asking them to evaluate their child because of concern about their youngster's suspected suicidality. Only a few students were referred for emergent evaluation off-site, and the parents of those requiring that level of evaluation were asked to come to the school and transport their child. School personnel helped families with inadequate insurance identify mental health services willing to see their children for evaluation and treatment. A meeting was held after the first day of intervention to provide classroom staff with helpful information about screening for suicidal ideation and risk. The press was again contacted to reiterate the suggestions for parents that had been published following the first death by suicide. A community meeting was scheduled for parents and interested community members to hear from experts in crisis intervention, at-risk behaviors among teenagers, and suicide. More than 400 parents attended.

As comparison of the preceding vignettes illustrates, the presence of a preexisting comprehensive crisis response plan will assist a school in anticipating and meeting the needs of its students, staff, and the larger community at the time of crisis. Although crisis can be disruptive to the educational process and be associated with short- and long-term psychological effects, these consequences can often be ameliorated if adequate support is provided at the time of crisis (Kline, Schonfeld, & Lichtenstein, 1995). These support services are more likely to be provided at school if a systematic school crisis response plan is already in place.

Schools have as their principal focus educational goals. Whereas schools are required to have a fire evacuation plan and to conduct regular fire drills, they less commonly have developed and implemented a plan for attending to the psychological and emotional needs of students and staff at the time of crisis. Many within schools (as well as many professionals outside of school systems) view these latter concerns as clinical issues that fall outside the realm of an educational institution. As a result, many schools remain unprepared for a crisis and fail to mobilize optimally the clinical and support resources both within the school and within the broader community to support students and staff when a crisis occurs.

Although schools may attempt to assemble an ad hoc crisis plan and team to address an acute episode, at the time of the crisis many staff members respond to the event in ways that do not allow them to take a thoughtful, broad, and long-term view of the needs of students and staff (Klingman, 1988). An effective crisis response requires prior preparedness and a systematic organizational response that is both flexible enough to be applicable to a broad range of crisis situations and specific enough to provide guidance at the time of a particular crisis.

The plan should address three broad areas: safety and security; obtaining, verifying, and disseminating accurate information to staff, students, parents, and the general public (when appropriate); and the emotional and psychological needs of those involved. All three domains must be addressed concurrently or none will be addressed effectively. This is unlikely to occur in the absence of an organizational school crisis response plan, prior training of school staff, and dedicated response staff and resources within the school.

An effective response should validate typical reactions to traumatic events and provide the mechanisms for students and staff to express and begin to resolve their personal reactions to the event. An organizational plan for systematic school crisis preparedness and response allows schools to remain proactive and ahead of unfolding crises by anticipating needs, assessing developing hazards, and identifying the resources available to respond to a crisis, as well as any service gaps that should be addressed. Relying exclusively on external resources to address a crisis may result in a sense of disempowerment among the staff, may contribute to the public's misperception of the capacity of school personnel to address the psychological and emotional needs of students, and may lead to a failure to anticipate and meet the long-term needs of students and staff subsequent to the initial intervention that may be provided by an external response team. While mental health resources from the community play a vital role in assisting a school in its response to a crisis, primary interventions should be provided by school staff because they already have some history with their students, and they will continue to be with the students—and the school—long after the crisis is over.

THE REGIONAL SCHOOL CRISIS PREVENTION AND RESPONSE PROGRAM

In 1991, the Regional School Crisis Prevention and Response Program was formed to address how schools might best prepare for crises. The organizing group, representing the fields of education, pediatric medicine, psychiatry, psychology, social work, and police, included members from Yale University School of Medicine, Department of Pediatrics and Child Study Center, and the Consultation Center; four area school systems; and the New Haven Police Department.

The group set three initial goals: (a) to develop a systematic organizational protocol (Schonfeld, Kline, & Members of the Crisis Intervention Committee, 1994; Lichtenstein, Schonfeld, Kline, & Speese-Linehan, 1995) that would define and anticipate the types of crises that may impact the student body and the local community, identify interventions that would be most effective in reducing long-term trauma, and create a structure to ensure a rapid, reliable, and replicable response mechanism with preliminary definition of personnel and responsibilities; (b) to provide the necessary training to prepare school staff in delivering services based upon the model; and (c) to increase the collaborative relationships between schools and community mental health and social service providers. To date, the program has trained more than 7,000 school and community staff in the use of the model, consulted to more than 300 district- and school-level crisis response teams, and provided technical assistance to schools during more than 175 crisis situations. The Regional School Crisis Prevention and Response Program has been integrated recently within the Child Development–Community Policing Program at the Yale Child Study Center (Marans, Berkowitz, & Cohen, 1998; Marans et al., 1995) and will be providing training and technical assistance to school and mental health staff at national replication sites.

CRISES BENEFITING FROM A TEAM RESPONSE

Not all crises affecting school children require or benefit from a team response. Generally, circumstances involving issues of privacy and confidentiality, such as child abuse in the home or a sexual assault, are better handled through student assistance teams, unless information about these events has become widely known and generated considerable concern among many members of the school community. Crises that involve significant numbers of students or school staff that typically benefit from a team response include situations involving loss and grief (e.g., the death of a student or staff member); when there is a perceived threat to personal safety (e.g., a school bus accident, an abduction, or a fire); environmental crisis (e.g., a hurricane, a chemical spill on a nearby road, or a gas leak in the school); and when there is a perceived threat to emotional well-being (e.g., a bomb threat, hate-crime graffiti left at the school, or public disclosure of sexual misconduct of staff or students). The organizational model as outlined in this chapter provides a general response plan that is applicable across specific crisis contexts. In special situations, such as suicide postvention (Brent, Etkind, & Carr, 1992; Davidson, Rosenberg, Mercy, Franklin, & Simmons, 1989; Schonfeld et al., 1994), adaptations of the model are indicated in order to address their unique contingencies.

LEVELS OF INTERVENTION

The Regional School Crisis Prevention and Response Program developed its protocols within a hierarchical framework. A regional resource team made up of representatives from mental health, police, academic, school administration, and support agencies meets on a quarterly basis to review program activities, improve mechanisms for training school staff, address service deficits in target areas, and provide support and technical assistance to representatives from the district-level teams. The regional resource team also operates as an information clearinghouse on school crisis prevention and response and related topics.

The next level within the hierarchy is the district-level team, which provides crisis response oversight for the individual school system. This team is generally composed of central office administrators and mental health staff.

It establishes relevant districtwide policies and oversees resource allocation, staff training and supervision, and technical assistance for schools within the district at the time of crisis.

The third level in the hierarchy is that of the school-based team, which is generally composed of the school's administrator(s); nursing, social work, psychology, and guidance/counseling staff; classroom staff; and others. Some schools may include a parent representative to assist in contacting parents more rapidly and to provide a liaison between the school and parents. This team is most capable of anticipating the reactions and needs of the students and staff, and is therefore most suited to provide the direct services to students and families at the time of crisis. This team can draw upon additional resources through the district-level team, such as supplemental counseling staff from other schools. Since school-level teams will provide the most direct services to students, they will also experience the greatest level of stress. These teams in particular must have a proactive plan to address the needs of staff providers who may experience vicarious traumatization or compassion fatigue.

The organizational model utilizes a structure of seven roles. Although each role has its own set of tasks and responsibilities, each member of the team should be cross-trained in anticipation of absences. The roles include crisis team chair, assistant team chair, coordinator of counseling services, media coordinator, staff notification coordinator, communication coordinator, and crowd management coordinator (Schonfeld et al., 1994; Lichtenstein et al., 1995). Table 9.1 outlines specific responsibilities for each role.

NOTIFICATION/COMMUNICATION

A team member who is notified of a crisis involving one of its students should immediately notify the chair of the crisis team and inform him or her of what is known to date and whether or not the information has been confirmed. It is preferable that confirmation not be obtained from the family of the victim; rather, the purpose of contact with the family should be to offer condolences and support. Liaison with the local or regional police facilitates timely and accurate confirmation of crisis events, as well as assisting in the coordination of services. A contact person within emergency services, when indicated, should be established to assure that the school system is updated as the event unfolds. The chair will assure that the remaining members of the school and district crisis teams are notified when indicated and decide whether to contact the rest of the school staff before the next school day. The staff notification coordinator will facilitate the contact with all school personnel through the use of a preestablished telephone tree. Before contact is made with the general staff, the crisis team should meet or consult by telephone to determine what initial steps will be taken to meet anticipated needs and will make this information available to the staff notification coor-

Table 9.1   Roles of Crisis Team Members

Member	Role
Crisis team chair	Chair all meetings of the crisis team and oversee the broad and specific functioning of the team and its members.
Assistant team chair	Assist the chair in all functions and substitute in the event of the unavailability of the chair.
Coordinator of counseling services	Determine the extent and nature of counseling services indicated by a particular crisis and (along with counterpart on District Team) mobilize community resources as needed. Oversee training and supervision of staff providing counseling services. Identify and maintain ongoing liaison with community resources.
Media coordinator	Serve as the sole contact person (along with counterpart on District Team) for all media inquiries. Prepare a brief press release, if indicated, and appropriate statements, in collaboration with other members of the team, for staff, student, and parent notification.
Staff notification coordinator	Establish, coordinate, and initiate a telephone tree for notification of team members and other school staff after school hours.
Communication coordinator	Oversee all direct in-house communication. Screen incoming calls and maintain a log of phone calls related to the crisis. Assist the staff notification coordinator and help maintain an accurate phone directory of community resources and district-level staff.
Crowd management coordinator	In collaboration with local police and fire departments, plan mechanisms for crowd management in the event of various potential crises and directly supervise the movement of students and staff in the event such plans are initiated. A crowd control plan must include arrangements to cordon off areas with physical evidence, to assemble students and faculty for presentations, and, in the event of an actual threat to the physical safety of students, to assure the safe and organized movement of students in order to minimize the risk of harm.

Source: Adapted with permission from Schonfeld, D., Kline, M., & Members of the Crisis Intervention Committee. (1994). School-based crisis intervention: An organizational model. Crisis Intervention and Time-Limited Treatment, 1, 158.

dinator. The crisis team chair or designee will make contact with the victim and/or family to offer support and assistance.

Following notification of a crisis, staff should meet, either at the end of the day or prior to the beginning of the next school day, depending on the circumstances and timing. Table 9.2 outlines a sample agenda for this meeting. The crisis team needs to ensure that all information pertinent to the crisis is obtained and disseminated to students and staff in a fashion that facilitates their processing the information and their reactions in the most

Table 9.2   Emergency Staff Meeting Agenda

Share all current information about the crisis event and response, as well as any memorial plans that have already been established.

Provide a forum for teachers and other staff to ask questions, share their own personal reactions or concerns, and offer feedback about reactions they anticipate or have noticed among the student body.

Distribute notification announcements and finalize plans for notifying students and contacting parents (when appropriate).

Inform staff of specific activities to support students, staff, and parents.

---

meaningful way. The school should identify those students closest to the victim(s) and arrange for them to be notified in a quiet and supportive location where their grief can be expressed in private. For the remainder of the student body, announcements should be structured to provide the information to all classes at approximately the same time, thereby reducing the potential problems that may arise should students with different amounts of information meet and compare notes. Rumors and speculation should be corrected as quickly as possible. In general, public address announcements should be avoided because of their depersonalized and disaffected quality and because they cannot anticipate or respond to students' reactions. If it is a staff member who has died, it is best to use a classroom teacher who is already known to the students and has an established relationship with them to cover the class on a short-term basis. A substitute can be used for this second class but would face enormous challenges if assigned to the grieving classroom.

Notification of parents is usually addressed through printed material sent home with students on the day of notification. In addition to providing information about the crisis event, written material can offer guidance on how parents can help their children deal with their reactions to the crisis and provide information on community mental health resources. Handouts providing suggestions on how to help children of different developmental levels deal with grief, bereavement (Schonfeld, 1993), trauma, or loss, and outlining typical and atypical reactions, as well as guidelines for when to seek additional mental health services, should be prepared prior to any crisis event and placed on file within the school or school district. For those children who are provided individual counseling or services within the support room, contact should be made directly with parents, usually by phone.

If it is likely that media attention will be generated by the event, the media coordinator should contact media representatives and provide them with the appropriate information by way of a press release. Suggestions concerning how the media can best help, and be least disruptive to the students and staff, should be offered. Interviews should be discouraged on school grounds, except those provided by the media coordinator.

MEMORIALIZATION

Teams will need to address both the content and the timing of memorialization. Often, questions regarding memorial activities will be raised within hours of notification of the crisis event. This may divert attention from addressing the acute emotional and psychological needs of the students and staff. The team may need to address early on how best to handle graffiti tags, posters, signs, buttons or T-shirts with a picture of the deceased, and quasi-sanctified memorial areas that draw numbers of students. In some situations, early discussion of memorialization may prompt premature closure of the crisis response.

Spontaneous public displays in hallway shadow boxes or postboards should be discouraged. Rather, students and staff should be given the opportunity to understand and express their needs through more thoughtful interventions. Using school resources and facilities to make multiple copies of newspaper articles, generating buttons commemorating the victim, or other activities that create semipermanent reminders that may persist in the community long after the initial trauma has worn off, should be avoided. For longer term memorial projects, schools should consider that the special acknowledgments of naming permanent objects after the person or dedicating a yearbook may set a precedent that will then be expected when another member of the school community dies. Memorial responses are more successful if they involve an assembled acknowledgment with some ritual content, such as a moment of silence or the lighting of a single candle. When a death involves suicide or another cause of death that bears a stigma (e.g., death by automobile accident while under the influence of alcohol), staff will need to help students acknowledge the loss of the individual student or staff member while taking care not to glamorize the means of death (Schonfeld et al., 1994; Brent et al., 1992).

The team should address how to handle the deceased's desk, locker, personal possessions, assignments hung up for display, and so forth. The team should anticipate that the deceased's locker may be utilized by other students as an informal memorial site, where they will post messages, place flowers, or otherwise acknowledge the loss. These spontaneous expressions should be monitored regularly to detect any unexpected reactions. The team can work with the student's class to help them identify how they would like to deal with the child's empty desk.

The team should remember that it is not the content of the memorial activities that is most important; rather, it is the process of engaging the members of the school community in the planning of a meaningful event. While raising money for a permanent memorial (such as a tree or plaque) may provide staff and students a means of "doing something" to show they care, it is far more helpful to facilitate an ongoing discussion among members of the school community about *how* they care about the deceased and for the survivors and what would be the most meaningful way(s) to express that concern prior to (or in place of) raising such funds.

SUPPORT ROOMS

The school should consider when it is appropriate to set up support rooms for those students requiring more intensive intervention than can be provided by teacher-directed class discussions. The crisis response plan should specify the staffing and location (e.g., in areas without heavy traffic) of support rooms. Support rooms are best for handling limited numbers of students who generally are sharing similar reactions and symptoms. Homogeneous groups of 3 to 6 participants work well, while larger groups of 7 to 10 can generally tolerate more variety in the reactions of participants. When several groups are manifesting different reactions, the school should consider using separate support rooms to meet the distinctive needs of each group. If a number of large groups seek services within the support room(s), more staffing may be required; the coordinator of counseling services should draw on counseling staff from other schools within the district, as well as community mental health resources, if appropriate. He or she should also determine if on-site assistance from community service providers will be necessary or if a direct referral system would work best. In many ways large groups (i.e., more than eight or nine participants) function similarly to classroom groups. If many groups of this size seek assistance through the support rooms, this may indicate that the interventions provided in the classrooms did not sufficiently meet the needs of many students, highlighting the need for further training and support of classroom teachers.

The support room staff, under the guidance of the coordinator of counseling services, should perform an initial assessment, following the principles of mental health triage, of students seeking to utilize the services offered in the support room. Those students with emergent mental health needs demanding immediate action should be referred directly to the appropriate community resources. Extensive evaluations and counseling services in the school setting prior to referral of these students should be avoided. Referring large groups of students to hospital emergency rooms to rule out suicidal risk is not an effective response plan and may only weaken the collaborative relationships between school and community mental health staff. Therefore, the crisis team needs to identify appropriate emergency services in the community that can respond immediately if needed at the time of crisis, as well as urgent services that can be provided within 48 hours for this purpose. Identifying students with needs requiring emergency treatment, such as those assessed as potentially suicidal, is a critical role of the counseling staff. Mental health staff in the support room should be identified as being available for specific, individualized tasks (e.g., one person may have the best assessment skills for suicidality and can be assigned for that purpose, whereas another may have advanced skills around grief work). Evaluations should be brief and goal specific, with the intention of screening students for the most appropriate level of service. The counseling staff should defer more lengthy evaluations and services until a later time, such as the next school day. Youngsters assessed as not requiring emergent mental health services should be offered limited immediate interventions, perhaps in a group setting. Support groups, which might continue to meet on an ongoing basis, may be a useful outcome of the support rooms (Lichtenstein et al., 1995).

Many students who might benefit from additional evaluation and intervention may not request, nor present themselves to support rooms for, these services. School staff may identify students as requiring further evaluation because of the circumstances of the crisis (e.g., if the student was a witness to the crisis or a close friend of the victim) or by their reactions upon notification (e.g., if the student has an extreme or atypical response). As a result, the general classroom staff will need to be able to determine who within their classroom may be at risk, and have a mechanism through which to refer these individuals for additional evaluation and intervention. Table 9.3 outlines risk factors that increase the likelihood that students will require additional services after a crisis event. These factors involve the nature and extent of the student's relationships with the victim, the quality of the student's coping with prior challenges, as well as the current crisis event, and the presence of predisposing factors and concurrent life stressors. Those staff who are part of early identification and intervention programs within the school (e.g., student assistance teams, mental health teams, child study teams) should be brought into the crisis response assessment and planning so that they are able to share their prior knowledge of those students who were experiencing difficulties before the crisis.

Individual services should, except on rare occasions, be directed toward either alleviating the dominant features or symptoms that prompted the need for individual attention or for the preliminary assessment regarding the need for referral to community mental health services (e.g., for students with severe suicidal ideation or profound decompensation). Although mental health resources within individual school districts vary greatly in the amount, extent, and nature of counseling services their staff can provide, all school districts need to establish relationships with local community services to provide supplemental or specialized mental health services for crisis situations.

School-based crisis intervention planning and response cannot occur in isolation from the community. A critical component of crisis preparedness planning involves identifying community resources, as well as service gaps, for addressing the emergent mental health needs of students and staff at the time of a crisis. Specific staff should be identified within community social service and mental health agencies to serve as liaisons with the school system. Through effective collaboration between schools and community men-

Table 9.3   Risk Factors for Students

Group affiliation with the victim
School staff should make themselves aware of the formal and informal social networks and the
    activities that the victim shared with other students: academic, shop, and special classes;
    afterschool clubs, teams, and extracurricular activities; community and social activities
    engaged in off-site; the victim's residential neighborhood.
A staff member should consider following the victim's schedule of classes for the first day(s). The
    crisis team should reach out to the external sites to offer support and guidance to the
    nonprofessionals who might have regular contact with peers (e.g., the scout leader, little league
    coach, or dance instructor).

Shared characteristics, interests, or attributes with the victim
Students who perceive themselves as sharing characteristics, interests, or attributes with the
    victim may be more inclined to have increased anxiety and distress.

Students with prior demonstration of poor coping
Social isolation
History of suicidal ideation/attempts
Prior history of arrests, acting-out behaviors, aggression, or drug/alcohol abuse

Students exhibiting extreme or atypical reactions
Students with grief reactions surpassing those of the general student body that would not be
    explained by close affiliation with the victim
Students with close relationships with the deceased that exhibit very little reaction to the news

Students with personal history related to the trauma
Former victims of crime or violence
Students who have threatened or acted violently in the past

Students with concurrent adverse personal situations
Family problems
Health problems
Psychiatric history
Significant peer conflicts

---

tal health providers, solutions can be developed to increase the community's
capacity to address mental health needs in a timely and effective manner at
the time of crisis. Such collaboration and community planning to improve
the mental health infrastructure will have clear benefit for members of the
school community even outside the context of a crisis event (e.g., when making referrals for students who have non-crisis-related issues that may require
ongoing counseling).

CLASSROOM INTERVENTIONS

To meet the emerging needs of students during a school's response to crisis,
interventions can be offered in classrooms. Classroom activities will reduce
the demands on individual counseling resources, allowing them to target
those students requiring more intensive intervention.

Additional in-service training is required to prepare teachers to provide
this service. The training should be general enough in nature (e.g., children's

developmental understanding of death and their responses to loss; Schonfeld, 1993) that it is clear to teachers (and administrators) that the skills learned can be applied more broadly than just at the time of major crisis events. Teachers may also need additional support and backup by school counseling staff in order to be able to provide this service within their classrooms. A crisis often awakens feelings related to a prior (or concurrent) crisis that may assume a primary focus for a particular child. At these times of stress, given an appropriate opportunity, children may be inclined to disclose a wide range of personal crises (e.g., prior deaths, unresolved issues regarding parent conflict or divorce). Teachers need timely access to appropriate backup services to address these "incidental" concerns (Schonfeld, 1989).

At the time of a crisis, teachers may benefit from additional briefing regarding the types of reactions that they may anticipate in their classrooms and some of the specific behavioral changes that are common following a crisis. Particularly when people are experiencing difficulty in identifying and expressing their feelings, teachers need to be attentive to nonverbal communication. Eye contact, posture, and energy levels may contribute valuable information for directing the flow of the discussion and determining whether a student's needs are being met through classroom interventions.

There are three general categories of classroom activities that can contribute to children's expression of their feelings and thoughts: discussions, written efforts, and art projects. Teachers will be most familiar with the developmental capabilities of their students, as well as their methods for coping with prior stressful situations, and should select the modalities that provide the best match.

Discussions are most effective when led by the teacher. However, if due to his or her personal connection with the crisis event the teacher feels unable to direct the classroom activity, it may be necessary for another staff person to guide the discussion initially while the teacher is allowed to observe and participate. Discussions should attempt to demystify the event and address any magical thinking that may be influencing the students' perceptions through efforts to correct rumors, provide logical explanations of what has transpired wherever possible, and draw out the impressions that students are forming so as to be able to reinforce accurate understanding and redirect mistaken impressions (Newgass & Schonfeld, 1996). Graphic details describing injuries and attendant imagery should be avoided; consideration of the developmental needs and capacities of students can guide how much information they need to process the experience without overwhelming their defensive structures (Yussen & Santrock, 1982).

During these discussions, teachers should not attempt to hide their own feelings and reactions but instead should be encouraged to model meaningful and compassionate ways to talk about feelings. Students will need assistance in focusing on their feelings, as opposed to behaviors or sensations, during these discussions. Teachers should consciously take time for themselves to become aware of their feelings and reactions. Opportunities should be provided for teachers to talk with their peers about how they are reacting to the incident and to their discussions with students.

Written activities are often used as a way of allowing students to express their angst and sorrow. If they are used excessively, or indiscriminately, their impact may be diluted. Entire classes are often assigned the "task" of writing a note or some other exercise, such as a poem or a recollection of a joyful time spent with the victim. However, this activity does not acknowledge the unique relationships that individual students may have or may have had with the victim of a trauma. Whereas some students may have very deep and meaningful relationships with the victim, others' relationships may be more distant or conflicted. An assignment that assumes all relationships are equivalent may reduce the effectiveness for those very students most in need of expressing their loss.

Written activities are most beneficial for students with better developed writing skills. Regardless of the assignment and its purpose (i.e., to be shared within the class, to be sent to the family in an effort to extend emotional support, or as an aid to individual processing of the event), all written assignments associated with responding to a crisis should be reviewed to identify any signs of extreme emotional distress or inappropriate content.

> Following the third death at the school mentioned in vignette 3, several staff worked together with groups of students to produce a notebook of poetry and reflections that might be presented to the parents of the child. When a number of students submitted contributions that reflected their confusion, hurt, and sorrow expressed in a way that may have been painful for the victim's family to read (e.g., "it was cruel of you to do this to us . . . you left us behind with the pain, while you get to escape it"), the staff guided students toward forming themselves into small peer review groups to read and reread each other's work and offer suggestions on alternate ways to express the intended emotional message. As one student commented, "Because we did this, I've found new ways to describe how I feel."

Art projects and manipulatives can also be used to facilitate emotional expression in a classroom setting. These generally take the form of pictures, banners, and temporary memorials. This intervention may be especially helpful for younger children, but all age-groups can use art-related activities to express their inner state. The benefits may expand as multiple sensory experiences are permitted through use of the medium; many students may benefit from finger painting because is employs multiple sensations (i.e., visual, tactile, auditory, and olfactory). Whatever the approach, it is important that the activity be used to elicit emotional responses and not to "diagnose" the students because of the content or structure of their artwork.

> In one of the classrooms at the school responding to the crisis in vignette 3, the art teacher invited students to draw a picture of their feelings. Sev-

eral media were available for the students' use, including pencils, crayons, tempera, and charcoal. After they had completed their drawings, the teacher asked each student to come forward and describe how the images on the paper illustrated their feelings. Several students became emotional as they talked, and the group spontaneously offered support, encouragement, and validating comments to one another. Several students commented that they were encouraged to hear others describe feelings that they themselves held but hesitated to share.

In adapting these interventions to special education classes, it may be helpful to allow additional "quiet time" and/or to alternate rest with physical activity (Axline, 1983). Music may help students relax so that they are better able to attend to their emotional reaction to a crisis. For some students, concrete methods that provide a framework are most effective, such as the use of a "feelings identification chart" to assist them in better identifying their feelings. Storytelling can also be used. The stories that may be most helpful depend upon the individual class and students. One technique is to tell a story in "rounds," wherein the teacher begins the story and the students take turns contributing elements, while the teacher offers modifications, if necessary. The teacher ultimately brings the story to a close with a straightforward solution that is reality-based yet hopeful.

In one classroom at the school that responded to the crisis in vignette 2, the individual leading the discussion asked if anyone could think of a story that would show how people can respond to tragedies. One youngster suggested starting the story with "A kid got shot." The facilitator added, "but she went to the hospital, where they are helping her to get better." Another child added, "She nearly died," and the facilitator contributed, "but everyone is pretty sure that she'll be all right in a few weeks." He went on to repeat the story as it had developed to that point: "A kid got shot, but she went to the hospital, where they are helping her to get better. She nearly died, but everyone is pretty sure that she'll be all right in a few weeks." He then asked if anyone wanted to add the next line, to which a girl replied, "And then she'll be able to come back to school." He once again repeated the story, now with a concluding sentence, and was able to use this as a means to examine the children's fears about the violence associated with guns, concerns of death, anxiety about hospitals, and their longing for the girl's return to school. This led to a more directed discussion about the students' worries and techniques to facilitate coping.

FOLLOW-UP AND STAFF SUPPORT

Children and adults grieve and respond to a crisis over time, and long-term reactions to significant events should be expected. Mechanisms need to be in place for referring students and staff for additional counseling outside of the school, if this proves to be necessary. A list of local community agencies, pediatricians, and private mental health providers should be available to staff and parents.

The staff members' responsibility to provide services to students at the time of crisis does not relieve them from experiencing their own reactions to the event. Acute reactions to crisis events among staff members should not be overlooked or discounted; rather, attempts should be made to normalize the distressing reactions that many will experience and provide opportunities for additional support. Unfortunately, mental health services and Employee Assistance Programs (EAPs) may bear a stigma in the minds of some staff. As part of their crisis protocol, schools should proactively identify any EAP contacts, along with necessary phone numbers and contact names, at the very beginning of a response and encourage staff to make use of their services. Frequent reminders about the service and the guarantee of confidentiality should be given throughout the time that crisis intervention services are offered. Following a crisis, a school system should speak with the EAP to see if its services were adequate to meet the needs of the staff; underutilization of the service may suggest the need for identifying an alternate means of providing staff support at the time of crisis.

Debriefing, a review of activities that has the goal of gaining a better understanding of a team's capacity, should be offered after the team has emerged from the response cycle. Whereas debriefing is intended to focus on the team's activities in executing the crisis plan, there is also an opportunity for team members to express their personal reactions to the event and to identify steps that might relieve stress during future crisis responses. In some cases, a debriefing session may include staff members outside of the crisis team, such as for a teacher whose classroom was most directly impacted by the crisis. The debriefing session will also allow the team to develop plans to evaluate and address ongoing issues, such as the possibility of posttraumatic and anniversary reactions among students and staff.

TRAINING AND TECHNICAL ASSISTANCE

Training of crisis response teams is most effective if it includes all members of the team, which often requires considerable planning. In addition to being most convenient for the trainer (thereby facilitating the involvement of outside consultants), the primary advantage is that team building will develop more predictably when all parties receive training together.

Training for a school crisis team should provide background knowledge on crisis theory and children's developmental understanding of and reactions to death (Schonfeld, 1993); introduce and familiarize the participants with the organizational model (Schonfeld et al., 1994); provide information on classroom interventions; and employ team-building activities. The importance of recognizing and addressing staff needs should be underscored throughout the training.

A vignette activity, wherein team members adopt roles from the model in order to address a school crisis situation, should be used to help the newly developing teams experience the manner of problem-solving and decision making that will confront them in a crisis. This vignette should provide the amount of information that might be available to schools at the time of an actual crisis. The subsequent processing of the experience with teams should clarify that there is no "right way" to respond. Rather, the training facilitators should elicit their reasons for making the structural decisions and draw out their rationale for intervention (Gallessich, 1990). The goal is to help the group learn how best to function as a team, and to appreciate both the complexity of responding to a crisis and how an organizational plan can help anticipate many of the issues and provide a mechanism for responding effectively.

It is often helpful to bring together several teams for training off-site (to minimize interruptions that may distract or remove participants from the training) in a full-day (i.e., 5- to 6-hour) workshop. The trainer/consultant can then follow up with individual teams to adapt the practices to the unique issues associated with each team's school. While providing the technical assistance, it is important that the unique cultural, economic, and environmental aspects of the school and its population be considered and that the plan be adapted to meet these unique circumstances. The individual providing technical assistance can also help identify unique vulnerabilities for a school. For example, a school serving a marginalized immigrant population should anticipate the need for increased translation and outreach services at the time of a crisis. Psychological vulnerabilities can also be considered, such as decreased support at home in communities with a high percentage of single-adult-headed households, or increased baseline stressors and decreased resources in disadvantaged communities.

CONCLUSIONS

A school-based crisis intervention team composed predominantly of school-based staff is ideally suited to coordinate crisis prevention activities and to provide intervention services to students at the time of a crisis. This chapter has discussed a systematic crisis intervention model to organize the activities of this team and has highlighted issues to consider in establishing and training school-based crisis teams. If representatives of community social service and mental health agencies are involved in the planning process, it is more likely that their services can be accessed at the time of a crisis for the mutual benefit of the students and the community. Planning for possible contingencies will facilitate optimal performance of the team while ameliorating the negative consequences impacting the students and the service providers, who, as members of the school community, will likely be reacting to the crisis themselves.

ACKNOWLEDGMENTS   The authors would like to acknowledge the contributions of the members of the Regional School Crisis Prevention and Response Program, including representatives of the public school systems of East Haven, New Haven, North Haven, and West Haven, Connecticut. We gratefully acknowledge the support of our program from the Community Foundation for Greater New Haven, the William Caspar Graustein Memorial Fund, the State of Connecticut (Office of Policy and Management), ACES (Area Cooperative Educational Services, Hamden, Connecticut), and the Office for Victims of Crime.

REFERENCES

Axline, V. (1983). *Play therapy*. New York: Ballantine.

Brent, D., Etkind, S., & Carr, W. (1992). Psychiatric effects of exposure to suicide among the friends and acquaintances of adolescent suicide victims. *Journal of the American Academy of Child and Adolescent Psychiatry, 31*, 629–640.

Davidson, L., Rosenberg, M., Mercy, J., Franklin, J., & Simmons, J. (1989). An epidemiologic study of risk factors in two teenage suicide clusters. *Journal of the American Academy of Child and Adolescent Psychiatry, 262*, 2687–2692.

Gallessich, J. (1990). *The profession and practice of consultation*. San Francisco: Jossey-Bass.

Kline, M., Schonfeld, D., & Lichtenstein, R. (1995). Benefits and challenges of school-based crisis response teams. *Journal of School Health, 65*, 245–249.

Klingman, A. (1988). School community in disaster: Planning for intervention. *Journal of Community Psychology, 16*, 205–216.

Lichtenstein, R., Schonfeld, D., Kline, M., & Speese-Linehan, D. (1995). *How to prepare for and respond to a crisis*. Alexandria, VA: Association for Supervision and Curriculum Development.

Marans, S., Adnopoz, J., Berkman, M., Esserman, D., MacDonald, D., Nagler, S., Randall, R., Schaefer, M., & Wearing, M. (1995). *The police–mental health partnership*. New Haven, CT: Yale University Press.

Marans, S., Berkowitz, S., & Cohen, D. (1998). Police and mental health professionals: Collaborative response to the impact of violence on children and families. *Child and Adolescent Psychiatric Clinics of North America, 7*, 635–651.

Newgass, S., & Schonfeld, D. (1996). A crisis in the class: Anticipating and responding to student's needs. *Educational Horizons, 74*, 124–129.

Schonfeld, D. (1989). Crisis intervention for bereavement support: A model of intervention in the children's school. *Clinical Pediatrics, 28,* 27–33.

Schonfeld, D. (1993). Talking with children about death. *Journal of Pediatric Health Care, 7,* 269–274.

Schonfeld, D., Kline, M., & Members of the Crisis Intervention Committee. (1994). School-based crisis in-tervention: An organizational model. *Crisis Intervention and Time-Limited Treatment, 1,* 155–166.

Yussen, S., & Santrock, J. (1982). *Child development: An introduction.* Dubuque, IA: Wm. C. Brown.

10

Crisis Intervention With School Violence Problems and Volatile Situations

GORDON MACNEIL

CHRIS STEWART

The following are examples of precipitating events that result in crisis situations:

- A ninth grader is verbally harassed because she doesn't wear "cool" clothes.
- A group of "jocks" bully a high school freshman at the bus stop, pushing and tripping him.
- A student who informed on another student who ditched classes is beaten up in their subsequent fistfight.
- On their way home after a football game, a group of middle school students are beaten by fans from a rival school.
- A high school senior is stabbed for making derogatory comments about another student's girlfriend.
- A student is fatally shot when he fails to pay another student for drugs.

Case Studies

John Hanson is a 17-year-old Asian American male. He attends Boca Vista High School, where he is a junior. John is a good student, with an overall grade point average of 3.6. John has had little trouble at school. His greatest transgression was when he was caught skipping school to attend a concert. He plans to attend college and become an engineer. He has a supportive family and has good relationships with both parents and his younger sister. John has been a witness to a tragic event at school. Two days ago a fellow student, who John did not know personally but recognized from some shared classes, shot several students and a teacher before committing suicide. One of the students was a close friend of John. John is experiencing extreme grief and is not able to speak with his parents about his feelings.

Jack Fujimoto is a 13-year-old White male attending Prairie View Middle School. Jack has reasonable grades, with an average of 2.5 in all subjects. Jack is small for his age. His parents have been divorced for 3 years, and he currently lives with a supportive mother. He has been the victim of an ongoing campaign by some other students. Several of the school athletes have been bullying Jack for several months because he is a member of the drama club. These students call him "fag" and steal his lunch money on a regular basis. In this last meeting the boys beat Jack, causing moderate harm, though no bones were broken. Jack is generally a quiet person and likes acting because it provides an avenue for expressing his feelings.

Aretha Jackson is a 16-year-old African American female. She attends Andrew Jackson High School, where she is a sophomore. She attends school regularly and has earned a grade point average of 3.0. She lives with her mother and grandmother. She has one younger brother and one older brother. She receives good support from both her mother and grandmother. Her father left her mother when Aretha was very young, and she has no recollection of him. Aretha has experienced a violent episode when changing classes. Another girl threatened her with a box cutter. Aretha had unknowingly trespassed into an area that "belonged" to the girl and her friends. Aretha escaped without injury but is upset about the event and fears it may happen again.

In this chapter we will discuss two principle forms of school violence: The first form includes acts of violence ranging from larceny and robbery to simple assaults and homicide; the second form includes those catastrophic outbursts against schoolmates and school personnel typified by recent shootings in Colorado, Arkansas, and Kentucky. These catastrophic school violence events have a powerful impact on the communities in which they occur. However, we think the more common form of violence, while not garnering the media attention of catastrophic events, is of greater concern due to the chronicity and frequency of these violent acts and the greater numbers of students, teachers, parents, and other school personnel directly affected by these acts in schools nationwide. Both forms of school violence require intervention by human service personnel (or trained school personnel). In particular, comprehensive crisis intervention services should be readily available for those victimized by the violence or exposed to it. This chapter presents a crisis intervention strategy targeting survivors of school violence that employs Roberts's crisis intervention model (Roberts, 1991, 1996) in combination with cognitive therapy.

In writing this chapter we address school violence in a general sense; we do not identify interventions for specific violent acts (such as rape or aggravated assault). We purposefully neglected two areas of violence: We have limited our discussion to violence against persons, thus omitting aggression toward property such as vandalism, arson, and bombing school buildings. Neither have we targeted violence of a sexual nature—rape—other than considering these as acts of violence.

DEFINITION OF THE PROBLEM

School violence encompasses a tremendous array of behaviors, ranging from verbally abusing a peer to deliberately bombing persons in a school building or shooting groups of persons with semiautomatic weapons. Despite their diversity, these are all overt, aggressive acts that result in physical or psychological pain, injury, or death (Frederick, Middleton, & Butler, 1995). Definitions of *school violence* have ranged from verbal acts of disrespect to teachers and administrators, theft, and physical assaults (Kelly & Pink, 1982) to the federal government's inclusion of only rape, robbery, and simple and aggravated assaults (Bastian & Taylor, 1992). This more restrictive definition is intended to provide a narrow focus for research studies (Alexander & Curtis, 1998).

Astor (1998) suggests that social workers adopt a definition of violence presented by Straus, Gelles, and Steinmetz (1980): Violence is "an act carried out with the intention, or a perceived intention, of causing physical pain or injury to another person. The physical pain can range from a slight pain such as a slap, to murder" (p. 20). Astor promotes this definition because it includes milder forms of aggression common in elementary schools. He contends lax rules about aggression, or tolerance for milder forms of aggression, in lower grades fosters more severe aggressive acts in later grades. He points out that changing our definition of violence can lead to increased awareness of the problem, as occurred in the 1970s and 1980s with domestic violence (Astor, 1998). For our discussion, we ascribe to the operational definition that *school violence* is any intentional verbal or physical act producing pain in the recipient of that act while the recipient is under the supervision of the school.

SCOPE OF THE PROBLEM

Events of the past few years have focused national attention upon the problem of school violence. Tragic, catastrophic incidents have served as vehicles for the popular press to identify this as a critical issue. The events in Jonesboro, Arkansas; West Paducah, Kentucky; Pearl, Mississippi; Edinboro, Pennsylvania; and, most recently, Columbine, Colorado, have become examples of what might happen in quiet, "good" communities. Had these events occurred in inner-city neighborhoods, they might have been no less tragic but perhaps less surprising (Wetzstein, 1998). Consequently, many questions have been raised regarding the nature and scope of the school violence issue. Parents and community officials alike are concerned about the perceived level of violence in the nation's schools (Goldstein & Conoley, 1997).

Determining the nature and scope of school violence in America, as with most complex social phenomena, is not an easy task. Violence in schools is a multidimensional issue highly related to the presence of violence in society. Violence exists in society and leaks into the school environment (Crews & Counts, 1997). As Goldstein and Conoley (1997) stated, "High levels of aggression in our homes, our streets, and our mass media rapidly find parallel expression in our schools" (p. 16). A federal government report in 1993 found that almost 3 million crimes in schools were reported annually, which translates to almost 16,000 crimes per school day (Goldstein & Conoley, 1997). Statistics demonstrated a recent increase in violent crime for youths under the age of 18, which rose 29.1% between the years of 1988 and 1992 (Goldstein & Conoley, 1997). Another report found that 10 percent of all public schools reported at least one incident of serious violence (including murder, rape, suicide, or physical attack with a weapon) to law enforcement officials in the 1996–1997 school year (Heaviside, Rowand, Williams, & Farris, 1998).

These findings are not without controversy. Some researchers claim these statistics are being used by the media to "scare" concerned parents into watching specific broadcasts (Wetzstein, 1998, p. 2). It is reported that there have been 220 deaths on school property since 1992. This is an average of 37 deaths per year, or 1.5 deaths per 1 million students, which is fewer deaths than those reported on some public transportation in some cities (Wetzstein, 1998). Further, it is reported that in the 1996–1997 school year 47% of schools reported no crime of any kind, and those that did usually reported thefts or fistfights (Kleinz, 1998). In fact, many schools have been proven to be safer than their communities (Poland, 1997).

Although the implications of these statistics are in question, they do seem to indicate an increase in the number and severity of violence in reported incidents of school violence (Agron, 1999; Sheley & Wright, 1998). Such an increase in the nature of school violence can be linked directly to the availability of and willingness to use weapons, such as guns (Crews & Counts, 1997; Dryfoos, 1998; Sheley & Wright, 1998). It is evident that most students have access to almost any form of weapon they desire, including automatic assault rifles (Current Health, 1998; Crews & Counts, 1997; Goldstein & Conoley, 1997). Most school-related incidents involving guns take place in high schools, and most (65%) are intentional shootings (Goldstein & Conoley, 1997). So, while the true scope of school violence remains controversial, the evidence indicating a rise in the type and severity of violence in school settings seems to cause the greatest public concern.

Administrators and students have responded to this perceived fear. Several schools now include drills that simulate gunfire along with the traditional natural disaster drills (Astor, 1998). Similarly, one report found an increase in the number of students who avoided specific places in their school because of fear (Kaufman et al., 1998). Another poll found that one in nine teens missed school because of the fear of violence (Current Health, 1998). This poll also reported that nearly half of the 2,000 sampled teens made some change in their daily activity because of the fear of imminent violence.

RISK AND PROTECTIVE FACTORS

From a prevention perspective, it is important to understand the factors that may contribute to aggressive and delinquent behavior in a general sense. Several factors have been identified that contribute to participation in aggression and delinquency (Dryfoos, 1998; Kazdin, 1995; Williams, Ayers, & Arthur, 1997). One set of these risk factors encompasses an adolescent's environment and includes such variables as family income level, neighborhood substance use patterns, the local availability of drugs and alcohol, and the degree of neighborhood crime and disorganization. A second group of risk factors includes biological and psychosocial characteristics such as an adolescent's degree of impulse control, the age at which an adolescent first engages in illegal behavior, the age at which an adolescent experiments with drugs or alcohol, an adolescent's family history regarding alcoholism, and the degree to which an adolescent is subject to genetic disorders. Research with genetics and other biological factors continues to produce promising results despite the current lack of concrete findings.

Another set of related risk factors concern the social world of the adolescent, including interpersonal relationships. These factors include such things as a lack of adequate parental supervision, inconsistent or overly harsh disciplinary practices, higher rates of drug and alcohol use by peers and family members, lack of interest in school on the part of the youth and/or the youth's parents, and poor academic performance.

INTERVENTIONS

Most of the literature related to intervening in school violence focuses on prevention efforts. Prevention is easier, cheaper, and more effective than actually curing the results of violence once it has been perpetrated (Rich, 1992). Many components of school violence prevention models can serve as points of departure for post-occurrence interventions with the perpetrators. A number of reviews of school violence prevention programs have been published (see Allen-Meares, Washington, & Welsh, 1996; Dryfoos, 1998; Goldstein & Conoley, 1997), and we encourage readers attempting to prevent or avert school violence in their communities to become familiar with the multitude of available prevention program options. However, for two reasons, this chapter does not address prevention programs: First, they focus on the perpetrators of violence, whereas we choose to focus on intervening with the victims of violence. Second, this text focuses on crisis intervention, and while there may be a national "crisis" with regard to school violence, we are limiting our topic to interventions pertinent to individual victims of violence.

Crisis Intervention Application

School settings provide unique environments for conflict among students. Because the student population in most schools is reasonably small, individuals commonly interact with the same peers repeatedly throughout the day. Although this familiarity has positive aspects, it can exacerbate tensions between individuals who may not be able to avoid others with whom they are having difficulty. Crisis intervention plans would necessarily have to address this issue.

Youth in middle school and high school experience intense developmental changes. Not least of these is their creation of a self-identity. During middle school and high school years, youth commonly affiliate with subgroups (such as "brains," "jocks," and "stoners"). The labeling associated with these groups can lead to stigmatization, and individual identity is sometimes subsumed by group identity (Crews & Counts, 1997). There is often tremendous peer pressure to adhere to group norms, and members commonly become intolerant of those who do not share their values or beliefs. Consequently, crisis intervention efforts need to assess the victim's self-identity and degree of subgroup assimilation in order to produce changes consistent with the individual's values. Proposed changes that conflict with the norms of the client's group need to be evaluated with regard to the client's willingness to challenge those norms.

Another factor that can contribute to difficulty in using a crisis intervention model is the common imposition of authority by school faculty and personnel through the use of fear and force. Strict rules and degrading experiences have been associated with violence against teachers as well as school property (Regoli & Hewitt, 1994). It is widely held that adolescents are distrustful of adults. A reckless imposition of authority can result in the youth's unwillingness to take advantage of services provided by adults (Curcio & First, 1993).

Although some trainers or educators adhere to a specific therapeutic model for intervening in crises, the diversity of acts constituting "school violence" indicates that an array of therapeutic models be considered. Roberts's seven-step crisis intervention model (Roberts, 1996) has garnered wide acceptance in the social work and social service practice community. It is applicable to a broad spectrum of populations and problems. Other chapters of this text present the model in detail, so we direct the reader to those chapters rather than restating its general principles.

It has been our experience that Roberts's crisis intervention model is most useful as an organizing structure or overriding framework in combination with a supplemental therapeutic intervention. Specifically, youth experiencing initial trauma responses to victimization respond well to behavioral interventions followed by cognitive therapy. Those who are not experiencing severe trauma do well with cognitive interventions (Wells & Miller, 1993). Cognitive therapy is one of the most widely used intervention methods in social work practice (Hepworth, Rooney, & Larsen, 1997). It is often used in conjunction with other interventions such as assertiveness training and desensitization (Hepworth et al., 1997). The following is a brief description of the basic principles of cognitive therapy and an illustrative application of the method within the overarching structure of Roberts's crisis intervention model with one of the cases presented at the beginning of the chapter. Included is a brief discussion of special concerns and considerations practitioners should note when applying Roberts's model to victims of school violence.

Cognitive Therapy

Judith Beck (1995) presents the following set of 10 principles upon which cognitive therapy is based.

1. Cognitive therapy is based on an ever-evolving formulation of clients and their problems in cognitive terms. The worker is reminded that current thinking is of paramount importance because it is the present that can be altered. Identifying precipitating factors and historical developmental events is tremendously important, particularly in the context of school violence, but their primary importance is in maintaining thoughts that impede the client from full functioning.

2. Cognitive therapy requires a sound therapeutic alliance. Consistent with training texts in most social service professions, the therapist-client "relationship" is of primary importance. Demonstrating empathetic interpersonal skills and requesting feedback concerning the relationship are encouraged. There may be difficulties in establishing a positive alliance due to the role differences between the worker and the adolescent, but our experience suggests that those truly in crisis quickly dismiss their "attitudes" when they are physically moved from their peers, who can serve as an audience, and when the worker is able to accurately identify their emotional and cognitive state.

3. Cognitive therapy emphasizes collaboration and active participation by both the worker and the client. Consistent with principle 6, the therapist may be more active and directive in the initial stages of therapy, and may allow more freedom and exploration by the client as therapy progresses.

4. Cognitive therapy is goal oriented and problem focused. Many victims of school violence are overwhelmed by the traumatic experience and are unable to identify their "problem." Using a cognitive approach in conjunction with the crisis intervention model can provide a tremendous opportunity to enhance clarity for our clients. Depending on clients' ability to problem-solve, they may need little more assistance than identifying their problem. This is particularly the case when the client identifies a goal of ceasing to ruminate about the event.

5. Cognitive therapy initially emphasizes the present. Although a significant transgression creates difficulty for clients responding to particular acts of school violence, it is the cognitive processing of those events that serves as an enduring problem. As Beck states, "Resolution and/or a more realistic appraisal of situations that are currently distressing usually lead to symptom reduction" (1995, pp. 6–7).

6. Cognitive therapy is educative, aims to teach the client to be his or her own therapist, and emphasizes relapse prevention. In educating clients about the cognitive model, the worker provides clients with a means of helping themselves. Consistent with crisis intervention values, clients are empowered to help themselves rather than becoming dependent on the worker.

7. Cognitive therapy aims to be time limited and posits several goals that are consistent with this aim. The goals of cognitive therapy are to provide symptom relief, facilitate a remission of the disorder, help clients resolve their most pressing problems, and provide clients with tools so that they can help themselves in the future. Given that the precipitating problem for the client is external (interpersonal), cognitive therapy tends to be effective and efficient in relieving distress in adolescent clients. This time-limited structure is congruent with the overarching structure of Roberts's crisis intervention model.

8. Cognitive therapy sessions are structured. Reviewing the client's progress since the previous meeting, setting an agenda for the session, getting feedback from any homework, discussing agenda items, giving new homework assignments, and summarizing the session are common tasks used in cognitive therapy sessions.

9. Cognitive therapy teaches patients to identify, evaluate, and respond to their dysfunctional thoughts and beliefs. Through Socratic questioning or guided discovery, the worker and client discover irrational or dysfunctional thoughts that maintain behaviors serving to impede the client from full functioning. By identifying these thoughts and critically evaluating their validity and usefulness, the client is taught to create new schemas that lead to healthier adaptive behaviors.

10. Cognitive therapy uses a variety of techniques to change thinking, mood, and behavior. Although Socratic questioning and guided dis-

covery are central tools for cognitive therapy, techniques from other therapeutic approaches are employed as well.

These principles are applied through a process in which the worker (a) assists clients in accepting that their self-statements, assumptions, and beliefs largely mediate their emotional reactions to the precipitating event; (b) assists client in identifying dysfunctional beliefs and patterns of thoughts that underlie their problems; (c) assists the client in identifying situations that engender dysfunctional cognitions; (d) assists clients in substituting functional self-statements in place of self-defeating cognitions; and (e) assists clients in rewarding themselves for successful coping efforts (Hepworth et al., 1997).

In the case of survivors of school violence, some of the client's thoughts may be rational—there may be real threats of subsequent violence. There may be times when life really is so hard that an appropriate response is to become clinically depressed or anxious. In fact, these responses may be part of a natural grieving process (Moorey, 1996). In either event, a primary problem may be that the client, finding out that he or she is unable to carry out tasks in the same way as previously, gives up and does little more than retreat from life. Clients may generalize their lack of control about one part of their life to all areas of their life. Reversing this pattern becomes the primary goal of cognitive therapy—and of the crisis intervention. In achieving this goal, the therapist allows the client to accept the negative thoughts (such as "When I am around those people, I may be in danger"), but either challenges the negative *automatic* thoughts of the client (such as "I automatically think that whenever I see them I am in danger. But maybe that isn't so. Maybe I'm just worried that I might be in a situation where they could jump me again") or develops strategies to facilitate the client's distracting himself from them and challenging their implications (Moorey, 1996).

APPLICATION OF ROBERTS'S CRISIS INTERVENTION MODEL WITH COGNITIVE THERAPY

Assessing Lethality

In assessing the case of Aretha Jackson, presented at the beginning of the chapter, we would be concerned that she is safe from further threats of violence. Crisis intervention for persons victimized by school violence should begin with a comprehensive assessment of the incident and persons involved. Ensuring that the victim is safe is of paramount importance. Whereas the specific perpetrator of the violence may be removed from the scene, members of that person's subgroup may be cause for concern. We would need to know if the girl who threatened Aretha still poses a threat to her. For instance, we would need to find out if she continues to bring a weapon to school. In the case of box cutters or other weapons, simply disarming the perpetrator may not be sufficient because the weapon can be easily replaced.

Determining if Aretha is a member of a group would be important. Assessing her membership in an organized gang is essential, but it is also important to determine if she is a member of any informal groups (geeks, brains, etc.). We might make these inquiries by asking about who Aretha associates with if we are familiar with most of the student population. We also need to try to assess the client's degree of assimilation into the group at the outset of the first interview.

The client's accounting of pertinent events preceding the altercation should be carefully noted. If possible, the worker should obtain school information specific to individual students because intervening after violent events is enhanced by knowledge of the participants: their family situations, specific stressors and strengths, social supports, and so on (Striepling, 1997). In Aretha's case, we would try to access her school records prior to meeting with her. We value her accounting of the violent event, but we also try to gather background information so that we can contextualize her comments.

We are concerned with three aspects of potential lethality in Aretha's case. First, how likely is it that she will commit harm to herself as a result of the victimization? Many adolescents are concerned with "saving face" and not losing the respect of their peers. If the individual fears that he or she will be humiliated or disgraced by being victimized, the threat of lethality is increased. We are more concerned with older adolescents in this regard than we are with early adolescents or younger children. In Aretha's case, we do not think this risk is great, as she readily came forth for help. Second, what is the threat that Aretha will think about personally redressing the wrong done to her? The common inability of adolescents to think temporally beyond "today" and to delay gratification can often increase the possibility that they will react to "even the score." Aretha's fear that the threat will be repeated suggests that this risk is not great. The third aspect of lethality the worker should assess is the degree to which there is a viable threat of recrimination by the perpetrator's subgroup. In Aretha's case, we are indeed concerned and will employ the school's administration and security personnel to intervene on her behalf. We will also work with her to identify potential dangerous situations she should avoid.

Establishing Rapport and Communication

As noted, many adolescents have a general distrust of adults. The victim may think that he or she can "handle the situation" without adult interference. However, it has been our experience that students are willing to trust persons in position of authority when they are in crisis situations.

We will pay attention to our use of effective interviewing microskills (attentive listening, body language, paraphrasing, etc.) and strive to project an aura of professionalism without being authoritarian with Aretha. Although it does not appear to be the case with Aretha, it is often the case that the "victim" played an active part in creating the situation that resulted in violence. Nonetheless, the worker should view the client in the "victim" role for the purposes of crisis intervention. Assuming an authoritarian role will certainly undermine any rapport that has been established between the worker and the client. As noted by Dziegielewski and Resnick (1995), de-emphasizing the term *victim* and instilling the idea that the client is a *survivor* may be helpful.

Identifying Major Problems

Precipitating events must be identified if the client is to successfully process the violent event. This information may be difficult to obtain, particularly if the violent act was an indiscriminate, aggressive act against a representative of a group rather than a specific individual. Many times the individual unknowingly provokes the attack. In these instances it is fruitful for the worker to use his or her professional knowledge to help identify possible causes of the attack. It appears that Aretha unknowingly or unintentionally provoked the threat against her. Helping her understand why the other girl reacted the way she did will help Aretha process the "meaning" of the threat. If we are unaware of this "meaning," we sometimes contact school security personnel or administrators to find out their perception of the interaction. Whereas it may be possible to get this information directly from the perpetrator, we have found that the school personnel may have already done so.

A second reason for gathering additional information about the violent act is that adolescents, even when not engaged in a crisis situation, are not known to be particularly good witnesses or reporters of events to which they are a part, so working to gather other "views" of the event may be helpful in assisting the client to understand what really happened. This understanding, in turn, may help the client identify or reframe his or her actual problems.

Many violent events are the culmination of a series of negative encounters between the victim and the perpetrator. These bullying situations are similar to a person being stalked, as the victim may have taken all known steps to avoid an altercation, to no avail. As Roberts and Roberts (1990) state, when these steps fail, the client is likely to enter an active crisis state. Although the client is likely to desire answers to the question of why he or she has been targeted, the worker should remain focused on the nature of the interpersonal behavior pattern because that is the client's problem.

Entering this active crisis state can provoke a sense of disequilibrium or disorganization, but it also is indicative of the client's generating resources to begin overcoming the crisis-provoking event (Roberts & Dziegielewski, 1995). It is at this point that cognitive therapy can be applied. At this point, the victim has begun to make self-statements that may be interfering with normal behaviors. Aretha may be considering her role in the violent interaction as something she should have known about, or something she did herself. Her fears may be causing her to become overly cautious.

During the first couple of sessions with Aretha, we will try to make sure she is not ruminating about the past event. We will work to identify those problems that impede her ability to function as she did prior to the violence. Specifically, we will help her understand that it is her cognitive responses that restrict her after the violent event.

Dealing With Feelings and Providing Support

Social service providers need to be attentive to social withdrawal of children exposed to traumatic violent events, because inhibition of their normal activity can serve as an indicator of their degree of stress. Children's grief responses are often more delayed than adult responses. Still, if children are being quiet, polite "angels," this may indicate that they are having difficulty adjusting to the aftermath of the precipitating event (Ursano, Fullerton, & Norwood, 1999).

Students typically feel fear, anger, frustration, powerlessness, embarrassment, and shame when they have been victimized by violent aggressors. If they are witness to another's victimization, they may also feel guilty for not responding more assertively or effectively. Providing attentive, nonjudgmental support allows the client to work through his or her emotional responses to the event. Normalizing the client's experience facilitates this process. Reconciling the mixture of feelings that result from being victimized allows the client to move toward applying energy to actively engaging in problem solving.

We will work with Aretha to help her understand that her fearful reaction to being threatened is normal and reasonable. If her emotional vocabulary is limited, we may try to help her broaden it so that she does not fall prey to the common problem of youngsters reporting being only "angry" or "sad" because they have not identified other emotions.

Exploring Possible Alternatives

Once the client's level of emotional distress has been reduced, he or she can begin to generate alternative solutions to the problem(s). The worker can help develop a list of viable alternative responses that will achieve the client's goals. It is important when working with adolescents to prod the client to persist and to brainstorm possibilities rather than accepting the first idea that comes to mind.

It is at this stage that we begin to help the client challenge his or her irrational cognitions or mediate emotional reactions to the precipitating event. We work with the client to explore if his or her perceptions are accurate reflections of what is going on in the external world. We acknowledge the protective function of these thoughts, but we also help the youth see that there are other ways of thinking about the current situation and that the past is the past. Translating these concepts to young children is sometimes quite challenging, and we often remind ourselves that patience is indeed a virtue.

Formulating an Action Plan

In this step, goals should be clearly formulated. Brower and Nurius (1993) suggest that the goals should be concrete, specific, and measurable. If they are not collaboratively established, there is a risk that the client will not be invested in achieving the stated goals. Providing a mechanism for the client to actively direct treatment goal setting can provide a model for subsequent self-empowerment activity (Roberts & Dziegielewski, 1995).

The worker is cautioned to remember that school students may lack the cognitive or emotional maturity (or the verbal acumen) to identify the steps necessary to carry out a plan that will achieve the identified goals. We have found that employing a problem-solving model such as the task-centered model (see Epstein, 1992) can provide a structure for articulating this plan. Cognitive behavioral interventions are compatible with the task-centered model, and the time-limited nature of the model has been amenable to using it in school settings.

Although we have, by this time, already begun our cognitive intervention by challenging the client's self-talk and beliefs, we use this step to direct the client to demonstrate behavioral tasks that indicate that she is achieving her goals. In Aretha's case we will make sure that she is again doing things that she avoided in the wake of the violent threat. We are very supportive of all efforts (no matter how small) that indicate she is making progress toward overcoming whatever impediments she had immediately following the violent event. We are particularly concerned that Aretha reward herself for her progress, because school victims are often reluctant to acknowledge their progress; we want them to be aware of their progress and of how they have overcome their own problems. If our cognitive intervention is to be educational, the client needs to be aware of her progress in order to replicate it later.

Follow-Up Measures

As in other interventions, the active phase of treatment can vary in duration. By definition, a "crisis" is time-bound, and there comes a point at which the crisis aspect of the problem diminishes; either the intervention has been effective and the client will terminate services, or continued services need to be contracted. Our cognitive intervention, imbedded in Roberts's crisis intervention model, typically focuses on only one or two dysfunctional beliefs or thoughts that are constricting the client from full functioning. However, we recognize that many clients had cognitive or emotional difficulties prior to their victimization that may impede their full recovery. Although successful treatment in crisis intervention is typically defined as the client's return to previous levels of functioning (Roberts & Dziegielewski, 1995), the trauma of being victimized by or exposed to school violence may require treatment beyond the intervention necessary to address the crisis aspect of the problem. In these cases, the client should be referred to service providers for this additional help. Ethical practice standards indicate that after terminating with the client, the worker should follow up to ensure that the client is maintaining satisfactory mental health.

Our work with Aretha continued for 3 weeks while she responded to being threatened by her peer. During that time she overcame her irrational fear of other girls in her school who belonged to organized gangs. She respected the potential for violence these girls presented but also recognized that she was not being singled out as a target for aggression. Aretha no longer avoided public areas of the school. She was able to identify irrational self-talk and challenge these thoughts. As a consequence, Aretha became pleased that she was able to address her own fears and conduct her social activities in the same way she had prior to her violent altercation with her peer. We should note that the perpetrator of the violence had been suspended from school for 1 week, and that school security personnel had been vigilant in their surveillance of the girls the perpetrator had been hanging out with.

SPECIAL CONSIDERATIONS

The crisis intervention provider should be aware of a few special considerations: First, there are numerous cultural considerations that impact one's successfully engaging clients. It is beyond the scope of this text to elaborate on specific practice techniques for intervening in specific cultures; the reader is directed to the vast literature emerging in this area (see Cartledge & Johnson, 1997; Castillo, 1997; McGoldrick, Giordano, Pearce, & Giordano, 1996). Second, workers should be sensitive to gender issues when attempting to provide crisis intervention services. We have found that same-gender relationships are most comfortable for students.

A growing area of concern regards secondary trauma responses on the part of service providers, school personnel, and even parents. Literature emanating from research on posttraumatic stress disorder indicates that those vicariously exposed to traumatic events are susceptible to experience trauma themselves (Figley, 1995; Hudnall, 1996). The risk of secondary trauma is higher for those repeatedly exposed to persons who have experienced trauma. Therefore, workers providing crisis intervention services need to take steps to ensure their own health (see Figley, 1995; Hudnall, 1996).

CATASTROPHIC EVENTS

The greatest special consideration in the area of school violence is what we term *catastrophic events*. Although, as noted earlier, the number of catastrophic events is essentially inconsequential in the context of all school violence, the heinous nature of multiple homicides in recent years, as well as the impact these events have on entire communities, has galvanized the media's attention on this phenomena.

The media's unwavering attention to the catastrophic homicidal school violence events of the past few years provides a profusion of anecdotal information about the perpetrators, victims, and societal responses to these events, but no systematic research has been presented that provides an understanding of this phenomenon. As in the previous section, our discussion is limited to the crisis intervention aspects of this phenomenon, focusing on the victims of the event rather than the perpetrators. Further, our discussion is limited to post-occurrence interventions. These emanate from literature on disaster relief, but they provide the best information relative to treating survivors of these devastating events.

Assessment/Risk Factors

A primary goal in helping survivors of catastrophic school violence is to restore and promote normative cognitive, emotional, and interpersonal functioning to those adversely affected by trauma and grief (Murphy, Pynoos, & James, 1997). In doing so, service providers should remember that individuals differ in their capacity to adjust to catastrophic events.

Freedy, Resnick, and Kilpatrick (1992) have developed a risk factor model for disaster adjustment. They suggest that workers perform short clinical assessments of factors thought to predict adjustment difficulties in the days and weeks following the disaster. Their identified high-risk individuals include those who have experienced high numbers of negative life events within the past year, and those with mental health problems prior to the disaster. Experiences during the phenomenon that indicate high risk for poor adjustment include threats of personal injury (including death), personal injury, exposure to grotesque sights, and the loss of a family member or loved one (witnessed or not). Ursano et al. (1999) suggest that the single best predictor of the probability and frequency of postdisaster psychiatric problems is the severity of the disaster, as indicated by the number of injured and the types of their injuries. Having effective cognitive coping skills and a social support network that promotes personal control and competence prior to the disaster are thought to be protective factors that can mediate the risk for poor adjustment to disasters (Freedy et al., 1992).

Post-Occurrence Interventions

We are proponents of an integrated model that combines Roberts's crisis intervention model and cognitive therapy. However, we recognize that catastrophic events require additional consideration. For instance, the needs of individuals following a disaster can be considered in the context of Maslow's hierarchy of needs (Maslow, 1968), suggesting that initial intervention efforts focus on establishing safety and physical health. Social and psychological interventions should follow. A crucial intervention component should be to educate members of the community about "normal responses to abnormal events" (Ursano et al., 1999). These responses are physical, cognitive, and emotional. Physical responses usually begin with a sense of shock and disorientation. This commonly triggers a "fight or flight" response, which manifests with increased heart rates and breathing and increased sensory perception. Because this intense response cannot be maintained for a long period, exhaustion follows (Young, 1991, 1995).

Cognitive and emotional responses are similar to the physical responses, with shock and disbelief manifesting initially, perhaps including denial and a sense of suspension of reality. This shock is followed by emotional turmoil as the individual engages emotions such as anger, frustration, guilt, and grief in responding to the losses resulting from the crisis (Young, 1991, 1995). It may take weeks or months to proceed through the shock and emotional turmoil responses, leaving the person mentally and emotionally exhausted. This emotional exhaustion commonly leaves the individual feeling as though he or she is on an emotional roller coaster: at one moment overwhelmed by emotion, and the next moment devoid of emotion. Some persons erect defenses to this phenomenon by constricting their range of emotional involvement in the world around them (Young, 1991). The goal of crisis intervention can be seen as facilitating the client's journey through this process and emerging as a "fully-responsive, fully-involved" person. It is often appropriate to include family members or friends in counseling sessions, because they can reinforce messages and provide ongoing support. This is the case even if those family members or friends also have been traumatized by the event. Peer support groups can also be helpful in the aftermath of catastrophic events (Young, 1991).

The National Organization of Victim Assistance (NOVA) has been responding to catastrophic school violence events for almost two decades (Young, 1991, 1995). Those administering postevent services will welcome NOVA's expertise, particularly its group debriefing process. We refer the reader to chapter 3 in this text detailing Mitchell and Everly's model of critical incident debriefing and note that it is an important mechanism for moving groups of survivors through steps 3 (identifying major problems) and 4 (dealing with feelings and providing support) of Roberts's crisis intervention model.

NOVA's intervention addresses the complicating factor of an entire community's being overwhelmed by the catastrophic event. In these instances it becomes important for survivors and their service providers to form a protective barrier against intrusive external forces, including media personnel. Using adults as buffers against external forces is appropriate, provided the adults themselves are not overwhelmed by the trauma. One method of accomplishing this is to facilitate crisis intervention with the adults so that they can then attend to their children. As noted previously, the grief response in children is typically delayed (in comparison with adult reactions). This period of shock or denial can be problematic if it lasts for an extended period, but it does provide a window of time when attention can be focused on adult care providers. We are not suggesting that necessary crisis intervention services be withheld from children, and we acknowledge that adults' ability to provide care for their children while they are in the midst of a trauma response should be assessed as well.

In addition to the trauma experienced by those directly exposed to the violent event, the social networks of these victims are also affected by the violence. In particular, parents and siblings of youth are at risk for secondary trauma responses. Social service workers need to be aware of potential interpersonal difficulties manifesting in families exposed to school violence in the weeks and months following the occurrence. Distributing literature that offers supportive services can be helpful to those who are not educated about the symptoms of secondary stress reactions, or those who have minimized their psychological or social problems subsequent to the violent event.

Finally, social workers and other crisis intervention providers are reminded that persons providing relief services may need psychiatric help as well, particularly police, medical personnel, hot line workers, insurance claims settlers, and community leaders. Special attention should be paid to "heroes," who often are under tremendous pressure to serve as spokespersons for the survivors or relief workers. These heroes may experience conflicting feelings of guilt, satisfaction, and anxiety that their actions do not justify their "hero" status.

The case of John Hanson exemplifies the need for crisis intervention in a catastrophic event. The assessment of John's situation is of critical importance. The length of time John was exposed to traumatic events and the nature of the events he witnessed will help determine the type and length of his treatment. Those students who witnessed shootings or were placed in hostage situations will need special consideration and are more likely to exhibit chronic symptomatology than those who were not present or who witnessed peripheral events.

The need for involvement by NOVA would be stressed, as would the need for a group debriefing. Because this event affects the entire community, it would be important to include John's parents and close friends to empower them to help in the healing process. Educating John's parents and other support network members about normal reactions to abnormal situations would be a primary goal, because those closest to John would need to be prepared for these reactions. In working with John directly, we would use a cognitive intervention similar to that described in treating Aretha Jackson. Emphasizing John's fears about his lack of control in the violent situation and the possibility of repeated catastrophic events would require his addressing irrational thoughts that impede his posttraumatic event functioning. While we work with him to address his cognitive distortions, we also remain supportive of his emotional recovery. Through these interventions it is likely that John would learn to cope with the catastrophic situation.

CONCLUSION AND POLICY RECOMMENDATIONS

Although continued efforts and resources need to be devoted to prevention programs directed at creating safe schools, there will always be a need for crisis intervention programs as well. In addition to violence between individuals, tensions between student subgroups in schools have always resulted in aggression between these groups, and crisis interventions with individuals are appropriate for dealing with these skirmishes or transgressions. If these tensions escalate, they can lead to devastating events that traumatize whole schools, if not whole communities. In these instances, disaster-relief models of crisis intervention are most appropriate. School district administrators, as well as social service agency administrators, would be well advised to establish both prevention and post-occurrence plans to address the issue of school violence.

REFERENCES

Agron, J. (1999). Safe havens: Preventing violence and crime in schools. *American School and University,* 71(6), 18–23.

Alexander, R., & Curtis, C. (1995). A critical review of strategies to reduce school violence. *Social Work in Education,* 17(2), 73–82.

Allen-Meares, P., Washington, R. O., & Welsh, B. L. (1996). *Social work services in schools* (2nd ed.). Boston: Allyn and Bacon.

Astor, R. A. (1998). School violence: A blueprint for elementary school interventions. In E. M. Freeman, C. G. Franklin, R. Fong, G. L. Shaffer, & E. M. Timberlake (Eds.), *Multisystem skills and interventions in school social work practice* (pp. 281–295). Washington,

DC: National Association of Social Workers Press.

Bastian, L. D., & Taylor, B. M. (1991). *School crime: A national crime victimization survey report (U. S. Department of Justice, Bureau of Justice Statistics, NCJ-131645)*. Rockville, MD: US Department of Justice.

Beck, J. S. (1995). *Cognitive therapy: Basics and beyond*. New York: Guilford.

Braaten, S. (1997). Creating safe schools: A principal's perspective. In A. P. Goldstein and J. C. Conoley (Eds.), *School violence intervention: Practical handbook* (pp. 46–57). New York: Guilford.

Brower, A. M., & Nurius, P. S. (1993). Social cognition and individual change: Currrent theory and counseling guidelines. Newbury Park Oaks, CA: Sage.

Cartledge, G., & Johnson, C. T. (1997). School violence and cultural diversity. In A. P. Goldstein and J. C. Conoley (Eds.), *School violence intervention: Practical handbook* (pp. 391–425). New York: Guilford.

Castillo, R. J. (1997). *Culture and mental illness: A client-centered approach*. Pacific Grove, CA: Brooks/Cole.

Crews, G. A., & Counts, M. R. (1997). *The evolution of school disturbance in America: Colonial times to modern day*. Westport, CT: Praeger.

Curcio, J. L., & First, P. F. (1993). *Violence in the schools: How to proactively prevent and defuse it*. Newbury Park, CA: Sage.

Current Health. (1998, April–May). When violence comes to school. *Current Health, 24*(8), 6–7.

Dryfoos, J. (1998). *Safe passage: Making it through adolescence in a risky society*. New York: Oxford University Press.

Dziegielewski, S. F., & Resnick, C. (1995). A model of crisis intervention with adult survivors of incest. *Crisis Intervention and Time-Limited Treatment, 2*(1), 49–55.

Epstein, L. (1992). *Brief treatment and a new look at the task-centered approach*. New York: Mcmillan.

Figley, C. R. (1995). *Compassion fatigue: Coping with secondary traumatic stress disorder in those who treat the traumatized*. Psychosocial Stress no. 23. New York: Brunner/Mazel.

Frederick, A. D., Middleton, E. J., & Butler, D. (1995). Identification of various levels of school violence. In R. Duhon-Sells (Ed.), *Dealing with youth violence: What schools and communities need to know* (pp. 26–31). Bloomington, IN: National Educational Service.

Freedy, J. R., Resnick, H. S., & Kilpatrick, D. G. (1992). Conceptual framework for evaluating disaster impact: Implications for clinical intervention. In L. S. Austin (Ed.), *Responding to disaster: A guide for mental health professionals* (pp. 3–24). Washington, DC: American Psychiatric Press.

Goldstein, A. P., & Conoley, J. C. (1997). Student aggression: Current status. In A. P. Goldstein and J. C. Conoley (Eds.), *School violence intervention: A practical handbook* (pp. 3–22). New York: Guilford.

Heaviside, S., Rowand, C., Williams, C., & Farris, E. (1998). *Violence and Discipline Problems in U.S. Public Schools: 1996–97* (U.S. Department of Education. National Center for Education Statistics, NCES 98-030). Washington, DC: U.S. Government Printing Office.

Hepworth, D. H., Rooney, R. H., & Larsen, J. A. (1997). *Direct social work practice: Theory and skills* (5th ed.). Pacific Grove, CA: Brooks/Cole.

Hudnall, B. (1996). *Secondary traumatic stress: Self-care issues for clinicians, researchers, and educators.* Lutherville, MD: Sidran Press.

Kaufman, P., Chen, X., Choy, S., Chandler, K. A., Chapman, C. D., Rand, M. R., & Ringel, C. (1998). *Indicators of school crime and safety, 1998.* U.S. Departments of Education and Justice. NCES 98-251/NCJ 172215. Washington, DC: 1998.

Kazdin, A. E. (1995). *Conduct disorders in childhood and adolescence* (2nd ed.). Newbury Park, CA: Sage.

Kleinz, K. H. (1998). *Never say never: Violence and tragedy can strike anywhere.* National Association of Elementary School Principals Online. *http://www.naesp.org/misc/violence.htm.*

Larke, P. J., & Carter, N. P. (1995). School violence: Preparing preservice teachers. In R. Duhon-Sells (Ed.), *Dealing with youth violence: What schools and communities need to know* (pp. 45–51). Bloomington, IN: National Educational Service.

Maslow, A. H. (1968). *Toward a psychology of being.* New York: Van Nostrand Reinhold.

McGoldrick, M., Giordano, J., Pearce, J. K., & Giordano, J. (1996). *Ethnicity and family therapy* (2nd ed). New York: Guilford.

Moorey, S. (1996). When bad things happen to rational people: Cognitive therapy in adverse life circumstances. In P. M. Salkovskis (Ed.), *Frontiers of cognitive therapy* (pp. 450–466). New York: Guilford.

Murphy, L., Pynoos, R. S., & James, C. B. (1997). The trauma/grief focused group psychotherapy module of an elementary school–based violence prevention/intervention program. In J. D. Osofsky (Ed.), *Children in a violent society* (pp. 223–255). New York: Guilford.

Poland, S. (1997). School crisis teams. In A. P. Goldstein and J. C. Conoley (Eds.), *School violence intervention: A practical handbook* (pp. 127–159). New York: Guilford.

Regoli, R. M., & Hewitt, J. D. (1994). *Delinquency in society: A child-centered approach.* New York: McGraw-Hill.

Resnick, P. A., & Mechanic, M. B. (1995). Brief cognitive therapies for rape victims. In A. R. Roberts (Ed.), *Crisis intervention and time-limited cognitive treatment* (pp. 91–126). Newbury Park, CA: Sage.

Rich, J. (1992). Predicting and controlling school violence. *Contemporary Education, 64*(1), 35–39.

Roberts, A. R. (1991). Conceptualizing crisis theory and the crisis intervention model. In A. R. Roberts (Ed.), *Contemporary perspectives on crisis intervention and prevention* (pp. 3–17). Englewood Cliffs, NJ: Prentice-Hall.

Roberts, A. R. (1996). Epidemiology of, and definitions of acute crisis in American society. In A. R. Roberts (Ed.), *Crisis management and brief treatment: Theory, technique, and applications* (pp. 16–33). Pacific Grove, CA: Brooks/Cole.

Roberts, A. R., & Dziegielewski, S. F. (1995). Foundation skills and applications of crisis intervention and cognitive therapy. In A. R. Roberts (Ed.), *Crisis intervention and time-limited cognitive treatment* (pp. 3–27). Newbury Park, CA: Sage.

Roberts, A. R., & Roberts, B. (1990). A comprehensive model for crisis intervention with battered women and their children. In A. R. Roberts (Ed.), *Crisis intervention handbook: Assessment, treatment, and research* (pp. 106–123). Belmont, CA: Wadsworth.

Sheley, J. F., & Wright, J. D. (1998). *High school youths, weapons, and violence: A national survey.* National Institute of Justice: Research in Brief. Washington, DC: U.S. Government Printing Office.

Straus, M., Gelles, R., & Steinmetz, S. K. (1980). *Behind closed doors: Violence in the American family.* New York: Anchor Press/Doubleday.

Striepling, S. H. (1997). The low-aggression classroom: A teacher's view. In A. P. Goldstein and J. C. Conoley (Eds.), *School violence intervention: A practical handbook* (pp. 23–45). New York: Guilford.

Ursano, R. J., Fullerton, C. S., & Norwood, A. E. (1999). *Psychiatric dimensions of disaster: Patient care, community consultation and preventive medicine.* American Psychiatric Press Online (*www.psych.org/pract_of_psych/disaster.html*).

U.S. Department of Education, National Center for Education Statistics. (1998). *Violence and discipline problems in U.S. public schools, 1996–97.* NCES 98-030. Washington, DC: U.S. Government Printing Office.

Young, M. A. (1991). Crisis intervention and the aftermath of disaster. In A. R. Roberts (Ed.), *Contemporary perspectives on crisis intervention and prevention.* Englewood Cliffs, NJ: Prentice-Hall.

Young, M. A. (1995). Crisis response teams in the aftermath of disasters. In A. R. Roberts (Ed.), *Crisis intervention and time-limited cognitive treatment* (pp. 151–187). Newbury Park, CA: Sage.

Wells, D., & Miller, M. J. (1993). Adolescent affective aggression: An intervention model. *Adolescence, 28,* 781–791.

Wetzstein, C. (1998, July 6). Make aware or scare? *Insight on the News, 14*(25), 37–38.

Williams, J. H., Ayers, C. D., & Arthur, M. W. (1997). Risk and protective factors in the development of delinquency and conduct disorder. In M. W. Fraser (Ed.), *Risk and resilience in childhood: An ecological perspective* (pp. 140–170). Washington, DC: National Association of Social Workers Press.

11

An Application of Crisis Intervention to Situational Crises Frequently Experienced by Adult Survivors of Incest

PAMELA VALENTINE

Case Stories

Debra, an attractive, sophisticated African American woman of 29 years, presented in therapy with symptoms of depression and "unexplained anxiety" shortly after she was married. While compiling her psychosocial history, the therapist discovered that Debra was a victim of childhood sexual abuse. Debra's new sexual relationship with her husband was triggering memories of the childhood abuse.

Patsy, a 32-year-old physical therapist, came to therapy complaining of migraine headaches and suicidal ideation. Her younger brother had just died of AIDS. The deceased brother was *not* the older brother who had sexually exploited Patsy when she was an adolescent.

Marsha was 30 years old and worked part-time in a department store. She came to therapy at the behest of her partner, who complained that Marsha never showed any emotions other than anger. Marsha described herself as "happy, busy, and productive." A thorough psychosocial history did not dispute her story. The only evidence that indicated that Marsha's childhood history might be different from that which she presented was the periodic "crash" that Marsha experienced every 6 to 9 months for no apparent reason. She would "hit a wall," feel depressed, and refuse to go to work for a week. By the week's end, however, Marsha would garner her strength and be back to her old self again. This pattern continued until Marsha's partner decided to leave her. Marsha did not go into crisis at this point but, for the first time, was ready to engage in regular therapeutic sessions. She wanted to explore why she felt virtually no emotions. As a deeply religious woman who combined therapy sessions with her faith in God, Marsha told God that it was okay if she began to feel. Within 1 week of that statement, Marsha began having disturbing "visions" that threw her into crisis. She needed several-time-a-week sessions and reassurance that she was not going crazy. Quickly, the "visions" became regular dreams and nightmares. Marsha's whole world was turning upside down.

Debra, Patsy, and Marsha had one thing in common: They were adult women who, as children, had experienced intimate sexual relations with significantly older male family members. In short, they were victims of incest. Like many incest victims, they did not present in therapy until another external precipitating event overwhelmed their normal coping strategies.

Treating crisis clients who have a history of childhood sexual abuse presents challenges for several reasons: (a) Victims' coping skills are naturally compromised by the incest, and practitioners, unaware of clients' histories of incest, will likely view clients as "resistant" when they fail to comply with simple directives; (b) worse are clients who engage in self-harmful practices such as wrist slashing or suicide attempts, leaving therapists perplexed and wondering why crisis intervention is deteriorating rather than progressing as expected; and (c) practitioners may even grow to dislike clients whom they perceive as resistant. This is especially true if clients fail to remember and/or reveal the incest to the therapist. (Incest victims' failure to remember is the result of the mind's attempt to protect them from overwhelming feelings [Coulson, Wallis, & Clark, 1994].)

Treating crisis clients with a history of childhood sexual abuse is challenging even when incest survivors tell the therapist about the incest. The nonchalant manner in which many victims speak of incest leads practitioners to believe that victims' pasts have no bearing on their present inabilities to cope with crisis precipitators. Even when practitioners are aware that childhood sexual abuse compromises adult coping strategies, they must be prepared to pace with the client, attempt first-order rather than second-order changes, and suffer through inevitable failures until the client is ready to link coping deficiencies with prior sexual abuse.

Crisis intervention with adult survivors of childhood incest is further jeopardized by therapists' tendency to refer out incest victims. Practitioners most often do this because they believe that incest is beyond the purview of a crisis interventionist. Treatment of adult incest survivors in crises is not a simple two-session endeavor, but drawbacks for referring out clients do exist. One is the revolving door that crisis clients experience, leaving them feeling rejected by their therapists. In time, incest victims who present in crisis come to believe that their situations are so unique or so bad that no one can help them or that no one really cares. Therapists need to be aware of the negative impact of referring out incest victims.

This confounding, confusing, dissatisfying, and all-too-frequent picture of crisis intervention can be altered by the therapist's knowing the ways in which a history of childhood sexual abuse affects coping strategies of adult survivors who are facing crisis-precipitating situational factors. This chapter gives an overview to the mind-set and coping strategies of adult survivors of childhood incest who present in crisis. There is no pat formula for treating incest victims in crisis, but to be unaware of the prevalence and effects of incest on adult coping strategies is to be uninformed about a large portion of the mental health population who present in crises. Foremost this chapter examines treatment issues surrounding adult survivors of childhood sexual abuse, applying Roberts's (1991) seven-stage model of crisis intervention. Also, it illustrates situational factors that accompany incest. Additionally, this chapter defines incest and reveals the prevalence, symptoms, and theory regarding why incest affects victims' coping strategies.

PRECURSORS TO CRISIS EPISODES AMONG ADULT SURVIVORS OF INCEST

Adult survivors of incest are predisposed to experience more crises than most people. The residual effects of incest leave victims with compromised coping strategies. Most often, incest victims take years to even reveal the incest to another person, much less to process the meaning of the event. Without successful resolution (making meaning of the incest), a large portion of a victim's normal day-to-day energy in adult life is channeled toward defense mechanisms such as denial, repression, projection, and transference. Consequently, current situational factors easily throw victims off center. Further, many ordinary life events trigger memories of the earlier incest. The triggers raise victims' anxiety level, and victims try to move the conscious memory back into the unconscious. This process requires energy and leaves victims deplete when crisis-precipitating factors arise.

Situational factors that bring about crises in adult victims of childhood incest vary. The factors may be substantial ones such as the death of a brother (as in Patsy's case), the imprisonment of a mother, the relocation of a friend, or the separation from a partner (as in Marsha's case). On the other hand, the precursors to crisis episodes may be mundane events such as bathing, sleeping, or urinating. (Much abuse happens in bathrooms. Besides fondling victims while they bathe, abusers commonly try to gain control of their victims' bodies, and the control that perpetrators seek often entails the victim's elimination of bodily waste. Therefore, upon remembering the abuse, something as routine as "needing to go to the bathroom" can throw some incest victims into a crisis state. They fear urination because of grotesque events that happened while they were urinating or defecating on command.)

Trying to go to sleep can also throw an incest victim into crisis. Sleeping is problematic because memories of abuse may come during the night while the subconscious mind is free to express itself. Dreaming a sexual dream could also throw an incest victim into crisis, since some victims cope by trying to be asexual. In fact, *anything* sexual could throw an incest survivor into crisis—the sight of a biker in tight clothes, the sight of a naked body (as in the case of newlywed Debra viewing her husband's body), or the sexual (and/or violent) content of a television show or movie. Marsha used to awake convinced that she had a penis. This delusion threw her into a crisis state and led her to become agoraphobic. She feared being seen in public, feeling certain that others could discern her penis beneath her clothes. Until the therapist and client can connect the precipitator with the childhood sexual abuse, confusion abounds. Roberts's seven-stage model for crisis intervention partializes many of the steps involved in untying the Gordian knot of crisis intervention with adult incest survivors.

DEFINITION OF INCEST

Incest has been defined as "any exploitative sexual behavior occurring between relatives" (Unger & Crawford, 1996, p. 521). Hazzard, Rogers, and Angert (1993) operationalize the term *exploitative sexual behavior* as "any unwanted sexual contact," and they operationalize *relatives* as persons "too close to marry" (p. 453). Hargett (1998) includes *nonfamily* members as perpetrators in his definition of incest. He writes that incest is "sexual activity forbidden because of a spiritual relationship, as between godparent and godchild" (p. 93). This definition encompasses the unwanted advances of, say, a high school basketball coach toward one of her players. Take Anna, for instance. Anna was a high school freshman who possessed basketball skills well beyond her years. The coaches placed her on the varsity team and let her be a starter. Anna ran into problems when the head coach fondled her before a game and told Anna that if she told anyone, she would not be allowed to start. Anna played the game, but poorly. Her mind was preoccupied with the molestation and the concomitant threat. After the game, Anna experienced humiliation from both her teammates and the fans. The next day, she attempted to end her life by overdosing on sleeping pills.

The degree of contact is an issue in defining incest. Incest may include contact ranging from fondling to sexual intercourse or *noncontact* sexual activity such as the viewing of pornography or others' sexual activities. To define incest as "unwanted sexual contact," however, excludes siblings' mutual exploration. The commonality between definitions is that, upon discovery, the intimacy of incest is damned by all. It is filled with shame, collusion, and guilt.

Finkelhor (1980) examined factors associated with negative outcomes of sex between siblings. He found that acts wherein one party was 5 or more years older than another and where force was used constituted the two variables that best explain whether sibling sex is regarded as adverse. Siblings who are forced into sibling sex are approximately four times as likely to view the experience as negative as those who experience sibling sex without force. Nelson-Gardell (1997) found these same two seminal factors in her work with teenagers who had been sexually abused: violence and perpetration by a significantly older family member. Other factors associated with severe disturbance due to incest are having been abused by a number of people and having been abused by a father figure. For the purposes of this chapter, the words *incest*, *childhood sexual abuse*, and *sexual exploitation* will be used interchangeably. The commonalities are victims under the age of 18 years and a sexual experience that was perceived as abusive. Also, since the majority of victims of incest are females, the feminine pronoun will be used most often in this chapter.

PREVALENCE OF INCEST

Since incest is pervasive and is linked to an increased likelihood of clients presenting in crises, the following section outlines the prevalence of incest. Incest has always existed across all cultures. The right to be free from sexual abuse often has *not* been considered a human right, and societies have most often protected children only from pornography and prostitution (Coulson, Wallis, & Clark, 1994). Sexual maltreatment and exploitation of children, therefore, is a problem of global proportions (Levesque, 1994). Between 1976 and 1992, there was a 331% increase in reporting of sexual maltreatment. Estimates of child sexual abuse range from 360,000 to 408,000 annually. Finkelhor, Hotaling, Lewis, and Smith's (1990) national survey of the prevalence of reported childhood sexual molestation revealed that 27% of adult women and 16% of adult men had experienced childhood sexual abuse, much of which consisted of actual or attempted intercourse (Rowan & Foy, 1993). Russell (1996) randomly surveyed 930 women in San Francisco and found that 38% had been victims of incest. Lubin and Johnson (1997) report similar proportions for women, but the proportion among men is 1 in 10. Finally, 60% of outpatient psychiatric patients report having engaged in sibling incest when they were children (Bess & Janssen, in DiGiorgio, 1998).

The reported prevalence of childhood sexual abuse is startling, yet, even so, underreporting of incest is certain, since incest involves a "web of secrecy" (Levesque, 1994, p. 990). Finkelhor's survey of college women revealed that *none* of those who had been exploited sexually had reported it to anyone. Finkelhor postulates that fear, secrecy, and shame added to an already painful experience. DiGiorgio-Miller (1998) writes a compelling story of homophobia and the lack of social support for adolescent males who were being sexually abused by one of their schoolteachers. The story follows.

DiGiorgio-Miller went to various high schools to present an assembly program on childhood sexual abuse. At one particular program, she invited girls who wanted to talk after the presentation to gather on one side of the auditorium and boys on the other. The girls quickly revealed to her that they were being molested by various male family members; each girl was willing to see a counselor. When DiGiorgio-Miller subsequently spoke with the boys individually, she found that each of them was being molested by a teacher in that school and that each of them refused to see a counselor. The boys spoke of having to drop out of school, leave town, or leave the country should anyone ever discover their connection with the sexual exploitation.

Disturbed by this interaction, DiGiorgio-Miller decided to conduct an experiment in her next high school presentation. Before beginning the speech, she asked a coach volunteer to be her helper. Quickly one coach jumped to his feet and came forward. She told him that she was going to ask him some questions, and that he was simply to say the first thing that came to his mind. He readily agreed. She asked, "What would you do if you discovered that one of the boys on your team was being sexually exploited by one of your coaches?" He hesitated. She reminded him that he was to respond immediately. The coach stated that he would "kick" the "fag" off the team and tell all the other players about the incident to teach them not to be "perverts" like the boy and the coach. DiGiorgio-Miller writes that silence filled the auditorium. After thanking the coach and telling him that he could sit down, she told the audience that this was a poignant illustration of why sexual abuse goes unreported. (In fact, sexual abuse *had* gone unreported in that very school for years!) DiGiorgio-Miller suggests that societal attitudes partially explain victims' reluctance to report incest.

EFFECTS OF INCEST ON VICTIMS

Incest often leaves its victims with enduring, chronic effects. These effects do not constitute a crisis, but they weaken victims' resilience to situational factors, making victims more vulnerable to crises. It is important to understand the basic constitution that an incest victim has *out* of crisis in order to understand her response to situational crises.

The effects of childhood sexual abuse are many. Feelings associated with incest include emptiness, loneliness, boredom, and confusion (Ogata et al., 1990). Feelings of disconnectedness and distrust result in social isolation. Protracted depression follows (Herman, 1992a). Another disconcerting feeling that incest victims often experience is that of ambivalence toward the perpetrator; they don't know whether to love or hate him, to be repulsed or to feel sexually attracted. Incest victims feel uncertain, even of their own thoughts. They suffer from "an inability to turn off a stream of consciousness that has become its own enemy" (Kroll, 1993, jacket cover). Their minds race to pictures of the abuse, flooding them with feelings of self-hatred, blame, and dread of the incest recurring. Finally, incest victims may fear that they will genetically pass an "incest trait" on to their children.

Uncertainty is another feeling reported by incest victims. Uncertainty comes from their trying to reintegrate into a world unlike their childhood environment. Herman (1992) writes that the experience is similar to that of an immigrant who has just arrived in the new "homeland." All that she has known has been left behind. While there can be a sense of wonder, there is also bewilderment (Herman, 1992a). Victims have to learn the rules of "this world" from scratch. Their previous worldviews were shaped by a perpetrator who taught them by example that "the strong can do as they please, without regard for convention" (Herman, 1992b, p. 196). Victims who must learn ordinary procedures and rules of interaction from "normal" people can be "woefully ignorant" of simple, everyday matters.

Long-Lasting Effects of Incest

The long-lasting effects of incest tilt the scales of emotional stability in the direction of crises (Herman et al., in Pribor & Dinwiddie, 1992; Russell, 1996). Within the population of incest victims there is a propensity for suicidal ideation (and/or attempts), substance abuse, self-destructive behavior, impulsive behavior, nightmares, sleep difficulties, nervousness, aggression, reenactment of trauma, low self-esteem, guilt, self-blame, depression, a lack of trust in interpersonal relationships, and a tendency to be revictimized (Cole & Barney, 1987; DiGiorgio-Miller, 1998; Hazzard et al., 1993; Lubin & Johnson, 1997; Ogata et al., 1990; Randall, 1995; Rowan & Foy, 1993). Other symptoms include self-mutilation, sexual problems, and symptoms that mirror posttraumatic stress disorder (PTSD; Hazzard et al., 1993).

For people who survive prolonged and severe childhood incest (where the victim is under the control of the perpetrator and unable to flee), the effects of traumatization are much more grave (Herman, 1992; Lindberg & Distad, 1985, in Rowan & Foy, 1993). Herman writes that victims of prolonged, severe abuse frequently suffer from *ego fragmentation*. In fact, it is quite common for victims to develop multiple personality disorders (dissociative disorders) and/or borderline personality disorder.

Additional symptoms of prolonged and repeated trauma involve somatization, dissociation, and affective disorders. *Somatization*, occurring in as many as 55% of adult survivors, manifests itself in tension headaches, gastrointestinal problems, back pain, tremors, choking sensations, and/or nausea (Morrison, 1989, in Herman, 1992a). (Patsy experienced headaches, and

Debra, choking sensations.) Dissociation is a coping mechanism that helps individuals tolerate pain and shame, distorting their sense of time and preserving their notion that parents are good (Herman, 1992a). People who dissociate often stay in another's presence physically but feign attention to what is being said; their minds are miles away. They have "checked out" mentally. Most often, affective changes are manifested as prolonged depression. Such depression comes about because the child-victim could not express anger, lest the perpetrator respond in rage. Repressed anger, plus disruptions in attachment, contributes to feelings of isolation, hopelessness, indifference, social withdrawal, and "paralysis of initiative" (a restricted sense of one's ability to take risks, to learn by trial and error; Herman, 1992a, p. 382). Other symptoms of prolonged, severe abuse include victim vulnerability to repeated harm, either self-inflicted or caused by others. (Victims of childhood sexual abuse frequently slash their wrists, attempt suicide, or engage in harmful sexual addictions, any of which constitutes a crisis.)

Victims of prolonged, severe abuse are likely to develop PTSD, and people with PTSD are likely to suffer from a series of crisis episodes. (PTSD symptoms consist of intrusive thoughts [nightmares], hypervigilance [i.e., startle responses], and avoidance [i.e., blunted affect to avert all reminders of the incident].) PTSD occurs when a person perceives an event as life-threatening and/or when the experience challenges her notions of fairness and justice (Janoff-Bulman, 1992). Incest does not always involve physical injury or life threat, but it is most often regarded as emotionally traumatic for those who experience it (Rowan & Foy, 1993); incest shatters assumptions about fairness and justice.

Cognitively, victims have difficulty making sense of the event, especially when the perpetrator is a trusted family member. Children observe the way that their perpetrator acts as if nothing happened (returning to the den, fixing himself iced tea, and watching his favorite TV show), and they may wonder if they are crazy. They grow unsure that the event actually happened.

The age and gender of the incest victim mediate the coping strategies of adult victims who face crises. People who were severely abused at young ages are more likely to use dissociation (Herman, 1992b) and amnesia (Rowan & Foy, 1993) as coping mechanisms. Further, children ranging from infants to 5 years old do not know that the incest is wrong, and the pleasurable sensations associated with incest confuse victims. Child-victims add sex to their repertoire of coping behaviors. Later, when they find out that incest is wrong, they feel guilt. As adults, they may continue to engage in compulsive sexual behavior to cope with anxiety and/or guilt. DiGiorgio-Miller (1998) writes that it is particularly difficult for therapists to help victims reshape values when pleasure and guilt are linked.

When the incest occurs between ages 6 and 13, children feel especially guilty. They know incest is wrong, and they feel unclean. Such feelings often lead to either frigidity or promiscuity (Philadelphia Child Guidance, in DiGiorgio-Miller, 1998). (For adolescent boys, the effects of incest are more severe and longer-lasting, presumably due to homophobic attitudes and a lack of social support. Boys fear shame and alienation should their sexual victimization ever be exposed.)

A woman's being confused about femininity is another effect of incest (Lubin & Johnson, 1997). Undergoing trauma as a child imprints deep, negative images of oneself. Women victims of incest are confused about issues of femininity because they equate femininity with a loss of control—the same loss that they experienced as children when they were forced into intimate relations by trusted family members.

Comorbidity as an Effect of Incest

Unfortunately, incest victims do not merely present in crisis or have a substance abuse problem or have PTSD. Many times, incest victims present with multiple diagnoses (more than twice the lifetime diagnoses of depressed patients [Pribor & Dinwiddie, 1992]). Having multiple, coexisting diagnoses is referred to as comorbidity. Two common diagnoses associated with incest victims are borderline personality disorder (BPD; Ogata et al., 1990) and multiple personality disorder (MPD) or dissociative disorder (Putnam et al., in Pribor & Dinwiddie, 1992). Other common diagnoses are agoraphobia, alcohol abuse or dependency, depression, panic disorders, PTSD, simple phobia, and social phobia. The number of possible diagnoses is daunting.

Crisis precipitators are abundant within the population of incest victims diagnosed with either MPD or BPD. Patients with BPD have trouble either modulating emotions or expressing affect. Aroused emotions lead patients with BPD to respond either too much (i.e., disproportionately to the stimulus) or too little (i.e., constricted affect). Responding too much mirrors intrusion, and responding too little mirrors avoidance. An example of responding too much is slashing one's wrist upon reading about a recent airplane crash. An example of responding too little is staying in the presence of abusive people and doing nothing to protect oneself from abuse.

CRISIS INTERVENTION: ROBERTS'S SEVEN-STAGE MODEL

Crises produce a state of both urgency and readiness to change. Urgency arises from an inherent, present danger concomitant in a crisis precipitator. Clients feel an ardent need to avoid both the danger and the inevitable disequilibrium brought about by a crisis. They seek to return their ecosystems to a state of equilibrium. This mind-set produces a readiness to change. Clients' readiness to change stems, in part, from a systemic disequilibrium that weakens their confidence in their habitual, "tried-and-true" coping strategies. In times of crisis, clients entertain the notion that their accustomed coping skills are failing or have failed them, and so they become more open to change.

Roberts's (1991) seven-stage model of crisis intervention outlines steps that help practitioners seize the opportunity to bring about change and reestablish equilibrium. A systematic change model helps practitioners respond with speed and thoroughness to their clients' emergency situations. Assessment of lethality is the first step to crisis intervention, as outlined by Roberts. This first stage is especially appropriate with vulnerable and often self-destructive victims of childhood sexual abuse.

Stage 1: Assessing Lethality

Practitioners must take the initiative in assessing for lethality whether or not they know clients are victims of childhood sexual abuse. Both the prevalence and the effects of incest (secrecy and vulnerability to self-harm) mandate that practitioners routinely assess for lethality (Hazzard et al., 1993). Failure to do so places both practitioners and clients in danger. If a client were to commit suicide while under the therapist's care and if the therapist had failed to assess for lethality and take appropriate measures, the practitioner could be held responsible for the client's death.

Assessing for lethality entails asking about suicidal ideation, prior suicide attempts, and the feasibility of carrying out suicidal ideation. Contrary to popular myths, frank discussions of suicide do not "put suicidal thoughts into clients' heads" (Lukas, 1993, p. 115). Instead, open discourse communicates that the therapist is someone who deals comfortably with reality and who cares enough to be honest and careful. Rather than feeling offended if a therapist mentions suicide, clients often feel reassured that someone is willing to broach an uncomfortable topic for their good. In other words, assessing for lethality (step 1 of Roberts's seven-stage crisis intervention model) facilitates stage 2 of his model, establishing rapport and communication.

To assess for lethality, a practitioner must ask if the client has any *thoughts* of harming herself, and, if so, the frequency, intensity, duration, and degree of pleasurableness of those thoughts (Lukas, 1993). (The more pleasurable the thought of suicide, the greater the likelihood of the client enacting the thought.) Second, the practitioner needs to ask the client if she has a *plan* for harming herself, and, if so, what are the means by which she would do so. Next, the practitioner needs to assess the feasibility of the client's successfully carrying out that plan. Finally, knowing that prior suicide attempts increase the likelihood of successful completions, the practitioner needs to take a *history* of previous suicidal attempts. Some practitioners contract with a client that she contact the practitioner and/or a crisis help line should she consider suicide while under the practitioner's care. Whatever rules apply to assessing for lethality also apply to dealing with self-mutilating behaviors, which are common in incest victims.

Stage 2: Establishing Rapport and Communication

Establishing rapport and communication is the second step in Roberts's seven-stage model of crisis intervention. Accomplishing this step with an incest victim is particularly challenging and important for several reasons. It is challenging because initially incest victims will distrust authority figures (the therapist represents authority to the victim). Having lived in unsafe environments as children, adult survivors are sensitive to any words that could be construed as judgmental. Judgment communicates rejection to the adult survivor of incest, for the survivor has never experienced the privilege of being wrong *and* being loved and accepted.

Establishing rapport with adult survivors of childhood sexual abuse is also challenging because survivors are likely to transfer to therapists their ambivalent feelings toward their perpetrators—feelings of fear, distrust, and desperate need (Unger & Crawford, 1996). Residual fear and distrust of their childhood perpetrator inspires incest victims to try to win the approval of their therapists (Herman, 1992a). Next, incest victims tend to form a dependence on therapists, feeling hopeless and helpless without them. When a therapist tries to enforce therapeutic boundaries, a victim may become enraged and revert to infantile splitting, believing that the therapist is either all good or all bad. Incest victims are terrified of both abandonment and domination. In short, they know no "range of moderate engagement or risk for relationship"; they approach "relationship as though questions of life and death are at stake, oscillating between intense attachment and terrified withdrawal" (Herman, 1992, p. 385).

Establishing relationship with incest victims is important because they may never before have been in relationship with a trustworthy person. Relating to one trustworthy person could change their lives. In a relationship with a therapist and/or a group of fellow incest survivors, an adult survivor of incest could find her first reliable life model. The therapist's responsibility, therefore, is enormous, daunting, and extremely important.

At stage 2 of Roberts's model, the knowledgeable crisis interventionist will understand that establishing rapport with an adult survivor of incest resembles the patterns of an authoritative parent—a combination of allowing "children" to participate in decision making and consistently enforcing therapeutic boundaries. Once an adult survivor of incest realizes that the therapist is a safe person who supports her, does not judge her, and allows her to make her own decisions, she is likely to feel very grateful, enthusiastic, and loyal to the therapist.

The first step of establishing rapport and communication has been completed, but stage 2 is not over. Although the client no longer resembles a "resistant" client but rather a loyal follower, this attitude is not without challenges. The client's enthusiasm can lead to idealized notions of the therapist. Dependency follows and underscores the need to further enforce boundaries. In short, stage 2 of Roberts's crisis intervention model is much like a dance, moving between setting limits and metaphorically embracing the wounded adult victim of childhood incest.

Stage 3: Identify Major Problems

When an adult victim of childhood incest presents in crisis, the therapist should assess for lethality, join with the client, and then strive to identify major problems. In striving to identify major problems, practitioners must be mindful that *presenting* problems and *major* problems are not necessarily synonymous. The presenting problem as identified by the adult survivor of incest will most likely be a situational factor, not a problem related to incest. In the case of Debra, the situational factor that threw her into crisis was her "discomfort" with intimate relations with her new husband; with Patsy, it was the death of her brother; and with Marsha, it was the loss of a relationship. None of these women presented in therapy with disquiet regarding childhood sexual abuse. Nor did they make any progress toward therapeutic goals until the history of childhood sexual abuse was discovered and treated.

In stage 3 of Roberts's crisis intervention model, identifying major problems, the practitioner should perform several steps: (a) take the presenting problem at face value; (b) operationalize it; (c) take other stated problems as they come up and operationalize them; (d) prioritize the identified problems; and (e) identify and operationalize the goal(s) of therapy. These steps constitute the elements of a therapeutic contract.

A therapeutic contract holds both the practitioner and the client accountable to work on specified goals either until the goals are reached or until the client changes her mind about the importance of reaching a given goal. The contents of contracts need to be spelled out in *operational* terms so that the client, therapist, and/or supervisor have a common understanding of major problems and treatment goals. This common understanding as stated in a therapeutic contract facilitates therapy's moving at a metered, focused, purposeful, and constructive pace. To operationalize a problem is to define it—to assure that the client's and the practitioner's use of and understanding of the problem are the same. A shared understanding of the problem is best facilitated by having the client describe the presenting problem in *countable* behaviors.

For the new crisis interventionist, operationalizing problems takes practice. To enhance operationalization, the practitioner can use a metaphor of a video camera recording a client's stated presenting problem. What would the camera record? In Debra's case, the camera would record Debra first kissing her husband passionately and then recoiling suddenly when he removes his clothes. His attempts to "keep the moment" would be "filmed," with her bursting into tears and locking herself in the bathroom for 2 to 3 hours. On another occasion, the camera would record Debra approaching her husband affectionately and then threatening to kill him should he touch her. (The therapist would then assess for lethality [stage 1 of Roberts's seven-stage model of crisis intervention] to see if Debra had a plan and the means to kill her husband.) Another segment of the "film of Debra's discomfort with intimate relations" would constitute her waking in the middle of the night, screaming, gagging, trembling, perspiring, and feeling breathless.

While Debra's symptoms were later revealed to be associated with her having been sexually exploited (having to repeatedly perform oral sex on her uncle and his friends), initially the symptoms served strictly to facilitate goal-making. For example, Debra established a goal that said that she would recognize having successfully completed treatment when she was aroused by her husband's naked body. Second, she would recognize successful treatment when she slept peacefully through the night (without having nightmares). The operationalization of Debra's other problems and solutions proceeded in similar fashion, with the therapist having Debra state the frequency, intensity, and duration of each behavior. It was important that the practitioner allow Debra to both identify and operationalize the solution, because clients feel empowered when they do most of the work (Valentine & Smith, 1998).

Since one can more easily strive for the attainment rather than the absence of a behavior, *and* since clients will often state goals in terms of the absence of a behavior, it is important that therapists instruct clients to state goals as the presence of a behavior. In Debra's case, she wanted to state her goal as being that she would neither recoil at the sight of her husband nor try to assault him. When the therapist asked Debra, "What will take the place of recoil and aggression?" Debra responded, "Arousal." Debra found it much more satisfying to strive toward arousal in regard to her husband's body than simply the absence of repulsion and aggression.

Prioritizing client problems, goals, and solutions both strengthens and simplifies therapeutic intervention with crisis clients, establishing focus and clarity. It strengthens intervention because it allows the therapist to attend to safety first and then to the need that the client views as most pressing. A question that facilitates prioritizing client problems follows: If you could find resolution to only one of the problems you have listed, which one would it be? The client's answer sets the stage for intervention.

Step 3 of Roberts's seven-stage model of crisis intervention entails not only identifying, operationalizing, and prioritizing major problems and goals but also the use of brokering and/or educational skills for the "easier" problems. The practitioner can give clients information and/or make appropriate referrals. Practitioners should be careful *not* to strive to fill every therapeutic gap in a treatment plan, especially gaps in which practitioners are ill-prepared. Adult victims of childhood incest are sensitive to unfulfilled promises, so when practitioners try to fake expertise or overextend themselves, incest survivors are hasty to interpret the unfulfilled promise as deception or betrayal. Feelings of betrayal activate incest survivors, creating tension, doubt, and hostility. These hostile feelings compete with the safety the client first experienced during stage 2 of Roberts's model. Therefore, it is important that therapists accurately assess their own strengths and availability and take small, attainable steps when dealing with adult survivors of childhood incest.

Stage 4: Dealing with Feelings and Providing Support

Dealing with feelings and providing support is an important part of Roberts's model of crisis intervention. Whereas this step may seem straightforward with many client populations, with adult survivors of incest, it is not. The step is complicated by adult survivors' reluctance to *recognize*, *acknowledge*, or *accept* feelings.

Adult survivors are reluctant to recognize emotions for at least two reasons. First, the abusive, powerful relationship in which they were locked for extended periods of time restricted their ability to feel. Perpetrators' punitive and threatening actions and words produced a paralysis of initiative that encompasses even the "right to feel." Victims grew fearful of feelings; they learned to trust the perpetrator's voice more than their own. In their desperate efforts to please the perpetrator, survivors learned to fake socially acceptable emotions. Even in adulthood, survivors tenaciously cling to that well-practiced repertoire of "emotions." Second, because of feeling out of control in their childhood, adult incest survivors feel a strong *need to* "be in control." One primary way of feeling in control is to deny feelings, to live as if feelings do not exist.

Practitioners can help incest survivors recognize feelings in several ways: First, they can give clients *permission to feel* by eliminating the judgment associated with feelings. Incest victims have difficulty believing that it is truly therapeutic to feel angry toward their perpetrators. Second, practitioners can be angry *for* the client. In other words, they can *model anger* for the client, which may inspire the client to try out the feeling—a feeling that otherwise would be totally foreign to express toward an authority figure. (The purpose of feeling angry is to facilitate recognition that the blame for the incestuous relationship rests with the perpetrator, not the victim.) Finally, practitioners can ask a client where she learned to feel a certain way. This question highlights *historical experience(s)* associated with a particular feeling. Both practitioner and client can learn to recognize the voice of the abuser and choose to resist it. In summary, to facilitate the recognition of feelings, practitioners need to state support of whatever feelings a client expresses; hold her in unconditional positive regard; and validate her feelings even if there is no family member who will agree with her.

Although *recognition* of feelings is the first step toward completing stage 4 of Roberts's crisis intervention model, practitioners need to be aware that, for incest survivors, crises may *follow* the recognition of feelings. Soon after Marsha allowed herself to feel, memories flooded her consciousness, and she went into crisis. She began being "triggered" by memories, sights, smells, sounds, and/or comments made by the therapist. For example, Marsha was triggered by the therapist's nonsexual use of the word *coming*. Rather than telling the therapist that she was triggered, however, Marsha tried to "respect authority" and keep her reactions to herself. Between sessions, however, she would call her therapist, either paralyzed, alarmed, or angry. For Marsha, one trigger would lead to another. Soon she was experiencing a full-blown crisis.

Marsha's failure to indicate that she was triggered *during* a session resulted in a breakdown of trust on the therapist's part. The therapist felt betrayed, having believed that a session ended on a positive note, only to learn later that her perception was false. Marsha was so accustomed to faking it that she had fooled both herself and the therapist. Two problems identified by the therapist were (a) that the therapist had difficulty determining which demeanor of Marsha's was real, and (b) that resolving the troubling feelings after time had passed meant that conversations had to be "resurrected" and reconstructed to identify triggers and gain an understanding of their meaning. This process was more difficult than attending to triggers as they happened.

Dealing with the feelings of adult incest survivors often requires more specific techniques than providing therapeutic support. One technique is to keep adult survivors in the "therapeutic window" (Cole & Barney, 1987), which is that space between intrusion and denial. Intrusion produces *undercontrolling* of emotions, whereas denial yields *overcontrolling*. The therapeutic window constitutes the frame of mind in which clients are not triggered, but rather are operating with a proactive stance, not a reactive one. "Grounding" facilitates the maintenance of the therapeutic window. According to Cole and Barney (1987), "Grounding is any technique that keeps the survivor in touch with her immediate adult reality" (p. 606). Triggered women's affective states feel so real and so strong that they fear becoming "stuck" in the past.

Group treatment for adult survivors is the most common form of providing grounding. Groups can be considered "interpersonal experimentation" (Hazzard et al., 1993). The group structure reconstructs the family experience, allowing members to learn to appreciate different styles of coping and different timings of disclosing members' pasts to other group members. Groups also allow adult survivors to view an incident through the eyes of an adult rather than those of a child. Groups facilitate the client's focusing on the incident rather than denying it, and they serve to diminish the stigma associated with incest. Further, groups operate within time boundaries, providing structure that was often absent in the client's family of origin. Finally, groups have been shown to instill hope, facilitate catharsis, and increase connectedness to others. (See Ogata et al. [1990] for specific procedures for screening clients for group inclusion.)

Stage 5: Exploring Possible Alternatives

After assessing for safety, joining with a client, naming and operationalizing major problems, and dealing with feelings, the next step in Roberts's seven-stage model for crisis intervention is to explore possible alternatives to the problems. This sequential and logical step presents special challenges when treating adult survivors of incest. Adult survivors, due to the paralysis of initiative, may be slow to explore new options. In fact, they may feel as if there *are* no new options. Survivors often are perfectionists who fear failure, and this fear leads them to restrict their range of options. They forgive others for the very mistakes for which they could never forgive themselves.

To deal with paralysis of initiative, practitioners may need to employ specialized therapeutic techniques or refer out to other practitioners who employ such techniques. Traumatic Incident Reduction (TIR; Gerbode, 1989), an open-ended session that most closely resembles imaginal flooding (Valentine & Smith, 1998) and group treatment are two modalities that have proven effective in helping incest survivors generate new options.

Before exploring other options (reestablishing systemic equilibrium by employing different coping strategies), many clients seek answers to disturbing questions such as: Were my parents monsters? Did Mom know and do nothing to protect me? Was I an accomplice to the abuse? Did I enjoy the abuse and "ask for it"? Can I accept and forgive myself? Can I feel proud of myself? How can I learn to trust and to relate intimately to another human being? Can I ever acknowledge sexual feelings? Both TIR and group treatment have been tested and found effective in assisting clients in answering old questions and generating new options.

Patsy asked such questions when she underwent a TIR session in which she "relived" the death of her younger brother enough times for her to examine her own belief systems regarding his death. She discovered that, being a health practitioner, she perceived his death as an emphatic statement that she was "no good." If she were any good, she could have saved his life; she could have kept him from dying of AIDS.

Where, one might question, does an intelligent person get such a belief system? For Patsy, it stemmed from a prior traumatic experience. By listening and refraining from speaking, a practitioner learned (along with the client) the source of Patsy's belief system. (Under *no* conditions should a therapist point out the obvious—that AIDS is presently incurable and that the best physicians in the world cannot save a man who is dying of AIDS.) The therapist learned that Patsy's tying her self-worth to saving her brother stemmed from her having been verbally abused (called "chicken shit") by her father when he discovered that Patsy and her older brother were engaging in sibling sex. Her younger brother, who later died of AIDS, came to Patsy's defense when her father was berating her. Later, when this brother was dying, Patsy wanted to return the favor; she wanted to befriend him in his most critical moment. She also wanted to prove her father wrong.

Patsy's story provides a poignant example of how a crisis interventionist can help a client with a history of incest to generate new options. Particular interventions such as TIR are often needed to access schemas that were altered during traumatic events and to give the client the chance to decide for herself that she no longer needs that schema for everyday living. An effective intervention can release a client from destructive, stuck thought patterns and free her to explore new alternatives.

Stage 6: Formulating an Action Plan

Stage 6 of Roberts's crisis intervention model consists of formulating an action plan, based on the alternatives generated in stage 5. It cannot be overstated that adult victims of incest need to generate their own solutions. Therapy and/or groups should teach clients to take care of themselves. Adult survivors of incest are prone toward dependence on practitioners and/or group members. The dependency stems from two therapeutic ingredients: (a) The therapeutic relationship offers more safety and consistency than a client has previously experienced, and (b) a natural bonding transpires during times of heightened physiological state (Straton, 1990).

Prendergast (1994) believes that the client's forming a dependency on the therapist is inevitable. He also believes that because of this inevitability, therapists need to take extreme caution to avoid furthering dependency, even to the point of avoiding making suggestions. (Putting forth options is part of the work of a therapist, but it differs from stating opinions about which option is best.) TIR has been found to be especially suited for fostering independence and empowerment (Valentine & Smith, 1998). For example, upon completion of a TIR session, Patsy told her therapist that, prior to the session, she had not believed that TIR would work. Patsy said, "I didn't think that you could do it." Smiling, she added, "I guess I was right; you didn't do it; I did all the work!" This is the kind of empowering attitude that most crisis interventionists want. It belies the dependency that is too often common in working with adult survivors of childhood incest.

Stage 6 of Roberts's model as applied to adult incest survivors can be summed up in several steps. The steps to exploring new alternatives include returning control to the survivor; allowing the survivor to ventilate the anger fully; creating a safe environment for full disclosure of the abuse; forming new images of self and of one's past; reassessing values; arriving at thought-out stances versus reactive, fearful ones; beginning to take risks; learning to forgive oneself for mistakes; learning to glory in mistakes, knowing that one is changing, growing, and becoming fully human; learning to live in the present; learning to plan for the future; and making provisions for follow-up (Prendergast, 1994).

Stage 7: Follow-Up

The last stage of Roberts's seven-stage model for crisis intervention is follow-up. Follow-up is necessary to measure whether therapeutic gains have been maintained. It also serves as a transition between intense therapy and the cessation of a therapeutic relationship. For many clients, some continued contact with the practitioner feels comforting. This is especially true for adult survivors of incest.

For the incest survivor, the timing and pacing of termination are critical. Termination, alone, can throw into crisis an incest survivor who is extremely sensitive to appearances of abandonment. Termination feels like rejection. Termination, itself, can trigger feelings of shame, low self-worth, and alienation. Therefore, for the adult survivor, follow-up becomes a means *toward* termination.

In order to terminate, both the client and the therapist should know that therapeutic gains are real. With incest survivors' lifetime habits of pleasing others, they often will fool themselves and their practitioners into believing that the work of therapy is done. Only talk of termination reveals whether the therapeutic gains are real or pretend.

Practitioners can become frustrated by the two-steps-forward-and-three-steps-back routine that is common with incest survivors. Practitioners have difficulty knowing which client profile is real—the healthy, insightful, capable, and independent one or the extremely emotional, self-blaming, desperate, childlike, and hopeless one. The merry-go-round of affect propels a practitioner to ask, "Will the real client please stand up?" The answer is that both presentations of the client are real. She often will vacillate between those two extremes. Normalizing this vacillation helps both the practitioner and the client: It braces the practitioner for extreme changes in client affect, and it removes the guilt and the self-blame profiles that adult survivors are quick to assume.

Although there is no formula by which a practitioner may determine the sincerity of a client's affect, some pointers may be helpful. Listen to the client. Listen to yourself. Maintain professional boundaries, especially when the client is pushing exceptionally hard for the dismissal of boundaries. Inform the client of other emergency sources of help. Refer the client to participate in a group so that her support base grows. Bring the client's attention back to the original therapeutic contract and the behavioral indicators of goal attainment. Above all, be patient. Termination should be gradual, and follow-up consistent. (Pen-and-paper measures, a phone call, or office visits facilitate follow-up.)

Careful, explicit, insightful planning from the beginning facilitates the timely termination and follow-up of a client. A therapeutic plan that allows practitioners to avoid burnout is essential to a well-placed termination and follow-up. Use-of-self, monitoring emotions, and maintaining boundaries are essential for practitioners working with adult survivors of incest. Practitioners must avoid suddenly burning out and dismissing a client, lest all therapeutic gains be lost.

SUMMARY AND CONCLUSION

Treatment can heal or distress crisis clients as they strive to abate the negative psychological effect of childhood incest (Cole & Barney, 1987). Besides a typical 40% dropout rate in the first five sessions of group therapy (Blake-White & Kline, in Cole & Barney, 1987), another indicator that treatment often distresses patients is presented by Hazzard et al. (1993). They found that patients who had *not* been previously hospitalized in a psychiatric unit were more likely to complete treatment than those who had been hospitalized. Further, 83% of the incest victims who had seen at least one mental health professional prior to their treatment reported that treatment was unhelpful (Pribor and Dinwiddie, 1992). (Of those who had previously seen a psychiatrist, only 5.8% found the psychiatrist helpful with psychological problems.) These statistics underscore the necessity of *effective* treatment for adult survivors of childhood incest.

Dealing effectively with adult incest survivors who present in crisis means knowing the client population, understanding how seemingly small things can precipitate a crisis in this population, devising a collaborative plan to address a client's most pressing problems, and following that plan.

One final note in crisis intervention with adult survivors of childhood incest: Personal coping styles make an impact on client recovery. Coping is a way of dealing with a stressor. It consists of "efforts made in response to stimuli experienced as threatening or stressful—efforts aimed both at reducing the anxiety that those stimuli create and at reducing the interference of the stimuli with one's capacity to function" (Runtz & Schallow, 1997 p. 212). In short, coping entails efforts to "master, tolerate, or reduce demands that exceed the person's resources" (Hiebert-Murphy, 1998, p. 425).

Some coping styles are more effective than others. Clients who blame themselves for their incestuous past often have poorer long-term adjustment (Coffey, Leitenberg, Henning, Turner, & Bennett, 1996). On the other hand, clients who take an active stance, problem solve, cognitively process the event, and even confront the abuser often experience fewer symptoms (Chaffin, Wherry, & Dykman, 1997). Clients who engage rather than disengage cope better with childhood sexual abuse. (Clients who were severely abused are more likely to disengage.) The work of practitioners who engage with adult survivors of incest, then, is to facilitate active rather than passive coping stances with their clients. Facing the abuse is essential for good health.

From stage 1 through stage 7 of Roberts's model, practitioners need to be aware of the large probability that as many as one in three of their women clients may have a history of childhood sexual abuse. Knowing the prevalence and the concomitant symptoms of many adult survivors of long-enduring sexual abuse undergirds assessment, joining, problem solving, intervention choices, and termination decisions. Although practitioners cannot assume responsibility for their clients' full recovery, careful planning and knowledge-based practice can serve to free clients to cope with life's exigencies. Effective work with adult survivors has resulted in clients' having a higher locus of control, a lower avoidance of stimuli related to traumatic events, higher self-esteem, and lower trauma symptoms and psychopathology (Hazzard et al., 1993)

Finally, treating the adult survivor of childhood incest can be highly rewarding. Effective treatment of these "victims" often results in practitioners' seeing these clients as heroes, overcomers, survivors, and role models. Few childhood histories present such handicaps in everyday coping; yet, with the help of a skillful practitioner, many of the victims learn to live with great freedom. Effective crisis intervention, as outlined in Roberts's seven-stage model for crisis intervention, begins the process of recovery. Such therapeutic accomplishments yield rich rewards.

REFERENCES

Alexander, P., Neimeyer, R., Follette, V., Moore, M., & Harter, S. (1980). A comparison of group treatment of women sexually abused as children. *Journal of Consulting and Clinical Psychology, 57*, 479–483.

Browne, A., & Finkelhor, D. (1986). Impact of child sexual abuse: A review of the research. *Psychological Bulletin, 99*, 66–77.

Chaffin, M., Wherry, J. N., & Dykman, R. (1997). School-age children's coping with sexual abuse: Abuse stresses and symptoms associated with four coping strategies. *Child Abuse & Neglect, 21*, 227–240.

Coffey, P., Leitenberg, H., Henning, K., Turner, T., & Bennet, R. (1996). The relation between method of coping during adulthood with a history of childhood sexual abuse and current psychological adjustment. *Journal of Consulting and Clinical Psychology, 64*, 1090–1093.

Cole, C. H., & Barney, E. E. (1987). Safeguard and the therapeutic window: A group treatment strategy for adult incest survivors. *American Journal of Orthopsychiatry, 57*, 601–610.

Coulson, K., Wallis, L., & Clark, H. (1994). The diversified team approach in the treatment of incest families. *Psychotherapy in Private Practice, 13*(2), 19–43.

Daly, M., & Wilson, M. (1991). A reply to Gelles: Stepchildren *are* disproportionately abused, and diverse forms of violence can share causal factors. *Human Nature, 2* , 410–426.

DiGiorgio-Miller, J. (1998). Sibling incest: Treatment of the family and the offender. *Child Welfare, 77,* 335–346.

Finkelhor, D. (1980). Sex among siblings: A survey in prevalence, variety and effects. *Archives of Sexual Behavior, 9,* 171–195.

Finkelhor, D. (1986). *A sourcebook on child sexual abuse.* Beverly Hills, CA: Sage.

Finkelhor, D., Hotaling, G., Lewis, I. A., & Smith, C. (1990). Sexual abuse in a national survey of adult men and women: Prevalence, characteristics, and risk factors. *Child Abuse and Neglect, 14,* 533–542.

Gerbode, F. (1989). *Beyond psychology: An introduction to metapsychology.* Palo Alto, CA: IRM Press.

Hargett, H. (1998). Reconciling the victim and perpetrator in sibling incest. *Sexual Addiction and Compulsivity: The Journal of Treatment and Prevention, 5*(93), 93–106.

Hazzard, A., Rogers, J., & Angert, L. (1993). Factors affecting group therapy outcomes for adult sexual abuse survivors. *International Journal of Group Psychotherapy, 43,* 453–468.

Herman, J. L. (1992a). Complex PTSD: A syndrome in survivors of prolonged and repeated trauma. *Journal of Traumatic Stress, 5,* 377–391.

Herman, J. (1992b). *Trauma and recovery: The aftermath of violence—from domestic abuse to political terror.* New York: Basic Books.

Hiebert-Murphy, D. (1998). Emotional distress among mothers whose children have been sexually abused: The role of a history of child sexual abuse, social support, and coping. *Child Abuse and Neglect, 22,* 423–435.

Hoey, H. (1994). Sibling incest in a clergy family: A case study. *Child Abuse and Neglect, 18,* 1028–1035.

Janoff-Bulman, B. (1992). *Shattered assumptions.* New York: Free Press.

Kilpatrick, D., & Best, C. L. (1990, April). Sexual assault victims: Data from a random national probability sample. Paper presented at a symposium at the meeting of the Southeastern Psychological Association, Atlanta.

Kroll, J. (1993). *PTSD/borderlines in therapy: Finding the balance.* New York: Norton.

Levesque, R. (1994). Sexual use, abuse and exploitation of children: Challenges in implementing children's human rights. *Brooklyn Law Review, 60,* 959–998.

Lubin, H., & Johnson, D. (1997). Interactive psycho-educational group therapy for traumatized women. *International Journal of Group Psychotherapy, 47,* 271–289.

Lukas, S. (1993). *Where to start and what to ask: An assessment handbook.* New York: Norton.

Morrison, J. (1989). Childhood sexual histories of women with somatization disorder. *American Journal of Psychiatry, 146,* 239–241.

Nelson-Gardell, D. (1997). Child report of treatment issue resolution: Pilot of a rapid assessment instrument. *Child Abuse and Neglect, 21,* 309–318.

Ogata, S., Silk, K., Goodrich, S., Lohr, N., Westen, D., & Hill, E. (1990). Childhood sexual and physical abuse in adult patients with borderline personality disorder. *American Journal of Psychiatry, 147*, 1008–1013.

Pelcovitz, D., van der Kolk, B., Roth, S., Mandel, F., & Risick, P.(1997). Development of a criteria set and a structured interview for disorders of extreme stress. *Journal of Traumatic Stress, 19*, 3–16.

Prendergast, W. (1994). Initial steps in treating child and adolescent survivors of sexual abuse. *Young Victims, Young Offenders, 89*–115.

Pribor, E., & Dinwiddie, S. (1992). Psychiatric correlates of incest in childhood. *American Journal of Psychiatry, 149*, 52–56.

Randall, D. (1995). Curative factor rankings for female incest survivor groups. *Journal for Specialists in Group Work, 20*, 232–239.

Roberts, A. R. (1991). *Contemporary perspectives on crisis intervention and prevention.* Englewood Cliffs, NJ: Prentice-Hall.

Roth, S., & Lebowitz, L. (1988). The experience of sexual trauma. *Journal of Traumatic Stress, 1*, 79–107.

Rowan A., & Foy, D. (1993). Post-traumatic stress disorder in child sexual abuse survivors: A literature review. *Journal of Traumatic Stress, 6*, 3–20.

Runtz, M., & Schallow, J. (1997). Social support and coping strategies as mediators of adult adjustment following childhood maltreatment. *Child Abuse and Neglect, 21*, 211–226.

Russel, D. (1996). *The secret trauma: Incest in the lives of girls and women.* New York: Basic Books.

Schwarz, R., & Prout, M. (1991). Integrative approach in the treatment of post-traumatic stress disorder. *Psychotherapy, 28*, 364–373.

Straton, D. (1990). Catharsis reconsidered. *Australian and New Zealand Journal of Psychiatry, 24*, 543–551.

Unger, R., & Crawford, M. (1996). *Women and gender: A feminist perspective* (2nd ed.). New York: McGraw-Hill.

Valentine, P. V., & Smith, T. E. (1998). A qualitative study of client perceptions of Traumatic Incident Reduction (TIR): A brief trauma treatment. *Crisis Intervention and Time-Limited Treatment, 4*, 1–12.

Valentine, P. V., & Smith, T. E. (in press). Evaluating Traumatic Incident Reduction (TIR) therapy with female inmates: A randomized controlled clinical trial. *Research on Social Work Practice.*

IV

CRISIS ASSESSMENT AND
CRISIS INTERVENTION IN
HEALTH-RELATED AND MENTAL
HEALTH–RELATED CRISES

12

Crisis Intervention Application of Brief Solution-Focused Therapy in Addictions

KENNETH R. YEAGER
THOMAS K. GREGOIRE

This chapter examines the application of Roberts's seven-stage crisis intervention model in working with substance-dependent individuals. Roberts's model will be combined with strengths perspective and brief solution-focused therapy.

Case 1

Dennis is a 41-year-old White male who progresses rapidly through crack cocaine dependence. Consumed by overwhelming cravings for cocaine, Dennis abandons his wife, children, business, and responsibilities. As he seeks comfort in crack cocaine and sex, he progresses into a repetitive cycle of craving, use, and pornography. Having lost all that is important in his life, Dennis presents seeking stabilization from his addiction.

This case demonstrates practical application of Roberts's model as a method to stabilize the individual and how this model can be utilized to develop effective treatment planning within the time constraints of a managed care treatment climate.

The second case of Susan examines Roberts's model in combination with the strengths perspective in addressing opioid addiction in the chronic pain client.

Case 2

Susan's pain is the result of several automobile accidents. Her chronic pain serves as the backdrop for compulsive behaviors rooted in her preoccupation with minimizing her pain while at the same time feeding her addiction. Susan presents in crisis, fearing legal consequences and being cut off from her supply of pain medications.

In this case application, Roberts's model demonstrates effective methods for brief interventions building on the strengths of the addicted chronic pain patient. Application in this case deflects the client's natural defense structures, assisting her to build on her supports rather than remaining entrenched in the agony of her injuries.

Case 3

Scott is a 20-year-old polysubstance-dependent individual who presents in acute withdrawal from several substances, including cocaine, heroin, and methamphetamine. Scott's use began at age 12 and has progressed to complete loss of control. At this point Scott has been asked to leave the university he has been attending and not to return to his parents' home after stealing a large amount of money from his parents. Scott presents in active withdrawal to the treatment center accompanied by his grandfather, who hopes the center can assist his grandson in reclaiming all aspects of his life through the process of recovery.

This case demonstrates how Roberts's model is combined with solution-focused theory to lead the client toward a greater assumption of self-responsibility in the development of a self-directed program of recovery. It demonstrates application of the miracle and exception questions in day-to-day practice as Scott moves through the stages of crisis intervention. Scott's story illustrates the effectiveness of combined solution-focused theory and Roberts's crisis intervention model in addressing issues that reach beyond the issue of dependence to move the patient through the process of recovery.

CRISIS OVERVIEW

The experience of crisis is an inescapable reality. For some, crisis may occur only infrequently. For others, crisis occurs frequently, with one crisis leading to another. Just as crises occur at varying intervals for individuals, there are variances in an individual's ability to cope with crisis (Roberts & Dziegielewski, 1995). Some are able to "work through" their perceptions and reactions to the event with little intervention. For many, however, successful resolution of a crisis event requires skillful intervention to clarify the individual's response to the event (Roberts, 1990).

Crisis intervention consistently occurs when one is addressing substance dependence. Persons presenting for substance dependence treatment frequently find themselves seeking assistance following a crisis or possibly a series of crises. Psychiatrist, psychologist, and social workers functioning within the managed care delivery system have been challenged to provide cost-effective treatment within the least restrictive environment. Professionals practicing in addiction treatments are finding that crisis intervention skills combined with brief solution-focused intervention strategies are effective when applied in today's abbreviated lengths of stay.

Managed care has hastened a fundamental shift in substance abuse treatment delivery. Increasingly, outpatient treatment has supplanted residential treatment, and programs now experience greater variation in both lengths of stay and types of interventions (Book et al., 1995). Cost savings attained in the private sector have led a number of states to implement similar approaches with public programs (Gartner & Mee-Lee, 1995). At least 40 states currently have some type of managed behavioral health care program for public mental health and/or substance abuse, and 5 other states have programs in development (Toff-Bergman, 1998).

However, a number of authors have expressed concern about the consequences of managed care programs for clients. Etheridge, Craddock, Dunteman, and Hubbard (1995) documented substantial declines in treatment services provided over the past decade. Their findings included a considerable increase in the number of clients reporting unmet service needs. Ford (1998) suggested that managed care approaches restrict treatment emphasis to short-term needs. Additional studies of public managed care programs have identified increased levels of client severity (Beinecke, Callahan, Shepard, Cavanaugh, & Larson, 1997) and a reduction in level of care occurring independent of severity (Thompson, Burns, Goldman, & Smith, 1992). Other authors have questioned whether the managed care approach can meet the needs of vulnerable populations (Platt, Widman, Lidz, Rubenstein, & Thompson, 1998; Rivers, 1998; Kusher & Moss, 1995; Wells, Astrachan, Tischler, & Unutzer, 1995). Despite these concerns, many program administrators anticipate making further reductions in the intensity of service because of continuing funding limitations (Rivers, 1998).

Managed care challenges addiction practitioners to rethink treatment strategies. Treating clients in longer term residential settings seems increasingly to be a bygone luxury. Practitioners in the addiction treatment field will continue to experience pressure to provide brief time-limited treatments, and to increase their ability to respond to clients in crisis in a timely, effective manner. In the future, expertise in crisis intervention may become the defining characteristic of the effective addiction counselor.

ESTIMATES OF THE SUBSTANCE DEPENDENCE PROBLEM IN AMERICA

Substance dependence treatment as a profession is in a state of transition, struggling to develop cost-effective treatment approaches as the prevalence of alcohol and drug use and abuse continues to escalate in the United States. The Substance Abuse and Mental Health Services Administration (SAMHSA) indicates that increasing numbers of individuals are reporting the use of mood-altering substances (SAMHSA, 1998). These reported results are the culmination of the National Household Survey on Drug Abuse, an annual survey that is conducted by SAMHSA and reports estimates of the prevalence of use of a variety of illicit drugs, alcohol, and tobacco. The survey is based on a nationally representative sample of civilian noninstitutionalized persons age 12 years and older.

In 1997, the National Institute on Drug Abuse Survey reported approximately 111 million persons age 12 or over were current alcohol users, which was about 51% of the total population age 12 and older. Approximately 31.9 million persons (15.3%) engaged in binge drinking, and approximately 11.2 million (5.4% of the population) were heavy drinkers (SAMHSA, 1998).

The National Household Survey estimated that 13.9 million Americans were current users of illicit drugs. The term *current users* was defined as a person who has used an illicit drug sometime in the 30 days prior to the survey interview. Of those identifying as current substance users, nearly 1 in 10 youth age 12 to 17 reported current use of marijuana. The number of youth identifying as marijuana users more than doubled from 1992 to 1997 (SAMHSA, 1998).

There has been an increasing trend in the use of heroin since 1992 as well. Estimates of heroin use ranged from 68,000 persons in 1993 (less than 0.1% of the population) to approximately 325,000 persons in 1997. Estimates of current use of cocaine remain steady, with approximately 1.5 million persons reporting current use. This number represents 0.7% of the population age 12 and older (SAMHSA, 1998).

Additionally, more than half of all youth age 12 to 17 reported that marijuana was easily obtained. Approximately 21% of the same group reported that heroin was easy to obtain. Overall, approximately 15% of the youth population reported being approached by someone offering to sell them drugs within the 30 days prior to the survey (SAMHSA, 1998).

The following list summarizes the prevalence of diagnosis and treatment considerations within the population presenting to the treatment center where these composite case examples were developed:

Substance	Presenting (%)
Alcohol, only	42.0
Polysubstance	58.0
Cocaine	41.6
Opioid	27.2
Sedative hypnotic	14.1
Cannabis	12.5
Other	4.6

These diagnoses were by percentage of Ohio State University Hospitals East Talbot Hall patient population, average of fiscal years 1997 and 1998.

DEFINITIONS OF DEPENDENCE, ACUTE STRESSORS, AND CRISIS EVENT

Crisis events within the substance-dependent population vary somewhat from traditional models of crisis, yet there remains one overwhelming similarity. This is the failure of an individual's coping strategies to ameliorate a current crisis. Frequently, within the substance-dependent population physiological factors work to precipitate crisis as the individual experiences loss of control over his or her use.

Crisis events within the substance-dependent population vary somewhat from the experience of crisis in other disciplines. Persons with addiction problems are highly motivated to maintain the status quo, at least with respect to their substance use. Addicts often make excessive use of denial and other defense mechanisms to avoid crisis and protect their lifestyle. Consequently, practitioners often see clients only in extreme distress and may experience a brief window in which to engage the client. It is at this time that the individual's temporary loss of control creates a willingness to engage in new behaviors to address the crisis event. The applications of brief crisis models, such as that described here, are very advantageous in assisting individuals with an alcohol or other drug problem (Ewing, 1990; Parad & Parad, 1990; Norman, Turner, & Zunz, 1994).

Definitions of substance dependence have varied over the years. For many, the "disease concept" of substance dependence is the primary diagnostic tool. Two examples of diagnostic definitions for substance dependence are those of the World Health Organization and the American Psychiatric Association, which to this day remain the primary diagnostic criteria for substance dependence.

- World Health Organization (1974) A state, psychic and sometimes also physical, resulting from the interaction between a living organism and a drug, characterized by behavioral and other responses that always include a compulsion to take the drug on a continuous or periodic basis in order to experience its psychic effects, and sometimes to avoid the discomfort of its absence.

The American Psychiatric Association's DSM IV (1994), the accepted diagnostic tool for the profession of social work, defines substance abuse and dependency with varying criteria for each category. It is of interest to note that the DSM-IV separates dependence with physiological dependence from substance dependence without physical dependence. This distinction is an addition to the criteria of dependence. This is likely because of the prevalence of crack cocaine and the recent reemergence of hallucinogenic drugs that do not appear to cause physical dependence. Two components separate abuse from dependence.

A simplistic definition of *substance dependence* is: "If alcohol/drugs are causing problems in your life, . . . then you likely have a problem with alcohol/drugs." This is the case when approaching addiction from a crisis intervention perspective. Persons entering treatment frequently report that the coping mechanisms they used in the past are not working. If the individual could "control" her or his use or life circumstances, there would be no need to seek assistance. Wallace's (1983, 1989) biopsychosocial model of addiction highlights the pervasiveness of alcohol and other drug problems. Crisis for persons with this disorder is just as likely to be precipitated by intrapsychic discomfort, social conflict, or the physiological consequences of continued substance use. Effective evaluation of the crisis mandates that practitioners attend to each area.

APPLICATION OF ROBERTS'S SEVEN-STAGE CRISIS INTERVENTION MODEL AND ANALYSIS OF RISK AND PROTECTIVE FACTORS

Within Roberts's crisis intervention model applied to substance dependence, the social worker must be aware of the delicate balance between stabilization and removal of motivation for treatment. Chemical-dependent persons use maladaptive defense structures combined with numerous irrational beliefs to minimize the extent and severity of their dependence. Crisis intervention often involves addressing the individual's rationalizations, justifications, catastrophizing, and use of negative self-talk to work his or her way out of treatment (Roberts, 1990; Dattilio & Freeman, 1994; Greene, Lee, & Trask, 1996).

To this end, there are differences between the substance-dependent population and the general population seeking assistance. Roberts initially reported the seven-stage model, which identified establishment of rapport as the first stage. In a review of Roberts's work as applied by professionals in clinical practice, one can see the ongoing development of this model. Subsequent publications by Roberts recommend interchanging assessment of le-

Table 12.1 Roberts's Seven-Stage Model and Solution-Focused Applications

Stage	Application
Make psychological contact.	Acceptance, Support, Empathy, Mirroring nonverbal communication.
Examine the dimensions of the problem in order to define it.	Scaling, Examination of resilience factors, Empowering the patient, Assess support factors.
Encourage exploration of feelings and emotions.	Acceptance, Support, Empathy.
Explore and assess past coping attempts.	Exception question, Scaling question, Past success.
Generate and explore alternatives and specific solutions.	Miracle question, Exception question, past success, Prediction task, Track current success.
Restore cognitive functioning through implementation of action plan.	Scaling, Empowerment, Exception question, Past success tracking, Track current success.
Follow-up.	Scaling in the form of outcome studies.

Note: This chart is a representation of techniques to use with each stage of Roberts's model. The absence of assessment of lethality as presented in additional publications by Roberts is due to the use of solution-focused therapy as persons progress through the process of recovery. This is not indicative that patients presenting for substance dependence may not experience lethality issues. Work with persons who are substance dependent requires ongoing mental status assessment.

thality (stage 2) with establishment of rapport (stage 1), depending on the presenting problem(s) of the patient (Roberts, 1996).

This is particularly true of cocaine-dependent persons, who experience tremendously intense crises in short periods of time, yet because there is little withdrawal, cocaine-dependent persons may mistake crisis stabilization as an all clear to resume use (Yeager, 1999). The inertia of the recovery environment is extremely powerful; when combined with the powerful cravings frequently associated with crack cocaine, the equation is complete for the relapse process. Second, special emphasis must be placed on examination of the dimensions of the problem (stage 2), exploration of feelings and emotions (stage 3), and exploration of past coping attempts. Emphasis on these steps will assure the substance-dependent individuals of remaining connected with treatment. The following example of crisis intervention with a cocaine-addicted individual demonstrates this process (Roberts, 1990). Table 12.1 provides an overview of Roberts's seven-stage model and compatible solution focused interventions.

Case Study 1: Dennis

Dennis E., Cocaine Dependent

Dennis is a 41-year-old self-employed chemical researcher who presented following "being pattern" episode of cocaine use. Dennis reported being sober for a 10-year period following treatment for alcohol dependence. Dennis eventually began to taper off his attendance of 12-step support meetings as his family and business grew. Dennis is married with two children, age 8 and 11. His younger daughter was diagnosed with leukemia 1 year ago. Dennis reports being very close to his daughters, stating that he reads to them every evening and never misses a doctor's appointment with his younger daughter. Dennis is extremely successful in his work. He reports having secured government contracts for the next 5 years that total millions of dollars of profits for his company. He reports that at this time last year he was receiving an award for "researcher of the year." His plan was to celebrate with a glass of wine.

Following this event, there were no apparent consequences. Approximately 1 week later, Dennis drank again, this time at a ball game, to the point of intoxication. Again, there were no consequences. The next day he was extremely tired and was faced with deadlines in his work. He purchased a gram of cocaine, worked 27 hours straight, and completed two projects, including a million-dollar grant application.

Dennis believed he had successfully found the "old Dennis," the one who could work for hours with no breaks. Dennis states, that his relapse was "a major memory event." He reports his thinking instantly reverted to where his thoughts were in his previous addiction to alcohol. His use of cocaine rapidly increased. Within a 1-month period, he was using 3 grams of cocaine daily. In an attempt to save money, he began to smoke crack cocaine.

The introduction of crack cocaine led to isolative patterns of use. Dennis recalls the panic he felt at 3:00 A.M. when he realized that his staff would be returning to work in a few hours, knowing that he would not be able to continue to use cocaine within the confines of his office. Acting on impulse, Dennis removed his computer from his office and drove to a motel with approximately $3,000 of cocaine. With nothing to do in the motel, Dennis began visiting pornographic sites on the Internet. He reports becoming preoccupied with these sites. Caught in a cycle of crack cocaine use, he found that sexual fantasy, paranoia, and isolation began to dominate and control his behaviors. He was particularly occupied with an interactive XXX site; he reports engaging in fantasy, substituting acquaintances for the persons with whom he was interacting. It was not until the supply of cocaine was depleted that the cycle was broken.

Dennis was missing for 4 days before returning home. He had missed two doctor's appointments with his daughter and reports pending separation between him and his wife. Dennis identifies the separation as the precipitating event for seeking treatment. Within the initial contact, he acknowledged hoping his heart would explode so he would not have to face the disappointment of his family following his relapse. He quickly added that death would have been easier to face than having to look at the sadness in his daughter's eyes.

Seeking to understand the severity of Dennis's situation, fears, and feelings led to the rapid establishment of a working relationship (Roberts, 1990). Making psychological contact with Dennis consisted of showing a genuine interest in and respect for him and offering hope. Dennis, like many cocaine addicts, found it easy to share where he had been. What is difficult for many in early recovery is the ability to see a way out of the insanity associated with their cocaine dependence. Letting Dennis know that he was not the first to present with this problem simply did not reduce his anxiety. He was in need of hearing that there are common symptoms associated with cocaine dependence, including physical, mental, and emotional preoccupations with the drug. Although this discussion was helpful, remarkable anxiety remained. There was no significant reduction in tension until discussion of sexual preoccupation occurred. At this point, it became clear that cocaine use had taken Dennis to a place he had not anticipated. Avoiding pushing Dennis away by discussing this issue in detail, the therapist assured him that many authors had discussed the concurrent sexual component with cocaine dependence (Hser, Chou, Yih-ling, Hoffman, Chih-Ping, & Anglin, 1999; Balsheim, Oxman, Van Rooyen, & Girod, 1992). Offering to provide Dennis with information related to this topic, and connecting him with a cocaine-specific group to address this issue seemed to provide a combination of understanding and awareness of resources. This minimized the anxiety carried into the initial session.

The second step in crisis intervention as outlined by Roberts is "examining the dimensions of the problem in order to define it." In this area, a couple of issues required further examination. First was gaining a greater degree of insight into the precipitating event that led Dennis to the treatment center on this date. The therapist used probing questions to expand the information provided initially (Roberts, 1990).

Q: Dennis, you said the pending separation was what led you to seeking help. Can you tell me more about what happened?

A: When I did finally go home, there weren't any questions of "Where were you?" "Are you all right?" or "Thank God you're home!" There was only silence and sadness. When the silence was broken, it was by the sobs of Tiffany. She was trying hard not to . . . but there was no way she could hold back. I knew she was torn between her mother's instructions and her wanting to make sure I was O.K. God just knowing that my daughter . . . after all she had been through . . . was worried about me, she was a victim of my use . . . I just couldn't take it. I asked Donna to take me to treatment. There was no answer. Instead, she handed me separation papers and said, "We had an agreement. If you use, we have to leave." I knew she was right, so I got in the car and drove myself. I can't bear the thought of living my life without them.

This account provided much more information and understanding than the previous answer of pending separation. There was greater understanding of the pain Dennis and his family were experiencing. It also provided information surrounding Donna's willingness to do what was best for herself and the children. Dennis knew this was what needed to happen, but he acknowledged that knowing what needed to happen did not make it any less painful (Roberts, 1990; DeJong & Miller, 1995).

Contained within the information provided by Dennis is the third step of Roberts's seven-stage crisis model. While examining the dimensions of the problem, Dennis was encouraged to express his feelings and emotions (stage 3). Dennis clearly expressed the pain associated with the realization that his wife and children had become the victims of his addiction. Further exploration of this issue at this time was not necessary. Dennis had experienced the impact of the feeling, and it was important to encourage him to move beyond this feeling. Dennis noted that it was important for him to stand still and feel this hurt, because it will be necessary to remember this pain when he experiences cravings to use in the future (Roberts, 1990).

Dennis reports that "only the pain associated with the consequences of use is powerful enough to thwart relapse." A basic tenet of solution-focused therapy when applied in crisis intervention is that one does not need to know the cause or function of the problem in order to resolve it (O'Hanlon & Weiner-Davis, 1989). In this case recognizing that Dennis knew best how to cope with his cravings provided a powerful tool for treating his cravings. Because of the respect between the counselor and the patient, and the counselor's willingness to listen, Dennis taught his counselor how to address cravings (Berg & Jaya, 1993).

Clinical Issues/Interventions/Special Considerations

Since Dennis has been sober previously, the fourth step of Roberts's model, exploring and assessing past coping attempts, became a vital part of the ongoing recovery plan. Assigning specific tasks assisted in reestablishing equilibrium. Dennis was given the assignment to list the right and the wrong ways he had treated his disease in the past. For example, his alarm going off in the morning had provided the opportunity to hit the snooze button four or five times, waking up late and rushing to work. Alternatively, he could get up, fix a healthy breakfast, read his morning meditation books, and begin the day with a plan for recovery. Giving Dennis a clear-cut way to measure coping strategies provided him with a tool to build upon his strengths and to work toward a solution (Fortune, 1985; Levy & Shelton, 1990; Roberts, 1990).

Upon completing the assignment, Dennis identified any specific areas that presented within his recovery environment as high risk. Understanding the reciprocal processes between an individual and his or her recovery environment is crucial for understanding how a patient uses environmental resources in the problem-solving process and how the environment creates challenges for the individual (Pillari, 1998; Zastrow, 1996; Newman & Newman, 1995). Dennis was able to identify three primary areas. First was payday: "It's a very simple equation for me: *Time plus money equal cocaine.*" The second area he identified was Internet pornography; and the third was his uncontrollable mood swings.

Dennis was asked to rank the three high-risk situations on a scale of 1 to 10, with 10 being remarkable cravings and 1 being no cravings at all. Scaling provides a clear measure of the problem at hand when working to resolve a crisis (Saleebey, 1996). Dennis rated having money as a 10; his rationale is that there was not a time when he did not experience remarkable cravings when he had money. He rated his Internet pornographic fixation as a 7, stating, "I don't always have to be high to go there." When asked if he felt this required further addressing, Dennis replied, "Absolutely. It's still a very real trigger for my addiction. The third area of mood swings posed more of a problem. Initially Dennis rated this as a 5; after a few minutes of thought, however, he changed it to a 9, reporting, "I never know when it's going to hit. Sometimes it's nothing, other times I'm a raging lunatic." For the sake of argument, it was agreed upon that this would remain a "9." Dennis agreed to address the potential for rage at the worst possible level so as not to minimize the extent and severity of the mood swings.

Following the discussion, the therapist instructed Dennis to list alternatives or possible solution-oriented actions he could take to minimize the impact of each high-risk situation. This took situations previously seen as negative out of the control of the patient and provided the opportunity to assume an active role in minimizing the impact of these issues (Berg, 1994).

Special Considerations of Treatment Planning

Dennis returned with a plan that was simple and applicable in each area. In an effort to control money as a trigger, he agreed to relinquish control of his finances to his business partner. Dennis had contacted with this person, who agreed to take over his checkbook and to manage his finances. Dennis and his partner agreed that he would receive an allowance of $10 per day for lunch and incidentals. A company or bank check would be used for larger transactions.

The issue of the Internet was a bit more complicated because Dennis completed a great deal of his research on the Internet. Two changes were agreed upon. First, Dennis was to move his computer into the main lab, an area that was public and provided sufficient observation to minimize the accessing of Internet sites that contained pornographic material. The second was utilization of a "Net nanny" program that blocked access to pornographic sites. However, all quickly agreed that Dennis was smart enough to work around this if he wanted. The last agreed change was that Dennis would work between the hours of 8:00 A.M. and 6:00 P.M., because there was no real reason for him to be spending excess time in the office. He agreed that the evenings required his focusing on recovery.

The area of mood swings was more abstract and thus required different planning skills. Dennis presented a list of recovering persons whom he agreed to contact daily to minimize the possible occurrences of mood swings. He further agreed to keep this list with him at all times and to contact these persons if he began to experience a mood swing. Dennis noted the need for ongoing treatment and agreed to attend the intensive outpatient program four evenings per week, including a specialized cocaine group one evening per week. Dennis then stated he felt it would be in his best interest to enter a sober living house rather than seeking an apartment on his own, acknowledging that his mood swings occurred primarily when he was alone. Again, the emphasis is placed on the importance of addressing triggers in the person's recovery environment (Pillari, 1998).

In approximately 2½ days, Dennis had stabilized. He developed a plan of action to address the major threats to his recovery and agreed to participate in ongoing outpatient treatment and to move into a sober living arrangement. Treatment had capitalized on Dennis's strengths. He developed the treatment plan and agreed that he was now ready to move ahead with his plan. When asked to report on his level of comfort as scaled on his treatment plan, Dennis reported being extremely comfortable with his recovery plan; he felt ready to move to an intensive outpatient level of care.

Analysis of Risk and Protective Factors (Dennis)

The recovery dimensions outlined by the American Society of Addiction Medicine (Hoffman, Halikas, Mee-Lee, & Weedman, 1991) represent a useful framework for analyzing this case. Such an approach requires the clinician to consider risk and protective factors in each area. Biomedical risks include family history and physical health factors. Relapse potential responses are closely tied to craving or cue reactivity, which are the physiological responses addicts experience when exposed to prior cues for using. The issue of cue reactivity is particularly important when working with persons addicted to cocaine because cues to resume use have been described as "perhaps more powerful than any other drug" (Chiauzzi, 1994). In this case, it would appear that overwork and compensating for becoming intoxicated served as cues for the resumption of cocaine use. Fueled partially by a need to compensate for the physical consequences of his intoxication, and in an effort to increase his energy level, Dennis quickly reverted to a destructive pattern of use.

Psychological or emotional behavioral risk factors include the role of expectations with regard to the perceived positive consequences of further drug use, a lack of effective coping skills, and the presence of psychopathology (Chiauzzi, 1991). Clearly, Dennis approached his first use of cocaine with positive expectations, which initially were rewarded with an increase in his productivity. In describing intrapersonal relapse risk factors, Cummings,

Gordon, and Marlatt (1980) noted that both extreme negative and positive emotions might contribute to relapse. Both were operating in Dennis's case. Dennis had been tremendously successful in the workplace, with a growing business that had high profits. In fact, his initial use of alcohol occurred in response to receiving a recognition award. Chiauzzi (1994) noted that the assessment of relapse risk often overlooks the contribution of positive emotions. Just as in extreme negative experiences, extreme highs contribute to upsetting one's equilibrium, often a precipitating event in a crisis. At the same time, Dennis's younger daughter suffered from a potentially fatal illness. By the time Dennis sought help, the paranoia and isolation created by cocaine use and his shame at relapsing had exacerbated his crisis.

Persons in crisis and those in relapse share many characteristics (Chiauzzi, 1994). These include the general loss of equilibrium brought on by extreme emotions, and the consequent compression of one's coping repertoire. At the time of initial consultation, Dennis's ability to contemplate a way out of his crisis was limited to hoping for his own death. However, his affect and mood swings represented an additional psychological risk factor. At presentation, Dennis was extremely depressed. Addressing these mood symptoms was essential to ensuring his ability to remain drug free. Brown et al. (1998) found higher levels of depressive symptoms associated with greater urge to use cocaine, alcohol, and other drugs in high-risk situations.

Social risk factors requiring inquiry included the stability of family relationships, the presence of negative life events, and a lack of supportive social contact (Chiauzzi, 1991). The recent binge by Dennis had led his wife to threaten him with separation. In addition, although he had been tremendously successful at work, his recent crisis had created substantial problems in that setting. The presence of employment and family problems account for a significant amount of variance in posttreatment adjustment (McClellan et al., 1994). In choosing to taper off his attendance at self-help group meetings, Dennis had reduced his contact with the appropriate social support. Havassy, Hall, and Wasserman (1991) found that a lack of social support for a continuing goal of abstinence predicted subsequent relapse.

Case Autopsy: Follow-Up (Dennis)

As planned, Dennis transitioned into a sober living arrangement. He successfully completed a 6-week intensive outpatient treatment consisting of 3 hours of education and group therapy four evenings per week. Dennis again became active in the fellowships of Alcoholics Anonymous (AA) and Cocaine Anonymous (CA). Dennis and his family did reunite; however, his daughter died shortly after his first-year anniversary of recovery. Dennis was able to cope with her death without using mood-altering substances. He reported that the support from his friends in the "program" was tremendous during the time of his loss.

Dennis did experience one relapse after 18 months of remaining clean. At the time, he reported drinking approximately 24 beers at a concert. He reported that being overconfident and eliminating the majority of 12-step support meetings from his schedule contributed to his relapse. Following this use, Dennis presented for one individual session, where he reviewed the plan he had developed to reestablish his recovery. In this session, Dennis worked on stages 2 through 6 of Roberts's model without prompting from the therapist. Using the skills he had learned in previous treatments, Dennis examined the dimensions of the problem; he explored his feelings and emotions, and discussed what he needed to "get back to his program of recovery." Dennis discussed several alternatives and specific plans to resolve issues with Donna should she not accept him back into the home. Upon leaving he successfully implemented this plan. Because of this single self-directed intervention Dennis was able to limit this relapse to a single use episode. At this time, Dennis has been clean for over 2 years. He was elected businessman of the year last year and reports that he is hopeful that he will not return to use.

Case Study 2: Susan

Susan C., Opioid Dependent

Almost 6 years ago to the day, Susan C. brought her brother-in-law to the center for treatment for his cocaine dependence. She was disgusted by his antics, including how he had given up all responsibilities and had placed his family at risk by taking illegal drugs. On this date Susan C. was brought to treatment by the same brother-in-law, who is now 4 years clean and sober. The onetime schoolteacher sat in the assessment office, a mere shadow of herself.

Susan explained: I was in four car wrecks in a little over 3 years. I have two compressed discs in my spine, which cause a great deal of pain. Initially my physician prescribed Darvocet and Percodan. These worked well for a while. But little by little the pain came back; it always comes back. It may have been the result of sleeping wrong or jerking while stepping down a step; there always seems to be something to aggravate the pain. For a while I was able to tolerate the pain. Now I can't seem to cope with it. My use of medication has steadily increased. Now I'm using Oxycodone and Oxycotin along with Ultran, Tylenol 3, Percocet, and Darvocet to tolerate the pain.

I've been seeing other doctors and getting prescriptions from them too. It all started out somewhat innocently when I was seeking a second opinion for the pain. I discovered that if I didn't tell them the visit was for a second opinion, they would prescribe the same or similar medications. The next thing I know I'm seeing five or six doctors and all are prescribing similar medications. I used to save them just in case I needed them . . . you know for vacations or whatever. As time progressed I needed more and more pills. Now I'm taking all that are prescribed. It's become a nightmare. I'm having trouble keeping straight in my head what prescription goes with what doctor and what pharmacy. I think my insurance company and the pharmacy are on to me.

Yesterday, one pharmacist refused to fill my prescription without consulting my physician first. He wasn't going to give the prescription back. I raised so much hell he reluctantly gave it to me. I immediately went to another pharmacy in the same chain, and they did fill it. Now I'm scared. I wonder what happens to the prescriptions when they have been filled? Where do they go? Do they go back to the doctor? If they do, I'm in deep trouble. You see, I was so afraid that I wouldn't get the prescription filled that I changed the number from 20 to 50. I know it wasn't right, but I was desperate.

My pain is real . . . and the medication I take comes from doctors. I know I need this medication. If I don't have it, the pain becomes too great to deal with. After all, it was the physicians who got me hooked on them. What I really need is a doctor who will give me something strong enough to deal with the pain I'm experiencing. It's not like I'm some sort of a street bum. I'm not some rum dumb who is just crawling out from under a bridge. I have a genuine problem with pain! They can't send me to jail because I have a legitimate health problem . . . can they?

Susan's was not an uncommon problem; one study found just fewer than 28% of a pain clinic's patients met three or more criteria for substance abuse (Chabal, Erjavec, Jacobson, Mariano, & Chaney, 1997). Women often use more socially acceptable substances, such as prescription drugs, and often abuse them in medicinal ways (Nichols, 1985). This case will demonstrate the effectiveness of combining both Roberts's crisis intervention model and the strengths perspective approach. In working with Susan, the establishment of psychological contact takes the form of genuine respect for her chronic pain issues, combined with acknowldgement of the need to develop new coping skills to address her pain (Saleebey, 1996; Sullivan & Rapp, 1991; Miller & Berg, 1995). Roberts's first step in crisis intervention and the strengths perspective fit nicely together because they both work to maintain the dignity and integrity of the patient. Both approaches recognize the individual's innate ability to establish recovery and seek to build on previous effective coping skills (Roberts, 1990; Saleebey, 1992, 1996).

In this case, the therapist could assure Susan of the program's ability to address her pain issues. However, there was also the need to caution her that seeking several prescriptions from several different physicians was not legal and that there could be consequences associated with doing this. With that proviso, the therapist assured Susan that the action she was now taking was the single best step she could take to minimize any potential legal consequences.

When combining Roberts's model and the strengths perspective, the initial question was not "Do you believe or think that you might have a drug problem?" Instead, it became "You have been functioning up to now under some very difficult circumstances. What are you doing that has helped you to keep going despite the pain?" This approach moves the client toward an approach that focuses on today rather than on yesterday and all the pain of the past (Roberts, 1990; Rapp, 1992; Saleebey, 1996).

The initial interview should focus on the patient's strengths. For example, instead of asking "what brought you to treatment today," the question becomes "What is it that gave you the courage to ask for help today?" In the case of chronic pain, focusing on pain will only serve to keep the client focused on the perceived need to medicate their pain. A focus on what life could be like if the pain was minimized will eventually lead the client to seek alternative methods for addressing the pain.

Providing the client with an opportunity to examine both coping skills and environmental supports, when combined with the client's strengths, becomes a viable approach within Roberts's second and fourth stage of crisis intervention. The goal was to capitalize on the client's view of her problem as a medical issue rather than as an addiction, which eliminated resistance to entering the recovery process. The desired outcome was to assist the patient in minimizing her dependence on pain medication rather than to force the admission of addiction.

Helpers should assure clients who are entering detoxification from pain medications that they are expected to participate in activities that support pain management through methods other than medication. They should also be informed that medication is given only in response to withdrawal symptoms—for example, elevated pulse, temperature, and blood pressure.

In addition to the limits placed on the client in relation to the use of medication to address pain issues, the therapist asked Susan to develop her personal plan of alternative solutions, step five of Roberts's crisis intervention model. When possible, the client should be encouraged to collaborate with persons in her recovery environment who she has identified as supportive (Benard, 1994; Mclaughlin, Irby, & Langman, 1994). Susan identified several persons as supportive; however, she had little insight as to how these persons could help. In addition, Susan neglected to identify several important persons. To address this, the helper asked Susan to identify persons who she may have omitted from her support person's list and asked her to describe her rationale for omissions from the previous list. There were several false starts before completion of this assignment. Susan's list grew to include her mechanic, plumber, paperboy, and garbage collector; however her physicians, employer, and recovering brother-in-law did not make several of the revised lists. Eventually, Susan resolved to include her physicians, pharmacists, and even her brother-in-law to the list. Susan's list included one brief explanation for the omissions, it read, "OK, OK, I now understand how I am trying to hold on to my old ways!"

Once this task had been completed, Susan was asked to compile a letter to each person on her list, seeking their support for her efforts and requesting suggestions on how she might cope with pain by methods other than medication. Given the possible legal issues involved, the helper cautioned her to provide only vague information related to what prompted this call for assistance. Susan completed 15 letters and agreed to mail 3 per day. The goal was to amplify the patient's individual resilience by increasing awareness of informal networks of support and encouragement (Benard, 1994; Berg & Miller, 1992).

The response was overwhelming. As each letter, card, bouquet of flowers, and telephone call arrived, Susan became less and less defensive. She began to acknowledge how her reliance on the medication as her solitary coping mechanism had led to isolation from the very persons who were the most willing to help her. In addition, Susan became increasingly aware of the sadness, frustration, anger, and fear she was experiencing. Exploration of these feelings, Roberts's third step, led her to becoming the person she felt she was before the accidents and the onset of her problems (Roberts, 1990).

Using the suggestions provided to Susan by her strengths-based support group led to the development of her action plan. Susan incorporated each suggestion into (a) a daily plan for recovery, (b) a list of actions to be taken in high-risk situations, and (c) a medical management plan developed with the assistance of her primary physician and the physician who completed her detoxification.

With this plan in place and demonstration of medical stability, Susan was discharged from the detoxification program 5 days after her initial presentation. She received a prescription for decreasing amounts of Clonopin to ensure successful completion of her detoxification on an outpatient basis and weekly follow-up individual appointments with her counselor on the detoxification unit.

Analysis of Risk and Protective Factors (Susan)

In assessing Susan's case it was important to recognize that physical dependence and tolerance were an expected component of her long-term opioid use for pain. Sees and Clark (1993) noted that determining the existence of dysfunctional behavior is the salient point in the diagnosis of addiction. However, as this case demonstrated, the need for continued pain medication can occur independently of the physical health problem. Ultimately Susan discovered that much of her pain was unrelated to her long-standing injury. This was consistent with Robinson's (1985) suggestion that for some persons pain continues to exist after the physiological process has ameliorated because of the continued reinforcement provided by drug use.

Accessing Susan's social network represented a step toward engaging an important protective factor. Women with addiction problems commonly have fewer social supports than men (Kaufmann, Dore, & Nelson-Zlupko, 1995) and are often more likely to use in isolation. Kail and Litwak (1989) suggested engagement of relatives, and friends contributed to reducing the likelihood of prescription medicine abuse. Other authors have empirically demonstrated the important role of social support in maintaining the benefits of treatment (Bell, Richard, & Feltz, 1996; Havassy et al., 1991).

Perhaps partly because of her brother-in-law's experience, Susan was ambivalent about characterizing her use of drugs as addictive. A strengths-based approach represented an effective mechanism for overcoming the initial denial that might have impeded engagement in substance abuse treatment (Rapp, Kelliher, Fisher, & Hall, 1994). The choice to eschew pressuring Susan to label herself as addicted also contributed to the therapist's ability to create a collaborative relationship. Miller (1995) observed that self-labeling was not an important determinant of subsequent outcomes. Instead, the goal of the initial interview is to "create a salient dissonance or discrepancy between the person's current behavior and important personal goals" (Miller, 1995, p. 95).

Case Autopsy: Follow-Up (Susan)

Following discharge, Susan maintained weekly appointments for a 1-month period. She then began biweekly sessions for a 2-month period and finally finished the remainder of the year with sessions once per month. As time progressed, Susan acknowledged that the symptoms of pain she had experienced were most likely withdrawal from the medication. She noted that she had not used mood-altering substances to address her pain, finding that the nonsteroidal anti-inflammatory medications work extremely well for her.

Following her first drug-free year, with a level of pain that was expected and seen to be reasonable, Susan returned to work. Three years after the crisis, Susan has completed a master's degree in education and is a principal in an inner-city high school. She is an extremely strong advocate of prevention programming to keep teens away from drugs. To this day Susan reports she is not certain if she is an "addict"; however, she quickly acknowledges that her use of medication was the basis of her problems.

Case Study 3: Scott

Scott S., Polysubstance Dependence

Scott presented at the treatment facility accompanied by his grandfather, who reported seeking substance-dependence treatment at this facility 20 years ago and had remained abstinent from all mood-altering chemicals since that time. Scott related to the interviewer that he felt he was "at the end of his rope." His parents have disowned him after he took approximately $4,500 from their business and spent it on a week long binge.

Scott reported using intravenous heroin, alcohol, and cocaine for the past 14 days. His recent binge began when the university he had been attending refused to admit him to classes. Scott returned to campus for the January term only to find he was placed on academic suspension after not meeting the requirements of academic probation from the previous semester. Scott remained on campus with friends rather than returning home to his parents.

Scott's first experience with mood-altering substances was LSD, which he first took at approximately age 12. He remembered being asked if "he wanted to take something that would make him giggle and laugh all night long." He began to smoke pot shortly after this use. Scott reported being an avid "head" throughout high school, having used cannabis daily since age 13. He began to use alcohol on a regular basis at age 14, drinking up to six beers per day in conjunction with one eighth of an ounce of cannabis per day.

Scott said he can best be described as a "garbage head," explaining, "That's a person who has taken about everything." Scott has experimented with sedative hypnotics, amphetamine, and inhalants. His favorites are LSD, cocaine, heroin, and alcohol. Scott had experienced over 200 acid trips, using everything from liquid LSD 25 to four-way windowpane, to designer drugs. The majority of this use occurred between the ages of 14 and 17.

At age 16 Scott began to use powder cocaine. His initial use was limited to weekends; however, it progressed rapidly to near-daily use following graduation from high school. His peak tolerance was $300 of per day intravenous cocaine combined with up to one fifth of alcohol (whiskey). Scott felt his use was out of control, and he wanted to stop the cocaine use. Also during this time Scott was using crystal methamphetamine. He said, "Now that's a drug that will steal your soul." Scott stated this was the only time that he became fearful when he was using. He reported a period of time when he became extremely violent and out of control as a result of his crank use.

Scott said, "The high is so intense, it never seems to end. Once in a while you get a chance to catch your breath, but this doesn't last very long." Scott noted it was during this time that he became involved in stealing and "boosting" in order to support his habit. He indicated that when he was using this drug he just did not care: "The stuff makes you feel invincible. There are a lot of violent and crazy people out there, and the worst are doing crank!"

A friend introduced Scott to heroin when he was following the band Phish. His initial use was intranasal, but he quickly progressed to IV. Scott noted his use has progressed to three $65 bags per day. His liver enzyme tests were all elevated to approximately 10 times normal, indicating possible hepatitis. Scott noted his alcohol consumption had decreased to two 40-ounce beers daily.

He was currently facing legal consequences for "bad checks" and shoplifting. Scott did not expect to be readmitted to the university, which he reported is particularly frustrating to his father, since both he and Scott's grandfather graduated from the school. Scott stated he is becoming dope sick and really doesn't care about the stupid college. He has tried to stop on his own and has failed each time, as the "jones" (withdrawal) becomes more intense.

Scott noted that while driving to the hospital he had seen at least three places where he could cop. He felt that if he was not admitted quickly, he would likely leave and find some dope. He reported that he is not craving, but he is going to have to have something to keep the sickness away or he will find and use heroin. Scott is angry and frustrated that his grandfather has to pay for his admission; however, he acquiesced following his grandfather's insistence that he get help today or walk away from all of the family. The grandfather also reminded Scott that he may well be Scott's last advocate. Scott acknowledged that he has tried everything he knows to establish recovery and had failed. Feeling that he had no other options, Scott agreed to be admitted to the treatment program.

Scott's pattern of use was not atypical of young adults. Use of heroin by American teenagers has increased in recent years. According to the Monitoring the Future Study (Johnston, O'Malley, & Bachman, 1998), the percentage of high school seniors reporting heroin use, while still a small figure, has risen 133% from 1990 to 1997. The pattern of Scott's substance use presented a number of risk factors. Polydependence on alcohol and cocaine has been linked to more acute dependence, an increase in the likelihood of leaving treatment early, and poorer long-term outcomes (Brady, Sonne, Randall, Adinoff, & Malcolm, 1995). Scott's family history of alcoholism and his early age of first use also placed him in a high-risk group for greater psychopathology, increased recidivism, and continued negative consequences (Barbor et al., 1987; Penick et al., 1987).

Scott was not a person who trusted very easily. Therefore, the worker emphasized the process of gaining psychological contact with Scott during assessment. When the worker asked Scott to decide if his grandfather would be involved in the assessment process, Scott chose to "do this on his own." The assessing clinician sought to establish a positive relationship, beginning by examining Scott's resilience factors rather than his problems; resilience factors include skills, abilities, knowledge and insight into what needs to occur to develop a plan for mitigating the crisis (Roberts, 1990). In doing so, the assessor established a relationship with Scott, which led him to feeling a part of the recovery process rather than having a process thrust upon him. Scott requested medication to help with the physical withdrawal he had experienced in the past, but he did not want to take anything that might continue his dependence. He reported a previous methadone detoxification and stated he felt one drug was a substitute for another. Scott asked if there would be a drug detoxification that could minimize the physical symptoms without maintaining his dependence. He was assured that detoxification could be accomplished with a combination of clonidine used as a patch and orally for the extrapyramidal side effects (e.g., anticholinergic effects); Buprinex to minimize cravings and withdrawal symptoms; Bentyl to minimize cramping associated with opioid withdrawal; Motrin to address aches and pains; and Immodium to address diarrhea (Ginther, 1999).

While not pretending to understand the detoxification process, Scott agreed that it seemed to him that his request would be granted, and he entered detoxification with the stipulation that if he felt like a zombie he would leave. Program staff respected and agreed with this stipulation.

In individual meetings with Scott, his social worker sought to further define and examine the parameters of the problem (Roberts, 1990) by eliciting Scott's definition of it. The goal in this case was to assist Scott's awareness of the tensions and conflicts that were present in his life by providing acceptance, empathy, and mirroring nonverbal communication in an environment free from confrontation (Greene et al., 1996). When defining the problem, it is important to allow the patient to explore her or his feelings and emotions surrounding the issues, which is Roberts's third step (Roberts, 1990).

In this case, Scott quickly identified feeling oppressed by his parents, believing that they were trying to force him into a role that he did not want. He spoke of feeling like an abused child:

> Not in the classic sense of abuse. It's like they never listen to my wants and needs, they believe if they give me everything they think I should have, then I will be happy. In all honesty, they could have kept all of the shit they gave me and just listened for a few minutes. That would have really made me happy. Instead they keep throwing things at me that make me; the right clothes, the right club memberships, the right college, what they think I should be instead of hearing what I really want to be!

Scott shared that as he progressed through school toward a business degree, he felt as though he was "selling out" and was being forced to become everything that he hated. He reported feeling conflict between being relieved that he did not have to continue in his classes and the fear of telling his father about his expulsion from school.

Roberts's fourth stage of crisis intervention, exploring past coping attempts (Roberts, 1990) addresses the fine line between solution-focused treatment and sustaining motivation without providing the client with justification for his or her illness. This stage merges well with solution-focused theory because it provides the opportunity to apply the exception question (Koslowski, 1989; Koslowski & Ferrence, 1990; Greene et al., 1996). In this case, the worker asked Scott to examine the right and wrong ways he has treated his disease in the past. This is an inventory of what worked for Scott and what did not when he had attempted to stay sober in the past. Scott was encouraged to develop his list of behaviors that supported his previous attempts at abstinence.

By this point, Scott had progressed into the second day of his detoxification and was quite agitated. He was frustrated and was resistant to examination of strengths or weaknesses. This provided an opportunity to apply scaling questions with the exception questions. The worker used the scaling question to provide Scott with a mechanism to mark his progress. This question asked the client to rank the problem he was experiencing on a scale of 1 to 10, with 10 being the most desirable state and 1 being the least desirable outcome (De Jong & Miller, 1995; Miller & Berg, 1995).

At times it is possible to use the scaling question in combination with the exception question or the miracle question (DeShazer, 1988; De Jong & Miller, 1995; Greene et al., 1996). For example, when meeting in medical rounds, the physician asked Scott:

Physician: On a scale of 1 to10 [as described above] how do you feel today?
Scott: I feel like shit. . . . I'm sick, my head is pounding, my stomach is cramped, my nose is running, I'm either hot or cold and sweating all the time. It could be a little worse, so I'll say I'm about a 3 today.
Physician: When is the last time you felt this lousy and didn't use?
Scott: [Silence] Never!
Physician: You must be doing detox exactly right. If you have never made it beyond this point without using before, you are definitely doing something right! Your addiction is real angry with you, and it is attempting to get you to self-medicate. Just keep doing what you are doing, and we will get you through the worst of the detoxification.

This supportive interaction provided Scott with an opportunity to notice progress that otherwise would have been overlooked. He was also encouraged to learn that, despite feeling poorly, he was doing his detoxification exactly right. Each subsequent interaction with the physician began with the scaling question and follow-up supportive feedback. Roberts's fifth stage, exploring alternatives and specific solutions, provided a format for the miracle question. The miracle question directed Scott to set new and unimagined goals for his recovery (DeShazer, 1988). For example, his social worker asked Scott: "Suppose after this meeting you fell asleep, and while you were sleeping a miracle happened and your problems were suddenly resolved. Because you were asleep, you are not aware that the miracle has happened. What will be the signs that tell you the miracle has occurred?"

From this question, Scott identified three clear indicators. First, "I wouldn't be dope sick. Second, I really wouldn't give a damn what my parents said or did. And third, I would be living my life clean, accomplishing the goals I really wanted." Follow-up questioning attempted to develop a clearer understanding of coping mechanisms and alternative behaviors Scott might apply. Scott indicated that if his parents permitted him to seek education in an area of interest, he would not likely be failing school. If he were not failing and was studying what he wanted, he would be making progress toward his life dream of becoming a marine biologist. From this discussion Scott developed the following goals:

1. Doing whatever he needs to do to finish his detox
2. Telling his parents that he was leaving the school he was attending
3. Making independent living arrangements
4. Enrolling in a college other than where he had been and completing his basic education requirements
5. Seeking acceptance into the University of Florida Marine Biology Program

Using the miracle question to define Scott's goals provided the format for the development and implementation of recovery-specific goals. Shortly after discussing this with his social worker, Scott became an active member in groups. He seemed to have a greater interest in the recovery process. Scott selected a sponsor in the 12-step fellowship of Narcotics Anonymous (NA). He began seeking permission to attend additional NA meetings and to spend time with his sponsor. Scott wrote a letter to his parents explaining his removal from the university. This generated an angry yet predictable response from his father; nevertheless, Scott used his growing sober support system to work his way through this problem. Because of these interactions, over a 4-day period Scott requested placement with a long-term halfway house facility where he could practice independent living skills and from where he could apply to the university.

Scott was now involved in the sixth stage of Roberts's model, the restoration of cognitive functioning. Scott had actively examined the events that contributed to the crisis. He was in the process of developing a clear understanding of the process of addiction and its progression over time. Scott began to verbalize awareness of the overgeneralizations, shoulds, projections, catastrophizing, and self-defeating behaviors that led to his maladaptive dependence on mood-altering substances.

Finally, Scott was replacing his irrational beliefs with new recovery-supported cognitions, using his sponsor and support group to think out his thoughts before turning these into action. Scott reported using the sober support group to increase his awareness of the behaviors that will be required to support his recovery and to facilitate the development of a self-directed program of recovery.

Following a 6-day detoxification and medical stabilization, Scott made the transition to a 3- to 6-month halfway house program. He was developing and implementing his plan for recovery. Scott was "cautiously optimistic" when he left the detoxification center, saying, "This is the first time I've taken the risk to do something out of the shadow of my family. It feels great!"

Analysis of Risk and Protective Factors (Scott)

Among the factors that contributed to Scott's current crisis were the fear of his parents' reaction to his school failure and his general conflict with them over his educational goals. To some extent, Scott's crisis was exacerbated by his need to emancipate from his parents. Paradoxically, his drug and alcohol addiction only further delayed development, including the task of developing his own agenda for his future. Bentler (1992) empirically demonstration that drug and alcohol use by young people impedes many of their important developmental tasks.

The therapist's attention to Scott's cognitive function and negative thought patterns was an important step in helping Scott on the road to recovery. Carroll, Rounsaville, and Gawin (1991) demonstrated that cognitive treatment was highly effective with cocaine-dependent persons, and was particularly beneficial among the more severe cases. Benefits gained from cognitive treatment are maintained over a long time (O'Malley et al., 1994).

Scott's willingness to embrace 12-step groups was a very positive step toward resolving his crisis. The literature is replete with the benefits of these approaches. Weiss et al. (1996) reported a positive association between self-help participation and short-term outcomes among cocaine-dependent patients. Other authors have published similar findings on the general efficacy of 12-step groups when working with alcohol and other drug-dependent clients (Stevens-Smith & Smith, 1998; Johnsen & Herringer, 1993). In fact, Humpreys and Moos (1996) found no significant differences among health outcomes at 1 or 3 years for persons who participated in AA groups only versus those who received outpatient treatment. The benefits of participation in self-help groups seem to have a long-term effect. One study found that ongoing participation in self-help groups was associated with better outcomes even after 3 years (Longabaugh, Wirtz, Zweben, & Stout, 1998).

Participation in self-help groups has also been associated with improvements in other life areas. In addition to finding that participation predicted better posttreatment substance-use outcomes, Morgenstern, Labouvie, McCrady, Kahler, and Frey (1997) determined that 12-step participation was positively associated with increased self-efficacy, motivation to change, and improved coping ability.

Involvement in self-help groups has the potential to influence the social domain as well. Persons who participated in 12-step groups were found to have more close friends, as well as fewer friends who were using alcohol and other drugs (Humphreys & Noke, 1997). Persons participating in an aftercare program had significant reductions in job absenteeism, inpatient hospitalizations, and arrest rates (Miller, Ninonuevo, Klamen, Hoffmann, & Smith, 1997).

Case Autopsy: Follow-Up (Scott)

Scott was discharged from the detoxification level of care and moved into the partial hospitalization program for 10 additional days. During this time, he worked to solidify his self-diagnosis while building his sober support network. Scott developed concrete plans to address high-risk situations, including arranging to enter a sober house near the university. Scott left the treatment center after a total of 16 days in the hospital. He continued his treatment in the intensive outpatient program for 6 weeks, after which he attended aftercare for 3 additional months.

Scott's awareness of the provoking nature of his relationship with his family led to the development of what he called his "family of choice" within the recovery community. He was extremely proud of his involvement in the local recovery fellowships, which provided the opportunity to realize and use his assets and abilities. The input he provided to his peer group complemented his awareness of the need for peer input into his recovery. Scott notes, "My thinking for myself stinks, but my ability to give others feedback is great. I can see exactly what they need. Just as they can see exactly what I need. As a collective, we are doing great things in recovery." Working within the recovery community provided for exponential growth for Scott's recovery from addiction and in his development of mature problem-solving strategies.

Scott applied for, and was accepted into, a marine biology program. He obtained grants and student loans to facilitate his transition. Approximately 6 months after entering detoxification, Scott had realized his goal of studying marine biology. He had also become active in the student union, providing guidance to students who are experiencing problems with substance abuse and dependence. Scott has now been sober for nearly 3 years. Every year Scott visits the treatment center, and last year he and his grandfather attended the 24th anniversary of the treatment center. He continues to communicate with his counselor and peers in recovery by telephone and e-mail.

CONCLUSION

The challenge facing social workers in substance-dependence treatment is to balance cost against quality. A completely new dimension of substance-dependence treatment is emerging. This dimension is crisis intervention and brief treatment, designed to stabilize patients as quickly and effectively as possible (Edmunds et al., 1997).

Roberts's crisis intervention model, combined with brief solution-focused therapy and a strengths perspective, provides extremely flexible, practical approaches to intervention with substance-dependent individuals in crisis. The established routes of Roberts's model provide clear guidelines for intervention and progression through detoxification and into a meaningful recovery process. This approach facilitates the development of a self-directed plan of recovery that capitalizes on the individual's strengths rather than taking the approach of more familiar problem-focused models utilized by traditional substance-dependence programs (Day, 1998).

As a result of using the crisis intervention/solution-focused approach, patients experienced rapid normalization and return to their recovery environment. Crisis response in this format sought to place the substance-dependent person in their environment as soon as they are medically stable. The goal was to facilitate greater utilization of the system of community support and relationships that are present in day-to-day life. Keeping the substance-dependent individual in contact with his or her community while participating in outpatient programming provided greater opportunity to address relapse traps and triggers as they occurred.

Links between the crisis and the patient's life history were identified and examined in a manner that maintained the patient's historical and existential continuity. The focus on community supports provided patients the opportunity to reframe what once was perceived as a using environment to an environment where sober support was found. The end result is a treatment process that allows patients to pass through the crisis event while maintaining their dignity, sense of strength, pride, trust, spirituality, and personal identity.

Substance-dependence treatment has traditionally placed a great deal of emphasis on outcome. Meaningful outcome studies have been undertaken to evaluate the effectiveness of treatment modalities for over 25 years. Examination of crisis intervention combined with solution-focused therapy outcomes will need to be examined. It will be important to identify the outcomes that this type of treatment can be expected to bring about, in both short- and long-term goals (e.g., detoxification and stabilization versus maintenance of established recovery goals over extended periods of time). Examination of outcomes within the solution-focused crisis intervention approach will be important for several reasons.

First, emphasis on customer-driven quality improvement may provide the opportunity to respond to what consumers and their families desire in the treatment of substance dependence. Substance dependence, by nature, is disempowering. Many of the systems established for the treatment of substance dependence have resulted in patients experiencing further disempowerment (Day, 1998). It will be important to fully understand how a solution-focused crisis intervention approach impacts outcome.

Second, this model is consistent with policy development and behavioral health care management systems that have been established over the past decade. This model is designed to incorporate individualized treatment planning, utilization of community support, capitalization on consumer strengths, and consumer choice. This model can provide a framework to examine the effectiveness of brief intervention within the recovery environment.

Finally, the model has the potential to accomplish the goals not only of the consumer but also of the payers and system administrators within the public and private sectors. That goal is to reduce the risk and exposure to unplanned increases in costs. Application of the crisis intervention solution-focused approach at this time appears to meet this challenge by (a) reducing hospital days, (b) reducing emergency services, (c) increasing utilization of community support, and (d) reducing relapse potential.

This chapter is not intended to present Roberts's seven-stage model as a replacement for traditional approaches to substance-dependence treatment. The intention is to provide an alternative framework that can be applied within the substance-dependence treatment setting. We hope that this approach will be considered, applied, refined, and researched as a viable alternative when social workers are faced with increasingly complex cases combined with reduced resources.

REFERENCES

American Psychiatric Association. (1994). *Diagnostic and statistical manual of mental disorders* (4th ed.). Washington, DC: Author.

Babor, T., Hoffman, M., DelBoca, F., Hesselbrock, V., Meyer, R., Dolinsky, Z., & Rounsaville, B. (1992). Types of alcoholics, I: Evidence for an empirically derived typology based on indicators of vulnerability and severity. *Archives of General Psychiatry, 49,* 599–608.

Balsheim, K., Oxman, M., Van Rooyen, G., & Girod, D. (1992). Syphilis, sex and crack cocaine: Images of risk and mortality. *Social Science and Medicine, 31,* 147–160.

Barbor, T. F., Korner, P., Wilbur, P., & Good, F. (1987). Screening and early intervention strategies for harmful drinkers: Initial lessons learned from the Amethyst project. *Australian Drug and Alcohol Review, 6,* 325–339.

Beinecke, R., Callahan, J., Shepard, D., Cavanaugh, D., & Larson, M. (1997). The Massachusetts mental health/substance abuse managed care program: The provider's view. *Administration and Policy in Mental Health, 23,* 379–391.

Bell, D., Richard, A., & Feltz, L. (1996). Mediators of drug treatment outcomes. *Addictive Behaviors, 21,* 597–613.

Bentler, P. (1992). Etiologies and consequences of adolescent drug use: Implications for prevention. *Journal of Addictive Diseases, 11*(3), 47–61.

Berg, I. K. (1994). *Family-based services: A solution-focused approach.* New York: Norton.

Berg, I. K., & Jaya, A. (1993). Different and same: Family therapy with Asian-American families. *Journal* of Marital and Family Therapy, 19, 31–38.

Berg, I. K., & Miller, S. D. (1992). Working with the problem drinker: A solution-focused approach. New York: Norton.

Blume, S. (1992). Alcohol and other problems in women. In J. Lowinson, P. Ruiz, & R. Millman (Eds.), Substance abuse (pp. 794–807). Baltimore: Williams and Wilkins.

Book, J., Harbin, H., Marques, C., Silverman, C., Lizanich-Aro, S., & Lazarus, A. (1995). The ASAM and Green Spring alcohol and drug detoxification and rehabilitation criteria for utilization review. American Journal on Addictions, 4, 187–197.

Brady, K., Sonne, E., Randall, C., Adinoff, B., & Malcolm, R. (1995). Features of cocaine dependence with concurrent alcohol abuse. Drug and Alcohol Dependence, 39, 69–71.

Brown, R., Monti, P., Myers, M., Martin, R., Rivinus, T., Dubreuil, M., & Rohsenow, D. (1998). Depression among cocaine abusers in treatment: Relation to cocaine and alcohol use and treatment outcome. American Journal of Psychiatry, 155, 220–225.

Carroll, K., Rounsaville, B., & Gawin, F. (1991). A comparative trial of psychotherapies for ambulatory cocaine abusers: Relapse prevention and interpersonal psychotherapy. American Journal of Drug and Alcohol Abuse, 17, 229–247.

Chabal C., Erjavec, M., Jacobson, L., Mariano, A., & Chaney, E. (1997). Prescription opiate abuse in chronic pain patients: Clinical criteria, incidence, and predictors. Clinical Journal of Pain, 13, 150–155.

Chiauzzi, E. (1991). Preventing relapse in the addictions: A biopsychosocial approach. New York: Pergamon Press.

Chiauzzi, E. (1994). Turning points: Relapse prevention as crisis intervention. Crisis Intervention, 1, 141–154.

Cummings, G., Gordon, J., & Marlatt, G. (1980). Relapse: Prevention and prediction. In W. Miller (Ed.), Addictive behaviors: Treatment of alcoholism, drug abuse, smoking, and obesity (pp. 291–321). Oxford: Pergamon Press.

Dattilio, F., & Freeman, A. (1994). Cognitive-behavioral strategies in crisis intervention. New York: Guilford.

Day, Stephen L. (1998). Toward consumer focused outcome and performance measurement. In K. M. Coughlin, A. Moore, B. Cooper, & D. Beck, 1998 Behavioral outcomes and guidelines sourcebook: A practical guide to measuring, managing and standardizing mental health and substance abuse treatment (pp. 179–185). New York: Fulkner and Gray.

DeJong, P., & Miller, S. D. (1995). How to interview for client strengths. Social Work, 40, 729–736.

DeShazer, S. (1985). Keys to solution in brief therapy. New York: Norton.

DeShazer, S. (1988). Clues: Investigating solutions in brief therapy. New York: Norton.

Edmunds, M., Frank, R., Hogan, M., McCarty, D., Robinson-Beale, R., & Weisner, C. (1997). Managing managed care: Quality improvement in behavioral health. In K. M. Coughlin, A. Moore, B. Cooper, & D. Beck, 1998 Behavioral outcomes and guidelines sourcebook: A practical guide to measuring, managing and standardizing mental health and substance abuse treatment (pp. 134–143). New York: Fulkner and Gray.

Etheridge, R., Craddock, S., Dunteman, G., & Hubbard, R. (1995). Treatment services in two national studies of community-based drug abuse treatment programs. *Journal of Substance Abuse, 7,* 9–26.

Ewing, C. P. (1990). Crisis intervention as brief psychotherapy. In R. A. Wells & V. J. Giannetti (Eds.), *Handbook of brief psychotherapies* (pp. 277–294). New York: Plenum.

Ford, W. (1998). Medical necessity: Its impact in managed mental health care. *Psychiatric Services, 49,* 183–184.

Fortune, A. E. (1985). The task-centered model. In A. E. Fortune (Ed.), *Task-centered practice with families and groups* (pp. 1–30). New York: Springer.

Gartner, L., & Mee-Lee, D. (1995). *The role and status of patient placement criteria in the treatment of substance use disorders.* Publication No. (SMA) 95-3021. Rockville, MD: U.S. Department of Health and Human Service.

Ginther, C. (1999, April). Schuckit addresses state-of-the-art addiction treatments. Special report: Addictive disorders. *Psychiatric Times,* April, 55–57.

Greene, G. J., Lee, Mo-Yee, Trask, R. In addition, Rheinscheld, J. (1996). Client strengths and crisis intervention: A solution focused approach. *Crisis Intervention, 3,* 43–63.

Havassy, B., Hall, S., & Wasserman, D. (1991). Social support and relapse: Commonalties among alco-holics, opiate users, and cigarette smokers. *Addictive Behaviors, 16,* 235–246.

Hoffman, N., Halikas, J., Mee-Lee, D., & Weedman, R. (1991). *Patient placement criteria for the treatment of psychoactive substance use disorders.* Chevy Chase, MD: American Society of Addiction Medicine.

Hser, D., Chou, Yih-ling, Hoffman, Chih-Ping, & Anglin, V. (1999). Cocaine use and high-risk behavior among STD clinic patients. *Sexually Transmitted Diseases, 26,* 82–86.

Humphreys, K., & Moos, R. (1996). Reduced substance-abuse-related health care costs among voluntary participants in Alcoholics Anonymous. *Psychiatric Services, 47,* 709–713.

Humphreys, K., & Noke, J. (1997). The influence of post-treatment mutual help group participation on the friendship networks of substance abuse patients. *American Journal of Community Psychology, 25,* 1–16.

Johnsen, E., & Herringer, L. (1993). A note on the utilization of common support activities and relapse following substance abuse treatment. *Journal of Psychology, 127,* 73–77.

Johnston, L., O'Malley, P., & Bachman, J. (1998). *National survey results on drug use from the Monitoring the Future study, 1975–1997. Vol. 1: Secondary school students.* NIH Publication No. 98-4345. Rockville, MD: National Institute on Drug Abuse.

Kail, B., & Litwak, E. (1989). Family, friends and neighbors: The role of primary groups in preventing the misuse of drugs. *Journal of Drug Issues, 19,* 261–281.

Kaufmann, E., Dore, M., & Nelson-Zlupko, L. (1995). The role of women's therapy groups in the treatment of chemical dependence. *American Journal of Orthopsychiatry, 65,* 355–363.

Koslowski, L. T., & Ferrence, R. G. (1990). Statistical control in research on alcohol and tobacco: An example from research on alcohol and mortality. *British Journal of Addiction, 85,* 271–278.

Koslowski, L. T., Henningfield, R. M., Keenan, R. M., Lei, H., Leigh, G., Jelinek, L. C., Pope, M. A., & Haertzen, C. A. (1993). Patterns of alcohol, cigarette, and caffeine and other drug use in two drug abusing populations. *Journal of Substance Abuse Treatment, 10,* 171–170.

Kusher, J., & Moss, S. (1995). *Purchasing managed care services for alcohol and other drug treatment: Essential elements and policy issues.* Publication No. (SMA) 95-3040. Rockville, MD: U.S. Department of Health and Human Service.

Levy, R. L., & Shelton, J. L. (1990). Tasks in brief therapy. In R. A. Wells & V. J. Gianetti (Eds.), *Handbook of the brief therapies* (pp. 145–163). New York: Plenum.

Longabaugh, R., Wirtz, P., Zweben, A., & Stout, R. (1998). Network support for drinking, Alcoholics Anonymous and long-term matching effects. *Addiction, 93,* 1313–1333.

McClellan, A., Alterman, A., Metzger, D., Grisson, G., Woody, G., Luborsky, L., & O'Brien, C. (1994). Similarity of outcome predictors across opiate, cocaine, and alcohol treatment: Role of treatment services. *Journal of Consulting and Clinical Psychology, 62,* 1141–1158.

Miller, N., Ninonuevo, F., Klamen, D., Hoffmann, N., & Smith, D. (1997). Integration of treatment and post-treatment variables in predicting results of abstinence-based outpatient treatment after one year. *Journal of Psychoactive Drugs, 29,* 239–248.

Miller, S. D., & Berg, I. K. (1995). *The miracle method: A radically new approach to problem drinking.* New York: Norton.

Miller, W. (1995). Increasing motivation for change. In R. Hester & W. Miller (Eds.), *Handbook of alcoholism treatment approaches: Effective alternatives* (2nd ed., pp. 89–104). Boston: Allyn and Bacon.

Morgenstern, J., Labouvie, E., McCrady, B., Kahler, C., & Frey, R. (1997). Affiliation with Alcoholics Anonymous after treatment: A study of its therapeutic effects and mechanisms of action. *Journal of Consulting and Clinical Psychology, 65,* 768–777.

Newman, B. M., & Newman P. R. (1995). *Development through life: A psychological approach* (6th ed.). Pacific Grove, CA: Brooks/Cole.

Nichols, M. (1985). Theoretical concerns in the clinical treatment of substance-abusing women: A feminist analysis. *Alcoholism Treatment Quarterly, 2,* 79–90.

Norman, E., Turner, S., & Zunz, S. (1994). *Substance abuse prevention: A review of the literature.* New York: State Office of Alcohol and Substances Abuse Services.

O'Hanlon, W. H., & Weiner-Davis, M. (1989). *In search of solutions:*

A new direction in psychotherapy. New York: Norton.

O'Malley, S., Jaffe, A., Chang, G., Rode, S., Shottenfeld, R., Meyer, R., & Rounsaville, B. (1994). Six-month follow-up of naltrexone and coping skills therapy for alcohol dependence. *Archives of General Psychiatry, 53,* 217–224.

Parad, H. J., & Parad, L. G. (1990). Crisis intervention: An introductory overview. In J. J. Parad & L. G. Parad (Eds.), *Crisis intervention book 2: The practitioner's sourcebook for brief therapy* (pp. 3–68). Milwaukee, WI: Family Service America.

Penick, E., Powell, B., Bingham, S., Liskow, V., Miller, M., & Read, M. (1987). A comparative study of familial alcoholism. *Journal of Studies on Alcoholism, 48,* 136–146.

Pillari, V. (1998). *Human behavior in the social environment.* Pacific Grove, CA: Brooks/Cole.

Platt, J., Widman, M., Lidz, V., Rubenstein, D., & Thompson, R. (1998). The case for support services in substance abuse treatment. *American Behavioral Scientist, 41,* 1050–1062.

Rapp, C. A. (1992). The strengths perspective of case management with persons suffering from severe mental illness. In D. Saleebey (Ed.), *The strengths perspective in social work practice* (pp. 45–48). New York: Longman.

Rapp, R., Kelliher, C., Fisher, J., & Hall, F. (1994). Strengths-based case management: A role in addressing denial in substance abuse treatment. *Journal of Case Management, 3,* 139–144.

Rivers, J. (1998). Services for substance abusers in a changing health care system. *American Behavioral Scientist, 41,* 1050–1062.

Roberts, A. R. (1990). Overview of crisis theory and crisis intervention. In A. R. Roberts (Ed.), *Crisis intervention handbook: assessment, treatment, and research* (pp. 3–16). Belmont, CA: Wadsworth.

Roberts, A. R. (1996). Battered women who kill: A comparative study of incarcerated participants with a community sample of battered women. *Journal of Family Violence, 5,* 291–304.

Roberts, A. R., & Dziegielewski, S. F. (1995). Foundation skills and applications of crisis intervention and cognitive therapy. In A. R. Roberts (Ed.), *Crisis intervention and time-limited treatment.* Thousand Oaks, CA: Sage.

Robinson, J. (1985). Prescribing practices for pain in drug dependence: A lesson in ignorance. *Advances in Alcohol and Substance Abuse, 5,* 135–162.

Saleebey, D. (1992). Introduction: Power in the people. In D. Saleebey (Ed.), *The strengths perspective in social work practice* (pp. 3–17). New York: Longman.

Saleebey, D. (1996). The strengths perspective in social work practice: Extensions and cautions. *Social Work, 41,* 296–305.

SAMHSA. (1998). Preliminary results from the 1997 National Household Survey. *http://www.* Samhas.gov/oas/nhsda97/nhsda976-990.htm.

Sees, K., & Clark, H. (1993). Opioid use in the treatment of chronic pain: Assessment of addiction. *Journal of Pain and Symptom Management, 8,* 257–264.

Stevens-Smith, P., & Smith, R. L. (1998). *Substance abuse counseling: *Theory and practice.* Upper Saddle River, NJ: Merrill.

Sullivan, W. P., & Rapp, C. A. (1991). Improving clients outcomes: The Kansas technical assistance consultation project. *Community Mental Health Journal,* 27(5), 327–336.

Thompson, J., Burns, B., Goldman, H., & Smith, J. (1992). Initial level of care and clinical status in a managed mental health program. *Hospital and Community Psychiatry,* 43, 599–603.

Toff-Bergman, G. (1998). *Managed behavioral healthcare updates: State and local activity.* SAMHSA Managed Care Tracking Report, 1(1).

Wallace, J. (1983). Alcoholism: Is a shift in paradigm necessary? *Journal of Psychiatric Treatment and Evaluation,* 5, 479–485.

Wallace, J. (1989). A biopsychosocial model of alcoholism. *Social Casework,* 70, 325–332.

Weiss, R., Griffin, M., Najavits, L., Hufford, C., Kogan, J., Thompson, H., Albeck, J., Bishop, S., Daley, D., Mercer, D., & Siqueland, L. (1996). Self-help activities in cocaine dependent patients entering treatment: Results from NIDA collaborative cocaine treatment study. *Drug and Alcohol Dependence,* 43, 79–86.

Wells, K., Astrachan, B., Tischler, G., & Unutzer, J. (1995). Issues and approaches in evaluating managed mental health care. *Milbank Quarterly,* 73, 57–75.

World Health Organization (1981). Nomenclature and classification of drugs and alcohol-related problems: A WHO memorandum. *Bulletin of the World Health Organization,* 59, 225–242.

World Health Organization Expert Committee on Drug Dependence. (1974). *Twentieth report* (Tech. Rep. Series No. 5(51). Geneva, Switzerland: Author.

Yeager, K. R. (in press). The role of intermittent crisis intervention in early recovery from cocaine addiction. *Journal of Crisis Intervention and Time-Limited Treatment,* 5.

Zastrow, C. (1996). *Introduction to social work and social welfare* (6th ed.). Pacific Grove, CA: Brooks/ Cole.

13

The Crisis of Divorce

Cognitive-Behavioral and Constructivist Assessment and Treatment

DONALD K. GRANVOLD

Case Example

Velia, a 46-year-old Hispanic woman, presented for therapy shortly after filing for a divorce from her husband of 28 years. The mother of five children ranging in age from 10 to 27, Velia reported extreme unhappiness with the relationship over the past 10 years. She had experienced repeated periods of separation, the last of which began 18 months ago. During this last separation period, Velia become involved in a sexual relationship with a family friend. The love relationship, now terminated, lasted 8 months and ended with an ultimatum from her lover to end the marriage or end the love relationship. Velia, ill-prepared to made a final decision about her marriage at the time, broke off the love relationship. About 2 months later, immediately prior to presenting for treatment, a family member informed Velia's husband and children of Velia's involvement outside the marriage. Velia felt extremely violated by the disclosure. Two of her adult offspring verbally attacked her and subsequently withdrew from her. All four adult children began acting very distant toward her and blamed her for the problems in the marriage. Despite Velia's explanation that her marital unhappiness had lasted over 10 years, the children held their mother solely responsible for the marital distress due to the extramarital relationship. Velia's husband, Jorge, remained willing to "work things out" and actively enlisted the children in trying to convince their mother to remain in the marriage. Velia felt no romantic feelings for Jorge, although she did feel love for him as the father of their children. While currently committed to the divorce, Velia was concerned with her children's coldness toward her and their strong views that her wrongdoing was account-able for the marital unhappiness. Although not suicidal, Velia experienced extreme depression primarily related to her children's negative judgments of her and her own self-recrimination for allowing herself to love another. She felt a sense of hopelessness and saw her future as empty of possible joy or personal well-being. She felt that she could not go back into the marriage, nor could she gain happiness outside it. *Velia's crisis was the disclosure by her sister and the subsequent loss of respect from her children and their physi-cal and emotional withdrawal from her.*

The following are brief examples of separation/divorce-related crises.

- Janet initiated a separation from Terry and has filed for divorce. She and their three children came by the house to pick up some picnic sup-plies and found Terry lying dead in the back yard next to a bottle of Jack Daniels and his shotgun. A suicide note inside the house detailed that Terry could not stand the thought of another man parenting his children or having sex with the "only woman I have ever loved."
- Lois separated from her husband, Alex, upon learning that she has geni-tal herpes, contracted from Alex. The discovery led to Alex's disclosure that he has been having sex with their neighbor.
- Bob returned home early from a business trip to find his wife having sex with two men in the den. Shattered by this violation of trust, Bob filed for divorce.
- Sam has been in and out of several substance abuse treatment programs during the 15 years of his marriage to Toni. Immediately after release from each program, he has resumed drinking, stating that he is different from those "alcoholics" in that he can control his drinking. After yet another episode of Sam (in a state of inebriation) becoming physically violent with their 10-year-old son, Toni painfully decided that she could no longer tolerate Sam's alcohol abuse and filed for divorce.
- Norma's 7-year marriage to David has been punctuated by a series of episodes of physical abuse, each one followed by David's expressions of remorse, commitment to get help with his jealousy and anger, and assur-ance that he will never hurt Norma again. Last weekend, in an unpro-voked jealous rage, David physically attacked Norma and broke two of her ribs, blackened her eyes, and bruised her arms. After her release from the hospital emergency room, Norma moved out and filed for di-vorce.
- Carrie understood that Todd, her husband from whom she separated 6 months earlier, agreed that after their divorce she would maintain man-aging conservatorship (custody) of their two preschool children. Carrie's attorney called to report that Todd has counterfiled, seeking custody of the children. Carrie suspects that his action related to the fact that she has begun dating. Whatever the motivation, she feels extremely threat-ened by the action.
- Sue received a letter from the IRS indicating that her ex-husband had

failed to file joint income tax returns for the past 3 years. This was information about which she had no prior awareness, since she had signed income tax returns each year with the understanding that her husband forwarded them to the IRS. The IRS letter went on to state that her share of the liability for past taxes, interest, and penalties is $14,000. Her annual income is $19,000.

- Joe has worked hard to overcome the pain of his divorce from Cathy, a woman with whom he wanted to remain married despite his concerns about her stability at times. He has a strong relationship with his 5-year-old daughter and enjoys being a father. He has seen his daughter at every opportunity both during regular visitation and whenever Cathy allows it. He received a telephone call from Child Protective Services, informing him that he has been charged by Cathy with sexual abuse of their daughter and that an investigation is under way.
- Tommy thought that he had successfully completed the "letting go" process regarding his ex-wife, Mary, who had initiated their divorce a year ago. Tommy has seen Mary infrequently during the past year. Last Saturday night, at a local fund-raiser, he observed Mary romantically engaged with another man. Tommy went into an "emotional tailspin" and reinitiated therapy.

The dissolution of a marital relationship or a similarly committed couple relationship is among the most stressful life circumstances. Divorce is a process characterized by peak periods of stress, extreme loss, and pervasive change demands, and the challenges to activate robust coping capacities are great. The pain of marital dissolution is extreme for most. Both those who make the decision to divorce and those who have the decision imposed on them suffer painful consequences.

Divorce is not a singular event; rather, it is a process characterized both by discreet stressful events and by a cumulative set of losses and adaptation demands. The self-system and family system are thrust into an extreme state of disequilibrium as pervasive change demands are realized. Individuals engaged in the divorce process are at risk of crisis in a multitude of ways. Typically, the emotional trauma is highly intense, episodes are repetitive, and crisis opportunities occur not only during the divorce process but long after the divorce is legally final. For some, the intensity of the crisis reaches life and death proportions. As evidence of divorce crisis intensity and lethality risk, recently a physician from the east coast followed his physician ex-wife to Texas where she traveled to visit his sister. He accosted her on a jogging path, murdered her, and moments later killed himself. His crisis was related to an imminent loss of easy access to his children for visitation. His ex-wife of two years, and managing conservator of their two children, planned to relocate her practice to the Midwest. His recent petition to gain managing conservatorship of his children had been denied by the court. To effectively treat divorcing/divorced clients, therapists must be skilled in crisis assessment and intervention.

This chapter addresses the application of cognitive-behavioral and constructivist crisis intervention procedures to divorce crises. Particular attention is given to the definition of crisis; the types and nature of divorce crises; the psychosocial needs of divorcing individuals; risk assessment; resilience and strengths assessment; and the application of the Roberts's (1990, 1996) intervention model to divorce crisis resolution.

PREVALENCE OF DIVORCE AND MENTAL HEALTH CONSEQUENCES

Divorce is a commonplace phenomenon in the United States and in many countries throughout the world. In America, the breakup of the family is a familiar theme, resounding across a range of divergent arenas from political conventions to mental health conferences. The preoccupation with divorce is a reflection, in part, of the pervasive consequences of divorce specifically to the couple and their children, and also to many others in their personal domain. Family members must somehow survive the crisis of the breakup, and the paths of their survival often lead to mental health professionals.

Divorce Rates

The U.S. divorce rate spiraled upward during the 1960s and 1970s, reaching a record high in 1981 when 1.21 million people divorced (5.3 per thousand population), affecting some 3 million men, women, and children (National Center for Health Statistics, 1986). There were 1,182,000 divorces in the United States in 1990, 4.7 per thousand population, and 20.9 per 100 married women age 15 and over (Monthly Vital Statistics Report, 1990). According to 1997 provisional data, there were 1,163,000 divorces annually, or 4.3 per thousand population. Data released by the United States Census Bureau in early 1999 show the U.S. divorce rate at around 50%, up from 43% in 1988. Despite the moderate decline since the 1981 high, divorces continue to occur at a remarkable rate in the United States.

An international comparison of divorce rates shows the United States to have a significantly higher rate than other nations, although the United Kingdom retains a strong second-place standing (4.44 per thousand U.S. population, compared with 2.97 per thousand population in the United Kingdom). (See Table 13.1.) These comparative data provide evidence that divorce is occurring at significant rates in many other countries as well, although Italy has a relatively low rate of divorce.

Factors Influencing the Rise in the Divorce Rate

As I have stated elsewhere (Granvold, 1989), a variety of factors have been identified as influential in the burgeoning failure rate of marriage in the

Table 13.1   International Comparison of
Divorce Rates

Country	Year	Divorce Rate per 1000
Japan[a]	1997	1.78
United States[b]	1995	4.44
Germany[b]	1995	2.07
France[b]	1996	1.90
Italy[b]	1994	0.48
United Kingdom[b]	1994	2.97
Sweden[b]	1996	2.40

a. *Vital Statistics of Japan*, The Statistics and Information Department, Minister's Secretariat, Ministry of Health and Welfare (Feb. 5, 1999). 1-2-2 Kasumigaseki, Chiyoda-ku, Tokyo 100-8045.

b. *Demographic Yearbook* 1996 Edition, United Nations Secretariat, Deptartment for Economic and Social Information and Policy Analysis, Statistical Division Room (1998). DC 2-1462-70, New York, NY 10017, USA.

United States from the 1950s to the present, including the liberalization of divorce laws (no-fault divorce); the desacralization of marriage (Weiss, 1975); the shifting roles of women, including their greater economic independence; the greater social acceptance of divorce concomitant with the increasing frequency rate (divorce begets divorce); a shift away from the intrinsic permanence-of-marriage ethic toward a more "pragmatic" view based on internal and external reward/cost factors (Scanzoni, 1972); and, perhaps most important, the trend toward greater satisfaction of personal goals, interests, and desires along with higher expectations for marital happiness (Weitzman, 1985). People are no longer willing to remain "long-suffering" in an unrewarding or abusive relationship. For many, the opportunities for success and comfort after divorce are considered to be too great in American society to choose to remain unhappily married.

Divorce and Mental Health

It is well documented that couple relationship problems are among the life stresses most highly associated with psychological disorders (Beach, Sandeen, & O'Leary, 1990; Epstein & Schlesinger, 1994; Michelson, 1987). Divorce among men and women is one of the most highly rated risk factors associated with major depression (Anthony & Petronis, 1991; Gallo, Royall, & Anthony, 1993; Weissman, Bruce, Leaf, Florio, & Holzer, 1991). Furthermore, the presence of a satisfying, committed couple relationship has been found to be associated with low rates of depression (Costello, 1982).

The suicide rate of separated and divorced individuals is significantly higher than that of their married counterparts (Cantor & Slater, 1995; Trovato, 1986). A recent study by the National Institute for Healthcare Research in Rockville, Maryland, found that divorced people in the United States are *three times* as likely to commit suicide as married people. Divorce currently ranks as the number one factor linked with suicide rates in major cities. In a recent Australian study, separated males were found to commit suicide at 6.2 times the rate of married males, and separated females were found to commit suicide at 1.7 times the rate of married females (Cantor & Slater, 1995). It can be concluded that marital separation and divorce pose significant mental health risks. The consequences are meaningful not only to the divorcing couple but also to their children, extended family, friends, and society at large.

DEFINITION OF CRISIS

A number of definitions of the term *crisis* have been posited (Bard & Ellison, 1974; Burgess & Holstrom, 1974; Freeman & Dattilio, 1994; Goldenberg, 1983; McCubbin & Patterson, 1983; Olson, 1997; Roberts, 1990; Slaiku, 1990). A crisis can be thought of as consisting of three elements: (a) the presence of a precipitating stressful, life-changing or life-threatening event or circumstance; (b) the individual's perception of the event or circumstance as a significant threat; and (c) the individual's current inability to cope with the threat or to mobilize the psychological and/or physical resources to facilitate resolution. To consider an event to be crisis precipitating, the individual must cognitively *appraise* the event as a significant threat to the self-system. Consistent with Lazarus (1989), the degree of threat is the consequence of primary and secondary appraisals. *Primary appraisals* establish the relevance of an event to one's well-being or steady state (dynamic homeostasis), whereas *secondary appraisals* reflect the individual's coping capacities and available resources to meet the demand. Hence, to consider an individual in crisis involves a precipitating circumstance that is perceived by the individual as posing a psychosocial accommodation significantly beyond the individual's belief in his or her capacity to cope, adjust, or integrate. The personal consequences of a crisis may take the form of emotional and psychological unrest, as well as physical trauma and detrimental somatic outcomes. And beyond these outcomes, many times personal crises have a detrimental impact on social relationships.

It is noteworthy that a crisis may evolve from an event that many would judge to be positive. Winning the lottery, receiving a promotion, and making a desired move to a new community are events with obvious positive meaning. Curiously, each event may become a crisis for the individual (and family) should the changes associated with it be greater than the individual's (family's) current capacity to accommodate change. Also, positive life events may occasion opportunities for or stimulate associated challenges that reach crisis proportions. For example, a long-sought promotion may require travel, posing unique changes in family dynamics, division of labor task performance, and child care.

It is also important to acknowledge that a crisis arising from a problematic circumstance has the potential to stimulate extremely positive outcomes (Boss, 1988; Slaiku, 1990). An individual may discover coping abilities and resilience far beyond precrisis self-views. Meaningful relationships may develop or become strengthened or expanded through crisis resolution. Unforeseen skills and talents may be cultivated and new behaviors learned as the individual lives through the crisis.

Capsule Summary

Based on the tripartite definition of crisis delineated here, a stressor becomes a psychological crisis only when the individual experiences a threat to self so intense that his or her *characteristic* capacities to cope and resolve distress are surpassed, or, alternatively, the individual's characteristic capacities to cope and resolve distress are so markedly compromised that an otherwise manageable challenge becomes a *crisis*. In either circumstance, the individual's cognitive functioning and the availability of social and instrumental resources play critical roles in distinguishing a manageable stressor from a crisis. Conceptualizing crises in this way lends great viability to the use of cognitive-behavioral and constructivist treatment both as a preventative approach for clients in a sea of crisis opportunities and as a means to facilitate a coping repertoire, sense of empowerment, and the proactive mobilization of personal and social resources for those in crisis.

DIVORCE AS CRISIS

The process of divorce may reach crisis status in two ways. First, the individual may experience a *discrete event* in the couple relationship that results in an extreme perturbation to the self-system. Second, the *cumulative effects* of loss and adaptation demands may limit and impair coping abilities rendering the individual more likely to experience a stressor as a crisis.

Discrete Event Crises

Discrete stressful events may occur: (a) as precipitants of the decision to divorce, (b) during the transition phase of divorce, or (c) well past the finalization of the divorce. Examples of specific life events that *precipitate* the decision to divorce include the discovery of infidelity, an acute escalation of conflict or physical violence, death of a family member (particularly a child) or close friend, evidence of physical and/or sexual child abuse, disclosure or discovery of gross financial irresponsibility, excessive use of alcohol or prescription drugs, use of illicit drugs, and episodic violation of trust (e.g., dishonesty, deceit, lying).

For many, the crisis of divorce is realized during the transition phase, when resolution of property settlement and child custody or visitation are being sought. This period, after the decision to divorce has been made and before the divorce is legally final, is punctuated by extreme levels of emotion, including acute feelings of loss across many categories (e.g., personal, intimate, moral/ethical, status, lifestyle, financial, physical), rejection and abandonment, hurt, anger, guilt, anxiety, worry, fear, and disappointment. Emotional consequences such as these, coupled with decision making, planning, and the mobilization of environmental and lifestyle change, seriously compromise the coping capacities of divorcing individuals. These individuals are strongly predisposed to psychological crisis.

Subsequent to the decision to divorce and many times well after the divorce is legally final, divorced individuals experience a crisis in relation to the ex-mate. Examples of life events in this category include seeing for the first time the ex-mate with a new mate, learning of predivorce relationship-violating behavior (infidelity; failure to file joint income tax return), acute conflict over parallel parenting (e.g., ex-mate's failure to pick up or return child on time; child not available for scheduled visitation; telephone access to child blocked), failure to receive child support, episodic family and kin side taking against the individual, and episodic discrimination socially and in the work place. While the marital relationship may be over, the ex-mates often remain interconnected in some fashion, particularly when children are involved. The on-going relationship between ex-mates is typically replete with opportunities for conflict, hurt, and protracted loss.

Cumulative Effect Crises

The second way in which the divorce process can reach crisis status is as a consequence of the *cumulative effects* of divorce. Divorce thrusts the individual into a state of distress, disorganization, and greater uncertainty about life and the future. Divorcing individuals experience highly meaningful and pervasive losses. Dealing with loss effectively reduces coping ability (Freeman & Dattilio, 1994). Although the experience of loss is a constant in one's ongoing evolution, the loss associated with marital dissolution and the revisioning, restructuring, and reordering of oneself as a single person pose immediate and long-term challenges. Neimeyer (1998) notes that the passing of another from one's life poses an identity challenge in the form of "reinventing" oneself. Inasmuch as one's sense of self is socially embedded, the loss of the mate through divorce results in both a void within and a modification in the nature of one's relationships with all others. One is no longer part of a dyad and therefore sees self and is seen differently by others. Beyond dealing with loss and identity re-formation, there are other responsibilities of a more practical nature that are physically and emotionally taxing. A change in marital status, for most, poses changes in practical needs (e.g., bank account, charge cards, will) and physical needs (e.g., relocate, replace furnishings). For those who had not been previously employed outside the home, it may require job hunting or academic preparation or training for enhanced entry into the workforce. The very activity of seeking a job may become a crisis given the challenges of job interviewing, mounting economic need during unemployment, and potential rejection inherent in the process, coupled with the individual's depleted coping capacities associated with postdivorce adjustment.

The ultimate consequence of the cumulative effects of the divorce process is that events and circumstances that heretofore would have been effectively met and accommodated may become elevated to crisis status. Many clinical anecdotes could be identified in which relatively "minor" events or life experiences become crises. An auto accident of "fender bender," noninjury proportions, an argument with a family member or friend, and a child's failure to call home from camp in a timely manner are all circumstances that would require coping and resource mobilization. Events such as these, however, become insurmountable, extraordinary challenges when the divorce process is consuming the individual's emotional and psychological resources.

PSYCHOSOCIAL NEEDS OF DIVORCING/DIVORCED CLIENTS

A number of "stage theorists" have collapsed generally common divorce-related experiences into categories (Bohannan, 1971; Brown, 1976; DeFazio & Klenbort, 1975; Everett & Everett, 1994; Fisher, 1973; Froiland & Hozman, 1977; Kaslow, 1984; Kessler, 1975; Kressel, 1980; Storm & Sprenkle, 1982; Weiss, 1975). The conceptualization of the divorce process in stages has been criticized as failing to "highlight the complexity of the processes involved in marital dissolution" (Ponzetti & Cate, 1988, p. 3). As I have noted elsewhere (Granvold, 1994), although therapists must be sensitive to the divorcing/divorced client's unique experience, there is facility in broadly subdividing the divorce process to better specify common objectives and tasks associated with a given period in the process. Consistent with Kaslow (1984) and Storm and Sprenkle (1982), divorce is conceptualized as being composed of three overlapping stages: *decision making, transition,* and *postdivorce recovery.* Each stage has its unique stressors and challenges.

Decision Making

The decision to divorce is not an easy one for most people. Typically, one or both partners continue their marriage in a state of high dissatisfaction and protracted indecision before ultimately arriving at a decision to divorce.

The state of indecision is stressful in itself, characterized by high levels of frustration, anxiety, uncertainty, fear, worry, insecurity, distrust (particularly for the mate who is more greatly committed), hurt, resentment, depression, hopelessness and impending doom, and feelings of disempowerment. There is often an erosion in feelings of love, intimacy, sexual desire, and sexual satisfaction. Individuals who are emotionally fragile, are highly dependent upon the mate, and/or lack self-esteem, often experience situation-specific crises as the couple move more closely toward a final decision. This individual, typically more committed and less likely to decide to leave the relationship, is far more vulnerable to crisis responses.

The decision to divorce may *be* the crisis event, or, as noted earlier, a relationship-related crisis may *stimulate* the actual decision to divorce. In either situation, heightened emotion surrounds divorce decision making for most. Whether the decision is unilateral or shared, or one is the initiator or the one being left, there is pain and disruption associated with the imminent coming apart (Everett & Everett, 1994; Granvold, 1989; Sprenkle, 1989).

Transition From Married to Single

When the decision is made to divorce, the spouses are thrust into a major life transition. The psychological and emotional responses of the divorcing couple and their children and the behavioral manifestations of these responses during the transition phase may be extreme. A multitude of very significant decisions flow from the decision to divorce (Granvold, 1994; Propst & Fries, 1989; Sprenkle, 1989). During this period, children and family members may be informed of the plan to divorce; often friends and associates are informed as well. Physical separation must be achieved, which requires the determination of who is going to move, and the location and setting to which the departing mate is to go. The legal system must be accessed either through attorneys or through no-fault unilateral legal actions. The process of filing for a divorce or the experience of being served a divorce petition is commonly unpleasant. These events all too often mark the beginning of an adversarial process punctuated by great acrimony between the divorcing couple. Property settlement and child custody–child visitation determinations are often highly emotionally charged deliberations. Opportunities for interpersonal crises abound at this time.

Postdivorce Recovery

Separation and divorce force the individual to accommodate pervasive change. "Against a backdrop of ambivalence and oscillating emotions, the individual is challenged to integrate: (1) the stress of wholesale change; (2) redefinition of self and object loss trauma; (3) role loss, disorientation, and restructuring; and (4) life-style adjustment" (Granvold, 1989, p. 198). Clients typically struggle with the pain of emotional separation from the mate.

Even for those who have experienced an erosion of love, there tends to be a persistence of attachment to the ex-mate, which exacerbates the letting go process (Weiss, 1975). Self-esteem and feelings of self-worth diminish during the entire process of divorce, particularly for the mate who has been rejected. In response to low self-appraisals and feelings such as depression, hurt, loss, and hopelessness, those in recovery often withdraw and become isolated. Loneliness and preoccupation with loss prevail. Common maladaptive coping strategies involve the excessive use of alcohol and drugs (prescribed and illicit), oversleep, overexercise, and overinvestment of time and energy in work. Although grieving is a necessary, adaptive process, and unique from person to person, it may become debilitating to those who allow it to become "all-consuming."

One of the greatest challenges during postdivorce recovery is reestablishing one's identity as a single person. Compounded by the process of overcoming the loss of the mate, one must formulate a sense of self independent of the ex-spouse. For some, this is appealing. However, for others who have enjoyed the dyadic identity and connection with the ex-mate, identity reformation may be a crisis in itself. Role changes such as single parent, sole financial provider, and social single contribute to the evolving sense of self as a single person. These new roles facilitate change but are typically stress provoking.

Divorce does not terminate peoples' human desires for closeness, intimacy, and sexual gratification. The world of dating and courtship is one in which skills from the past are once again called into play. Many approach dating with a sense of trepidation, distrust, anxiety, fear, and uncertainty, whereas others find it exciting, rejuvenating, fun, and provocative. Unresolved issues from the dissolved marriage can be stimulated in dating relationships and thrust the individual into crisis. Also, the depletion of coping resources during divorce recovery may render the individual more vulnerable to stressful and crisis responses in newly forming relationships.

Dating naturally leads to opportunities for sexual activity. The loss of one's mate (love object) leaves the individual without a partner for sexual gratification. The availability of multiple, new sex partners coupled with normal sexual desire is highly likely to lead to sexual activity in dating relationships. Frequently, recently divorced individuals enjoy their sexual freedom by having a series of sexual partners. For some individuals, having sexual relations with several partners across time functions to prevent deep involvement with any one person. This pattern is perceived to be a form of self-protection. The obvious risk of having sex with many partners is the possibility of contracting a sexually transmitted disease (STD). Neff and Mantz (1998) suggest that those recently separated or divorced individuals who are dealing with postdivorce recovery issues (loneliness, isolation, depression, or low self-esteem) may fail to adopt rational "safe sex" practices, increasing their risk of disease. They maintain that, in an era in which HIV/

AIDS has increasingly become a heterosexual phenomenon (Centers for Disease Control, 1990), the separated and divorced are a possible risk group for HIV infection. I would add to the combination of postdivorce recovery, available multiple sex partners, and the epidemic status of HIV/AIDS and other STDs, the disinhibitory effects of alcohol consumption and "recreational" drug use on sexual behavior. Although the Neff and Mantz study found inadequate evidence to support the disinhibitory contributions of alcohol use on sexual behavior during marital disruption, they suggest that the lack of evidence is counterintuitive and may be partly explained methodologically. In my clinical experience, alcohol and drug use often have been reported as factors in accounts of indiscriminate and "unprotected" sexual encounters. Despite rational commitments to "safe sex" practices, substance abuse, in combination with the emotional and coping challenges of postdivorce recovery and desires for sexual gratification, results in people putting themselves at risk. It can be concluded that, on occasion, attitudes and beliefs are poor predictors of human behavior. Many who profess the wisdom of "safe sex" practices do not practice it.

RISK ASSESSMENT

As noted, the vulnerabilities of individuals experiencing marital disruption and divorce include low self-esteem, depression, hopelessness, anxiety and fear of the unknown, substance abuse, loneliness, isolation, and sexually transmitted disease. This combination of vulnerabilities and a depletion in coping abilities makes this population particularly at risk of suicide. In rare instances there is risk of homicidal action.

The divorced/divorcing individuals in crisis are at high risk of depression, suicide, and substance abuse. Reinecke (1994) notes that risk assessment should include the identification of risk factors associated with a particular outcome, such as suicide. Risk factors are defined as experiences, events, or propensities that make a particular outcome more likely. Assessment of risk, then, requires exploration of those factors that are known to be associated with a particular outcome.

Depression

Whereas most individuals in the process of divorce or in postdivorce recovery experience some degree of depression, vulnerability to severe clinical depression may be determined by making an assessment of risk factors. Among the relevant risk factors to be assessed are self-esteem level, social involvement/withdrawal, social support from family and friends, history of depression, depression in family of origin, financial problems, parenting problems, substance abuse, and feelings of hopelessness. Both clinical interview and standardized measurement instruments should be used to assess for risk and to determine current status of depression. Recommended self-report instruments for depression include Beck Depression Inventory–Second Edition (BDI-II; Beck, Steer, & Brown, 1996), Zung Self-Rated Depression Inventory (Zung, 1965), and the Generalized Contentment Scale (Hudson, 1992). Additionally, the Beck Hopelessness Scale (Beck & Steer, 1988) is highly useful in gaining access to the client's cognitive schemas related to negative expectancy about the short- and long-term future. This psychological construct has been found to underlie various mental health disorders (Beck & Steer, 1988). Specifically, hopelessness is a core construct in depression and has been found to be an important mediator of suicide (Beck, Rush, Shaw, & Emery, 1979; Clark, Beck, & Alford, 1999; Reinecke, 1994).

Lethality

The most critical risk assessment is the determination of lethality. As noted earlier, the likelihood of suicide among separated and divorced men and women is significantly greater than among married individuals. The pain of coping with the loss of love is excruciating for many. Compounding this loss are many change demands that can propel the individual into crisis. Suicide over love loss is a familiar theme. An infrequent but extremely tragic occurrence is murder/suicide among separated, recently divorced, and couples in extreme marital distress. With regard to homicidal intention, statements of desire for the estranged or ex-spouse to experience pain or death should be explored regardless of the emotional state of the client at the time. That is to say, expressions made during extreme anger and rage should not be dismissed lightly as anger-driven, misrepresentative, unrealistic, or unintentional statements. Furthermore, when a client expresses fear for her safety, the therapist should guide the client in mobilizing protective systems and resources. Now, let us consider suicidality.

Specialized skills are required to recognize a client as suicidal and to assess suicidal risk (Beck et al., 1979; Clark, 1995). Beck and his colleagues recommend that the assessment cover four components: intent, planning, resource availability, and motive. First consider intention. They note that even the mildly depressed individual may commit suicide. Thus, our appraisals of intention must be finely discriminating. The therapist must be sensitive to the indicators of suicide in terms of behaviors, emotional states, and verbalizations. The client who suddenly puts his or her affairs in order (e.g., completes a will, organizes and clears his desk at work, contacts friends and family with whom he has had no recent contact) may actually be preparing for death. Other potential indicators of suicidal intent are depression; a sense of overwhelming grief; loss of love, parenting opportunities, and meaning in life (emptiness); hopelessness that life will improve (Beck, 1987); and coldness, hostility, and anger. Listen for and explore verbal statements such as the following: "I can't live without her/him"; "I'll never be happy again";

"I can't stand the thought of her/him making love with anyone else"; and "I have to stop this hurt."

Should the client admit to suicidal planning or you surmise it from indicators of intention, make an inquiry into the way or ways the client has considered committing suicide. Following this exploration, determine the resources available to the client to fulfill the plan (e.g., knowledge of lethal levels of drugs, access to firearms). Exploration of motive may expose objectives such as the desire to escape from life or to seek surcease, to retaliate through creating pain in the life of the rejecting ex-mate, and manipulation of significant others through suicidal attempts (Beck et al., 1979).

Reinecke (1994) aptly notes that, "if there is a truism in psychology, it is that the best predictor of future behavior is past behavior. So it is with predicting suicidal risk" (p. 75). Accordingly, determine the strength of past suicidal thinking, degree of past planning and mobilization of resources, and actual suicide attempts. Determine whether other family members or close friends have committed or attempted suicide.

Finally, it is important to consider the interactive effects of variables that may contribute to suicide. Substance abuse, depleted coping capacity and intensity of the love loss, social isolation, lack of support system, poverty or financial problems, and history of psychological instability collectively may produce a lethal effect.

The use of self-report instruments may further facilitate suicidal risk assessment. See Beck's Scale for Suicide Ideation (Beck et al., 1979). Other relevant instruments may be located in Fischer and Corcoran (1994).

Substance Abuse

Substance abuse is a coping strategy frequently employed by separated and divorced individuals. Alcohol and drugs are effective in reducing stress, assuaging guilt and remorse, and numbing one's emotional pain. Although perhaps effective to these ends, the undesirable consequences of substance abuse are extreme. Depression and suicide, highly associated with substance abuse, are among the major vulnerabilities (Beck, Wright, Newman, & Liese, 1993). On the basis of the preceding information, it is important to assess the risks of substance abuse among separated and divorced clients. In addition to interview assessment, several viable substance use/abuse assessment instruments are available (Beck et al., 1993; Fischer & Corcoran, 1994).

CLIENT STRENGTHS, RESILIENCE, AND PROTECTIVE STRATEGIES

Before addressing specific strategies that can be implemented in divorce crisis recovery, a statement about philosophy is in order. The intervention model promoted in this chapter is a constructivist approach to human functioning and human change in which individual strengths and assets are emphasized, stimulated, and expanded (Franklin & Nurius, 1998; Granvold, 1996, in press; Mahoney, 1991, 1995, in press; Neimeyer & Mahoney, 1995; Saleebey, 1992). Saleebey (1992) has identified three essential assumptions that undergird the strengths perspective as follows:

> First, it is assumed every person has an inherent power that may be characterized as life force, transformational capacity, life energy, spirituality, regenerative potential, and healing power. . . . Second, a strengths perspective assumes that the power just described is a potent form of knowledge that can guide personal and social transformation. . . . Third, there is a crucial pragmatic presumption about the nature of change . . . that when people's positive capacities are supported, they are more likely to act on their strengths. (p. 24)

Constructivist psychotherapy is optimistically focused on possibilities. Individual strengths (both active and potential), resources, and competencies are collaboratively identified with the client, emphasized, and prompted toward greater activation. Life is viewed as "an ongoing recursion of perturbation and adaptation, disorganization and distress, and emerging complexity and differentiation—a process of evolutionary self-organization" (Granvold, 1996, p. 346). Consistent with this conceptualization of life span development, human disturbance and distress are considered "normal." Problems are construed as opportunities for constructive change. The resilience and creative potential of all people are emphasized.

Pragmatically, this means that crisis assessment and intervention are focused on the personal, social, and community resources available to the client. An essential personal resource is the client's belief in his or her right and ability to be *empowered* (Freeman & Dattilio, 1994). Client self-efficacy plays a crucial role in empowerment; low self-efficacy impedes empowerment, while high self-efficacy effects it. Hence, if lacking, an early goal of therapy is the development of efficacy expectations. Efficacy expectations not only are meaningful in crisis resolution but also have been found to be associated with postdivorce adjustment (Bould, 1977; Pais, 1978; White, 1985; Womack, 1987).

Basco and Rush (1996, p. 214) have generated the following list of internal resources useful in coping with stress that are worthy of consideration in developing a crisis intervention treatment plan:

Intelligence	Resourcefulness
Practicality	Energy
Analytical-mindedness	Stamina
Common sense	Creativity
Fortitude	Self-esteem
Assertiveness	Money

322 Health- and Mental Health—Related Crises

Sensitivity	Confidence
A sense of humor	Self-perceived competency
Time	Ability to seek out and accept help
Personableness	from others
Organizational ability	Perserverence

Turning now to external coping resources, it has been found that those with active support systems are better adjusted to divorce than those without support (Granvold, Pedler, & Schellie, 1979; Spanier & Casto, 1979; Wallerstein & Kelly, 1980). It is recommended that individuals in divorce crisis remain active socially through involvement with family and friends, or through participation in interest groups (e.g., Sierra Club) and singles groups. Also, many communities offer psychoeducational seminars focused on postdivorce recovery or grief recovery (Granvold & Welch, 1977; Salts, 1989). Alienation and isolation, feeling disconnected from caring others, and social withdrawal are major contributors to human disturbance and dysfunction. Every effort should be made to promote client involvement in the community.

The client's past history in resolving crises and life dilemmas should be explored as a means of activating coping and adaptive skills, instilling resilience, and mobilizing protective strategies. The risk factors identified earlier, along with other maladaptive responses to the crisis, should be addressed through the identification of the cognitive, behavioral, and emotional responses that have effectively reduced risk in the past. This may involve the exploration of compensatory actions, the activation of a support system, or the development of novel interests and life goals.

Finally, resilience is represented not only by overt behaviors but also by attitude. The therapist should access the client's self-views regarding his or her capacity to "bounce back" and return stronger than before. Explorations should be made into self-esteem and self-reliance conceptualizations that support or undermine views of self as resilient. Interventions should be initiated consistent with these findings.

INTERVENTION

In this section the Roberts (1990, 1996) seven-stage model of crisis intervention will be discussed and applied to clients in the process of divorce. Although a client may move in and out of crisis while in counseling during the process of postdivorce adjustment, the intervention highlighted here is crisis focused.

Engagement and Relationship Formation

Clients who present for therapy in crisis must feel free to express the specific details of the stressful event and their range of emotional responses with a therapist who is open, an active and careful listener, nonjudgmental, talented in Socratic questioning, and an expert in the crisis area. During extreme crises, regardless of the stage of therapy (initial session or much later), clients may evidence an array of thoughts, emotions, and behaviors that are highly uncharacteristic of them when they are not in crisis. For others, the crisis event may activate or amplify characteristic maladaptive responses. Therapists can expect to hear (a) highly irrational thinking ("I'll never recover"); (b) emotionally driven statements ("I'd like to smash his face in"); (c) expressions of extreme and uncontrollable emotion (crying, anger, anxiety, panic); (d) emotionally charged content with flat affect; (e) perseveration—words, phrases, gestures, images ("I'm so bad, I'm so bad, I'm so bad," etc.); (f) incoherent, disjointed, and spotty accounts of events; and (g) dissociation ("I felt numb; it was as if I was observing someone else"; "I felt nothing, nothing at all as he hit me again and again").The therapist must be prepared for expressions such as these, to rapidly assess the client's verbal and nonverbal behavior, and to respond with clinical wisdom. Each type of expression enumerated here obligates the therapist to activate strategic responses that compliment the client's expression. For example, when a client expresses irrational thoughts during the engagement phase of crisis intervention, it would be inappropriate to attempt cognitive restructuring or cognitive elaboration at that time. It is far more desirable to listen carefully and seek an understanding of the client's thoughts and images, to gain a more global awareness of the crisis situation through Socratic questioning, to elicit feeling states, to reflect content and feelings, to offer strategic empathic expressions, and to display *human emotion* consistent with the nature of the client's crisis. For the client who expresses incoherent, disjointed, and spotty accounts of a stressful circumstance, the therapist may find it effective to use combinations of Socratic questioning, guided imagery, deep muscle relaxation, and repetitive iterations of increasingly complete accounts. In each of these examples, therapist responses complement the client's expressions, promote the therapeutic alliance, and further the treatment endeavor.

Although it is highly important to maintain focus on the crisis, the engagement process requires that the therapist ultimately ascertain the client's treatment goals and expectations of the therapist, as well as explicate therapist-held expectations (Garfield, 1998; Granvold, in press; Kanfer & Schefft, 1988). Early on, the therapist should act in ways that establish that treatment is a *collaborative* effort between client and therapist. As Freeman and Dattilio (1994) point out, however, "the collaboration is not always 50 : 50 but may, with the crisis patient be 30 : 70 or 90 : 10, with the therapist providing most of the energy or work within the session or in the therapy more generally" (pp. 6–7). The client should come away from the first session with the understanding that the therapist expects the client to be active in the treatment process, and with the awareness that the therapist will actively participate as well. Genuine expressions of empathy, complementary responses to idiosyncratic expressions, structuring the roles of client and therapist, assuming a collaborative stance, and the expression of content about the crisis event and characteristic human responses (therapist knowledge-based expertise) are all meaningful ingredients in establishing a therapeutic alliance and building rapport.

Initial Risk Assessment

When a client presents for treatment in crisis, it is imperative that a risk assessment be completed before ending the session. The therapist should gain an understanding of the crisis situation and establish the severity of the crisis. The next step is to assess the client's strengths, coping capacities, resources (personal, social, financial), and vulnerability to lethal or health-threatening responses. Focused attention should be given to both suicidal and homicidal ideation, including intent, planning, resource availability, and motive. As noted in the preceding section on risk assessment, a cursory exploration of the client's thoughts about suicide and homicide is inadequate. It is advised that the potential be explored more than once in the session to limit the perfunctory or deceptive denial and to allow greater opportunity to expose indicators of lethality.

Problem Definition

The therapist seeks an understanding of the client's meaning constructions regarding the crisis situation. Recall that a crisis may develop in such challenges as the process of dissolving a marital union; identity reformation as a single person; assumption of altered role relationships; and return to dating, mate selection, and potential reconstitution of the family with a new mate. These life transitions have unique meanings to each individual. Understanding these meanings may provide the therapist with clinically relevant contextual information useful in crisis intervention. For example, the individual who holds the view that he must stay married at all costs (intrinsic permanence view of marriage) is more likely to experience the day when the divorce is final as a greater crisis partly *because* of this view. In a sense, the therapist seeks a determination of *why a crisis is a crisis*.

In recognition of the idiosyncratic nature of meaning constructions, the therapist and client collaborate in generating the meaning of the crisis. The client may have difficulty articulating his or her thoughts about the circumstance. Exploration of the crisis circumstance through Socratic questioning may allow articulation of what took place and expose the client's views of and responses to the event or circumstance. It may be appropriate after gaining an understanding of the client's current thinking to guide the elaboration of meanings as a means of extending possibilities. This process is a necessary prerequisite to proceeding to the generation of alternative paths of action.

Constructivist intervention focuses on the *viability* of meaning constructions. Viability is a function of the *consequences* of the construct to the individual and society, as well as its *coherence* with prevailing personal and social beliefs (Neimeyer, 1993). To clarify, consider the client who states that the divorce is the worst that could happen to him and that he has no reasons to go on living. These meanings, while perhaps consistent with his current thoughts, lack viability because they promote (or at least imply) actions with dire negative consequences to the individual and to society. The clinical objective in this situation is to expand and elaborate possible meanings of the divorce in order to arrive at meanings that may promote more viable consequences. Merely modifying the view from "It's the worst" to "It's *one* of the worst" achieves greater viability. Other meanings that might be generated with this client include, "It hurts so bad"; "I never thought she'd leave me"; "I believe in 'love is forever'"; and "Divorce is wrong." All of these views may have unappealing consequences to a degree, but they may be *less* destructive than the client's initial construct. Gaining access to specific beliefs, as noted earlier, and determining other relevant constructions regarding divorce and the transition to single life may contribute greatly to the formulation of an intervention strategy to meet the crisis.

In the initial interview with Velia, information gathering was focused on formulating the problem specifically through (a) discovering the crisis circumstances and her beliefs that strongly contributed to the crisis, (b) conducting a risk assessment, and (c) gaining a preliminary understanding of her current coping abilities.

The weekend prior to Velia coming in for treatment she had seen a family happily interacting at a local park. She longed for the laughter, sharing, and warm interaction visible in that family. She returned home deeply depressed and realized that she must seek help. In defining the problem, I learned that warm family relationships and mutual respect and admiration between children and parents were paramount in Velia's value system. The core meanings of being a mother were to protect her children from pain and discomfort, and to always "be there" for them. Her estrangement from her adult children prevented her from fulfilling these roles and threatened her "purpose in life." She held despicable views toward herself for the infidelity. I learned that Velia was a survivor of incest, having been abused by her biological father. She loved her mother dearly but felt deep hurt over her mother's failure to protect her from her father. She was now confronting her own "failure to protect her children" from the pain of her infidelity and the impending divorce. Although Velia had demonstrated remarkable coping abilities in the past, she questioned her current strength. Assessment of additional stressors in her life revealed underemployment and resulting financial hardship, a condition that further depleted her coping resources. Velia reported no suicidal ideation now or at any time in her past, and there were no indicators of suicidal intention. She denied any substance abuse or use of prescription drugs. This information, along with the content reported in the introductory vignette, helped define Velia's crisis and gave direction to the intervention.

Explore Emotions and Promote Ongoing Development

Traditional therapeutic approaches have tended to consider emotions such as anger, anxiety, depression, worry, sadness, and the like to be "negative," and goals of treatment correspondingly have been to control, alter, or terminate such emotions (Granvold, 1996). Constructivists, social constructionists, and other postmodernists conceptualize emotions as agents of change, adaptation, and self-development (Greenberg & Safran, 1989; Guidano, 1991a, 1991b; Mahoney, 1991, in press; Safran & Greenberg, 1991). I believe that exploring emotions with clients in crisis should be done with the view, consistent with constructivism, that emotions and their expression are crucial to the process of change.

In some circumstances it is highly appropriate to assist clients in curbing or controlling intense emotion. For example, consider the deeply depressed client whose depression is jeopardizing his or her job or parenting performance, or there is evidence of strong suicidal ideation or planning. Intervention should focus on protective strategies, behavioral activation, and cognitive changes designed to ensure safety and to prevent incapacitation and dysfunction in fulfilling key responsibilities.

Many contemporary views of emotion emphasize the personal meaning constructions associated with emotionality: "The ways individuals think, feel, speak, and act are integrally tied to the concepts they use to categorize their emotions and make them meaningful" (Nunley & Averill, 1996, p. 226). It is important not only to determine clients' views of the crisis circumstance to which they are emotionally responding but also to gain an understanding of their beliefs about their feelings and emotional expressions. For example, some clients believe themselves to be "seized" by emotion and hold the view that they have little control over their feelings (Nunley & Averill, 1996). Others believe themselves to be "going crazy," to be weak, or see themselves as worthless *because* they are experiencing and expressing extreme emotion. Clients may greatly benefit from the view that there is honor in being emotional—that it is "normal," and not necessarily to be considered negative (although extreme and enduring feelings and emotional expressions carry some level of discomfort for most people). Restructuring client views of emotion from negative and undesirable to positive and viable in the process of human change and adaptation will shape clients' tolerance and appreciation for their emotionality.

As a further means of gleaning positive inputs from emotionality, I have found it useful to guide clients in externalizing their feelings and emotional expressions (White & Epston, 1990). This may be accomplished by asking questions like, "What do you think your depression is trying to tell you?" "If your tears had a voice, what would they be saying?" Questions such as these give rich access to client cognitions and client awareness of behavioral and lifestyle changes that are, truly, in their best interests. Furthermore, the process of externalization reinforces the belief that feelings are useful.

For clients who express flat affect or report little emotional responsivity to crisis events that typically prompt emotional reactions, it is important to employ methods to access feelings and stimulate emotional expressiveness. Experiential techniques have been found to be highly effective with these clients.

> The purpose of these techniques varies, including the stimulation of feelings related to a life event, a preparatory rehearsal of a behavior (e.g., assertive expression), to gain a better understanding of another's thoughts or feelings (e.g., role reversal), and to process negative or ambivalent thoughts or feelings regarding past or more contemporary experiences. (Granvold, 1996, p. 354)

Methods to access affective states and to stimulate emotional arousal include role-playing, psychodrama, behavior rehearsals, imagery and guided discovery, imaginary dialogues (empty-chair technique), and therapeutic rituals. The timely use of techniques such as these may facilitate the arousal and expression of emotions in the divorcing client who, although in crisis, is unemotional.

As established earlier, divorce is about loss—not one loss, but a variety of losses. The accommodation of loss in divorce recovery, as with other traumatic events, requires meaningful expressions of emotion for successful adaptation. Treating the crisis of divorce, therefore, must focus on human emotion as a change process.

Velia: I have been upset since I spoke with Jorge on the phone last weekend.

Don: You say that you've been upset. What feelings make up being upset?

Velia: I feel so guilty . . . and I feel resentment toward him because he's using the children to get me to come home.

Don: So, you're feeling guilty and resentful. Are you feeling any other feelings?

Velia: I guess I am. I'm really angry with Jorge, and overall I just feel depressed. I wish that things were different.

Don: Are there any other feelings here, or do these pretty much cover it?

Velia: I think that's all . . . there's too much here.

Don: It can get a bit overwhelming at times. There's a lot to your situation. . . . Suppose we explore each one of these feelings. Perhaps if we take each one we can arrive at some conclusions that may bring a bit of relief.

Velia: Okay.

Don: You first said that you felt guilty. What was it about the phone call that resulted in your feeling guilty?

Velia: Jorge always tries to make me feel guilty. He tells me how much he loves me and how he can forgive me for what I've done. Then he brings the children into it. He says that we can all be back together as a family. It hurts so much.

Don: So, first there's guilt, followed closely by hurt.

Velia: Yes, that's what usually happens anyway.

Don: Velia, sometimes people have a tendency to allow guilt to immobilize them. As we've discussed before, if you were to consider guilt as a *motivator,* what actions might you consider taking?

Velia: Well, I could first think that I'm not going to buy into his attempts to make me feel guilty.

Don: That sounds good. So when he makes statements as he did on Saturday night, you will begin telling yourself, "I'm not going to allow him to make me feel guilty."

Velia: Yes, that's what I plan to do. Also, I am going to use the guilt as a *reminder* that I must stay committed to seeing this divorce through, even though Jorge and the children don't want me to do it.

Don: So you are not going to allow feelings of guilt or hurt to deter you from following through with the divorce, an action that you truly believe is best for you.

Explore and Assess Past Coping Attempts

As noted earlier, the divorce-related crisis may be the result of a distinct event or the consequence of the cumulative effects of loss and adaptation demands. In either condition, it is important to assess the coping and adaptation capabilities of the client. Gathering information about loss, coping, and adaptation requires the exploration of the client's developmental history. Goals of this exploration should be focused on uncovering client strengths as well as limitations. Often, clients in crisis (and many not in crisis) do not recognize legitimate strengths among their personal resources. There is a tendency to ignore or minimize abilities and to attribute past successes to chance, others' efforts, or the circumstances. Also, clients are inclined to maintain that their talents and their demonstrated coping capacities are uncharacteristic responses; therefore, they are viewed as invalid. Insight into these views will be most helpful to the therapist in promoting greater client self-efficacy.

The therapist may gain an understanding of client coping capacities through interviewing or by means of journaling. Through either means, past successes in problem solving, coping, and adaptation, along with current self-appraisals of coping capacities and resource availability, should be identified and elucidated. During crisis, it can be expected that clients' efficacy expectations become reduced. In response, the therapist should guide explorations into the client's demonstrated and potential coping capacity and resource management. Various means that the client has used to cope in similar crisis situations should be specified and the client queried regarding the possibility of incorporating the same coping measures in the current crisis. Cognitive restructuring, cognitive elaboration, problem solving, and therapist support are all viable approaches in the enhancement of client self-efficacy and in crisis management.

Don: Velia, you have said that coping with your children's reactions to you has been tremendously difficult for you, that you've felt extremely depressed. I understand that you are a *survivor*, that you have suffered terrible abuse but handled it. Do you see yourself as a survivor?

Velia: Yes, I do.

Don: What does that mean to you? . . . that you're a survivor.

Velia: I guess that it means that I haven't let what Dad did to me stop me from being happy, to fall in love, . . . and to pretty much *trust* people.

Don: That says a lot about you, Velia. I'm really pleased for you. Can you see that you must have used tremendous coping skills to get through the abuse and survive as you have?

Velia: I've never really thought about it, but I guess that I have. I'm pretty good, aren't I?!

Don: Yes, you are, Velia. I'm impressed . . . really. Now what do you think would allow you to access those same coping abilities to deal with your current crisis?

Velia: Mmm, good question. I'll have to think about it. But I see where you are headed with this. If I did it before, I can do it again!

Don: Exactly! You have demonstrated that you can cope, and cope well. We will continue to explore your past and uncover the specific strategies you used.

Generate and Explore Alternatives and Solution Seeking

The therapist should promote the view that there is no one way or "right" way to work through a crisis. The task at hand is to generate alternative approaches to the current crisis with the objective to tailor the solutions specifically to this client at this time. Obviously, the more alternatives generated, the greater the likelihood of creating change strategies that are more appealing to the client and of greater promise in producing effective outcomes. Once alternative strategies are determined, the perceived consequences (viability) of each should be explored. Once again, consider Velia as an illustration of this process.

Velia felt stuck with regard to her relationship with her children. She continued to write to them but received no letters in return. She felt an extreme sense of loss, and her deep depression continued. We explored in session many alternative actions that she could take to improve her relationship with her children. Possible consequences of each option were discussed. She considered the following alternatives: have a family reunion at her home; appeal to Jorge to talk with the children on her behalf; meet with each one individually; talk with her daughter, Maria, who is least upset with her mother and enlist her to accompany Velia in meeting with the other children individually; take no action and allow time to heal the hurt; and involve her brother, highly respected by Velia's children, in talking with each of them individually with Velia. The perceived consequences of each action were considered. Velia chose to approach her daughter, Maria, first. She had in mind asking Maria to go with her when she went to meet individually with her other children. Once this decision was made, the focus of the intervention turned to what Velia hoped to accomplish in face-to-face interactions with her children, the determination of the specific content to be shared and discussed, and the establishment of realistic expectations.

Restoration of Cognitive Functioning Through Implementation of an Action Plan

Divorce-related crises, like other crises, have the potential of promoting healthy change, empowerment, and creative and novel life experiences. As clients put their change efforts into effect, they realize outcomes well beyond the resolution of the current crisis. Successful crisis resolution has the potential of "proving" to the client that relatively rapid and pervasive changes can be accomplished. Additionally, a multitude of cognitive benefits are possible. Several outcomes are likely in the category of self-views. The potential exists that divorced individuals learn to view the process of divorce as having meaningful positive as well as negative consequences. Divorce isn't *all* negative. This contradicts the tendency to engage in "all-or-nothing" thinking or dichotomous thinking (Granvold, 1994). The client may develop a sense of greater inner strength and self-reliance. A new or renewed sense of self-confidence and self-efficacy is possible as the individual takes on new responsibilities, fulfills novel roles, and makes independent decisions. Client coping capacities are severely tested during the crises of divorce. The result is an expansion of coping strategies and an overall increase in coping ability. Many who did not seek the divorce ultimately report a sense of rejuvenation, excitement about life, and joy in experiencing greater novelty both in relationships and in activities.

Another highly significant cognitive outcome is that clients learn the benefits of expanding their meanings about crisis events. They learn that many meanings exist for any event or circumstance in life. Furthermore, they develop *skills in cognitive elaboration* through therapist-guided practice in sessions and self-generated cognitive elaboration *in vivo*. Journaling, thought records, and verbal accounts in therapy are useful methods in developing these skills.

Another important outcome is that clients learn to view their emotions as instrumental and necessary in the process of change. Rather than viewing feelings of loss, depression, fear, and anxiety as *negative,* these emotional states and their expressions are to be viewed as positive and meaningful in their effects. Emotions are viable agents of change; they serve us well in achieving truly painful transitions. They can be useful guides in activating steps toward healing, renewal, and an evolving self.

Follow-Up

Follow-up is one element of relapse prevention, an aspect of intervention that is important in all forms of treatment, including crisis intervention (Granvold & Wodarski, 1994; Greenwald, 1987; Marlatt & Gordon, 1985). Follow-up telephone calls or follow-up cards or letters are appropriate methods to gain information about the client's status following treatment. Useful information may also be gleaned from client feedback with regard to the meaningful aspects of the treatment experience (and aspects of the counseling effort that the client did not find useful). Therapist-initiated 3- and 6-month follow-up contact is appropriate. At termination, the therapist should make it clear that he or she is always available for future contacts, should the client so desire. It is also important to stress that a booster session may be appropriate and that a follow-up session is not necessarily a sign of dependency or major relapse in recovery.

As I have identified throughout this chapter, in the divorce process there are many opportunities for the individual to experience a crisis. Successful crisis recovery does not protect the individual from encountering future stressful events that may reach crisis proportions. A crisis may actually develop in another aspect of the recovery process well past treatment termination for the original crisis. Recently, a divorcing father who had successfully resolved the crisis of separation and impending divorce was charged by his estranged wife with the sexual abuse of their daughter. The client returned to therapy in crisis regarding the consequences of these allegations. Crisis intervention was implemented as the client was evaluated by social and legal system representatives. Although all parties concluded that the allegations were false, the client was in crisis throughout the entire process.

CONCLUSION

The crisis of divorce has been noticeably absent from the crisis intervention literature. Taking only the suicide rate as an indicator of the *intensity* of the crisis of separation/divorce, and the high divorce rate as representative of the *magnitude* of the problem, one can conclude that mental health professionals should consider this population to be significantly at risk. The crisis intervention strategies and techniques discussed in this chapter, and those detailed elsewhere, should be given strong consideration in meeting the therapeutic needs of the multitudes in our society who are in the throes of "coming apart" as a couple or family, and attempting to revision their lives.

REFERENCES

Anthony, J. C., & Petronis, K. R. (1991). Suspected risk factors for depression among adults 18–44 years old. *Epidemiology, 2,* 123–132.

Bard, M., & Ellison, K. (1974). Crisis intervention and evidence of forcible rape. *The Police Chief, 41,* 68–73.

Basco, M. R., & Rush, A. J. (1996). *Cognitive-behavioral therapy for bipolar disorder.* New York: Guilford.

Beach, S. R. H., Sandeen, E. E., & O'Leary, K. D. (1990). *Depression in marriage.* New York: Guilford.

Beck, A. T. (1987). Hopelessness as a predictor of eventual suicide. *Annals of the New York Academy of Sciences: Psychobiology of Suicidal Behavior, 487,* 90–96.

Beck, A. T., Rush, A. J., Shaw, B. F., & Emery, G. (1979). *Cognitive therapy of depression.* New York: Guilford.

Beck, A. T., & Steer, R. A. (1988). *Beck hopelessness scale manual.* San Antonio, TX: Psychological Corporation.

Beck, A. T., Steer, R. A., & Brown, G. K. (1996). *BDI-II manual.* San Antonio, TX: Psychological Corporation.

Beck, A. T., Wright, F. D., Newman, C. F., & Liese, B. S. (1993). *Cognitive therapy of substance abuse.* New York: Guilford.

Bohannan, P. (1971). The six stations of divorce. In P. Bohannan (Ed.), *Divorce and after.* New York: Doubleday/Anchor.

Boss, P. (1988). *Family stress management.* Newbury Park, CA: Sage.

Bould, S. (1977). Female-headed families: Personal fate control and the provider role. *Journal of Marriage and the Family, 39,* 339–349.

Brown, E. (1976). Divorce counseling. In D. H. Olson (Ed.), *Treating relationships.* Lake Mills, IA: Graphic.

Burgess, A., & Holstrom, L. (1974). *Rape: Victims of crisis.* Bowie, MD: Robert J. Brady.

Cantor, C. H., & Slater, P. J. (1995). Marital breakdown, parenthood, and suicide. *Journal of Family Studies, 1*(2), 91–104.

Centers for Disease Control. (1990). Update: Acquired immunodeficiency syndrome United States, 1989. *Mortality and Morbidity Weekly Report, 39,* 81–86.

Clark, D. A., Beck, A. T., & Alford, B. A. (1999). *Scientific foundations of cognitive theory and therapy of depression.* New York: Wiley.

Clark, D. C. (1995). Epidemiology, assessment, and management of suicide in depressed patients. In E. E. Beckham & W. R. Leber (Eds.), *Handbook of depression* (2nd ed.; pp. 526–538). New York: Guilford.

Costello, C. G. (1982). Social factors associated with depression: A retrospective community study. *Psychological Medicine, 12,* 329–339.

DeFazio, V. J., & Klenbort, I. (1975). A note on the dynamics of psychotherapy during marital dissolution. *Psychotherapy: Theory, Research and Practice, 12,* 101–104.

Epstein, N., & Schlesinger, S. E. (1994). Couples problems. In F. M. Dattilio & A. Freeman (Eds.), *Cognitive-behavioral strategies in crisis intervention* (pp. 258–277). New York: Guilford.

Everett, C., & Everett, S. V. (1994). *Healthy divorce.* San Francisco: Jossey-Bass.

Fischer, J., & Corcoran, K. (1994). *Measures for clinical practice: A source book* (vol. 2). New York: Free Press.

Fisher, E. O. (1973). A guide to divorce counseling. *The Family Coordinator, 22,* 56–61.

Franklin, C., & Nurius, P. S. (Eds.). (1998). *Constructivism in practice: Methods and challenges.* Milwaukee, WI: Families International.

Freeman, A., & Dattilio, F. M. (1994). Introduction. In F. M. Dattilio & A. Freeman (Eds.), *Cognitive-behavioral strategies in crisis intervention* (pp. 1–22). New York: Guilford.

Froiland, D. J., & Hozman, T. L. (1977). Counseling for constructive divorce. *Personnel and Guidance Journal, 55,* 525–529.

Gallo, J. J., Royall, D. R., & Anthony, J. C. (1993). Risk factors for the onset of depression in middle age and later life. *Social Psychiatry and Psychiatric Epidemiology, 28,* 101–108.

Garfield, S. L. (1998). *The practice of brief psychotherapy* (2nd ed.). New York: Wiley.

Goldenberg, H. (1983). *Contemporary clinical psychology* (2nd ed.). Monterey, CA: Brooks/Cole.

Granvold, D. K. (1989). Postdivorce treatment. In M. Textor (Ed.), *The divorce and divorce therapy handbook* (pp. 197–219). Northvale, NJ: Jason Aronson.

Granvold, D. K. (1994). Cognitive-behavioral divorce therapy. In D. K. Granvold (Ed.), *Cognitive and behavioral treatment: Methods and applications* (pp. 222–246). Pacific Grove, CA: Brooks/Cole.

Granvold, D. K. (1996). Constructivist psychotherapy. *Families in Society: The Journal of Contemporary Human Services, 77*(6), 345–359.

Granvold, D. K. (in press). Constructivist theory and practice. In P. Lehmann & N. Coady (Eds.), *Theoretical perspectives in direct social work practice. An eclectic-generalist approach.* New York: Springer.

Granvold, D. K., Pedler, L. M., & Schellie, S. G. (1979). A study of sex role expectancy and female postdivorce adjustment. *Journal of Divorce, 2,* 383–393.

Granvold, D. K., & Welch, G. J. (1977). Intervention for postdivorce adjustment problems: The treatment seminar. *Journal of Divorce, 1,* 82–92.

Granvold, D. K., & Wodarski, J. S. (1994). Cognitive and behavioral treatment: Clinical issues, transfer of training, and relapse prevention. In D. K. Granvold (Ed.), *Cognitive and behavioral treatment: Methods and applications* (pp. 353–375). Pacific Grove, CA: Brooks/Cole.

Greenberg, L. S., & Safran, J. D. (1989). Emotion in psychotherapy. *American Psychologist, 44,* 19–29.

Greenwald, M. A. (1987). Programming treatment generalization. In L. Michelson & L. M. Ascher

(Eds.), *Anxiety and stress disorders* (pp. 583–616). New York: Guilford.

Guidano, V. F. (1991a). Affective change events in a cognitive therapy system approach. In J. D. Safran & L. S. Greenberg (Eds.), *Emotion, psychotherapy, and change* (pp. 50–79). New York: Guilford.

Guidano, V. F. (1991b). *The self in process.* New York: Guilford

Holmes, T.H., & Rahe, R. H. (1967). Social adjustment rating scale. *Journal of Psychosomatic Research, 11,* 213–218.

Hudson, W. W. (1992). *The WALMYR assessment scales scoring manual.* Tempe, AZ: WALMYR Publishing.

Kanfer, F. H., & Schefft, B. K. (1988). *Guiding the process of therapeutic change.* Champaign, IL: Research Press.

Kaslow, F. W. (1984). Divorce: An evolutionary process of change in the family system. *Journal of Divorce, 7,* 21–39.

Kessler, S. (1975). *The American way of divorce: Prescriptions for change.* Chicago: Nelson-Hall.

Kressel, K. (1980). Patterns of coping in divorce and some implications for clinical practice. *Family Relations, 29,* 234–240.

Lazarus, R. S. (1989). Constructs of the mind in mental health and psychotherapy. In A. Freeman, K. M. Simon, L. E. Beutler, & H. Arkowitz (Eds.), *Comprehensive handbook of cognitive therapy* (pp. 99–121). New York: Plenum.

Mahoney, M. J. (1991). *Human change processes: The scientific foundations of psychotherapy.* New York: Basic Books.

Mahoney, M. J. (Ed.). (1995). *Cognitive and constructive psychotherapies: Theory, research, and practice.* New York: Springer.

Mahoney, M. J. (in press). *Constructive psychotherapy: Exploring principles and practical exercises.* New York: Guilford.

Marlatt, G. A., & Gordon, J. R. (Eds.). (1985). *Relapse prevention.* New York: Guilford.

McCubbin, H. I., & Patterson, J. M. (1983). The family stress process: The double ABCX model of adjustment and adaptation. In H. I. McCubbin, M. B. Sussman, & J. M. Patterson (Eds.), *Social stress and the family: Advances and developments in family stress theory and research* (pp. 7–37). New York: Haworth Press.

Michelson, L. (1987). Cognitive-behavioral assessment and treatment of agoraphobia. In L. Michelson & L. M. Ascher (Eds.), *Anxiety and stress disorders: Cognitive-behavioral assessment and treatment* (pp. 213–279). New York: Guilford.

Monthly Vital Statistics Report. (1990). Vol. 43, No. 9, Supplement.

National Center for Health Statistics. (1986, September 25). Advance report of final divorce statistics. In *1984 Monthly Vital Statistics Report, 35*(6) (Supp. DHS Pub. No. PHS 86-1120). Hyattsville, MD: U.S. Public Health Service.

Neff, J. A., & Mantz, R. J. (1998). Marital status transition, alcohol consumption, and number of sex partners over time in a tri-ethnic sample. *Journal of Divorce and Remarriage, 29*(1), 19–42.

Neimeyer, R. A. (1993). An appraisal of constructivist psychotherapies.

Journal of Consulting and Clinical Psychology, 61, 221–234.

Neimeyer, R. A. (1998). *Lessons of loss: A guide to coping.* New York: Primis.

Neimeyer, R. A., & Mahoney, M. J. (Eds.). (1995). *Constructivism in psychotherapy.* Washington, DC: American Psychological Association.

Nunley, E. P., & Averill, J. R. (1996). Emotional creativity: Theoretical and applied aspects. In H. Rosen & K. T. Kuehlwein (Eds.), *Constructing realities: Meaning-making perspectives for psychotherapists* (pp. 223–251). San Francisco: Jossey-Bass.

Olson, D. (1997). Family stress and coping: A multi-system perspective. In S. Dreman (Ed.), *The family on the threshold of the 21st century: Trends and implications.* New York: Lawrence Erlbaum.

Pais, J. S. (1978). Social-psychological predictions of adjustment for divorced mothers. Unpublished doctoral dissertation, University of Tennessee, Knoxville.

Ponzetti, J. J., & Cate, R. M. (1988). The divorce process: Toward a typology of marital dissolution. *Journal of Divorce, 11,* 1–20.

Propst, L. R., & Fries, L. (1989). Problems and needs of adults. In M. Textor (Ed.), *The divorce and divorce therapy handbook* (pp. 45–60). Northvale, NJ: Jason Aronson.

Reinecke, M. A. (1994). Suicide and depresion. In F. M. Dattilio & A. Freeman (Eds.), *Cognitive-behavioral strategies in crisis intervention* (pp. 67–103). New York: Guilford.

Roberts, A. R. (1990). An overview of crisis theory and crisis intervention. In A. R. Roberts (Ed.), *Crisis intervention handbook* (pp. 3–16). Belmont, CA: Wadsworth.

Roberts, A. R. (Ed.). (1996). *Crisis management and brief treatment.* Chicago: Nelson-Hall.

Safran, J. D., & Greenberg, L. S. (1991). *Emotion, psychotherapy, and change.* New York: Guilford.

Saleebey, D. (1992). Introduction: Power in the people. In D. Saleebey (Ed.), *The strengths perspective in social work practice* (pp. 3–26). White Plains, NY: Longman.

Salts, C. J. (1989). Group therapy for divorced adults. In M. Textor (Ed.), *The divorce and divorce therapy handbook* (pp. 285–300). Northvale, NJ: Jason Aronson.

Scanzoni, J. (1972). *Sexual bargaining.* Englewood Cliffs, NJ: Prentice-Hall.

Slaiku, K. A. (1990). *Crisis intervention* (2nd ed.). Boston: Allyn and Bacon.

Spanier, G. B., & Casto, R. F. (1979). Adjustment to separation and divorce: An analysis of 50 case studies. *Journal of Divorce, 2,* 241–253.

Sprenkle, D. H. (1989). The clinical practice of divorce therapy. In M. Textor (Ed.), *The divorce and divorce therapy handbook* (pp. 171–195). Northvale, NJ: Jason Aronson.

Storm, C. L., & Sprenkle, D. H. (1982). Individual treatment in divorce therapy: A critique of an assumption. *Journal of Divorce, 6,* 87–98.

Trovato, F. (1986). The relationship between marital dissolution and suicide: The Canadian case. *Journal of Marriage and the Family, 48,* 341–348.

Wallerstein, J. S., & Kelly, J. B.

(1980). *Surviving the breakup: How children and parents cope with divorce*. New York: Basic Books.

Weiss, R. S. (1975). *Marital separation*. New York: Basic Books.

Weissman, M. M., Bruce, M., Leaf, P., Florio, L., & Holzer, C. (1991). Affective disorders. In L. Robins & E. Regier (Eds.), *Psychiatric disorders in America* (pp. 53–80). New York: Free Press.

Weitzman, L. J. (1985). *The divorce revolution: The unexpected social and economic consequences for women and children in America*. New York: Free Press.

White, J. J. (1985). The effect of locus of control on post-divorce adjustment. Unpublished master's thesis, University of Texas at Arlington.

White, M., & Epston, D. (1990). *Narrative means to therapeutic ends*. New York: Norton.

Womack, C. D. (1987). The efects of locus of control and lawyer satisfaction on adjustment to divorce. Unpublished master's thesis, University of Texas at Arlington.

Zung, W. W. K. (1965). A self-rating depression scale. *Archives of General Psychiatry, 12*, 63–70.

14

Crisis Intervention With HIV-Positive Women

SARAH J. LEWIS
DIANNE F. HARRISON

This chapter is intended to provide an overview of crisis intervention with women who test positive for the human immunodeficiency virus (HIV) and the many factors that must be considered when working with this population. In order to provide stabilization during a time of crisis, it is necessary for clinicians to have an understanding of not only the emotional, social consequences of being HIV-positive, but the physical consequences as well. Because HIV disproportionately affects minority women, it is imperative that clinicians also understand the cultural ramifications of living with HIV as well as cultural coping strategies.

There are several phases of the HIV trajectory in which women typically incur disequilibrium that may require intervention: at the time of HIV-positive diagnosis; disclosure of HIV status; deterioration of the immune system; commencement of antiretroviral therapy; application for disability and/or termination of employment; and at the time of a diagnosis of acquired immunodeficiency syndrome (AIDS) (Poindexter, 1997). The continual uncertainty that results from these events can precipitate situational, developmental, social, or compound crisis states individually or simultaneously (Poindexter, 1997).

Approximately 50% of the women who have been diagnosed with AIDS are African American, 25% of the females are White, and 25% are Hispanic (CDC, 1999). Because of the heterogeneity of the female HIV-positive population, it is important to consider the cultural health beliefs as well as historical racism and sexism with which these women have been plagued. Many of the crises associated with HIV are related not to illness but to the social and developmental consequences of HIV, a stigmatized disease.

Clients with HIV are often affected by twin epidemics that are compounded by biopsychosocial factors: substance abuse and HIV. Substance abuse may inhibit access to medical care, producing a negative impact on quality of life (Israelski, Eversley, Janjus, & Smith, 1998). Social workers must be willing to address substance abuse issues with HIV-positive clients so that the client may rise to a higher level of functioning.

CASE VIGNETTES

The following cases are typical of those that face social workers working within a community-based AIDS organization that provides case management.

Case 1

Mary J., a 22-year-old African American daycare center worker, was referred to a social worker for case management by her OB-GYN after her husband called the doctor and reported that Mary had not gotten out of bed since her last appointment the prior week. At Mary's last appointment with the OB-GYN she had found out that she was HIV-positive after routine testing during the first trimester of her pregnancy.

When Mary's physician presented Mary with the consent form for HIV testing, explaining that all pregnant females should be tested, she chuckled and stated, "The HIV test is one test I have worked hard to fail." Mary had participated in no high-risk behavior except for having unprotected sex with her husband. Mary's husband, however, had had several sex partners prior to marriage and had never been tested for HIV.

Mary was not prepared for, and was totally devastated by, the news of her infection and felt as though her world as she knew it had come to an end. She had always believed that if she worked hard and had love in her heart and a strong faith in God, her life would be protected from atrocity. She felt betrayed by her husband and too dirty and infectious to be around the children she worked with, and she didn't know whether to continue carrying the baby that she desperately wanted. When she sat down in the social worker's office she was in shock, unable to comprehend that everything could change in an instant.

Case 2

Linda B. was a 26-year-old White crack cocaine addict. She was arrested while prostituting herself in order to support her drug habit, and the judge presiding over her case ordered that she be tested for HIV. Although Linda had been a sex worker since she left home at age 16 because of physical abuse by her parents, she was shocked that she tested HIV-positive. Linda told no one of her HIV status for fear of being rejected by her friends who were also sex workers. Linda attempted to stop smoking cocaine but was unsuccessful. Her health began to deteriorate, and a year after her initial diagnosis she collapsed in an alley and was taken to the local hospital with pneumonia and diagnosed with AIDS.

The drug combination that could drastically reduce HIV viral load and strengthen her immune system required strict adherence and monitoring. Linda's doctor believed that Linda would continue using cocaine when she was released and was therefore unwilling to start her on the drug combination. The doctor attempted to explain to Linda that if she could stop using drugs, keep clinic appointments, and regularly take the medication, she could look and feel healthy for several years, but without medication she would probably not live more than 2 years.

When the doctor left the hospital room, Linda called for the nurse to come in. She was afraid of her doctor, but she trusted her nurse. Linda asked the nurse if she would die without the medication, and the nurse confirmed, in a much gentler manner, what the doctor had stated. Linda panicked. She did not want to die, but she did not have the coping skills necessary to live. She was at a turning point. The nurse gave Linda the phone number of a local AIDS case management organization and told her that they might be able to help but that she would have to make the call.

DEFINITION OF CRISIS

Crisis is defined as a "subjective reaction to a stressful life experience that compromises the individual's stability and ability to cope" (Roberts, 1990, p. 328). A defining characteristic of a crisis is that it is time limited, lasting from 4 to 6 weeks; however, HIV-positive clients may experience serial crises. Although a stressful or hazardous event precipitates the crisis, it is the perception of the event and the individual's inability to cope with the perceived consequences of the event using previous coping strategies that designate a crisis.

Poindexter (1997) explains that because HIV is a chronic illness that has physical, emotional, social, spiritual, and developmental consequences, an HIV-positive person may experience multiple and cumulative crises over time. Crisis states can be the result of developmental, situational, or social conflict (Kanel, 1999; Poindexter, 1997). Each major event throughout the HIV trajectory may precipitate a crisis in the life of an HIV-positive woman. The following are examples of these events:

- Original HIV diagnosis
- Issues related to external and internal stigma

- Issues related to partner infidelity or other trust issues
- Issues related to role definition (being a woman, partner, mother, etc.)
- The decision to divulge, or not divulge, HIV status to family and peers
- First clinical signs of a compromised immune system
- Issues related to antiretrovirals or other treatment
- Issues related to pregnancy
- AIDS diagnosis

The concept of developmental crisis stems from ego psychology, specifically from Erik Erikson (Pillari, 1998). Erikson proposed eight stages through which a person passes in his or her lifetime. Each stage presents a conflict or crisis that must be mastered in order to successfully develop or move on to the next stage. When an individual faces a chronic or terminal illness in young adulthood, the length of time to master each stage is shortened or otherwise disrupted (Kanel, 1999). The dramatic shift in role perception can also have an impact on developmental tasks.

A situational crisis is not a normal stage of development but an event that is extraordinary. A situational crisis can be precipitated by events such as a violent crime, a sudden death, a natural disaster, or the diagnosis of a chronic or terminal illness. The event can challenge the fundamental assumptions that underlie the individual's worldview (Parad & Parad, 1990; Roberts, 1996). According to Roberts (1996), "a person's vulnerability to a stressful life event is dependent to a certain extent on the newness, intensity, and duration of the stressful event" (p. 22).

Opportunities for situational crises abound throughout the HIV trajectory, resulting in what can be considered a "chain of life stressors" (Roberts, 1996, p. 23). A diagnosis of being HIV-positive often changes the way a person imagines his or her world is in the present and will be in the future. Dreams can vanish in an instant, and life plans can suddenly turn into uncertainty. Because HIV-positive individuals can have a long asymptomatic period, the first signs of immune system depletion or the diagnosis of an AIDS-defining illness can also trigger a crisis. The interpretation of these events by the HIV-positive individual is often that death is imminent.

Social crisis is brought about by societal or cultural events or responses (Poindexter, 1997). These events or responses can be racism, sexism, homophobia, or other discriminatory beliefs and their accompanying behaviors. Crisis arises in a cultural sense when cultural identity is challenged. Unfortunately, HIV triggers most of society's negative "isms." Individuals with HIV face a level of discrimination that is far worse than that experienced by individuals with other chronic or terminal diseases (Poindexter, 1999). Even when one does not disclose one's HIV status, one can still be impacted by internalized stigma. Internalized stigma does not require overt mistreatment, but it can occur simply by accepting perceived societal judgment and threat of rejection.

SCOPE OF THE PROBLEM AND PSYCHOSOCIAL VARIABLES

HIV is transmitted through body fluids such as blood, semen, vaginal secretions, and breast milk and leads to suppression of the immune system. Until 1993, a diagnosis of AIDS was given only if an individual was HIV-positive and had 1 of 26 opportunistic infections. In January 1993, case definitions were changed to include other clinical markers such as a CD4+ T-lymphocyte count of less than 200 per milliliter of blood or a CD4+ percentage of less than 14, and diagnosis of pulmonary tuberculosis, recurrent pneumonia, or invasive cervical cancer. Opportunistic infections are mostly ubiquitous infections that are generally thought to be benign in individuals with healthy immune systems. However, when depletion of the immune system occurs, these infections take the "opportunity" to propagate and then can be deadly.

Case reporting of surveillance data related to HIV and AIDS has recently gone through several changes. Before 1993, only AIDS cases as defined by the preceding criteria were reported to the Centers for Disease Control (CDC). Immune-system depletion to the point of susceptibility to opportunistic infection can take 10 years or longer, and because of this the epidemiological picture was quite distorted. Only approximations of HIV infection rates have been available because HIV per se was not reportable; only the outcome of HIV (i.e., AIDS) was reportable.

Through June 1998, 28 states had regulations requiring confidential reporting of HIV and of individuals who had AIDS. Three additional states require AIDS reporting for adults and HIV infection reporting only for children. All other states require confidential reporting of cases meeting the criteria of an AIDS diagnosis only. Because of these unstandardized surveillance requirements, HIV infection surveillance data must be interpreted with caution (CDC, 1998). Figures 14.1 through 14.6 present information on overall AIDS cases in the United States between 1992 and 1997 or 1998.

In 1997, the death rate for AIDS in the United States was the lowest in a decade—almost two-thirds below rates from just 2 years previous. The decrease is attributed to a new class of drugs known as protease inhibitors. New complex, multidrug regimens, labeled "cocktails," which include a protease inhibitor in combination with one or two other classes of antiretroviral drugs, are capable of lowering viral loads to the point of nondetection, allowing T cells to resume healthy levels. Unfortunately, as many as 50% of those with HIV cannot take the drugs or, if they do take the drugs, will have limited success. One of the main contributors to this limitation is drug-regimen adherence (Ungvarski, 1997).

As of June 1998, 108,032 women with AIDS, and an additional 17,728 with HIV, had been reported to the CDC. The HIV infection rate among women is the fastest growing of any group, and 78% of newly reported HIV cases are among Black or Hispanic women. Even though AIDS incidence

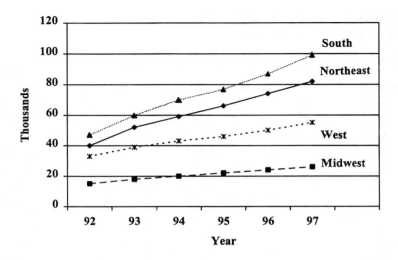

Figure 14.1 Estimated persons living with AIDS by region and year of diagnosis, 1992–1998, United States

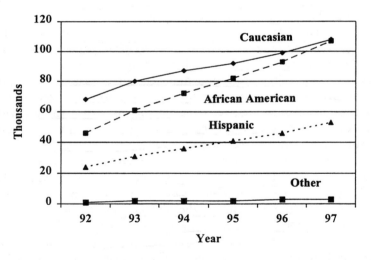

Figure 14.2 Estimated persons living with AIDS by race/ethnicity and year of diagnosis, 1992–1997, United States

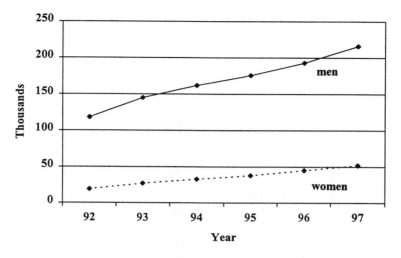

Figure 14.3   Estimated persons living with AIDS by gender and year, 1992–1997, United States

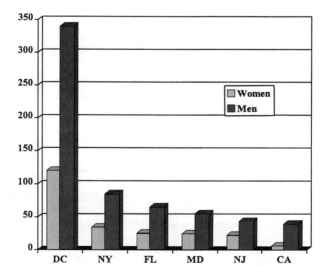

Figure 14.4.   Adult/adolescent annual AIDS rates per 100,000 population, for cases reported in the continental United States, 1999

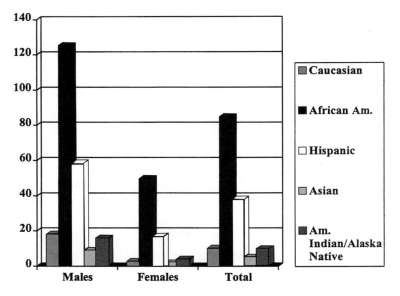

Figure 14.5.   AIDS cases and annual rates per 100,000 population, by race/ethnicity and gender reported in the continental United States, 1999

dropped in all groups from 1996 to 1997, the decrease was smaller among women (8%) than men (16%). Women who seek treatment early tend to have the same survival rates as men; however, women have historically been less likely to receive an early diagnosis. Often the impetus for women to get tested is pregnancy.

Pregnancy and HIV

Federal guidelines now require doctors to counsel pregnant women about HIV and encourage them to test voluntarily for HIV. The rationale behind these guidelines is that if women know their HIV status, they can participate in antiretroviral therapy (drugs that fight the virus) during pregnancy and lower HIV transmission risk to the fetus. Vertical transmission rates (from mother to fetus) have dropped dramatically.

Approximately 7,000 HIV-positive women give birth each year. Although each of the babies is born HIV-antibody-positive, by 18 months, most of them seroconvert to HIV-antibody-negative after they develop their own immune systems. The vertical transmission rate of women on antiretroviral therapy is less then 8%, which is down from over 25% without therapy. The Bay Area Perinatal AIDS Center (BAPAC), an example of one program that provides case management, counseling, education, and the latest in antiretroviral therapy, has reduced transmission rates to virtually zero.

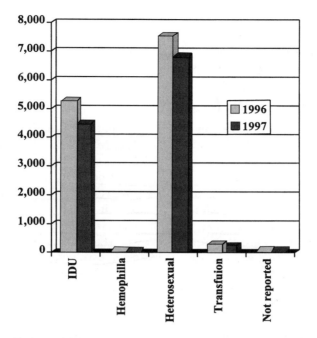

Figure 14.6.   Estimated female adult/adolescent AIDS incidence, by exposure category and year of diagnosis, 1996–1997, United States

It is important to recognize philosophical and cultural perspectives about women and childbirth when considering the topic of women and HIV. The cultural identity associated with motherhood and women's place in society is threatened by the possibility of vertical transmission of the virus. In cultures that place a high value on childbirth, HIV mothers are put in double jeopardy: Have a child and possibly expose it to the virus—making the woman a bad mother; or don't have a child—and have diminished value as a woman.

Prostitution

Because of the various definitions of prostitution and the often-illegal nature of the trade, it is difficult to estimate the number of persons who currently work as prostitutes. There is a social hierarchy of female prostitutes. Escort services or call girl establishments recruit the younger, most attractive women, whereas women who work the street are considered to be the lowest level in the hierarchy.

  Studies suggest that HIV transmission is up to four times higher among prostitutes who are intravenous drug users (IDUs) as opposed to those who are not IDUs, suggesting that occupational exposure via heterosexual transmission is the not highest reported risk category for sex workers. Sex workers who use crack cocaine tend to have more paying as well as nonpaying sex partners with whom they will have unprotected sex in order to obtain drugs or charge additional money.

Drug Abuse and HIV

Drug abuse and HIV have gone hand and hand since the beginning of the AIDS epidemic in the United States. Surveillance data do not accurately describe the impact of drug abuse on HIV exposure because drug use is a contributing factor in exposure via method of delivery, not a risk factor in and of itself. Intravenous drug use, therefore, is the only reported indicator of the drug abuse/HIV correlation. Although it is impossible to determine exact numbers, studies suggest up to 80% of HIV-positive women were infected directly or indirectly through drug use (Ferrando, 1997). Up to 90% of HIV-positive drug abusers have a comorbid psychiatric illness.

Drug abuse and/or psychiatric illness exacerbates psychosocial stresses associated with the HIV disease trajectory and must be considered throughout any intervention. Even though it may seem impossible, it is imperative that treatment of substance abuse and or mental illness be provided concomitantly with medical treatment. If substance abuse and/or psychiatric illness is not addressed initially, sabotage of medical intervention as well as client-worker relationships is likely. Although there are several reasons for addressing these concurrent problems, possibly the most important are the severe individual and societal consequences associated with nonadherence to multidrug regimens.

Consequences of Nonadherence

Nonadherence to protease inhibitors is directly related to the development of antiretroviral drug resistance (Chessney, 1997; Mirken, 1997; Vanhove, Schapiro, Winters, Merigan, & Blaschke, 1996). Poor adherence can be a problem with any chronic illness; however, as early as 1996, the issue of nonadherence was recognized as a potential disaster with protease inhibitors (Vanhove et al., 1996).

HIV replicates hundreds of millions of times a day, creating approximately 10 billion viral particles. Every replication is a potential for mutation (Mirken, 1997). When no antiretroviral is being used, these mutations are mostly random natural accidents and make no meaningful difference. When an antiretroviral is stopped and started, as is the case with nonadherence, Darwinian selection pressure is exerted, giving the mutated virus an advantage to survive. The mutations become systematic because the particles that are most drug-susceptible are killed, leaving only drug-resistant particles to replicate.

The strength of the multidrug regimen is what makes it so susceptible to resistance through viral mutation. A weak regimen like Zidovudine (AZT) monotherapy does not completely halt viral replication, so mutation is not necessary for the virus to survive. When regimens are stronger and completely halt the replication process, only particles that have mutated around the medication survive and replicate. Even though resistance to AZT does happen, it usually takes 18 months to 3 years; resistance to multidrug cocktails happens much more quickly (Mirken, 1997). There is a serious gap in the literature regarding how much nonadherence is too much nonadherence; however, some believe that less than 90% adherence is unacceptable.

Viral mutation has both personal and societal consequences. The first level is that of increased viral burden in the patient with the mutated virus. Currently only 11 protease inhibitors have been approved by the Food and Drug Administration (FDA), and the virus may form resistance to several of these at one time. This leaves few options for effective regimes.

The societal consequence is a result of an individual who has developed resistance to all available treatments infecting others. The newly infected individuals will acquire the mutated virus, which is resistant to all treatment, leaving them with no treatment options (Mirken, 1997). This new resistant strain of the virus has the potential to start a whole new phase of the AIDS epidemic.

RESILIENCE AND PROTECTIVE FACTORS

At most AIDS service organizations that provide case management, clinicians attempt to prepare clients for possible future events in order to prevent crisis situations. During the intake, myths are dispelled by educating the client about the disease spectrum, constitutional symptoms, what to do and not to do to stay healthy, and strategies for safer sex. Suggestions for keeping the immune system healthy usually include nutritional facts, information on support groups, hotlines, counselors for stress management and other mental health issues, medication adherence issues, and spiritual support. There are remarkable Internet megasites to help clients and clinicians keep up with new clinical trials, news briefs, and the history of the AIDS crisis. (See Table 14.1.)

SEVEN STAGES OF ROBERTS'S CRISIS INTERVENTION MODEL

Roberts's seven-stage model of crisis intervention provides an excellent framework for working with HIV-positive individuals who are experiencing a crisis state. The seven stages of intervention are as follows:

Table 14.1   HIV/AIDS Internet Mega-Sites

Site	Content
http://www.aegis.com	Information for clients and clinicians; excellent library that is a valuable resource; site map easy to navigate. Should be a top choice when looking for something quickly.
http://thebody.com	Multimedia site that, like aegis, can be considered a megasite. Updated at least once a day, so outdated information is rare. Another excellent site to bookmark.
http://www.cdc.gov	Centers for Disease Control. Must navigate around a bit to find information on HIV, but for health care, it is worth the visit.
http://www.medscape.com	More clinical; however, has the most up-to-date information on new important findings in the medical community.

- Assessing lethality and safety needs
- Establishing rapport and communication
- Identifying the major problems
- Dealing with feelings and providing support
- Exploring possible alternatives
- Formulating an action plan
- Providing follow-up

It is important for the clinician to remember that what separates a crisis from a difficult situation is the lack of tools and the perception of danger. For example, when a person gets a flat tire in his or her car, if one has the tools, a spare tire, and a safe place to change the tire, the flat is a mere inconvenience. However, if that person is alone on a dark, deserted highway and there is no lug wrench, a feeling of crisis begins to stir. The event, the flat tire, is not the crisis. The perception of danger generated by the lack of tools to ameliorate the situation and the feelings aroused by that perception are the crux of the crisis. The clinician's acknowledgment and assessment of the perceived danger are the starting point for crisis intervention. Roberts's seven-stage model is meant to be a flexible framework for practice, providing guidelines for crisis intervention without rigidity.

Lethality Assessment and Building Rapport

An assessment of suicidal or homicidal ideation should be a part of every crisis intervention even if it is informal and brief. In someone who is newly diagnosed with HIV, the crisis does not usually involve homicidal or suicidal ideation but instead a strong desire to live. Therefore, the assessment of lethality is usually informal and done within the context of rapport building. If, however, it is suspected that a client could possibly be in immediate danger, a more in-depth lethality assessment is necessary. When danger is suspected, the clinician must ask the client directly whether she has intention to hurt herself or someone else. The directness of this approach may be uncomfortable for the practitioner; however, it gives the client permission to talk about her intentions. The following questions must be answered:

1. Do you want to harm yourself or someone else?
2. Have you ever attempted to harm yourself in the past?
3. Has anyone close to you ever committed suicide or homicide?
4. Do you have a plan? (Clinician must determine if the plan is realistic.)
5. Do you have the (pills, gun, etc.) to carry out the plan?

All agencies and private practitioners should have protocols on safety procedures in place before ever being faced with a homicidal or suicidal client. If the answer to question 1 and any additional question is yes, the clinician must follow through with the aforementioned protocols. Each affirmative answer indicates an increase in the risk of physical harm.

For the most part, crisis intervention with HIV-positive women generally begins with the stage of rapport building, or relationship building. The tools or assets that the clinician needs in this stage are a nonjudgmental attitude, the ability to understand verbal and nonverbal communication, sincerity, objectivity, and a sense of humor.

When attempting to build rapport, it is important for the clinician to remember the stigma that is often attached to an HIV-positive status. The clinician will be asking the client to reveal very personal actions that are not customarily talked about with anyone, let alone strangers. After working with the HIV-positive population for a while, it is easy to forget the discomfort associated with topics such as sex and drug use. These topics become a part of the everyday experience of the practitioner; however, the discomfort may remain for the client. The practitioner must provide a safe and respectful atmosphere for such disclosures; this can be done through modeling a level of comfort with sensitive material often considered taboo.

It is during this stage of assessment that most information gathering will be done. Most agencies have a routine intake form consisting of several pages of questions. These questions are generally used to collect demographic information (place of residence, family size, income, etc.), possible HIV exposure routes, method of payment for medical services, some medical information, and information about the client's family system or other avenues of support. A succession of rapid-fire questions can severely hinder the attempt to build a mutually respectful relationship because there is no give-and-take between parties: The client is doing all the giving. Such one-way communication sets up a dynamic where the clinician is the one with all the power, diminishing the client.

When clinicians are familiar with the intake and assessment process, it is much easier to guide the client to tell his or her story as opposed to giving one-sentence answers to a series of questions. This storytelling provides both a more relaxed atmosphere for the client, as well as an opportunity for the clinician to assess cognitive functioning. A moderately scheduled guide is used to assure the collection of all needed information. The guide does not have to be an actual object (although that may be helpful in the beginning) but instead a way of thinking or arranging the interview. The format of the guide is funnel shaped, meaning the interview starts with very open questions that lead to more direct questions. For example:

- So, Mary, what brings you in to see me today?
- Is this your first pregnancy?
- What are your fears about keeping this baby?

Each question in the preceding sequence gets more focused. There may or may not be several questions between these questions, depending on the depth and breadth of Mary's responses. The guide is moderately scheduled because it gives an outline, not the exact questions or timing of the questions. All the information needed by the agency must be gathered, but it can be gathered in a time frame agreed upon by both the client and the clinician.

Assessment of the Problem

The primary challenge for clinicians working with HIV-positive individuals is resisting the urge to become enthralled by the crisis. Because death is so embedded in societal consciousness as the ultimate negative consequence of danger, it is hard to recognize that death is not a crisis. A sign on the wall of the employee lounge in one AIDS service organization reads: "There is no such thing as a crisis." This is to remind clinicians that no matter what the circumstance, when individuals have the tools they need, there is no crisis. The questions and issues that the practitioner needs to identify and assess are shown in Table 14.2 for each of the two case illustrations.

When working with HIV-positive clients, it is important to always consider possible cognitive impairment of a physiological nature. This is not to imply that the social service clinician should attempt to medically diagnose a client with HIV brain involvement; however, the clinician should be able to recognize telltale signs in order to make immediate medical referrals. These signs may include, but not be limited to, memory impairment, illogical or disorganized thinking, severe headaches, blurred vision, a change in speech, or a change in gait.

Because of the heterogeneity of the HIV-positive population, practitioners should take every opportunity to learn about the cultures and customs of the people they serve. For example, many African American members of some fundamentalist religious groups believe that fate and God have a great impact on health (Bekhuis, Cook, Holt, & Scott-Lennox, 1995). African American students have been found to have group-specific thoughts about providers of health services and their own mental health (Millet, Sullivan,

Table 14.2   Aspects of Current Crisis and Coping Strategies

Aspects of Current Crisis	Positive and Negative Coping Strategies

What is the perceived danger?
  MARY: Not being able to have children
  LINDA: Eminent death
Is the danger physical or emotional?
  MARY: Emotional
  LINDA: Emotional
How will the client's life be affected?
  MARY: Change in perceived life story
  LINDA: Must make a conscious decision to live
	What strategies (both negative and positive) have been attempted to resolve similar dilemmas in the past?
	  MARY: Reliance on faith and family
	  LINDA: Drugs and self-reliance
	What tools are presently necessary to resolve the dilemma?
	  MARY: Knowledge of vertical transmission risks, faith, and family
	  LINDA: Knowledge of disease spectrum and adherence issues, trust in someone other than herself, a support system, and drug treatment

Schwebel, & Meyers, 1996). Not all cultures follow or place the same importance on stages of development or life events, and it is important to consider the presenting crisis within the context of the client's cultural identity.

The clinician must assist the client to rank order or prioritize the major problems, as well as the perceived danger that these problems evoke. Although this may seem obvious, it is mentioned as a reminder to the reader of the ease with which projection can occur. The clinician may prioritize the presenting problems differently from the client; however, it is the client who is feeling the distress. If the practitioner believes that groundwork must be laid before tackling the prioritized problem, he or she is obligated to work through these issues with the client.

For example, Mary identified her main problem as the moral dilemma of keeping her baby and possibly infecting it with HIV, or having an abortion, which was against her religious beliefs. Her cultural identity as a woman was challenged by the belief that she was not fit to bear children, and she was experiencing a tremendous amount of internalized stigma. Although Mary was experiencing several other issues, this was the order of priority that she felt was most important.

In the case of Linda, she needed both medical treatment and drug treatment. Linda recognized that she did not want to die. She knew there was some medicine that could give her a chance but also knew the doctor wouldn't give it to her if she continued using crack. Linda, who could not imagine life without crack, identified the main problem as the physician who would not prescribe the medicine for her. The clinician's role was to help Linda understand the true nature of the problem and to assist her in finding a workable solution.

Exploration of Feelings

Women who are newly diagnosed could be experiencing one or more of many feelings:

- Shame: "I caught this disease through drug use or sex."
- Betrayal: "I can't believe that he was cheating on me."
- Anger: "That no good so-and-so gave this to me."
- Loss: "I won't be able to have sex, or a baby, ever again."
- Fear: "I am afraid I am going to die soon."
- Guilt: "I may have given HIV to someone else."

Throughout this chapter, perceptions and thoughts have been presented as the driving force behind crisis. Emotions, according to cognitive theorists, are also driven by cognitions. A primary objective in crisis intervention, therefore, is to provide information to correct distorted ideas and provide better understanding of the precipitating event. This is not to be done in an emotionless vacuum but instead in a supportive environment that emphasizes the client's strengths.

The clinician must actively listen during this cathartic phase and gently keep the client on track by asking open-ended questions. The clinician's job at this point is to not only actively listen to the client but also see the client within the client's system. This will provide tools for the next stage, where solutions are explored. In order to see the larger client system, the practitioner must constantly keep in mind five things: (a) the stage of development of the client (e.g. Erikson or some other developmental theorist), (b) stage of disease, (c) place in family or support system, (d) cultural norms, and (e) strategies that have worked in the past in similar situations.

In the first case illustration, Mary had several issues to contend with: being pregnant and HIV-positive, internalized stigma, inability to fill a cultural role, and dashed dreams. Mary also had very little knowledge about HIV, and some of her perceptions were formed by misconceptions about the disease. Mary had an amazing support system consisting of both an extended family and the church of which she was an active member. Her feelings were exacerbated by her limited knowledge about the disease spectrum and misinformation about vertical transmission.

Linda had a tremendous amount of fear. She had not trusted anyone since she was 16 years old and left an abusive home to live on the street. She did not have a legal means to support herself, and she did not know how to stop smoking crack cocaine. Linda's fear presented as anger: anger at the doctor for not giving her the medicine, anger at whoever gave her the virus, anger at cocaine for having a grip on her, and anger at the case manager for not being willing to talk the doctor into prescribing the medicine.

Exploration of Solutions and Action Plan

Throughout the assessment process, information is gathered in order to explore solutions. By this point in the intervention, the clinician has determined whether the client is suicidal or homicidal, has established rapport, has investigated the major problem(s), and has explored feelings and thoughts the client is experiencing as a result of the problem(s). Finding a workable solution and developing an action plan are the next two steps. The solution(s) must be tailor-made for the client and must take into account the tools with which she has to work. It is also important that the solution provide some immediate relief for the client.

When finding a workable solution, the clinician often has to take an active role. Because of the crisis, the client is experiencing disequilibrium and is unable to identify tactics or skills to alleviate the situation. The client may not recognize that she has overcome similar or more difficult hurdles in the past, and it is the role of the practitioner to point out these strengths and accomplishments.

The action plan must contain identifiable steps. It is a good idea to write down each step on a piece of paper in the presence of the client. Draw a vertical line down the paper. On one side of the paper write down the objective or task; on the other side write down who is to accomplish the task and the time frame in which it is to be accomplished. The client may only be able to make one phone call a day. This may not seem like much of an accomplishment, but it starts a momentum toward the goal.

In the case of Mary, education about vertical transmission and the HIV disease trajectory was the first step. Although the needed education could begin in the office with the clinician, it was important for Mary to see a physician who specialized in prenatal HIV care. Just obtaining knowledge of available treatments that can greatly reduce the probability of vertical transmission helped to ameliorate much of the crisis state that Mary was experiencing. An appointment was made from the clinician's office for the first prenatal visit with the HIV specialist, and the clinician offered to sit with Mary and her husband when Mary told him about her HIV-positive status. The clinician also suggested that Mary make an appointment with her pastor, who had provided her with spiritual counseling since she was a child. The counselor recognized the pastor's name as a member of the local HIV pastoral network and knew that he would provide a great deal of comfort to Mary.

Linda had a completely different set of needs and skills with which to work. She had survived on the streets for many years and had a strong desire to live. She needed a safe, structured environment in order to change her drug-abusing lifestyle, but before that she needed someone to explain to her in layperson terms why the doctor could not prescribe medication to her if she could not maintain adherence. Another major issue was that Linda had no legal means of supporting herself and, without such, was likely to feel the need to continue her work in the sex trade. Linda's list of things to do consisted of (a) application for disability (which would provide income and health insurance), (b) education about disease spectrum and adherence issues, and (c) referral for inpatient drug treatment.

Follow-Up

The last step of every action plan should be some form of follow-up with the crisis intervention counselor. A set appointment or follow-up contact with the clinician gives the client an incentive to accomplish each task on the objective list and also provides assurance that she does not have to do it all on her own. During the follow-up contact, the problem and steps taken to overcome the problem are reviewed. If the problem still exists, additional possible solutions are investigated. If the problem has been resolved, it is important for the clinician to affirm the client's accomplishment. This affirmation will help anchor these newly found coping strategies for future use.

CONCLUSION

Even though the number of deaths from AIDS-related illnesses has decreased in the recent past, the number of new HIV infections has not declined. Minority women, who are often already marginalized, make up the fastest-growing group of new HIV infections. Because of the nature of the virus and the stigma associated with it, these women may face serial crises.

When working with HIV-positive women, crisis intervention clinicians must consider not only psychosocial variables but also physiological complications. The crisis counselor often is the first person to provide factual information to the client in layperson terms. This education helps to form the foundation from which the client can begin to restore cognitive functioning and make informed decisions.

Clinicians must be sensitive to cultural norms, including the roles that women tend to play within each culture. The crisis intervention assessment should be within a cultural context that considers the client's system of support. It is important to recognize the client's strengths and successful coping strategies utilized in the past.

The final word on Mary is a positive one. Mary had her baby, which was HIV-antibody-positive but seroconverted to HIV-antibody-negative at 18 months. Mary discovered that her husband had acquired the virus before he had even met her, and the couple decided to stay together. Mary is employed by a women's peer education program through her church, where she tells her story to young African American women to help prevent the further spread of HIV. Mary's life is different now than it was before, but, according to Mary, it is better.

Linda's story has a positive yet poignant ending. Linda discontinued her drug use in a treatment center and finally began to trust someone other than herself. She found meaning in life and other people who cared a great deal about her. Linda's immune system, however, was unable to recover from the damage done by HIV and years of abuse. Before Linda died, she recognized that healing had taken place and that she had the tools and inner strength to deal with anything.

REFERENCE

Bekhuis, T., Cook, H., Holt, K., & Scott-Lennox, J. (1995). Ethnicity, church affiliation, and beliefs about the causal agents of health: A comparative study employing a multivariate analysis of covariance. *Health Education Research, 10,* 78–82.

Centers for Disease Control (1999). *HIV/AIDS surveillance report.* Atlanta, GA: Author.

Chesney, M. A. (1997). New antiretroviral therapies: Adherence challenges and strategies. *HIV Newsline 3*(3), 65–66.

Cocores, J. A., & Gold, M. S. (1990). Recognition and crisis intervention treatment with cocaine abusers: The Fair Oaks Hospital model. In A. R. Roberts (Ed.), *Crisis intervention handbook: Assessment, treatment and research.* Belmont, CA: Wadsworth.

Ferrando, S. J. (1997). Substance use disorders and HIV illness. *The AIDS Reader, 7*(2), 57–64.

Israelski, R., Eversley, R., Janjua, S., & Smith, S. (1998). Race, HIV symptoms, recovery from drug abuse, and appointment adherence are associated with quality of life (QOL) among HIV infected women [on-line]. AIDSLINE . Abstract from Int Conf AIDS. 1998; 12:1075.

Kanel, K. (1999). *A guide to crisis intervention.* Pacific Grove, CA: Brooks/Cole.

Katz, A. (1996). Gaining a new perspective on life as a consequence of uncertainty in HIV infection. *Journal of the Association of Nurses in AIDS Care, 7*(4), 51–61.

Linn, G. L., Anema, M. G., Hodess, S., Sharpe, C., & Cain, V. A. (1996). Perceived health, HIV illness, and mental distress in African-American clients of AIDS counseling centers. *Journal of Association of Nurses in AIDS Care, 7*(2), 43–52.

Linsk, N. L., & Keigher, S. M. (1997). Of magic bullets and social justice: Emerging challenges of recent advances in AIDS treatment. *Health and Social Work, 22*(1), 70–75.

Millet, P. E., Sullivan, B. F., Schwebel, A. I., & Meyers, L. J. (1996). Black Americans' and white Americans' views of etiology and treatment of mental health problems. *Community Mental Health Journal, 32,* 235–242.

Mirken, B. (1997). How much does it really matter if you take your pills on time? *Bulletin of Experimental*

Treatments for AIDS [on-line].
DOCN: BE970902. Available at
http://www.sfaf.org

Parad, H. J., & Parad, L. G. (1990).
Crisis intervention: An introductory overview. In H. J. Parad & L.
G. Parad (Eds.), *Crisis intervention, book 2: The practitioner's
sourcebook for brief therapy.* Milwaukee, WI: Family Service
America.

Pillari, V. (1998). *Human behavior in
the social environment: The developing person in a holistic context.*
Pacific Grove, CA: Brooks/Cole.

Poindexter, C. C. (1997). In the aftermath: Serial crisis intervention for
people with HIV. *Health and Social Work, 22*(2), 125–132.

Poindexter, C. C. (1999). HIV-related
stigma in a sample of HIV-affected
older female African American
caregivers. *Social Work, 44*(1),
46–55.

Roberts, A. R. (1990). An overview
of crisis theory and crisis intervention. In A. R. Roberts (Ed.), *Crisis
intervention handbook: Assessment, treatment and research.* Belmont, CA: Wadsworth.

Roberts, A. R. (1996). Epidemiology
and definitions of acute crisis in
American society. In A. R. Roberts

(Ed.), *Crisis management and brief
treatment: Theory, technique, and
applications* (pp. 16–33). Chicago:
Nelson-Hall.

Roberts, A. R., & Burman, S. (1998).
Crisis intervention and cognitive
problem-solving therapy with battered women: A national survey
and practice model. In A. R. Roberts (Ed.) *Battered women and
their families: Intervention strategies and treatment programs* (2nd
ed.). New York: Springer.

Siegel, L., & Korcok, M. (1989).
AIDS: The drug and alcohol connection: What health care professionals need to know. Center City,
MN: Hazelden.

Ungvarski, P. J. (1997). HIV/AIDS:
New knowledge, new treatments,
and the challenges for nursing.
*Journal of the Association of
Nurses in AIDS Care, 8*(4), 5–6.

Vanhove, G. F., Schapiro, J. M., Winters, M. A., Merigan, T. C., &
Blaschke, T. F. (1996). Patient compliance and drug failure in protease
inhibitor monotherapy. *Journal of
the American Medical Association,
276,* 1955–1956.

Winiarski, M. G. (1991). *AIDS-related psychotherapy.* Boston: Allyn
and Bacon.

Mobile Crisis Units

Frontline Community Mental Health Services

JAN LIGON

Gloria

Late Friday afternoon a caseworker from the outpatient mental health center received a call from Gloria, a long-standing client. Gloria was to see the worker and psychiatrist that morning but never came. She was very agitated on the telephone and told her caseworker that she did not intend to return to the mental health center, stating "Don't call me anymore or you might be sorry you did." Gloria's diagnosis is schizophrenia, and she has been hospitalized many times over the years when her symptoms would exacerbate, usually because she had stopped taking her medications. She lives alone in an apartment and receives health benefits, monthly income, rent supplements, and reduced rate passes for public transportation. The outpatient office was closing for the weekend, so the caseworker called the crisis center, to convey what Gloria had said. All clients have access to the crisis center, and caseworkers often call to relate concerns they have about clients who may call or need services after hours. Gloria did call the crisis center about 10:00 P.M. that night and told the hotline worker "I'm telling all of you that if you don't leave me alone somebody's going to get hurt." The hotline worker immediately contacted the mobile crisis unit (MCU) by cellular telephone to relate the details of the telephone call and to provide information maintained on the computer about the client, diagnosis, medications, and treatment history. The MCU proceeded to Gloria's apartment, the last of five calls it would make that shift.

Cindy

It was a hot, humid summer night, when tempers often run short. The Mobile Crisis Unit received a radio call from the county police to advise about a domestic disturbance on an isolated road in the county. The police stated that Cindy, age 19, shot a high-caliber gun into the ceiling of her grandmother's house. The grandmother ran to a neighbor's and called the police. Cindy and her father live in another county. She had not been following curfew rules, and he told her, "You can just go to your grandmother's because I'm done with you here." After a few days with her grandmother, Cindy began to call her father to try to work things out, but he reinforced that he had reached his limit with her. That night, after he hung up on Cindy, she became very upset, grabbed a gun in the house, and shot it into the ceiling several times. The police contacted the Mobile Crisis Unit for assistance, and on arrival there were five police cars and numerous neighbors who had walked over from their modest houses along the road. Cindy's father had been contacted and would arrive soon. Mental health computer records had no previous history to report.

Michael

This evening had been a quiet one for the MCU when a radio communication came in from the county police SWAT team. The team had received a call from Amanda, who advised that her husband, Michael, was in the house with her, armed and threatening to kill himself. Upon arrival, the SWAT team learned that the man had a painful and debilitating physical condition that had become worse. He was very despondent and wanted to die. Amanda stated, "I've talked him down from these states before, but this time things are much worse. He wants to die, but he doesn't want me to be left alone. Our parents are deceased, and we have no children. We're really all each other has." Although the SWAT team was requesting a backup consultation from the Mobile Crisis Unit, the scene quickly became one that required negotiation not only with the client but also with the intervening teams.

As behavioral health services for mental and substance abuse problems have shifted from institutional and inpatient settings to community services and programs, methods for dealing with crisis episodes are changing. In the past, many crisis episodes were addressed by involuntarily transporting clients to an emergency receiving facility such as a psychiatric hospital. However, with the declining influence of institutional inpatient facilities and the growing impact of managed care, it is becoming increasingly likely that crises will now be addressed at the community level. One promising approach to crisis intervention, the MCU, has been utilized in a number of communities to literally intervene at the local level, often in the client's home.

OVERVIEW OF THE PROBLEM

In the United States up to 30% of the population per year may be affected by a mental health or substance abuse problem, and 21% of the population has experienced both problems during their lifetimes. One fourth of the population will experience an anxiety disorder during their lives, 19.3% will experience an affective disorder, and over 2 million people in the United States suffer from schizophrenia. The U.S. Department of Health and Human Services, Substance Abuse and Mental Health Services Administration (SAMHSA) provides extensive information through its annual compilation of statistics (Rouse, 1998) and the Internet <http://www.samhsa.gov>.

Personal and societal costs related to mental health and substance abuse problems exceed $400 billion per year including health care and lost productivity. Although the number of alcohol-related traffic fatalities is declining, 40% of crash-related deaths involve alcohol; for drivers age 21 to 24 the rate is over 50%. Substance abuse is heavily related to crime. For example, of those individuals convicted of burglary, 40% were under the influence of drugs at the time of the crime. Alcohol and other drug use is a factor in over 500,000 emergency room episodes per year and accounts for 11% of the preventable deaths annually. Suicide rates are highest for White and American Indian/Alaskan Native males, while males in the general population who have a psychotic disorder are at almost twice the risk of committing suicide as those having nonpsychotic disorders. Mental disorders are listed as a contributing factor to the cause of death on 7.6% of death certificates (Rouse, 1998).

EXPANSION OF COMMUNITY CRISIS SERVICES

Reding and Raphelson (1995) note that as early as the 1920s psychiatrists in Amsterdam provided home-based psychiatric services with the belief that the care was more effective than that received in an inpatient hospital ward. During that same period, emergency psychiatric services began to appear in the emergency wards of general hospitals as "essentially an on-the-spot adjustment to situational exigencies" (Wellin, Slesinger, & Hollister, 1987, p. 476). Emergency services in urban psychiatric hospitals were begun in the 1930s, followed by community-based services in the 1950s. As documented by Roberts in the overview chapter, crisis services became available in the community following passage of the Community Mental Health Center (CMHC) Act of 1963, which required that all centers receiving federal funds offer 24-hour crisis and emergency services as one of five mandated categories of services.

The CHMC Act focused on moving mental health services from institutional settings to the community, and early intervention was an important component of these programs. With ongoing federal support, these services continued to expand in the 1970s, and the total number of community mental health centers offering emergency services expanded 69% from 1976 to 1981 (Wellin et al., 1987). Between 1969 and 1992, the number of mental health episodes per year doubled, the number of admissions to outpatient and partial care facilities tripled, and the rate of inpatient admissions remained constant. The number of admissions to state and county mental hospitals declined 45% from 1975 to 1992, and the number of admissions to substance abuse treatment facilities receiving public funds remained constant from 1993 to 1996. Over 50% of the funding for substance abuse treatment is from public sources, and 90% of treatment is outpatient (Rouse, 1998).

As an increasing number of clients become covered by various forms of managed care, it is likely that the trend to utilize outpatient and community-based services will expand even further. Community-based crisis intervention presents a unique challenge to both practitioners and administrators of behavioral health services. The need for crisis services continues to grow, while inpatient and institutional supports continue to decline. Therefore, it is essential that community programs develop and implement services that are congruent to community needs. While describing the disappointments and setbacks of federal mental health policy implementation, Kia Bentley (1994) also reports that "cumulative gains have been made, largely because of the family and consumer movements and legislation they helped to create" (p. 288). Georgia is one example of a state in which mental health services have been reformed based on legislation that was primarily driven by consumers of services and their families.

MENTAL HEALTH REFORM IN GEORGIA

In 1993 the Georgia General Assembly passed House Bill 100 (HB100) to reorganize mental health, mental retardation, and substance abuse services in the state into 28 community service boards. The community boards were originally overseen by 19 regional boards; however, the number of regional boards has now been reduced to 13. The law requires that a minimum of 50% of all board members must be consumers of services or their families. The 13 regional boards receive funding, determine needs, contract for the provision of services, and monitor the outcomes of services provided. Additional details about the Georgia reform are available elsewhere (Elliott, 1996). Since the 1993 reform in Georgia, services for residents of DeKalb County, located in metropolitan Atlanta, are now provided by the DeKalb Community Service Board (DCSB), based in Decatur, Georgia. DCSB provides a wide range of services to over 10,000 of the county's 600,000 residents. The county has a long history of committment and advocacy for addressing mental health, mental retardation, and substance abuse issues. Services had previously been provided through outpatient programs, and inpatient treatment was provided through one of the state's eight psychiatric hospitals.

CRISIS SERVICES

Following the passage of HB100, DeKalb County began to offer inpatient services for crisis stabilization in the community. This was consistent with the wishes of consumers and their families that services be provided in the community so that the need for hospitalization could be reduced. The facility's interdisciplinary team of physicians, psychiatrists, nurses, social workers, paraprofessional health workers, dietary workers, and volunteers provide around-the-clock access to assessments, physical examinations, medication, treatment, and case management services. Treatment approaches include individual therapy, 12-step groups, and education groups. In addition, many clients are transported to specialized community programs such as dual diagnosis and day treatment programs or are sent to halfway house and residential programs in the community. The crisis facility also serves as the base of operation for the county's crisis telephone service. In addition, since 1994 a MCU has been in continuous service and provides essential intervention and support services that were not available prior to its inception.

DEVELOPMENT OF MOBILE CRISIS UNITS

Mobile crisis units (MCUs) can be broadly defined as a community-based program, staffed by trained professionals who may be summoned to any location to deliver services. A number of programs have been previously documented in the literature, and early efforts focused on in-home psychiatric services (Chiu & Primeau, 1991). Other programs were specifically intended to avoid hospital admissions (Bengelsdorf & Alden, 1987; Henderson, 1976) and for providing training to psychiatric residents (Zealberg et al., 1990). More recent efforts have included programs that target the homeless mentally ill (Slagg, Lyons, Cook, Wasmer, & Ruth, 1994), with the ability to offer "medications that would otherwise be administered by court order in a hospital" (Reding & Raphelson, 1995, p. 181).

Although the specific features of MCUs vary, Zealberg, Santos, and Fisher (1993) identify a number of advantages offered by mobile crisis units, including increased accessibility of services, the benefit of assessing in the "patient's native environment" (p. 16), and the ability to intervene without delay, to avoid unnecessary arrests or hospitalizations, and to offer crisis training opportunities to mental health professionals. Because police officers are often the first source of contact and response to community crises, the authors also note that MCUs offer the opportunity to collaborate with the law enforcement system.

ROLE OF LAW ENFORCEMENT

Police activities related to mental health and substance abuse are particularly problematic for law enforcement because these calls can be very time-consuming and frequently are not perceived as "real police work" (Olivero & Hansen, 1994, p. 217) compared with activity associated with criminal behavior. Zealberg et al. (1993) note that police officers have little training in mental health issues and "techniques that were developed for use with criminals are often not applicable to nor successful with psychotic patients" (p. 17).

Law enforcement agencies and behavioral health care services are systems that may be prone to clash (Kneebone, Roberts, & Hainer, 1995). For example, in the past law enforcement was integrally involved in providing assistance for the involuntary admissions of mental health and substance abuse patients to psychiatric hospitals. However, the current system has become more restrictive concerning involuntary commitments (Olivero & Hansen, 1994) while favoring community-based interventions. Efforts to support community treatment and avoid psychiatric hospitalizations are congruent with the intent of deinstitutionalization However, there has been a corresponding increase in the number of persons with a history of mental problems who are jailed rather than hospitalized, a systemic shift that has been referred to as "transinstitutionalization" (Olivero & Hansen, 1994, p. 217). As noted by Zealberg et al. (1993), "Mobile crisis teams can alleviate the anxiety of law enforcement personnel and can prevent police overreaction" (p. 17).

DIFFERENCES IN MCU STAFFING AND SERVICE DELIVERY

MCUs have varied greatly in staffing and service delivery approaches. Gaynor and Hargreaves (1980) note that some mobile units were more likely to use mental health professionals, with psychiatrists available on a consultant basis, whereas Chiu and Primeau (1991) describe a team approach that includes a psychiatrist, a registered nurse, and a social worker. Some MCUs have been positioned as support and consultant services, which are called for assistance by the law enforcement or mental health systems (Bengelsdorf & Alden, 1987; Henderson, 1976; Zealberg, Christie, Puckett, McAlhany, & Durban, 1992). Other programs have been based in vans or other vehicles and offer outreach services to targeted populations (Chiu & Primeau, 1991; Slagg et al., 1994).

Community MCUs differ with respect to staffing and objectives, and the role of law enforcement in these programs also varies. Programs have been described that are designed to increase the knowledge and effectiveness of police officers when working with mental health issues (Dodson-Chaneske, 1988; Tesse & Van Wormer, 1975), as a collaboration with police and psychiatric services (Zealberg et al., 1992), or as a team consisting of police officers and mental health professionals (Lamb, Shaner, Elliott, DeCuir, & Foltz, 1995). On the other hand, many programs have focused on the delivery of services without law enforcement collaboration (Bengelsdorf & Alden, 1987; Chiu & Primeau, 1991; Slagg et al., 1994). Deane, Steadman, Borum, Veysey, and Morrissey (1999) surveyed urban police departments concerning their method of response to situations involving mental health issues and found no significant differences in four approaches to the calls.

MOBILE CRISIS SERVICES IN DEKALB COUNTY, GEORGIA

Prior to 1994, many crises involving mental health and substance abuse problems in DeKalb County were addressed by police department officers who responded to these calls. If necessary, individuals could be arrested, or they could be transported involuntarily by the sheriff's department to the state psychiatric hospital. Community residents, family members, and mental health advocates were very vocal about their displeasure with this arrangment for several reasons. First, the opportunity to resolve the situation at the location of the incident was limited by the expertise of the officer who responded. Second, many arrests and incarcerations were for behavior that was directly related to a mental health issue and were potentially avoidable. Finally, when clients were assessed at the psychiatric hospital, it was not uncommon for the facility to make decisions that conflicted with the judgment and opinions of community providers and family members. With the consumer and family focus of the reform in Georgia, it was now possible for county residents to secure services that were desired, including the MCU.

The MCU operates from 3:00 to 10:30 P.M., 7 days per week, and pairs a uniformed police officer with a mental health professional who operate from a regular marked police car. Each team works 4 days per week, with the operations based at the county's mental health and substance abuse crisis center, which includes the 24-hour crisis telephone service, walk-in services, and inpatient crisis stabilization and detoxification unit. About half of the referrals to the MCU are made by police dispatchers or other officers through the police radio communications system. The other half of the referrals come from the crisis unit or other mental health workers via cellular telephone and pager. Police officers have continuous access to field supervisors, and the mental health worker has direct access to consultation, including administration and staff psychiatrists. In addition, client histories are available through both the law enforcement and the mental health information system. The MCU responds to a wide range of calls that occur in homes, public places, and schools. About half the calls involve a psychotic episode, 25% are related to suicidal individuals, and about one fourth include a substance abuse problem as well. About six calls are completed per shift, which includes a combination of crisis calls and prearranged client and family follow-up calls.

APPLICATIONS OF ROBERTS'S SEVEN-STAGE MODEL

Roberts (1991) provides a highly practical approach to crisis intervention that is consistent with the needs of members of mobile crisis teams. It is important to address each of the seven stages in the model, beginning with stage 1, assessing lethality and safety needs, followed by stage 2, establishing rapport and communication. Stage 3 involves identifying the major problems, followed by stage 4, dealing with feelings and providing support. Possible alternatives are explored in stage 5, followed by the formulation of a plan in stage 6, and follow-up during stage 7. Roberts (1991) aptly stresses the importance of using sound judgment in sequencing the model's stages. For example, an MCU call involving a frightened mental health client could begin with stage 2 to establish rapport, whereas a call concerning an actively suicidal client would begin with assessing lethality, stage 1.

Case Application: Gloria

In the case of Gloria, assessing the lethality of her threats is consistent with stage 1 and began with contacts to the outpatient case manager and the telephone crisis worker. These were both excellent resources to determine from their experience and case records if any history of violence toward self or others was evident. In stage 2 the telephone crisis worker had already spoken with Gloria at her apartment as well as to her neighbor, who was with her and considered a supportive person. In stage 3 it was determined that Gloria's threats were consistent with her not being properly medicated. In the past this usually resulted in being transported to the psychiatric hospital and involuntarily admitted.

On this call, the team consisted of a uniformed officer and a licensed master's-level social worker, who proceeded to the apartment. In stage 4 the crisis telephone worker had begun the process of offering support to Gloria and her neighbor and provided an opportunity to express feelings. However, given Gloria's level of hostility, this dialogue was of limited benefit, and her neighbor was very relieved to know that the MCU was en route. As the MCU team entered her apartment, Gloria became very fearful about the presence of a uniformed officer. It was now important to go back to stage 1 in order to specifically make sure there were no weapons in the apartment and to assess Gloria's intent to harm herself or someone else. Although a full discussion of assessing suicidal and homicidal intent is beyond the scope of this chapter, a more thorough review of risk factors and assessment techniques is available elsewhere (Sommers-Flanagan & Sommers-Flanagan, 1995).

Continuing to stages 2, 3, and 4, Gloria was calmed by the team and encouraged to relate to it the details of her missing her usual appointment, the status of her medications, her recent appetite and sleep patterns, and any recent events or circumstances that may have impacted her mental status. In stages 5 and 6 it was important to consider the input of both Gloria and her neighbor as well as the previous feedback from the case manager and telephone worker. The team was able to acquire her trust, and she provided helpful input in developing a plan. Gloria had not stopped taking her medications, but she was running low on her supply and attempting to stretch what she had, which led to her decompensation. Although one option was to transport her to the crisis center for further evaluation, her neighbor was willing to stay with her for the night. If there were any difficulties she could contact the telephone crisis line. In stage 7 the neighbor was willing to bring Gloria to the outpatient mental health center for a walk-in meeting with her case worker and the psychiatrist and to replenish her medications at the center pharmacy.

This case illustrates several benefits of the mobile crisis unit. First, the combination of a law enforcement officer and a mental health worker is of tremendous benefit in assessing safety and providing the option of involuntary transportation, if needed. Second, the appearance of a uniformed officer and a plainclothes worker has the effect of balancing the need for authority and empathic support in crisis work. This is not always possible if an officer is working solo and may have to move swiftly to an arrest that could have been avoided. By the same token, it may not be safe for a mental health professional to attempt such a call alone. Finally, there was significant benefit in addressing the crisis from a contextual perspective in Gloria's home. This includes her physical environment and also makes it possible to more accurately assess the viability of her neighbor as an action plan alternative. There was no further contact until the next morning, when Gloria arrived with her neighbor at the mental health center.

Case Application: Cindy

In the case of Cindy, the assessment of lethality in stage 1 had been addressed by law enforcement officers prior to the arrival and in many cases MCUs. The MCU is not the first responder to police calls but is summoned by officers when appropriate. The MCU was contacted by officers on the scene via police radio. On this shift, the mental health worker was a licensed clinical social worker who had the authority to sign, if necessary, an involuntary order to transport the woman to the psychiatric emergency receiving facility. Although the objective is not to arrest or hospitalize individuals, it is beneficial for the authority to initiate an involuntary intervention to be present. In stage 2, since her father had arrived, team members met separately with Cindy and her father, and in stages 3 and 4 both felt comfortable with sharing their feelings and relating their views of the problems. Options in stage 5 included arrest, involuntary transportation to the psychiatric hospital, or transportation to the crisis center, which is a voluntary status facility. It was agreed that the client would come to the crisis center for further evaluation. Given her age and the lack of any client history, she was admitted for overnight observation, was reevaluated the next morning, and was referred to the outpatient mental health division for both individual and family therapy. For stage 7 a telephone call was placed to the father; it was determined that Cindy had returned home, and she and her father did follow-up with outpatient services.

This case description illustrates several benefits of MCUs reported by Zealberg, Santos, and Fisher (1993). First, the ability to observe and interview on-site "allows for the most complete assessment with the least trauma to the patient" (p. 16). In this case it was also possible to interview Cindy and her father individually and to then converge the information obtained to determine similarities and differences reported. Second, mobile units can respond quickly, prevent situations from escalating, and avoid unnecessary arrests or hospitalizations. Third, a well-executed mobile crisis call "allows for better public education about mental health issues and resources" (p. 17). Fourth, potential cost savings to the county include not only the avoidance of unnecessary arrests or hospitalizations but also the opportunity for "officers to return to duty more quickly" (p. 17).

Case Application: Michael

This evening had been a quiet one for the MCU when a radio communication came in from the county police SWAT team. It had received a call from Amanda, who advised that her husband, Michael, was in the house with her, armed and threatening to kill himself. Upon arrival, the SWAT team learned that the man had a painful and debilitating physical condition that had become worse. He was very despondent and wanted to die. Amanda stated, "I've talked him down from these states before, but this time things are much worse. He wants to die, but he doesn't want me to be left alone. Our parents are deceased, and we have no children. We're really all each other has." Although the SWAT team was requesting a backup consultation from the MCU, the scene quickly became one that required negotiation not only with the client but also with the intervening teams.

The case of Michael points out the importance of stage 1 in assessing both lethality and past experiences with coping behaviors. Although his wife was not being held hostage, this case presented an element of extreme risk and danger to Michael and Amanda and required the use of negotiation skills (Strentz, 1995). On this evening, the team consisted of the uniformed police officer and a registered nurse, and computer records found no criminal or mental health information on Michael. After consultation with the SWAT team, it was agreed that the nurse would, consistent with stage 2, attempt to first establish rapport with Amanda and use her alliance to connect with Michael. The problems (stage 3) were clear, so the predominant effort on this call was to connote empathy and provide support (stage 4). Given the severity of Michael's physical and mental conditions, the only alternative in stages 5 and 6 would be to arrange for his hospitalization. The dialogue between the MCU nurse and the couple went extremely well, and Michael voluntarily surrendered the gun and agreed to go with the MCU to the hospital. A follow-up call to the hospital for stage 7 confirmed that Michael was safe and stabilizing in the hospital.

Although the outcome of this case was positive, it was important to note the difference between this call and others handled by the MCU and SWAT teams. A follow-up meeting was held with the SWAT team and a mobile crisis worker to review the call. The SWAT team members expressed the need for additional training around mental health and substance abuse issues, which was subsequently provided. As noted by Strentz (1995), "The element of danger coexists with the opportunity for successful resolution and personal growth" (p. 147). Therefore, it is also essential to provide cross-training about SWAT team interventions to team members of mobile crisis units.

OUTCOMES OF MCUs

Outcome information about MCUs is limited, and Geller, Fisher, and McDermeit (1995) note that "beliefs about mobile crisis services far outnumber facts" (p. 896). Although Reding and Raphelson (1995) reported a 40% reduction in hospital admissions during a 6-month period, a study by Fisher, Geller, and Wirth-Cauchon (1990) did not "support the numerous claims regarding the ability of mobile crisis intervention to reduce the use of hospitalization" (p. 249). However, Fisher et al. (1990) go on to report that "some mobile crisis teams may be very effective in reducing hospitalizations because they function as part of a system which has other key services available for treatment and diversion" (p. 250).

In addition, Fisher et al. (1990) note that these units often reach people in need of hospitalization, so "that the unnecessary hospitalizations prevented by mobile crisis units are offset by the admission of individuals needing inpatient care who are discovered" (p. 251). Another problem is that "large numbers of persons who have committed minor crimes are taken to jails instead of to hospitals or other psychiatric treatment facilities" (Lamb et al., 1995, p. 1267). Lamb et al. (1995) conducted a follow-up study in Los Angeles of clients having a history of criminal and mental problems who had received outreach services from a police-mental team and found that "remarkably, only two percent of the group were taken to jail" (p. 1269).

INITIATING AND SUSTAINING MCUs

The future of MCUs is dependent on the ability of multiple systems to perceive their value and to then collaborate in a manner that will assure quality services that can be sustained in the community. While it is impossible to document how many MCUs have opened and closed over the years, a number of factors can influence these programs. First, crisis work can be dangerous when interventions occur in neighborhoods and homes with persons who may exhibit or have histories of violent behavior (Zealberg et al., 1993). Second, the behavioral health and law enforcement systems are rife with conflicts between the two systems (Dodson-Chaneske, 1988; Teese & Van Wormer, 1975), so "constant attention must be given to such collaboration" (Zealberg et al., 1992, p. 614). Finally, the larger political and turf factors that exist in any community can, unfortunately, lead to premature cuts despite a program's efficacy (Diamond, 1995; Reding & Raphelson, 1995).

The political and organizational environments in which these units operate will no doubt present both obstacles and opportunities. It is also essential to work closely with law enforcement and to include ongoing supervision and training opportunities for police officers and mental health workers. In addition, consumers of services and their families must be involved in the development and refinement of MCUs. One study (Ligon, in press) found that in one urban program family members who received services from the MCU rated the services higher than client ratings of three different crisis services, including the MCU. As stated by DCSB director, R. Derrill Gay, "Families see Mobile Crisis Units as essential services in community mental health and these are the people who need it, use it, and value it" (personal communication, May 19, 1999). The support of mental health advocacy groups at the national, state, and local levels is also beneficial in the further development of mobile crisis units.

FUTURE OPPORTUNITIES

Although the application and outcomes of mobile crisis units are encouraging, there are a number of opportunities to improve these services and to expand their availability. Zealberg, Hardesty, Meisler, and Santos (1997) identify several key areas of concern that include medical issues and the need for technology to support these units. The authors note that "one of the more frustrating aspects of mobile crisis work involves patients whose presenting symptoms include medical as well as psychiatric diagnoses" (p. 272). Ambulance and EMS services can assist with medical problems, but collaboration with these operations may be problematic due to multiple providers of these services in communities or poor communication capability with MCUs. Because MCUs often address issues related to physical health and medications, the DeKalb unit has found that coupling psychiatrically trained registered nurses with the police officer can be very beneficial. In addition, the DeKalb MCU has added a limited number of antipsychotic and side effects medications, which are carried onboard, ordered by the unit psychiatrist, and administered by the onboard nurse.

Technology offers immense opportunities to improve mobile crisis services. First, equipment is increasingly portable and more affordable, and it is feasible to equip MCUs with computers, cellular telephones, and other emerging products. Second, the ability to merge sources of information is improving, and it is possible for MCUs to determine any criminal and mental health history on clients quickly and efficiently. Finally, technology enables team members of MCUs to enter data and update records without burdensome paperwork and forms. This can include outcome data, new client information, and instructions for other services concerning follow-ups.

Virtually all the MCUs that have been documented are based in urban areas, which is understandable given the concentration of population and availability of resources. However, rural areas are extremely underserved; 21% of all rural counties have no mental health services, compared with only 4% in urban counties. The situation is much worse if overnight care is required; 78% of rural counties have no overnight services, compared with 27% in urban counties (Rouse, 1998). Coupled with the lack of public transportation in rural areas, MCUs offer the potential not only to provide services where needed but also to initiate any follow-up services that may be required.

Although the costs of operating MCUs are a significant concern to communities, Zealberg et al. (1997) note that indirect cost savings must be considered, including the reduced loss of time for police officers, court costs that are avoided when situations are resolved without arrests, and avoidance of high-cost inpatient care in many cases. In addition, behavioral health care is increasingly provided under managed care models. Therefore, managed care organizations are also in a position to gain from such cost savings as avoiding hospitalizations and need to partner with the public sector in developing and supporting MCUs.

MCUs operate across a wide range of geography and sites and encounter very diverse populations. Based on the experience of an MCU based in New York City, Chiu (1994) provides case examples and suggestions on working with Asian, Hispanic, African American, and other diverse groups. In addition, Lyons, Cook, Ruth, Karver, and Slagg (1996) note that the inclusion of consumers of mental health services on MCU teams may be beneficial when responding to calls across a variety of settings, including homes and public places. For example, the authors found that "consumer staff were more likely to do street outreach than were non-consumer staff" (p. 38) and go on to note that consumer experience "can be an advantage for mobile crisis assessment with persons with problems of mental illness and housing instability" (p. 40).

MCUs can be of tremendous benefit to communities when they are carefully staffed and supported by all stakeholders, including consumers of services and their families, law enforcement, and both public and private providers of behavioral health services. However, more research needs to be conducted to determine what combinations of staffing, services, technology, and intervention techniques are most effective and in what settings. It is also important to learn more about working with diverse populations and to investigate the benefits to rural residents through the implementation and evaluation of programs in these underserved areas.

ACKNOWLEDGMENTS   The author appreciates the input and support provided by Dr. R. Derrill Gay, Director of the DeKalb Community Service Board, Decatur, Georgia, and to the staff of the Mobile Crisis Unit in the development of this chapter.

REFERENCES

Bengelsdorf, H., & Alden, D. C. (1987). A mobile crisis unit in the psychiatric emergency room. *Hospital and Community Psychiatry, 38*, 662–665.

Chiu, T. L. (1994). The unique challenges faced by psychiatrists and other mental health professionals working in a multicultural setting. *International Journal of Social Psychiatry, 40*, 61–74.

Chiu, T. L., & Primeau, C. (1991). A psychiatric mobile crisis unit in New York City: Description and assessment, with implications for mental health care in the 1990s. *International Journal of Social Psychiatry, 37*, 251–258.

Deane, M. W., Steadman, H. J., Borum, R., Veysey, B. M., & Mor-

rissey, J. P. (1999). Emerging partnerships between mental health and law enforcement. *Psychiatric Services, 50*, 99–101.

Diamond, R. J. (1995). Some thoughts on: "Around-the-clock mobile psychiatric crisis intervention." *Community Mental Health Journal, 31*, 189–190.

Dodson-Chaneske, D. (1988). Mental health consultation to a police department. *Journal of Human Behavior and Learning, 5*, 35–38.

Elliott, R. L. (1996). Mental health reform in Georgia, 1992–1996. *Psychiatric Services, 47*, 1205–1211.

Fisher, W. H., Geller, J. L., & Wirth-Cauchon, J. (1990). Empirically assessing the impact of mobile crisis capacity on state hospital admissions. *Community Mental Health Journal, 26,* 245–253.

Gaynor, J., & Hargreaves, W. A. (1980). "Emergency room" and "mobile response" models of emergency psychiatric services. *Community Mental Health Journal, 16,* 283–292.

Geller, J. L., Fisher, W. H., & McDermeit, M. (1995). A national survey of mobile crisis services and their evaluation. *Psychiatric Services, 46,* 893–897.

Henderson, H. E. (1976). Helping families in crisis: Police and social work intervention. *Social Work, 21,* 314–315.

Kneebone, P., Roberts, J., & Hainer, R. J. (1995). Characteristics of police referrals to a psychiatric unit in Australia. *Psychiatric Services, 46,* 620–622.

Lamb, H. R., Shaner, R., Elliott, D. M., DeCuir, W. J., & Foltz, J. T. (1995). Outcome for psychiatric emergency patients seen by an outreach police–mental health team. *Psychiatric Services, 46,* 1267–1271.

Ligon, J. (in press). Client and family satisfaction with brief mental health, substance abuse, and mobile crisis services in an urban setting. *Crisis Intervention and Time-Limited Treatment.*

Lyons, J. S., Cook, J. A., Ruth, A. R., Karver, M., & Slagg, N. B. (1996). Service delivery using consumer staff in a mobile crisis assessment program. *Community Mental Health Journal, 32,* 33–40.

Olivero, J. M., & Hansen, R. (1994). Linkage agreements between mental health and law: Managing suicidal persons. *Administration and Policy in Mental Health, 21,* 217–225.

Reding, G. R., & Raphelson, M. (1995). Around-the-clock mobile psychiatric crisis intervention: Another effective alternative to psychiatric hospitalization. *Community Mental Health Journal, 31,* 179–187.

Roberts, A. R. (1991). Conceptualizing crisis theory and the crisis intervention model. In A. R. Roberts (Ed.), *Contemporary perspectives on crisis intervention and prevention* (pp. 3–17). Englewood Cliffs, NJ: Prentice-Hall.

Roberts, A. R. (1995). *Crisis intervention and time-limited cognitive treatment.* Thousand Oaks, CA: Sage.

Roberts, A. R. (1996). *Crisis management and brief treatment.* Chicago: Nelson-Hall.

Rouse, B. A. (Ed.). (1998). *Substance abuse and mental health statistics sourcebook.* Washington, DC: U.S. Government Printing Office.

Slagg, N. B., Lyons, J. S., Cook, J. A., Wasmer, D. J., & Ruth, A. (1994). A profile of clients served by a mobile outreach program for homeless mentally ill persons. *Hospital and Community Psychiatry, 45,* 1139–1141.

Sommers-Flanagan, J., & Sommers-Flanagan, R. (1995). Intake interviewing with suicidal patients: A systematic approach. *Professional Psychology: Research and Practice, 26,* 41–47.

Strentz, T. (1995). Crisis intervention and survival strategies for victims of hostage situations. In A. R. Roberts (Ed.), *Crisis intervention and time-limited cognitive treatment* (pp. 127–147). Thousand Oaks, CA: Sage.

Teese, C. P., & Van Wormer, J. (1975). Mental health training and consultation with suburban police. *Community Mental Health Journal, 11,* 115–121.

Wellin, E., Slesinger, D. P., & Hollister, C. D. (1987). Psychiatric emergency services: Evolution, adaptation, and proliferation. *Social Science and Medicine, 24,* 475–482.

Zealberg, J. J., Christie, S. D., Puckett, J. A., McAlhany, D., & Durban, M. (1992). A mobile crisis program: Collaboration between emergency psychiatric services and police. *Hospital and Community Psychiatry, 43,* 612–615.

Zealberg, J. J., Hardesty, S. J., Meisler, N., & Santos, A. B. (1997). Mobile psychiatric emergency medical services. In S. W. Henggeler & A. B. Santos (Eds.), *Innovative approaches for difficult-to-treat populations* (pp. 263–274). Washington, DC: American Psychiatric Press.

Zealberg, J. J., Santos, A. B., & Fisher, R. K. (1993). Benefits of mobile crisis programs. *Hospital and Community Psychiatry, 44,* 16–17.

Zealberg, J. J., Santos, A. B., Hiers, T. G., Ballenger, J. C., Puckett, J. A., & Christie, S. D. (1990). From the benches to the trenches: Training residents to provide emergency outreach services: A public/academic project. *Academic Psychiatry, 14,* 211–217.

16

The Comprehensive Crisis Intervention Model of Community Integration, Inc. Crisis Services

YVONNE M. EATON
BARB ERTL

Community Integration, Inc. Crisis Services is recognized as a model program by the Pennsylvania State Office of Mental Health. Five types of crisis intervention are available 24 hours per day, 7 days per week, to anyone experiencing a crisis within Erie County, Pennsylvania. A *crisis* is defined very broadly and includes anyone who is experiencing a disturbance of mood, thought, emotion, behavior, or social functioning. Some examples include suicide (ideation, attempts, and completed), psychiatric decompensation, situational stressors, family discord, substance abuse, domestic violence, and bereavement. The structure and functioning of the crisis team results in effective, successful intervention to those in crisis. The five basic services are telephone crisis services, walk-in crisis services, mobile crisis services, access to crisis residential unit, and Critical Incident Stress Management. These services will be discussed using case scenarios to illustrate techniques of crisis intervention.

ORGANIZATIONAL STRUCTURE AND FUNCTIONS

There are 23 crisis services staff scheduled around the clock who have a variety of educational and experiential backgrounds. All staff members complete a month of orientation with subsequent required weekly in-services/

training. Ongoing education is essential in ensuring staff are kept current on clinical intervention strategies and community resources. Training is video-taped for those not on shift at the time it is given. All staff are also certified in Nonviolent Crisis Intervention through the Crisis Prevention Institute, Inc. Staff attend individual clinical supervision sessions twice monthly to review cases and interventions. Field evaluations, in which the clinical supervisor accompanies workers on cases, are conducted frequently to assess clinical and intervention skills, and 24-hour accessibility to a psychiatrist and administrator are provided to all staff. Staff includes 2 telephone triage specialists, 13 crisis workers, 6 shift supervisors, 1 clinical supervisor, and 1 director. Telephone triage specialists provide much of the phone crisis counseling, information, referrals, and telephone triage. They also provide phone support to suicidal callers until the mobile crisis worker arrives on the scene. Telephone triage specialists are based at the office for the duration of their shift. Crisis workers provide full crisis assessments and face-to-face intervention to individuals and significant others either at the scene of the crisis or on a walk-in basis. These workers utilize techniques of crisis intervention to assist consumers in accessing and utilizing resources to resolve the crisis situation. These workers report to the office but are quickly dispatched to respond to crisis calls by the shift supervisor. Shift supervisors, who also remain in the office, provide clinical and administrative direction to the crisis staff on their shift. They assure all requests for services are responded to in a timely manner as dictated by policy. They conduct documentation reviews and juggle the various demands on their shifts. The clinical supervisor and director are responsible for the hiring, training, clinical supervision, administrative direction, and discipline of all crisis staff. They are also responsible for the administrative duties of the agency (policies, budget, etc.). An additional 40 per diem staff, the Erie County Critical Incident Stress Management Team, are utilized as needed for the provision of Critical Incident Stress Management. These team members have a minimum of Basic CISM as certified by the International Critical Incident Stress Foundation.

TELEPHONE CRISIS SERVICES

Crisis Services receives more than 2,000 phone calls per month. Crisis calls result in crisis counseling and support, information and referrals, and crisis screening and triage. Crisis staff engage all callers with empathic responses and supportive listening skills. Professor Roberts (1996) offers a comprehensive text for crisis intervention strategies, which includes hotline work. Many callers choose to remain anonymous or, with phone support only, effectively resolve their crises. A screening/triage form is completed for all callers who request further services or face-to-face contact. This essential form addresses both clinical information (such as suicide or homicide risk) and safety issues (such as weapons on the scene and legal history). All calls are assigned an intervention priority code, which allows the shift supervisor to prioritize these multiple requests on a clinical basis. Priority I calls require immediate intervention because of an individual's significant risk of harm to self or others. Some examples of Priority I calls include suicide attempts in progress, police on scene or en route, and suicidal or homicidal ideation with intent and means readily available. Priority II calls require timely intervention because of an inability to cope with current stressors. Risk of harm to self or others is not pressing at the time of contact due to the presence of reliable supports or lack of feasible plan, intent, or method. Some examples include hallucinations, delusions, and suicidal or homicidal ideation with lack of plan or intent. Priority III calls require intervention because of a moderate level of dysfunction. There is no identified risk of harm to self or others. Some examples include impaired ability to meet basic needs (shelter, hygiene), impairment in ability to meet family, educational, or occupational roles, and mood disturbance or other significant vegetative disturbances. Priority IV calls require intervention because of subjective distress and/or mild level of dysfunction or difficulty coping with current stressors. Some examples include minor mood disturbance and relational conflict. Regardless of the intervention priority assigned, all requests for services are addressed as quickly as possible, and every request for service is addressed within 24 hours.

Case Scenario

A phone call was received from an anonymous male caller. This individual was very reluctant to provide information to crisis services. However, it was determined that the consumer had overdosed on 20 Prozac and 20 Ambien. The caller would not provide any demographic or identifying information, and the call had to be traced. While the trace was being completed, the caller became nonresponsive, and the phone was heard dropping to the floor.

Roberts's (1996) seven-stage crisis intervention model was initiated.

Stage 1: Assess Lethality. It was quickly determined via the suicide risk assessment (on the Crisis Services triage form) that the caller had already overdosed on a significant amount of medications, making this a highly lethal/urgent situation.

Stage 2: Establish Rapport. Through the use of rephrasing, paraphrasing, questioning, empathy, and supportive listening, the crisis worker was able to keep the client engaged while the trace was being completed. Establishing rapport with the client was essential because if the client terminated the call, he would likely have died. The triage form utilized by Crisis Services provides workers with structure for questioning,

Table 16.1   Sample Triage Questions

Suicidality	Are you/client having thoughts of self harm?	( ) yes	( ) no	( )unknown
	Have you/client done anything to hurt self already?	( ) yes	( ) no	( )unknown
	If yes, describe:			
	How long have you/client had thoughts to hurt self?			
	How might you/client hurt self?			
	Have you/client made any preparations to hurt self?	( ) yes	( ) no	( )unknown
	What keeps you/client from hurting self?			
Homicidality	Are you/client having thoughts to hurt others?	( ) yes	( ) no	( )unknown
	Who do you think about hurting?			
	Have you/client hurt anyone already?	( ) yes	( ) no	( )unknown
	If yes, describe:			
	How long have you/client had thoughts to hurt others?			
	What keeps you/client from hurting others?			

which is particularly helpful in these stressful situations. Some excerpts from the triage appear in Table 16.1.

Stage 3: Identify Major Problem(s). The number one identified problem was a known overdose, which was complicated by the secondary problem of the client's refusal to provide identifying information.

Stage 4: Deal With Feelings. The worker first allowed the client to tell his story about why he felt so bad at this point in his life. The worker began to address those feelings but was unable to do much work in this area because the client became nonresponsive.

Stage 5: Explore Alternatives. Because of the critical nature of the case and the client's unconsciousness, there was no opportunity to explore alternatives or develop an action plan with him in collaboration with Crisis Services.

Stage 6: Develop Action Plan. The crisis worker had to take control of this situation. The following steps were completed:

1. The trace was completed and the address was obtained.
2. A crisis worker and the police were dispatched to the scene.
3. The client was observed through the window lying still on the floor.
4. The police gained entry.
5. The ambulance was called, and the client was transported to the hospital.
6. Because of the client's earlier refusal of crisis assistance and mental health treatment, Crisis Services petitioned for an involuntary commitment, and this was approved.
7. The client was given medical treatment.

Stage 7: Follow-Up. The next morning, a follow-up phone call was made to the hospital, which indicated that the client had been admitted to the mental health unit following his medical stabilization.

WALK-IN CRISIS SERVICES

Any individual may appear at the office for services. Crisis staff will complete a crisis assessment encompassing the evaluation of the individual in crisis, as well as the social context in which the crisis is occurring. The psychosocial format of the evaluation enables the worker to determine the extent and acuity of all reported problem areas, the appropriate therapeutic response for crisis de-escalation, and any referrals indicated for ongoing treatment.

Case Scenario

A 19-year-old male was brought into the office by his parents because he was becoming "bizarre." The consumer was collecting urine in a bottle, collecting used female sanitary products, and making drawings of elaborate machinery. He also began talking about death and harmful effects of heavy metal music and was found burying heavy metal CDs in the backyard. This individual had no previous mental health history.

Roberts's (1996) seven-stage crisis intervention model was initiated.

Stage 1: Assess Lethality. The client's father phoned Crisis Services, expressing concern over bizarre behaviors exhibited by his son. There was no evidence of risk of harm to self or others but obvious evidence of a thought disorder. The father opted to bring his son into the office for a walk-in assessment.

Stage 2: Establish Rapport. Upon the client's arrival, it quickly became apparent that he had not been informed of the purpose of his visit. It was essential that the worker gather the client's perceptions of any difficulties he was having and seek his point of view on the issues mentioned by his father. The use of the worker's empathic communication skills allowed the client to express his thoughts, feelings, and experiences.

Stage 3: Identify Major Problem(s). The assessment of the client included information regarding his mental status. The identified problem was the emergence of a serious thought disorder. It was discovered through the parents' contributions that a diagnosis of mental illness, specifically schizophrenia, existed within the family history.

Stage 4: Deal With Feelings. The crisis worker focused on the thought processes of the client. The client was somewhat insightful at the time of assessment, indicating a realization that others viewed his behaviors as illogical. He, however, explained his delusional beliefs and behavior to the worker. The worker was able to communicate concerns in a nonjudgmental and nonconfrontive way to the client, who was agreeable to seeking inpatient mental health treatment. The client was, however, very fearful. The crisis worker dealt with the client's immediate feelings of fear by explaining the admission process and treatment in detail, as well as offering to accompany the client and family to advocate for their needs. This alliance between the worker and the client was an essential component in getting the client to accept further services.

Stage 5: Explore Alternatives. Various alternative treatment options were discussed with both the client and the family, including two inpatient treatment facilities. The crisis residential unit was also explained as another option if hospitalization was denied.

Stage 6: Develop Action Plan. The crisis worker, client and his parents decided on the following action plan:

1. Hospitalization at one of the inpatient facilities would be pursued.
2. The client was admitted to the inpatient mental health unit.
3. Support group information through AMIECO (Alliance for the Mentally Ill) was provided to the family.
4. Outpatient referrals were given to the client.

Stage 7: Follow-Up. Upon phone follow-up with the client's parents, it was learned that the client had started medications and was responding well. The parents were working actively with the hospital staff to assist in discharge planning.

MOBILE CRISIS SERVICES

Mobile crisis services may be provided by an individual crisis worker or by a team of two crisis staff members at the scene of the crisis. This service shows most clearly the social context in which the crisis is occurring, giving the worker extremely beneficial information and insights. A crisis assessment is completed at the scene, with the goal of quickly determining the most appropriate disposition to meet the individual's needs and obtain relief from distress. Recommendations will include a disposition in the least restrictive setting appropriate for the individual and the presenting crisis.

Case Scenario

Crisis Services received a call from a 30-year-old female who claimed to be calling for someone else. Her speech was slurred, and the information given was inconsistent. The caller did provide an address of the apparent individual in crisis. Because of possible safety issues and unknowns, Crisis Services responded with the police. The consumer was not answering her apartment door, but the landlord assisted us in gaining entry. The consumer was discovered unconscious with a suicide note, an empty bottle of lithium, and 12 serious self-inflicted stab wounds.

Roberts's (1996) seven-stage crisis intervention model was initiated.

Stage 1: Assess Lethality. During the initial phone contact, the client was providing misinformation to Crisis Services, claiming to be calling for a relative in distress. The crisis worker heard various inconsistencies in her story and also noticed the phone number from where the call was originating was also the phone number the caller was claiming to be her "relative's." The caller's slurred speech was another warning sign. The crisis worker did attempt to ask direct questions to assess suicidality, but the caller refused to respond to these questions. The only information gathered about this alleged relative was that she was going to kill herself by overdosing.

Stage 2: Establish Rapport. Through the worker's attentiveness, accurate listening skills, reassurance, and support, the caller was kept engaged and eventually provided an address. While the initial worker was attempting to elicit more information, another worker was able to identify with police assistance that the address provided was in fact the residence that was connected with the incoming phone number; therefore, it was determined that the caller was in fact the one in distress.

Stage 3: Identify Major Problems. Because of various inconsistencies and misinformation provided by the client on the initial phone contact, the major problems were unknown at the time of dispatch. It was not until the crisis worker and the police officer arrived on the scene that the critical nature of the problem was identified. The client would not answer her apartment door, but heavy, labored breathing was heard on the other side. The police forcefully gained entry to find the client naked and unresponsive on the bed with 12 serious self-inflicted stab wounds to her chest area. A suicide note and an empty bottle of lithium were found on the dresser.

Stages 4 and 5: Deal With Feelings and Explore Alternatives. Because of the client's unconscious state and critical condition, the crisis worker was unable to deal with the client's feelings or mutually explore treatment options.

Stage 6: Develop Action Plan. The police officer and crisis worker took control of the situation by doing the following:

1. The police immediately called for an ambulance.
2. The police and crisis worker attempted to stop the bleeding from the client's wounds.
3. The ambulance arrived and transported the client to the hospital.
4. Crisis Services petitioned for an involuntary commitment on an anonymous female (because her true identity was unknown), and this was approved.
5. The client was treated and medically admitted.

Stage 7: Follow-Up. A follow-up phone call was made to the hospital the next day, but the client was still in the intensive care unit (ICU). On day 2 the hospital revealed the client's identity to Crisis Services and reported that the client had eloped from a mental health unit earlier that week. The client was eventually transferred to the original hospital from which she had eloped because her family wanted to assist with her treatment and discharge planning.

Face-to-face contact with individuals in crisis may be provided either by a walk-in or by a mobile service. Crisis Services currently sees more than 350 individuals per month.

ACCESS TO CRISIS RESIDENTIAL UNIT #4

The crisis residential unit (CRU) provides residential accommodations and continuous, 24-hour supervision for individuals in crisis. This essential resource is another option in providing effective crisis intervention options. CRU is a truly collaborative program between Community Integration Inc, Crisis Services and Stairways (a separate community mental health provider). Crisis Services admits individuals to this unit after a thorough crisis assessment has been conducted and a physician's order from the on-call crisis physician has been obtained. In order to be considered for admission, the individuals must be medically stable, voluntary, and at least 18 years of age, and must present no overt threat to him- or herself or others. The CRU program is an eight-bed facility staffed and run by Stairways, Inc. CRU provides brief treatment (up to 5 days) as an alternative to hospitalization which focuses on problem solving and crisis management.

Services

The following services are provided at CRU (Stairways, 1999):

Assessment: A thorough assessment is conducted to identify and address an individual's emotional needs. In addition, a nursing health assessment is conducted to determine one's physical health needs.

Psychiatric assessment: Each client sees the psychiatric consultant on a daily basis in order to plan and monitor the best course of treatment.

Crisis counseling: Each client receives individual counseling to assist him or her in better understanding the crisis process and ways to effectively cope with the crisis situation. This involves initial problem identification and the development of a rehabilitation plan with a staff member.

Stabilization: The CRU program offers a safe, therapeutic environment in which clients in crisis may feel secure and better able to address their problems with as little stress as possible.

Medication monitoring: CRU offers medication monitoring and education to all clients so that the most appropriate medication regime can be developed.

Programming/psychoeducational groups: The following groups are provided:

1. *Stress reduction:* Reviews the effects of stress on the body and teaches clients to practice one of four techniques to alleviate the symptoms of stress. In addition, assertiveness and goal planning are taught so the clients might feel better able to take control over stressful life events and implement healthy coping strategies during times of stress.

2. *Conflict resolution:* Assists clients in learning how to objectively recognize, evaluate, and execute a healthy course of decision making for daily living. It also helps the client to examine the primary conflict or crisis that resulted in his or her CRU admission so that a prevention plan can be developed.

3. *Symptom management:* Offers suggestions to assist clients in coping with symptoms associated with mental illness. Symptoms covered during this group are modified to meet individual needs.

4. *Recreation:* Aims planned, structured, regular group activities at promoting social interaction and introducing new time-structuring ideas.

Program Steps

Admission

CRU's short-term program utilizes a problem-solving model to resolve crisis situations in the shortest time possible. The maximum stay in most cases will be 5 days; however, the treatment team has the authority to authorize an additional 5 days with clinical rationale. Crisis Services, with a signed release, provides CRU with a copy of the crisis assessment, the safety contract indicating the client's ability to maintain safety, and a verbal report. Crisis Services brings the client, clothes, and medication to the unit. Upon admission, CRU staff count and secure medications, search belongings for weapons or pills, review paperwork, determine the comfort needs of the client (need for food, bath, etc.), and orient the client to the unit and his or her assigned room (Bryan Hickman, personal communication, May 5, 1999).

Treatment Team

The treatment team is run by the clinical supervisor of Crisis Services and includes the supervisor of CRU and an administrative case manager from Case Management Support Services (who authorizes admissions and extensions). A homeless case manager is always in attendance to address the placement needs of the homeless. Additional providers are always welcome to attend to provide their input and recommendations.

The treatment team meets three times per week to review the client's progress, make recommendations for treatment needs, and make plans for discharge. Under certain situations, when there is a clinical need for additional stabilization, an extension of an additional 5 days may be granted by the majority vote of the three main members.

Hospitalization and/or Termination

If it is determined that a client is not making adequate progress at CRU, other accommodations may be necessary. If a client presents an immediate danger to him- or herself or others, Crisis Services will be contacted immediately to pursue hospitalization. Clients who are consistently unable or unwilling to follow the rules at CRU may be discharged after treatment team review and approval (Stairways, 1999).

Discharge

Discharges generally occur when the following conditions exist:

1. Short-term treatment goals are sufficiently met.
2. A client's psychiatric condition or level of functioning has been raised to allow him or her to move to a less restrictive setting.
3. Discharge planning and follow-up are arranged. (Stairways, 1999)

Individuals who choose to leave the unit against clinical advice (ACA) are asked to sign an ACA form. Crisis Services is contacted with every discharge and sent a discharge summary. Crisis Services attempts to follow up on all clients who left ACA.

EMERGENCY PSYCHIATRIC CRISIS STABILIZATION: CASE APPLICATION

Case Scenario

A 35-year-old male with a history of schizophrenia was referred to Crisis Services by another provider after being denied hospitalization. He was very paranoid and delusional, believing that people were attempting to break into his apartment at night. His speech was rapid and tangential, with loose associations. He talked about killing Jeffrey Dahmer and Hannibal Lecter and believed that he was a disciple of Satan. At times he was responding to internal stimuli, whispering to himself and making unusual gestures.

Roberts's (1996) seven-stage crisis intervention model was initiated.

Stage 1: Assess Lethality. By conducting a thorough crisis assessment, it was determined that the client was experiencing nihilistic delusions but was able to contract for safety, indicating he would seek help before acting on any thoughts to hurt himself or others. He had no previous assaultive history nor any current drug or alcohol use. Although psychotic, the client was cooperative and did not appear in danger of impulsively acting out; he did, however, present in a heightened state of anxiety. It seemed that he could benefit from a structured, supervised setting.

Stage 2: Establish Rapport. Understanding and support were two of the most essential skills utilized by the crisis worker in establishing rapport with the client. When intervening with a psychotic client, it is essential to not challenge his or her delusional system or "play along" with it. Challenging this fixed belief system will only create a sense of distrust by the client. Playing along with delusions or hallucinations could incite violence or mistrust when the worker is not aware of or fails to respond to those perceptions that the client is experiencing. The use of attending behavior (Kanel, 1999), such as active listening and supportive posture, were extremely helpful in letting the client know the worker was interested and was there to help.

Stage 3: Identify Major Problem(s). Several problems were identified during the crisis assessment. The client was psychiatrically decompensating. He was not on any medications and was not receiving any outpatient treatment at the time.

Stage 4: Deal With Feelings. The crisis worker, rather than focusing on the delusional beliefs, focused on the client's feelings of anxiety and fear of being alone in his apartment. The worker was able to address these feelings and suggest that together they explore options to make the client feel more comfortable.

Stage 5: Explore Alternatives. Because hospitalization was already denied, other alternative treatment options had to be explored. The CRU was described to the client, who was agreeable to being admitted to this unit. The client also signed a safety contract, indicating his ability to maintain control. The crisis worker received an admission order through the crisis psychiatrist on call, and the client was transported to CRU.

Stage 6: Develop Action Plan. Once the client admitted to CRU, the staff formulated an action plan with him. The following goals were discussed:

1. The client would start medications as prescribed by the CRU consulting psychiatrist.
2. The client would be given an intake appointment for ongoing outpatient services.

3. The client would participate in individual supportive counseling at CRU.

Stage 7: Follow-Up. At the CRU treatment team meeting (2 days after admission), it was determined that the client had started antipsychotic medication, and an intake appointment was scheduled for that day. On the fifth day, the usual day for discharge, the client's progress was discussed, and an extension was granted for an additional 5 days so that the client could get linked up with other mental health services and stabilize further. At the end of the 10-day stay, the client was transferred to a Stairways Group Home (Community Rehabilitation Residence), was on a waiting list for a case manager, was taking psychotropic medication, and had an outpatient follow-up appointment.

CRITICAL INCIDENT STRESS MANAGEMENT

Critical Incident Stress Management (CISM) is an integral part of any crisis intervention program. CISM includes a wide variety of techniques and interventions for individuals exposed to life-threatening or traumatic events (Mitchell & Everly, 1993). According to Everly (1995), CISM aims to prevent traumatic stress, mitigate the effects of the critical incident, and maximize recovery. The seven core components of CISM (see chapter 4, pp. 86–90) include the following:

1. *Precrisis preparation:* Educational programs are available on topics of stress, stress reactions, coping strategies, disaster response, and so on, to assist in mental preparedness.
2. *Individual crisis intervention:* Support services and individual crisis intervention.
3. *Large groups:* Large group crisis intervention and demobilization.
4. *Critical Incident Stress Debriefing (CISD):* A group meeting/discussion about a critical incident provided to those directly involved in the incident.
5. *Defusing:* A shortened version of a CISD that takes place about 12 hours after the event.
6. *Family CISM/organizational consultation:* A variety of services and education can be tailored for significant others whose loved one has experienced a critical incident.
7. *Follow-up/referral:* Telephone outreach, station visits, and various referrals can be made.

Case Scenario

At 9:38 P.M. on April 24, 1998, 14-year-old Andrew Wurst allegedly shot and killed teacher John Gillette at a middle school dance. Reportedly, he then proceeded to point the gun at the school principal and threatened to kill her. In just under 10 minutes, Andrew Wurst allegedly wounded another teacher, shot two fellow students, and changed the lives of thousands of people forever.

Everly and Mitchell (1999) have defined a "critical incident" as any event that can exert such a stressful impact so as to overwhelm an individual's usual coping mechanisms. A critical incident may also be thought of in the context of a traumatic event (i.e., an event outside the usual realm of human experience that would be markedly distressing to most individuals) and clearly has the potential to develop into an acute crisis (Everly & Mitchell, 1999).

Clearly, a middle school shooting, as described here, is a critical incident. On Saturday April 25, 1998, the Critical Incident Stress Management team was called upon to help deal with the aftermath of the James W. Parker Middle School shooting. Initially, 10 individuals specially trained in the core components of CISM (Mitchell & Everly, 1993) were dispatched to the school. They were to join a group of previously identified mental health professionals and clergy who were to provide crisis intervention services to the witnesses, families, faculty, staff, and community.

Beginning with a large group informational briefing conducted by the General McLane School District administration in collaboration with the Pennsylvania State Police, an overview of the events of the previous night was provided to the parents of the students and other interested community members. Information on such topics as the confirmation of John Gillette's death; the identification, condition, and location of those wounded; the identification and status of the perpetrator; and initial plans for intervention services was given. An opportunity to have questions answered was provided, and information about the reopening of the school was presented. Approximately 300 people were involved in the large-group briefing.

Immediately following the large-group informational briefing, small-group defusings were conducted. The defusings were used to provide participants with an opportunity to begin to process the information received during the large-group briefing, as well as to ask questions germane to their children. Information on "normal reactions to abnormal events" was presented and discussed. Information on stress management and coping techniques was reviewed.

The defusings were also used to begin to identify certain high-risk groups and individuals for more immediate or more intensive outreach and intervention. Defusings were done in groups of 3 to 10 individuals and lasted approximately 45 minutes. About 150 of the original 300 people involved in the large-group informational briefing were defused.

On Monday, April 27, the students of James W. Parker Middle School returned to classes. Prior to the start of the school day, a full faculty and staff meeting was held to discuss the crisis intervention services available. The logistics for obtaining services and for identifying particular needs and problems were discussed. Services were provided to teachers and staff by bringing people into the classrooms and by referring certain students or groups of students elsewhere. Teachers and other staff members were reminded that they, too, might need crisis intervention services, including respite from their classrooms. All were encouraged to take advantage of the services and support available.

During the first 2 weeks following the tragedy, members of the Crisis Services team provided a wide range of services in conjunction with other crisis responders. A few crisis workers served as triage specialists by identifying those exhibiting severe stress reactions and linking them to appropriate resources. These specialists also provided outreach by telephone to those students who initially did not immediately return to school. Parents were provided with information and support upon request.

In the days preceding John Gillette's funeral, the focus of the crisis responders was on small-group defusings and one-on-one interventions. Following the funeral, the efforts shifted to debriefing those most impacted by the tragedy. Priority was given to the chaperones and students at the dance, John Gillette's teaching team, the owners of the facility at which the dance was held, and the family of the wounded students. Other groups that received debriefing included the eighth-grade students not in attendance at the dance, the servers and caterers at the dance, and other teachers and staff.

Approximately 6 days after the shooting, the extent of the impact on the community as a whole started to become evident. At that point the administration of the General McLane School District began receiving telephone calls from other school districts that had either students and/or faculty members who were reacting to the shooting. For example, it was discovered that a church youth group from a neighboring community had been on an outing at a miniature golf course adjacent to the dining facility where the dance was held. Many of those students and adults witnessed either John Gillette's murder or the panic it caused. The CISM team provided these people with debriefing as well.

The faculty of two other neighboring school districts also required assistance. During John Gillette's long and distinguished career as a teacher, adviser, and coach, he had developed friendships throughout the area. He had also been employed by three different school districts during his tenure. Efforts were made to provide crisis intervention services for all those requesting it. When all was said and done, 37 debriefings were held for approximately 500 people.

Periodically throughout the subsequent weeks and months, additional crisis intervention services have been required, particularly during the ensuing legal proceedings. Follow-up services in the form of support groups and family counseling have been provided by other agencies. Many people have taken advantage of individual counseling services, although the exact number may never be known. In addition, members of Crisis Services and the CISM team continue to provide consultation to the General McLane School District administrators as they wrestle with life without their colleague and friend, John Gillette.

In the aftermath of the James W. Parker Middle School shooting, Crisis Services and the CISM team joined forces with other school and community responders to provide services to those affected by the shooting. A variety of crisis intervention techniques were utilized to mitigate the negative effects of this incident, including large-group information briefings, defusings, debriefings, one-on-one interventions, family and organizational consultation and referral, and follow-up services.

No other incident in the region has required as massive a response as this. In all, hundreds of people were impacted by this one critical incident. Long-term symptom relief for those involved has required the continued collaboration and cooperation of various crisis responders and the provision of a comprehensive array of group and individual intervention services.

Taking Care of Your Own: CISM for Crisis Workers

It is essential that crisis workers exposed to traumatic events be provided with CISM services when appropriate. CISM allows workers the opportunity to discuss the traumatic event, promotes group cohesion, educates them on stress reactions and coping techniques, and shows that the Crisis Services employer cares about the welfare of its employees.

As Maggio and Terenzi (1993) state, administrators must review potential critical incidents and pinpoint particular vulnerabilities of their agency. The following critical incidents have warranted the use of CISM techniques with the crisis workers of Crisis Services:

Nature of Incident	CISM Service
Suicide by gunshot (three times)	CISD
Suicide by hanging (two times)	CISD
Suicide attempt—severe stabbing	CISD
Dead body—several days old	CISD
Threat and assault on crisis worker	CISD
Shooting at crisis worker	Individual consult

Policies indicating response to these critical incidents, as well as aftercare and stress management for the crisis workers, should be in place in all crisis intervention agencies.

REFERENCES

Everly, G. (1995). *Innovations in disaster and trauma psychology: Applications in emergency services and disaster response.* Ellicott City, MD: Chevron.

Everly, G., & Mitchell, J. (1999). *Critical Incident Stress Management—a new era and standard of care in crisis intervention* (2nd ed.). Ellicott City, MD: Chevron.

Gilliland, B., & James, R. (1997). *Crisis intervention strategies* (3rd ed.). Pacific Grove, CA: Brooks/Cole.

Kanel, K. (1999). *A guide to crisis intervention.* Pacific Grove, CA: Brooks/Cole.

Maggio, M., & Terenzi, E. (1993, December). The impact of critical incident stress: Is your office prepared to respond? *Federal Probation, 57,* 10–16.

Mitchell, J., & Everly, G. (1993). *Critical Incident Stress Debriefing: An operations manual for the prevention of traumatic stress among emergency services and disaster workers.* Ellicott City, MD: Chevron.

Roberts, A. (1996). *Crisis management and brief treatment: Theory, technique and applications.* Belmont, CA: Wadsworth.

Stairways. (1999). *Crisis residential unit: A program handbook for clients, their family and friends.* Erie, PA: Author.

17

Crisis Intervention in the Hospital Emergency Room

MARY BOES
VIRGINIA MCDERMOTT

Case 1

When paramedics found Mary Winston, age 68, face down in a pool of blood after answering the call for "code 52," a shooting, they didn't expect to find any signs of life. They had entered the darkened house with flashlights, for there was no electricity. Six through-and-through gunshot wounds had pierced her body: two in her neck, one in each arm, and two in her abdomen. As they turned her over from the puddle of thick, congealed blood, she slowly took a breath and continued shallow breathing, her eyes wide open. "We can see you're a strong lady, Mary."

Once Mary was in the emergency room (ER), the social worker was called to notify the family. Soon a large crowd of people of all ages gathered in the ER waiting area. Before security could be called, two daughters rushed into the trauma room screaming and crying. One rolled over and over on the floor, impeding the medical team's work. The other jumped up and smashed all the windows in the ER door. Mary Winston was the sole matriarch of an extended family. She raised 13 grandchildren as her own. She was the only nurturing presence and figure of stability in a neighborhood where drug lords reigned over the night and poverty and hunger ruled the days.

Upon hearing "Mary might not make it," 30 people reacted in their joint grief by stampeding through the hospital, banging on patients' doors. One

13-year-old who fainted in the bathroom was assisted to a stretcher by a registered nurse, but when he woke up he punched her in the stomach. "You're killing Grandma!" he yelled. He misinterpreted the emergency procedures the medical staff were doing in the ER as signs they were hurting Mary. While Mary was rushed to surgery, this chaotic crisis enveloped the hospital. The family believed the very foundation of their lives was being threatened.

Case 2

One hectic, rainy night, paramedics of Philadelphia, Pennsylvania, were called to the scene of a car crash. By assessing the severe damage of the vehicle, which had rolled over, they realized that any victim would be severely injured, if not dead. They rushed to the side of Chris Jones, age 35, who was covered with blood, screaming, "I can't breathe!" and cursing at their struggles to help him. Upon closer examination the paramedics found a deep laceration on the back of Chris's head and blood coming from his left ear. They immobilized his neck and back, in case there were any spinal fractures. Intoxicated and driving at high speed, he had been thrown from the car, smashing head first through the windshield and then banging his head on the pavement.

"Do you remember what happened?" "No," he replied. A loss of consciousness at the time of crash could imply a severe concussion or massive head injury. (Cambell, 1994)

Case 3

Mark Smith, a 30-year-old construction worker, had just undergone a highly contested and painful divorce. After drinking one third of a bottle of Jack Daniels and 6 beers, he passed out on his sofa. His still-smoldering cigarette fell from his fingers onto the cushions. By dawn, the couch ignited, engulfing Mark in flames. He never regained consciousness. The fire spread rapidly through the small house. A neighbor on his way to work heard Mark's 9-year-old son, Paul, screaming in panic at the front window. Racing to the porch, he smashed the glass and pulled the child to safety. The fire company and paramedics had been called by this time, and they rushed Paul, suffering from severe smoke inhalation and second degree burns, to the ER. Some of his clothing and skin were still smoldering.

These three cases portray a type of "quick trajectory" that can occur at any time and any place. A person in good health may suddenly become the victim of an automobile accident, a small child may fall into a swimming pool, an "unloaded gun" may discharge, a restaurant patron may choke, a person with a history of heart disease may suffer another attack. These are just some emergency situations that can result in death.

Several types of problems are more likely to arise when there is a life-or-death emergency in a community setting as compared with a health care facility:

- Panic: "What's happening? What should we do?"
- Inappropriate action: "Let's get him on his feet . . . "
- Misinterpreting the situation: "Stop whining and go back to bed!"
- Minimizing the danger: "I don't need a doctor. It's just a little indigestion."
- Preoccupied by own concerns: "I'd better clean this place up before I call anybody."

Glaser and Strauss are among those who maintain that the American hospital system is best prepared to cope with emergencies. Human and technological resources are mustered most impressively when there is an acute life-or-death crisis. The ER, the intensive care unit (ICU), and the perpetual readiness of specialists to rush to the scene are lifesaving resources that Americans have come to expect from the modern medical center.

Time truly is of the essence when a patient is defined as being on an expected quick trajectory. The staff organizes itself with precision to make the most effective use of the time that remains on the side of life. This contrasts vividly with the more leisurely, almost drifting pattern that surrounds a patient on a lingering trajectory. As staff members devote themselves to the patient's urgent needs, there may be a series of redefinitions in their minds—for example, "He is out of immediate danger but probably will not survive very long" changes to "I think he has passed the crisis point and has the possibility of complete recovery."

The crisis trajectory imposes another condition on both the patient and those concerned. The patient is not in acute danger at the moment, but his or her life might suddenly be threatened at any time. This creates an especially tense situation that will persist until the patient's condition improves enough so that he or she is out of danger or until the crisis actually arrives and rescue efforts can be made.

Different from all of these is the will-probably-die trajectory. The staff believes that nothing effective can be done. The aim is to keep the patient as comfortable as possible and wait for the end to come, usually within hours or days. This might be the accident victim who is beyond saving or the individual whose suicide attempt failed to end life immediately but did result in a terminal course.

These are not the only types of expected quick trajectories, but they illustrate the range of experience and situations that exist among those who face death in the near future. There are also some common problems that arise in connection with the expected quick trajectory. The family, for example, is likely to be close by the patient. Glaser and Strauss emphasize the possible disruptive effects of this proximity based upon their direct observations. The presence of the family confronts the staff with more demand for interaction and communication. What should those people in the waiting room be told? Who should tell them? Is this the time to prepare them for the bad news, or can it be postponed a little longer? Should all the family be told at once, or is there one person in particular who should be relied on to grasp the situation first? The staff must somehow come to terms with the needs of the family while still carrying out treatment. Obviously, this is a situation to challenge the ER social worker's judgment and interpersonal skills. ER staff traditionally have kept a barrier between the patient and the rest of his family as medical lifesaving procedures are under way.

The family are relegated to the waiting room. More enlightened establishments now permit family to be at the bedside and even to remain there during the event of a "code" if they express this wish. The Emergency Nurses Association supports family-witnessed resusitation. "Family" includes any person who has an established, mutual relationship with the patient (Goldsworth & Bailey, 1998).

The significance of the interpersonal setting in which dying takes place is emphasized again by the unexpected quick trajectory. Personnel in the ER, for example, expect to be called on for immediate life-or-death measures. The experienced ER team adjusts quickly to situations that might immobilize most other people. But in other areas of the same hospital the staff is likely to have a pattern of functioning and a belief system that are less attuned to a sudden turn of events: "The appearance of the unexpected quick trajectory constitutes crisis. On these wards there is no general preparation for quick dying trajectories—at least of certain kinds—and the work and sentimental orders of the ward blow up when they occur" (Glaser & Strauss, 1968, p. 121).

Emergency rooms prime their staff for the sudden onset of medical/surgical distress. Time is of the essence in treatment in order to save lives. Emergency rooms serve as portals for the most vulnerable members of our population. Early identification in the ER of individual and family psychosocial stressors, which are often the precipitants to an acute crisis, can lead to crisis stabilization and thereby avert a full-blown crisis at a later stage. Crisis social workers can be integral in helping hospitals develop programs that minimize the chance that victims of abuse or sudden trauma are overlooked (Myer & Hanna, 1996).

This chapter begins with an overview of crisis intervention in the ER. Objective data are presented concerning the type and frequency of ER visits. Next we will consider the subjective reality. A highlight of this chapter is the presentation of protocol for crisis intervention in the ER, a protocol devised from one of the author's 8 years of social work experience in an inner-city hospital emergency services department. Throughout this chapter, the focus is on the role of the social worker in situations ranging from moderate to severe crisis.

OVERVIEW

For the purposes of determining the nature of ER work today, one of the authors constructed a brief questionnaire, which was sent to 25 hospitals across the United States. The nonrandom sample was of health care settings as diverse as a 65-bed hospital with one social worker in a town with a population of 9,000 in Caribou, Maine, to Cedar-Sinai Health System in Beverly Hills, California, a 1,200-bed hospital with 30 social workers and 20 case managers. Eleven hospitals responded. Respondents were asked to list the most common urgent and nonurgent problems encountered in the ER.

Urgent conditions are those requiring immediate attention within a few hours; there is possible danger to the patient if medically unattended. Disorder is acute (Weinerman, 1966). In order of most to least common, hospital staff listed motor vehicle accidents, gunshot wounds, child abuse, domestic violence, and self-inflicted injuries as the most common reason for coming to an ER.

SOCIAL WORK STAFFING

In Caribou, Maine, there is only one social worker assigned to the entire 65-bed hospital. There is also only one social worker scheduled from 3:00 P.M. to 11:30 P.M. Thursday through Monday in the Emergency Department at University Hospital and Medical Center in Stony Brook, New York. However, the Social Work Services at Stony Brook employs 30 full-time social workers (all MSW level or higher). Twenty-two social workers are assigned Emergency Department rotation to cover on weekdays when the assigned social worker is absent or not scheduled to work. In addition, on-call/recall coverage is provided by social work staff for overnight coverage to the Emergency Department (and hospital-wide).

The Emergency Department at Stony Brook consists of triage to immediate care (fast track). In the main emergency room and shock-trauma area all of the nurses have at least an RN degree. The Emergency Department employs an Administrative Duty Nurse (ADN) and 2 nurse educators. Nurses assigned to the shock-trauma area are highly trained and exceptionally well skilled. Within the shock-trauma area (the trauma centers), the social worker is frequently called upon to address issues of grief, bereavement, crisis intervention, locating family of patients, and informing relatives of patients' situations. The Shock Trauma area receives many traumatic injuries and traumatic illnesses, including motor vehicle accidents, cardiac arrest, burn injuries, overdoses, falls, pedestrians struck by cars, and so on. Adjacent to the Emergency Department is the Comprehensive Psychiatric Emergency Program (CPEP), which is staffed with five psychiatric social workers and psychiatric nurses. Following medical clearance from the Emergency Department, patients who have inflicted self-harm or experienced altered mental status are evaluated by CPEP staff. CPEP also receives patients from triage who have no medical needs and patients from other psychiatric facilities.

INCIDENCE AND
PREVALENCE ESTIMATES

Data from the National Hospital Ambulatory Care Surveys for 1995 reveal that trauma is the number one killer of Americans under the age of 37 and the fourth-leading cause of death overall (U.S. National Center for Health Statistics, 1997). Common examples of life-threatening trauma which are pervasive are gang-related shootings, domestic violence, and child abuse.

Motor vehicle accidents alone kill more than 43,000 people each year, and over 4 million car crash victims end up in the ER. Burns are one of the most traumatic injuries sustained by the body. The following statistics reveal just how devastating this one example of trauma can be.

Each year in the United States, approximately 2 million burn injuries occur, and half of these require medical attention. Approximately 70,000 of those patients seeking medical attention suffer potentially life-threatening injuries, either from the high percentage of skin area involved or from complications from smoke inhalation and other concomitant injuries. Of the other 1 million people with burns who do not seek medical attention, about 10,000 die at the scene of the accident (Demling & LaLonde, 1989). The rest of the injuries are minor, and treatment with basic first aid at home is adequate.

Burns are the third-leading cause of accidental deaths in the United States, and causes vary among different age-groups. The highest risk is among those 18 to 30 years old. Males are twice as likely to be burned as females (Beare & Myers, 1994).

A severe thermal injury can be one of the most devastating physical and psychological injuries a person can suffer. The fire death rate in the United States (57.1 deaths per million population) is the second highest in the world and the highest of all industrialized countries—almost twice that of second-ranking Canada (29.7 deaths per million).

Table 17.1 gives a breakdown for general characteristics of persons treated in ERs across the United States. Data are for nonfederal short-stay and general hospitals.

Typically, ER patients can be prioritized by placing them in one of four categories (Sheehy, 1998). The emergent group requires immediate attention and includes cardiac arrest and trauma codes. Urgent and nonurgent cases fall into the intermediate categories. Urgent are problems that should be treated as soon as possible—generally within 1 to 2 hours; these include obvious fractures and acute abdominal pain. Nonurgent are problems that need to be treated sometime today and not necessarily in the ER; these include sore throat and simple laceration. The "delayed" group can be transferred to a "walk-in" location; these include conditions that do not require ER care at all and can be seen at any time, like most rashes or a previous

Table 17.1   Visits to Hospital Emergency
Departments: 1995 and 1996

Characteristic	1995	1996
All visits	96,545	90,347
Age		
Under 15 years old	22,709	20,872
15 to 24 years old	15,681	14,366
25 to 44 years old	30,086	28,036
45 to 64 years old	13,978	13,745
65 to 74 years old	6,057	5,945
74 years old and over	8,033	7,382
Sex		
Male	46,501	42,473
Female	50,044	47,873
Race		
White	74,593	68,702
Black	19,284	19,604
Asian/Pacific islander	1,963	1,639
American Indian	705	401
Expected Source of Payment[a]		
Insurance[b]	75,890	70,514
Blue Cross/Blue Shield	10,987	10,084
Other private insurance	25,056	24,314
Medicare	14,949	14,462
Medicaid	22,041	19,884
Worker's Compensation	3,776	3,058
Other source of insurance	4,544	4,254
Unknown source of insurance	3,474	2,978
Self pay	16,113	15,188
No charge	519	1,097
Other	2,471	1,874
Unknown source of payment	1,552	1,674

a. More than one reported source of payment may be reported.

b. Equal to all visits minus self-pay, no charge, other source, and no answer

Source: U.S. National Center for Health Statistics: Advance Data Nos. 293 and 294. December 17, 1997, and prior issues.

wound that needs checking (Emergency Nurses Association Nursing Practise Committee, 1992). Table 17.2 provides a more detailed list of conditions included in each triage category.

Social work services in the ER are critical because this is the time when nurses and physicians are being overwhelmed by the traumatic and emergency surgical needs of the patient. Soon after or at the same time that the person is medically stabilized, the social worker needs to begin psychosocial

Table 17.2   Care in the Hospital Emergency Room

Emergent	Urgent	Nonurgent	Delayed
Cardiac complaints like chest pains	Acute abdominal pain	Common cold	Exams
Codes	Acute headache	Minor injury	Prescription refill
Conditions associated with airway compromise (e.g., foreign bodies, dystonia allergic reactions, and angioedema)	Cellulitis	Simple laceration	Rash
	Major laceration	Sore throat	Request for a work slip
	Nonurgent complaint in a patient with an underlying medical condition like diabetes, cancer, hypertension, or AIDS	Sprains or strains	Suture removal
Eye injuries		Toothache	Wound check
Falls or jumps of more than 20 feet			
Hemodynamic instability	Obvious fracture		
Hypo- or hyperglycemia	Sexual assault		
Inhalation injuries			
Limb amputations			
Respiratory distress			
Seizures and post-seizure states			
Serious motor vehicle accident cases			
Stroke			
Trauma, including major facial injuries and penetrating injuries to the head, neck, chest, abdomen, axilla, shoulder, groin, or buttocks			

protocol. For instance, a greater variety of social issues present to the ER. It is through the ER that problems such as homelessness, domestic violence, rape, and drug abuse have been documented (Centers for Disease Control and Prevention, 1993; Padgett & Brodsky, 1992). In addition, ER social work demands quick, immediate attention—the time frame for assisting a patient is short, and the patient is invariably in a state of crisis. For these reasons, accurate assessment and intervention are essential for effective ER social work.

The following is a protocol used to ensure continuity of social work coverage in one ER of the two hospitals used in a previous study by the author (Boes, 1997). Where locally available resources are provided, social workers would use the resources provided in their own communities. Telephone numbers were listed in the actual protocol, but they were deleted for this chapter.

PROTOCOL FOR CRISIS INTERVENTION IN THE EMERGENCY ROOM

I. Code/Trauma

ASSESSMENT

In a code or trauma situation, the assessment will vary according to the patient's medical severity. You will need to monitor the patient's medical condition and intervene accordingly.

INTERVENTION

If the family members are present:

- Your goal is to keep them calm and informed. Obtain any possible medical information on the patient's status (even if it is only "they are running several tests now") to relay to the family for reassurance. Try to keep them calmly in the waiting room. Inform them that a physician or nurse will speak to them as soon as possible.
- It is also helpful to refocus their anxiety. Encouraging them to talk is often helpful. Ask them who they are, what their relationship to the patient is, what happened, how they got there or learned of it, if there are other family members or clergy that need to be contacted.

If the patient is unidentified or no family or friends are present:

- Check with the ambulance/police/fire rescue that brought in the patient. Inquire where the patient was found, if anyone at the scene knew the patient, and so on, for clues.
- Check the hospital's records for any previous admissions that could provide name, address, or phone numbers.
- It may be necessary to search the patient's belongings for a piece of information. Use gloves to prevent contact with blood or body fluids.
- Use the Coles Directory. This will provide phone numbers for a given address. You can then proceed to contact neighbors.
- If the patient's address does not have a phone number, it is possible to send a police officer to the home with a message. You need to contact the appropriate district to request this service.

If the code or trauma has resulted in the patient's death:

- Provide emotional support.
- Offer to call any family members or clergy if they desire, or explain that they are free to make unlimited telephone calls and accompany them.
- If family members wish to view the body, accompany them for support. It is helpful to prepare them for what they may see (i.e., tubes, discoloration), as well as providing tissues, chairs, or anything that might aid with their immediate comfort.
- Explain that they need only contact the funeral home when they feel able; the funeral home will then locate and retrieve the body from the morgue or the medical examiner's office if they requested an autopsy.
- Make sure that the patient's belongings or valuables are given to the appropriate person.

- If possible, ensure that a spouse or family member does not go home alone or to an empty house.

II. Protective/Abuse

ASSESSMENT

Visually assess the patient for the following suspicious injuries:

- Bruises of several colors (indicating they were sustained at different times)
- Bruises that have odd shapes, are clustered, or are located in unusual places for an accident to occur
- Retinal damage (from being shaken)
- Orbital or facial fractures (if patient was not in a car accident, suspect domestic abuse)
- Rope burns or marks from restraints
- Signs of hair pulling (bald spots, loose hair, or swollen scalp)
- "Fearful behavior" (the patient may speak very softly, look around when answering, question the confidentiality of the interview)

Verbal inquiries:

- Conduct a patient interview without family present, then conduct an interview with the accompanying person to see if there is a conflict of information.
- What were the events that led to the patient's admission?
- Who comprises the patient's household (obtain the ages and health of members)
- Were any family members ever treated for mental health problems?
- What is the patient's past medical history? (you are looking for a pattern of "doctor hopping" or similar injuries in the past)
- How does their caretaker express anger?

INTERVENTION

If child abuse is suspected:

- Patient will be stabilized and transferred to Children's Hospital for further treatment.
- We are required by law to report if abuse is suspected. We also must inform the caretaker that we are doing so. There is no liability for any report made in good faith. Referrals should be made to the state child abuse hotline, as well as the local child protective service agency.

  ▨ CHILD ABUSE STATE HOTLINE: _____

  ▨ CHILD ABUSE CITY HOTLINE: _____

- Interview the mother privately to ascertain if she is also a victim of abuse.

If spousal abuse is suspected:

- Encourage the victim to file a police report.
- Explain that for her safety, the victim could have the abuser arrested and held in custody and/or take out a Protection Against Abuse order on a 24-hour basis for up to 1 year.

- Encourage the victim to call a hotline from the ER; accompany and assist her.

  ▨ WOMEN AGAINST ABUSE: _____
  (24-hour counseling, shelter for women and children, and legal counsel)

  ▨ WOMEN IN TRANSITION: _____
  (24-hour counseling)

- Be alert for abuse and neglect in the children.

If elder abuse is suspected:

- Follow the same procedures as you would for spousal abuse and make a refer-ral to elder abuse protective services and a hotline for advocates for the rights of the infirm elderly.

  ▨ PCA ELDER ABUSE PROTECTIVE SERVICES: _____

  ▨ CARIE (Coalition of Advocates for the Rights of the Infirm-Elderly) HOTLINE: _____

If the patient alleges rape:

- Patient will be medically stabilized and transferred to a rape crisis treatment center if not available at the hospital.

  ▨ WOAR (Women Organized Against Rape): _____

III. Psychiatric

ASSESSMENT

- *Is the patient exhibiting behavior that would pose a danger to him- or herself or others?* If so, contact the nurses to determine if restraints are necessary.
- Review patient's chart, consult with accompanying person and with physicians regarding the patient's condition and past mental health history.
- Observe and interview patient for signs of mental illness (agitation, depression, suicide attempt/overdose, disorientation, etc.).
- Obtain the usual historical information on the presenting problem (what are the symptoms, how long has the victim been experiencing them, what is the victim's living situation, what were the precipitating events leading to admis-sion, any history of drugs, alcohol, arrests, medical treatment, etc.).

INTERVENTION

If the patient is medically cleared:

- And they indicate an acute threat to harm themselves or others, you MUST CALL FOR a psychiatric consult for evaluation.
- If psychiatry feels the patient requires inpatient treatment and the patient is willing to enter treatment VOLUNTARILY:
  * If the patient does have insurance, the psychiatrist will arrange for place-ment.
  * If the patient does not have insurance, social work will arrange for placement though the catchment system. The patient's catchment area cannot refuse placement for any reason.

* Provide the patient with a "201" (voluntary commitment) form (located in the emergency room), which they are required to sign.
* If the psychiatrist has evaluated for inpatient treatment and the patient is resistant, the following procedure is for INVOLUNTARY placement:
  * Obtain a "302" (involuntary commitment) form.
  * The petitioner for placement *must* be the ER physician (if no family member who has witnessed the patient's behavior over the past 30 days is available or willing to petition); the "examining physician" portion is to be filled out by the psychiatrist. SOCIAL WORKER IS NOT TO FILL OUT ANY PARTS OF THIS FORM.
  * Contact the Mental Health Delegate (M–F: #_____, Weekends: #_____) to arrange for a receiving facility.
  * The patient must be transferred to the facility by ambulance.

If the patient is not medically cleared (admitted):

* And the patient is admitted to the hospital VOLUNTARILY:
  * It is only necessary to call a psychiatrist if you, in consult with the ER physicians and nurses, feel suicidal precautions are necessary. Psychiatry will then make the ultimate determination if one-on-one companionship is required.
* If the patient REFUSES medical admission:
  * Contact an administrator. The administrator will need to contact City Hall, which will find a judge on call to issue an emergency medical commitment.

If the patient is homeless with a chronic mental illness:

* You can contact the Mobile Mental Health Unit, which places this population in supervised shelters.

IV. Shelter

ASSESSMENT

* First ascertain where the patient stayed last night or if he or she has friends or family in the area who can provide shelter.
* How long has the patient been without shelter?
* Has he or she ever been to a shelter before? If so, which one?
* Would he or she be willing to go to a shelter now if a bed were available? (Patients must be ambulatory for the shelter to accept them).

INTERVENTION

* If the patient is willing, contact a shelter (a comprehensive listing of shelters is posted in the ER) to see if a bed is available.
* If there is evidence of a mental health problem, contact the city's Mobile Mental Health Unit to arrange for evaluation.
* The Ridge Avenue Shelter (for men only) will always accept people for emergency shelter between 5:00 P.M. and 10:00 P.M., even if it is full because it sends them out to other shelters.
* If there are no beds available anywhere, you can call the Office of Service to Homeless Adults (OSHA): Monday–Friday, #_____; after 4:00 P.M. and weekends, #_____ for outreach. Shelters are available for men only; for women and children; and for families. Referrals for emergency shelter can be made during the evening as well as daytime hours.

V. Substance Abuse

ASSESSMENT

- When was the substance last used? What was it? How much was used? What was the method (IV, smoked, snorted, in combination with other substances)?
- How often does the patient use? How long has he or she been drinking or using?
- What physical symptoms is he or she experiencing (i.e., shakes, blackouts, seizures)?
- Has the patient ever been in detoxification or rehabilitation? When, where, and what was the result?
- Is the patient interested in or willing to enter a detoxification or rehabilitation program right now? If so, does he or she want an inpatient or outpatient program?
- What type of insurance does the patient have? The patient must have him or her insurance card as proof of coverage.
- If the patient does not have insurance, the one place that will accept his or her is DRC (Diagnostic and Rehabilitation Center).
- Be alert for unsafe environment for children.

INTERVENTION

If the patient is interested in entering a detoxification or rehabilitation program:

- Make sure he or she is medically cleared by the medical staff
- Make sure that the patient is willing to go immediately from the ER. We will provide a cab voucher if he or she unable to pay.
- Contact the patient's insurance company (HMO, Blue Cross, Healthpass, etc.) for precertification. The insurance company will determine where the patient will be referred. The insurance company will call the facility to find a bed and confirm admission; however, this is something we often do to expedite the admission process.

If the patient is uninterested in detoxification or rehabilitation at this time, or would like outpatient help, or it is after hours and facilities are no longer admitting:

- Provide the patient with the pertinent information (the name, address, phone number, and contact person at the agency) and explain the procedure so that he or she can follow up the next day or whenever ready.

There are assessment and intervention protocols for domestic violence in hospitals and mental health settings. The reader is referred to chapter 8 in this book. In addition, for a comprehensive examination of the emerging roles for the ER social worker and clinical nurse specialist with battered women, see Boes (1998).

APPLICATION OF ROBERTS'S SEVEN-STAGE CRISIS INTERVENTION MODEL

It is paramount that the ER social worker be present from the first moment that the crisis presents to the ER. The social worker must be considered an integral part of the trauma team, and when the words "trauma alert" are heard paged throughout the hospital, the social worker, as well as doctors, nurses, respiratory therapists, and lab technicians, will race to the scene. The social worker must promptly initiate interventions after a quick assessment. Effective intervention with trauma survivors in crisis requires a careful assessment of individual, family, and environmental factors. A crisis by definition is short term and overwhelming. According to Roberts (1990), a crisis can be described as an emotionally distressing change that interferes with one's ability to function.

Roberts (1996, pp. 26–29), describes seven stages of working through crisis: (a) assessing lethality and safety needs, (b) establishing rapport and communication, (c) identifying the major problems, (d) dealing with feelings and providing support, (e) exploring possible alternatives, (f) formulating an action plan, and (g) providing follow-up. Roberts's seven-stage model applies to a broad range of crises. This model provides a sturdy framework for the accurate assessment and immediate intervention, essential for ER social work.

> Crisis workers, however, should recognize that this model is not set up to be rigidly followed in a step-by-step fashion. Instead, the model should be viewed as fluid and adaptable for work in emergency departments. For example, as new information is made available, such as a patient's condition unexpectedly deteriorating, the patient, family members, and even staff may experience further reactions. Crisis workers, therefore, must be attentive to changes in the clients and the environment that might influence reactions to the crisis event. As changes occur, crisis workers must be flexible in moving to that part of the model that best corresponds with current circumstances. (Myer & Hanna, 1996, p. 42)

Use of such a fluid model is invaluable in consideration of the three case studies presented in this chapter.

(Mary Winston)

The case of Mary Winston, gunshot victim, readily lends itself to an application of Roberts's model, beginning with assessing lethality and safety needs. Immediately, the social worker would need to call security to remove the daughter who smashed the ER windows, as well as the one who dropped onto the floor thus interfering with the work of the trauma team. It takes all of the interpersonal skills that a social worker can muster to reach out to enlist the daughters' cooperation to come with her to a private room. The urgency of the situation may necessitate a call to the nursing supervisor to evaluate the girl to determine if a sedative may be warranted so that the team may continue its efforts.

Security would again need to be alerted to the fact that 30 people are stampeding through the hospital banging on patients' doors. A neutral location needs to be established, perhaps the hospital dining room, which could accommodate 30 people at once, so that they are removed from the patient floors to assure safety for themselves and patients within the hospital. The main problem with regard to establishing rapport and communication is that Mary had been such an integral part of so many lives. The level of emotion is so intense, and the ability to absorb so many crises simultaneously is indeed a challenge to say the least.

Once the 30 people are assembled, an immediate priority is that of answering as many concerns as may be addressed. The social worker needs to establish guidelines (e.g., two people at a time could visit Mary in the trauma room). Before anyone could enter the trauma room, the social worker would need to have the visit okayed with the "code captain," the physician in charge of running the "code," the resuscitation effort. Once this permission was granted, the ER social worker would accompany two people into the trauma room, where chairs would be available should anyone look faint and tissues would be available for the family's use. In the meantime, the remaining people could be assigned a task such as writing their name, address, phone number, and relationship to Mary. The assigning of a small task may be useful in refocusing attention. While Mary is in surgery, beverages and snacks could be provided to assist with comfort. In establishing rapport, the social worker will encourage the family to tell stories about Mary or to recount how they learned of Mary's tragedy and will determine who the spokesperson or spokespersons for the family will be.

Mary made it through surgery and was now in the recovery room. The surgeons were notified that Mary's family was in the dining room. The surgeons came to the dining area and informed the family that Mary would be transferred from the recovery room to the intensive care unit. It was explained to the family that only two people could spend the night. Beds were made up for two visitors to stay in the patient lounge overnight; provisions were made for transportation home for the other family members, and consideration was given so that no one would be alone.

As the family was about to leave the hospital, Mary died, and her death initiated a crisis all over again. One of the girls vomited, and the social worker took her to the ER for treatment. The family was offered the option of viewing the body, which everyone wished to do. The social worker accompanied two people at a time to the room. An option of calling any clergy was also provided by the social worker, as well as a discussion of whether the family wished for an autopsy. The specifics of what would occur next were explained to the family. If they wanted an autopsy, the body would be transported to the funeral home from the medical examiner's office; if not, it would be picked up from the morgue in the hospital. The social worker offered to call any funeral home and provided the family with telephone use to speak with anyone they wished to at that time.

Due to the suddenness of Mary's death, there was extreme shock and anger. As he was about to leave, one of the boys said that he would be back with a gun. The Philadelphia police were notified of this threat, and came to the hospital. The main problem appeared to be that Mary was so important to so many people that it seemed she was indispensable. How would the 13 grandchildren whom she had raised cope with such a great loss? The ER social worker helped the family deal with the immediate crisis and offered assistance in the days to come. Fortunately, Mary's family was large, and numerous options were available to them. The social worker dealt with the feelings of the young boy who thought the doctors were killing his grandmother. The social worker explained to the boy that his grandmother's chest had to be cracked so that the physician could massage her heart to help it start beating again. Although it looked like the doctor was torturing his grandmother, he was doing his best to save her life.

Many of the situations in which an ER social worker finds him- or herself are extremely complex and complicated. The task, as was true in this case, was to continually prioritize many crises that were occurring simultaneously. Many alternatives were explored, from attempting to provide as much support, comfort, and privacy to the family as possible during the time at the hospital to trying to identify who may care for whom when the family left the hospital.

A very important stage of Roberts's model that can be easily overlooked, especially by an ER social worker who is continually dealing with crisis within the hospital, is that of follow-up. The emotional and physical demands are such that if not given careful consideration, this most important final step can be easily neglected. The family has begun to trust someone who so quickly fades from their lives. Due to this most demanding work, it may be rare that a social worker will take time to attend a funeral, send a sympathy card, or make the crucial follow-up phone calls to assure that the family is safe and to also acknowledge their sadness and assist with referrals and emotional support as needed.

Chris Jones

For the social worker to intervene effectively, the seven stages of Roberts's crisis intervention model are followed.

Plan and Conduct a Thorough Assessment: Assess Lethality and Safety Needs

As paramedics immediately exchange with the medical team the status of Chris's condition, he says, "I can't breathe." The social worker can help with identification of the client through a search of the patient's belongings. Chris was incoherent, and it was difficult to ascertain whether it was effects of the intoxication or of severe head injury. Chris's orbital area and facial structure were all freely mobile and fractured. A CAT scan revealed that he had swelling in his brain. Chris's conditoin could quickly deteriorate as "head trauma is an evolving injury, the product of many secondary insults, not just the primary lesions" (Jastremski, 1998, p. 42). Someone must promptly try to notify his next of kin. Chris's wallet contains the address of his father, and that number is unlisted. The social worker uses the Coles Directory, a directory organized by address block, to call the next-door neighbor. The neighbor agrees to attempt to establish contact with his father, and his effort is successful. Chris has suffered a severe skull fracture, and his brain is swelling; he is lapsing into a coma.

Establish Rapport and Communication

The social worker first meets the family in a private room with the doctor to describe the dimension of the problem. The social worker uses warmth, acceptance, empathy, caring, and reassurance to provide support and convey the feeling that he or she is on the family's side and will be a helping person. Crying or angry outbursts are not discouraged but rather are seen as a positive release of feeling. Only when feelings seem out of control, such as in extreme rage or despondency, should the social worker shift to help the family member concentrate on thinking rather than feeling (Stuart & Sundeen, 1995).

Identify the Major Problems

Helping to ease the impact of the initial wave of shock and grief reaction to the crisis, the social worker escorts the family to the bedside after first warning them that the sight of all the lines and tubes can be distressing. Sensing the family's feeling of powerlessness, she will encourage communication between the family and Chris through nonverbals such as hand holding and touch. They first are afraid to go near him. Even if he cannot respond, she emphasizes, perhaps he can still hear them, so it is important to talk hopefully and lovingly.

Returning the patient and his family to their previous level of functioning is the goal of crisis intervention. Yet it is uncertain whether Chris will ever emerge from his coma. Even if he should recover, the rehabilitation process will be long, slow, and difficult. Initially, Chris's mood and affect will be erratic, with many angry outbursts. He might even have some amnesia, with a permanent change of his personality. All this needs to be explained to the family.

He might have to relearn basic skills such as reading, writing, and walking through long months of therapy. His role as breadwinner for the family is threatened for the short term and, perhaps, permanently. "During this phase, the clinician should help the family to focus on the most important problem, as they see it, by having them rank and prioritize several problems and the harmful or potentially threatening aspect of the number one problem. It is important and most productive to help the clients ventilate about the precipitating event: This will lead to problem identification" (Roberts, 1996, p. 28).

Deal With Feelings and Provide Support

This stage involves active listening, communicating with warmth and reassurance, nonjudgmental statements, and validation with accurate empathic statements. The family in crisis might have multiple mood swings throughout the crisis intervention; therefore, Roberts suggests the use of verbal counseling skills to help the clients explore their emotions. These verbal responses include reflecting feelings, restating content, using open-ended questions, summarizing, giving advice, reassurance, interpreting statements, confronting, and using silence.

Throughout this long, uncertain vigil Chris's parents, wife, and children will need further intervention in dealing with their grief. A referral is made to the in-house social worker for daily contact with the family. The elderly parents remain the most hopeful and stay at Chris's bedside daily. They will need encouragement to take turns to rest and to spend time caring for themselves. While the doctors gave a dire prognosis, doubting Chris would ever recover and emerge from his coma, his parents are proved to be ultimately correct. Within 2 weeks, Chris grasps his father's hand, and after 3 weeks is able to give a "thumbs-up" signal.

Generate and Explore Alternatives

Since the clients are emotionally distressed and consumed by the aftermath of the crisis episode, it is very useful to have an objective and trained clinician assist them in conceptualizing and discussing adaptive coping responses to the crisis. During this potentially highly productive stage, the social worker and clients collaboratively agree upon appropriate alternative coping methods.

Chris's wife lives 200 miles from the hospital. After discussion of options, the social worker arranges for her and the children to stay at the local Ronald McDonald House. The family wants Chris placed in a rehabilitation center near his home. The children need counseling to understand the changes in their dad's personality.

The social worker had quickly assessed the high level of the wife's panic and distress and has promptly utilized all the available community resources. This helped allay the wife's fears that the entire family unit would collapse.

Develop and Formulate an Action Plan

This will ultimately restore cognitive functioning for the clients. The precipitating event of Chris's car accident has threatened the family with the loss of a son, husband, and father. Many clients have great difficulty mobilizing themselves and following through on an action plan. It is imperative that the clients be encouraged and bolstered so they will follow through. The social worker provides support and an opportunity to freely ventilate feelings and move on to explore their options. The clinician continues to act as a liaison between the family and the medical staff so as to break down all medical jargon into lay language. The family sit numbly, apparently listening to the doctors, but in their state of anxiety they cannot recall specifics or fully understand. The social worker's action plan will be to support the use of healthy, adaptive defenses, while helping the family take a more active role in exploring solutions on how to best cope. Ultimately, the parents, wife, and children decide to band together while Chris recovers in a rehab center in their hometown. This eliminates the wife's panic and worry about how to pay all the bills and feed and care for the children. While still supporting Chris by visiting him, his father will call Chris's workplace to ascertain his disability coverage and file the necessary papers.

Provide Follow-Up

Stage seven in crisis intervention should involve an informal agreement or formal appointment between the social worker and the family to have another meeting at a designated time, either in person or on the phone, to gauge the client's success in crisis resolution and daily functioning 1 week, 2 weeks, or 1 month later. The family decide to initiate the first phone call in 2 weeks and report they are returning to this precrisis level of functioning and continue to rely on adequate support systems while using constructive coping mechanisms.

Paul Smith

Let us now turn to the case of Paul, the 9-year-old burn and smoke-inhalation victim whose injuries resulted from his father's lit cigarette. First, the ER nurses carefully examine Paul as a recent burn victim to ensure that all burning has been stopped and cooled. Events within the first hour after injury can make the difference between life and death in a thermally injured patient. During the emergent phase, immediately after injury, medical care focuses on the stabilization of the patient's condition. Simultaneously, Roberts's (1990) seven-stage model for crisis intervention provides an excellent guide for crisis workers in the emergency departments. During the emergent phase of this crisis, the social worker makes the required referrals to the police and child protective services. Then she turns her attention to the grieving and hysterical family members.

In this severe emergency, as in all such crises, the social worker must play a dual role. He or she must gather and record pertinent information about the circumstances that led to the injury and at the same time offer much-needed psychological support to prevent traumatization and promote healing at a later stage. "A severe burn may have psychologic, physiologic, and social consequences that permanently alter the quality of a person's life" (Beare & Myers, 1994, p. 2118). By all means, an accusatory demeanor must be avoided. Sometimes in a family crisis such as this, the surviving parent will lash out at their troublesome and troubled children. In such a situation, the social worker, as an objective arbiter, can help enormously to subdue the children's pain and provide an element of calm and caring in a moment of catastrophe. Research shows that the initial encounter between a crisis survivor and a trusted individual, especially one in an authority role, has more impact on his or her eventual recovery than almost anything else (van Wormer & Bartollas, in press).

RESILIENCE AND THE RESOLUTION OF CRISIS

Working through a crisis event involving sudden trauma, loss, or new diagnosis of cancer can shatter one's prior way of life and alter one's perception of the world. According to Moyers (1993), most crises

> call into question the way you live and what's important. This wake up call leads to "whole reshifting of values. We suddenly realize that very little is random or trivial, and that life is full of opportunities to love and connect and grow in wisdom. We're not a special group of people here, we're just human beings, frightened, lonely, hurting, and able to grow in response to crisis." (pp. 359–360)

Feelings of powerlessness awaken panic, which darkens one's powers to effectively cope through a crisis. Panic is like the pessimistic person who turns out all the lights just to see how dark it is. One would never attempt to drive at night down a steep, treacherous cliffside road without headlights. Paradoxically, at the very moment of crisis, when one needs to summon all reservoirs of courage and clearheaded decision making, the person can be rendered least capable of doing so.

The social worker's belief in the capacity for growth-oriented change (Saleebey, 1997) is the first step in reestablishing people's faith in their capacity to recover from the crisis event and to return to a precrisis level of functioning. A more ambitious expected outcome would be for the patient to recover from the crisis event to a higher than precrisis level of functioning and to an improved quality of life (Stuart & Sundeen, 1995).

The Kennedy family is often alluded to as having great resilience—the ability to "bounce back" bravely, still vitally immersed in facing life's challenges after suffering so many violent and premature losses of family members. Yet, according to Saleebey (1997):

> It is not a specific group of individuals who are resilient; rather, each individual has the capacity for resilience, at least potentially. It was formerly thought that resilience was an exclusive property of certain kinds of people blessed with particular genetic/constitutional characteristics, interpersonal relationships, traits and environments. Now the effort is to discover the processes by which anyone might rebound or regenerate following adversity or decline. (p. 202)

As Mahrer (1978) explains, "In achieving higher levels of actualization, the aim is to bring into the realm of experiencing the potentials which are present within the person. . . . Sometimes to a very large extent . . . this calls for guts, courage and hard work" (p. 568).

Before crisis threatens to overwhelm an individual, the social worker using Roberts's seven-stage crisis intervention model alleviates anxiety and supports the emergence of the client's inner strength. This model facilitates the early identification of crisis precipitants and promotes problem solving and effective crisis resolution.

From the first intense moment of acknowledging the pain, grief, rage, and confusion that stem from a precipitating crisis through to follow up: "the purpose is to cement the foundation of strengths, to insure the synergy of the continuing development and articulation of strengths, and to secure a place for the person to be" (Saleebey, 1997, p. 56).

CONCLUSION

As emergency rooms increasingly have become the only access to care available, some means is required to identify and alleviate those conditions that produce, precipitate, and perpetuate poor physical and emotional health. One way to achieve early identification and remediation is by crisis intervention, and a hospital ER provides one obvious setting for the initiation of this type of service. Yet because of the volume of patients to be seen and the acute nature of medical treatment, ER medical staff are often unable to provide the level of psychosocial care required by patients and/or their families. Social work coverage and services in ERs are invaluable in meeting patients' long-term and short-term needs. Roberts's seven-stage model of crisis intervention is an excellent model for ER social workers.

REFERENCES

Beare, P., & Myers, J. (1994). *Principles and practice of adult health nursing* (2nd ed.). St. Louis: Mosby.

Boes, M. (1997). A typology for establishing social work staffing patterns within an emergency room. *Crisis Intervention, (3),* 179–185.

Boes, M. (1998). Battered women in the emergency room. In A. Roberts (Ed.), *Battered women and their families* (2nd ed., pp. 205–229). New York: Springer.

Cambell, J. E. (1994). *Basic trauma life support* (3rd ed.). Paramus, NJ: Prentice-Hall.

Centers for Disease Control and Prevention. (1993). *Journal of the American Medical Association,* 270 (2), 1174.

Demling, R. H., & LaLonde, C. (1989). *Burn trauma.* New York: Thiene Medical Publishers.

Emergency Nurses Association Nursing Practice Committee. (1992). *Triage: Meeting the challenge.* Chicago: Emergency Nurses Association.

Glaser, B. G., & Strauss, A. (1968). *Time for dying.* Chicago: Aldine.

Goldsworth, J., & Bailey, M. (1998). Where's the family? *Nursing 98,* 52.

Jastremski, C. (1998). Head injuries. *R.N.,* 61 (2), 40–44.

Mahrer, A. (1978). *Experiencing a humanistic theory of psychology and psychiatry.* New York: Brunner Mazel.

Moyers, B. (1993). *Healing and the mind.* New York: Doubleday.

Myer, R. A., & Hanna, F. J. (1996). Working in hospital emergency departments: Guidelines for crisis intervention workers. In A. Roberts (Ed.), *Crisis management and brief treatment: Theory, technique, and applications* (pp. 37–59). Belmont, CA: Wadsworth.

Padgett, D., & Brodsky, B. (1992). Psychosocial factors influencing non-urgent use of the emergency room: A review of the literature and recommendations for research and improved service and delivery. *Social Science and Medicine,* 35, 1189–1197.

Roberts, A. R. (1990). An overview of crisis theory and crisis intervention. In A. R. Roberts (Ed.), *Crisis intervention handbook: Assessment, treatment and research* (pp. 3–16). Belmont, CA: Wadsworth.

Roberts, A. R. (1991). Conceptualizing crisis theory and the crisis intervention model. In A. R. Roberts (Ed.), *Contemporary perspectives on crisis intervention and prevention* (pp. 3–17). Englewood Cliffs, NJ: Prentice-Hall.

Roberts, A. (1996). Epidemiology and definitions of acute crisis in American society. In A. R. Roberts (Ed.), *Crisis management and brief treatment: Theory, technique, and applications* (p. 28). Belmont, CA: Wadsworth.

Saleebey, D. (1997). *The strengths perspective in social work practice* (2nd ed.). New York: Longman.

Sheehy, S. B. (1998). *Emergency nursing principles and protocols* (4th ed). St. Louis: Mosby.

Stuart, G., & Sundeen, S. (1995). *Principles and practice of psychiatric nursing* (5th ed.). St. Louis: Mosby.

U.S. National Center for Health Statistics (1997, December 17). Advance Data Nos. 293 and 294.

van Wormer, K., & Bartollas, C. (in

press). *Women and the criminal justice system: Gender, race, and class.* Boston: Allyn and Bacon.

Weinerman, E. R., Ratner, R., Robbin, A., & Lavenhor, M. A. (1966). Yale studies in ambulatory medical care: Determinants of use of hospital emergency services. *American Journal of Public Health, 56,* 1037–1056.

18

A Model of Crisis Intervention in Critical and Intensive Care Units of General Hospitals

NORMAN M. SHULMAN
AMY L. SHEWBERT

Historically, when a patient in a medical-surgical hospital is recognized as having a need for psychological support as a result of a medical crisis, the attending physician requests a consultation from a psychiatrist, psychologist, or other mental health professional. Although this professional can provide important diagnostic information on the immediate mental status of the patient, usually little, if any, consideration is given to the patient's ongoing emotional needs. Typically, directives for medication and possibly a referral to another mental health or social service professional are given. Generally, only if a patient becomes a behavior management problem will daily psychological intervention be ordered. When such services are not available, behavior management is frequently left up to nursing, case management, or clerical staff, who often do not have the time or training to attend to these problems, which can be very disruptive. It is thus our assertion that this lack of proper attention to a patient's psychological needs results in an unnecessary burden for the immediate staff and frequently leads to an exacerbation of the patient's crisis. A standing psychological consult available to critical care and other areas of a general hospital would provide the means for giving proper attention to the patients' mind-body experience, while alleviating stressors which the staff is neither trained nor compensated to address. As a result, potential crisis situations can be minimized and in some cases prevented.

DEFINITION AND SCOPE OF
MEDICAL CRISIS

Medical crises are an inevitable part of the human experience. Although the definition of a medical crisis is subjective, the drastic change in lifestyle resulting from the crisis is a common theme. Pollin and Kanaan (1995) defined a medical crisis as "a time of unusual emotional distress or disorientation caused by the onset of, or a major change in, the medical condition" (p. 15). Another definition of a medical crisis is the reaction of a person resulting from a substantial variation in experiences differing from the person's usual view of the world (Shulman, 1999). These emergencies create such instability and chaos in the person's life that normality, as the patient previously experienced it, ceases to exist. People in a crisis state demonstrate the following identifiable characteristics (Roberts, 1990):

1. Perception of a meaningful and threatening event
2. Inability to cope with the impact of the event
3. Increased fear, tension, or confusion
4. Subjective discomfort
5. Rapid progression to a state of crisis or disequilibrium

The stress involved with medical crises is typically temporary, yet it can have lifelong effects. The individual's coping skills, cognitive processes, typical affective processes, and history of psychopathology not only determine the degree to which life is affected but also define the medical crisis itself (Roberts, 1996).

The medical crisis generates stress that is universal to all persons in crisis regardless of age, gender, race, and so on. Situational factors, including medical emergencies, life-threatening and chronic illnesses, family health problems, crime, and natural disasters, often incite a medical crisis (Roberts, 1996). Roberts (1996) cites valuable statistics provided by the U.S. Department of Justice establishing the prevalence of medical crises as initiated by medical emergencies. For example, as a result of acute psychiatric or medical emergencies, 254,820 people visit emergency rooms daily; these medical crises also include between 685 and 1,645 suicide attempts per day in a year (Roberts). Regarding life-threatening disease, medical professionals diagnose 3,205 new cancer cases per day, and 140 AIDS patients die each day. Chronic illnesses also account for a great deal of the medical problems experienced by persons in crisis. For instance, a 1991 national health interview survey concludes that some 36 million Americans limit daily activities because of long-term sickness (Pollin & Kanaan,1995). In addition, 56.5 million individuals suffer problems caused by cardiovascular disease; other chronic illnesses that contribute to the high incidence of medical crises include arthritis, cystic fibrosis, multiple sclerosis, and diabetes mellitus (Pollin & Kanaan, 1995). Family health problems, consisting of child abuse, drug abuse, domestic violence, and so on, relate directly to the origin of medical crises (as cited in Roberts, 1996). Finally, violent crime estimates also illustrate the high incidence of crises in society today. Data based on the Bureau of Justice statistics indicate that 357 persons are victims of forcible rape every day of the year (Roberts, 1996). Medical crises arbitrarily affect all humans, thus creating a scope of immense proportions.

DIAGNOSTIC DESCRIPTORS OF PATIENTS AND FAMILY

Persons in a crisis state frequently experience similar emotions, reactions, and periods of vulnerability. The medical crisis produces stress for the patient and family. Furthermore, examination of patients in specialized hospital units indicates the same characteristics identifying persons in medical crisis.

Certain characteristics and vulnerabilities identify the patient in crisis. High-risk patients often have suppressed or agitated affect, or "frozen fright," which describes the inability to react entirely (Pollin & Kanaan, 1995). Suicidal ideation combined with depressive symptoms clearly indicates a person with high-risk qualities. Depression is among the most prevalent psychological responses among patients in medical crisis. Goldman and Kimball (1987) report that 25% of patients admitted to critical care units experience symptoms of depression. Four common types of depressed states among special risk patients are: (a) major depressive illness, (b) adjustment disorder, (c) dysthymic disorder, and (d) organic affective disorder (Goldman & Kimball). A contributory factor to the depression is low self-esteem. Patients report feeling dehumanized by the lack of privacy during treatment times (Rice & Williams, 1997).

Additional common concerns of the patient include quality of life, death, and dying. Other traits of crisis patients consist of inadequate communication with caregivers and inadequate cognitive assimilation of the crisis (Pollin & Kanaan, 1995). Control, self-image, dependency, abandonment, anger, and so on are issues that must be dealt with by the patient in crisis. These descriptors contribute to a patient's vulnerability during the traumatic event. At a time of extreme stress as produced by a medical crisis, patients are susceptible to emotional changes. The degree of vulnerability depends on the "newness, intensity, and duration of the stressful event" (Roberts, 1996 p. 26). Physical and emotional exhaustion, previous crisis experience, and available material resources (Roberts, 1996) are important considerations when determining the risk of the patient in medical crisis.

The family of a person in medical crisis cannot be disregarded when considering the effect on lifestyle change. Family members frequently deny the severity of the situation (Pollin & Kanaan, 1995). A new role as the primary caregiver during hospitalization and after discharge can be an overwhelming responsibility for a family member not properly prepared emotionally. Daily care for people with chronic illness occurs in informal, noninstitutional settings in 70 to 95% of the situations necessitating such activities (as cited in Pollin & Kanaan, 1995). Difficulty with living arrangements and financial commitments create a new burden for all persons involved.

Changes in the family dynamic resulting from differing coping styles in response to the crisis provide an additional stress. Tension between family members can escalate, introducing another problem for the family and patient in crisis that must be resolved. The unpredictability and obscurity of the medical problem are perhaps most difficult for the family. Rice and Williams (1997) describe the exacerbation of family members' fears and anxieties caused by the presence of intimidating equipment and the proximity of critically ill patients. Furthermore, emergency and intensive medical treatment is typically swift and may appear impersonal to a concerned family member. Dealing with life-sustaining issues, life-or-death decisions, and the possibility of death elicit familial emotional complications (Rice & Williams, 1997). The psychological distress of families may also include guilt as a result of the medical crisis.

Specific Intensive Care Unit Symptoms

Patients of specialized intensive care units experience similar symptoms; for example, rehabilitation hospitals provide services for patients with injuries that embody great potential for psychological distress (Bleiberg & Katz, 1991). As a result of medical problems with varying degrees of impairment, disability, and handicap, patients must cope with issues of autonomy, loss, self-concept, and cognitive capacity. Medical intensive care unit (MICU) patients exhibit symptoms of the high-risk patient. Patients diagnosed with cancer experience psychological distress involving matters regarding quality of life, possibilities of disfigurement or disability, pain, and changes in personal relationships (Rozensky, Sweet, & Tovian, 1991). Matus (as cited in Creer, Kotses, & Reynolds, 1991) attests that psychological precipitants (emotional arousal), psychological symptoms (panic), and psychological factors (secondary gain, low self-esteem, etc.) are operants with asthma patients. End-stage renal disease (ESRD) patients, whose treatment often requires up to 12 to 21 hours of dialysis per week, are disturbed by the constant threat of death and increasing dependency.

MICUs are treating increasing numbers of patients with human immunodeficiency virus (HIV) who require psychosocial services for themselves as well as their families and loved ones. Cardiac intensive care units (CICUs) also provide an arena for crisis patients in need of psychological treatment. Thompson (1990) indicates a reduction of anxiety and depression in crisis patients being treated for coronary disease who receive psychological services. Finally, the pediatric intensive care units (PICUs) are the domain of children in crisis coping with a traumatic event. A sense of desperation involved with treating a sick child elicits heartfelt stressors for the staff and families (DeMaso, Koocher, & Meyer, 1996).

A MODEL OF COMPREHENSIVE CARE

This section focuses on how an already established program in a general hospital increases the resilience and reduces the impact of risk factors on patients suffering from a medical crisis. The section will examine how the traditional consult system has proven to be ineffective in helping a patient recover from a crisis. The rationale for a more effective and accessible system will be proposed, followed by a detailed description of the model, including how it interfaces with the rest of the hospital and the social support network.

The Failure of the Traditional Consult System

The traditional consult system continues to fail within most hospitals, and therefore many medical crises that could be prevented are not. For example, in teaching hospitals, where psychiatric residents depend on mental health consults to gain experience, all too frequently several unprepared students respond to a consult and overwhelm an already vulnerable patient. A balance of the patient's emotional needs and the residents' educational needs can be affected with a modicum of sensitivity and forethought, but, unfortunately, this scenario is more the exception than the norm.

The stigma attached to the public's perception of mental illness continues to pervade the general society, and hospitals are no exception. This prejudice creates an indirect negative impact on patient care because hospital staffs often feel that suggesting psychological consultation may be interpreted as an insult by the patient. In fact, this perspective affects staff to the degree that the patient's emotional needs may never by considered. The social stigma attached to mental illness, coupled with the reality of an intense medical perspective of doctors and nurses, facilitates the psychological neglect of patients with psychological needs, especially those in critical care. This phenomenon occurs even when medical conditions are affected by a patient's mental and emotional status. Depression of the chronic type (e.g., dysthymic disorder) can contribute to hostility and behavioral management problems in critical patients.

Finally, physicians' inclinations to divert immediate attention from psychological treatment adversely affect the consult system in a variety of ways. Because physicians in critical care areas are trained specifically to identify and treat medical conditions, a patient's total care tends to remain unaddressed. A physician's professional agenda may also be threatened by a mental health clinician's involvement in the case, especially if it is not asked for, thus resulting in rejections of a psychological consultation. The end result is that all too many patients spend their hospital days without proper psychological help even in intensive care units. This neglect often complicates and exacerbates a patient's existing medical problems to crisis proportions.

Rationale for the Standing Consult

Increasing volumes of evidence demonstrate the efficacy of mental health interventions during a patient's hospital stay for medical or surgical crises. For example, MICUs employ mental health consultants in cancer treatment centers. Rozensky, Sweet and Tovian (1991) describe the therapeutic efficacy of psychological consultation for cancer patients. Assessment of the patient's physical and social environments, psychological strengths and weaknesses, and response to the diagnosis and treatment of cancer, as well as assessment of the patient's personality and coping styles, provide a unique perspective that is integrated into individualized treatment strategies. It is essential that medical professionals realize the value of a holistic approach to treatment as essential within critical care areas, including psychological consultation and ongoing treatment. Such intervention during the patient's hospital stay defies the standard of the "one time only" consult and includes the provision of ongoing supportive and adjustment psychotherapy. This trend to consider a patient's continuing needs includes family therapy, particularly when treatment is compromised by unhealthy family interactions. Additional services include arranging for psychological testing and referrals to related specialists (e.g., neuropsychologists and outpatient aftercare community medical professionals).

Given the traumatic nature of a serious or critical illness or injury and the treatment necessary for patients in these conditions, it seems appropriate to adhere to a comprehensive approach to recovery. The vision of a standing psychological consult embodies the perspective of the mind-body interaction—specifically, that a patient's mental health directly correlates to length of stay and potential for recovery. The model proposed here includes ongoing attention to fluctuations in mental stability as a result of traumatic injury or severe medical conditions.

The following model (see Fig. 18.1) has been established at the Texas Tech University Medical Center in Lubbock, Texas. It includes the burn intensive care unit, transitional care center, rehabilitation, and neonatal and pediatric intensive care units. (The Southwest Cancer Center and the bone marrow transplant unit are covered in a similar fashion by an independent clinician.) The standing consult was approved on these units with the authorization of the acting chief of surgery, John T. Griswold, M.D., of the Texas Tech University Medical School after the model was proposed to him in 1992.

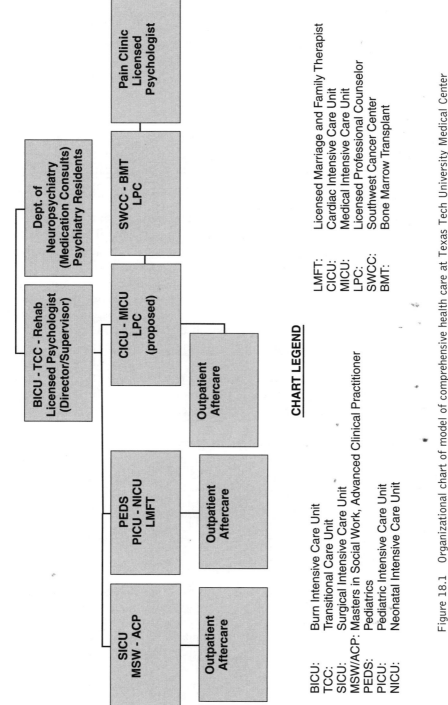

CHART LEGEND

BICU:	Burn Intensive Care Unit
TCC:	Transitional Care Unit
SICU:	Surgical Intensive Care Unit
MSW/ACP:	Masters in Social Work, Advanced Clinical Practitioner
PEDS:	Pediatrics
PICU:	Pediatric Intensive Care Unit
NICU:	Neonatal Intensive Care Unit

LMFT:	Licensed Marriage and Family Therapist
CICU:	Cardiac Intensive Care Unit
MICU:	Medical Intensive Care Unit
LPC:	Licensed Professional Counselor
SWCC:	Southwest Cancer Center
BMT:	Bone Marrow Transplant

Figure 18.1   Organizational chart of model of comprehensive health care at Texas Tech University Medical Center

Dr. Griswold had been thinking at the time the proposal was made that only half of a patient's needs were attended to at discharge from critical care areas. The Department of Psychiatry, the likely option to turn to regarding the provision of psychological support on these units, did not consider this to be part of its curriculum agenda. Its consultation role had been narrowly defined to include assessment and pharmacotherapy only. On rare occasions, a patient would be followed a few times until discharge, but usually the extent of the consultation ended after one interaction, if a consultation was requested at all. There was also a problem of responsiveness in that frequently a patient would be discharged before a psychiatric resident saw the patient. Unfortunately, when this problem was added to the understandable lack of attention to psychological issues by hospital staff, an inordinate number of patients never had an essential aspect of their treatment attended to.

Traditionally, automatic consults in general hospitals have been limited. Once the resistance to the standing psychological consult was overcome by Dr. Griswold's insistence to the staff of the importance of the program, it was instituted as a component of overall health care. The mental health professional, in this case a licensed psychologist, was able to systematically evaluate every patient admitted to the six-bed burn intensive care unit, the first unit on which it was tried.

The initial assessment included the patient's mental status, internal and external coping resources, degree of family support, and premorbid mental health history. The evaluation included a determination not only of the patient's need for services but also whether the patient and family would accept those services. Psychological interventions were never imposed on a patient (or family), and it was the patient's (or family's) prerogative to terminate the relationship at any time. The attending physician always retained power over the course of treatment, including the option to cancel the intervention.

Rounds were made daily on the burn unit and on weekends when indicated. In addition, the attending physician or staff would call in the clinician at any other time if the situation warranted it. Deference to medical personnel was always given if a procedure was in process or needed to be done at the time of the session. The patient's condition was also taken into consideration in the sense that the patient was never pushed to tolerate more than he or she could handle. As it turned out, the length of the sessions increased as the patient's condition improved. Once a patient stabilized, less time was then required until discharge.

Patient needs were also informally determined by any physician, resident, intern, nurse, therapist, or aide who detected and then passed on important information to the psychologist. Formally, his attendance at weekly staffings provided input regarding the degree and type of interventions. Frequently, the psychologist, with and without his colleagues, would consult with other professionals who might shed more light on a patient's status. The psychologist was in a unique position to subsequently consult a psychiatrist for medication issues, a neuropsychologist, a substance abuse expert, or any other professional who could contribute to the comprehensive care of a patient.

Since a systems approach is utilized, family support was also given on a regular basis, particularly when a patient could not be communicated with directly. The psychologist made it a priority to either convey information himself or encourage physicians working on the case to keep a patient's family updated with concrete and realistic information, even if it was less than positive. Anecdotally, it is safe to say that the overwhelming majority of critical care patients and their families appreciated the consistent presence of a caring mental health professional on an intensive care unit—even in cases where death is imminent. This professional can serve to help a patient maintain dignity with a sense of purpose while facing death. Patients and families were also satisfied with the continuity of psychotherapeutic care made available. They realized that there were times when a patient needed to talk to a neutral party about issues that may not be easily shared with significant others, even clergy.

The unit psychologist was clearly in a unique position to prevent problems from occurring and to be available to respond to occasional conflicts among patients, family members, and professional caregivers, including physicians. Physicians open to the psychologist's role with the treatment team benefited from input not normally made available, as well as from not having to commit valuable time and energy to nonmedical issues. In general, the entire scope of a patient's needs was treated more effectively and efficiently.

While a hospital nonaffiliated psychiatrist was used as a consultant on medication issues, this model suggests the ideal arrangement of pairing a psychiatrist with a psychologist to work in tandem on critical care units. Questions regarding psychiatric medications and follow-up maintenance need not be the concern of the attending and resident physicians alone.

As opposed to the limited consultation offered by existing models, a psychiatric counterpart to the psychologist can also follow a medicated patient daily. Such a professional liaison proves to be efficient for all members of the treatment team. For example, many times issues of drug interactions and the psychologial effects of medication routinely administered to critical care patients can be handled by the specialist most uniquely qualified to address these issues. A psychiatrist experienced in the area of critical care is an invaluable member of the team, allowing other physicians to be free to concentrate on their specific areas of expertise.

At the Texas Tech University Medical Center intensive care and rehabilitation units, the psychological needs of patients are no longer neglected by the absence of integrated treatment. Treatment is now more comprehensive, with issues of compliance, treatment interference, and patient-family-staff conflicts being dealt with quickly and as a function of overall care, since the psychologist is already involved. In this manner, demands on the staff to perform duties outside of their job description are minimized. After discharge, another advantage to the patient is the increased tendency to follow through with outpatient aftercare either with the unit psychologist or with another professional in the community.

The psychologist is also available to staff members whose equilibrium may be disturbed by the extraordinary demands of critical-care. Individual and group interventions are useful either for ongoing support or in response to a traumatic event on the unit. As a result, the staff gains a measure of solidarity and security with the knowledge that a trusted professional is readily available to respond to their professional and personal needs.

CASE ILLUSTRATIONS

Case 1

T. is a 35-year-old Hispanic female seen to evaluate her emotional response to traumatic double leg amputations. The patient was injured in an automobile accident, which also involved her 16-year-old son, who was driving and had fallen asleep at the wheel. The patient's son had informed her prior to the accident that he was very tired and that he wanted her to drive. Shortly thereafter, the accident occurred, and the patient's legs were crushed beyond repair. The boy suffered only minor injuries.

The first intervention was agreed to by the patient's husband, who wanted his son seen. This was to allow the boy to see his mother and determine that she was going to live, and to give her an early opportunity to absolve him of any guilt. Once this was accomplished, the patient was talked to daily and encouraged not to give up because her prognosis was good, given current rehabilitation capabilities. These interventions constituted the initial cognitive reframing efforts.

The importance of employing a systems approach is exemplified in this case. As the inpatient psychotherapy progressed (eventually over a course of 65 sessions covering two admissions, over a 5-month period), it came to the therapist's attention that the patient's husband and other son (age 17) were in the midst of their own crises. This information necessitated that family and individual therapy be done with various combinations of family members collaterally with the treatment of the identified patient.

Adjustments and readjustments of coping styles have had to be made over the past several months as minor crises have erupted. For example, the father and one of the sons began drinking more to numb their pain over their loved one's condition. Second, the patient became recurrently depressed during the difficult physical rehabilitation she had to endure. In addition, she was forced to face the hard reality that an above-the-knee amputation posed extremely difficult prosthetic complications. Third, the other son considered dropping out of college, against his mother's wishes, because of his inability to concentrate.

At the time of this writing, the family members are still struggling to balance their respective means of coping. Overall, the situation has been partially reframed successfully in that some positive adaptations have been made. For example, T. returned to graduate school to get a master's degree in counseling so that she can help others. Her husband has stopped drinking, and the boys are being seen individually to facilitate their resolving any residual guilt, resentment, and substance abuse issues.

In the best of all possible circumstances, the family would have accepted the assistance of antidepressant medication, but the patient and her family wanted to work without its potential benefits. They remain committed to working together to complete their collective resolutions and should continue their treatment as outpatients until it is no longer indicated. It is important to note that much of the success of therapy was attributed to the early and consistent interventions provided by the standing consult in place at the time in the surgical intensive care unit where the patient was initially treated. She was then able to be seen subsequently on the regular floor and later as an outpatient, thus ensuring an essential continuity of care.

Case 2

N. is a 43-year-old White male referred for a mental status exam pursuant to several days of unconsciousness caused by a propane explosion. When he was initially seen, the patient had only a sketchy memory of the incident and could remember no details. He was oriented to person but not to place or time. Since one suspected cause of the explosion was a suicide attempt by purposely igniting the propane tank, an assessment of suicidal risk had to be done. However, because of the nature of his mental status, a risk assessment had to be done frequently during the first 2 weeks of his stay in the burn intensive care unit. The patient vehemently denied that he was trying to kill himself, and he never changed his response.

It became imperative that the patient be seen frequently (a total of 32 sessions over a 4-month period) because of his mental health history. Shortly after admission, it became clear from the medications he was taking that he had a premorbid condition of bipolar disorder (depressed). Upon intubation, the patient was unable to receive his psychotropic medications, which included Serzone and Restoril. Therefore, it was feared that when he regained consciousness, he may present behavioral management problems and possible attempt suicide, which he did have a history of.

During the course of his hospitalization, rapport was developed and maintained as a hedge against any disruptive behavior on the floor or suicidal ideation. At times the patient did become agitated and difficult to manage, but with the assistance of psychiatry, a proper administration of his psychotropics restored him to stability. Prior to discharge, contact was made with a physician in his hometown, where treatment (pharmacotherapy and psychotherapy) could continue without interruption.

The standing consult again proved to be invaluable in preventing a crisis from evolving as the patient was seen shortly after admission and regularly after that until discharge. Rather than be treated with heavy sedation alone after becoming a behavior management problem, the patient did not fall between the cracks and his psychological needs were consistently attended to. His mental illness was quickly and properly addressed, and he passed through the hospital with only minimal disturbance to the patient and staff.

APPLICATION OF ROBERTS'S SEVEN-STAGE CRISIS INTERVENTION MODEL IN CRITICAL CARE AREAS

Roberts's (1996) seven-stage crisis intervention model can be applied in hospital settings where initial intervention with health emergencies and other traumatic events naturally occur. However, performing crisis intervention in critical care areas of general hospitals poses unique problems that must be considered. For example, in Case 2, a thorough assessment, including an assessment of lethality, could not be done until well after admission. Since a suicide attempt was suspected, close contact with the medical staff had to be maintained so that this critical assessment could be made as soon after extubation as possible. At this point, if suicidal ideation persisted, the proper suicide prevention protocol could be implemented on the unit, in this case, burn intensive care.

Regarding Case 1, in spite of the fact that a suicide attempt was not the cause of the accident, the patient's despondence in the aftermath of the double amputation had to be considered and a lethality assessment done until it was determined beyond any doubt that T. posed no threat to herself. The "captive audience" reality of the inpatient setting allows for lethality assessments to be made at least daily or, if necessary, multiple times daily by different staff members. Any change in the degree of the lethality is reported to the unit mental health clinician, who would alter the treatment plan as indicated.

Another distinguishing feature of the inpatient crisis intervention is the necessity of establishing rapport (Roberts's, stage 2) with a patient over a sometimes inordinate extended period. Mind-altering pain medications, pain itself, disorientation caused by ICU isolation (resulting in a phenomenon known as ICU psychosis), and the difficulty of determining staff identity due to masks and gowns all contribute to a difficult period of rapport building.

In addition, frequent interruptions from medical staff for the application of intensive care procedures necessarily shorten time with the patient and interrupt the therapeutic flow.

Both N. and T. were unable to communicate until well after admission. Once the interventions began, rapport was established with both patients piecemeal and over several days. At times, information had to be repeated because of the patients' relatively incoherent mental status early in their medical care. In time (longer with N. than with T. because of mental illness), rapport was successfully established.

In both case examples, identification of the crisis precipitant (stage 3) was readily apparent (i.e., the accidents). Although premorbid issues with both N. and T. certainly affected their individual responses to crisis, it is clear that the interventions were necessitated by the patients' misfortunes. In the cases of most ICU patients, the crisis begins and continues to resolve as their physical condition improves. However, in the case of T., who would suffer numerous physical and family-related emotional setbacks, each new precipitant had to be dealt with aggressively and in a timely manner. The already established rapport with her made subsequent interventions that much easier for her to take advantage of.

The majority of time with both patients was spent dealing with their various feelings about what had happened to them (stage 4). Active listening techniques, as well as conveyance of validation, empathy, warmth, and reassurance, were used to help the patients understand that they were being heard by a caring professional. Basic counseling skills were employed in the course of the supportive psychotherapy to foster their exploration of their emotions about what had happened to them and the potential consequences that awaited them during and after their recoveries. T. required more and longer sessions because of her many concerns about her husband and two children, who complicated her recovery. Their difficulties coping with T.'s amputations and its meaning to them initially created secondary crisis precipitants for her, such as reactive drinking and depression. N.'s adaptations were relatively straightforward and uncomplicated.

In the course of helping T. and N. explore their feelings, various alternatives were generated and explored (stage 5). T. benefited greatly from being aware of the resources available to amputees that would allow her to resume a relatively normal life. The physical rehabilitation protocol for amputees was reviewed with her shortly after she was able to communicate her feelings about the loss of her legs. She received much reassurance from knowing what to expect regarding her physical recovery (which would be done in her hometown), the fitting of prostheses, learning how to walk again, and gradually being able to resume her teaching career. She was also greatly relieved that her family would be worked with individually and collectively to focus on their various problems. This allowed her to focus on her rehabilitation and to spend less time and energy on issues she had no control over.

N. received comfort from learning that the unit was aware of his history of mental illness, was in contact with his treating doctors and family, and therefore would be able to maintain his medication schedule and his stable mental status. In addition, contact with his ex-wife, who remained a valuable source of support in his life, was encouraged and facilitated. This person was especially important because she was N's only nonprofessional support, whereas T. had a multitude of supportive family, friends, and wel-wishers.

As a result of the extended stays of both patients, ample time was available for the development and formulation of their respective action plans (stage 6). Prior to discharge, the hospital assisted in setting up the medical and psychiatric resources that would ensure cognitive and affective stability. With N. several conversations were held with his treating professionals and his ex-wife, who had an investment in assuring that N. would be referred back to his mental health providers upon his return home. The patient participated in developing the discharge plan and knew exactly what was expected of him (i.e., compliance), and what resources were available to him.

T. also had a clear idea of the postdischarge phase of her recovery. The mental health phase was offered to her in the form of aftercare psychotherapy for her and her family members in various combinations. She was pleased with the predictability and availability of the discharge plan and knew she could inquire about it with several different professionals and receive a straight answer.

Both patients agreed to follow-up plans (stage 7). Since T. and her family would return to the hospital where the initial crisis was treated for medical and psychological care, follow-up was easily confirmed. At these times the progress of her medical and emotional rehabilitation was discussed, as well as what she could next expect and have to cope with. N.'s follow-up care, on the other hand, was arranged where he was currently being treated. Phone calls to his providers near his home were made shortly after discharge to ensure follow-through.

Roberts's seven-stage model is well adapted to serving the psychological needs of patients in critical care areas. One can safely assume that crisis intervention with most of these patients is indicated by virtue of their need for intensive care. Although the model's application has to be tempered by the specific demands on units of this kind, the essential elements of the seven stages have universal utility. As a result, patients' crises are alleviated by timely intervention (i.e., as close to the time of the precipitating event as possible). In addition, future crises can be prevented because of the adaptive learning that takes place during the daily, intensive interventions.

CLINICAL CONSIDERATIONS AND IMPLICATIONS

Several special direct service intervention considerations must be taken into account when working with patients in crisis in critical care areas. First, deference to medical staff has to be a priority. Because of the nature of intensive care medical services, there may never be a convenient time for a proper assessment or intervention. It is commonplace for several interruptions to occur during the course of as little as 10 to15 minutes, making the atmosphere less than conducive for crisis management.

At times the therapist has to do his or her best to prioritize the treatment issues and address them in the time available. This becomes especially important when assessing suicidal risk or any other self-destructive behavior that may complicate treatment. In practical terms, this may mean that several brief interventions have to be done before a clear picture of the patient's functioning can be ascertained. The patient's tenuous condition, which can limit the effectiveness of a session, is frequently more of a reason for brief intervention than procedural interruptions.

A second consideration is the indicated emphasis on performing the initial crisis intervention as close to the time of the crisis as possible. As with any crisis, a medical crisis, especially a traumatic event, needs to be processed as early as possible before defenses have the opportunity of reconstituting. This issue becomes most relevant with posttraumatic stress disorder, which if not treated early can fester and manifest its myriad symptoms months or even years later. Therefore, if possible, it is recommended that the patient be seen as soon after admission as possible—for example, shortly after extubation or regaining consciousness.

Another advantage of early intervention is the forging of relationships even when a patient may be initially asymptomatic. Once a bond has been established, the patient will be far more inclined to talk about an emergence of symptoms when they do occur, sometimes well after discharge. It is not unusual for a patient to contact a therapist for issues of PTSD or depression months after the first contact and request outpatient therapy. This, of course, is not as likely to occur without the initial formation of the therapeutic relationship. Creation of this early tie is particularly essential when the impact of heavy sedation, which has the capacity of masking psychopathological symptoms, is considered.

A third consideration is the importance of integrating a family systems model into one's crisis intervention techniques. A critical illness or accident affects an entire family, or extended family because these relatives become victims as well. Effective crisis intervention considers the needs of the overall family, which can be used to further the emotional healing of a patient if correctly directed.

When doing critical care crisis intervention, much of the work takes place in the waiting areas or in the corridors of the hospital talking to family members forced to cope with the consequences of a serious illness or accident. Frequently, they become as much or even more in need of crisis services as the patient. Therefore, time and attention should be focused on them in order to maintain family equilibrium for its own sake, as well as for the ultimate recovery of the patient.

A fourth consideration is the potential for burnout of the crisis intervenor performing daily crisis intervention services in repeated life-and-death situations, not to mention with patients who are severely maimed or disfigured. It is imperative that the demands placed on the crisis professional are not excessive and that the intervenor has adequate supervision and emotional support. A high tolerance for stress and multiple available coping resources are prime factors for the crisis professional to have access to while working in a critical care area.

The two case studies presented earlier are informative for crisis intervenors because they are reflective of the ICU patients who are seen as a matter of course. They represent more the rule than the exception. All four of the clinical considerations (i.e., treatment priority given to medical issues, early intervention, a family focus, and staff burnout potential) had to be taken into consideration when working with both patients. In fact, it is unusual to have a patient in critical care when less than all of these intervention themes are present. Occasionally, lack of family involvement becomes a problem. However, the absence of this coping resource usually exacerbates the potential for burnout because the intervenor's role becomes more demanding as involvement with the patient necessarily increases.

Managed Care

Managed care poses unique problems regarding insurance reimbursement for the work performed on the ICUs described earlier. The brunt of inpatient care must be precertified before an insurance carrier is willing to pay for psychotherapeutic services. Unfortunately, the precertification process is often cumbersome, and several days may pass before permission is given. One would think that any patient suffering from severe illness or injury would be automatically certifiable for at least an initial assessment, but this is not the case.

All too often, billing for time spent doing crisis intervention is nonreimbursable because the sessions were not precertified. However, waiting for precertification would be anathema to the maximum efficacy of crisis intervention. Although there is no pat resolution to this issue, professional ethics dictate that the patient must be seen as soon as medically feasible. Hopefully, efforts to retrocertify will be successful on the basis of the logic of the argument. Perhaps someday a limited number of diagnostic evaluation sessions will be automatically precertified for patients victimized by accidents or some other trauma, but until that time comes, struggles with managed care will continue.

Two potential means of reimbursement may be explored to compensate for the denied sessions. One is for the hospital to provide a supplementary stipend to a clinician working in critical care areas. The amount could be based on the average number of nonreimbursable sessions combined with the average number of sessions spent with nonfunded patients. The second alternative is for the facility to apply for grants to foundations specializing in funding innovative medical programs. In fact, both of these options are being explored at University Medical Center in Lubbock, Texas, where the comprehensive, integrated psychological support program mentioned earlier is in the process of being developed in all of its critical care units.

CONCLUSION

It only makes sense for the psychological needs of patients in general hospitals to be attended to along with their physical problems. The general trend in medicine is to recognize this logical, inseparable connection in patients. Although individual physicians and, on a larger scale, certain critical care units integrate treatment successfully, the premise of this chapter is that the successful integration of treatment can be effected in an entire hospital.

If such treatment is properly implemented, patients, families, staff, and the facility should benefit in a variety of ways, not the least important of which is the predicted reduced length of stay (and reduced associated costs). Research soon to be published (Shulman, 1999) should validate this hypothesis, among others, such as the predicted use of less medication, fewer psychological problems, and reduced stress on staff.

Common sense dictates that an essential aspect of health care is the prevention and minimization of potential psychological crises, which complicate and exacerbate ongoing and later treatment. A comprehensive model of crisis intervention in critical and intensive care units is a sensible means of bringing about this necessary improvement in overall health care.

REFERENCES

Bleiberg, R. C., & Katz, B. L. (1991). Psychological components of rehabilitation programs for brain-injured and spinal-cord-injured patients. In R. H. Rozensky, J. J. Sweet, & S. M. Tovian (Eds.), *Handbook of clinical psychology in medical settings* (pp. 375–400). New York: Plenum.

Creer, T. L., Kotses, H., & Reynolds, R. V. (1991). In R. H. Rozensky, J. J. Sweet, & S. M. Tovian (Eds.), *Handbook of clinical psychology in medical settings* (pp. 497–516). New York: Plenum.

DeMaso, D. R., Koocher, G. P., & Meyer, E. C. (1996). Mental health consultation in the pediatric intensive care unit. *Professional Psychology: Research and Practice, 27(2),* 130–136.

Goldman, L. S., & Kimball, C. P. (1987). Depression in intensive care units. *International Journal of Psychiatry in Medicine, 17(3),* 201–212.

Pollin, I., & Kanaan, S. B. (1995). *Medical crisis counseling.* New York: Norton.

Rice, D. G., & Williams, C. C.

(1997). The intensive care unit: Social work intervention with the families of critically ill patients. *Social Work in Health Care, 2(4)*, 391–398.

Roberts, A. R. (1990). Assessment and treatment research. *Crisis intervention handbook*. Belmont, CA: Wadsworth.

Roberts, A. R. (1996). Epidemiology and definitions of acute crisis in American society. In A. R. Roberts (Ed.), *Crisis management and brief treatment: Theory, technique and application* (pp. 16–31). Belmont, CA: Brooks Cole.

Rozensky, R. H., Sweet, J. J., & Tovian, S. M. (1991). *Handbook of clinical psychology in medical settings*. New York: Plenum.

Shulman, N. M. (1999). The relative impact of an open consult system of psychological intervention on burn intensive care patients and staff. Unpublished research data.

Thompson, D. R. (1990). Efficacy of counseling for coronary patients and partners (Doctoral dissertation, Loughborough University of Technology, 1990). *Dissertation Abstracts International, 50*. (50–10B) 4450 pg. #

19

Crisis Intervention With Culturally Diverse Families

ELAINE P. CONGRESS

Case 1

The Marshall family consists of 30-year-old Jerome, 28-year-old Sadie, their 12-year-old son, Samuel, from Sadie's first marriage and their 2-year-old son, Thomas, who was recently diagnosed with a developmental disability. This African American couple had been married for 3 years. Jerome taught physical education in the local high school, and Sadie worked as a bank clerk. Sadie came from a poor family in which she never knew her father, and she and her five siblings had grown up on welfare. She had been born in the rural South, but her family had moved to the South Side of Chicago when she was 2. She had married her first husband when she was 18, when she was already 3 months pregnant with Samuel. Her husband was abusive and used drugs, and Sadie and he separated when Sam was 1 year old. Sadie was determined that her child would not grow up on welfare as she had. She took her GED exam and enrolled in a bank training program, after which she obtained a position as a bank clerk. Jerome had come from a middle-class background and had grown up in suburban Chicago. Both his parents were teachers, and they had supported him through college and an M.Ed. program.

The Marshall family first came to Somerset Mental Health Clinic with the complaint that Samuel was acting out both in school and at home. At school he would not listen to his teachers and often fought with other kids. His grades had slipped from B+ to C−. At home he refused to talk to his parents and spent all his time in his room listening to rap music. He was especially hostile to Jerome, whom he said was not his real father and so could not discipline him.

After the initial appointment had been made, but before the family could be seen, Jerome substained serious injury as a victim in a robbery attempt. He was placed on disability, and it was uncertain when he would be able to return to work.

Case 2

This Hispanic family consists of Juan Sanchez (50 years old), his wife, Maria (40), their four children, Juan Jr. (22), Carlos (16), Carmen (16), and Juanita (6), and Maria's 70-year-old mother, Sabrina Cruz. Maria was born in Puerto Rico but had lived in New York since she was 5. Juan had come from Mexico when he was 25 to visit a sick relative but never returned. All four children lived at home. Maria had struggled for many years with severe depression. She occasionally visited a mental health program to receive medication, but with a diagnosis of adjustment disorder, she had not been able to receive supplementary security income (SSI). The family was supported by welfare. Because of Juan's undocumented status and alcohol abuse, he had never been able to work regularly. Under welfare reform Maria had been informed that she must seek work. Maria, however, had left school after the sixth grade. Because of an untreated learning disability, she could barely read or write; thus the only work opportunities available tò her were housekeeping and baby-sitting jobs.

The family was very proud of Juan Jr. because he was enrolled in a computer technician program at a local community college. Carlos, on the other hand, was a continual source of concern. He had been picked up by the police on several occasions when he was suspected of selling drugs, but the charges had been dropped. He was rarely at home, choosing to spend his time hanging around the street corner with his friends. Sabrina, Maria's mother, had always been helpful in raising the children, especially when Maria was too depressed and Juan too intoxicated. There had been increasing concern, however, that she had become too forgetful. Recently when she had been caring for Juanita, she had left a pot burning on the stove. It was Juanita who had called the fire department to extinguish the fire. The Sanchez family were particularly concerned that Carmen do well in school and marry a nice boy. Recently they had been concerned that she seemed less interested in her schoolwork, preferred to hang around with her friends, and had become obsessed about her appearance. Maria had noticed that Carmen had lost 10 pounds and now wore a size 3.

The presenting problem at the Somerset Mental Health Clinic was Carmen's rape by an alcoholic friend of Juan. The incident had occurred when Maria was out working on a housekeeping job and Sabrina was caring for Juanita. Juanita had fallen down the stairs on the stoop; because she was bleeding, Sabrina rushed her to the emergency room, leaving Carmen alone with her father and his friend. Juan had gone out to the local liquor store, and during his absence the rape had occurred.

The proceeding examples demonstrate the types of crisis situations that some families encounter and that lead them to seek mental health treatment. Crisis can take many forms: acute situational crisis, as in Jerome's injury and subsequent disability and Carmen's rape, or developmental crisis, as with Sam's behavior changes as he enters adolescence or Sabrina's cognitive changes with increasing age. No family is immune to crisis, regardless of their income, class status, or racial/ethnic background. This chapter will explore crisis theory and treatment for culturally and racially diverse families. The incidence of common stressors and crisis events will be explored. Special focus will be placed on resilience and protective factors that support families of color in coping with crisis and stress. Roberts's seven-stage model of crisis intervention will be applied to the examples to provide greater understanding of how the clinician could use crisis intervention treatment in work with culturally diverse families. The implications of providing crisis intervention services to such families in a managed care environment will be discussed. The chapter will conclude with guidelines for the clinician in work with diverse families within a rapidly changing mental health/behavioral health system.

Although there are many definitions of crisis and different views on its effects on individuals and families, the precipitating event is usually a hazardous event or a developmental stage (Golan, 1986; Parad, 1990; Roberts, 1990, 1996). These events are not sufficient, however, as two other factors must be present for the individual to experience a crisis. First, the individual must perceive the event as causing considerable distress; second, the individual must not be able to use previous coping skills. Whereas some may view a particular incident as producing a significant crisis reaction, others may not interpret the same incident as a crisis at all. Even an event that most people may interpret as a crisis, such as a loss of job, may not be seen as a crisis by the person who perceives the job loss as providing an opportunity to explore new vocational opportunities.

Most of us, although we may not credit ourselves with the skill, are masters at handling crisis events. Adults, for the most part, have successfully mastered developmental crises for different stages of childhood. All have weathered the crises events of births, marriages, and deaths of family members.

In a previous work, I discussed types of crisis that families encounter (Congress, 1996). Some crisis events that affect families are precipitated by "bolts from the blue" stressors (Pittman, 1987). These stressors can be a death, sudden or otherwise, of a family member, a loss of employment, or illness. "Bolts from the blue" are often not negative. Even positive "bolts from the blue" such as winning the lottery or receiving a big promotion at work can be experienced as crisis events. "Bolts from the blue" may affect individual family members differently than the family as a whole. For example, Jerome's injury following a robbery attempt certainly has a greater effect on him and less on other family members. However, the loss of him as a breadwinner and his constant presence within the household certainly will be a crisis for the whole family.

Crisis events of both types (unexpected and developmental) may have different meanings for different individuals and families. For example, the loss of a job may be very traumatic for many individuals and families because of loss of status and income. Another family may experience a loss of job as providing an opportunity to try a new field or move to a new location. In terms of developmental crisis, a young adult's leaving home may be seen as positive and providing new opportunities for both the departing child and the parents who remain behind.

CULTURALLY DIVERSE FAMILIES

In work with diverse families, many clinicians make generalizations based on their own backgrounds or previous work with White, middle-class American families from Western European backgrounds. Families need to be looked at individually, with the expectation that each group will relate differently to the world in general and to crisis events in particular. Much has been written recently about working with culturally diverse families (Congress, 1997; Green, 1995; Ho, 1987; McGoldrick, Pearce, & Giordano, 1996; Lum, 1992). Some literature has focused on general characteristics (McGoldrick et al., 1996) of different ethnic groups, but in crisis work it is essential to individualize the culturally diverse families. The clinician must assess the impact of the crisis event in different stages of development, as well as the positive crises of graduations, promotions, and births, and the sadder crises of deaths in the family and rejections from job and school possibilities.

STRENGTHS AND COPING OF CULTURALLY DIVERSE FAMILIES

Although clinicians have long used a deficit model that focus on clients' problems and shortcomings, a focus on strengths and coping skills is often more useful (Saleebey, 1997). Culturally diverse families have strengths that have enabled them to cope successfully with past crisis events. The clinician needs to focus on what families are doing right and what they have accomplished (Kaplan & Munoz, 1997). Because of strengths and previous successful experience in handling crisis, most families are able to cope with new crisis events. This approach may be especially useful in working with culturally diverse families who, despite the stresses of immigration and discrimination, often are able to cope with multiple crisis events. Family support may be a unacknowledged source of strength for the immigrant family. The support of family members may build resilience to help in coping with present and future crisis events. At times, however, the crisis event (acute event or developmental stage) is such that previous coping skills do not work. This constitutes a crisis event, which makes the individual and family vulnerable yet capable of positive growth through crisis intervention treatment.

CRISIS PRECIPITANTS FOR CULTURALLY DIVERSE FAMILIES

The author has identified the following crisis precipitants that most commonly affect immigrant families.

Unemployment

Fathers in immigrant families may have difficulty in finding jobs that are comparable in income and status to positions they held in their homelands. Unemployment and underemployment may produce stress within the family. Often the family crisis is manifested though substance abuse and/or domestic violence as demonstrated by the Sanchez family.

Changed Gender Roles

In the United States, married women have much more freedom than in many other parts of the world. This changed social norm may be stressful for the immigrant family, especially when women find work more easily than their husbands. For culturally diverse families from traditional backgrounds, a role reversal occurs when the wife becomes the breadwinner. Family conflict, substance abuse, or domestic violence may result and lead the family to seek crisis intervention treatment.

Intergenerational Conflict

Because of school and peer contacts, children and adolescents often become more quickly acculturated than their parents. This may produce family conflict and consequent crisis when children want to behave the same as their American peers (Congress, 1994, 1997). For example, adolescent daughters of immigrants may want to spend free time with their peers, whereas their parents expect them to care for younger siblings and help with household tasks as they did in their country of origin.

School Failure

Most immigrant families are very child focused and concerned that their children should use their educational experience in the United States to advance and achieve success. Thus, a family crisis often can occur when a child, because of the stresses of immigration and adjusting to a new culture

(Congress & Lynn, 1994), does not succeed academically. It is important that the crisis intervention clinician be cognizant of the impact of school failure on immigrant families who have focused many of their hopes and dreams on their children's academic success (Congress, 1990). The Sanchez family case example demonstrates how families adjust to differing academic achievement among different family members.

DEVELOPMENT AND USE OF THE CULTURAGRAM

In previous work with students and professionals, I became increasingly aware that many clinicians generalize about families from different cultural backgrounds. Cultural sensitivity involves much more than identifying that a family is Hispanic. There are many cultural and familial differences between the Hispanic Puerto Rican family, who have lived in New York City for 30 years and who work as teachers, as compared with the Hispanic Mexican undocumented family, who arrived in the United States last week and are day agricultural workers in Texas. To help workers become more aware of the cultural differences between families even from the same ethnic background, I developed the *culturagram* (Figure 19.1), which can readily be applied to work with culturally diverse families (Congress, 1994, 1997).

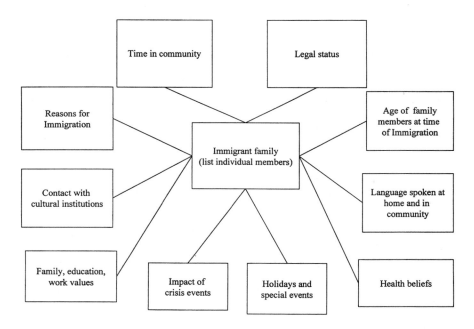

Figure 19.1   Culturagram

The culturagram has also been used with specific populations, including the elderly (Brownell, 1997) and victims of domestic violence (Brownell & Congress, 1998).

Culture has been defined not as a singular concept but rather as incorporating "institutions, language, values, religious ideals, habits of thinking, artistic expressions, and patterns of social and interpersonal relationships" (Lum, 1992, p. 62). In developing the culturagram, culture was used as a generic term under which ethnicity, race, national origin, and religion were subsumed. The culturagram examines the following 10 aspects of a family's culture.

1. Reasons for immigration
2. Length of time in the community
3. Legal status
4. Age of members at time of immigration
5. Language spoken at home and in the community
6. Health beliefs
7. Impact of crisis events
8. Holidays and special events
9. Contact with cultural institutions
10. Values about family, education, and work

Knowledge about these areas helps the worker better understand the culturally diverse areas, assess strengths, empower the family, and point to areas for possible social work intervention. All the aspects are relevant for the social worker who wishes to apply a crisis intervention model in working with culturally diverse families.

The reasons for immigration may precipitate a family crisis. A refugee family that has had to leave home because of religious and political prosecution or has had its home destroyed by war has faced a crisis event of loss and displacement. Many families come because of poverty in their homelands, but they may experience a crisis when they learn that economic opportunities in America are not what they anticipated. Some can readily return home and often travel back and forth for holidays and special occasions. Others experience a crisis because they can never go home again.

Economic and social differences between the country of origin and the United States can precipitate a crisis for immigrant families. For example, in America, latency-age children attend large schools, often far from their communities, and begin to develop peer relationships apart from their families. For culturally diverse families coming from backgrounds in which education was limited and even young children were supposed to work and care for younger siblings, the American school system, with its focus on individual academic achievement and peer relationships, may precipitate a crisis that is often first seen in the school setting (Congress & Lynn, 1994).

A second main part of a culturagram assessment involves learning the ages at which different members came to America. Age may be related to how individual families react to the crisis of immigration and relocation. Usually the family members who have arrived earlier are more assimilated than other members. Because of attending American schools and developing peer relationships, children often become more quickly acclimated than their parents. This may lead to a family crisis when conflicts develop because of role reversals in which children, because of their understanding of English, assume a leadership position within the family. A current phenomenon involves mothers first immigrating to the United States and then sending for their children. This certainly can create a crisis both for parents and for the children, who are first separated when they are very young and then reunited much later.

The legal status of a family may precipitate a crisis. If a family is undocumented and fears deportation, both individual members and the family as a whole may become secretive and withdrawn. Latency-age children and adolescents will be discouraged from developing peer relationships because of the fears of others knowing their immigration secret (Congress & Lynn, 1994). Many families may not be forthcoming about sharing about their legal status because of lack of trust of the clinician. Families may fear that their clinician is connected with the Immigration and Naturalization Service and will promote their deportation. Yet learning this information can be helpful because the worker can then help refer the family for legal assistance or to other community resources that can help with this problem.

Language is the mechanism by which families communicate with each other. Often families may use their own native language at home but may begin to use English in contacts with the outside community. Sometimes children begin to prefer English as they see knowledge of this language as most helpful for survival in this country. This may lead to conflict in families. A most literal communication problem may develop when parents speak no English and children only minimally speak their native tongue (Congress, 1996).

Families from different cultures have varying beliefs about health, disease, and treatment (Congress & Lyons, 1992). Often health issues impact on family functioning, as, for example, when the primary wage earner with a serious illness is no longer able to work, a family member has HIV/AIDS, or a child has a chronic health condition such as asthma or diabetes. Mental health problems also can negatively affect families. Families from different cultures may encounter barriers in accessing medical treatment, or they may prefer alternative resources for diagnosing and treating physical and mental health conditions (Devore & Schlesinger, 1996). Many immigrants may use health care methods other than traditional Western European medical care involving diagnosis, pharmacology, X rays, and surgery (Congress & Lyons, 1992). The social worker who wishes to understand families must study their unique health care beliefs.

Each family has particular holidays and special events (McGoldrick,

Pearce, & Giordano, 1996). Some events mark transitions from one developmental stage to another, as, for example, a christening, a bar mitzvah, a wedding, or a funeral. It is important for the social worker to learn what are important holidays for the family because they indicate what families see as major transition points in their family development.

Contact with cultural institutions often provides support to an immigrant family. Family members may use cultural institutions differently, as, for example, when the father belongs to a social club, the mother attends a church where her native language is spoken, and adolescent children refuse to participate because they wish to become more Americanized.

All families have differing values about work, education, and family. The social worker must explore what these values are in order to understand the family. For example, employment in a middle-class position may be very important to the male breadwinner. It may be especially traumatic for the immigrant family when the father can find no work or only work of a menial nature. Sometimes there may be a conflict in values. This occurred when an adolescent son was accepted with a full scholarship to a prestigious university 1,000 miles away from home. Although the family had always believed in the importance of education, the parents believed that the family needed to stay together and that they did not want their only child to leave home even to pursue higher education.

The family's reaction to crisis is most relevant in work with culturally diverse families. Similar to all families, culturally diverse families encounter developmental crisis as well as "bolts from the blue" crisis (Congress, 1996). Clinicians need to examine the impact of the specific crisis on the culturally diverse family with whom they are working. Developmental crisis occurs when the family transits from one stage of development to the next. For example, a child's leaving home may mark a significant transition stage for the family. For many culturally diverse families this stage may not occur at all, because single and even married children continue to live in close proximity to the parents. If separation is forced, this developmental crisis might be especially traumatic.

Families also deal with "bolts from the blue" crisis in different ways. A family's reactions to crisis events are often related to their cultural values. For example, a father's accident and inability to work may be especially traumatic for an immigrant family in which the father's providing for the family is an important family value. Rape is certainly traumatic for any family, but the rape of a teenage girl may be especially traumatic for a family that values virginity before marriage.

DEMOGRAPHICS

Many culturally diverse families experience "bolts from the blue" crisis events that may lead them to seek treatment. Crisis events of infant and maternal mortality, school dropout, lower life expectancy, and unemployment seem to disproportionately affect culturally diverse families. Infant mortality, which certainly precipitates a crisis in any family, is disturbingly high in the United States as compared with other industrial nations (Miringoff & Miringoff, 1999). Culturally diverse families in the United States are twice as likely as White American families to experience the death of an infant (Ginsberg, 1995), and four times as likely to experience maternal death (Miringoff & Miringoff, 1999).

A primary crisis event for any family is the death of a member. In general, individuals from culturally diverse families have a much shorter life expectancy than those from White families. White women have a life expectancy at birth of almost 80 years, whereas in some urban areas in the United States, Black men have a life expectancy of 57.9 years, which is as low as in many places in nonindustrialized countries in Africa (Miringoff & Miringoff, 1999.) Family crisis often occurs because of the unexpected death of a child or adolescent. Suicide of Black adolescent males has increased dramatically (Miringoff & Miringoff, 1999). Although Blacks constitute only 13% of the national population, a recent study indicated that there were more deaths of Black adolescents than Whites (Ginsberg, 1995).

Although, fortunately, most crisis events are not as final as death, culturally diverse families also experience other crisis events. Early school dropout, which is certainly experienced as a crisis event for immigrant families, especially those with high educational expectations, happens more frequently with culturally diverse families, especially Hispanic adolescents. Nationally 34.5% of Hispanic youth as compared with 12.5% of White do not complete high school (Miringoff & Miringoff, 1999). Unemployment for culturally diverse families, especially Black members is almost double the national average (Miringoff & Miringoff, 1999).

Although an examination of the incidence of crisis events that impact on culturally diverse families may be discouraging, it is important to look at the strength and resilience factors that protect families and help them weather crisis events. First, in terms of life expectancy, there is a crossover effect: As both Whites and those from other cultural backgrounds reach old age, there is less difference in life expectancy; in fact, for those who survive to 80, Blacks may have higher life expectancies. One explanation for this fact may be the resilience of many Black women who have lived through and surmounted stresses of poverty and prejudice (Congress & Johns, 1994). The role of the Black church in providing support for older Black women has been seen as enhancing their strength and resilience to cope with crisis events (Boyd-Franklin,1989). Another factor contributing to the strength of culturally diverse families in coping with crisis has been seen as family relationships. Whereas many White American families are influenced by an individualistic perspective, culturally diverse families are often more family oriented. Families can provide much support to individuals experiencing crisis. Also, extended families members often provide support to families experiencing crisis. For example, the number of AIDS orphans (100,000) in the United States is staggering (Romano & Zayas, 1997), yet many families have dealt with the crisis of parental death by having a grandparent assume parenting roles (Cohen, 1997).

Families of color often have incomes that are below or near the poverty line. Being poor often places families at high risk for substance abuse, homelessness, and domestic violence. Many practitioners focus on the problems of multicultural families, but it may be more helpful to look at their strengths and resilience. Families provide much support that protects individuals from the deleterious effects of poverty and all too frequent social problems. In working with a multicultural family facing a crisis, it is often most helpful to focus on their strengths—that thus far they have survived the stresses of immigration and may be living with very limited resources in a dangerous community.

Culturally diverse families, especially immigrants, may underutilize professional services. First, many families come from backgrounds where family problems, as well as physical and mental conditions, were handled within the family or, if this failed, the larger lay community. For many culturally diverse families there may be shame associated with seeking professional help. Attending a mental health program may be seen as announcing to the world that the problem cannot be resolved, that there are no family members who can help resolve the crisis. Furthermore, many families from diverse backgrounds may seek alternative forms of care. For example, the crisis of an unfaithful marital partner may lead a Dominican woman to seek the services of a spiritualist, or the illness crisis of a family member may lead a Chinese person to seek an acupuncturist. It is important for the professional to be respectful of families' right to choose the type of care they wish. While we acknowledge the importance of crisis intervention as a professional treatment, we know that some clients improve, some remain the same, and some emerge worse from the crisis even with treatment. It should be noted that many families are able to cope with crisis by calling upon family and community resources.

Other culturally diverse families would use crisis-intervention treatment if it was available. Since I first wrote about culturally diverse families and crisis (Congress, 1990), agencies have become much more culturally sensitive. Students in all the professions now study cultural issues, and agencies frequently provide in-service training in cultural competency. Yet there continue to be access issues that may limit culturally diverse families' use of crisis intervention services. Programs may have intake procedures that stigmatize or reject culturally diverse families. If families are asked to complete lengthy application forms in English, a language they do not understand, their use of crisis intervention services may be curtailed even before it begins. The lack of bilingual and bicultural staff may also detrimentally affect access for the culturally diverse family.

An increasing amount of professional care, including crisis intervention services, is administered under the rubric of managed care plans. Culturally diverse families will increasingly be seen in this way, especially as Medicaid managed care spreads through the nation. One issue for culturally diverse families is whether they will be covered, especially with welfare reform and undocumented status. Another concern is that crisis intervention services may not be authorized or may be authorized only after a significant delay. Yet early and immediate professional care is essential in crisis intervention treatment. A major concern about managed care is that often treatment protocols are used. For culturally diverse families that are very unique, one prescribed length or type of treatment may not be ideal. Whereas most crisis intervention treatment usually spans 8 sessions and no more than 12 (Cournoyer, 1996), some families may need less time for intervention and others may need more. The short-term nature of crisis work corresponds well to the current focus on brief treatment within a managed care world.

APPLICATION OF ROBERTS'S SEVEN-STEP CRISIS INTERVENTION MODEL

Because of its comprehensiveness and its flexibility, Roberts's seven-step model can be used effectively in working with culturally diverse families (Roberts, 1990, 1996). This model will be discussed in terms of the families in crisis presented earlier in this chapter.

The first step in Roberts's crisis intervention model, and an important initial step in all therapeutic work, is to plan and conduct a thorough assessment (including lethality, dangerous to self and others, and immediate psychosocial needs). Lethality, both imminent and potential danger, must be assessed. As a result of crisis, people are often unable to use emotional resources that have helped them cope in the past. Emotional reactions to crisis may take the form of depression, anger, or anxiety. Those for whom the reaction is that of depression have a much higher risk for suicide. Because the suicide rate is increasing, especially among adolescents, clinicians must be very aware of potential suicide risk. Sometimes a suicide attempt following a crisis event may precipitate a family seeking crisis intervention treatment. Then the clinician must make an assessment about whether a referral for inpatient treatment is necessary or whether outpatient treatment will be sufficient.

In making a suicide assessment, the clinician must consider whether there is a history of suicides in the family, whether the individual has made previous suicide attempts, the degree of hopelessness, the proximity of means, and the presence of a developed plan. The clinician must take very seriously any comments the client makes about suicide, because this is often a significant cry for help. Different ethnic groups may have differing rates of attempted and successful suicides. For example, Hispanic adolescent girls have a high rate of suicide attempts. Thus, the clinician must be very attuned to this potential risk when working with a Hispanic family. In the case example, Carmen may be at increased risk for a suicide attempt. She has lost weight, which can be a sign of depression or anorexia. Whereas depression is directly linked to suicide, anorexia could involve a slow type of suicide in which 10 to 15% of its victims die. The precipitating crisis event—that of Carmen's rape—can also lead to a suicide attempt, especially if the family blames the victim and increases her feelings of guilt and low self-esteem.

There is also a risk for increased violence toward others when an individual and family have experienced a crisis. In the preceding cases, Jerome may want to seek vengeance on the person he suspected injured him. Juan may want to seek retribution for the rape of this daughter. There is also increased risk for domestic violence, child abuse, and elder abuse. Because of Jerome's unemployment and conflict with his stepson, there may be escalating violence between the marital couple. Juan's alcohol problem also can contribute to domestic violence in the Sanchez family.

When families are under stress, having experienced current and ongoing crisis, there is an increased possibility of child abuse, and elder abuse. Often the victims of abuse are the most vulnerable—for example, children with special needs, such as 2-year-old Thomas Marshall, or elderly people who require constant care, such as 70-year-old Sabrina Cruz.

The third component of a crisis intervention assessment involves attention to immediate psychosocial needs. Because many culturally diverse families have limited incomes, and welfare reform has decreased the amount of social service benefits, families have increasing difficulty meeting their basic needs. In the preceding example, Maria Sanchez has been cut off from welfare and must go to work. Yet her educational and psychiatric background make it difficult for her to secure and maintain a job that can support the family. The Marshall family also may need help in securing social security disability benefits. The crisis intervention must be attuned to economic factors that contribute to the family's crisis.

Assessment must be done immediately during the first interview. Gone are the days during which the assessment process took place over many weeks. Crisis intervention work demands brief assessment. This works well with culturally diverse families, who may have very specific current problems that require immediate identification and intervention. The focus on the present for immediate assessment is most helpful in work with culturally diverse families.

The second step in Roberts's model involves establishing rapport and developing the relationship through a demonstration of genuine respect and concern for the client. The family needs to be reassured that they can be helped. In establishing rapport the clinician must be attuned to the family's cultural values. Because Hispanic families may expect a personal relationship (*personalismo*) with their therapist (Congress, 1990), the therapist who relates to the family in a personal way is more likely to establish rapport with the family. The clinician must not be overly formal and demand facts and dates. He or she also must be willing to listen to the family. Minuchin (1984) has described this process as "joining" or using the same language as the family and entering into their life space. Only after this has occurred can the worker proceed with crisis intervention treatment. Whereas many culturally diverse families, especially Hispanics, welcome *personalismo*, this is not true for all families. Some families may be suspicious of a worker who does not maintain formal relationships. For example, the Marshall family may interpret informality as a sign of disrespect and prejudice given the legacy in this country of racism, with accompanying infantilism and condescension, toward African Americans. The clinician must be very sensitive to verbal and nonverbal cues about the best way to establish rapport with families.

The third step is to have the family members identify their problems (Roberts, 1990). The clinician must help the family to prioritize the many problems they may have experienced. It is helpful to identify the precipitating problem that brought the family into treatment. The clinician who is working with a family must try to learn this from each member, not only the family spokesperson, because each member may be experiencing crisis in a different way. Families may tell their problems in different ways. A tendency for all families, including culturally diverse families, is to focus on one problem, usually related to a child. The Marshall family came to seek crisis intervention because of 12-year-old Samuel's behavior, whereas the Sanchez family came because of their 16-year-old daughter's rape. These were precipitating events, "the straw that broke the camel's back." The crisis intervention worker, however, must be sensitive to the cumulative effect of past and present crises on families. Other recent crisis events for the Marshall family has been Mr. Marshall's sudden injury and consequent inability to work, as well as Thomas's recently diagnosed developmental disability. Mr. Sanchez's alcoholism, Maria's chronic depression, and Sabrina's increasing need for care are chronic crisis events. The effect of cumulative crisis often has a deleterious effect on a family's ability to cope with "bolts from the blue" crises, such as Carmen's rape.

The fourth step of Roberts's model involves dealing with family members' varied feelings and emotions. The clinician must adopt a nonjudgmental stance and communicate care and reassurance to all family members. Some culturally diverse families may not trust the crisis intervention clinician, fearing that the worker will be critical and judgmental. Undocumented families may be reluctant to discuss their real feelings with the worker. It may be necessary to inform the family at the outset that the clinician does not work for the government and will not contribute to their deportation. Family members may express their feelings in different ways. For example, Mrs. Marshall, who has striven to be middle-class, may be ashamed to expose her son's problems to the outside world. Mrs. Sanchez may be depressed and may blame herself for her daughter's rape. Mr. Sanchez may be angry and belligerent.

Therapy may be a new phenomenon for many culturally diverse families. To discuss their feelings with a professional may have been unheard of in their countries of origin, and any emotional problem may cause the family to feel shame. Men, especially if their status has been undermined in America, may find it especially difficult to share their feelings with the therapist. In crisis intervention work with culturally diverse families, the therapist must move at a pace that is comfortable for the family and the individual members. Much good listening and positive reassurance will be necessary to help the family share their feelings regarding the crisis event.

The next step involves generating and exploring alternatives. Because the family members probably have had many years of experience in coping with and managing other stresses, the clinician should try to generate some alternatives from them. This is particularly true for many culturally diverse families for two reasons: (a) Culturally diverse families often have had much experience in coping with crisis events, and (b) Culturally diverse families often can generate alternatives that are particularly helpful for them.

The Marshall family, for example, discussed an alternative of sending Samuel to live with his great aunt in the South. Sometimes families are too anxious to generate alternatives, and in these cases the clinician can be helpful. Often the clinician can be most helpful in generating alternatives that are specific and concrete, as well as culturally and linguistically sensitive. For example, Mr. Marshall's disability benefits from his job were almost depleted, and the clinician was prepared to refer him for Social Security disability benefits.

The Sanchez family had been so upset and ashamed by Carmen's rape that they had not sought medical attention. One alternative the crisis intervention worker discussed was arranging for Carmen to visit a gynecologist. The family was concerned that Carmen was too young to see a gynecologist. The clinician presented the alternative of her seeing a female Puerto Rican doctor who would be culturally and linguistically sensitive to the Sanchez family. The clinician also told the family about a day program for Hispanic senior adults in the community that could provide some respite for the family and about Spanish Alcoholic Anonymous (AA) meetings in a local church.

The sixth step involves developing and formulating an action plan. Just as the culturally diverse family was involved in generating alternatives, so, too, should they participate in the final action plan. The family must choose among the various alternatives. For example, Mr. Marshall decided that he did not want to apply for Social Security disability benefits but instead preferred to enter a vocational rehabilitation program to learn new skills to prepare him for a more sedentary job. The Marshalls planned to send their son Samuel south to live with his great aunt, but then wanted him to return in the fall. If there were still problems after Jerome had begun a new career, the family planned to enter into family therapy.

The Sanchez family took advantage of some of the alternatives that had been generated by the crisis intervention worker. Juan, however, continued to deny that he had an alcohol problem and refused to become involved with AA. Mrs. Sanchez did not seek mental health treatment for her depression, but she did join a Hispanic Alanon group from which she received ongoing support. Carmen became involved in an activity group at school for adolescent girls.

The final step in crisis intervention work necessitates a plan for follow-up. After experiencing a crisis, a family can get better, get worse, or continue at their precrisis level of functioning (Parad & Parad, 1990). After 8 to 12 weeks of crisis intervention treatment, many families feel and function better. The majority of families may never return for crisis intervention treatment. Yet the clinician should stress availability if the family chooses to return. Sometimes it is helpful to call the family a month later to check how it is doing. During the last session the family should be informed that this is planned, so that a call a month later does not seem like an unwelcome intrusion.

Crisis intervention treatment is by definition a short-term model, and thus ideal for the current managed care environment in which briefer treatment is preferable. Crisis intervention also works well for culturally diverse families who seek specific results within a short period of time.

In working with culturally diverse families using a crisis intervention model, the following guidelines are helpful:

1. Assess the impact of the crisis on individual members and the family as a whole. Families from different countries often have different values. What is a crisis for one family may not be one for another.

2. Acknowledge strengths and previous successful coping. Many culturally diverse families have had many years of experience in coping with crisis without assistance from professionals. Yet in America they may feel stigmatized and their previous achievements minimized. Crisis work with immigrants should involve building up self-esteem by recognizing past successes.

3. Develop a treatment plan that is very specific and concrete. Many culturally diverse families come from countries in which mental health problems are seen as a source of shame. They are more likely to appreciate crisis intervention work that is relevant and related to their problem.

4. Use natural support systems such as family and community. In crisis work with culturally diverse families, the crisis worker should try to mobilize existing support systems. Often culturally diverse families will be most trusting of this type of help. Also at a time of diminished government support and agency care, informal support systems may be the only support available.

5. Develop alternatives that are linguistically and culturally sensitive. In this way families are more likely to utilize alternatives to help them cope with crisis.
6. Normalize crisis experiences. Often the family undergoing crisis feels very isolated and believes no one else has had a similar experience. This may be particularly true for the culturally diverse family, which may have recently suffered the losses and separation connected with immigration. Helping a family to see that they are not the only ones to have experienced this crisis is often helpful.
7. Empower the family in crisis to generate alternatives and to develop an action plan to help them survive the crisis. This demonstrates to the family that the clinician has confidence in their ability to survive the crisis. Culturally diverse families may especially need to be empowered, since much of their experience in the American social environment may have contributed to their feelings of lack of control and power.

CONCLUSION AND IMPLICATIONS FOR FUTURE STUDY

During the next century the majority of Americans will be from backgrounds other than Western European (Congress, 1994). What crisis events will these new Americans face? The last years of the twentieth century have witnessed the dismantling of the safety net and cutbacks in public welfare benefits. In most states, welfare benefits for both legal and undocumented immigrants have been eliminated. In a managed care environment, health care benefits for the insured have been curtailed. Many working Americans have no health insurance and thus are not able to access minimal health care. Unskilled jobs are rapidly being eliminated, and technical knowledge and advanced education may be needed to secure many jobs. Many new Americans may have difficulty securing employment in a highly competitive job market.

Unemployment, underemployment, lack of health care, and lack of welfare benefits may contribute to stress and crisis reactions in culturally diverse families. Economic hardships also often contribute to domestic violence and substance abuse among culturally diverse families. In the current social and economic environment, it can be predicted that the incidence of crisis precipitants for the culturally diverse family will increase as we enter the next century.

Can crisis intervention treatment make a difference with culturally diverse families? Although there has been research on the efficacy of the crisis intervention treatment model in general, its specific usefulness in work with such families has been minimally studied. Crisis intervention treatment does and will continue to appeal to culturally diverse families for several reasons:

1. Crisis intervention treatment addresses the family's immediate greatest needs. For many culturally diverse families, a treatment method that focuses on their specific needs is preferable.

2. Crisis intervention treatment focuses on strengths and resilience. Culturally diverse families find this model empowering, in contrast to other methods that stress problems, deficits, and limitations.
3. Crisis intervention treatment is solution focused. This will appeal to culturally diverse families, who may be wary of traditional talk therapies.
4. Crisis intervention treatment is short-term. Culturally diverse families with little income and limited health insurance will benefit from a treatment method that is time limited.

Although crisis intervention treatment seems most appropriate for culturally diverse families, the effectiveness of this model for diverse populations needs to be further addressed. The following are some important questions for future study:

1. Does a general crisis intervention model work effectively with all culturally diverse families, or should there be variations for different racial, cultural, and ethnic groups?
2. What is the impact of multiple crisis events, which often seem to plague culturally diverse families?
3. Since culturally diverse families are often very family oriented, how can crisis intervention services be developed for working with families?
4. Does the cultural background of the clinican make a difference in the effectiveness of crisis work with diverse families?
5. Should the crisis intervention clinician maintain the same professional distance with culturally diverse families as with other families? In an earlier edition of this book, I described *personalismo* (i.e., a personal relationship) as being essential in developing a positive therapeutic relationship with the client (Congress, 1990).
6. How effective is crisis intervention treatment with culturally diverse families? Do individuals and/or the family have improved functioning immediately after treatment? After a year has elapsed? At the point a new crisis occurs?

Future research on these questions will help professionals assess the value of crisis intervention services with the rapidly increasing number of culturally diverse families.

REFERENCES

Boyd-Franklin N. L. (1989). *Black families in therapy: A multisystems approach*. New York: Guilford Press.

Brownell, P. (1997). The application of the culturagram in cross-cultural practice with elder abuse victims. *Journal of Elder Abuse and Neglect, 9*(2), 19–33.

Brownell, P., & Congress, E. (1998). Application of the culturagram to assess and empower culturally and ethnically diverse battered women. In A. Roberts (Ed.), *Battered women and their families: Intervention and treatment strategies* (pp. 387–404). New York: Springer.

Cohen, C. (1997). The impact of culture in social work practice with groups: The "Grandmothers as mothers again" case study. In E. Congress (Ed.), *Multicultural perspectives in working with families* (pp. 311–331). New York: Springer.

Congress, E. P. (1990). Crisis intervention with Hispanic clients in an urban mental health clinic. In A. R. Roberts (Ed.), *Crisis intervention handbook: Assessment, treatment, and research* (pp. 221–236). Belmont, CA: Wadsworth.

Congress, E. (1994). The use of culturagrams to assess and empower culturally diverse families. *Families in Society, 75(9)*, 531–540.

Congress, E. P. (1996). Family crisis: Life cycle and bolts from the blue: Assessment and treatment. In A. Roberts (Ed.), *Crisis management and brief treatment: Theory, technique, and applications* (pp. 142–159). Chicago: Nelson-Hall.

Congress, E. P. (1997). Using the culturagram to assess and empower culturally diverse families. In E. P. Congress (Ed.), *Multicultural perspectives in working with families* (pp. 3–16). New York: Springer.

Congress, E., & Johns, M. (1994). Aging and ethnicity. In I. Gutheil (Ed.), *Working with older persons: Challenges and opportunities.* (pp. 65–84). New York: Fordham University Press.

Congress, E., & Lynn, M. (1994). Group work programs in public schools: Ethical dilemmas and cultural diversity. *Social Work in Education, 16(2)*, 107–114.

Congress, E., & Lyons, B. (1992). Cultural differences in health beliefs: Implications for social work practice in health care settings. *Journal of Social Work Practice in Health Care, 17(3)*, 81–96.

Cournoyer, B. (1996). *The social work skills handbook*. Pacific Grove, CA: Brooks/Cole.

Devore, W., & Schlesinger, E. (1996). *Ethnic-sensitive social work practice.* New York: Macmillan.

Ginsberg, L. (1995). *Social work almanac.* Washington, DC: NASW Press.

Golan, N. (1986). "Crisis" theory. In F. J. Turner (Ed.), *Social work treatment: Interlocking theoretical approaches* (3rd ed) (pp. 296–340). New York: Free Press.

Green, J. (1995). *Cultural awareness in the social services.* Englewood Cliffs, NJ: Prentice-Hall.

Ho, M. (1987). *Family therapy with ethnic minorities.* Newbury Park, CA: Sage.

Kaplan, C., & Munoz, M. (1997). Poor minority adolescents and their families. In E. P. Congress (Ed.), *Multicultural perspectives in working with families* (pp. 3–16). New York: Springer.

Lum, D. (1992). *Social work practice and people of color: A process-stage approach.* Pacific Grove, CA: Brooks/Cole.

McGoldrick, M., Pearce, J., & Giordano, J. (1996). *Family therapy and ethnicity.* New York: Guilford.

Minuchin, S. (1984). *Family kaleidoscope.* Cambridge MA: Harvard University Press.

Miringoff, M., & Miringoff, M. L. (1999). *The social health of the na-*

tion: How America is really doing. New York: Oxford University Press.

Parad, H. J. (1965). *Crisis intervention: Selected readings.* New York: Family Services Association of America.

Parad, H., & Parad, L. (1990). *Crisis intervention: The practitioner sourcebook for brief therapy.* Milwaukee, WI: Family Service Association.

Pittman, F. (1987). *Turning points: Treating families in transition and crisis.* New York: Norton.

Roberts, A. (1990). An overview of crisis theory and crisis intervention. In A. Roberts (Ed.), *Crisis intervention handbook: Assessment,* *treatment, and research* (pp. 3–16). Belmont, CA: Wadsworth.

Roberts, A. R. (1996). Epidemiology and definitions of acute crisis in American society. In A. R. Roberts (Ed.), *Crisis management and brief treatment: Theory, technique, and applications* (pp. 16–33). Chicago: Nelson-Hall.

Romano, K., & Zayas, L. (1997). Motherless children: Family interventions with AIDS orphans. In E. Congress (Ed.), *Multicultural perspectives in working with families* (pp. 109–124). New York: Springer.

Saleebey, D. (Ed.). (1997). *The strengths perspective in social work practice.* New York: Longman.

V

RESEARCH

20

Research on Crisis Intervention and Recommendations for Future Research

JACQUELINE CORCORAN
ALBERT R. ROBERTS

Crisis intervention programs and centers exist in a managed care environment of budget constraints and increased demands for accountability and outcome measures. Research on program effectiveness and outcome data can document which types of crisis intervention programs work best, with trained and experienced staff, for particular target groups. Behavioral health care and other managed care organizations strongly challenge administrators, program directors, and clinicians to demonstrate the efficacy of crisis intervention and time-limited treatment. Historically, the crisis intervention paradigm has been at the core of the professions of community psychiatry, community psychology, and social work. The current managed care arena fosters an emphasis on symptom reduction through medication management rather than cognitive restructuring and crisis mastery. In this cost-conscious climate we have a golden opportunity to demonstrate both the cost-effectiveness and the value to humane care of crisis intervention as a practice model. It is important to include crisis intervention programs in the continuum of care options available for patients in both psychiatric and situational crisis. Crisis intervention research and the growth of 24-hour mobile crisis units can provide the antidote to inhumane care and abandonment of persons in dire need of frontline mental health services.

The importance of future research on crisis intervention in the managed care era of accountability is aptly addressed by Virginia Richardson, professor of social work at Ohio State University. First and foremost, crisis intervenors should emphasize treatment planning and the application of a particular type of treatment protocol, such as Roberts's seven-stage crisis intervention model. Measuring behavioral outcomes of clients, such as crisis resolution and improved social functioning, should not be too burdensome and time-consuming. The key to rapid assessment is the use of brief instruments or scales that are easily administered and scored, and that include concise questions and computer-scannable response forms. Although many crisis counselors identify intervention strategies based on intuition, tradition, and conjecture, most crisis workers value data obtained from research, including findings that reveal which crisis techniques work best, when they should be used, and with which clients. More research is needed, especially on the efficacy of reflective listening, brief assessments, and specific crisis intervention techniques. We also lack consensus on how well the suicide lethality index predicts suicide in clients of different ages; which scales accurately measure symptom reduction and crisis resolution; when to incorporate cognitive techniques; and the differences between directive and nondirective treatments. Managed care and the need for accountability demand that crisis counselors better document the outcomes of their work. Despite the many obstacles inherent in crisis intervention research, such as limited time, immediate intervention, and distressed clients, more research in this area ultimately will enhance empirically based practice in crisis intervention. It will also generate valuable resources that crisis counselors can refer to and use in their practice (Richardson, 1999).

A step-by-step model of program evaluation for assessing crisis intervention units in mental health agencies and psychiatric hospitals has been recommended by Michael J. Smith, a professor at Hunter College, of the City University of New York (see Smith, 1990, for further information). Smith recommends that mental health agencies start small with a staged-in approach to evaluation. The aim is to establish a commitment to evaluation. This commitment to evaluation will place the agency in a positive position with federal, state, and local regulatory bodies.

> The starting place should not be experimental studies or impact assessment studies which evaluate a causal link between intervention and outcomes. The starting place should be monitoring studies or systematic examinations of service delivery. According to Roberts's (1995) national survey of the organizational structure and functions of 107 crisis intervention units and centers, the most frequent presenting problems were depression, substance abuse, suicide attempts, and marital crises. Monitoring studies will help us establish the service context in a particular agency by helping us answer basic questions about the crisis intervention service: Who is being served? What are the main problems they are experiencing? What combination of problems or issues do they have? How were they referred to the service? What interventions did they receive? Do service providers think the program is working? Have the families been involved in the service?

Available case record data such as management information system (MIS) data could be used to answer many basic questions such as: How many patients are being seen? What are the primary problems? Small follow-up surveys of client groups can be used to determine if the crisis unit was successful at linking crisis cases to needed services in the community. The program goals of a crisis unit may never be reached if monitoring studies that assess basic questions of service delivery and the implementation of interventions are never conducted.

After developing a commitment to evaluation through monitoring studies, the research agenda should proceed to more of a focus on goal-oriented evaluation, whether or not program goals are being achieved? Are symptoms being reduced? Are client conditions being stabilized. Is long-term rehabilitation being achieved? Are families being strengthened? The follow-up research strategy can be used to focus on whether or not these goals are being achieved by the crisis unit. As a crisis unit achieves a certain expertise in a particular type of case, such as treatment of depression, substance abuse, etc., then quasi-experimental studies in which different types of cases are assigned to different forms of intervention can be conducted. (Smith, 1999)

As the evaluation agenda develops, Smith (1999) suggests that some new approaches in the context of evaluation may be useful. Empowerment evaluation (Fetterman, 1996) could be a useful approach in crisis centers. Clients or patients who come to crisis centers can be among consumers with the fewest resources and the least power. Staff and evaluators may want to recognize that clients are the most profound stakeholders in the evaluation process. Their fate is literally in the hands of the service provider and the staff they use. Program staff also need to be empowered so that their interventions are understood by those doing the evaluation. An outright recognition of the political nature of evaluation can bring issues of power and decision-making out in the open so that evaluation studies can be conducted and their results fed back into a program planning process.

Evaluability assessment (Wholey, 1981) is another useful trend in evaluation that emphasizes evaluation as a participatory process. An evaluability assessment includes questions such as "Can the program be evaluated given its current level of implementation?" This type of question is especially relevant in measuring the effectiveness of the program paradigm or model, along the lines of Roberts's seven-stage crisis intervention model presented in this book. In evaluability assessment, practitioner interviews and direct observation of program participants are utilized to refine the intervention model. Both approaches—empowerment evaluation and evaluability assessment—are contextual overlays that can be utilized in either monitoring studies or goal-oriented evaluations to promote evaluation and better program planning (Smith, 1999).

Allen Rubin, Bert Kruger Smith Centennial Professor of Social Work at the University of Texas at Austin, strongly recommends the use of randomized experimental or quasi-experimental designs when evaluating the effectiveness of crisis intervention:

> My rationale for preferring a randomized experimental design is simply that it is the strongest design for inferring causality. Quasi-experimental designs are also acceptable, if they are done in a rigorous fashion, and often must be used instead of experimental designs when evaluating crisis intervention because it may be unethical to withhold services for control group purposes for people experiencing crises. Since there are several different crisis intervention models, an experiment could randomly assign some clients to Roberts's crisis intervention program and other clients to a program using a different crisis intervention modality—to see which of the two modalities is more effective. (Rubin, 1999).

OUTCOME MEASURES AND RECOMMENDED ASSESSMENT INSTRUMENTS

The editor of this volume interviewed a panel of research professors each of whom has taught graduate courses on research methods, evaluating clinical practice, single-subject design, program evaluation, and/or qualitative research for approximately 25 years, or a total of 150 years. These experts have also directed research grants and published their findings in peer-reviewed professional journals. All of the research authorities agreed that there is a critical need for a multifaceted crisis assessment scale. The editor of this volume, in collaboration with Sara Lewis, is completing such a scale.

The Lewis-Roberts Multidimensional Crisis Assessment Scale (Lewis-Roberts MCAS), currently under development, is intended to be a multidimensional instrument that measures the severity or magnitude of personal and/or social dysfunction associated with a crisis state. The Lewis-Roberts MCAS will not measure or score crisis events, but instead the individual's functioning level associated with the perception of crisis. The two primary goals of the instrument are rapid clinical assessment and standardized measurement for group research.

One use of rapid assessment instruments (RAI) is to assist clinicians in the assessment and monitoring of clients. By administering an instrument upon intake and periodically throughout treatment, clinicians can determine client progress or setbacks. Another use of RAIs that is equally important is standardized measurement. There are currently no multidimensional instruments reported in the crisis literature that allow researchers to measure personal and social functioning associated with a crisis state. The Lewis-Roberts MCAS will open the doors to stronger research in the field of crisis intervention. Until the Lewis-Roberts MCAS is developed and incorporated into the rapid assessment intake completed by mental health centers and other crisis intervention programs, we will have to rely on a combination of several of the older scales used to measure symptomatology according to the research experts.

In the words of Virginia E. Richardson (1999): "Outcomes include symptoms of crisis and clients' self-reports that the intervention helped. Roberts (1995) identifies depression, substance abuse, suicide attempts, and marital crises as the most frequent presenting problems in crisis intervention." Richardson suggested the following assessment instruments, which have been standardized and evaluated for their reliability and validity:

- Brief Psychiatric Rating Scale (BPRS) (Faustman, 1994).
- Brief Symptom Inventory (BSI) (Derogatis, 1993).
- Hamilton Anxiety Rating Scale (HARS) (Hamilton, 1959).
- Self-Rating Anxiety Scale (Zung, 1971).
- Hamilton Rating Scale for Depression (HRSD) (Hamilton, 1960).
- Beck Depression Inventory (BDI) (Beck, Ward, Mendelson, Mock, & Erbaugh, 1961).
- Scale for Suicide Ideation (Beck, Kovacs, & Weissman, 1979).

According to Tom Jackson (1999), professor of Psychology and director of Clinical Training at the University of Arkansas, and chair of the Committee on Accreditation of the American Psychological Association, the salient outcome measures represent those that would demonstrate the purported effectiveness of the crisis intervention unit—that is, measures of changes in depression, suicidality, general psychological symptoms, anxiety or panic, and problem-solving skills. These measures would be in addition to client-rated satisfaction with the services. Sampling techniques would likely include individual test administration, telephone survey follow-up, and, potentially, reports from significant others. Several useful and fairly brief scales or instruments are Beck's face valid measures (Beck Depression Inventory II, Beck Hopelessness Scale, Beck Scale for Suicide Ideation); Derogatis's Symptom Checklist 90-R or its brief version; and Spielberger's State-Trait Anxiety Inventory and State Trait Anger Expression Inventory. The consumer satisfaction questionnaires should be fairly easy to construct if the agency has not already developed them. The point of the research is to provide comprehensive measures of effectiveness involving behavior and symptom change as well as consumer satisfaction (Jackson, 1999).

According to Susan Matorin, director of the Intensive Out-patient Program (IOP) of the Cornell Psychiatry Department and the Payne Whitney Clinic at New York Presbyterian Hospital, research on the effectiveness of crisis intervention should be conducted

in a natural setting in which a practitioner-researcher partnership organizes already available data. Research to define patient characteristics, impact of interventions, level of skill of clinician, and follow-up data would be invaluable in the clinician-insurer dialogue. One viable research design could utilize a chart review of currently existing computerized records for a sample supplemented by a follow-up interview by a rater and a patient satisfaction tool.

Optimally, one would describe the sample with regard to age, sex, DSM-IV multiaxial diagnosis, source of referral (e.g., emergency room, inpatient unit, private practice therapist), and payment source. The study should examine how quickly crisis patients are evaluated and provided with service. Because the computerized record allows for clear documentation of in-person and collaborative contacts, it would be important to track not only actual "visit counts" regarding service, but other interventions as well. For example, many of these clients maintain phone contact with the clinician between visits. All patients are given a global assessment score (GAS) at intake. Unfortunately, no other scales are currently utilized. However, charts should be studied for attention to psychiatric and social risk variables (i.e., suicidality, substance abuse, eviction threats, domestic violence, and confounding medical illnesses). An additional variable that merits attention is the subgroup of clients who enter the intensive outpatient program from prior "failed" community-based treatments, often split arrangements in which the nonmedical therapist and psychiatrist collaboration failed to intervene rapidly enough to avert a crisis. (Matorin, 1999)

Although this statement from one of the master clinician/research experts seems harsh, it is often an accurate description in New York City, where many thousands of individuals experience acute crisis episodes after being either dropped or ignored by a mental health agency. In sharp contrast to the 24-hour comprehensive mobile crisis units in DeKalb County, Georgia, and Erie, Pennsylvania (see Chapters 15 and 16 in this book for further detailed information), it is very difficult to have an in-person emergency appointment with a psychiatrist or licensed clinician after 5:00 P.M. during the week or anytime on weekends in many cities. The 24-hour mobile crisis units are the exceptions, since they regularly do home visits when the crisis caller is physically or mentally immobilized and homebound. Crisis intervention units of local mental health centers and emergency hospital-based psychiatric services are usually available by phone 24 hours a day and on weekends. However, in the majority of programs, the psychologists and social workers leave by 5:00 P.M., and they rely on trained volunteers and graduate student interns to rapidly intervene with the most difficult cases. On the positive side, many of the established crisis intervention programs and centers have licensed clinicians on call in the evening and on weekends for suicidal, domestic violence, and other dangerous crisis episodes.

RESEARCH LITERATURE ON CRISIS INTERVENTION

Although crisis intervention is used in many areas of direct practice, a search of the literature indicates that little empirical outcome research has been conducted. Only certain areas have studies to represent them: crime victimization, suicide prevention, psychiatric emergencies, and child abuse. In this section recent research (from the last 15 years) is organized according to problem area. Following a discussion in each section, recommendations on how to improve future evaluation efforts will be explored.

CRIME VICTIMIZATION STUDIES

In response to the needs of crime victims, many victim assistance programs have been developed in the last three decades of the twentieth century, and most programs have as their basis crisis intervention (Roberts, 1990, 1998). As documented in chapter 1 of this volume, the number of programs operating nationally is now estimated at 9,000. Despite the large number of programs, many of which receive federal and state funding, few have published evaluations of their efforts. For brief summaries of the studies we located, see Table 20.1.

Two studies describe a crisis intervention approach in which counselors provided assistance to victims of domestic violence at the scene of an assault (Allen, 1998; Corcoran, Stephenson, Allen, & Perryman, 1999). Both studies were based in urban southwestern police departments. Patrol officers in the two programs referred victims for the following services: counseling; providing information about criminal justice system policies and procedures; explaining victims' rights; explaining protective orders; giving legal referrals; and collaborating with battered women's shelters. The two programs differed by the role of the service providers. In Allen (1998), the response team consisted of a detective from the police family violence unit and a trained crisis intervention volunteer. The police detective was responsible for gathering evidence, conducting an investigation, filing charges, and sending the case to the district attorney's office. In Corcoran et al. (1999), the team was composed of a staff victim assistance counselor and a trained volunteer.

In the Allen and Corcoran (1999) study, family violence calls after the crisis team was developed were compared with calls from the preceding year, in which no team was in operation, and certain differences were found. Victim cooperation was greater when the team did not respond than when it did. Perhaps the intervention was utilized more frequently on calls when the victim was hostile or resistant. The number of arrests at the scene was greater when the team approach was utilized: 84% (of 77 cases) in the team approach compared with only 36% (of 80 cases) when only patrol officers responded. It may be that the team was called more regularly to those scenes in which a suspect had been apprehended. One reason may have been that the detective in the team was responsible for investigating, taking statements, and completing the paperwork once a suspect had been arrested. To avoid the confounding of law enforcement policy and crisis intervention by trained

Table 20.1   Crime Victimization

Author/Model	Design/Sample	Measures	Results	Limitations
Corcoran (1995) Victim assistance for child sexual abuse	Posttest only, $N = 91$ respondents (mostly parents of sexual abuse victims) Majority parents (84%); majority female (90%); 51% white, 18% African-American, 25% Hispanic; 23% alleged sexual abuse involved a natural parent, 19% by family friend, 11% by stepparent, 10% by acquaintance, 8% by neighbor, 7% by grandparent, 4% by aunt/uncle, 4% by stranger	Nonstandardized survey on satisfaction with services and utilization of community counseling referrals	50% of parents reported they had been in counseling, as were 65% of their children; in majority of cases (70%), respondents reported positive or somewhat positive change in children and/or family as a result of attending counseling; most respondents (92%) professed satisfaction with services at victim assistance unit	Small response rate (8%); no pretest; nonstandardized measurement instrument; lack of uniform follow-up time

Davis (1987) Victim assistance program, NYC (1) crisis intervention with supportive counseling; (2) crisis intervention with cognitive restructuring (3) material/concrete assistance only; (4) no-service control 91% of those in crisis counseling condition and 82% in cognitive restructuring treatment	Quasi-experimental design, pretest, follow-up (3 months) N = 249 victims randomly assigned to groups	Affect Balance Scale; Impact of Event Scale; Symptom Checklist 90-R	At 3-month follow-up, no differences between experimental and control groups	No posttest; pretest within 1 month of crime; lack of demographic information
Allen & Corcoran (1999) Police–crisis intervention team approach to working with domestic violence victims at scene of crime	Quasi-experimental, comparing calls in which team responded vs. those in which they did not N = 154 56% female; 53% African-American, 19% white, 5% Hispanic	Offense reports	More arrests were made with team cases; less cooperation from victims in team cases	Intervention had just begun 2 months prior to data collection; bias toward intervention in that comparison of all experimental cases was made against random selection of cases from year before; history bias; lack of standardized measures; possible bias of crisis intervention with mandatory arrest and direct file procedures; lack of follow-up

(continued)

Table 20.1 *Continued*

Author/Model	Design/Sample	Measures	Results	Limitations
Corcoran et al. (1999)	Posttest only N = 219 patrol officers	Utilization of and satisfaction with victim assistance family violence response team survey	67% had called out response team; majority (54%) had called out team 2–10 times; 79% found team helpful; suggestions for improvement: available more hours (32%); can respond to calls other than domestic violence (19%); provide education and awareness of program to patrol officers (22%)	No pretest; no standardized measures; no comparison group

volunteers, it might be more helpful (and less expensive for law enforcement agencies) to assess the effectiveness of social service responses at the scene rather than also having the presence of a police detective.

However, few patrol officers seemed to refer victims to the team crisis intervention approach. For instance, when cases in a 6-month period the first year after program implementation were randomly selected, only 1% of 80 cases had crisis team intervention. It could be that officers were unaware of the program or were unfamiliar with its potential benefits at this stage of program implementation.

The other crisis intervention approach with domestic violence victims examined patrol officers' opinions toward the domestic violence team (Corcoran et al., 1999). The 219 patrol respondents were generally positive toward the team: 69% had used the team, with most using the team between two and ten times; 79% found the team helpful. When asked how services could be improved, officers requested an expansion of efforts. As a result of survey opinions, the victim assistance program altered its hours to increase availability and to respond to other victims of crime, such as robbery and homicide survivors.

Another study of crime victims examined the use of crisis intervention with child sexual abuse victims and their families (Corcoran, 1995). A follow-up survey of victim assistance services was sent to 1,200 households. Of those who responded (8%), a majority of parents (92%) were very satisfied or somewhat satisfied with these services. The study also looked at the use of referral information because one such function of crisis intervention involves referral to ongoing services in the community (Young, 1990). Half the parents reported attending counseling sessions, with a higher percentage of their children (65%) also going to counseling sessions. A majority of parents (70%) attributed at least a somewhat positive change in their children and/or their families to these services.

A final study in the area of crime victimization involved victims who had experienced different types of crimes; here the focus was on the kinds of crisis intervention methods that were most helpful for recovery (Davis, 1987). In this study, 249 victims were randomized to crisis intervention with supportive counseling, crisis intervention with cognitive restructuring, the provision of material assistance and concrete services only, or a control group that did not receive any services. A three-month follow-up indicated that both crime-related problems and psychological functioning improved significantly, although few differences were found between any of the experimental conditions and the control group. However, there were some limitations that might have contributed to this finding. The second author had planned and implemented this research project (funded by the National Institute of Justice) in New York City. He indicated that the pretest and intervention took place not right after the crime victimization but usually within 2 to 3 weeks after the incident, whereas crisis intervention is usually defined as intervention occurring immediately (or within 72 hours) after the crisis event has taken place (see chapters 1 and 8 in this volume). Bureaucratic delays in the Police Commissioner's Office for the New York City Police Department (NYPD) and poor record-keeping at several of the police precincts caused some of the delays in contacting crime victims. The biggest obstacle was that the researchers were not allowed to telephone the crime victims; instead, they had to send a postcard inviting the victim to call and make an appointment with the designated offices of Victim Services. Since an assumption of crisis intervention is that crises can be resolved within 4 to 6 weeks of a traumatic event, it also could well be that the crisis of the crime was reaching resolution by the time intervention occurred. In addition, follow-up administration took place at 3 months. It is difficult to know how a single counseling contact (a majority of clients attended only one session) contributed to functioning at the 3-month follow-up, considering the many factors that may be enacting an influence. Nevertheless, most victims claimed they found crisis intervention helpful.

Recommendations for Future Research in Crisis Intervention with Crime Victims

Recommendations involve, first, supplementing client satisfaction with assessment of individual functioning due to the almost universal tendency for clients when queried to report high satisfaction with services (Larsen, Attkisson, Hargreaves, & Nguyen, 1979). Although sensitivity to victim distress should take prime consideration, a standardized assessment measure can be taken at the initial contact once a client has stabilized sufficiently. Initial scores can then be compared against the same measure administered at a follow-up contact. One such measure is the Impact of Events Scale, a 15-item, self-report instrument that assesses the degree of distress an event causes (Horowitz, Wilner, & Alvarez, 1979).

Follow-up, whether through face-to-face, telephone, or mailed contact, should be administered at a uniform period, so that a better understanding of program effects on victims can be established. When satisfaction is assessed, workers must probe for what was helpful (e.g., "How well do you feel the counselor understood you?" [Neimeyer & Pfeiffer, 1994] and unhelpful (e.g., "What was least helpful about what the counselor said or did?" [Neimeyer & Pfeiffer, 1994]) about the initial contact. Further questions may need to be tailored to the needs of the specific victim (Neimeyer & Pfeiffer, 1994) regarding the particular problems that have been resolved as a result of contact, and the needs that are still outstanding. However, this method may be limited by people's tendency to present socially desirable responses. One option, therefore, is that an independent evaluator conduct telephone interviews or that anonymous mailed surveys be distributed, although a potential problem with mailed surveys is the low response rate.

SUICIDE PREVENTION AND CRISIS INTERVENTION RESEARCH

In order to examine the effects of suicide prevention centers on community suicide rates, Lester (1997) reviewed 14 studies published in the last few decades (Bagley, 1968; Lester, Saito, & Abe, 1996) from a variety of countries: England (Bagley, 1968; Jennings, Barraclough, & Moss, 1978; Lester, 1980, 1990, 1994); West Germany (Riehl, Marchner, & Moller, 1988); Canada (Leenaars & Lester, 1995); Taiwan (Huang & Lester, 1995); Japan (Lester et al., 1996); and the United States (Bridge, Potkin, Zung, & Soldo, 1977; Lester, 1974, 1993; Medoff, 1984; Miller, Coombs, Leeper, & Barton, 1984; Weiner, 1969). (See Table 20.2.) Part of the Lester (1997) review included a meta-analysis in which an overall program effect of −.16 was reported. This effect, although representing a positive association between the presence of programs and decreased suicide rates in communities, is very small (Cohen, 1977).

When populations were broken down according to gender and age groups, certain populations seemed to reap more benefit from the presence of suicide prevention centers. People aged 15 to 24 and 55 to 64 and females showed the most positive impact from crisis intervention centers. The effect for females may be due to a few different but related contributing factors: the higher risk of suicide attempts among women (with men more likely to successfully suicide) [e.g., Carnetto, 1997; Carnetto, 1998]; females' greater likelihood of depression (American Psychiatric Association, 1994); and females' greater propensity for help-seeking behavior (Congress, 1995). Societal prohibitions against males seeking help may begin by adolescence. One study found that even boys at high suicide risk reported that they would not utilize school-based crisis lines and other services to prevent suicide, preferring instead to handle their crises alone (Evans, Smith, Hill, Albers, & Neufeld, 1996).

Table 20.2   Suicide Intervention

Author/Model	Design/Sample	Measures	Results
Lester (1997)	Meta-analysis on the effects on community suicide rates of suicide prevention-centers. 14 studies, published from the 1960s to the 1990s	Suicide rates; presence of center; duration of center; centers per area; number of centers; centers per capita	An overall program effect of −.16 was reported; females and individuals aged 15 to 24 or 55 to 64 had the most positive impact from crisis intervention centers

Recommendations for Research in Crisis Intervention with Suicide Prevention

Recommendations for future study of suicide crisis intervention centers have been made. First, routine data collection at suicide prevention centers should involve client demographic characteristics, such as gender, age, and socio-economic status (Lester, 1997). These characteristics affect utilization of services by certain groups, which influences the centers' effectiveness in preventing suicide.

Studies also do not have to be only retrospective. For instance, A-B-A designs could be established in which rates of suicide and suicidal behaviors, such as cutting, shooting, or drug overdoses reported from hospital records, are established prior to an intervention, whether it is a school- or university-based suicide prevention program or a poison control hotline (Neimeyer & Pfeiffer, 1994). Particular programs could address the needs of certain populations at risk, such as adolescents, young women, or older adults. A program can then be pilot-tested and the effects on suicidality assessed. Removal of the pilot test will further show its impact on suicidal behavior to determine whether the program needs to be fully implemented.

Lester (1997) has also suggested that using the number of centers in a particular area to determine the effect of crisis intervention may represent too crude a measure; instead, the number of people providing such services or the volume of clients using services should be employed. One study in this vein examined contacts to crisis telephone hotlines in a western state, which constituted a total of 97,000 calls over a 6-year period (Albers & Foster, 1995). Only a small proportion (8-12% of calls) were related to suicide, with the largest percentage of calls (40%) involving interpersonal problems. Therefore, attention must be paid not only to the impact of crisis intervention on suicidal thoughts and behaviors but also to resolution of crises related to various interpersonal and/or family crises.

For assessing the more immediate effects of crisis intervention (as opposed to distal measures such as the number of suicides in a certain area), Neimeyer and Pfeiffer (1994) recommend borrowing from psychotherapy research in which a number of sessions are studied for their effect on outcome. In some cases, callers may have more than one contact with a suicide prevention agency while resolving a particular crisis, and the cumulative impact of these contacts can be assessed. The authors suggest administering a relevant standardized scale, such as the Beck Depression Inventory (Beck, Rush, Shaw, & Emery, 1979; Beck et al., 1961), either by telephone or by mailing surveys on a weekly basis.

Neimeyer and Pfeiffer (1994) further argue that evaluation of suicide intervention staff is crucial. Their review of the literature indicated that crisis counselors fail to consistently demonstrate Rogerian counseling skills, such as warmth, empathy, and genuineness, in role-play situations. In order to assess the basic skills of service providers, Neimeyer and Pfeiffer (1994) have developed the Suicide Intervention Response Inventory. Such tests may also be administered to crisis line workers prior to and after training to measure how much progress has been made in the acquisition of knowledge and skills. Tests may also be used to discern the helpfulness of training or what combination of didactic or experiental training modules is most beneficial.

RESEARCH ON PSYCHIATRIC EMERGENCIES

Crisis intervention efforts have also been applied in response to psychiatric emergencies (see Table 20.3). The nature of the psychiatric problem has varied according to the program. For example, Andreoli, Frances et al. (1993) studied people suffering from depression; Anthony (1992) implies that the focus of his study involved schizophrenic patients; and the criteria for inclusion in the Cluse-Tolar (1997) study involved presentation in a general hospital emergency room for a psychiatric problem. Crisis intervention programs also appear to vary by different psychiatric settings, although one limitation is that such programs are often not described (e.g., Anthony, 1992; Blouin et al., 1985; Cluse-Tolar, 1997). One exception involves a program at a psychiatric center in Switzerland (Andreoli, Frances et al. 1993; Andreoli, Muehlebach et al. 1991). The intervention generally lasted 6 weeks and comprised a week of inpatient treatment, followed by outpatient treatment, involving medication if needed and two to three sessions per week of time-limited treatment.

Another program detailed was from a study conducted in Italy (Mezzina & Vedoni, 1996), although length of treatment was not provided. Treatment comprised the following: (a) individual support psychotherapies or family counseling; (b) involvement of the social network; (c) specific resocialization treatment, such as group therapy, art therapy, self-help groups, or occupational therapy; (d) legal advocacy; (e) job training or new employment; (f) self-care management and housing support; (g) cooperation with other welfare and health services; and (h) medication.

In crisis intervention studies with psychiatric emergencies, control or comparison groups are typically lacking. In an attempt to make comparisons, authors have differentiated groups of psychiatric patients on certain characteristics. For example, Andreoli, Frances et al. (1993) studied individuals with depression ($N = 35$) and whether they also had an accompanying personality disorder. Those without personality disorders had briefer episodes of depression and fewer relapses compared with those with personality disorders at 1- and 2-year follow-up. Individuals in the sample also could have had additional treatment during this time period, although the extent and type of treatment services were not delineated. A factor associated with poor

Table 20.3 Psychiatric Emergencies

Author/Model	Design/Sample	Measures	Results	Limitations
Andreoli et al. (1993) Andreoli et al. (1992) Geneva, Switzerland Average length of crisis intervention = 6 weeks	Pretest, posttest follow-up (1, 2 years) N = 39 patients seeking inpatient psychiatric care for depression 29% male, 31% female; mean age = 39 years Those with personality disorders compared against those without	Clinician ratings based "on a number of clinical and psychosocial change areas . . . according to the additional scales of the Health-Sickness Rating Scale" (p. 390)	Depressed individuals without personality disorders tended to have positive outcomes in terms of briefer episodes of depression and few relapses in comparison with those with personality disorders; factors associated with poor outcome for those diagnosed with personality disorders include poor therapeutic relationship and/or having had less long-term treatment at 2-year follow-up	No comparison/control group; information on standardization of measure was not given
Anthony (1992)	Posttest, comparing those who were discharged to their homes and those who required inpatient psychiatric stay N = 69 patients admitted to program Majority male; majority high school graduates; majority unemployed	Chart records Discharge	59% successfully discharged to their homes; 41% needed transfer to inpatient psychiatric unit; treatment compliance and family support were correlated with successful discharge	No pretest; no comparison/ control group; nonstandardized measures; lack of information on program

Study	Sample/Design	Measures	Findings	Limitations
Blouin et al. (1985)	Posttest only, N = 67 referrals to an outpatient crisis intervention (Canada) Average of 3 sessions Mean age = 30; 64% females; 36% males; 37% single; 30% married; 30% divorced, separated, widowed; 50% had completed high school or beyond, with 50% completing only elementary school or less	Treatment engagement Rating on 1–5 scale by therapist whether client had improved as a result of crisis intervention	High SES individuals dropped out of treatment significantly less often and benefited more; age was significantly related to outcome in that older patients improved more than young adults; higher dropout rate and less positive outcome for those with marital difficulties rather than general difficulties	Nonstandardized measure; therapist bias in reporting; no pretest; no comparison/control group
Cluse-Tolar (1997)	Pretest, posttest N = 54 presenting to a hospital emergency room for psychiatric emergency 69% female; 32% male	Brief Symptom Inventory	Females tended to improve but males did not	Lack of information on program; lack of demographic information; no comparison/control group
Hartmann & Sullivan (1996)	Follow-up of 96 (40% response rate) 64% of admissions were women Schizophrenia (22%), major depression (20%), bipolar disorder (17%) and adjustment-reaction disorder were predominant categories; substance abuse was a primary or secondary diagnosis in 21% of cases.	Belief they would have been hospitalized; satisfaction with services	61% believed they would have been hospitalized; 55% were highly satisfied with services; 24% were satisfied; 7% were dissatisfied or highly dissatisfied	Referral source and process unclear; average length of stay not provided; no pretest; biased follow-up in terms of who had been contacted; no comparison/control group; no standardized measures; actual hospitalization rates were not provided; period of follow-up was not given

(continued)

Table 20.3 *Continued*

Author/Model	Design/Sample	Measures	Results	Limitations
Hartmann & Sullivan (1996)	Follow-up of 96 (40% response rate) 64% of admissions were women Schizophrenia (22%), major depression (20%), bipolar disorder (17%) and adjustment-reaction disorder were predominant categories; substance abuse was a primary or secondary diagnosis in 21% of cases.	Belief they would have been hospitalized; satisfaction with services	61% believed they would have been hospitalized; 55% were highly satisfied with services; 24% were satisfied; 7% were dissatisfied or highly dissatisfied	Referral source and process unclear; average length of stay not provided; no pretest; biased follow-up in terms of who had been contacted; no comparison/ control group; no standardized measures; actual hospitalization rates were not provided; period of follow-up was not given
Mezzina & Vidoni (1996) Italy Crisis intervention comprised the following: (1) individual support psychotherapies or family counseling; (2) involvement of social network; (3) specific resocialization treatment; (4) legal advocacy; (5) job training or new employment; (6) self-care management and housing support; (7) cooperation with other welfare and health services; (8) medication	4-year follow-up Criteria for entry into crisis center: (1) severe acute symptomatology; (2) social withdrawal; (3) refusal of treatment but accepting contact; (4) total refusal of contact; (5) situation of alarm in family or social network 59% women; 50% over 55; 67% lived with their family; majority had at least a junior high education	Semistructured interview	Of those who had never had psychiatric contact prior to crisis services, none needed additional treatment; of those who had previous psychiatric contact, 18.5% needed treatment	Nonstandardized measures; no posttest; no comparison/ control group; unspecified referral source or process

470

Study	Design	Outcome measure	Results	Comments
Redding & Raphelson (1995) 24-hour on-site crisis intervention team, including a psychiatrist	Time-series analysis of data from state and private hospital admissions for 6-month program period, 1 year prior, and 1 year post-program .	State and private hospital admissions	Decline occurred in state hospital admissions during program period compared with two previous years and following year	Study focused on involvement of psychiatrist rather than the rest of the team
Ruffin et al. (1993) Crisis stabilization program within a child and adolescent program at a local mental health center	Pretest, posttest	State hospital admissions	During first year of program, 51% (from 117 to 58) reduction in admissions to state psychiatric facility for children and adolescents; second year of operation, 19% (58 to 47) reduction in admissions; cost savings also present with crisis intervention vs. hospitalization	No other measures of functioning discussed; no comparison/control group; not known whether program accounted for change in hospital records

outcome in the group with personality disorders involved less long-term treatment at 2-year follow-up. Apparently, crisis intervention alone was not enough to prevent relapse of depression in those with personality disorders. Similarly, Mezzina and Vidoni (1996) found that those with previous psychiatric assistance were more likely to need treatment after crisis intervention at 4-year follow-up.

Anthony (1992) examined the effect of a crisis intervention program on those who required transfer to a long-term care unit and those who were discharged into the community. An examination of hospital records showed that both increased treatment compliance and family support were significantly associated with successful discharge.

Cluse-Tolar (1997) looked at response to a crisis intervention program, comparing men and women who presented for a psychiatric emergency. When assessed over a 6-week period on psychological functioning, women improved; the men did not, although men also made up a minority of the sample. Cluse-Tolar (1997) argued that psychological services are generally unresponsive to the needs of men, and that a substantial barrier involves societal prohibitions against help-seeking for men.

A Canadian study compared types of problems and certain crisis techniques in an outpatient crisis intervention program that referred individuals from a hospital emergency room (Blouin et al., 1985). The major source of crises involved interpersonal difficulties, particularly those associated with a relationship partner (45%). At the same time, dropout for marital cases was high: 52% before the third session. These cases also seemed to benefit less overall from the crisis intervention program. The authors suggest that marital problems may require a longer-term and more intensive approach. In general, the authors found that an approach involving ventilation of emotions and education about feelings associated with the crisis was more helpful than either cognitive techniques focusing on maladaptive negative thoughts or psychodynamic techniques focusing on past relationships and events.

Other studies examined the effects of crisis intervention programs on hospital admission rates rather than on individual functioning. Redding and Raphelson (1995) discussed a mobile crisis intervention unit, with an emphasis on the role of the psychiatrist. A decline in state hospital admissions occurred during the program period, as well as the following year, when compared with the two previous years. Similarly, a reduction was found in hospital admissions after the implementation of a crisis stabilization unit for children and adolescents (Ruffin, Spencer, Abel, Gage, & Miles, 1993). A 50% reduction in admissions was found the first year, and almost a 20% decrease occurred the second year.

Another study looked at individuals' beliefs about whether they would have been hospitalized rather than actual hospitalization rates at follow-up. Although it is unknown at what point data on follow-up were collected (Hartmann & Sullivan, 1996), it may have been a long time after intervention given that only 40% of the sample was interviewed. A majority of those interviewed (61%) reported they would have been hospitalized if they had not received the crisis intervention program.

In sum, positive results were found for crisis intervention with psychiatric emergencies in terms of preventing additional treatment and for improving symptoms. It appears that those with more severe disorders (personality disorders and those with prior treatment) may require more than just crisis intervention, although crisis intervention may still be helpful for postponing relapse and rehospitalization in these individuals.

Recommendations for Research in Crisis Intervention with Psychiatric Emergencies

Future studies could be strengthened by, first, providing clearer descriptions of the crisis intervention program, which would allow programs with similar characteristics, to be compared across studies. Studies also could be strengthened by including standardized assessment of individual functioning at pretest, posttest, and follow-up, along with rehospitalization rates. One suggested measure is the Brief Symptom Inventory (Derogatis, 1993), which assesses several domains of psychological adjustment, as well as providing global ratings of symptom distress.

A third recommendation involves comparison groups. Although researchers often attempted to create comparison conditions within sample groups (those with and without personality disorders, men and women, type of problem), whenever possible, a true comparison group condition should be created. One naturally occurring comparison group could involve a "treatment-as-usual" control group (no crisis intervention), while comparison conditions should also be outlined so that it is clear how crisis programs differ from alternative treatments.

CHILD ABUSE RESEARCH

Another area of research for crisis intervention involves family preservation programs for child abuse victims and their families (see Table 20.4). Specifically, the "Homebuilders" program (Kinney & Dittmar, 1995; Kinney, Haapala, & Booth, 1991) follows a crisis intervention model. Families come to the attention of family preservation because of placement risk due to child abuse and/or neglect, and the main goal of the program is to prevent such placement. However, family preservation has also been used with the families of children with behavior disorders and with juvenile offenders (e.g., Henggeler, Melton, Brondino, Scherer, & Hanley, 1997).

Crisis intervention is a common approach to family preservation. Respondents to a Child Welfare League survey from 1996 indicated that a little over half of all states (53%) report their family preservation programs are

Table 20.4 Crisis Intervention with Family Preservation of Child Abuse and Neglect

Author/Model	Design/Sample	Measures	Results	Limitations
Bath, et al. (1992) Washington Average hours of service = 65.8	Posttest only (1 year after intake) N = 1,506 children represented 1,112 families referred from child welfare workers due to imminent risk of placement; low-income; majority white Ages 0–2 (6.9%); 3–9 (18%); 10–17 (76%)	Outcome: out-of-home placements 12 months after intake Independent variables: nonstandardized checklist of child and family characteristics	At case termination, success of avoiding placement: 98.5%; at 3 months: 91.4%; 83% avoided placement	Pre-to-post not tracked; lack of control/comparison group; age groupings were not clearly laid out in demographic information; nonstandardized measures
Feldman (1991) After Homebuilders (four sites in New Jersey) 5.35 weeks	Experimental design, randomization to intensive treatment (N = 96) if availability of family preservation slots or community service (N = 87), 1-year follow-up N = 183 families recruited from child welfare, county family-juvenile crisis units, crisis mental health units; mean age of child = 13; majority single-parent; 45% white; 36% African-American; 20% Hispanic; 90% at two lowest SES groups	Placement; Family Environment Scale; Child Well-Being Scales; Life Event Scale (nonstandardized); Interpersonal Support Evaluation List; Goal Attainment Scale; Community SES	Family preservation group did significantly better avoiding out-of-home placement from case termination to 9-month follow-up; then effect dissipated Experimental group did not do significantly better on standardized measures from pretest to follow-up	22 were "turnbacks" after randomization (didn't meet program selection criteria, caretaker refused to participate, children had to be removed)

| Fraser et al. (1991)
Pecora et al. (1991)
Pecora et al. (1992)
Spaid & Fraser (1991)

Homebuilders

2 sites in Utah (60 days); 4 sites in Washington (30 days) | Pretest, posttest, follow-up (12 months) with overflow comparison group (N = 27 children) from the Utah sites

N = 581 children from 446 families at imminent risk of placement (within 1 week)

Percentages of families referred by CPS: Washington (45.5%), Utah (59%); families referred by family reconciliation, youth services, or juvenile court: Washington (54.5%), Utah (40.2%); of ethnic minority families: Washington (18.3%), Utah (13.5%); of single-parent families: Washington (42.5%), Utah (38.3%); majority income below $20,000 | Placement defined as outside the home for at least 2 weeks in a nonrelative setting

Family Risk Scales; FACES-III; Social Support Inventory (adapted from Inventory of Socially Supportive Behaviors)

Nonstandardized: parent ratings of family problems; global family ratings by parents | 93.9% of children were in home at case termination (Washington); 90.7% (Utah); children experienced placement during study (nonrelative or continuous runaway behavior for at least 2 weeks): 32% (Utah), 22.5% (Washington)

Only 263 families served early enough to participate in 12-month follow-up: placement prevention rate 58.8% for Utah (compared with 14.8% for comparison group), 70.2% for Washington

No significant changes on FACES-III; positive significant changes in Family Risk Scales for child, parent, and family environment; significant positive changes for aversive social interactions between spouses and empathic friendships with extended kin and network members changes for parent ratings of changes

Oppositional and older youth at higher risk of placement | Small comparison group; bias for therapist ratings; social desirability for parent ratings of improvements; some measures nonstandardized; only 29% of Utah and 71% of Washington sample tracked for the full 12-month follow-up |

(continued)

475

Table 20.4 *Continued*

Author/Model	Design/Sample	Measures	Results	Limitations
Fraser & Haapala (1987–1988) Homebuilders	Qualitative survey method—"critical incidents" during intervention and helpfulness of services related to placement (3 months after termination of services) N = 41 families referred for child abuse and/or neglect, psychiatric impairment, disruptive behavior Mean age of child = 13.9 Half were single-parent families	In-home placement defined as children continuously being in the home from pretreatment to 3 month follow-up Interview guide to discover client (independent children) and therapist versions of "critical incidents" during treatment sessions.	Client perceptions of global helpfulness of treatment not related to placement outcome; neither were any therapists' reports related to outcome; the provision of concrete assistance was related to positive outcome; although interruptions in home were rated by mothers as unhelpful, they were significantly related to positive outcome, since may have given therapists opportunities for teaching families	Although Homebuilders model was described generally as lasting between 2 and 5 months duration of services, service time here not defined; no racial or SES information provided; posttest assessment delayed until 3 months

476

Scannapieco (1994)	Pretest, posttest, divided by risk (high-risk: child at risk of placement outside the home)	Placement prevention; family functioning (nonstandardized); completion of program; improvement of problem areas (nonstandardized)	Low-risk families made progress on identified problem area 89% of time compared with 58% of the high-risk family cases. No statistically significant differences between high- and low-risk families' family functioning, program completion; 59% of high-risk families completed, compared with 56% of low-risk); or placement prevention (achieved in 82% of high-risk cases compared with 72% of low-risk cases).	"High risk" not defined; no specific intake criteria for program; measures nonstandardized; race not given; although 80 cases selected, only 45 engaged in services—low engagement/high dropout of concern; although services were said to be delivered intensely between 3–6 months, average length of services not given
	$N = 80$ families randomly selected from 480 cases, only 45 families engaged in services			
	40% receiving welfare assistance			
	Referral reasons: physical abuse (42%), sexual abuse (22%), child neglect (27%), drug abuse (53%), domestic abuse (13%), mental illness (24%)			

(continued)

Table 20.4 *Continued*

Author/Model	Design/Sample	Measures	Results	Limitations
Walton (1996) Walton et al. (1993) Modified Homebuilders Utah 90 days	Randomization to treatment (family preservation) or comparison group (once-monthly visits and provision of resources so that child could return home), posttest (90 days), follow-up (6 months) N = 110 children from computer-generated list of children in out-of-home placement; primarily white; mean age = 10.7; Neglect was the most frequent reason for the initial out-of-home placement (32.7%), followed by child disruptive behavior (18.2%), physical abuse (14.5%), and sexual abuse (14.5%); hall of sample were divorced/separated; half of caretakers has annual income less than $10,000	Placement McMasters Family Assessment Device; Index of Self-Esteem; Index of Parental Attitudes; Consumer Outcome and Satisfaction Survey; Six Month Follow-up Survey (latter two developed by authors)	No significant differences on groups of parents on standardized measures; significant differences were noted between groups on Six Month Follow-up Survey, favoring family preservation; children in family preservation group were more likely to be returned to the home and stayed in the home longer than control children; at 90 days, 93% of family preservation group had been returned, compared with 28.3% of control children; at 6 months, 75% of family preservation families remained together, compared with 49% of control group (differences between groups at both time periods were significant)	Standardized measures not administered at 6-month follow-up, just at 90 days; no pretest information; measures by authors not standardized

Wood et al. (1988) Northern California 4–6 weeks	Quasi-experimental, with casework-as-usual services, provided to overflow comparison group, pretest, 1-year follow-up $N = 50$ families referred by CPS in which child was "in danger of being removed from the home" 50% received public assistance year prior to referral but range in income from working poor to affluent; 72% mothers white, 12% African-American, 11% Hispanic, 7% Asian; 57% boys, 43% girls; children in in-home group older (mean = 8.9 years) than in comparison group (mean = 5.4 years)	Family Adaptability and Cohesion Scale-II (results to be published in another study) Placement	At 1 year, 74% of children in family preservation group remained in home, compared with 45% in casework-as-usual group. Costs for family preservation group were also lower	No randomization to groups; lack of information on casework-as-usual services; no posttest; selection bias found in referrals (some units were enthusiastic supporters of in-home services and many referrals; some units were not supportive and made few referrals or none)

based on the Homebuilders model (Petit & Curtis, 1997). Consistent with the crisis intervention assumption that a critical short-term period is involved in restabilization to a former, more adaptable level of functioning, workers provide immediate services (within a day of referral) in the home with 24-hour availability of workers (Kinney & Dittmar, 1995; Kinney, Haapala, & Booth, 1991), and clients are usually seen for a brief period (between 4 and 6 weeks). In addition to counseling services, workers provide a variety of concrete resources and make community referrals so that families meet basic needs for food, clothing, housing, and medical care (Nelson et al., 1990; Pecora, Fraser, & Haapala, 1992).

Prevention of placement of children has been the major outcome for services, and programs have been successful in this regard. Pretest, posttest-only designs have found placement prevention rates ranging from an average of 77% (Scannapieco, 1994) to nearly 99% (Bath et al., 1992) at case termination and from 65% (Fraser, Pecora, & Haapala, 1991) to 83% (Bath et al., 1992; Yuan, Struckman, & Johnson, 1991) at follow-up.

Quasi-experimental designs with random assignment to family preservation or casework-as-usual services (Feldman, 1991; Walton, 1996; Walton et al., 1993) or the use of overflow comparison groups (Wood, Barton, & Schroeder, 1988) have also shown high placement prevention rates for the family preservation group, although rates tend to dissipate over time. Despite the success for placement prevention, in the couple of cases in which standardized self-report measures were used, no significant differences were found between family preservation and casework-as-usual services (Feldman, 1991; Walton, 1996). Therefore, although family preservation programs may help keep children in the home, improved adjustment of family members may not also be reflected.

Research Recommendations in Crisis Intervention with Child Maltreatment

Although prevention of child placement seems to be averted through the use of crisis intervention services in the home, more clarification is needed on whether children are truly at risk for imminent placement when their families are assigned to family preservation. The term *imminent risk of placement* needs to be clarified and operationalized so that family preservation services are delivered only to families that are truly at risk of placement (Tracy, 1991; Rossi, 1992; Wells & Biegel, 1992). In addition, reliable and valid measures of a child's risk for placement need to be developed (Tracy, 1991; Wells & Biegel, 1992).

Moreover, quasi-experimental designs in which both experimental and comparison group subjects are at the same risk for placement are needed in order to establish the effects of family preservation. Whereas ethical considerations preclude the use of no-treatment control groups, casework-as-usual services provide an acceptable alternative (Rossi, 1992) as long as such services are detailed so that the differences between regular and family preservation services are clear. Families also need to be tracked after crisis intervention to discern if changes made at treatment completion are maintained over time.

Another recommendation involves the standardization of treatment. Although one tenet of family preservation is that treatment is individualized to the particular family (Kinney & Dittmar, 1995; Kinney et al., 1991), this orientation can still be maintained within manualized treatment (Henggeler & Borduin, 1990). The importance of adherence to a standardized treatment model was highlighted in a recent study on family preservation with juvenile offenders (Henggeler et al., 1997). Treatment adherence was associated with improved outcome in terms of prevention of rearrest and incarceration. Despite the potential importance of adherence to manualized treatment, the crisis intervention family preservation literature does not address efforts to ensure that therapists follow structured interventions.

A final recommendation involves the implementation of standardized measurement assessment at pretest, posttest, and follow-up and/or coded behavioral ratings by unbiased parties, rather than relying mainly on placement as an outcome measure or worker report (Barth 1988; Wells & Biegel, 1992). Rates of placement may not always be determined by crisis intervention programs, since many other contextual variables may influence placement decisions, such as the availability of placements, resources, and services, and prevailing community attitudes (e.g., Rossi, 1992). Recommendations for self-report measures for parents include the following: the Child Behavior Checklist (Achenbach, 1991), which assesses parents' perceptions of their children's internalizing and externalizing symptoms; the Parenting Stress Index (Abidin, 1983), which assesses parenting stress; the Child Abuse Potential Inventory (Milner, 1986), which assesses risk of child abuse; and the Brief Symptom Inventory (Derogatis, 1993), which measures psychological adjustment. Finally, recommendations for self-report measures for children include the following: the Child Depression Index (Kovacs & Beck, 1977); the Anger Response Inventory (Hoshmand & Austin, 1987); and the Trauma Symptom Checklist (Briere, 1995).

REFERENCES

Abidin, R. R. (Ed.). (1983). *Parenting Stress Index* (3rd ed.). Odessa, FL: Psychological Assessment Resources.

Achenbach, T. M. (1991) *Manual for the Child Behavior Checklist/4-18 and 1991 Profile.* Burlington, VT:

University of Vermont Department of Psychiatry.

Albers, E., & Foster, S. (1995). A profile of 97,100 crisis intervention contacts over a six-year period. *Crisis Intervention, 2,* 23–29.

Allen, S. L. (1998). *Effect of domestic*

assault response team on family violence. Unpublished master's thesis, University of Texas at Arlington, Arlington, Texas.

Andreoli, A., Frances, A., Gex-Farby, M., Aapro, N., Gerin, P., & Dazford, A. (1993). Crisis intervention in depressed patients with and without DSM-III-R personality disorders. *Journal of Nervous and Mental Disease, 181,* 732–737.

Andreoli, A., Muehlebach, A., Gognalons, M., Abensur, J., Grimm, S., & Frances, A. (1992). Crisis intervention response and long-term outcome: A pilot study. *Comprehensive Psychiatry, 23,* 388–396.

Anthony, D. (1992). A retrospective evaluation of factors influencing successful outcomes on an inpatient psychiatric crisis unit. *Research on Social Work Practice, 2,* 56–64.

Bagley, C. (1968). The evaluation of a suicide prevention scheme by an ecological method. *Social Science and Medicine, 2,* 1–4.

Barth, R. (1988). Theories guiding home-based intensive family preservation services. In J. Wittaker, J. Kinney, E. Tracey, & C. Booth (Eds.), *Improving practice technology for work with high-risk families: Lessons from the "Homebuilders" social work education project* (pp. 91–113). Seattle: Center for Social Welfare Research.

Bath, H., Richey, & Haapala. (1992). Child age and outcome correlates in intensive family preservation services. *Children & Youth Services Review, 14,* 389–406.

Beck, A. T., Kovacs, M., & Weissman, A. (1979). Assessment of suicidal intention: The scale for suicide ideation *Journal of Consulting*

and Clinical Psychology, 47, 343–352.

Beck, A. T., Rush, A. J., Shaw, B. F., & Emery, G. (1979). *Cognitive theory of depression.* New York: Guilford.

Beck, A. T., Ward, C. H., Mendelson, M., Mock, J., & Erbaugh, J. (1961). An inventory for measuring depression. *Archives of General Psychiatry, 4,* 561–571.

Blouin, J., et al. (1985). Effects of patient characteristics and therapeutic techniques on crisis intervention outcome. *Psychiatric Journal of the University of Ottawa, 10*(3), 153–157.

Bridge, T., Potkin, S., Zung, W., & Soldo, B. (1977). Suicide prevention centers. *Journal of Nervous and Mental Disease, 164,* 18–24.

Briere, J. (1995). *Trauma symptom checklist for children: Professional manual.* Odessa, FL: Psychological Assessment Resources.

Carnetto, S. (1997). Meanings of gender and suicidal behavior during adolescence. *Suicide and Life-Threatening Behavior, 27,* 339–351.

Carnetto, S. (1998). The gender paradox in suicide. *Suicide and Life-Threatening Behavior, 28,* 1–23.

Cluse-Tolar, T. (1997). Gender differences in crisis theory recovery: Rethinking crisis theory. *Crisis Intervention, 3,* 189–198.

Cohen, J. (1977). *Statistical power analysis for the behavioral sciences.* New York: Academic Press.

Congress, E. P. (1995). Clinical issues in time-limited treatment with women. In A. R. Roberts (Ed.), *Crisis intervention and time-limited cognitive treatment* (pp. 215–230). Thousand Oaks, CA: Sage.

Corcoran, J. (1995). Child abuse victim services: An exploratory study of the Austin, Texas, Police Department. *Family Violence and Sexual Assault Bulletin, 11*, 19–23.

Corcoran, J., Stephenson, M., Allen, S., & Perryman, D. (1999; under review). Police satisfaction with a domestic violence response team. *Families in Society.*

Davis, R. (1987). Studying the effects of services for victims in crisis. *Crime and Delinquency, 33*, 520–531.

Denkers, A., & Winkel, F. (1998). Crime victims well-being and fear in a prospective and longitudinal study. *International Review of Victimology, 5*, 141–162.

Derogatis, L. (1993). *Brief Symptom Inventory: Administration, scoring, and procedures manual.* Minneapolis, MN: National Computer Systems.

Evans, W., Smith, M., Hill, G., Albers, E., & Neufeld, J. (1996). Rural adolescent views of risk and protective factors associated with suicide. *Crisis Intervention, 3*, 1–12.

Faustman, W. O. (1994). Brief Psychiatric Rating Scale. In M. E. Maruish (Ed.), *The use of psychological testing for treatment and planning outcome assessment.* Hillside, NJ: Lawrence Erlbaum.

Feldman, L. H. (1991). *Evaluating the impact of intensive family preservation services in New Jersey.* Newbury Park, CA: Sage.

Fetterman, D. M. (1996). Empowerment evaluation: An introduction to theory and practice. In D. M. Fetterman, S. Kaftarian, and A. Wandersman (Eds.), *Empowerment evaluation: Knowledge and tools for self-assessment and accountability.* Thousand Oaks, CA: Sage.

Fraser, M., & Haapala, D. (1987–1988). Home-based family treatment: A quantitative-qualitative assessment. *Journal of Applied Social Sciences, 12.* 1–23.

Fraser, M. W., Pecora, P. J., & Haapala, D. A. (1991). *Families in crisis: The impact of intensive family preservation services.* Hawthorne, NY: Aldine de Gruyter.

Hamilton, M. (1959). The assessment of anxiety states by rating. *British Journal of Medical Psychiatry, 32*, 50–55.

Hamilton, M. (1960). A rating scale for depression. *Journal of Neurology, Neurosurgery, and Psychiatry, 23*, 56–62.

Hartmann, D., & Sullivan, P. (1996). Residential crisis services as an alternative to inpatient care. *Families in Society*, 496–501.

Henggeler, S. W., & Borduin, C. M. (1990). *Family therapy and beyond: A multisystemic approach to treating the behavioral problems of children and adolescents.* Pacific Grove: Brooks/Cole.

Henggeler, S. W., Melton, G. B., Brondino, M. J., Scherer, D. G., & Hanley, J. H. (1997). Multisystemic therapy with violent and chronic juvenile offenders and their families: The role of treatment fidelity in successful dissemination. *Journal of Consulting and Clinical Psychology, 65*, 821–833.

Horowitz, M. J., Wilner, N., & Alvarez, W. (1979). Impact of Event Scale: A measure of subjective stress. *Psychosomatic Medicine, 41*, 207–218.

Hoshmand, L., & Austin, G. (1987). Validation studies of a multifactor cognitive-behavioral anger control inventory. *Journal of Personality Assessment, 51*, 417–432.

Huang, W., & Lester, D. (1995). Have suicide prevention centers prevented suicide in Taiwan? *Chinese Journal of Mental Health, 8*, 27–29.

Jackson, T. L. (October 29, 1999). Personal communication with Albert Roberts.

Jennings, C., Barraclough, B., & Moss, J. (1978). Have the Samaritans lowered the suicide rate? *Psychological Medicine, 8*, 413–422.

Kinney, J., & Dittmar, K. (1995). *Homebuilders: Helping families help themselves.* Lincoln: University of Nebraska Press.

Kinney, J., Haapala, D. A., & Booth, C. (1991). *Keeping families together: The Homebuilders model.* New York: Aldine de Gruyter.

Kovacs, M., & Beck, A. T. (1977). An empirical-clinical approach toward a definition of childhood depression. In J. G. Schulterbrandt & A. Raskin (Eds.), *Depression in childhood: Diagnosis, treatment, and conceptual models* (pp. 1–25). New York: Raven Press.

Larsen, D. L., Attkisson, C. C., Hargreaves, W. A., & Nguyen, T. D. (1979). Assessment of client/patient satisfaction: Development of a general scale. *Evaluation and Program Planning, 2*, 197–207.

Leenaars, A., & Lester, D. (1995). Impact of suicide prevention centers on suicide in Canada. *Crisis, 16*, 39.

Lester, D. (1974). Effect of suicide prevention centers on suicide rates in the United States. *Health Services Reports, 89*, 37–39.

Lester, D. (1980). Comment: Suicide prevention centers. *Social Science and Medicine, 14A*, 85.

Lester, D. (1990). Was gas detoxification or establishment of suicide prevention centers responsible for the decline in the British suicide rate? *Psychological Reports, 66*, 286.

Lester, D. (1993). The effectiveness of suicide prevention centers. *Suicide and Life-Threatening Behavior, 23*, 263–267.

Lester, D. (1994). Evaluating the effectiveness of the Samaritans in England and Wales. *International Journal of Health Sciences, 5*, 73–74.

Lester, D. (1997). The effectiveness of suicide prevention centers: A review. *Suicide and Life-Threatening Behavior, 27*, 304–310.

Lester, D., Saito, Y., & Abe, K. (1996). Have suicide prevention centers prevented suicide in Japan? *Archives of Suicide Research, 2*, 126–128.

Lindsey, D. (1994). Family preservation and child protection: Striking a balance. *Children and Youth Services Review, 16*, 279–294.

Matorin, S. (October 30, 1999). Personal communication.

Medoff, M. (1984). An evaluation of the effectiveness of suicide prevention centers. *Journal of Behavioral Economics, 15*, 43–55.

Mezzina, R., & Vidoni, D. (1996). Beyond the mental hospital: Crisis intervention and continuity of care in Triests: A four-year follow-up study in a community mental health centre. *International Journal of Social Psychiatry, 41*, 1–20.

Miller, H., Coombs, D., Leeper, J., & Barton, S. (1984). An analysis of the effects of suicide prevention facilities in the United States. *American Journal of Public Health, 74*, 340–343.

Milner, J. (1986). The Child Abuse Potential Inventory: Manual (2nd ed.). Webster, NC: Psytec.

National Organization of Victim Assistance (NOVA). http://www.try-nova.org/resources.html.

Neimeyer, R. A., & Pfeiffer, A. M. (1994). Evaluation of suicide intervention effectiveness. *Death Studies, 18,* 131–166.

Nelson, K. E. et al. (1990). Three models of family-centered placement prevention service. *Child Welfare, 69,* 3–19.

Norris, F. H., & Kaniasty, K. (1994). Psychological distress following criminal victimization in the general population: Cross-sectional, longitudinal, and prospective analyses. *Journal of Consulting and Clinical Psychology, 62,* 111–123.

Norris, F., Kaniasty, K., & Scheer, D. (1990). Use of mental health services among victims of crime: Frequency, correlates, and subsequent recovery. *Journal of Consulting and Clinical Psychology, 58,* 538–547.

Parad, H. J., & Caplan, G. (1960). A framework for studying families in crisis. *Social Work, 5,* 1–15.

Pecora, P. J., Fraser, M. W., & Haapala, D. A. (1991). Client outcomes and issues for program design. In K. Wells and D. E. Biegel (Eds.), *Family preservation services: Research and evaluation.* Newbury Park, CA: Sage.

Pecora, P. J., Fraser, M. W., & Haapala, D. A., (1992). Intensive home-based family preservation services: An update from the FIT project. *Child Welfare, 71,* 177–188.

Petit, M. R., & Curtis, P. A. (1997). *Child abuse and neglect: A look at*
the states: 1997 CWLA stat book. Washington, DC: CWLA Press.

Redding, G., & Raphelson, M. (1995). Around-the-clock mobile psychiatric crisis intervention. Another effective alternative to psychiatric hospitalization. *Community Mental Health Journal, 31,* 179–187.

Richardson, V. E. (October 28, 1999). Personal communication.

Riehl, T., Marchner, E., & Moller, H. (1988). Influence of crisis intervention telephone services ("crisis hotlines") on the suicide rate in 25 German cities. In H. J. Moller, A. Schmidtke, & R. Weiz (Eds.), *Current issues of suicidology* (pp. 431–436). New York: Springer-Verlag.

Roberts, A. R. (1990). *Helping crime victims.* Newbury Park, CA: Sage.

Roberts, A. R. (1995). Crisis intervention units and centers in the United States: A national survey. In A. R. Roberts (Ed.), *Crisis intervention and time-limited cognitive treatment* (pp. 54–70). Thousand Oaks, CA: Sage.

Roberts, A. R. (1998). *Battered women and their families: Intervention strategies and treatment programs.* New York: Springer.

Rossi, P. H. (1992). Assessing family preservation programs. *Children and Youth Services Review, 14,* 77–98.

Rubin, A. (October 29, 1999). Personal communication.

Ruffin, J., Spencer, H., Abel, A., Gage, J., & Miles, L. (1993). Crisis stabilization services for children and adolescents: A brokerage model to reduce admissions to state psychiatric facilities. *Community Mental Health Journal, 29,* 433–440.

Scannapieco, M. (1994). Home-based services program: Effectiveness with at-risk families. *Children and Youth Services Review, 16,* 363–377.

Smith, M. J. (1990). *Program Evaluation in the Human Services.* New York, N.Y.: Springer Publishing Company.

Smith, M. J. (October 29, 1999). Personal communication with Albert Roberts.

Spaid, W. M., & Fraser, M. (1991). The correlates of success/failure in brief and intensive family treatment: Implications for family preservation services. Special issue: Child welfare policy and practice. *Children and Youth Services Review, 12,* 77–99.

Thyer, B. (October 30, 1999). Personal communication.

Tracy, E. M. (1991). Defining the target population for family preservation services. In K. Wells & D. E. Biegel (Eds.), *Family preservation services: Research and evaluation* (pp. 138–158). Newbury Park, CA: Sage.

Walton, E. (1996). Family functioning as a measure of success in intensive family preservation services. *Journal of Family Social Work, 1,* 67–82.

Walton, E. Fraser, M., Lewis, R. E., Pecora, P., & Walton, W. K.

(1993). In-home, family-focused reunification services: An experimental study. *Child Welfare, 72,* 473–487.

Weiner, I. (1969). The effectiveness of a suicide prevention program. *Mental Hygiene, 53,* 357–363.

Wells, K., & Biegel, D. (1992). Intensive family preservation services research: Current status and future agenda. *Social Work Research and Abstracts, 28,* 21–27.

Wholey, J. S. (1981). *Evaluation promise and performance.* Washington, DC: Urban Institute.

Wood, S., Barton, K., & Schroeder, C. (1988). In-home treatment of abusive families: Cost and placement at one year. *Psychotherapy, 25,* 409–414.

Young, M. (1990). Victim assistance in the United States: The end of the beginning. *International Review of Victimology, 1,* 181–199.

Yuan, Y. Y., & Struckman-Johnson, D. L. (1991). Placement outcomes for neglected children with prior placements in family preservation programs. In K. Wells and D. E. Biegel (Eds.), *Family preservation services: Research and evaluation.* Beverly Hills, CA. Sage.

Zung, W. W. (1971). A rating instrument for anxiety disorders. *Psychosomatics, 12,* 371–379.

21

Designs and Procedures for Evaluating Crisis Intervention

SOPHIA F. DZIEGIELEWSKI
GERALD T. POWERS

The overall efficacy, popularity, and necessity of brief, time-limited therapeutic encounters, including crisis intervention approaches, focus clearly on
ascertaining the variables that can be linked directly to client change (Dziegielewski, Shields, & Thyer, 1998; Dziegielewski, 1997, 1996; Hartman &
Sullivan, 1996; Evans, Smith, Hill, Albers, & Neufeld, 1996; Roberts &
Dziegielewski, 1995; Mezzina & Vidoni, 1995; Koss & Butcher, 1986; Auerbach & Kilmann, 1977). To date, however, methodological limitations
inherent in most forms of time-limited intervention remain, particularly with
respect to the paucity of empirical evidence supporting significant differences
in the overall effectiveness of competing intervention approaches (Neimeyer & Pfeiffer, 1994). Historically, establishing treatment effectiveness in all
areas of counseling has often been met with resistance, especially since client
change behavior and the resulting therapeutic gains can be seen as subjective.

This subjectivity makes the task of establishing therapeutic effectiveness
and efficiency a complicated one (Koss & Shaing, 1994). In an effort to
formulate the evaluation process, it is useful to first identify two basic assumptions that underlie counseling efforts in the area of crisis management
and intervention, and then discuss why they can complicate the measurement
of intervention outcomes. First, in time-limited intervention of any type,
most counselors agree that the main effect of therapy is not curative but
rather one that directs, facilitates, and accelerates the pace of client progress
toward change. The experience is considered noncurative, and it must also

be time-limited in regard to service delivery. This makes the importance of early and brief intervention a consistent requirement, especially since clients typically remain in treatment fewer than six sessions (Dziegielewski, 1997). Crisis intervention strategies need to support and stabilize clients, as well as help them develop new coping strategies that allow them to adjust to the situational experience (Roberts & Dziegielewski, 1995).

Second, crisis is itself a multifaceted phenomenon that does not respond readily to traditional forms of therapeutic measurement and evaluation. Crisis situations are not experienced uniformly by those who encounter them. The nature, extent, and intensity of any given crisis are, in large measure, a product of the individual's construction of the social reality. The intervention, as well as the methods used to evaluate it, must vary accordingly. In the absence of any compelling evidence in support of long-term therapy as a more effective mode of practice, crisis intervention as a unique form of brief time-limited intervention is often preferred (Bloom, 1992; Koss & Shaing, 1994; Dziegielewski, 1996, 1997; Dziegielewski et al., 1998).

THE IMPORTANCE OF INTEGRATING RESEARCH AND PRACTICE

Helping professionals who routinely work with victims (or survivors) of crises report that several factors seem to be common to virtually all crisis situations. The first is the acknowledgment that the crisis situation often brings about a time-limited disequilibrium that must be addressed in order for the client to reach a homeostatic balance (Roberts & Dziegielewski, 1995). The disequilibrium associated with crises serves as a powerful motivational force that can heighten the client's susceptibility to intervention (Koss & Butcher, 1986). This is entirely consistent with the so-called strengths perspective, in which clients are believed to already possess the resources necessary to address stressful situations. They simply are not using them, are underusing them, or are currently unaware of how to best use them on their own behalf (Green, Lee, Trask, & Rheinscheld, 1996).

By nature, a crisis situation and the attendant reaction are self-limiting (Dziegielewski & Resnick, 1996; Roberts, 1990). Beginning with Lindemann's (1944) initial formulation of crisis intervention in his now classic study of the Coconut Grove nightclub disaster, crises have been characterized as time-limited phenomena that inevitably get resolved one way or another (with or without professional help) in a relatively brief period of time. The client's pressing need to resolve the crisis, and thus alleviate the associated pain, appears to heighten motivation, so much so that nominal levels of therapeutic intervention provided during the crisis period tend to produce positive and sometimes dramatic therapeutic results (Parad & Parad, 1990; Roberts & Dziegielewski, 1995).

Given this narrow window of vulnerability to change, it is considered essential that clients who experience crises must be provided immediate assistance in order to maximize the potential for constructive growth. Some authors, particularly those in the domestic violence field, believe that immediate intervention is so important that the postponement of appropriate help for more than 11 days places the client at greater risk of repeat victimization (Davis & Taylor, 1997).

According to Roberts and Dziegielewski (1995), Gilliland and James (1997), and other professionals in the area, positive life changes can be achieved following a crisis. Furthermore, the way a client handles a present crisis may have a profound and lasting impact not only on the individual's current adjustment but also on his or her capacity to cope with future crisis situations. From a research perspective, this suggests that practitioners should seek to understand and accurately explain the intervention approach being implemented. In addition, it is important to accurately identify the expected impact of the intervention and the anticipated adaptive responses. Unless outcome measures are clearly defined in operational terms, it is difficult to determine whether the intervention goals and objectives have been attained. The goals and objectives, in turn, must clearly be linked to positive life changes and methods of coping that enhance continued client functioning. Consequently, the central task of outcome-based research is to measure the presence and magnitude of both immediate and long-term changes that result from the counseling process (Lambert & Hill, 1994).

THE ROLE OF THE PRACTITIONER IN EMPIRICAL PRACTICE

From a clinical perspective, some of the important limitations associated with many of the studies that have traditionally compared short- and long-term intervention methods remain. In establishing an empirical basis for crisis intervention, similar to other forms of practice, one primary limitation rests in the fact that the independent variable cannot be adequately addressed in a homogeneous fashion alone. For example, when evaluating crisis intervention programs in particular, Neimeyer and Pfeiffer (1994) report that many researchers operate on the assumption that there are no important individual differences among clinicians with respect to what goes on during the therapeutic encounter. Limited attention is often given to ensuring that those who provide crisis intervention services have been adequately trained, and it is assumed that all practitioners have the same effect on client progress. This lack of attention to measuring the relative effectiveness of the social worker can clearly lead to myths that support some sort of global and homogeneous index of client improvement. These "uniformity myths," as Kiesler (1966) originally described them, deflect attention from possible important individual differences both within and between groups of clients and the therapists who treat them. Several studies provide ample evidence in support of the relative effectiveness of time-limited crisis intervention strategies (Neimeyer & Pfeiffer, 1994; Rudd, Joiner, & Rajab, 1995; Mezzina & Vidoni, 1995; Hartman & Sullivan, 1996; Davis & Taylor, 1997). Equally apparent, however, is the relative absence of any clear-cut preferences regarding the "impact of alternative treatments on alternative clinical problems with clients of varying characteristics and other manifold conditions that may mediate treatment" (Kazdin, 1994, p. 20). Simply stated, the critical issues to be addressed are essentially no different now than they were when Paul first issued his now famous dictum in 1966: "What treatment, by whom, is most effective for this individual with that specific problem, and under which set of circumstances?" (Paul, 1966, p. 111).

The purpose of this chapter is to present clinically grounded research models that are relevant for those in crisis situations and that remain sensitive to the three major variables of the therapeutic paradigm: the client, the social worker as a researcher/practitioner, and the outcome. Against a general background of group design or "nomothetic" research, we will consider several evaluation models, all of which emphasize what Chassan (1967) and others have referred to as "intensive" or "ideographic" designs of research. When used alone, none of them is foolproof. Together, however, they provide a useful set of assessment tools that can help social workers evaluate the efficacy of their practice and improve the quality of the services they provide.

MACRO- AND MICROANALYSES IN CRISIS INTERVENTION

Over the years, a variety of measurement strategies have been employed in an effort to assess various dimensions of the crisis intervention process. When viewed as a whole, they provide an intriguing array of designs, ranging from macro to micro levels of analysis. For example, in an attempt to assess the process and outcome of crisis intervention in terms of suicide interventions, Neimeyer and Pfeiffer (1994) attempted to chronicle the relative effectiveness of various suicide intervention strategies and how such strategies actually contributed to the therapeutic relationship. When effectiveness was measured from a macro perspective, these methods focused primarily on epidemiological data collected by local, regional, and national organizations. Some studies compared suicide rates before and after the implementation of a particular intervention program. Other studies employed quasi-experimental designs in which similar populations of treated and untreated suicide attempters were compared. In still other studies, cohorts of treated clients were compared with population parameters based on data derived from the

National Center for Health and Statistics within the United States. There are serious methodological problems inherent in the use of extant data, however, especially with respect to threats to internal validity as well as comparability across idiosyncratic samples. In an effort to address some of these apparent weaknesses, client or caller satisfaction methods are sometimes used to help validate client perceptions and support the intrinsic worth of the study. Based on these macro types of analyses, many suicide programs and crisis intervention services have failed to gather the kinds of information necessary to adequately establish program effectiveness (Neimeyer & Pfeiffer, 1994). Without such information, it is impossible to determine whether negative findings are the result of inadequacies in the practice theory or liabilities in the research methodology. For questions like this, there are no easy answers. The fact that a crisis is itself a dynamic and multifaceted phenomenon can also complicate the measurement process, particularly when it is done on an aggregate basis, or when it relies primarily on secondary sources. Further, studies that rely exclusively on self-reports, can also be problematic. For example, when looking specifically at rural adolescents at risk of suicide, Evans et. al. (1996) clearly established a relationship between characteristics such as the respondent's family dynamics, and whether there was a history of abuse. Regardless of how data is collected (via a data base, support lines, or self-report) crisis intervention strategies represent multi-faceted perspectives that consistently pose challenging assessment problems for the professional practitioner.

Some practitioners have argued that the most effective way to assess the efficacy of practice interventions at the micro level is to focus on the idiosyncratic interactions that take place between the worker and the client (Bloom, Fischer, & Orme, 1999). This approach typically combines both quantitative and qualitative methods that rely heavily on the client's personal constructions of the crisis experience. Such methods tend to minimize threats to internal validity, but they raise serious questions with respect to generalizability. In focusing on the rich detail of the client-worker transactions and subsequent outcomes, the search for scientifically objective generalizations is abandoned in favor of in-depth insights that can be attained only by exploring the individual case as it is subjectively experienced. Toward this end, the worker can employ a variety of evaluation strategies. It is generally agreed that no single measure can adequately capture all the relevant subtleties of the crisis intervention process. As a result, Denzin (1970) and others encourage the use of multiple measures. Through an evaluation strategy referred to as "triangulation," workers can arrive at a reasonably accurate approximation of what is actually going on in the intervention process.

When addressing service effectiveness on a much smaller scale or with a more individualized focus, the micro level of *intervention* becomes the primary locus of attention. For example, from a "micro" perspective, issues such as individual worker influences and the subsequent treatment effectiveness that results become paramount. To highlight this perspective, skills are sometimes measured through simulated calling experiences or formalized role-playing. In an attempt to quantify this more micro perspective, Neimeyer and Pfeiffer (1994) discuss the potential value of using specific instruments designed to directly measure the skill of the worker. When dealing with suicide prevention, these authors also suggest that one such instrument that could be utilized is the Suicide Intervention Response Inventory (SIRI-2), designed to measure forced responses of the professional helper in the crisis intervention setting. In fact, a variety of useful rapid assessment instruments have been designed and tested for use in crisis situations, including indices that measure life stress, negative expectations, depression, problem-solving behaviors and attitudes, personality characteristics, and other similar traits associated with psychiatric conditions, as well as other relevant crisis-related phenomena (see Buros, 1978; Corcoran & Fischer, 1999a, 1999b). The micro approach does not merely invite the use of these indices for the measurement of crisis behaviors—it virtually mandates it. However, the authors of these instruments tend to recommend caution in their use. They recognize that the evaluation of a crisis situation is a multifaceted undertaking that cannot be adequately assessed if one relies solely on a single instrument or focuses on a single dimension such as the worker's effectiveness. Overall, these authors warn that there is a paucity of literature from both a macro and a micro perspective. Very few studies address outcome-based measurement involving the evaluation of crisis intervention in general or suicide prevention services in particular (Neimeyer & Pfeiffer, 1994).

PREREQUISITES TO EFFECTIVE EVALUATION

Each of the chapters in this handbook discusses the application of crisis intervention strategies with a different population at risk. While the strategies have much in common with respect to many of the technical characteristics of the crisis intervention process, there is wide variability regarding various dimensions of the therapeutic experience. Crisis experiences can vary in terms of the identified problem, the client's reaction, the social worker's handling of the situation, the surrounding circumstances, and the expected outcome. Although some researchers have utilized the classic pretest/posttest design to measure practice effectiveness (Dziegielewski, 1991), others have concluded that such attempts at utilizing group designs remain problematic (Bergin, 1971). Similarly, Kazdin (1986, 1994) noted that investigations that involve groups, as well as conclusions about average client performance, can misrepresent or under- or overrepresent the effects of intervention on the individuals being served.

In discussing the need for specificity in conducting outcome research, Bergin (1971) cautioned that "it is essential that the entire therapeutic enterprise be broken down into specific sets of measures and operations, or in other words, be dimensionalized" (p. 253). This ideal is still supported and considered essential in crisis intervention as evidenced in the more recent work of Neimeyer and Pfeiffer (1994). This concept, however, remains complicated because in the measurement of crisis intervention, techniques that evaluate crisis situations require an intimate understanding between the social worker and the individual in crisis. The resulting assessment must also reflect the multifaceted assessment process that will be initiated. In viewing crisis intervention from an empirical standpoint, the various dimensions of the intervention experience need to be treated as a complex network of functional relationships within which there occurs a series of interactions among the primary factors (i.e., the independent and dependent variables). Simply stated, in any functional relationship, the independent variables operate as the presumed causes and dependent variables operate as the presumed effects. Therefore, in crisis intervention an important first step in the evaluation process is to sort out what are believed to be the causal connections operating in any given crisis situation. This involves identifying a series of interdependent problem-solving steps that logically flow from the presenting problem (Powers, Meenaghan, & Toomey, 1985). Embedded in the logic of this problem-solving process is an implied hypothesis, the calculus of which can be stated as follows:

> In crisis situations, if "X" (e.g., suicide prevention service) is employed as an intervention strategy (i.e., the independent variable) then it is expected that "Y" (i.e., a return to previous functioning level) will be the predicted outcome (i.e., the dependent variable).

Crisis intervention is no different than any other form of intervention. Inevitably, it involves, in one way or another, the testing of this implied hypothesis. For example, when it is believed that residential crisis services can serve as a supportive measure for those in crisis, thereby limiting hospitalization and increasing stabilization, specific steps to outline a plan of action become necessary.

Empirical practice requires that the clinician-researcher specify clearly what he or she intends to do with or on behalf of the client, as well as the expected consequences of those actions. In order to do this, both the intervention and the outcome must be defined in operational or measurable terms. To say that emotional support will result in enhanced client self-esteem or that ventilation will reduce depression—although on the surface both may appear very important in practice—simply is not an adequate statement of a testable hypothesis. As is true in all time-limited interventions, social work clinicians are expected to state exactly what is meant by concepts such as "emotional support" and "ventilation," as well as what changes are expected to occur as a result of their use (Dziegielewski, 1996, 1997).

Based on this premise, Hartman and Sullivan (1996) clearly established specific objectives for center staff working in residential crisis services. They maintain that the key objectives include stabilizing crisis situations efficiently by reducing presenting symptoms; maintaining or reducing the frequency of hospitalizations or preadmission levels; helping consumers return to previous levels of satisfaction and service, such housing and vocational status; and attaining high levels of consumer satisfaction with services.

Although the task of operationally defining concepts is not an easy one, most researchers concur that it is essential to the effective evaluation of empirically based practice, regardless of one's theoretical orientation (Bloom et al., 1999; Bisman & Hardcastle, 1999; Marlow, 1998). Furthermore, the value and subsequent recognition of our clinical practice efforts will prove to be only as good as the empirical observations on which they are based.

MEASURING GOALS AND OBJECTIVES

The brief and time-limited nature of crisis intervention presents some interesting challenges for the clinician who wishes to evaluate his or her practice. From the very outset, clients in crisis need to be convinced that change is possible and that they are capable of contributing to the change process. In so doing, they gain confidence and competence, attributes that should also be mirrored in the behavior of the helping professional. The development of this mutual respect and confidence in one another's abilities provides the necessary foundation for both practice and its evaluation. Basically, no matter what evaluation strategy one employs, it is likely to be meaningful only if it is initiated early and brought to closure fairly quickly. In addition, the methodology itself should not be experienced by the client as being in any way intrusive to the helping process. Ideally, the purposes of both the intervention and the evaluation should be compatible and mutually supportive.

This mutuality of purpose can be facilitated by the social work professional not only by helping the client to participate in the development of appropriate treatment goals but also by enabling the client to stay task oriented in regard to pursuing them. The social work professional can facilitate this process by helping the client establish specific and limited goals (Hepworth & Larsen, 1993). Simply stated, a *goal* may be defined as the desirable objective that is to be achieved as a result of treatment. Well-stated goals permit the practitioner to determine whether he or she has the skills and/or desire to work with the client (Cormier & Cormier, 1991).

Brower and Nurius (1993) suggest two key characteristics to be considered when designing effective intervention goals. First, goals need to be as clear and as behaviorally specific as possible. The more precisely they are defined in measurable terms, the easier it is to verify if and when they are achieved. Once the goals are defined, they may be further refined in terms of more specific immediate, intermediate, and long-term objectives. Second, both the helping professional and the client should mutually agree upon all goals and objectives. This may seem difficult during times of crisis, particularly when the helping professional is required to assume a very active role to help the client meet his or her own needs. This role, however, should always be one of facilitation, in which the client is helped to achieve what he or she has deemed essential in order to regain an enhanced homeostatic balance (Dziegielewski, 1997). Only the client can determine whether the goals and objectives sought are consistent with his or her own culture and values. It is up to the social worker to help the client structure and establish the intervention strategy; however, emphasis on mutuality is central to the development of goals and objectives.

Social workers have long realized the value of goal setting as a means of facilitating the intervention process. With the advent of managed care, however, pressures from both within and outside the profession have heightened awareness of the importance of documenting outcomes. A new performance standard has been established, one that requires practitioners to have mastered the technical skills necessary to evaluate the efficacy of their interventive strategies. For empirically based practice to be meaningful, social workers must be capable of establishing the kind of practice climate in which programmatic goals, and the specific objectives designed to meet them, are viewed as realistic, obtainable, and measurable. Given the complexities of contemporary practice, however, no one methodological approach is likely to prove appropriate for all types of crisis situations. The research challenge for crisis workers, as inevitably it is for practice in general, is to fit the method to the problem, and not vice versa. This requires a thoughtful selection of research strategies, the various threads of which can be creatively woven throughout the broader fabric of the overall intervention plan.

One evaluation model that has received widespread attention and use is Goal Attainment Scaling (GAS; Lambert & Hill, 1994). This type of scaling, which appears to be adaptable to a wide range of crisis intervention situations, was originally introduced by Kiresuk and Sherman (1968) as a way of measuring programmatic outcomes for community mental health services. It is discussed here as an example of an evaluation model that combines a number of very useful ideographic as well as nomothetic methodological features. GAS employs a client-specific technique designed to provide outcome information regarding the attainment of individualized clinical and social goals. Several researchers support the belief that in today's practice environment insight-oriented intervention strategy is limited (Dziegielewski, 1997, 1998; Koss & Butcher, 1986; Fischer, 1976; Bellak & Small, 1978). Therefore, these types of highly structured scaling methods, with their clear conceptualization and methodology, remain popular and necessary for practice survival in today's managed care environment. The structured nature of crisis intervention, organized around the attainment of limited goals with concretely specified objectives, articulates especially well with the methodological requisites of standardized measures such as the GAS.

The GAS requires that a number of individually tailored intervention goals or objectives be specified in relation to a set of graded scale points, ranging from the *least* to the *most* favorable outcomes considered likely. The net result of this scaling procedure is a transformation of each outcome into an approximate random variable, thus allowing the overall attainment of specific goals to be treated as standard scores, a feature that becomes important when GAS is used for program evaluation purposes.

This process is operationalized in the form of a Goal Attainment Guide. For example, the intervention objectives for a particular suicidal client may include (a) the elimination of suicidal ideation, (b) the alleviation of depression, and (c) the enhancement of self-esteem. Table 21.1 illustrates how these goals might be defined in terms of expected outcomes that are relevant to a specific client. Although goals can be tailored to each client's needs, a Dictionary of Goal Attainment Scaling is available to assist clinicians in their efforts to operationally define goals and construct Goal Attainment Guides (Garwick & Lampman, 1973).

Although somewhat dated, the definitions contained in the Goal Attainment Guide continue to be relevant to today's behaviorally based, outcome-focused practice environment, structured as it is with a specific time frame in mind. The definitions for the expected level of success (i.e., the midpoint of the 5-point scale) represent clinical predictions concerning client performance at some predetermined future date (e.g., 4 or 6 weeks following the formulations of the goals; Lambert & Hill, 1994). The amount and direction of goal attainment can then be measured by comparing baseline functioning with the level of functioning recorded on the identified target date. Specific weights can also be assigned to each goal or objective as a way of reflecting its relative importance or priority in the overall intervention plan. The actual numerical value of the assigned weight is of significance only when GAS is used as a basis for comparing the relative effectiveness of alternative intervention approaches within or between programs.

Any number of goals may be specified for a particular client, and any subject area may be included as an appropriate goal. Even the same goal can be defined in more than one way. For example, the goal of alleviating depression could be scaled in relation to self-reports or in relation to specific cutoff points on a standardized instrument such as the Beck Depression Inventory (Beck, 1967). It is essential, however, that all goals be defined in terms of a graded series of verifiable expectations in ways that are relevant to the idiosyncrasies of the particular case.

It should be emphasized that the use of GAS as a framework for the intensive study of a single case does not warrant inferences concerning causal

Table 21.1   Sample Goal Attainment Guide Illustrating Scaling Procedure for
Hypothetical Suicidal Client

Levels of expected attainment	Goals		
	Suicide Weight: 40	Depression Weight: 20	Self-esteem Weight: 10
Least favorable outcome thought likely (−2)	Commits suicide or makes additional suicidal attempt(s).		
Less than expected success (−1)	Preoccupied with thoughts of suicide as a possible solution to personal problems; says "life is not worth living."	Complains of being very depressed all the time; eating and sleeping patterns irregular; cries daily; not working.	Considers self a "bad person"; criticizes self; feels people would be better off without him or her.
Expected level of success (0)	Occasionally thinks about suicide, but is able to consider alternative solutions to personal problems.	Complains of being depressed all the time; eats at least two meals a day; sleeps at least six hours a night; cries occasionally; misses work occasionally.	Doesn't verbally criticize self, but says he or she is not very happy.
More than expected success (+1)		Only occasional feelings of depression; eating and sleeping regularly; no longer crying; working regularly.	
Most favorable outcome thought likely (+2)	No longer considers suicide a viable solution to personal problems; talks of future plans.		Reports he or she likes self and way of living and/or reports being "reasonably happy."

relationships between intervention and outcome. In fact, by stressing the importance of outcome factors, it tends to deflect attention away from concern for issues directly involving interventions. Although it cannot be concluded that the identified intervention is necessarily responsible for the attainment of goals, when expected goals are not realized it does raise serious questions concerning the efficacy of the intervention strategy. In summary, the GAS is given as an example of how goal or objective attainment can be specified in order to monitor, organize, and collect information on the assessment process as a means toward establishing empirically based practice. GAS suffers from many of the same limitations as other systems of measurement designed to treat data that are inherently ordinal in nature as if they possessed the characteristics of an interval or ratio scale.

USING MEASUREMENT INSTRUMENTS

Once the goals and/or objectives of intervention have been established, the difficult task of evaluating the clinical intervention in standardized or operationally based terms can be addressed. This task is simplified greatly when problems are articulated in terms of realistic goals and operationally defined objectives rather than in vague and nebulous language. Terms such as *stress*, *anxiety*, and *depression* are often used to describe important facets of a client's social or psychological functioning. Although commonplace in our professional jargon, such terms tend to carry subjective connotations. This semantic elusiveness makes it very difficult to establish reliable measures of change. Measuring practice effectiveness, as stated earlier, typically involves a process designed to determine whether, or to what extent, mutually negotiated goals and objectives have been met. Change is documented through some type of concrete measurement that is indicative of client progress. Hepworth and Larsen (1993) suggest that this process can be greatly facilitated by establishing clear-cut contracts with clients, which, in turn, provide a viable foundation for a variety of individual and/or group evaluation designs (Bloom & Fischer, 1982; Rosye, 1995; Rubin & Babbie, 1993). Once the contract is in place, standardized instruments can be used as repeated measures to gather consistent data from baseline through termination and follow-up. It is the responsibility of the social work professional, of course, to select, implement, and evaluate the appropriateness of the measurement instruments. Most professionals agree that standardized scales (i.e., those that have been assessed for reliability and validity) are generally preferred.

In recent years, social workers have begun to rely more heavily on standardized instruments in an effort to achieve greater accuracy and objectivity in their attempts to measure some of the more commonly encountered clinical problems. The most notable development in this regard has been the emergence of numerous brief pencil-and-paper assessment devices known as *rapid assessment instruments* (RAIs). As standardized measures, RAIs share a number of characteristics. They are brief; relatively easy to administer, score, and interpret; and require very little knowledge of testing procedures on the part of the clinician. For the most part, they are self-report measures that can be completed by the client, usually within 15 minutes. They are independent of any particular theoretical orientation, and as such can be used with a variety of interventive methods. Since they provide a systematic overview of the client's problem, they often tend to stimulate discussion related to the information elicited by the instrument itself. The score that is generated provides an operational index of the frequency, duration, or intensity of the problem. Most RAIs can be used as repeated measures, and thus are adaptable to the methodological requirements of both research design and goal assessment purposes. In addition to providing a standardized means by which change can be monitored over time with a single client,

RAIs can also be used to make equivalent comparisons across clients experiencing a common problem (e.g., marital conflict).

One of the major advantages of standardized RAI's is the availability of information concerning reliability and validity. *Reliability* refers to the stability of a measure. In other words, do the questions that constitute the instrument mean the same thing to the individual answering them at different times, and would different individuals interpret those same questions in a similar manner?

Validity speaks to the general question of whether an instrument does in fact measure what it purports to measure. There are several approaches to establishing validity (Chen, 1997; Cone, 1998; Schutte & Malouff, 1995; Powers et al., 1985), each of which is designed to provide information regarding how much confidence we can have in the instrument as an accurate indicator of the problem under consideration. Although levels of reliability and validity vary greatly among available instruments, it is very helpful to the social work professional to know in advance the extent to which these issues have been addressed. Information concerning reliability and validity, as well as other factors related to the standardization process (e.g., the procedures for administering, scoring, and interpreting the instrument), can help the professional make informed judgments concerning the appropriateness of any given instrument.

The key to selecting the best instrument for the intervention is knowing where and how to access the relevant information concerning potentially useful measures. Fortunately, a number of excellent sources are available to the clinician to help facilitate this process. One such compilation of standardized measures is *Measures for Clinical Practice*, by Corcoran and Fischer (1999a, 1999b), and another in *Sourcebook of Adult Assessment Strategies*, by Schutte and Malouff (1995). These reference texts can serve as valuable resources for identifying useful rapid-assessment instruments suited for the kinds of problems most commonly encountered in clinical social work practice.

Overall, the RAIs can serve as valuable adjuncts for the social work professional's evaluation efforts. In crisis intervention, however, more emphasis on their utility is needed. To date, the reviews and acceptance of this type of assessment tool have been mixed. For example, in the area of suicide risk, Jobes (1995) and Jobes, Eyman, and Yufit (1995) found that most professionals familiar with such instruments tended to use them only infrequently. Many of these same professionals believed that, when RAIs are used specifically to quantify behaviors and feelings in times of crisis, their utility was limited. Until these perceived shortcomings have been resolved, RAIs should probably be employed only as one aspect of a more comprehensively triangulated evaluation strategy.

One of the more notable deficits cited in the evaluation literature related to crisis intervention is the paucity of studies that look directly at social work practitioner effectiveness. A variety of tools are available that can help the social worker to measure his or her own perceived effectiveness (Fischer, 1976). This type of introspective practice assessment is intentionally designed to provide social workers with the kinds of timely feedback they need to enable them to modify and refine their techniques and strategies for future use in similar cases. Several scales and other concrete measurement indices have been designed to assist the social worker to do this (Corcoran & Fischer, 1999a, 1999b).

Finally, to further enhance the measurement of practice effectiveness, many social workers feel pressured to incorporate additional forms of measurement as part of the treatment plan (Dziegielewski, 1997). The pressure to incorporate individual, family, and social rankings is becoming more common. This requires a procedure capable of monitoring a client's functioning level that can be clearly measured and documented. To provide this additional form of measurement, an increasing number of professionals are turning to the DSM-IV (American Psychiatric Association, 1994) and providing Axis V (Generalized Assessment of Functioning) rating scores for each client served. In this method, ratings of a client's functioning are assigned at the outset of therapy and again upon discharge. The scales allow for assigning a number that represents a client's behaviors. The scales are designed to enable the worker to differentially rank identified behaviors from 0 to 100, with higher ratings indicating higher overall functioning and coping levels. By rating the highest level of functioning a client has attained over the past year, and then comparing it to his or her current level of functioning, helpful comparisons can be made.

Also, in the DSM-IV Criteria Sets and Axes Provided for Further Study there are two scales that are not required for diagnosis yet can provide a format for ranking function that might be particularly helpful to social work professionals. The first of these optional scales is the relational functioning scale termed the Global Assessment of Relational Functioning (GARF). This index is used to address the status of family or other ongoing relationships on a hypothetical continuum from *competent* to *dysfunctional* (American Psychiatric Association, 1994). The second index is the Social and Occupational Functioning Assessment Scale (SOFAS). With this scale, an "individual's level of social and occupational functioning that is not directly influenced by overall severity of the individual's psychological symptoms" can be addressed (American Psychiatric Association, 1994, p. 760). The complementary nature of these scales in identifying and assessing client problems is evident in the fact that all three scales—the GARF, GAF, and SOFAS—use the same rating system. The rankings for each scale range from 0 to 100, with the lower numbers representing more severe problems. The use of all three of these tools has been encouraging for obvious reasons. Collectively, they provide a viable framework within which social workers can apply concrete measures to a wide variety of practice situations. They also provide a multidimensional perspective that permits workers to document variations in levels of functioning across system sizes, including the individual (GAF), family (GARF), and social (SOFAS) perspective.

In summary, it remains obvious that the helping relationship is a complex one that cannot be measured completely through the use of standardized scales or social worker assessment measures. To facilitate measurement of effectiveness, specific concrete goals and objectives must incorporate a number of direct behavioral observation techniques, self-anchored rating scales, client logs, projective tests, Q-sort techniques, unobtrusive measures, and personality tests, as well as a variety of mechanical devices for monitoring physiological functioning. Together these methods can provide a range of qualitative and quantitative measures for evaluating practice. A number of excellent sources are available that discuss in detail the kinds of information one would need in order to make informed decisions regarding their selection and application to specific cases (Bloom et al., 1999; Rubin & Babbie, 1993; Powers et al., 1985).

CASE-RELATED OR MICRO DESIGNS IN CRISIS INTERVENTION

Intensive, as a specific type of microlevel design, is distinguished from extensive models of research because it is concerned primarily with the study of single cases (i.e., N = 1). In this chapter, the terms *single system* (Bloom, Fischer, & Orme, 1999), *single subject design*, and *single case design* (Bisman & Hardcastle, 1999) are used more or less interchangeably. Preference is noted, however, for the term single system or single case design because they allow for a broader definition of the case under study rather than simply referring directly to one specific client as a subject.

These intensive designs provide the means by which clinicians can evaluate the idiosyncratic aspects of their practice, while at the same time allowing for the generation of practice-relevant hypotheses suitable for testing via the more traditional extensive research approaches. Further, it is important to note that the distinction between extensive and intensive models of research relate directly to the long-standing controversy regarding the relative merits of nomothetic versus idiographic research as originally differentiated by Allport (1962).

Advocates of the nomothetic approaches emphasize the primacy of the confirmatory aspect of scientific activity, in which the ultimate goal is to discover the laws that apply to individuals in general. These researchers believe that the aggregate is of greater importance than are the individuals who comprise it. As a result, nomothetists devote their time to the study of groups in an effort to confirm or disprove hypothetical statements and thus to arrive at scientific generalizations concerning some aspect of the empirical world. In contrast, advocates of the idiographic approach tend to be more interested in the study of individuals as individuals. Rather than focusing their attention on the discovery of general propositions, they prefer to investigate the rich and intricate details of specific cases, including the deviant cases that prove to be exceptions to the rule. In crisis intervention, the acknowledgment of both approaches appears relevant and both contribute to the cushion of knowledge that informs our practice. Neither one should be seen as superior to the other and with some over-lap they can prove to be complementary.

The intensive or idiographic models of research are emphasized here simply because they lend themselves more directly to the primary purposes of the clinician—that is, the assessment of the social worker's own practice on a case-by-case basis. There is no intent to discount the importance of the extensive or nomothetic approaches. In fact, the probability of success in practice is likely to increase to the extent that more social workers can participate in studies that involve controlled observation and systematic verification. In this sense, the two approaches are indeed complementary: one generating scientific generalizations under controlled circumstances, and the other applying and evaluating their utility in the idiosyncratic crucible of practice. Ideally, in measuring the effectiveness of any time-limited crisis situation, the clinician-researcher needs to be able to identify with confidence a causal relationship between the independent variable (i.e., the intervention) and the dependent variable (i.e., the target behavior). For the social worker it is problematic when extraneous variables (those not directly related to the intervention) occur and cannot be clearly identified and controlled during the therapeutic process. These extraneous variables represent competing hypotheses that could be conceived as possible causes of change in the target behavior. To the extent that this occurs, it raises serious questions with respect to the internal validity of the intervention, thus reducing the level of confidence warranted by any causal inferences that might be drawn.

The classic work by Campbell and Stanley (1966) clearly describes a number of possible design weaknesses that pose threats to internal validity. For social workers engaging in empirically based practice, knowledge of these factors is essential for measuring effective and efficient services. It is important to remember that when a practice design can effectively control the influences and subsequent contamination from outside (extraneous) variables, it is said to be valid. Single case designs can offer the practitioner a means for measuring practice effectiveness; however, as Barlow and Hersen (1984) and other researchers (Bloom et al., 1999; Bisman & Hardcastle, 1999) openly point out, single case study designs vary widely with respect to their ability to accomplish this goal.

TIME-SERIES DESIGNS

The prototype for the intensive/idiographic model of practice research is the time-series design (Fischer, 1976). The process involves the measurement of change in some target behavior (usually the identified problem) at given intervals over a more or less extended period (Bloom et al., 1999). In this case, the successive observations made during the course of therapeutic intervention enable the clinician to systematically monitor the nature and extent of change in a target behavior. The actual observations, and/or the recording of those observations, may be done by the social worker, the client, or any other willing mediator with whom the client interacts of a regular basis, including, for instance, a family member, a friend, or a teacher.

Once a target behavior has been identified and an appropriate observational approach selected, it is a relatively simple matter to record any changes that occur during the course of intervention. The amount and direction of changes are usually portrayed in the form of a two-dimensional graph, as illustrated in Figure 21.1.

Basically, the practitioner identifies the target behavior and plots it in relation to gradations (in frequency, duration, or intensity) arranged along the vertical axis. Successive observations are similarly recorded at regular time intervals, as indicated along the horizontal axis. The points are then joined in a continuous line that reflects the pattern of behavioral change that has occurred over the intervention time period.

In all single-subject designs the preintervention observation phase is referred to as the *baseline period* and generally is labeled with an "A". The intent of the baseline is to determine whether the pattern of behavior observed during the baseline (i.e., Phase A) changes in the expected direction following the introduction of treatment (i.e., the treatment is referred to as Phase B). If changes occur during intervention, the social worker has some basis upon which to infer that the treatment may have had something to do with it.

In working with clients in crisis, however, collecting baseline data may not be practical, and the necessity of an immediate intervention may negate the luxury of gathering these data in advance of treatment. In most crisis situations delays in the initiation of treatment not only are likely to be viewed as theoretically questionable but also may pose serious ethical implications (Kazdin & Wilson, 1978). In crisis, often the best one can expect with respect to the collection of baseline information may be a retrospective reconstruction of relevant data as reported by the client or some other available informant.

It is apparent that the more rigorous the design, the more confidence one can have that threats to internal validity can be effectively ruled out. Unfortunately, the most rigorous designs require the use of baseline measures. Despite the limitations already noted, it is useful to understand some of the more sophisticated derivations of the time-series design. Although they may not always prove to be of practical value in the evaluation of particular crisis situations, they do provide useful models against which to compare the rigor of alternative approaches.

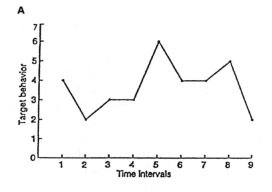

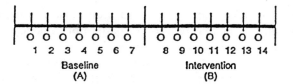

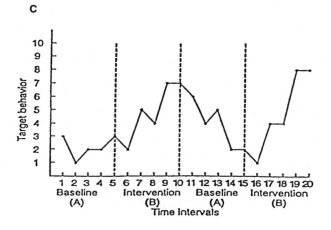

Figure 21.1   Changes in target behavior

Two of the most commonly encountered variants of the basic time-series design are the reversal design and the multiple baseline approach (Bloom et al., 1999). In the reversal design, intervention is introduced for a prescribed period and then abruptly withdrawn, with the resulting circumstances essentially approximating preintervention or baseline conditions. In the absence of intervention, certain types of client behaviors might be expected to move in the direction of preintervention levels. When this occurs, it is generally considered to support a causal relationship, especially when treatment is subsequently reinstated (A_1-B_1-A_2-B_2) with concomitant improvements in the client's functioning.

Suppose, for example, a clinician was employing cognitive therapy as a means of reducing anxiety associated with the inability to control violent tendencies. The theory supporting the use of intervention assumes that the inability to control one's temper is escalated by irrational thoughts, which in turn inhibit self-control and justify violence as a course of action. The clinician employs cognitive techniques and observes an improvement in the client's self-control during the intervention phase (B_1). The techniques are subsequently withdrawn, and the client returns to his or her former state of irrational thinking during the second baseline period (A_2) with a concomitant increase in anxiety and potential fear over loss of control. This return to baseline conditions and ultimately to a second intervention phase provides the rationale for naming the process a reversal design. As can be seen by this example, reversal designs can be problematic, especially when the behavior one is exhibiting is dangerous to self or others. In this case, once the client's "locus of control" becomes questionable, immediate reinitiation of the treatment phase is warranted.

In a second type of design the multiple baseline approach, like its A-B-A-B counterpart, is also used to minimize the possibility of behavior change due to chance. Unlike the reversal design, however, there is no withdrawal of intervention. Instead, baseline data are collected either (a) on more than one target behavior, (b) on the same target behavior but in more than one setting, or (c) on more than one but similar clients. Intervention techniques are applied in a sequential manner so that once a change in the initial target behavior is observed, the intervention is systematically introduced with the next target behavior or in an alternative setting (Bisman & Hardcastle, 1999; Mark, 1996; Fischer, 1976).

The sequential nature of the multiple baseline approach is especially useful in client interventions where more than one problem must be addressed or there is more than one target behavior that is expected to be affected by the intervention. This is true in most crisis situations, where the precipitating events typically affect various aspects of the client's overall social or psychological functioning. It is important to keep in mind, however, that the validity of any multiple baseline approach is based on the assumption that the selected target behaviors are themselves independent of one another. If changes in one behavior are somehow functionally interdependent, use of the multiple baseline approach would be discouraged.

Both the A-B-A-B design and the multiple baseline approach begin to approximate the level of confidence achieved in what Campbell and Stanley (1966) refer to as *true experiments*. However, they are the most difficult to implement and, with respect to the evaluation of crisis intervention, have only limited utility for the practical, ethical, and methodological reasons cited earlier.

A final note is in order before we conclude our discussion of the time-series designs. In most instances, it is possible to determine whether meaningful change has occurred by means of simple visual inspection of the two-dimensional graph. Sometimes, however, it is impossible to determine from visual inspection alone whether the shift that occurs between the baseline and the intervention phases is dramatic enough to constitute a significant change. This is due to the fact that time-series data tend to be serially dependent (Gottman & Leiblum, 1974). In cases in which the observed changes may be due to serial dependence, the worker can apply some fairly simple statistical procedures (referred to as *autocorrelation*) to help resolve the issue (Bloom et al., 1999).

As stated earlier, practice wisdom often dictates how best to proceed in helping a client, given the specific nature of the crisis situation and the surrounding circumstances. It can also help the practitioner decide when to apply and/or withdraw the various components of the treatment package throughout the course of the intervention process. Social work professionals are increasingly being called upon to balance practice skills with empirical techniques, techniques that in the end will yield more efficient and effective modes of service. For the crisis intervention worker, the use of measurement devices, such as structured questionnaires and psychometric instruments, needs to be supplemented with practice wisdom, theory, and, in the final analysis, life experience (Rittner, Smyth, & Wodarski, 1995).

SUMMARY AND CONCLUSIONS

The efficacy of crisis intervention as a viable alternative to the more traditional long-term models of therapy has been well documented. The question is no longer whether crisis intervention or short-term therapeutic measures work, but rather what techniques work best with what kinds of clients and problems, and under what set of circumstances (see chapters 3 and 20)? Managed care presents a type of service delivery never before experienced. Social workers must show that the time-limited brief services they provide are necessary and effective. This challenge has been a particularly vigorous one for crisis intervention advocates because of the fluctuating nature of any crisis response. In this arena, however, effectiveness must extend beyond merely helping the client. Ultimately, the process of validating the effectiveness of our practice dictates that we be able to demonstrate that the greatest concrete and identifiable therapeutic gain has been achieved, in the quickest amount of time, and with the least expenditure of financial and professional resources. This means not only that the treatment that social workers provide should be therapeutically necessary and effective but also that it should be delivered in a manner that is professionally competitive with other disciplines that claim similar treatment strategies and techniques.

Professional interest in the various forms of time-limited brief therapy has increased greatly and will most probably continue to increase in the coming years. Social work practice that operates within a framework of a planned, time-limited brief intervention format appears to be a viable and essential practice modality, especially in today's managed care environment. Health maintenance organizations and employee assistance programs generally favor highly structured brief forms of therapy, and as they continue to grow, so too will use of the time-limited models they support (Wells, 1994). Further, insight-oriented intervention strategies and cure-focused therapeutic approaches seem to have given way to more pragmatically grounded practice strategies.

It is important to realize that social workers, like their physician counterparts, rarely "cure" client problems—nor should they be expected to do so. What should be expected, however, is that we help clients utilize their own potential to help diminish or alleviate symptoms and/or states of being that cause discomfort. The prevailing emphasis on client individuality and time-limited concrete changes not only is accepted as a reasonable professional expectation but also is generally recognized as an essential element of "state-of-the-art" practice (see chapters 1 and 2).

Throughout this chapter, it has been argued that the best way to evaluate the relative effectiveness of our crisis intervention strategies is through the creative use of various intensive research designs. In recent years, a range of quantitative and qualitative research methods has evolved. These ideographically grounded methods are of particular value to the social work professional because they are specially designed for use in clinical practice situations where the primary unit of attention is a single client system (i.e., an individual, a family, a couple, or a group). For the most part, they are relatively simple, straightforward evaluation strategies that can be unobtrusively incorporated into the helping professional's daily practice routines. When used appropriately, they not only provide useful evaluative feedback but also enhance the overall quality of the intervention itself.

The micro or intensive designs of research make no pretense with respect to their contribution to scientific generalizations. They do, however, enable the social worker to test the utility of scientific generalizations within the crucible of practice. The time-limited nature of most crises is such that both the intervention and the evaluation must be initiated quickly. In many instances, it is necessary to proceed under less than optimal circumstances. The clinician is inescapably faced with the issue of somehow balancing the requirements of evaluation with those of practice, and, of course, in any apparent conflict between the two, the interests of the latter must always be accorded primary consideration. It is not surprising, therefore, that methodological purists may at times be critical of our evaluation efforts. But the methodological rigor of any research endeavor is inevitably a relative rather than an absolute condition. Each evaluation effort represents an imperfect attempt to arrive at a closer approximation of the truth. As such, research provides no guarantee of certitude. It simply helps us reduce the probability of error in the face of uncertainty. If we can tolerate its limitations and exploit its possibilities, we can almost certainly improve the quality of the services we provide our clients.

One final observation is in order. The delivery of any human service, regardless of its form, never takes place in an ethical and political vacuum. Professional actions should always be guided by an unequivocal set of professional values. All professional codes of ethics speak to the paramount importance of client rights, including self-determination and confidentiality—rights that are believed to play a critical role in the helping process.

REFERENCES

Allport, G. W. (1962). The general and the unique in psychological science. *Journal of Personality, 30,* 405–422.

American Psychiatric Association. (1994). *Diagnostic and statistical manual of mental disorders* (4th ed.). Washington, DC: Author.

Auerbach, S. M., & Kilmann, P. R. (1977). Crisis intervention: A review of outcome research. *Psychological Bulletin, 84,* 1189–1217.

Barlow, D. H., & Hersen, M. (1984). *Single-case experimental designs: Strategies for studying behavior change* (2nd ed.). New York: Pergamon.

Beck, A. T. (1967). *Depression: Clinical, experimental and theoretical aspects.* New York: Harper and Row.

Bellak, L., & Small, L. (1978). *Emergency psychotherapy and brief psychotherapy.* New York: Grune and Stratton.

Bergin, A. E. (1971). The evaluation of therapeutic outcomes. In A. E. Bergin & S. L. Garfield (Eds.), *Handbook of psychotherapy and behavior change* (pp. 217–270). New York: Wiley.

Bisman, C. D., & Hardcastle, D. A. (1999). *Integrating research into practice.* Belmont, CA: Brooks/Cole.

Bloom, B. L. (1992). *Planned short-term psychotherapy: A clinical handbook.* Boston: Allyn and Bacon.

Bloom, M., & Fischer, J. (1982). *Evaluating practice: Guidelines for the accountable professional.* Englewood Cliffs, NJ: Prentice-Hall.

Bloom, M., Fischer, J., & Orme, J. (1999). *Evaluating practice: Guide-*

lines for the accountable professional (3rd ed.). Boston: Allyn and Bacon.

Brower, A. M., & Nurius, P. S. (1993). Social cognitions and individual change: Current theory and counseling guidelines. Newbury Park, CA: Sage.

Campbell, D. T., & Stanley, J. C. (1966). Experimental and quasi-experimental designs for research and teaching. Chicago: Rand McNally

Chassan, J. B. (1967). Research designs in clinical psychology and psychiatry. New York: Appleton-Century-Crofts.

Chen, S. (1997). Measurement and analysis in psychosocial research. Brookfield, VT: Avebury.

Cone, J. D. (1998). Psychometric considerations: Concepts, contents and methods. In A. S. Bellack & M. Hersen (Eds.), Behavioral assessment: A practical handbook (4th ed., pp. 22–46). Boston: Allyn and Bacon.

Corcoran, K., & Fischer, J. (1999a). Measure for clinical practice: A sourcebook: Vol. 1. Couples, families, and children (3rd ed.). New York: Free Press.

Corcoran, K., & Fischer, J. (1999b). Measures of clinical practice: A sourcebook: Vol. 2. Adults (3rd ed.). New York: Free Press.

Cormier, W. H., & Cormier, L. S. (1991). Interviewing strategies for helpers (3rd ed.). Pacific Grove, CA: Brooks/Cole.

Davis, R. C., & Taylor, B. G. (1997). A proactive response to family violence: The results of a randomized experiment. Criminology, 35, 307–333.

Denzin, N. (1970). The research act. Chicago: Aldine.

Dziegielewski, S. F. (1991). Social group work with family members who have a relative suffering from dementia: A controlled evaluation. Research on Social Work Practice, 1, 358–370.

Dziegielewski, S. F. (1996). Managed care principles: The need for social work in the health care environment. Crisis Intervention and Time-Limited Treatment, 3, 97–110.

Dziegielewski, S. F. (1997). Time limited brief therapy: The state of practice. Crisis Intervention and Time-Limited Treatment, 3 217–228.

Dziegielewski, S. F. (1998). The changing face of health care social work: Professional practice in the era of managed care. New York: Springer.

Dziegielewski, S. F., & Resnick, C. A. (1996). A model of crisis intervention with adult survivors of incest. Crisis Intervention and Time-Limited Treatment, 2, 49–56.

Dziegielewski, S. F., Shields, J. P., & Thyer, B. A. (1998). Short-term treatment: Models, methods, and research. In J. B. Williams & K. Ell (Eds.), Advances in mental health research: Implications for practice (pp. 287–308). Washington, DC: NASW Press.

Evans, W., Smith, M., Hill, G., Albers, E., & Neufeld, J. (1996). Rural adolescent views of risk and protective factors associated with suicide. Crisis Intervention and Time-Limited Treatment, 3, 1–13.

Fischer, J. (1976). Effective casework practice: An eclectic approach. New York: McGraw-Hill.

Fischer, J., & Corcoran, K. (1994). Measures for clinical practice: A source book (2nd ed.). New York: Free Press.

Garwick, G., & Lampman, S. (1973). *Dictionary of goal attainment scaling*. Minneapolis, MN: Program Evaluation Project.

Gilliland, B. E., & James, R. K. (1997). *Crisis intervention strategies* (3rd edition). Pacific Grove, CA: Brooks/Cole.

Gottman, J. M., & Leiblum, S. R. (1974). *How to do psychotherapy and how to evaluate it*. New York: Holt, Rinehart and Winston.

Green, G. J., Lee, M., Trask, R., & Rheinscheld, J. (1996). Client strengths and crisis intervention: A solution-focused approach. *Crisis Intervention and Time-Limited Treatment, 3*, 43–64.

Hart, R. R. (1978). Therapeutic effectiveness of setting and monitoring goals. *Journal of Consulting and Clinical Psychology, 46*, 1242–1245.

Hartman, D. J., & Sullivan, W. P. (1996). Residential crisis services as an alternate to inpatient care. *Families in Society: The Journal of Contemporary Human Services,* (vol. 77, October), 496–501.

Hepworth, D. H., & Larsen, J. (1993). *Direct social work practice*. Pacific Grove, CA: Brooks/Cole.

Jobes, D. A. (1995). The challenge and the promise of clinical suicidology. *Suicide and Life Threatening Behavior, 25*, 437–450.

Jobes, David A., Eyman, James R., & Yufit, Robert I. (1995). Crisis intervention and time-limited treatment, Vol. 2, no.1, p. 1–12.

Kazdin, A. E. (1984). Statistical analyses for single-case experimental designs. In D. H. Barlow & M. Hersen (Eds.), *Single case experimental designs* (2nd ed., pp. 285–324). New York: Pergamon.

Kazdin, A. E. (1986). The evaluation of psychotherapy: Research designs and methodology. In S. L. Garfield & A. E. Bergin (Eds.), *Handbook of psychotherapy and behavior change* (pp. 23–68). New York: Wiley.

Kazdin, A. E. (1994). Methodology, design and evaluation in psychotherapy research. In S. L. Garfield & A. E. Bergin (Eds.), *Handbook of psychotherapy and behavior change* (4th ed., pp. 19–71). New York: Wiley.

Kazdin, A. E., & Wilson, G. T. (1978). *Evaluation of behavior therapy: Issues, evidence and research strategies*. Cambridge, MA: Ballinger.

Kiesler, D. J. (1966). Some myths of psychotherapy research and the search for a paradigm. *Psychological Bulletin, 65*, 110–136.

Kiresuk, T. J., & Sherman, R. E. (1968). Goal attainment scaling: A general method for evaluating comprehensive community mental health programs. *Community Mental Health Journal, 4*, 443–453.

Koss, M. P., & Butcher, J. N. (1986). Research on brief psychotherapy. In S. L. Garfield & A. E. Bergin (Eds.), *Handbook of psychotherapy and behavior change* (pp. 627–670). New York: Wiley.

Koss, M. P., & Shaing, J. (1994). Research in brief therapy. In A. E. Bergin & S. L. Garfield (Eds.), *Handbook of psychotherapy and behavior change* (4th ed., pp. 664–700). New York: Wiley.

Lambert, M. J., & Hill, C. E. (1994). Assessing psychotherapy outcomes and process. In S. L. Garfield & A. E. Bergin (Eds.), *Handbook of psychotherapy and behavior change*

(4th ed., pp. 72–113). New York: Wiley.

Lindemann, E. (1944). Symptomatology and management of acute grief. *American Journal of Psychiatry, 101,* 141–148.

Mark, R. (1996). *Research made simple: A handbook for social workers.* Thousand Oaks, CA: Sage.

Marlow, C. (1998). *Research methods for generalist social work.* Pacific Grove, CA: Brooks/Cole.

Mezzina, R., & Vidoni, D. (1995). Beyond the mental hospital: Crisis intervention and continuity of care in Trieste. A four-year follow-up study in a community mental health centre. *International Journal of Social Psychiatry, 41,* 1–20.

Neimeyer, R. A., & Pfeiffer, A. M. (1994). Evaluation of suicide intervention effectiveness. *Death Studies, 18,* 131–166.

Parad, H., & Parad, L. (1990). *Crisis intervention: The practitioner's sourcebook for brief therapy.* Milawakee, WI: Family Service America.

Paul, G. L. (1966). *Insight versus desensitization in psychotherapy.* Stanford, CA: Stanford University Press.

Powers, G. T., Meenaghan, T., & Toomey, B. (1985). *Practice-focused research.* Englewood Cliffs, NJ: Prentice-Hall.

Reynolds, S., Stiles, W. B., Barkman, M. et al. (1996). Acceleration of changes in impact during contrast-ing time-limited psychotherapies. *Journal of Consulting and Clinical Psychology, 64,* 577–586.

Rittner, B., Smyth, N. J., & Wodarski, J. (1995). Assessment and crisis intervention strategies with suicidal clients. *Crisis Intervention and Time-Limited Treatment, 2,* 71–84.

Roberts, A. R. (1990). *Crisis intervention handbook: Assessment, treatment and research.* Belmont, CA: Wadsworth.

Roberts, A., & Dziegielewski, S. F. (1995). Foundation skills and applications of crisis intervention and cognitive therapy. In A. Roberts (Ed.), *Crisis intervention and time-limited cognitive treatment* (pp. 3–27). Thousand Oaks, CA: Sage.

Royse, D. (1995). *Research methods in social work* (2nd ed.). Chicago: Nelson-Hall.

Rubin, A., & Babbie, E. (1993). *Research methods for social work* (2nd ed.). Pacific Grove, CA: Brooks/Cole.

Rudd, M. D., Joiner, T. E., & Rajab, M. H. (1995). Help negotiation after acute suicidal crisis. *Journal of Counseling and Clinical Psychology, 63,* 499–503.

Schutte, N. S., & Malouff, J. M. (1995). *Sourcebook of adult assessment strategies.* New York: Plenum.

Wells, R. A. (1994). *Planned short-term treatment* (2nd ed.). New York: Free Press.

Glossary

A-B-C model of crisis management: A three-stage sequential model for intervening with persons in crisis. The "A" refers to "achieving contact," the "B" to "boiling down the problem," and the "C" to "coping." (See chapter 8.)

Acquaintance rape: Nonconsensual sex between adults who know each other. (See chapter 7.)

Adolescence: Transitional period between childhood and adulthood, typically commencing with the onset of puberty, during which youth develop the physical, social, emotional, and intellectual skills necessary for adult functioning. (See chapter 10.)

Adolescent school subgroups: Naturally formed groups within school populations, commonly identified by ethnicity, activity, or year in school. Individuals may be associated with multiple groups. Examples include "jocks," "brains," "druggies," "homeboys," or "seniors." (See chapter 10.)

Adult abuse protocol: A detailed assessment and intervention guide for the abused adult, based on assessments made by multidisciplinary staff, such as a triage nurse, a physician, and a social worker. Using this protocol accomplishes two purposes: (1) It alerts the involved hospital staff to provide the appropriate clinical care, and (2) it documents the violent incident, so that if the victim decides to file a legal complaint, reliable, court-admissible evidence (including photographs) is available. (See chapter 8.)

Affective disorders: Affective disorders affect moods and are commonly called *mood disorders*. They comprise a wide spectrum of emotions, from elation to depression to mania, with depression dominating the clinical picture. Affective disorders also manifest themselves in physical symptoms, self-destructive behavior, loss of social functioning, and impaired reality testing. The frequency, intensity, and duration of the moods distinguish affective disorders from common, everyday moods. (See chapter 11.)

Aggression: Acting with intent to dominate or behave destructively; physical or verbal force directed toward the environment, another person, or oneself. (See chapter 10.)

AIDS service organization (ASO): A not-for-profit or for-profit community organization that may or may not provide health services. ASOs are generally funded through federal, state, and/or local dollars to provide psychosocial services to people with HIV and/or AIDS. (See chapter 14.)

Anticholinergic: An agent that blocks parasympathetic nerve impulses. Associated with medications utilized to minimize the discomfort associated with opioid withdrawal. (See chapter 12.)

Anticomplementary counselor responses: Counselor responses such as interpretations, reframes, and probes that are designed to "loosen" client's maladaptive cognitions or challenge dysfunctional behavioral choices. (See chapter 7.)

Antiretroviral therapy or antiviral therapy: Medication that slows, stops, or alters the production of viral particles. There are currently three classes of antiretroviral drugs: nonnucleoside reverse transcriptase inhibitors (NNRTI), nucleoside reverse transcriptase inhibitors (NRTI), and protease inhibitors. (See chapter 14.)

Baseline period: The period during a pre-intervention phase when a series of observations are made to monitor subsequent changes in the client's target behavior. It provides a basis on which to determine whether the behavior observed during baseline (i.e., phase A) changes in the expected direction following the introduction of treatment (i.e., phase B). (See chapters 20 and 21.)

Battered women's hotlines and shelters: The primary focus of these services is to ensure women's safety through crisis telephone counseling or provision of short-term housing at a safe residential shelter. Many shelters provide not only safe lodging but also peer counseling, support groups, information on women's legal rights, and referral to social service agencies. In some communities, emergency services for battered women have expanded further to include parenting education workshops, assistance in finding transitional and permanent housing, employment counseling and job placement, and group counseling for batterers. These crisis intervention and housing placements for battered women and their children exist in every state and in many large metropolitan areas in the United States. (See chapters 1 and 8.)

Bereavement: See "Normal bereavement" and "Uncomplicated bereavement."

Binge: A prolonged episode of continuous alcohol or drug use extending over a period greater than 24 hours. (See chapter 12.)

Brief therapy: A type of intervention based on the premise that a system in crisis is more open to change, and that certain and often brief intervention into the unstable system can result in lasting changes in how the system functions. (See chapter 21.)

Buprinex: A medication used in opioid detoxification that binds with opiate receptors in the central nervous system, altering both perception of and emotional response to pain through an unknown mechanism. (See chapter 12.)

Catastrophic events: Acute, localized violent occurrences producing widespread trauma in those experiencing or exposed to the event. These incidents commonly directly victimize groups of people and frequently include multiple fatal assaults. (See chapter 10.)

Code: Word used to alert the medical team to start resuscitation efforts (CPR) to revive a victim of cardiac and pulmonary arrest. Combined with different words to designate different types of emergencies at hospitals and broadcast over the PA system. Examples: CODE Blue for victim of cardiac arrest; CODE Red for fire. (See chapter 17.)

Cognitive elaboration: The generation of alternative conceptualizations of a given event, phenomenon, or stimulus condition. This process is completed in recognition that multiple meanings exist for all human experience. (See chapter 13.)

Completed suicide: See Suicide. *Suicide* and *completed suicide* are interchangeable terms. (See chapter 6.)

Construct: An individual's active processing or organizing experience (George A. Kelly). Personal constructs represent personal or shared meanings. (See chapter 13.)

Constructive: A term associated with "constructivism" or "constructive metatheory" in psychology, a tradition emphasizing the active participation of each person in his or her own life organization and development. (See chapter 13.)

Coping questions: Coping questions ask clients to talk about how they manage to survive and endure their problems. Coping questions help clients to notice their resources and strengths despite adversities. (See chapters 1 and 2.)

Cravings: A term defined in various ways related to drug use. Typically it refers to an intense desire to obtain and use a drug. (See chapter 12.)

Crisis: An acute disruption of psychological homeostasis in which one's usual coping mechanisms fail and there exists evidence of distress and functional impairment. The subjective reaction to a stressful life experience that compromises the individual's stability and ability to cope or function. The main cause of a crisis is an intensely stressful, traumatic, or hazardous event, but two other conditions are also necessary: (1) the individual's perception of the event as the cause of considerable upset and/or disruption; and (2) the individual's inability to resolve the disruption by previously used coping methods. *Crisis* also refers to "an upset in the steady state." It often has five components: a hazardous or traumatic event, a vulnerable state, a precipitating factor, an active crisis state, and the resolution of the crisis. (See chapters 1 and 3.)

Crisis call to domestic violence hotline: A telephone call to a hotline in which the caller is in imminent danger or has just been abused or battered by an intimate partner. (See chapters 1 and 8.)

Crisis intervention: The first stage of crisis intervention, also known as emotional "first aid," focuses on establishing rapport, making a rapid assessment, and stabilizing and reducing the person's symptoms of distress and the impact of a crisis. The next stages utilize crisis intervention strategies (e.g., active listening, ventilation, reflection of feeling, storytelling, reframing, and exploring alternative solutions) while assisting the individual in crisis to return to a state of adaptive functioning, crisis resolution, and cognitive mastery. This type of timely intervention focuses on helping to mobilize the resources of those differentially affected. Crisis intervention may be given over the telephone or in person. (See chapters 1 and 4.) For in-depth case applications of Roberts's seven-stage crisis intervention model to a range of urgent and acute crisis episodes, see chapters 5 through 19.

Crisis intervention service: These services provide a person in crisis with the phone numbers of local hotlines, community crisis centers, crisis intervention units at the local community mental health center, rape crisis centers, battered women's shelters, and family crisis intervention programs, which then provide follow-up and home-based crisis services. Crisis intervention services are available 24 hours a day, seven days a week, and are usually staffed by crisis clinicians, counselors, social workers, hospital emergency room staff, and trained volunteers. (See chapters 1, 3, and 12 to 18.)

Crisis-oriented treatments: Treatment approaches that apply to all practice models and techniques, which are focused on resolving immediate crisis situations and emotionally volatile conflicts with a minimum number of contacts (usually one to six), and are characterized as time-limited and goal-directed. (See chapter 1.)

Crisis residential unit: A 24-hour supervised setting for individuals experiencing any type of crisis who are 18 years of age or older, medically stable and no overt threat to themselves or others. This brief stay (up to 5 days) focuses on problem solving and crisis management through individual supportive counseling, group treatment, psychiatric and nursing services, as well as appropriate referrals. (See chapter 16.)

Crisis resolution: The goal of interventions given by trained volunteers and professionals to persons in crisis. Resolution involves the restoration of equilibrium, cognitive mastery of the situation, and the development of new coping methods. An effective crisis resolution removes vulnerabilities from the individual's past and bolsters the individual with an increased repertoire of coping skills that serve as a buffer against similar situations in the future. (See chapters 1 through 4).

Critical incident: An event that has the potential to overwhelm one's usual coping mechanisms, resulting in psychological distress and an impairment of normal adaptive functioning. (See chapter 4.)

Critical Incident Stress Debriefing: A seven-stage structured group meeting or discussion in which personnel who have been affected by a traumatic event given a chance to discuss their thoughts and emotions in a controlled manner usually, 1 to 10 days after an acute crisis and 3 to 4 weeks after a mass disaster. (See chapter 4.)

Critical Incident Stress Management (CISM): An integrated and comprehensive multicomponent program for providing crisis and disaster mental health services. A variety of stress management techniques/intervention provided to emergency services personnel, police, and/or firefighters who are exposed to life-threatening or traumatic incidents. This model was developed by Jeffrey Mitchell and George Everly (authors of chapter 4 and cofounders of the International Critical Incident Stress Foundation). (See chapters 4 and 16.)

Date rape: Nonconsensual sex between partners who date or are on a date. (See chapter 7.)

Date rape drugs: Sedative-type drugs, some of which are illegal substances, that render victims unable to defend themselves against sexual exploitation; alcohol, Rohypenol, and Ectasy are three of the most common date rape drugs. (See chapter 7.)

Debriefing at school: A meeting held soon after a crisis event to review the activities of a school crisis intervention team during a recent crisis response with the primary goal of supporting team members and ultimately improving the future functioning of the team as a whole and the quality of the interventions offered. (See chapter 9.)

Decompensation: Person having a chronic mental condition may periodically experience worsening symptoms such as depression or psychosis. This general decline in condition is called *decompensation*. (See chapter 15.)

Defusing: An approximately 1-hour, three-phase, structured small-group discussion provided within hours of a crisis for purposes of assessment, triaging, and acute symptom mitigation. (See chapter 4.)

Deinstitutionalization: The Community Mental Health Centers Act of 1963 required that mental health services be moved from inpatient institutions to community-based services. This transition is referred to as *deinstitutionalization,* and one of the services mandated by the act is crisis services. (See chapter 15.)

Delayed: Group that can be transferred to a "walk-in" location. These include conditions that do not require emergency room care at all and can be seen at any time, like most rashes or a previous wound that needs checking. (See chapter 17.)

Dependent variables: Variables that represent the presumed effect in any functional relationship. (See chapter 20.)

Disequilibrium: An emotional state that may be characterized by confusing emotions, somatic complaints, and erratic behavior. The severe emotional discomfort experienced by the person in crisis propels him or her toward action that will reduce the subjective discomfort. Crisis intervention usually alleviates the early symptoms of disequilibrium within the first 6 weeks of treatment, and hopefully soon restores equilibrium. (See chapters 1 and 3.)

Dismantling treatment strategy: A strategy involving the orderly removal of one or more components of the treatment package, accompanied by careful recording of the apparent effects. This systematic elimination, or isolation, enables the clinician to "determine the necessary and sufficient components for therapeutic change." (See chapter 20.)

Dissociation: A coping mechanism that helps individuals tolerate pain and shame, distorting their sense of time and preserving false notions of safety. (See chapter 11.)

District-level crisis intervention team: A school crisis intervention team composed of staff from the school district's central office to provide oversight, resources, and administrative support to school-based crisis intervention teams. (See chapter 9.)

Ego fragmentation: Ego fragmentations, sometimes referred to as *dissociative disorders,* are characterized by disturbances in normally integrated functions of memory, identity, or consciousness. They are found in diagnoses such as posttraumatic stress disorder, acute stress disorder, and somatization disorder. Harsh psychosocial stressors such as physical threat, wartime, and disasters predispose susceptible persons to ego fragmentations. (See chapter 11.)

Emergency room: A department in a hospital open 24 hours a day to victims of emergent and urgent situations. Treatment is provided by a medical team of doctors, nurses, respiratory therapists, lab technicians, and social workers. (See chapter 17.)

Emergent: Group that requires immediate attention and includes cardiac arrest and trauma codes. (See chapter 17.)

Exception questions: Questions that inquire about times when the problem is either absent, less intense, or dealt with in a manner that is acceptable to the client. (See chapter 2.)

Excitatory toxicity: Massive release of neurotransmitters that in high enough concentrations may damage or destroy the neural substrates they serve. (See chapter 4.)

Extensive designs of research: Designs that emphasize the primacy of the confirmatory aspect of scientific activity. The goal of these designs is to discover laws that apply to aggregates of individuals rather than to the individuals who constitute the aggregate. In this approach, the ultimate goal is to discover scientific generalization under controlled circumstances. (See chapter 21.)

Goal Attainment Scaling (GAS): This evaluation method measures intervention outcomes in which a number of individually tailored treatment goals are specified in relation to a set of graded scale points ranging from the least favorable to the most favorable outcomes considered likely. It is suggested that at least five points comprising a Likert-type scale is assigned with the "least favorable outcome" scored −2, the "most favorable outcome" scored +2, and the "most likely outcome" assigned a value of zero. (See chapter 21.)

HIV trajectory: The stages of HIV infection and the symptoms that accompany those stages. (See chapter 14.)

HIV viral load: The amount of viral particles per milliliter of blood (scientifically "quantitative plasma HIV RNA"). The viral load is an indication of prognosis, with a high load indicating that the virus is progressing rapidly. (See chapter 14.)

Idiographic research: This approach focuses on the study of individuals as individuals, rather than on the discovery of general propositions. Idiographic research investigates the rich and intricate detail of specific cases, including deviant cases that prove to be exceptions to the general rule. (See chapter 21.)

Imposter phenomenon: An internal experience of intellectual phoniness that persists despite independent, objective, and tangible evidence to the contrary. (See chapter 7.)

Incest: Exploitative sexual behavior (unwanted sexual contact) occurring between relatives (people too close to marry). Incest is sometimes delimited to relations wherein one person is at least 5 years older than the other (See chapter 11.)

Independent variables: Variables that represent the presumed cause of any functional relationship. (See chapter 21.)

Information and referral (I and R) services: The goals of I and R services are to facilitate access to community human services and to overcome the many barriers that may obstruct a person's entry to needed community resources. (See chapter 1.)

Intensive designs of research: Designs primarily concerned with the study of single cases. They provide the means by which clinicians can evaluate the idiosyncratic aspects of their practice. Intensive research models can serve to generate relevant hypotheses suitable for testing by the more traditional extensive research approaches. (See chapter 21.)

Internal validity: The level of confidence warranted by any causal inference. The designs that effectively control contamination from outside variables are said to be internally valid. (See chapter 21.)

Intervention period: The period of time, typically referred to as the B phase, in any time-series design during which treatment is purposefully administered. (See chapter 21.)

Intervention priority code: Method of prioritizing crisis requests on a clinical basis. Priorities range from I to IV, depending on clinical symptoms and presenting problems of the individual. These priorities dictate in which order cases should be responded to and in what time frame. (See chapter 16.)

IOP Intensive outpatient program: Outpatient substance dependence treatment, usually offered three evenings per week, 3 hours each evening. (See chapter 12.)

Lethality: Measuring the degree to which a person is capable of causing death. Assessing for lethality entails asking about suicidal ideation, prior suicide attempts, homicidal thoughts, and feasibility of carrying out suicidal ideation or homicide. (See chapters 1, 3, and 11.)

LSD (Lysergic acid diethylamide): A class of drugs referred to as the *serotonergic hallucinogens.* (See chapter 12.)

Maladaptive reaction: A codependent's tendency to continue investing time and energy to control a substance abuser's actions and behaviors despite repetitive adverse consequences. (See chapter 12.)

Managed care: A health care services delivery model that attempts to control the cost of services in two ways: first, by restricting services to approved providers who accept reduced payment levels; second, by restricting access to higher-cost services such as specialists or inpatient services by requiring referrals from primary care physicians and precertifications for certain services. (See chapters 3 and 15.)

Maslow's hierarchy of needs: A continuum of needs continually experienced by humans, as identified by Abraham Maslow. These hierarchically ordered needs include (from lowest to highest level): physiological needs, safety needs, belongingness and love needs, esteem needs, aesthetic and cognitive needs, and self-actualization needs. Lower-level needs must be satisfied before the next level of need can be addressed. (See chapter 10.)

Memorialization: Activities of grieving individuals and groups to remember and honor those who have died. (See chapter 9.)

Methamphetamine (methedrine, desoxyn): Synthetic stimulant drug. Acts to stimulate or mimic activity in the sympathetic branch of the autonomic nervous system (See chapter 12.)

Miracle question: Miracle questions help clients to construct a vision of life without the presenting complaint. A widely used format is: "Suppose that after our meeting today you go home and go to bed. While you are sleeping a miracle happens and your problem is suddenly solved, like magic. The problem is gone. How will you know a miracle happened? What will be the first sign that tells you that a miracle has happened and the problem is resolved?" (See chapter 2.)

Mobile crisis services: Crisis counseling, assessment, and intervention provided at the scene of the crisis (someone's home, other agencies, community, prison, etc.). (See chapter 16.)

Mobile crisis unit: A self-contained team of mental health and law enforcement professionals trained to respond to a crisis anywhere in the community, including residences, public places, and schools. (See chapter 15.)

Multiple baseline approach: A crisis intervention approach designed to minimize the possibility of behavior change due to chance. Baseline data are collected either (1) on more than one target behavior, (2) on the same target behavior but in more than one setting, or (3) on more than one but similar clients. Intervention techniques are then applied sequentially so that once a change in the initial target behavior is observed, the intervention is systematically introduced with the next target behavior or in an alternate setting. (See chapter 20.)

Net nanny: A brand-name computer software system for blocking access to certain Internet Web sites. (See chapter 12.)

Nonurgent: Problems that need to be treated sometime today and not necessarily in the emergency room (e.g., sore throat or simple laceration). (See chapter 17.)

Nonviolent crisis intervention: Variety of prevention and intervention techniques proven effective in resolving potentially violent crises. This model is taught by the CPI Crisis Prevention Institute, Inc. (See chapter 16.)

Normal bereavement: The reactions to loss of a significant person, which may not be immediate, but which rarely occurs after the first 2 to 3 months after the loss. Normal bereavement involves feelings of depression that the person regards as "normal," although professional help may be sought for associated symptoms, such as insomnia or weight loss. Bereavement varies considerably among people of different ages and cultural groups. (See chapter 5.)

Objectified case studies: Studies that attempt to relate the process of intervention (what the worker does) to the outcome of that intervention (whether what the worker does can be concluded to be effective). (See chapter 20.)

Outcome evaluation: A process aimed at establishing whether a program or intervention is achieving its objectives and whether the results are due to the interventions provided. (See chapter 20.)

Paralysis of initiative: Paralysis of initiative is a restricted sense of one's ability to take risks or to learn by trial and error. Incest is usually a precipitator to paralysis of initiative. (See chapter 11.)

Parametric treatment strategies: Strategies that attempt to determine in what quantity and/or in what sequence the components of a treatment package are likely to have their most beneficial impact. By systematically manipulating one or more of the components of a treatment package, it is possible to monitor the differential effects. (See chapter 21.)

Perturbation: A state of system disequilibrium characterized by disorganization and distress, resulting in adaptation and emerging complexity and differentiation. (See chapter 13.)

Postmodernism: Refers to philosophical reflection in which a conception of reality independent of the observer is replaced with notions of language actually constituting the structures of a perspectival social reality. (See chapter 13.)

Posttraumatic stress disorder (PTSD): A diagnosis given to people who experience symptoms of intrusion, avoidance, or hyperarousal after experiencing or observing serious injury, threat, or death of a close associate (after experiencing any event that is extremely traumatic and terrifying, and that provokes feelings of helplessness).

PTSD occurs when a person perceives an event as life-threatening and/or when the experience challenges his or her notions of fairness and justice. (See chapters 8 and 11.)

Postvention: Activities that take place in the aftermath of a crisis event to review the crisis response to date, with the primary goal of identifying ongoing needs of students and staff, as well as steps that can be taken to prevent the occurrence of comparable events (e.g., in suicide postvention, case finding for additional students at risk of suicide). (See chapter 9.)

Prevention: Efforts designed to avert inappropriate and antisocial behaviors prior to their occurrence. (See chapter 10.)

Primary adolescent suicide prevention: Programs offered in schools, churches, and recreational and social organizations, designed to serve as a deterrent to a suicidal crisis. These programs focus on education, peer counseling, and other prevention methods. Teaching about the prevention and identification of possible suicide attemptors may be part of these programs. (See chapters 9 and 10.)

Protocol: The step-by-step or sequential plan of a treatment. (See chapters 8 and 17.)

Psychosocial crises: Crises that are characterized primarily by psychosocial problems such as homelessness, extreme social isolation, and unmet primary care needs, and that may contribute to physical and psychological trauma and illness. (See chapter 1.)

Rape crisis programs: Programs that include specialized protocols for rape victims and that have been established by medical centers, community mental health centers, women's counseling centers, crisis clinics, and victim assistance centers. The protocol in these crisis intervention services generally begins with an initial visit from a social worker, victim advocate, or nurse while the victim is being examined in the hospital emergency room. Follow-up is often handled through telephone contact and in-person counseling sessions for 1 to 10 weeks following the rape. (See chapters 1 and 3.)

Rape-supportive attitudes: Stereotypic beliefs or societal "myths" about rape that result in the following: women being portrayed as sexual objects, discounting the impact of rape as a traumatically violent act, and absolving the perpetrator of full responsibility for committing rape. (See chapter 7.)

Rape victim: A person who reports having experienced a sexual assault that meets the legal criteria for rape. Forcible rape is unwanted and coerced sexual penetration of another person. (See chapter 3.)

Rapid assessment instruments (RAIs): Evaluation instruments that refer to any one of numerous assessment devices that are relatively easy to administer, score, and interpret and can be used to measure one or more dimensions of a client's target behavior. RAIs require very little knowledge of testing procedures on the part of the practitioner. The score that is generated provides an operational index of the frequency, duration, or intensity of the problem or target behavior. (See chapters, 1, 6, 8, 16, and 20.)

Regional resource team: A group of professionals representing a range of allied disciplines (e.g., educational, emergency response, law enforcement, medical, mental health) that meet on an ongoing basis and provide consultation and technical assistance to district-level crisis intervention teams in the development and implementation of school crisis intervention responses. (See chapter 9.)

Relapse prevention: A set of procedures designed to maintain therapeutic change and to facilitate accommodation of trauma with limited long-term negative effects. (See chapter 13.)

Relationship questions: Relationship questions ask clients how their significant others are reacting to their problem situation and progress in solution-finding. The establishment of multiple indicators of change helps clients develop a clear vision of a desired future appropriate to their real-life context. (See chapter 2.)

Reliability: An evaluation term that refers to the stability of a measure. One aspect of reliability is whether the questions that comprise an instrument mean the same thing to one or more individuals answering them at different times. (See chapter 20.)

Reversal designs: Designs that involve a process in which an intervention is introduced for a time and then abruptly withdrawn, with the resulting circumstances essentially approximating pre-intervention or baseline conditions. In the absence of intervention, certain types of client behaviors might be expected to move in the direction of the pre-intervention levels. (See chapter 21.)

Revictimization: Victims may experience this process when counselors, police officers, or prosecutors place themselves in the role of judging whether a reported rape or incest experience was "real," or whether they think the client "provoked" the attack. (See chapters 1, 3, 8, and 11.)

Safety contract: Written agreement between the crisis worker and client that acknowledges that the client has agreed not to harm himself or herself or anyone else; and are unable to resist that urge, the client will call for help first. (See chapter 16.)

Scaling questions: Question that ask clients to rank their situation and/or goal on a scale of 1 to 10. Scaling questions provide a simple tool for clients to quantify and evaluate their situation and progress so that they establish clear indicators of progress for themselves. (See chapter 2.)

School-based crisis intervention team: A team composed of school staff from one school to provide direct services to student and staff within that particular school. (See chapters 9 and 10.)

School crisis intervention team: A group of individuals formed, outside the context of a particular crisis event, with the purpose of developing plans and protocols to meet the needs of students and school staff in the event of a crisis affecting the school community. (See chapters 9 and 10.)

School violence: Aggression against property, or persons within a school context. Against persons, the term denotes an intentional verbal or physical act that produces pain, either physical or emotional, in the recipient of that act while the recipient is under the supervision of the school. Similarly, this operational definition is concerned primarily with violence that occurs within the school environment and not with general violent incidents involving adolescents. (See chapter 10.)

Secondary adolescent suicide prevention: Process involving the identification of the at-risk adolescent and his or her family. The at-risk adolescent is often difficult to approach and may have withdrawn from friends, school, and family. (See chapters 5 and 6.)

Secondary trauma responses: (Also known as *secondary victimization* or *compassion fatigue*.) Psychological aftereffects of traumatic victimization experienced by those who assist victims of violence. This vicarious traumatization commonly occurs in mental health workers who assist or treat victims of traumatic events. These responses can occur as reactions to short-term interactions with specific clients or as alterations of long-held beliefs that are challenged by interactions with multiple clients over time. (See chapter 10.)

Self-efficacy: The conviction that one can successfully execute the behavior required to produce desired outcomes. (See chapter 13.)

Single-system design: Crisis intervention approaches that focus on the study of individuals as individuals. These designs investigate the rich and intricate details of specific cases, including the deviant cases that prove to be exceptions to the general rule. (See chapter 20.)

Solution-focused approach: A solution-focused therapy is a time-limited treatment model aiming to assist people to find solutions to their concerns in as few sessions as needed. Rather than focusing on the history of the problems, such an approach emphasizes an individual's strengths and resources. (See chapter 2.)

Somatization: This term is synonymous with *somatic distress*. Somatization involves experiencing physical symptoms that suggest a medical condition but to which physiological causes are undetermined. It is usually assumed that psychological factors are connected to the multiple, recurring medical complaints. Somatization manifests itself in tension headaches, gastrointestinal problems, back pain, tremors, choking sensations, and sexual complaints. (See chapters 3 and 11.)

Steady state: A total condition of the system in which it is in balance both internally and with its environment, but which is in change; a moving balance or dynamic homeostasis. (See chapter 13.)

Strengths perspective: A practice perspective that looks at individuals, families, and communities in light of their capacities, strengths, talents, competencies, possibilities, and resources. (See chapter 2.)

Stress inoculation training (SIT): A useful treatment package for clients who have resolved many assault-related problems but continue to exhibit severe fear responses. A cognitively and behaviorally based anxiety management approach, SIT is designed to assist the client in actively coping with target-specific, assault-related anxiety. (See chapters 1 and 8.)

Student developmental tasks: Predictable challenges facing late adolescent college students that require some measure of successful resolution or adaptation. Typical age-related tasks include coordinating apparent contradictory aspects of self, managing emotions, achieving greater cognitive complexity, and forming mutually satisfying relationships characterized by autonomous interdependence. (See chapter 7.)

Suicidal behavior: Potentially self-injurious behavior for which there is evidence that the person intended at some level to kill herself or himself or wished to use the appearance of such an intention to obtain some other end. (See chapter 6.)

Suicidal ideation: Any self-reported thoughts of engaging in suicidal behavior. (See chapter 6.)

Suicidal intent: One's motive for engaging in suicidal behavior. (See chapter 6.)

Suicide: Death where there is evidence that the injury was self-inflicted and that the person intended to kill herself or himself. (See chapter 6.)

Suicide attempt: A potentially self-injurious behavior with a nonfatal outcome, for which there is evidence that the person intended at some level to kill herself or himself. (See chapter 6.)

Suicide prevention and crisis centers: Centers that provide immediate assessment and crisis intervention to suicidal and depressed callers. The first prototype for these centers was established in London in 1906 when the Salvation Army opened an antisuicide bureau aimed at helping suicide attemptors. The first federally funded suicide prevention center was established in 1958 in Los Angeles. The Los Angeles Suicide Prevention Center, codirected by Edwin Schneidman and Norman Farberow, provided comprehensive training to medical interns, psychiatric residents, and graduate students in psychology, social work and counseling. (See chapters 1 and 6.)

Suicidologists: Researchers who study suicidal behavior and suicide-related phenomena. The founder of the term *suicidology* was Edwin Schneidman. (See chapter 6.)

Surveillance data: Reports produced by the Centers for Disease Control (CDC) or state departments of health on the number of HIV and/or AIDS cases and the routes of transmission, age, race, and gender of those cases.

SWAT team: Special weapons and tactics teams are units based within police departments that receive focused training to deal with hostage situations. SWAT usually use state-of-the art equipment and communications technology, and team members are trained in hostage negotiation skills. (See chapter 15.)

Telephone crisis services: Crisis counseling, crisis stabilization, screening, information, and referrals provided to any individual calling in crisis or any significant other calling for someone else. (See chapters 1 and 16.)

Time-series designs: Research designs that involve the measurement of change in some target behavior (usually the identified problem) at given intervals over a more or less extended period of time. Successive observations made during the course of therapeutic intervention enable the practitioner to systematically monitor the nature and extent of change in a target behavior. Typically, the phases of the time-series are referred to as baseline (A) and intervention (B). (See chapter 20.)

Transdermal infusion system: A method of delivering medicine by placing it in a special gel-like matrix "patch" that is applied to the skin. The medicine is absorbed through the skin at a fixed rate. (See chapter 12.)

Transinstitutionalization: Movement of clients back and forth between systems. For example, it is common for people to move between the mental health and criminal justice systems. (See chapter 15.)

Treatment package strategy: A treatment evaluation strategy in which the impact of intervention is assessed as a total entity. In order to rule out potential threats to internal validity, such as changes attributable to motivation, spontaneous remission, intervening historical events, and the like, some sort of control or comparison condition must be incorporated into the research design. (See chapter 20.)

Triangulation: A process involving the use of several evaluation strategies simultaneously within or across client systems. When done intentionally, triangulation enables the clinician to use each strategy as a means of cross-validating the findings generated by alternative strategies. (See chapter 20.)

Trigger: A term used to describe environmental cues that lead the substance-dependent person to crave his or her drug of choice. (See chapter 12.)

24-hour hotlines: Telephone services, often staffed by volunteers, that provide information, crisis assessments, crisis counseling, and referrals for callers with various problems, such as depression, suicide ideation, alcoholism, chemical dependency, impotence, domestic violence, and crime victimization. Because of their 24-hour availability, they can provide immediate, though temporary, intervention. (See chapters 1 and 8.)

Two-factor model of acute crisis: A unifying model of acute crisis consisting of neurological hypersensitivity and psychological hypersensitivity. (See chapter 4.)

Uncomplicated bereavement: Grief that continues to be characterized by guilt that is associated with things done or not done by the survivor at the time of death. (See chapter 5.)

Urgent: Urgent conditions are those requiring immediate attention within a few hours; there is possible danger to the patient if medically unattended and the disorder is acute. Problem should be treated as soon as possible—generally within 1 to 2 hours. (See chapters 3 and 17.)

Validity: An evaluation term that refers to the question of whether an instrument measures what it purports to measure. (See chapter 20.)

Vertical transmission: The transmission of HIV from mother to fetus. (See chapter 14.)

Viability: The evaluation of a construct on the basis of its consequences to the individual and society, as well as its coherence with prevailing personal and social beliefs. (See chapter 13.)

Victim: An innocent person, such as someone who suffers as a result of a violent crime or a disaster, and who encounters physical injury, trauma, fear, acute anxiety, and/or loss of belongings. (See chapter 17.)

Violence risk factors: Biological, social, and familial characteristics or phenomena that have been shown to contribute to participation in adolescent aggression and delinquency. Although numerous risk factors have been identified, associating with negative peer groups; overly lax, inconsistent, or harsh parenting styles; and involvement with illegal substance use are among the most powerful factors associated with aggressive and violent behavior by adolescents. It is believed that increasing numbers of risk factors are associated with an increased likelihood of association with aggressive acts. (See chapter 10.)

Viral mutation: A change in the genetic structure of the viral particle. Mutation is a naturally occurring process in all living organisms and is dangerous in HIV when the new or mutated viruses are the only ones to survive and thrive, rendering the antiretroviral therapy ineffective. (See chapter 14.)

Walk-in crisis services: Crisis counseling, assessment, and intervention provided at the Crisis Services office. (See chapter 16.)

Weltanschauung: An individual's worldview regarding safety, security, or sense of self. (See chapter 4.)

Withdrawal: A definable illness that occurs with a cessation or decrease in use of alcohol or a drug. (See chapter 12.)

Index

CNS. *See* central nervous system
cocaine, 275–276, 280–288, 298
  in polysubstance dependence, 292,
    294
  sexual behavior and, 283
  statistics on, 278, 279
Cocaine Anonymous, 288
Coconut Grove fire, 11, 65, 488
codes
  ethical, 510–511
  priority, 394–395, 396, 520
  resuscitation, 392, 515
cognitive issues
  appraisal, 186–197
  elaboration, 329, 330, 515
  functioning, 20–21
  mastery, 20–21
  training, 108
cognitive therapy, 61, 66, 236, 463
  for divorce, 329, 330–331
  for school violence, 235–242
  Roberts's Seven-Stage Crisis Interven-
    tion Model and, 237–242,
    244–246
  for substance dependence, 297, 298
collaboration, 168, 184, 212–213, 236,
  323
college students, 152–173
  anxiety in, 164, 165
  assessment of, 159–160, 166–168
  developmental needs of, 152, 169,
    526
  rape and, 153–158
  social isolation of, 5, 169
  statistics on, 155–156
  violence and, 152, 155–156
combat neurosis, 12, 66
commitment, involuntary, 139, 362
communication, 69, 215–217, 260–
  261, 369
  suicidal clients and, 136–137,
    143–144
Community Integration, Inc. Crisis Services, 373–387
community mental health centers, 6–7,
  14, 24
Community Mental Health Centers Act
  of 1963, 14, 23, 359
community mental health services
  for AIDS, 347, 514

vs. emergency rooms, 390–391
evaluation of, 495
history of, 57, 359–360
home-based, 359, 361
mobile (*see* mobile crisis units)
school crises and, 212, 220–221
compliance (drug therapy), 341, 346–
  347, 354
compliments, 45–46, 50–51
Comprehensive Psychiatric Emergency
  Program, 393
conduct patterns, 11, 65
confidentiality, 157, 214
confrontation, 36, 168, 268
Congress, Elaine P., 430–449
constructivist therapy, 313, 320–321,
  324–325, 326–328, 515
Consumer Outcome and Satisfaction
  Survey, 478
continuity of care, 57, 71
contracts
  safety, 146, 524
  therapeutic, 261, 498
control, 47–48, 50, 244
  groups, 467, 468, 480–481
  locus of, 37, 38, 68, 185, 269
Copeland, Ellis P., 101–130
coping questions, 44–45, 515
coping strategies, 32, 65, 107, 108, 313
  adaptive, 7, 20, 112–113, 124
  of adolescents, 106–107, 119,
    122–124
  of adult survivors of incest, 251–252,
    257, 268–269
  of battered women, 184, 185–186
  of culturally diverse families, 433–
    434, 439, 445, 447
  for divorce, 317, 322, 328–329
  external, 322
  failure of, 9, 13, 31
  identifying, 19–20, 185–186
  impostor phenomenon and, 163, 166
  medical crisis and, 415
  of rape victims, 160
  school violence and, 221, 243–244
  in substance dependence, 280, 284–
    285, 295
  suicidal clients and, 112–113, 142,
    143, 144–145
  victimization and, 186–197

for rape victims, 159–162
for residential services, 382–384
for schizophrenia, 382–384
for school violence, 237–242,
    244–246
for sibling death, 121–125
for substance dependence, 275–278,
    280–288, 289–292, 294–298,
    299–301
for suicide prevention, 134–137,
    134–147
for walk-in crisis services, 376–378
Robinson, J., 291–292
Rogerian counseling, 466–467
Rohypnol, 153, 154
role playing, 327, 466
romance, 4–5
Rubin, Allen, 456
rural areas, 107, 369

safe sex, 318
safety
    contracts, 146, 524
    Maslow on, 81, 244
    school violence and, 244
    victim, 39, 159, 193
Saleebey, D., 409
sampling techniques, 457
Santos, A. B., 361, 366, 368–369
satisfaction, client, 464, 478, 491
Scale for Suicidal Ideation, 457
scales. See instruments
scaling questions, 41–42, 49–50, 296,
    524
schizophrenia, 357, 364–365, 467
    residential services for, 382–384
    statistics on, 359, 469
Schneidman, Edwin, 14
Schonfeld, David J., 209–228
school issues
    achievement, 163–164, 434–435, 439
    dropouts, 439
    subgroups, 238, 242, 246, 513
    teachers, 224–225, 255
school crisis intervention, 209–228,
    229–249
    classroom interventions, 221–224
    collaboration for, 212–213, 236
    protocols, 212–214
    response plans, 212–217

risk assessment in, 219–220, 221,
    233, 243–244
school crisis intervention teams, 214–
    215, 216, 525
    district level, 214–215, 518
    regional level, 214, 524
    school level, 215, 226–227
    training, 225–226
school violence, 229–249
    case studies of, 103, 121–125, 229–
        230, 384–387
    catastrophic events in, 243–246
    cognitive therapy for, 235–242
    Critical Incident Stress Management
        for, 384–387
    debriefing, 245, 386, 517
    definition of, 231, 525
    firearms and, 232–233
    gangs and, 238, 242, 246, 394
    interventions for, 233–234, 235–242,
        244–246
    postraumatic stress disorder and,
        242–243
    precipitating events for, 229, 235,
        239–240
    risk assessment for, 219–220, 221,
        233, 243–244
    statistics on, 105, 232–233
Schwartz, M. D., 156
secondary trauma responses, 245, 525
security systems, 200–203
self-blame, 109–110, 154, 186, 256,
    268
self-definition, 169, 292
self-destructive behavior, 138, 256, 259
self-efficacy, 321, 329, 525
self-esteem, 19, 142, 414
    in adult survivors of incest, 269
    in battered women, 182–183, 184,
        186
    in college students, 164
    in crisis reactions, 7, 66
    in divorce, 316
self-harm, 143, 251, 257
self-help groups, 63, 287, 298
self-report instruments, 491, 498
    for child abuse, 481
    for depression, 318–319
    for suicide, 144, 320
self-talk, 34, 168